SMALL
BUSINESS
MANAGEMENT

SMALL BUSINESS MANAGEMENT

THIRD EDITION

Hal B. Pickle
St. Edwards University

Royce L. Abrahamson
Southwest Texas State University

John Wiley & Sons
New York   Chichester   Brisbane   Toronto   Singapore

Text and cover design by Kevin J. Murphy

Cover photography by Michael Breskin/David Emberling

Location: Dianne B.
426 West Broadway, Soho, New York
Edward I. Mills, Architect

(Wiley series in management)

Copyright © 1976, 1981, 1984, by John Wiley & Sons, Inc.

Library of Congress Cataloging in Publication Data:

Pickle, Hal B.
  Small business management.

  Includes index.
  1. Small business—Management. I. Abrahamson,
Royce L. II. Title.

HD62.7.P52 1984   658'.022   83-16821
ISBN 0-471-89129-0

Printed in the United States of America

10 9 8 7 6 5 4 3 2

PREFACE

While we have written this book for students in the classroom, we have also written this book for prospective small business entrepreneurs and for those persons already operating small business firms who desire to improve the overall efficiency of their operations. The format of this book enables the classroom instructor to use one of several teaching methods: lecture, lecture with case assignment before class, case discussion in class, or a combined case-lecture method in class.

As in the first and second editions, the approach is practice oriented and the writing style is informal. But in this edition we have expanded our presentation of the techniques and methods used in day-to-day management of the small business enterprise. Responding to suggestions by users, we have made one basic change in the chapter sequence—by moving the chapter on sources of funds from Chapter 7 to Chapter 5. The chapter arrangement for the remainder of the book is that of the second edition.

Chapter 15, on "Computers in the Small Business," has been substantially expanded to reflect the growing significance of computers for the small business owner. The section on minicomputers and microcomputers has been enlarged, and a section has been included detailing the factors that should be evaluated when the small business owner selects a computer for the firm.

Many new features appear in each chapter of this edition to aid student comprehension of small business management.

Learning Goals are stated at the beginning of each chapter alerting the reader to major points in the discussion.

Key Words are listed at the start of each chapter. Each key word is highlighted in boldface type the first time it is defined in the text.

Small Business Profiles focus on successful entrepreneurs.

Special Interest Features pertain to some specific facet of small business management that requires further discussion.

Summary of Key Points is presented for each chapter to aid the students in reviewing chapter material. Each summary highlights the major concepts presented in the chapter.

Furthermore, new Student Projects have been added for a number of chapters, and Discussion Questions have been revised to stress the major concepts presented in the chapter. A Glossary has been included in which the key words are defined.

Approximately 50 percent of the cases are new to this edition. These cases are based on "real-world" small business situations and illustrate points made in the text discussion. Moreover, new or expanded topics, illustrations, and applications have been incorporated throughout the text. Some of these are listed here.

Stress and the small business owner

Time management

Women entrepreneurs

Results-oriented performance appraisal

Laws to aid small business owners engaged in international marketing

Government regulations

Government action to reduce paperwork load on small business owners

Impact of small business on the U.S. economy

Section 8 (a) of the Small Business Administration Act

Types of franchise arrangements

Location analysis for manufacturers

Purchasing procedures

Make or buy analysis

Value analysis

Impact of computers on people

Criteria for selecting a computer

Computer security

Trade associations

Alternative forms of international marketing

Methods of preparing advertising budgets

The prime interest rate and its relation to interest rates charged to small business

How to apply for a bank loan

Software capabilities for financial and inventory control

Product liability

Lie detectors

The Small Business Administration Office of Advocacy

Of special interest to students and entrepreneurs alike should be the list of Small Business Administration publications contained at the end of each chapter. We have listed both the "free" and the "for sale" publications pertinent to each chapter. In addition, a complete listing of the SBA publications and the field offices from which the publications may be obtained are found in the Appendix.

Finally, acknowledgment and thanks is given to those reviewers who have contributed valuable suggestions to this project: Professor George Eddy, University of Texas (Austin); Professor Roy Knab, Center for Business, New York Institute of Technology; Professor Jack Brandmier, San Francisco State University; Professor Edward Hamburg, Gloucester County College; Professor Joseph Barton-Dobenin, Kansas State University (Manhattan).

Hal B. Pickle
Royce L. Abrahamson

CONTENTS

SMALL
BUSINESS
MANAGEMENT

ENTREPRENEURSHIP, SMALL BUSINESS OWNERSHIP, AND FRANCHISING

SECTION ONE

CHAPTER ONE

ENTREPRENEURSHIP

After reading this chapter, you will understand:

1. What personal characteristics contribute to small business success.
2. What a small business is and that there are various ways of defining a small business.
3. The role and scope of small business in our private enterprise economy.
4. The advantages and limitations of the small business enterprise.
5. That there are many rewards, in addition to profit, that entrepreneurs derive from small business ownership.
6. That many small businesses are a family operation.
7. That a commitment to social activity and community involvement is required of both the entrepreneur and spouse in many small businesses.

KEY WORDS

Entrepreneur

Drive

Mental ability

Creative thinking

Analytical thinking

Human relations ability

Empathy

Communications ability

Technical knowledge

Committee on Economic Development (CED)

Small business

Small Business Administration (SBA)

Small business owner–manager

Section 8 (a) program

Regulatory Flexibility Act

Stress

SMALL BUSINESS PROFILE

Six Who Succeeded: The Long-Distance Man

No one, but no one, had ever taken on Ma Bell and won. So, in 1968, William McGowan decided to try. Says he: "The fact that it had never been done before made the idea all the more irresistible."

McGowan, 54, is the founder and head of MCI Communication Corp., and the idea was to compete with the world's largest company in the lucrative long-distance telephone market. And compete he has. MCI's revenues for 1983 are expected to top $1 billion. McGowan's stock alone is worth an estimated $96 million.

The leathery-faced McGowan was a self-employed management consultant when he began MCI with some $50,000 of his own money. He used it to buy the rights to the name of Microwave Communications Inc., a dormant Chicago firm with a yellowing 1963 proposal before the Federal Communications Commission. The proposition: to build a microwave voice communications link between Chicago and St. Louis.

McGowan had a bigger and bolder ambition: to form such a network nationwide. The fact that the government hadn't sanctioned competition in the long-distance market didn't stop him. Says he: "AT&T had never expressly been given a monopoly in this market. Everyone just thought they had."

In 1969 the FCC approved the Chicago-to-St. Louis link of the MCI network. Meantime, McGowan hit the road in search of capital. Says he: "I went to bankers and venture capitalists. I even hit my brother up for $15,000." He was a fund raiser extraordinaire. Within four years of acquiring MCI, he'd pulled in more than $100 million. He'd also opened the maiden link of his network and, most important, had got the FCC to endorse the concept of nationwide long-distance phone competition. McGowan expanded MCI as fast as he could. It turned its first profit—$345,000—in 1977.

All this came in the face of tough competition from AT&T. It fought MCI in the marketplace, before the FCC, in Congress and the courts. "Why do you think I moved the company to Washington, D.C., half a block from the Federal Communications Commission?" he asks.

AT&T's brawl with MCI has proved expensive for both sides but may be the more costly for Ma Bell. In June 1980, a federal jury in Chicago ruled Ma Bell guilty of antitrust violations and ordered her to pay MCI $1.8 billion in damages—the largest antitrust judgment awarded to a company in U.S. history. The case is under appeal.

Meantime, McGowan keeps to the 70-plus-hour workweeks that have marked his career. A lifelong bachelor, he devotes almost all of his time to MCI. His principal diversion: supervising the renovation of three townhouses he owns overlooking the Potomac in Georgetown, one of which he plans eventually to make his home.

Source   Marlys Harris, "Six Who Succeeded—The Long Distance Man," *Money*, vol. 11, no. 12 (December, 1982), p. 68. Reprinted by special permission, © 1982, Time, Inc.

Owning your own business offers you the opportunity to be independent.

The foundation of America's free enterprise economic system is found in small business. In our country's formative years, nearly all businesses were small. The advent of the Industrial Revolution saw the emergence of large-scale businesses and a corresponding decline in the production of goods and services by small businesses. Nevertheless, small business remains viable and continues to play a principal role in our nation's economy through the substantial contribution made in terms of employment opportunities and technological innovation.

Since the mid-1970s, small business owners have been confronted by problems caused by inflation, regulation, high interest rates, and other factors beyond their control. These conditions do not seem to create a climate for new business ventures. However, Dun & Bradstreet reports that new business incorporations rose to a record of nearly 600,000 in 1981 compared to half that number 10 years earlier.[1] And the number of self-employed Americans has risen to almost 7 million as reported by the Bureau of Labor Statistics. Thus, more and more Americans are deciding that they can achieve the quality of life they desire through small business ownership.

---

[1] *Wall Street Journal,* September 27, 1982, p. 22.

FIGURE 1–1

Entrepreneurs organize and operate small businesses for profit and psychological satisfaction.

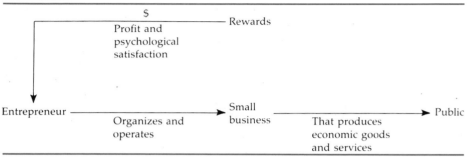

The individuals who initiate these businesses are called entrepreneurs. An **entrepreneur** is "one who organizes a business undertaking, assuming risks, for the sake of profit."[2] Entrepreneurs are the cornerstone of the American private enterprise system. They play a leading role in the identification of new ideas and products, which results in new business opportunities. Furthermore, entrepreneurs bring together the funds needed to initiate the business, organize it so that it is direct toward goal accomplishment, and often play the leading or major role in managing the business operation to provide economic goods and services for the public. Without a doubt, the success of the United States has resulted, in large measure, from the energy and the innovations of its entrepreneurs operating in an environment of private enterprise.

Thus, small business owners are in every way entrepreneurs. They assume risk, and usually the owners of small businesses organize all aspects of their business. Perhaps the only difference between small business owners and entrepreneurs, in view of our definition, is in terms of profit. For example, the psychological satisfaction owners derive from their business often rivals the profit satisfaction. (See Fig. 1–1.)

SPECIAL INTEREST FEATURE

What It Takes to Succeed in Business

I received a letter from Ed Sawicki, national sales manager of Dun and Bradstreet, pointing out that the small to medium-sized business is the backbone of this country, with large companies accounting for the muscle.

We hear so much hue and cry, so much clamor about big companies getting bigger, we tend to forget that this is basically a country of relatively small businesses.

---

[2]Webster's *New World Dictionary of the American Language.*

Forty-five percent of all business establishments reporting to Dun and Bradstreet have fewer than four employees; 30 percent have from four to 10; 11 percent, 10 to 20; and another 7 percent, from 20 to 50. Most of the working people in this country are employed in small companies.

And more people than ever before are going into specialty businesses. I have a friend, Bob Peterson, who is president of Perma Craft Boats in Hollywood, Florida. For a quarter-century, his company has been building 32-foot boats, one at a time. He is not interested in building more. He can turn out 12 handmade boats a year, which he then sells to boat nuts. They're good boats, exceptionally well built, as I said, by hand. Bob's wife does the interior decorating, and his kids work in the shop.

BE A CRAFTSMAN

It's a small business when you think of some of the giants in the field, but it's what Bob wants. For years, he's been trying to build himself a boat, and it gets his special loving care. But by the time it's finished, some customer has come along who wants it, and so Bob starts another one. I don't think he makes much money, but he's comfortable and happy doing the one thing in the world he most enjoys. He doesn't have the problems connected with big companies, and he can go fishing when he feels like it.

There's a big market out there for good ideas and good products.

Willie Loman in *Death of a Salesman* said, "You gotta know the territory." Willie was wrong. You gotta know the people, and you gotta give them what they most want.

My old friend, Irwin Premack, president of Premack Research Corporation of St. Petersburg, Florida, tells of the time when South Florida had been badly overbuilt with condominiums. Everyone and his brother was building a multistory condominium. It was like a crazy gold rush. Of course, the slump came along, and all the look-alike condos selling in the 30- to 50-thousand-dollar price range (this was some years ago!) lay inert upon the marketplace like so many rotting fish. You couldn't even rent them.

A newcomer came along, right in the middle of the worst market in years, and constructed a $20-million building full of condominiums and, as Irv put it, sold every one of them before the paint had dried.

KNOW YOUR PROSPECTS

How had he wrought such a seeming miracle? Before he did anything, he made a marketing study, and in doing so, he found a segment of the market that had gone begging. All the other apartments were in the same price range, a modest range as condominiums went at the time. The newcomer's units started at $250,000. By shrewd market analysis he found a sizable number of people in the area who wanted to live like millionaires for the simple reason that they were millionaires. But they didn't want the headaches of a mansion: grounds, pool, maintenance, security guards, and so on. With a quarter-of-a-million-dollar condominium, they could live like the wealthy people they were without the encumbrances.

Understanding the psychology of people can be of tremendous help in business. It can go a long way toward getting people to try your product or service. Of course, only real quality will bring repeat business.

As the size and complexity of the country grows, it offers more, not less, opportunity to those who want to go into business for themselves. There's always room for excellence. It's true that the cost of going into business has risen along with the costs of everything else, but it is still possible, depending on the nature of the enterprise, to begin quite small. If you've got a good thing, it will grow.

SUCCESS REQUIRES EFFORT

Remember, too, that you don't have to come up with a new or revolutionary idea; just improve on an old one or just be as good as the successful people in the old one, no matter what it might be. It may mean long, tedious hours, probably a seven-day week, 52 weeks a year, no fringe benefits, no pension and profit-sharing plans, no so-called security. But if you make it go, at least you're your own boss.

Risk? Yes, lots of it. Your chances of failing the first time are formidable. But they're better odds than you can find in Las Vegas, and thousands of people invest millions out there every week.

Source   Earl Nightingale, "What It Takes to Succeed in Business," *Salesman's Opportunity*, vol. 119, no. 6 (May 1982), p. 25. Copyright © 1982 Nightingale-Conant Corporation, Chicago. Reprinted from *Salesman's Opportunity* Magazine, 6 N. Michigan Avenue, Chicago, Ill. 60602.

PERSONALITY CHARACTERISTICS THAT CONTRIBUTE TO BUSINESS SUCCESS

Extensive research has been conducted in an attempt to identify the personality characteristics that contribute to business success. To date, no general agreement has resulted from this search. One research study of 97 small business managers did produce a correlation of .63 between success and five general characteristics: (1) drive, (2) mental ability, (3) human relations ability, (4) communications ability, and (5) technical knowledge.[3] (See Fig. 1–2.)

[3] Hal B. Pickle, *Personality and Success: An Evaluation of Personal Characteristics of Successful Small Business Managers* (Washington, D.C: Small Business Administration, 1964).

FIGURE 1–2

Contributors to small business success.

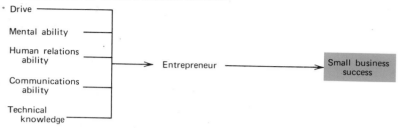

Drive

In general terms, **drive** is a person's motivation toward a task. It is comprised of such personality traits as responsibility, vigor, initiative, persistence, and ambition. Entrepreneurs must exert considerable effort in establishing and managing the business. The small business owners who conscientiously plan, organize, direct, and control their small business are more likely to have a successful business than the owner–managers who are lax and approach the management of the business haphazardly.

Of course, many entrepreneurs work long hours in their businesses at menial tasks, such as cooking in a restaurant, and still do not succeed because they fail to perform the more difficult management functions of planning, organizing, directing, and controlling. In fact, some small business managers perform menial chores in order to avoid managerial tasks because they feel inadequate or lack the knowledge necessary for functioning as an effective manager. By staying busy in the menial tasks, they convince themselves they don't have time to perform many management functions. It is not unusual to hear such comments as "I know I should be doing that, but I just don't have time."

Mental Ability

Mental ability that contributes to the succcess of the small business entrepreneur–manager consists of overall intelligence (IQ), creative thinking ability, and analytical thinking ability. Small business managers must be reasonably intelligent, able to adapt their actions to the needs of the business in various situations (**creative thinking**), and able to engage in analysis of various problems and situations in order to deal with them (**analytical thinking**). (See Fig. 1–3.)

Small business managers who are able to recognize the unique problems of their business and create innovative ways of solving them are much better equipped to succeed in small business than the individuals who are unable to perform these functions adequately. For example, some managers in retail

FIGURE 1–3
Mental ability is important to the entrepreneur.

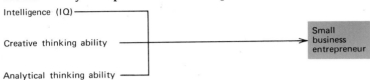

establishments use their intelligence to create unique promotional campaigns that are very effective in increasing patronage of their stores.

This is not to imply that a person with a high IQ will automatically be a success. Instead, it suggests that adequate intelligence, creative thinking, and analytical thinking are among the contributors to a person's success in small business management. Many people who have less than average intelligence have succeeded in small business, and many people with very high levels of intelligence have failed in small business ventures.

Human Relations Ability

Personality factors—such as emotional stability, skill in interpersonal relations, sociability, consideration, and tactfulness—are all important contributors to the entrepreneur's success in small business. One of the most important facets of **human relations ability** is **empathy.** By being empathetic, owner–managers show their ability to "put themselves in someone else's place" and know how the other person feels and perceives the situation.

Small business managers must maintain good relations with their customers if they are to create a relationship that will encourage customers to continue to patronize their business. They must also develop and continue good relations with their employees if they are to motivate them to perform their jobs at high levels of efficiency. In addition, they must be aware of the needs and motives of customers if they are to train employees adequately to retain good customer relations.

The entrepreneur who strives to develop and maintain good human relations with customers, employees, suppliers, creditors, and the community at large is much more likely to succeed in business than the individual who makes no effort to practice good human relations.

Communications Ability

Communications ability is the skill to convey both written and oral information effectively so that understanding is created between the sender and receiver. For example, the entrepreneur may give verbal instructions directly to an employee and assume that the message is understood. However, communication between the two may not have occurred because of psychological semantic barriers that cause understanding to be blocked.

Psychological barriers include various forms of incomplete information and problems revolving around interpersonal relationships. To illustrate, a psychological barrier exists when employees filter out negative information and pass on to the entrepreneur only the positive information they perceive is desired by the owner.

Semantic barriers occur as a result of the different meanings of words for people. Semantic barriers may arise in a number of ways—for example, when words are used that have many meanings and the sender assumes that they are understood in the way he or she understands them, or when terms are used with which the receiver is not familiar, such as technical terms.

Effective written communications are much more difficult to achieve than effective oral communications. The receiver does not have the sender's tone of voice and facial expressions to provide meaning. Also, there is not immediate feedback from the receiver to the sender to aid in clarification. To illustrate, a teacher might walk into class and in a pleasant voice, with a smile, say, "This class can go jump in the lake." Very few students would be offended although they might be puzzled. On the other hand, if the instructor wrote the same message on the blackboard and left it for the class to discover, the instructor would probably receive a wide range of reactions, from anger to amusement.

Small business managers who effectively communicate with customers, employees, suppliers, and creditors will be more likely to succeed than the managers who cannot. For example, a business firm may send a form letter to good customers who have let a payment deadline pass that states, "We have not received your monthly payment; please remit at once." The letter is intended only to remind the customers; however, they may interpret it as a dun and an implication that they are irresponsible in meeting their obligations. Some individuals may be offended enough to cease trading with the business, and the owner would never know why.

Technical Knowledge

If the small business is to succeed, it must offer an acceptable product or service. For example, in an eating establishment, the entrepreneur may be highly motivated, practice good human relations, be an effective communicator, and possess high mental ability. However, if quality food and service are not provided, the business will fail.

Technical knowledge is the one ability that most people can acquire if they put forth the effort. For example, a wise course of action for an entrepreneur who plans to open a restaurant is to obtain "hands-on" experience by working in that type of environment for a period of time to learn the technical aspects of the business, such as food preparation, equipment usage, and sources of supply.

Small business entrepreneurs who have high levels of drive, mental ability, human relations ability, communications ability, and technical knowledge stand a greater likelihood of success than their counterparts who possess low levels of these same characteristics.

WHAT IS A SMALL BUSINESS?

Answers to the question, "What is a small business?" would likely reflect a wide range of understandings. No doubt some would consider a business small if it had no more than a specified number of employees (i.e., 5 or 10). Others would likely believe that a small business is one that limits its scope of operations to the local market area. Others frequently classify businesses as small by the nature of the firm, such as the local drugstore, clothing store, service station, barbershop, or jewelry store.

Committee on Economic Development

To provide a framework of understanding of what a small business is, two of the more common definitions are presented. The **Committee on Economic Development (CED)** offers a definition that states that a business will be classed as a **small business** if it meets two or more of the following criteria:

1. Management is independent. (Usually the managers are also owners.)
2. Capital is supplied and ownership is held by an individual or a small group.
3. The area of operations is mainly local. Workers and owners are in one home community. Markets need not be local.
4. Relative size within the industry—the business is small when compared to the biggest units in its field. The size of the top bracket varies greatly so that what might seem large in one field would be definitely small in another.[4]

Small Business Administration

The **Small Business Administration (SBA)** was created by the Small Business Act of 1953 and is an independent agency of the federal government. The purpose of the SBA is to assist and counsel the small business owner–manager. The SBA attempts to help people get into business and stay in business. The definition of a small business used by the SBA is one that is independently owned and operated and not dominant in its field of operation.

The CED and the SBA definitions are similar. Both use qualitative guidelines for size classification. Each emphasizes independent ownership and management and relative small size in the field of operation as guidelines for

---

[4]*Meeting the Special Problems of Small Business* (New York: Committee for Economic Development, 1947), p. 14.

defining a business as small. These guidelines are appropriate for our definition of a "small business" as used in this text.

In addition, the SBA uses a quantitative size classification to determine if a firm is eligible for a loan and other assistance through the SBA. These standards are defined in Chapter 5, "Sources of Funds."

The Small Business Owner–Manager

In the text discussions, we refer to the manager, management, owner, owner–manager, entrepreneur, and entrepreneur–manager. Whenever such references are made, they are describing the **small business owner–manager,** the person in charge of a small business in either of the following situations: (1) where the owner is also the manager or (2) where the manager is a paid employee.

IMPACT OF SMALL BUSINESS IN THE ECONOMY OF THE UNITED STATES

Small business contributes significantly to our economy. The SBA classifies approximately 97 percent of all businesses in the United States—sole proprietorships, partnerships, corporations, part-time businesses, and unincorporated professional activities—as small businesses.

Small enterprise runs the gamut from corner news-vending to developing optical fibers. Small business people sell gasoline, flowers, and coffee-to-go. They publish magazines, haul freight, teach languages, and program computers. They make wines, motion pictures, and high-fashion clothes. They build new homes and restore old ones. They repair plumbing, fix appliances, recycle metals, and sell used cars. They drive taxicabs, run cranes, and fly helicopters. They wildcat for oil, quarry sand and gravel, and mine exotic ores. They forge, cast, weld, photoengrave, electroplate, and anodize. They also invent anti-pollution devices, quality control mechanisms, energy saving techniques, microelectronic systems—a list would go on for volumes.[5]

Nearly a third of all small businesses are in service industries, and nearly a quarter are in retailing. As a source of employment, small businesses provide jobs for about 50 percent of the American work force excluding farm employment. In terms of output, small businesses account for approximately 40 percent of the gross national product. The following facts give us some additional evidence of the dramatic influence of small business.

Small firms account for nearly $8 out of every $10 made by construction firms.

---

[5] *Report to the President, America's Small Business Economy* (Washington, D.C.: Agenda for Action, White House Commission on Small Business, April 1980), p. 16.

Small firms account for nearly $7 out of every $10 made by retailers and wholesalers.

The livelihood of more than 100 million Americans is provided directly or indirectly by small business.

Businesses with fewer than 20 employees create two out of every three new jobs. About 80 percent of new jobs were created by firms with 100 or fewer employees.

Nine out of 10 small businesses have fewer than 10 employees.

Four out of 5 U.S. businesses are sole proprietorships, and nearly all of these are small businesses.

Small businesses create more jobs than medium- and large-scale organizations. For example, in the period 1969–1976, medium- and large-scale concerns provided only about 13 percent of all new jobs created in the private sector. However, small businesses accounted for nearly 87 percent of all new jobs created in the private sector, and the majority of the new jobs were generated by the very small companies! The need for small business to play a more important role in generating new jobs is emphasized in the following statement issued by Congress.

The future of small business in our country is going to have a great deal to do with helping the United States economy remain strong as we come down after 25 years of cornucopian growth to a rather slow-growing economy. We are going to have to look to small business to pick up some of the slack to provide not only more jobs, but jobs which over the next decade absorb all the energy and talents of the biggest, best-educated, and potentially the most capable labor force in U.S. history.[6]

Another mark on our economy has been the contribution made by individual inventors and small company owners. An Office of Management and Budget study reports that over 50 percent of the major technological advances in the twentieth century came from these sources despite the fact that they received only about 3.5 percent of all federal research and development dollars. Some of the inventions that have resulted in new major industries and growth companies include:

Xerography	Frequency modulation radio
Insulin	Self-winding wristwatch
Vacuum tube	Helicopter
Penicillin	Mercury dry cell
Power steering	Shrink-proof knitted wear

[6]"Future of Small Business in America," *A Report of the Subcommittee on Antitrust, Consumers, and Employment Committee on Small Business* (Washington, D.C.: U.S. House of Representatives, November 9, 1978), p. 4.

Zipper	Kodachrome
Automatic transmission	Air conditioning
Jet engine	Polaroid camera
Cellophane	Ball-point pen

WOMEN ENTREPRENEURS

Today women are playing an increasingly important role in the labor force, and it is likely that this role will remain prominent. A significant aspect of this emerging role of women in the work force is their growing interest in entrepreneurship. The following facts give us some of the characteristics of the entrepreneurial woman.

1. Women-owned firms account for 7.1 percent of all business firms excluding large corporations.
2. These firms account for 6.6 percent of all sales.
3. Women who own businesses in the United States are likely to be first-time entrepreneurs with managerial experience who have sought to prepare themselves for their tasks through education.
4. Most of the women-owned businesses are small, and slightly more than half are operated from locations other than a residence.
5. More than 70 percent of these businesses have no full-time or part-time employees.
6. Women business owners are experienced as workers and managers. They report a median of 15 years as paid business employees and a median of 7 years of managerial experience.
7. More than three fourths have education beyond high school, with nearly twice as many concentrating on business subjects compared to other fields of study.
8. Nearly half (45 percent) of all women business owners are in the service sector of the economy, and another 30 percent are in retail trade.[7]

Some of the problems confronted by women entrepreneurs include difficulty in entering markets and obtaining commercial loans, government contracts, and management assistance. Women entrepreneurs also feel that many male entrepreneurs are not ready to accept them as equals. Nevertheless, an increasing number of women are opting to take a chance and start their own business despite these problems.

---

[7] *The State of Small Business: A Report of the President Transmitted to the Congress* (Washington, D.C.: Small Business Administration, March 1982), p. 49.

Consider the following successful female entrepreneur, Bette Graham.[8] The electric typewriter, introduced in the early 1950s, made the job of typing easier and faster. However, correcting typing errors was difficult. A young secretary and amateur artist, Bette Graham, discovered that she could use paint to cover the typing errors. Within 5 years, her product, Mistake Out, was in great demand. Later, the name of the product was changed to Liquid Paper.

At first, Graham and her son spent weekends filling orders from her kitchen. Soon they were selling 100 bottles a month by marketing Liquid Paper to office suppy dealers. Within 10 years, the Liquid Paper Corporation was producing more than 500 bottles a minute of the correction fluid for sales worldwide.

MINORITY-OWNED BUSINESSES

Minority-owned businesses account for approximately 5.7 percent of the total businesses in the United States, and sales of these businesses amount to about 3.5 percent of total sales. The minority-owned firms are concentrated in retail trade, services, and nonindustrial construction. These types of businesses are characterized by low growth and low profit margin.

Some of the problems faced by minority entrepreneurs are inadequate capital, insufficient management training, lack of opportunities to buy businesses, and difficulty of marketing outside the minority communities.[9]

The success of George Johnson is the story of one from among many successful black entrepreneurs.[10] Though familiar now, beauty care products designed especially for blacks were a novelty and much in demand in the early 1950s. George Johnson is given credit for recognizing this market. His introduction to the beauty aids business came in 1945, when he went to work for the Fuller Products Company. In 1954 he secured a $250 loan, and with the assistance of his wife and a barber friend, Johnson started his enterprise and sold a product that he had developed, Ultra Wave Hair Culture, from the back of his station wagon. By 1969, Johnson Products had become the largest black-owned manufacturing company in the country and was the first such company to be listed on a major stock exchange. Since then the business has expanded internationally with more than 500 employees producing 150 products.

[8]Example adapted from *A Century of Entrepreneurs* (San Mateo, Calif.: National Federation of Independent Business Research and Education Foundation, 1981). Reprinted with the permission of the National Federation of Independent Business Research and Education Foundation.

[9]*The State of Small Business: A Report of the President Transmitted to the Congress* (Washington, D.C.: Small Business Administration, March 1982), p. 66.

[10]This example was adapted from *A Century of Entrepreneurs* (San Mateo, Calif.: National Federation of Independent Business Research and Education Foundation, 1981). Reprinted with the permission of the National Federation of Independent Business Research and Education Foundation.

The SBA program designed to provide assistance to small businesses owned and operated by economically and socially disadvantaged persons is the **Section 8 (a) program** of the Small Business Act. The purpose of this program is to award noncompetitive contracts to economically and socially disadvantaged small business operators in order to assist them in becoming self-sufficient. Small business owners who participate in the Section 8 (a) program receive management, technical, marketing, and financial assistance.

REWARDS AND ADVANTAGES OF SMALL BUSINESS OWNERSHIP

The small business owner–manager realizes distinct rewards and advantages that are directly related to the size and the form of ownership. We now look at some of these rewards and advantages.

Profit Expectation

A key incentive for many small business entrepreneurs is profit. In this regard, some small businesses are extremely profitable. The *Wall Street Journal* reports, "Small business owners sometimes make far more than Fortune 500 chiefs."[11]

Profit is an important product of the small business because it reflects the success of the firm, it affords owners with the funds that they need to provide for the standard of living they desire for their families, it serves as the salary of the owner–manager, and it provides at least a part of the resources necessary for the stability and growth of the company. To a great extent, small business entrepreneurs control the amount of their income by their managerial expertise. Thus, earning a profit is one of the strongest motivators for initiating a small business. As shown in Figure 1–4, however, profit is certainly not the only reward small business entrepreneurs may receive from a successful small business.

Anticipation of Future Wealth

Many small business entrepreneur–managers work more for the future of their business than for their present well-being. Their dreams of building their business to achieve future wealth and status motivate them and contribute considerable personal satisfaction. Many never realize their dreams, but some do. J. C. Penney, Henry Ford, and King C. Gillette are just a few of the entrepreneurs who saw their small businesses grow into modern corporate giants.

The classic example of the small business owner who turned his company into a corporate giant is H. Ross Perot. Perot started his company, Electronic

---

[11] *Wall Street Journal*, November 8, 1982, p. 25.

FIGURE 1–4
Entrepreneur contributions and rewards.

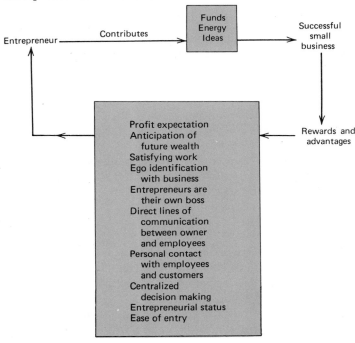

Data Systems, Inc., when he was 32 years old with $1000 and an idea. Just 7 years later, he was worth over $1 billion.

Many small business firms are operated as part-time activities by people who support themselves and often their business by working at other full-time employment. They create and operate these part-time businesses in expectation of creating a full-time business for themselves. Some realize their dreams, and others just go on supporting their part-time businesses for years with income from their full-time employment.

It should be noted that dreams for some people are more satisfying than the actual realization of the dreams. In this sense, small business firms that are not successful may provide considerable satisfaction to their creators for long periods of time.

Satisfying Work

Most people spend a third or more of their waking hours in a work environment. Unfortunately, many people derive little satisfaction from their work. Some dislike their work to the extent that they continually look forward to the weekend, dread the thought of the next workweek, and even develop psychological illnesses resulting from the dislike of their work. Conversely, people who experience a high level of job satisfaction approach their work more positively, demonstrate better physical and mental health, exhibit a higher level of commitment to the firm, and have a more constructive outlook on life in general.

Many small business owners realize a high level of personal satisfaction derived from working in their own business. The owner of a TV repair shop may derive a sense of accomplishment each time a set is repaired. However, the owner may gain even greater satisfaction from the management of the business. The challenge of creating a business and achieving the various tasks involved in its operation and growth can be very exhilarating to many people. As the owner of a small retail apparel shop observed, "The most important thing today is job satisfaction, and each day I find this is a more attainable goal through owning my own business rather than working for someone else. Owning a business provides me with the opportunity for personal achievement and personal fulfillment."

Ego Identification with the Business

Most owners of small businesses started the firms themselves, often as a result of considerable sacrifice and work. As a result, it is understandable that most of them feel a close ego identification with their business. Many entrepreneur–managers feel the firm is, in a sense, an extension of their own being. The authors realized early in their consulting experience with small business firms that any criticism of the operations of the firm had to be handled very tactfully because it was common for the entrepreneur–manager to take strong personal offense.

Almost all small business entrepreneur–managers who have established a successful small business exhibit a very strong sense of personal pride in their business, which is certainly justified. In fact, it is not at all uncommon for the entrepreneur–managers to want their children to carry on the family business because of personal pride.

Entrepreneurs Are Their Own Boss

A strong reason often given by small business owners for choosing to become an entrepreneur is, "I am my own boss." Making management decisions for the business represents a continuing challenge and provides a source of personal satisfaction for the entrepreneur. Entrepreneur–managers, in a real sense, feel that they control their own destiny and do not have to answer to anyone except themselves for their actions. And as we have observed, the rewards they receive are in direct proportion to their level of management performance in the business.

Some small business entrepreneurs have continued to operate their own business for years even though they could have earned considerably more money in the employment of someone else. Thus, the desire to be one's own boss is undoubtedly a primary motivator for these individuals.

Direct Lines of Communication
Between Owner and Employees

Since there is usually only one level of management in the small business enterprise, face-to-face contact is the norm between the manager and the employees when instructions are given or specific problems relating to the business are discussed. The one-to-one communication relationship significantly increases the chances of reducing or eliminating many common communications problems encountered in larger firms. In larger firms, for example, messages ordinarily must pass from the sender through several other persons in the chain of command before the person for whom the communications are intended finally sees or hears them. In this relaying process, messages can easily become distorted or misinterpreted.

Even though lines of communication are short and direct in small businesses, managers must exercise great care in communication. As we have already mentioned, they must be aware that it is quite possible for such common communication problems as semantic barriers, psychological barriers, and selective perception to persist even in face-to-face communication.

Small business owner-managers should recognize these barriers and take advantage of the opportunities they have to avoid them as a result of their strategic position in the communication chain. Furthermore, they should realize that direct oral communication with employees can eliminate much of the confusion or misinterpretation that so often results from written instructions, especially when employee feedback is encouraged.

In the small enterprise, effective use can be made of upward communication from the employees to the owner–manager. The bottom-to-top communication process is an effective method for improving understanding within the organization.

Effective utilization of the short lines of communication will enable the small business owner–managers to reduce many of the human problems caused by faulty communication. On the other hand, poor communication will have a negative influence on the organizational environment and consequently increase human relations problems.

Personal Contact with
Employees and Customers

Small business owners have the opportunity to develop and maintain harmonious working relationships with their employees. With only one level of management, direct interaction is possible between manager and employees. Through this personal relationship, owner–managers and employees have an opportunity to understand each other's position, needs, and wants better. Furthermore, the employees and the manager often work side by side on an informal rather than a formal basis. In this way, each participant learns to respect the other's viewpoints. In the small firm, it is especially vital that all members cooperate to form an effective work team.

One of the particular advantages of the small business firm is that it provides the type of environment in which close, personal customer relationships can be cultivated by the owner–manager. The owner–manager may know customers on a first-name basis, and the manager knows what products they are buying. Customers can be given personal, individualized consideration to fit their specific needs. The small business manager recognizes the value of such relationships to the success of the business. Customers appreciate this personal concern, and it is often a major reason why they patronize a particular business. The manager is also in a better position to handle customer complaints directly. By utilizing the opportunities they have for personal contact and by dealing fairly with their customers, small business owners can do much to ensure the success of the firm.

Centralized Decision Making

When there is only one level of management, the small business owner is directly involved in making all decisions affecting the firm. Whereas the manager of the larger firm often must refer matters to higher management for a decision to be made, the owner–manager can make decisions quickly—an especially important advantage when time is a critical factor for reaching a decision. By being able to respond quickly, the owner–manager can often take advantage of unexpected business opportunities that require a quick response.

For example, a small Texas firm was able to purchase the unwanted inventory of a large textile mill at an extremely low price. The mill offered the popular fabric at a 38 percent discount with 30-day credit terms. The small business bought 1000 yards and within two weeks turned them into finished goods and sold them. Because the firm was able to respond quickly, it was able to use part of the proceeds from selling the finished goods to pay for the fabric.[12]

Entrepreneurial Status

In most communities, the entrepreneur–manager ranks high in the work status hierarchy. There is a wide range of status even within the small business group. For example, the principal stockholder–president of the local bank is usually assigned a higher status in the community than the service station owner–manager. In spite of this range of status, the community usually perceives a higher status for the small business entrepreneur group than most forms of blue-collar and white-collar employment. In fact, in many small communities, small business owners are often assigned to the top of the status scale.

It should also be pointed out that perceived status is more important to an individual's satisfaction than actual status assigned by other people. Many

---

[12] *Wall Street Journal*, March 13, 1980, p. 24.

small business entrepreneur–managers feel they have high levels of status in their communities and derive considerable satisfaction from this impression, regardless of whether or not it is actually true.

Ease of Entry

An attractive feature of the small business operations, particularly the single proprietorship, is the ease with which one can go into business. All that is required to open the doors for business is a location, any special operating licenses required by city or state government, and some capital. No other restrictions are normally placed on entrance into small business.

SOME LIMITATIONS OF SMALL BUSINESS OWNERSHIP

As a means of presenting an objective, balanced perspective of small business ownership, some limitations are discussed here.

Lack of Specialization

Large firms have the financial resources available to hire individuals who possess the expertise needed to staff the variety of positions in the firm. Accountants maintain company financial records, salespeople make contacts to sell the company's products, and personnel staff members actively recruit the type of qualified persons needed to fill job vacancies.

In the small business, the owner–managers generally perform all or most of the functions because their monetary resources are limited. Hence, they must be generalists rather than specialists. They must be familiar with all phases of the firm's operations—general management, accounting, sales management, production management, personnel management, and any other necessary functions. Because they have many duties to carry out, they frequently do not have enough time to devote to long-range planning of the firm. Instead, most of their time is spent in dealing with the current day's activity or crisis. Thus, a disadvantage to many small firms is lack of resources for hiring and utilizing specialists in the functional areas of the business.

Confining, Long Hours of Work

Considerations on the positive side of owning a business include being one's own boss and profit expectations. One disadvantage is that managers of the small business must do most of the work themselves. For example, entrepreneur–managers are usually the first to arrive in the morning and the last to leave at night. If they become ill, they cannot call in sick to their boss. They cannot take off a few days without making special arrangements for someone to operate the business for them.

It is common for most firms to be open 6 days a week, and many are open

7. Owners work long hours—for example, the owner of a steak house who remains open from 11 A.M. to 9 P.M. 7 days a week. Added to this must be the time spent in preparation prior to opening and after closing.

Risk of Funds

Although there is the advantage of profit making, there is the risk of losing funds. Because funds invested in the firm are largely personal funds or borrowed funds, the owner may be personally liable for any and all debts. Hence, it is possible that the small business owner–manager may not only lose a lifetime's personal savings but may also build up liabilities that will take years to repay.

COMMON PROBLEMS OF SMALL BUSINESS FIRMS

A successful business offers too many monetary and psychological rewards to owners for them to be discouraged by the historical failure rate of small businesses. When a "going out of business" decision is made, it clearly was not the entrepreneur's objective when the business opened its doors. And the question that must be addressed is, Why did the business fail?

In this section, we examine some of the common problems of small business ownership. We were apprehensive about discussing the topic of business failure early in the text. However, we are convinced that the identification and analysis of the causes of these problems will enable the prospective small business manager to develop the management knowledge and skills necessary to avoid these problems in their firms.

Each year, Dun and Bradstreet reports on the causes of business failure for all sizes of businesses, and these causes are shown in Figure 1–5. As the data

FIGURE 1–5
Some common causes of business failure.

Causes		Percent of Total Failures
Inadequate management		94.8
Lack of experience in line	14.9	
Lack of managerial experience	16.1	
Unbalanced experience	19.7	
Incompetence	44.1	
Neglect		0.8
Fraud		0.4
Disaster		0.5
Reason unknown		3.5

Source Dun & Bradstreet.

indicate, over 90 percent of the business failures were directly attributed to the owners' lack of managerial skill. Inadequate management was demonstrated through lack of business experience and through incompetence. Only a small percentage of business failures are attributed to neglect, fraud, or disaster. The cause for a small percentage of failures was not available.

Inadequate Management

In today's dynamic business environment, entrepreneurs must be alert to rapidly changing conditions. For example, owner–managers must recognize and react to variables that impact on their specific firm, such as consumer habits, inflation, availability of energy, and technological change.

Failure to identify and respond to changing social, economic, and environmental conditions will lead to serious problems or eventual failure of the firm. A number of problems faced by small business managers caused by inadequate management are discussed in the following sections.

Lack of Experience in Line

Sometimes owner–managers may lack experience in the line of business they enter. They may have a strong background in one line of business but be unsuccessful in another owing to their unfamiliarity with the specific problems of the new line of business. A case in point is the mortician who sold his mortuary business and purchased a jewelry store. Within a year the jewelry store closed. The primary cause of this unsuccessful business venture was that the owner lacked experience in this completely different line of business.

Lack of Management Experience

Another form of inexperience is shown by a lack of management experience. There is a vast difference between being the best machinist, mechanic, or salesperson and being able to manage a machine shop, an auto repair shop, or a retail store. Whereas the manager of the firm usually has a specific job skill, the possession of a particular job skill in no way guarantees success in the new role as manager. Without proper management training, the skills and techniques necessary for effective management will not likely be attained.

Overconcentration of Experience

An overconcentration of experience in one function may present a problem to the small firm owner–manager. Owner–managers must have the ability to view the firm conceptually. This means they should be able to perceive the need for, interrelationship of, and contribution of each activity of the firm. If owner–managers concentrate a major portion of their time and energy on the one function that is their interest and speciality—either sales, production, or finance—and neglect the others, this approach will likely have an adverse effect on the total firm. For example, managers may focus their efforts on sales. In order to complete a sale, they may promise delivery of merchandise by certain dates when they know the firm does not have the productive capacity to meet such deadlines. When the firm is unable to make a delivery on the scheduled date, customers become irritated and may even cease doing business with the firm. Thus, small business managers must be aware that the health and vitality of the firm depend in large measure on giving balanced attention to all functions of the firm. In addition, this example underscores the need for all business managers to be honest with their customers. Ethical dealings with customers help to build repeat sales and enhance the small business owner's image in the business community.

Incompetence of Management
The major hazard of the small firm is the incompetence of the manager. Owner–managers are incompetent when they do not possess the leadership ability and knowledge necessary to operate their own firms.

Consequences of Inadequate Management

The causes of inadequate management discussed earlier—lack of experience in the line of business, lack of managerial experience, overconcentration of experience, and management incompetence—may be evidenced in various ways in the life of a company. If owner–managers lack proper management skills and knowledge, they may be unable to avoid such conditions for the company as (1) weak competitive position, (2) lack of proper inventory control, (3) inadequate credit control, (4) low sales volume, and (5) poor location.

Weak Competitive Position
Competition is the bulwark of our economy. Firms that cannot efficiently compete in such areas as services offered, prices charged, or quality of merchandise sold definitely have difficulty surviving. For example, a small restaurant manager may lower the price of the lunches served in order to match lower prices charged by competitors. However, as a result of lowering the price, the manager may have to serve smaller portions. If this action is needed to remain competitive, the outlook for the firm is bleak. Because most business firms and especially small businesses must depend on repeat patronage for survival and growth, reducing the size of portions or lowering the quality of the product will surely lessen patronage.

Inadequate Inventory Control
As small business managers must have general management skill to operate the total business, they may not possess some of the specialized and technical skills required for proper management of the firm, such as control of inventory. If too large an inventory is in stock, the result is that too much of the owner's capital is tied up or there is the possibility of inventory loss through spoilage or obsolescence. Where insufficient levels of inventory are stocked,

merchandise is not available to meet customer demand. For example, a farm equipment dealer in a small town made only a minimum effort to maintain control of his inventory. Consequently, he had no idea of stock availability or which were the high turnover items. When customers needed parts, they usually required them immediately. However, the equipment dealer was normally out of stock for most items, but would order the parts from the manufacturer, a process requiring several days for delivery. Because customers could not wait for replacement parts, they were forced to go elsewhere to fill their needs. As a result of the farm equipment dealer's policy on inventory, he lost many sales and the result was that the firm went out of business.

Lax Credit Controls

A concern of the small business manager is whether to extend credit. Firms that do grant credit must protect against the practice of extending too much credit. One small auto repair garage had at one time $10,000 worth of accounts receivable on the books. Much of the credit had been extended to "friends" of the owner. When bills came due, most were never collected because the friends had disappeared. Even though it was difficult or impossible for the owner to collect on these accounts, he could not postpone payment of his bills. Fortunately, the firm was able to survive. Survival was made possible by a reversal of credit policy. The owner no longer extends any credit. All sales are for cash only. And though the owner was uncertain as to the effect this policy would have on his customers, the results have been positive. Today, the firm is on sound financial ground.

Low Sales Volume

For all lines of business—manufacturing, wholesaling, retailing, construction, and commercial service—inadequate sales represent a common problem of the small firm. Income for the firm is generated by sales. Without income, the result is obvious—failure of the business. Many reasons contribute to a poor sales record. Some of the most commonly identified factors include a poor location, inferior products, ineffective advertising, prices out of line with those of competitors, and poor service.

Poor Location

Site selection frequently is not accorded the attention it should receive. Too often, a location is selected for some superficial reason, such as the availability of a building to rent or to buy, closeness of a facility to one's home, heavy traffic flow, or any other of a myriad of reasons. Yet none of these reasons may be the salient locational factors necessary to help make the business a success. For example, a heavy flow of pedestrian traffic past a site does not guarantee that shoppers will drop in, much less purchase merchandise. It is possible that the traffic flow is heavy simply because people are rushing by on their way to a bus stop or to their place of work and do not have time to stop and shop.

Neglect

Whereas only a small percentage of firms fail because of personal neglect, neglect is a particular problem of the small business owner–manager. Common reasons for personal neglect include improper use of time, poor health, laziness, marital problems, or apathy. Sometimes managers become too involved and devote too much time to community or other outside activities. Though these activities have merit, owner–managers must be careful not to place these activities ahead of the firm's interest. The owner–managers should establish priorities for themselves relative to their business. They must keep in mind the objectives of the firm and not become easily diverted by too many outside activities or disenchanted by minor business or personal setbacks.

Fraud

Fraud is the deliberate misrepresentation of the status of the business by the owner–manager in order to deceive others. Some means by which fraud is committed include using a misleading name for the company, issuing false and misleading financial statements, and disposing of the assets of the firm in an irregular manner.

Disaster

There are some circumstances over which the owner may have little or no control. Natural disasters, such as an earthquake, flood, or hurricane may wipe out the small business owner. Hurricane Agnes, in June of 1972, was the most destructive storm in U.S. history. Some $3 billion in property damage was reported, with many thousands of businesses damaged or destroyed. Hurricane Frederick caused some $2 billion damage along the Gulf coast in 1979. In May 1983, Coalinga, California was struck by a devastating earthquake, causing millions of dollars in damage to business firms and residences. Fire, labor problems, burglary, and theft of merchandise by employees are further examples of types of disasters that confront the small business owner. Some specific occurrences of disaster affecting businesses follow.

A pawn shop suffered some $6000 in damages to the building when the driver of a stolen car lost control of the vehicle and crashed into the show window.

A lawn mower repair-rental-sales firm burned on Christmas weekend, causing $25,000 damage to the store building, some 50 lawn mowers, tools, and accessories.

The bookkeeper of a small restaurant supply firm was arrested and charged with embezzling $23,591 over a 10-month period.

Insurance coverage and bonding of employees can provide some measure of protection against these occurrences and thus ease some of the burden of financial loss.

Government Regulations and Paperwork

Although not a specific cause of failure identified in the Dun & Bradstreet report and clearly not a problem limited to small businesses, the growing number of government regulations and required reports is placing a disproportionately heavier burden on the small business, due in large measure to their limited financial and personnel resources. The report prepared by the White House Commission on Small Business emphasized this point: "The most maddening obstacles to operating a small business are the inappropriate federal regulations and the overwhelming, often incomprehensible reporting requirements that go with them."[13]

Small business owners realize that some government regulation is necessary to maintain an orderly society. However, we have seen a dramatic upsurge in the number of regulations, particularly in the areas of affirmative action, hiring, energy conservation, and protection for consumers, workers, and the environment.[14] Currently, some 90 agencies issue thousands of new regulations annually, all of which have a major impact on the small business. One study on this critical subject noted the following impact in Small Business.

One of the threats to the continued existence of small firms is the requirement for major capital expenditures to meet environmental or workplace safety standards. Less frequent, but no less serious, are regulations that reduce the market for a firm's product, such as a ban on a product, or a performance standard that precludes the use of the product for its normal market application.[15]

The impact is particularly noted in the foundry industry. Chilton and Weidenbaum report that from 1968 through 1975 at least 350 foundries closed. In a survey of these companies, 35 percent indicated that the Environmental Protection Agency regulations were partly or totally the cause for the closing of the firm.[16]

The increase in required paperwork that accompanies the increased number of regulations is a major drain on the small business owner's time and energy. For example, some agencies require separate reports for local, re-

---

[13] *Report to the President, America's Small Business Economy: Agenda for Action* (Washington, D.C.: White House Commission on Small Business, April 1980), p. 29.

[14] Ibid., p. 29.

[15] Kenneth W. Chilton and Murray L. Weidenbaum, "Small Business Performance in the Regulated Economy," Working Paper no. 52 (St. Louis: Center for the Study of Small Business, Washington University, February 1980), p. 1.

[16] Ibid., pp. 16–17.

gional, and federal offices. And as we noted at the opening of this section, the small business firm does not have the personnel staff to interpret and complete the necessary forms. As the Advisory Committee on Industrial Innovation points out

It is virtually impossible for the struggling innovator to comply with the never-ending forms, mandated reports, applications, investigations, inspections, permits, licenses, standards, variances, checklists, guidelines, plans, study-sessions, public meetings, rule-makings, hearings, nonhearings, burdens of proof, appeals, etc. . . . to accommodate the rapidly growing enforcement budgets at all levels of government.[17]

The Small Business Administration estimates that small businesses spend $12.7 billion per year on paperwork. In a survey of 1,000 firms, the SBA learned that these companies had to deal with 305 million forms from 103 different agencies asking 7.3 billlion questions.[18]

Specific examples spotlight the problem faced by the small business owner. For example, one small manufacturer spends $12,000 and $15,000 annually responding to required government requests for information. Another small business owner estimates that one fourth of her time is spent filling out required reports, leaving much less time for performing the management functions needed to enhance the survival and growth possibilities of the firm.

The final report of the White House Commission on Small Business recognized the magnitude of the problems of regulations and paperwork. One of the major recommendations of this commission was to require all federal agencies to analyze the cost and relevance of regulations to small businesses. This action could then lead to the development of a specific regulatory policy for small business and could result in some businesses being exempt from some regulations and reporting requirements. Furthermore, when new regulations are proposed, small business representatives should have the opportunity to provide input before final regulations are adopted.

Some relief from the burden of rules and regulations has been gained by the small businesses with the passage of the **Regulatory Flexibility Act** or ''Regflex'' in the fall of 1980. The act went into effect in 1981, and its purpose is to require federal agencies to revise or drop excessive rules. The act requires government agencies to give public notice of impending major rules so that small business can comment, to weigh the effect of proposed rules on small business, to explain the need and objective of each proposed rule, and to review all existing rules within 10 years and to eliminate those that are not needed.

---

[17]"The Effects of Domestic Policies of the Federal Government upon Innovation by Small Businesses" (Washington, D.C.: Advisory Committee on Industrial Innovation, Final Report, U.S. Department of Commerce, September 1979), p. 257.

[18]"Government Paperwork and Small Business Problems and Solutions" (Washington, D.C.: Office of the Chief Counsel for Advocacy, United States Small Business Administration, December 1979).

Stress

All small business owner–managers face stressful situations not only in the day-to-day management of the firms but in their personal lives as well. **Stress** refers to how people respond to events in the environment that pose a threat. For example, the small business owner encounters stressful situations when sales are declining, when customers are not paying their bills, when employee productivity is declining, or when employee absenteeism and tardiness are increasing. Stressful situations in the personal life include a change in the goals of the small business owner, aging, children leaving home, or the death of parents.

A moderate level of stress is desirable because it keeps us alert as well as serves to motivate us. However, too much stress or stress handled improperly can lead to adverse physiological and behavioral consequences for the owner, such as heart disease, mental illness, or ulcers. Thus, if stress is not dealt with by the small business owner, it can result in serious health problems and eventually lead to bankruptcy of the firm.

A FAMILY OPERATION

Many small businesses are a family operation, and the business plays a central role in the daily existence of the family. Often all members of the family participate in some ways in the business, and business matters are a central part of family discussions.

It is common for the wife to work on a full-time basis on an equal footing with her husband in the business. In service firms, she performs secretarial and accounting functions. In retail establishments, she performs these same functions in addition to acting as a salesperson.

More and more women are becoming entrepreneurs. In these situations, the husband often works as a full-time employee for another firm. The husband's role in the small business involves physical activities, such as store maintenance.

Children of small business owners often perform some duties in the family business as soon as they are old enough. Making deliveries, cleaning up, waiting on customers, and operating a cash register are common tasks for children to perform. In skilled trades, children of the owner often learn trade skills as apprentices to their father. It has been common practice, in all nations throughout history, for many skilled trades to be passed down from father to son. In addition, small business firms are often passed down from parents to their children, and some have operated in the same family for generations.

There are many small businesses in operation that provide a service to customers that could not exist except as family operations. The profit of the firm is in reality a salary for the family. If many small business firms were forced to pay salaries to other people for work being performed by the family, it would be financially impossible for them to continue to exist.

SOCIAL AND CIVIC INVOLVEMENT

If they are to be successful, many small business entrepreneur–managers and their spouses must make a commitment to social activity to promote their business. Social activity is an excellent means of promoting contact. For example, the owner of an insurance agency usually depends on social contacts to provide many potential policy holders. The owner of a retail store often builds customer patronage for his or her store from acquaintances he or she meets socially. The advantages of social activity are particularly important to owners of service and retail establishments in small towns.

Many small business managers find it desirable to belong to such organizations as the local chamber of commerce, country clubs, and various civic organizations. Many spouses of small business managers also help the small business by belonging to various clubs and organizations. The wife or husband of a small business owner–manager can usually contribute considerably to customer patronage through social activity. It is not at all uncommon to find the small business manager or spouse or both engaged in various community projects sponsored by civic organizations.

SUMMARY OF KEY POINTS

1. Millions of Americans have fulfilled their dream of owning their own business, and this spirit has been the cornerstone for making America the most economically powerful nation in the world. Small business continues to provide avenues for individual creativity and self-expression.

2. Personality characteristics that contribute to business success include (a) drive, (b) mental ability, (c) human relations ability, (d) communications ability, and (e) technical knowledge.

3. The Committee on Economic Development defines a business as small when (a) management is independent, (b) capital is supplied and ownership is held by an individual or a small group, (c) the area of operations is mainly local, and (d) the business is small when compared to the biggest units in its field.

4. The SBA defines a small business as one that is independently owned and operated and not dominant in its field of operation.

5. Small business firms make a substantial contribution to the economy of the United States in terms of providing employment, accounting for a large share of our gross national product, and generating new products and services through research and development.

6. Women and minority entrepreneurs will play an increasingly strategic role in the small business economy.

7. Rewards and advantages of small business ownership include profit

expectation, anticipation of future wealth, satisfying work, ego identification with the business, being one's own boss, direct lines of communication between owner and employees, personal contact with employees and customers, centralized decision making, entrepreneurial status, and ease of entry.

8. Some limitations of small business ownership include lack of specialization, confining and long hours of work, and risk of funds.

9. Common problems of small business firms include inadequate management caused by lack of experience and incompetence, neglect, fraud, disaster, government regulations and paperwork, and stress.

10. Consequences of inadequate management are demonstrated by a weak competitive position, inadequate inventory control, lax credit controls, low sales volume, and poor location.

11. Many small businesses involve the total family in the operation of the firm.

12. The small business owner should make a commitment to becoming involved in social activities and civic affairs. These activities can greatly enhance the small business's image in the community.

13. Throughout this presentation, we have sought to underscore the significance of small business to the nation. In the future, the small business community will continue to make a significant contribution to the total economic system.

DISCUSSION QUESTIONS

1. What is the role of the entrepreneur in our society?

2. Identify some of the personality characteristics that are important contributors to the success of the small business entrepreneur–manager.

3. How do the Committee on Economic Development and the Small Business Administration define a small business?

4. Discuss the impact of small business on the economic system of the United States.

5. What are some of the characteristics of the entrepreneurial woman?

6. How significant are minority-owned small businesses in the United States?

7. Explain the advantages of small business ownership.

8. Identify the common problems of business failure. Which problems are the major cause of most failures?

9. What effect can stress have on the small business owner?

10. Are social activity and civic involvement important to some small business owners? Explain.

STUDENT PROJECTS

1. Prepare a short written report outlining the reasons why you would like to go into business for yourself. In addition, list three to five types of business in which you would be interested.

2. Prepare a list of reasons against going into business for yourself.

3. Interview the owner–manager of a local small business. Obtain all or any part of the following information.

   a. Why did you start the business?

   b. What personality characteristics do you feel are your strong points and those which need strengthening?
      (1) Drive
      (2) Mental ability
      (3) Human relations ability
      (4) Communications ability
      (5) Technical knowledge

   c. List in order of importance the following advantages you receive from small business ownership.
      (1) Profit expectation
      (2) Anticipation of future wealth
      (3) Satisfying work
      (4) Ego identification with the business
      (5) Being one's own boss
      (6) Direct lines of communication with employees
      (7) Personal contact with employees and customers
      (8) Centralized decision making
      (9) Entrepreneurial status
      (10) Ease of entry

   d. Does any member of the owner–manager's family work in the business? If so, what are his or her duties?

   e. Do the owner and the owner's spouse involve themselves in social and civic activities? Does the owner believe that this involvement increases customer patronage?

CASE A

Gould's Specialties

Aaron Gould, 57 years old, is married and has three children. A high school graduate, Gould appears quite intelligent. He dresses neatly, exhibits a pleasant personality, and is a very gregarious person.

Gould has spent most of his adult life working for various jewelry manufacturing firms, mainly in a supervisory capacity. For some time, though, he has been quite dissatisfied with his occupation, feeling that he was not "getting anywhere" in this line of work. His attitude about his work was expressed this way:

Well, I've been in factory work for many years now, and it was killing me. I've done everything, including production manager, and I could never relax. They were taking advantage of me. The older I got, the longer my hours were. I was doing everything— not only on the creative side, working with molders and casters—but I also had the production too—getting the stuff manufactured. They never let me relax, so I gave it up. I decided to do something where I could relax . . . I was under such tension that it just ruined my nervous system. So I decided to do something where I could relax and make a little money for myself.

One day, he saw an ad in the newspaper about a retail cookie business for sale. The idea of running a cookie store appealed to him. He went out to see the store and talk to the present owners of the business, and within two days he signed the lease to rent the building. For capital, he used his savings.

'Gould's Specialties' (his store) was located on a heavily traveled street in a neighborhood of lower-income homes and apartments, light industry, and some stores. He thought the population density, coupled with the fact that many of the residents didn't have cars and therefore would find it difficult to do their shopping downtown, would contribute to his business success. He wasn't particularly worried about the fact that parking was available only at meters or that delivery trucks had to park in front of his store or that there was a small supermarket 200 yards up the street. He knew that the interior of his store was clean, neat, and well lit; that his prices were low (especially for cookies in bulk); and that a lot of people went past his store every day.

So Gould had a sign painted on his storefront (which was hard to see if you were driving past the store); spent $5000 on new cookie containers, a cash register, and an impressive line of cookies; and opened for business.

He started losing money almost immediately, but knowing that it was important to wait out that initial slow period, he dipped further into his savings. Open from 8:00 A.M. to 7:00 P.M. (to be available to the going-to-work crowd and the going-home crowd), on a good day he had about 30 customers who bought an average of $1.85 worth of merchandise. On a bad day, he had as few as 10 customers.

When his business didn't start to pick up after six months of operation, Gould began to do some thinking. "Come to think of it," he mused, "I had more customers before the department store down the street closed."

He spent some money on newspaper ads, but didn't see much improvement. He ran a sale, advertising a 50 percent discount on all purchases over $5.00. Although more customers came in, Gould lost more money with the big discount. He hired neighborhood kids to distribute circulars around the neighborhood advertising his store (and paid them in cookies), leading to some improvement, but not much. Even repainting the outside of his store from white to tan with dark brown spots (like a huge chocolate chip cookie!) did not increase sales.

After a year in business, Aaron Gould had gone through $20,000 of his savings for start-up expenses, inventory replacements, operating expenses, and money to live on in the meantime. He finally gave up, and has sold his business—at a loss.

Source   Case adapted from *The First Two Years: Small Firm Growth and Survival Problems*, Small Business Research Series No. 2 (Washington, D.C.: Small Business Administration), pp. 172–176.

QUESTIONS

1. What was Gould's primary reason for starting a business of his own?
2. In your opinion, did Gould have the necessary personality characteristics that contribute to small business success? Explain.
3. Why did Gould believe he could be satisfied as the owner and operator of a small business?
4. What were the causes of the failure of Gould's Specialties?

CASE B

Reflections of a Small Business Owner

The following letter, written by a small business owner, are his reflections after 10 years of successful business operation.

As with most other things, the advantages and disadvantages of small business have drastically changed in the past 10 years. Many years ago there was more money to be made by owning your own small business than working for someone else and, because you were your own boss, there was more freedom as far as time off. Today many large companies, particularly those that are government-subsidized, are in a position to pay larger salaries, give more time off, and offer more benefits than the small business owner. Many changes have affected the potential profit for small business, some of which are higher minimum wage (normally with little or no additional volume or profit); the collection and disbursement of various taxes (sales taxes, etc.), which is costly at higher hourly wages and no profit; so much additional bookkeeping and reports required by government (small business cannot afford computers and many new aids because of cost). The trend now is to consumer protection, which has made it more difficult to meet government regulations on a small budget and small volume. Many of these regulations have actually increased the price to the consumer because the cost of complying with these rules and regulations must be added to the price with little or no benefit to the consumer. The trend as far as laws governing credit collection has also been to protect the consumer; therefore, the small business owner has more problems trying to collect when people refuse to pay for their purchases.

The advantages of owning and managing a small business as compared to working for a large concern are less in number but probably more satisfying personally. There is a sense of accomplishment that could not be attained otherwise. Small business managers have more opportunity to "do their thing" by expressing themselves in advertising, and in many other ways.

If I had it to do over again, I would still own my small business because of the personal satisfaction.

Very truly yours,

QUESTION

As a student of small business, evaluate what this small business owner is saying about the status of small business ownership.

SMALL BUSINESS ADMINISTRATION PUBLICATIONS*

Management Aids (Free)

Problems in Managing a Family-Owned Business
Business Plan for Small Manufacturers
Business Plan for Small Construction Firms
Can You Make Money with Your Ideas or Invention?
Checklist for Going into Business
Business Plan for Retailers
Thinking About Going into Business?
Management Checklist for a Family Business
Association Services for Small Business

Small Business Management Series (For Sale)

An Employee Suggestion System for Small Companies
Small Business and Government Research and Development

---

*At the conclusion of each chapter, a relevant list of the *free* and *for sale* publications offered by the Small Business Administration is included. A complete list of the SBA publications and the addresses of the SBA field offices from which these publications may be obtained can be found in the Appendix at the end of the book.

Management Audit for Small Manufacturers
Management Audit for Small Retailers
Management Audit for Small Service Firms
Management Audit for Small Construction Firms
Managing the Small Service Firm for Growth and Profit

Starting and Managing Series
(For Sale)

Starting and Managing a Small Business of Your Own

CHAPTER TWO

OWNERSHIP

LEARNING GOALS

After reading this chapter, you will understand:

1. The needs and characteristics of the business determine which form of ownership best fits the business.

2. The advantages and disadvantages of the sole proprietorship, the partnership, and the corporation.

3. You will understand the difference between general and limited partners.

4. What stocks and bonds are and the difference between preferred and common stock.

5. How a joint venture functions and where it is used.

6. How a business ceases to function through dissolution and bankruptcy.

7. The different ways forms of ownership are taxed and how Subchapter S may save you money if you are a small business owner.

KEY WORDS

Sole proprietorship	Preferred stock
Partnership	Par value
Joint venture	Common stock
General partner	Bonds
Limited partner	Dissolution
Corporation	Bankruptcy
Stockholders	Corporation tax
Dividends	Subchapter S corporations

SMALL BUSINESS PROFILE

Ron Mullen

Ron Mullen was born in Arlington, Texas, in 1939. After high school, he attended Abilene Christian College. He then married and went to work in the construction business. Later Ron worked nights as a police officer in San Antonio attending college in the daytime. The last year before he graduated from Southwest Texas State University, Ron started selling insurance to support his family.

After graduation, Ron sold insurance in San Antonio for a year and a half. He then moved to Austin to set up offices for the same insurance company. Starting with no employees, he has built the agency to one of the largest and most respected in the city. Ron also set up his own company, Ron Mullen & Associates, Inc., to offer a wide range of services to business. Since then, five companies have been added or affiliated with Ron Mullen & Associates, Inc. Ron has widespread investments in land, oil and gas wells, and various other business ventures. His current income is well in excess of $100,000 a year.

Over the years, Ron has served in many positions of leadership: vice-president of the Austin Symphony Orchestra, area governor of Toastmasters International, member of the Board of Directors of the Austin Jaycees, campaign chairperson of the March of Dimes, and so on. In 1977, Ron was elected to a city council position and served in this capacity until he was elected Austin's mayor in 1983. Ron has received many awards, such as National

Manager of the Year and Boss of the Year. Ron keeps physically fit by regular exercise, such as playing racquetball.

Ron feels it was natural for him to become a small business entrepreneur because his father also was a small business entrepreneur. His father was a successful contractor for many years, but he went broke and lost everything (he did not declare bankruptcy). The family was forced to move from a large expensive home to a house renting for $30 a month. Ron's father then made a deal to increase output of oil wells in which he was paid $1.00 for each barrel he increased production. The first well he increased by 80 barrels a day by injecting water under pressure into the well. From this, he started in rental trailer repairs and now owns one of the state's largest trailer-recreational vehicle sales, rental, and repair business.

When Ron was asked what had made him a success, he replied that two of the most important things were attitude and the ability to practice empathy and communicate with people. By attitude, Ron means he is willing to take a calculated risk, has the confidence that he can achieve what he is attempting, and has the ego drive to devote the effort necessary for success. Ron says that every morning he wants to go to work because he likes what he does. It is not like work; it is the opportunity to build something, achieve something, and to grow.

When asked what advice he would have for college students, Ron replied that first they should learn the principles and skills involved in managing a business. He also feels it is very important to learn to communicate with people—to understand not only what they are saying, but what they are feeling.

Ron has a strong feeling about ethics in business. What he is most proud of in business and politics is being open-minded and honest. He would rather tell people not to buy from him or lose a person's vote than tell an untruth. In the long run, people will respect you for honesty. He is amazed at people who will tell their employees to tell someone a lie, such as, "Tell him I am not here," and then expect those employees to respect and believe them. Ron feels that being consistently straightforward and honest is the only way to be successful because in the long run you will pay for it if you are not.

FORMS OF BUSINESS OWNERSHIP

There are three forms of business ownership: (1) the sole proprietorship, (2) the partnership, and (3) the corporation. In addition, the joint venture, technically an adaptation of the partnership form of ownership, is increasing in usage.

Small business owners often ask which is the best form of ownership. There is no one answer to this question because it depends entirely on the individual business. The corporation form of ownership is usually not suited to a "mom and pop" operation, and the sole proprietorship form of ownership would be completely impossible for a giant firm like General Motors.

FIGURE 2–1

Characteristics of each small business determine best form of ownership.

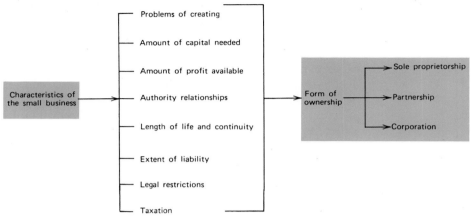

The needs and characteristics of each business dictate which form of ownership is most suited to that business (see Fig. 2–1). Some of the factors that should be considered when selecting a form of ownership are these.

1. The problems of creating the form of ownership.
2. The amount of capital needed in the business.
3. The amount of profit available for distribution.
4. The authority relationship in operating the business.
5. The length of life of the business and need for continuity of the business.
6. The extent of liability to the owners.
7. Legal restrictions of the form of ownership.
8. Taxation.

THE SOLE PROPRIETORSHIP

The **sole proprietorship** is the most common form of business ownership in the United States today, as shown in Figure 2–2. The sole proprietorship is owned by one person and has distinct advantages and disadvantages relative to other forms of ownership.

Advantages of the Sole Proprietorship

The advantages of the sole proprietorship are as follows.

1. It is the easiest form of ownership to establish. All the owner must do to create this form of ownership is to acquire the assets (permits are some-

FIGURE 2–2

Number of sole proprietorships, partnerships, and corporations in the United States.
Source *Statistical Abstract of the United States, 1982–83.*

Sale
proprietorship | 76% .... | 12,330,000

Partnership | 8% | 1,300,000

Corporation | 16% | 2,557,000

times required, such as a liquor license for a tavern) to begin the business and it is automatically a sole proprietorship.

2. All profits earned by the business belong to the owner and do not have to be shared with anyone else.

3. The owner of the business has total authority over the business.

4. There are no special legal restrictions on the sole proprietorship form of ownership. Only those general areas of civil and criminal law that apply to all forms of business ownership apply to the sole proprietorship.

Disadvantages of the Sole Proprietorship

1. The amount of capital available to the business is limited to the assets and credit of the one owner. The degree of the problem rests with the amount of capital needed in the business. Many people in the United States could finance a small hot dog stand in a rented building. However, no one could amass the wealth necessary to sustain General Motors, which has assets valued at over $40 billion.

2. Length of life of the business is dependent on the owner. In general terms, the owner may close his or her doors and go out of business at any time he or she chooses. In addition, technically, if the owner dies, the business ceases to exist. Of course, the assets are still in existence. The business may be sold, or a relative may take over the firm, at which time it then becomes a new sole proprietorship.

3. The owner has unlimited liability. The owner is liable not only for the amount invested in the business but also for all other assets owned. In cases of bankruptcy or legal judgments, all assets (except those exempted by state law, such as the owner's homestead) may be taken from the owner to satisfy legal claims.

THE PARTNERSHIP

A **partnership** consists of two or more people. The partnership may be established almost on any basis the partners may wish.

Although this is not required legally, it is best for partners to have legal counsel draw up an instrument called "articles of copartnership" (see Fig. 2–3). This agreement should state what each partner is to contribute to the partnership, what authority each partner has, and how the profit or loss is to be shared. If an articles of copartnership agreement is not created, the laws of the state in which the partnership exists determine distribution of authority, profit, and loss in cases of dispute.

Articles of copartnership should contain the following general information.

1. Effective date of the partnership.
2. Name of the firm.
3. Names and addresses of the partners.
4. Nature and scope of business activity of the partnership.
5. Location of all business activity.
6. Period of time the partnership is to exist.
7. Contributions of each partner.
8. Distribution of profit and loss.
9. Withdrawals and salaries of the partners.
10. Contribution of time by the partners to the business.
11. Authority relationship of the partners.
12. Partners' access to books and records of the partnership.
13. Terms and method of withdrawal of any partners.
14. Distribution of assets and name of business if dissolved.
15. A provision for arbitration of disputes.

Types of Partners

There are two basic categories of partners in a partnership—the general partner (sometimes called ordinary) and the limited partner (sometimes called special).

General Partner

There is no legal limit to the number of **general partners** a partnership may have, but there is usually a requirement that it have at least one. The general partner has unlimited liability. He or she may be held liable not only to the extent of his or her investment in the business but also any other assets he or she may own (excluding certain homestead items specified by state law). The general partner must also take an active part in the operations of the business.

Limited Partner

There is no legal requirement that a partnership must have any **limited partners**, and there is no limit to the number it may have. The primary difference between the general partner and the limited partner is that the limited partner

FIGURE 2–3

A section of a standard form for creating articles of copartnership.

107—Article of Co-Partnership.

JULIUS BLUMBERG, INC., LAW BLANK PUBLISHERS
80 EXCHANGE PLACE AT BROADWAY, NEW YORK

Articles of Agreement,

Made the   *day of*   *one thousand nine hundred and*

BETWEEN

WITNESSETH: *The said parties above named have agreed to become co-partners and by these presents form a partnership under the trade name and style of*

for the purpose of buying, selling, vending and manufacturing

and all other goods, wares and merchandise belonging to the said business and to occupy the following premises:

their co-partnership to commence on the   *day of*   *19*

and to continue

and to that end and purpose the said

to be used and employed in common between them for the support and management of the said business, to their mutual benefit and advantage. AND it is agreed by and between the parties to these presents, that at all times during the continuance of their co-partnership, they and each of them will give their attendance, and do their and each of their best endeavors, and to the utmost of their skill and power, exert themselves for their joint interest, profit, benefit and advantage, and truly employ, buy, sell and merchandise with their joint stock, and the increase thereof, in the business aforesaid. AND ALSO, that they shall and will at all times during the said co-partnership, bear, pay and discharge equally between them, all rents and other expenses that may be required for the support and management of the said business; and that all gains, profit and increase, that shall come, has limited liability. The limited partner can lose only his or her investment in the partnership. Other assets the limited partner may own cannot be seized to satisfy debts of the partnership. The three basic types of limited partners are these.

Secret partner   The public does not know the individual is a partner in the business.

Silent partner   The partner does not take part in the management of the business.

Dormant partner   The public does not know the person is a partner, and the person does not take part in the management of the business.

Advantages of the Partnership Form of Ownership

1. Creation of the partnership form of ownership requires little effort and involves little cost. Usually, the only cost in creating the partnership form of ownership is a legal fee for drawing up and recording the articles of copartnership. There also may be fees to obtain permits and/or licenses, such as a health permit.

2. Profit may be divided in any manner prescribed by the partners. Sometimes, formulas are created to divide profit on the basis of funds invested in the business or time spent in the business.

3. Usually, more capital may be raised by the partnership than by the sole proprietorship. The amount of capital that can be raised by the partnership is limited to the assets and credit of all the partners.

4. The partnership allows for limited partners who have limited liability. This is important not only to the limited partners but also to the capital-accumulating ability of the partnership. The protection of limited liability makes it easier to obtain investment funds from people who would not become general partners because of the risk involved.

5. Any type of authority relationship may be established in the partnership. Often, it allows people of widely diverse talents and skills to enter into a business. For example, one person may be a highly skilled technician in the production of a product but not have sales or management skills. Another person may have sales ability and management skills but not have sufficient technical skills to produce the product. Together in a partnership, they may be very successful, where alone they may have failed.

6. Usually, no special legal restrictions exist for partnerships that do not exist for the sole proprietorship.

Advantages offered by the partnership not offered by the sole proprietorship are (1) its ability to combine capital or skills or both of more than one person and (2) the limited liability of being a limited partner.

Disadvantages of the Partnership Form of Ownership

1.   Although the partnership usually has greater capital-accumulating ability than the sole proprietorship, it usually has far less potential than the corporation.

2.   There is a great potential for authority disputes in partnerships. Although the articles of copartnership generally spell out the authority of each partner, it is impossible to allow for all contingencies. There are usually areas of overlap of authority where conflict may arise. In addition, it is unusually difficult for even two people to function in the operations of a business without some friction. The addition of each person to the partnership geometrically increases the potential of friction. It is not at all unusual for a highly successful partnership to break up because of personality clashes in the operations of the business.

3.   General partners contribute a limited life to the partnership. The withdrawal or death of any general partner terminates the partnership. The remaining partners may settle claims of the withdrawn partner and start a new partnership. However, it can often be a real problem to obtain enough funds to buy the ownership of a partner. Limited partners aid continuity of the business because they may withdraw, die, or sell their ownership in the partnership without terminating the partnership.

4.   The unlimited liability of the general partners can be a serious disadvantage to the general partners. For example, suppose a person with extensive property holdings goes into business with another person to produce canned specialty food items. Also, imagine a negligent employee allowing canned fish to go out of the plant without sufficient cooking and causing several deaths (accidentally uncooked food products causing death has actually occurred). Court judgments against the partnership could cause the individual to lose all of his or her wealth and put the person into debt for the rest of his or her life. Of course, insurance and other methods of dealing with risk (Chapter 14) can help reduce losses.

Primarily, the partnership has disadvantages the sole proprietorship does not have in that it must generate sufficient profit for more than one person and there is considerable potential for dispute.

JOINT VENTURES

A **joint venture** is a specialized type of partnership. In the regular partnership, persons join together in a *continuous operation* of a business. In a joint venture, individuals join together in co-ownership for a *given limited purpose.*

For example, three men who purchase a tract of land for the sole purpose of developing it with apartments and then selling it for a profit would be engaging in a joint venture. On the other hand, if the three men contributed funds to the purchase and operation of a store on a continuous basis, it would be the creation of the usual partnership.

Although not nearly as common as other forms of ownership, joint ventures are increasing in frequency, particularly in real estate developments. The joint venture is taxed as a partnership. In addition, a formal, signed agreement should be drawn up by legal counsel to avoid future problems and disputes.

THE CORPORATION

The **corporation** form of ownership consists of three or more owners (in most states) who are known as stockholders. The corporation is in a legal sense an artificial being in that it may own property, enter into contracts, be liable for debts, sue and be sued, and conduct day-to-day business.

The corporation form of ownership comprises only 16 percent of all businesses; however, it accounts for 88 percent of all business receipts (Fig. 2–4).

Corporations are created by obtaining a charter from 1 of the 50 states. State laws vary in their requirements and taxation of corporations. Among other things, states usually require that a corporation have three or more stockholders, that the stockholders elect a board of directors, and that records are maintained at a designated location. The board of directors has overall responsibility for operating the corporation. The board of directors also appoints the officers of the corporation and establishes overall policy for the corporation.

The articles of incorporation usually contain such information as

1. Name of the corporation.
2. Period of time the corporation will exist (usually, perpetual).
3. Purpose of the corporation.
4. Number of shares of stock the corporation can issue and their par value.
5. Initial address of the corporation.
6. Names and addresses of the initial board of directors.
7. Names and addresses of incorporators.

FIGURE 2–4

Receipts of business by form of ownership.

Source *Statistical Abstract of the United States, 1982–83.*

Sole proprietorships	8%	$488 billion
Partnerships	4%	$258 billion
Corporations	88%	$5,599 billion

The corporation must also have its own bylaws, which give such information as

1. Stockholders' meetings.
   a. Place and time.
   b. Means of calling special meetings.
   c. Means of establishing a voting list.
   d. What constitutes a quorum.
   e. Voting of shares.
2. Board of directors.
   a. Number and means of election.
   b. Term of office.
   c. Means of removal.
   d. Method of filling vacancies.
   e. Quorum at meetings.
   f. Regular and special meetings—time, place, notification.
3. Officers of the corporation.
   a. Titles and duties of principal officers.
   b. Means of removal and filling vacancies.
   c. Method of fixing salaries.
4. Contracts, loans, checks, and deposits.
   a. Who may enter into contracts for the corporation.
   b. Who may borrow money for the corporation.
   c. Who may write checks and drafts.
   d. Place of deposit of corporation money.
5. Certificates for shares and their transfer (stock).
   a. Form of stock certificates.
   b. Methods of transfer of stock.
6. Fiscal year of the corporation (when it starts and ends).
7. Dividends (how they are declared and paid).
8. Description of the corporation seal.
9. Amendment of bylaws.

Corporations accumulate funds by selling stock (certificates of ownership) or bonds (certificates of debt) or both.

Stock

Ownership in a corporation may exist in two basic forms: preferred stock and common stock. Both preferred stock and common stock may be issued by the corporation with an almost unlimited combination of features available to them. However, most stocks issued do have certain features in common.

Stockholders receive payment from the corporation in the form of **dividends**. The board of directors of the corporation determine if a dividend will be paid and the amount of the dividend if it is paid. There is no legal requirement under normal circumstances that a corporation must pay dividends. One exception to this general rule occurred when stockholders forced Henry Ford to pay dividends after they proved in court that he was unreasonably holding back large profits to the detriment of the stockholders.

Some corporations have never paid a dividend. In fact, some stockholders do not want their corporation to pay dividends. They prefer to have earnings plowed back into the corporation to increase the value and growth of the corporation. This, in turn, almost always increases the value of their stock. Individuals must pay income taxes on all dividends received, and the dividends are treated as current income. This may be as much as 50 percent for some persons with large incomes. By holding the stock more than a year and selling it for more than they paid for it, they are required to pay income taxes on only 40 percent of the gain because it is considered a capital gain.

Preferred Stock

Preferred stock has several distinct characteristics, some of which, as its name implies, provide benefits that common stock does not receive. However, preferred stock usually has to give up some desirable features to obtain these benefits.

Par or No-Par Feature   Preferred stock may be either par or no-par stock. **Par value** of a stock is an arbitrary amount of value that is printed on the face of the stock certificate. Preferred stock with a par value usually exists in units of $100. The par value of the stock has no relationship to either the market value (the price it can be sold for on the open market) or book value (all assets minus all liabilities equals book value of all stock). For all practical purposes, it is simply a record-keeping device. Preferred stock may also exist as no-par; that is, it does not have a stated value printed on the certificate.

Preferred Payment of a Stated Amount of Dividend   Preferred stock usually has a stated amount of dividend that must be paid to the stockholder before any dividends can be paid to common stockholders. Usually, this stated dividend exists in the form of a stated percent of par value. For instance, it is relatively common for the dividend rate of preferred stock to be 6 percent of par. If the stock is 6 percent, $100 par, then the preferred stockholder must be paid $6.00 before common stock may receive any dividends. If the preferred stock is no-par, then the certificate will contain a statement as to a standard dividend that must be paid first. For instance, it may state on the face of the certificate that the preferred stockholder must receive $6.00 before any payment can be made to common stockholders.

Cumulative or Noncumulative   Preferred stock may be cumulative or noncumulative in terms of dividends. A cumulative feature is the most common.

Since there is no requirement that dividends be paid to stockholders each year, it would be possible for a corporation dominated by common stockholders to hold back all dividends for several years and then pay preferred stockholders for only one year and distribute the rest to the common stockholders. The cumulative feature prevents this in that it requires the corporation to pay not only the current year's dividend but also all past years' unpaid dividends to preferred stockholders before common stock can receive any dividends. Of course, noncumulative means that previous years' dividends that were not paid do not have to be paid before common stock receives dividends.

Voting or Nonvoting   Preferred stock usually does not have voting rights. It is a feature that is usually reserved for common stock. However, there is no legal requirement that prevents preferred stock from having voting rights, and it does have this privilege in some corporations. Stockholders in corporations often sign proxies that give another person the right to cast their vote in the corporation. Proxies are usually solicited by the existing board of directors.

Common Stock

There is more **common stock** than any other type of stock in most corporations, and in most small businesses it is the only type of stock.

Common stock usually has full voting rights. In addition, it usually is paid only after preferred has been paid. As a result, it is a higher risk stock than preferred. However, in a corporation with large profits, it often receives much larger dividends or increases in price per share or both than preferred.

A common-stock certificate.

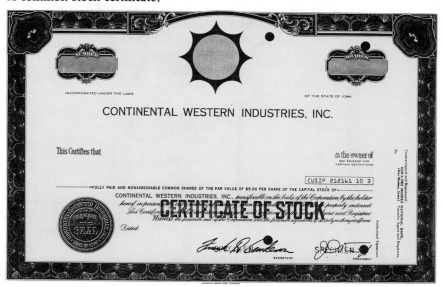

Common stock, as with preferred stock, may also be par or no-par. Also, it is an arbitrary figure that exists only for record-keeping purposes. More common stock has a par value of $1.00 per share than any other denomination. In fact, it is not unusual for a common stock to have a par value of $1.00 per share and have a market value of several hundred dollars per share. Some common stocks do not have an arbitrary value assigned to them and, as a result, are no-par common stock.

Bonds

Bonds are a certificate of long-term debt owed by a corporation. They are usually issued in amounts of $1000 each. Bonds have a maturity date, at which time the corporation must pay the face amount of the bond to the owner of the bond. In addition, the bond has an interest rate printed on the face of the bond. The corporation must pay the amount of the interest to the bondholder at the prescribed periods of time, usually once a year. For example, a bond with $1000 value and carrying an 8 percent interest rate must pay the bondholder $80 each year and $1000 at maturity. In addition, just because the bond has a face value of $1000 does not mean it is sold for that amount. Depending on the current interest rate, most bonds are sold at either above or below this face value. However, the face value is the amount that must be paid at maturity regardless of how much it brought when first sold.

The bondholders do not have voting rights unless the corporation fails to pay its yearly interest or its face value at maturity. In cases of forfeiture,

An example of a registered bond.

bondholders usually assume full voting rights, and all forms of stock lose their voting rights until the debt is satisfied.

Advantages of the Corporation Form of Ownership

1. The primary advantage of the corporation is its ability to accumulate capital. Many corporations have accumulated vast amounts of money for investment into assets through the sale of stocks and bonds. General Motors is an excellent example in that it has more than 1 million stockholders and assets in excess of $30 billion.

2. The length of life of the corporation is established in its charter. Most charters specify the life of the corporation to be to perpetuity (i.e., their life is without end). Ownership of corporations in the form of stock makes it easy to transfer ownership without disturbing the corporation. A father who owns a business may find it very hard to divide his business among his children under the sole proprietorship and partnership forms of ownership. In the corporation form of ownership, all he must do is divide the shares of stock.

3. In general, the corporation has limited liability, that is, all a stockholder can lose is the money the person paid for the stock. There are some exceptions to this general rule. If a very small corporation borrows money, lenders often require the owners to sign personal liability notes in order to obtain the loan. This means that the owners must repay the note with their own assets if the corporation is unable to repay the note. Another somewhat rare exception occurs when a stockholder is also an officer of the corporation and is guilty of fraud or neglect.

Disadvantages of the Corporation Form of Ownership

1. Creating the form of ownership of the corporation requires greater time and money than any other form of ownership. However, it is not an unreasonable amount in most cases. A charter must be obtained from the state. This requires time, legal fees, and state fees. It usually takes several weeks to process the charter application. The cost for attorney and state fees usually is from $500 up, depending on the state.

2. Taxation is sometimes a serious disadvantage, which will be discussed later in this chapter.

3. There are a wide range of legal restrictions on corporations. States have various legal requirements of corporations such as charter limitations, right to do business in other states, and some government supervision, which usually requires reporting to various agencies of the state. The federal government also has various legal restrictions on corporations that engage in interstate commerce. The corporation is also subject to all

Features of the sole proprietorship, partnership, and corporation form of ownership.

	Sole Proprietorship	Partnership	Corporation
Creation of form of ownership	One person starts a business	Two or more people sign articles of copartnership	Three or more people obtain state charter
Ability to accumulate capital	Assets and credit of one person	Assets and credit of all partners	Sale of stocks and bonds
Profit sharing	All to owner	To partners based on agreement	Stockholders
Authority	All to owner	Based on articles of copartnership	Board of directors
Life and continuity	Depends on owner	Depends on general partners	Usually perpetual life and transfer of stock provides continuity
Liability	Unlimited liability	Unlimited liability to general partners	Limited to amount of stockholder investment
Legal restrictions	No special ones	No special ones	Several state and federal restrictions

usual civil and criminal aspects of law to which the sole proprietorship and partnership are subject. Individuals operating the corporation are subject to the law in terms of their conduct in operating the corporation. For example, a few years ago several officers of electrical manufacturers were sentenced to terms in prison for price fixing in violation of the Sherman Antitrust law.

Figure 2–5 presents the different features of the three forms of ownership.

DISSOLUTION AND BANKRUPTCY

The form of ownership of a business may be terminated by either dissolution or bankruptcy. Although in a technical sense the business is dissolved in bankruptcy, dissolution is usually considered terminating the business when it is solvent. On the other hand, bankruptcy is always an act of terminating the business because of insolvency.

Dissolution

Dissolution of the sole proprietorship may result because of the death of the owner or as an act of the owner. The partnership form of ownership may cease owing to withdrawal of a general partner (such as by death), some condition stated in the articles of copartnership (such as a time limit for the partnership to exist), or by consent of the partners. A corporation may be dissolved because of a charter limitation (i.e., time limit) or vote of the stockholders (the charter usually specifies the number of votes necessary for dissolution, such as majority or two thirds).

Bankruptcy

Stated simply, the conditions exist for **bankruptcy** when the total amount of all liabilities exceed the total value of assets. Or to state it in another way, it is when there are not sufficient assets to pay all debts.

In a technical sense, a business is not bankrupt until it is declared to be bankrupt. A petition to the courts to declare the business bankrupt may be made by owners of the business (voluntary bankruptcy) or by creditors (involuntary bankruptcy). In cases of declared bankruptcy, the courts appoint a trustee who sells all assets of the business and divides it according to the order listed in dissolutions. The trustee receives a fee, which is deducted from the total funds before any are distributed.

In cases of bankruptcy, it should be remembered that the sole proprietor and general partner have unlimited liability, while the stockholder in the corporation has limited liability to the extent of the stockholder's investment in the corporation.

State laws prescribe the order in which various claims against the assets of the business are satisfied. Generally, they are satisfied in this order:

1. Any wages or claims of employees.
2. Any taxes due government agencies.
3. Creditors' claims.
4. Owners of the business.

In the case of the corporation form of ownership, creditors' claims would include all bondholders. Also, the par value (in the case of no-par, the value carried on the books) of the preferred stockholders would be paid first, and then common stockholders would receive all moneys that are left after the sale of assets.

TAXATION OF THE FORMS OF OWNERSHIP

There are some areas of government taxation that are common to all types of business ownership. Some of these common forms of taxation are local business licenses, licenses for sale of alcoholic beverages, property taxes (real estate and personal property), and payroll taxes.

In addition to these common areas of taxation, there are some taxes that vary according to the form of ownership (Fig. 2–6).

FIGURE 2–6
Taxation by form of ownership.

	Taxed
Sole proprietorship	As individual
Partnership	As individuals
Corporation	Corporation tax
	Dividends taxed to individuals
Subchapter S corporations	Under certain conditions small corporations taxed as partnership

Taxation of Sole Proprietorships

Usually, the only type of tax the sole proprietorship is subject to, other than those listed earlier as common taxes, is the federal income tax. All profit of the sole proprietorship is considered current income to the individual owner. All profit from the business is listed as "business income" in the owner's personal income tax return. All profit of the business is taxed in this manner even if the owner has not withdrawn it from the business. It is never considered as a salary and, therefore, is not an expense of the business.

Taxation of Partnerships

Partnerships are usually taxed differently from other forms of business ownership only in the area of federal income taxes. All profit earned by the partnership is considered personal income to the partners in the proportion of share of profits specified by the articles of copartnership. It does not matter whether or not the profits are withdrawn from the business. Even when the articles of copartnership specify a salary to one or more partners, it is still considered a distribution of profit rather than wages in the computation of federal income taxes. This treatment of federal income taxes is the same for both general and limited partners.

Taxation of Corporations

The corporation is subject to taxes that are not common with partnerships or sole proprietorships. One of these is the state corporation tax. State laws vary widely in their method and amount of taxation of corporations. However, most states tax corporations on profit and some on the basis of assets.

Corporations are also subject to a federal **corporation income tax**. The corporation income tax is computed on the basis of 15 percent of the first $25,000, 18 percent of the next $25,000, 30 percent of the next $25,000, 40 percent of the next $25,000, and 46 percent on all income above $100,000. For example, if a corporation had taxable income this year of $150,000, the tax would be computed as follows:

$$
\begin{array}{rl}
15\% \text{ of } \$25,000 &= \$\ 3,750 \\
18\% \text{ of } \$25,000 &=\quad 4,500 \\
30\% \text{ of } \$25,000 &=\quad 7,500 \\
40\% \text{ of } \$25,000 &=\quad 10,000 \\
46\% \text{ of } \$50,000 &=\quad \underline{23,000} \\
\text{Total tax} &\quad\ \ \$48,750
\end{array}
$$

Salaries of all employees and officers, regardless of whether or not they are stockholders, are considered an expense to the corporation. However, the salaries of the officers or employees are considered wages in their personal income tax computation. In addition, all dividends distributed by corporations are considered personal income to the individual. In a sense, this amounts to double taxation in that profit of the corporation is subject to a corporate income tax, and the dividends distributed from the remaining profit are also taxed as current income to the stockholder.

SPECIAL INTEREST FEATURE

Corporate Taxation Can Be an Advantage

The double taxation of the profits of the corporation would seem to be a serious disadvantage of the corporation form of ownership. Sometimes it can be an advantage to certain persons. For example, suppose you were earning a good salary and wanted to invest some of your savings in a new business venture with someone else. The business would start small, but you would want it to grow by reinvesting profit into the business. You would not want profits from the business until it has reached its full potential growth. If the business were a partnership, you would have to report the profit as personal income and pay federal income tax on it. Suppose the business made $100,000 profit the first year. As one of the partners, you would report $50,000 as personal income tax. If both of you were at the 50 percent tax bracket as a result of your salaries, together you would pay $50,000 in taxes on the income and only have $50,000 left to reinvest in the business.

However, as a corporation, the corporation would pay federal income taxes on the profit, and the rest could remain in the business, and you would not have to pay income tax on the profit. As a corporation, the first year profit would be taxed as follows:

$$
\begin{array}{rl}
15\% \text{ of } \$25,000 &= \$\ 3,750 \\
18\% \text{ of } \$25,000 &=\quad 4,500 \\
30\% \text{ of } \$25,000 &=\quad 7,500 \\
40\% \text{ of } \$25,000 &=\quad \underline{10,000} \\
& \quad\ \ \$25,750
\end{array}
$$

By being taxed as a corporation, you and your partner would leave $74,250 in the business for growth—a gain of $24,250 more than as a partnership. When the business reached its full potential and you began to take out profit from the business, you could elect *Subchapter S* (discussed later) and be taxed as a partnership.

SUBCHAPTER S CORPORATIONS

In an attempt to assist small businesses, Congress added Subchapter S to the Internal Revenue Code. Subchapter S permits corporations under certain conditions to be taxed as a proprietorship or partnership. These conditions are

1. It must be a domestic corporation (a corporation chartered by one of the 50 states).
2. It cannot have more than 35 shareholders.
3. It cannot be a member of an affiliated group of corporations.
4. All shareholders must be individuals or estates (not corporations or partnerships).
5. No stockholder can be a nonresident alien.
6. It has only one class of stock.

People are often confused by the title **Subchapter S corporation**. They mistakenly think it is a special form of corporation. It is a regular corporation chartered by 1 of the 50 states. It is eligible for and does elect to be taxed under Subchapter S of the Internal Revenue Code. In a year in which the corporation elects to be taxed under Subchapter S, all profits of the corporation (whether distributed or not) are *not* subject to the regular corporation tax. The shareholders (stockholders) have their share of the profit added to all their other income and are then taxed as individuals. If a corporation terminates their tax option status and elects to be taxed as a corporation, the stockholders must then wait 5 years (unless IRS consents) before electing to be taxed as a partnership again. Subchapter S can be of considerable value to a small business. The business gets to keep all the desirable features of the corporation form of ownership without the double taxation disadvantage. For example, if you had considerable wealth but still wanted to enter into a high risk business, you could possibly lose everything as a sole proprietor or general partner. However, if the corporation is a Subchapter S corporation, you would only risk your investment and still be taxed as an individual.

Some of the other potential benefits are these.

1. Income splitting. In a high profit year, a father may give stock to his children to take advantage of his lower income tax bracket without giving up control of the corporation.

2. Availability of fringe benefits for the stockholders. Employee benefit plans are often not available to sole proprietors and partners simply because they are employers, not employees. Fringe benefits to stockholders as employees (life and health insurance, pension plans, etc.) are a deductible expense to the corporation. Also, some executives may be uninsurable as individuals but insurable under group plans because all employees must be accepted in the plan.

3. A tax-free death benefit can be provided to selected stockholders. The company can provide up to $5000 to an employee's family at the time of the employee's death. The company can restrict the benefit to one or as many employees as the company chooses.

Subchapter S is rather complex and technical and the potential for tax savings so diverse, that no one should become a Subchapter S corporation without the advice and guidance of an accountant or attorney. On the other hand, the potential benefits are so great to many businesses that almost everyone operating a small business should investigate its potential for his or her business.

In conclusion, all the factors presented in this chapter must be considered by each individual business before an effective decision can be reached as to the best form of ownership for that business.

SUMMARY OF KEY POINTS

1. The needs and characteristics of each business determine which form of ownership is most suited to that business.

2. The advantages of the sole proprietorship are that (1) it is easiest to form, (2) profits belong only to the owner, (3) there is total authority over the business, and (4) there are no special legal restrictions.

3. The disadvantages of the sole proprietorship are (1) limited capital, (2) limited life, and (3) unlimited liability.

4. The partnership agreement is called "articles of copartnership."

5. There must be one general partner, but there can be any number of limited partners or none.

6. The advantages of the partnership are that (1) it is easy to form, (2) profits are divided as desired, (3) there is more capital, (4) it allows for limited partners, (5) there is any authority relationship wanted, and (6) there are no special legal restrictions.

7. The disadvantages of the partnership form are (1) less capital potential than corporations, (2) potential for authority disputes, (3) limited life of general partners, and (4) unlimited liability of general partners.

8. Corporations are chartered by the states and may issue preferred or common stock or both. They may also issue bonds.

9.   Advantages of the corporation form of ownership are (1) ability to accumulate capital, (2) perpetual life, and (3) limited liability.

10. Disadvantages of the corporation form of ownership are (1) time and cost of acquiring charters from the state, (2) taxation, and (3) legal restrictions.

11. Dissolution and bankruptcy are methods of terminating a business. Dissolution occurs when it is solvent, and bankruptcy occurs when it is not solvent.

12. Partnerships and sole proprietorships are taxed as individual income. Corporations pay a corporation income tax, and dividends to stockholders are taxed as income to the individual.

13. Under certain conditions, corporations can elect to be taxed as partnership under Subchapter S.

DISCUSSION QUESTIONS

1.   Because more businesses are sole proprietorships than any other form of ownership, the sole proprietorship must be the best form of ownership for small businesses. Evaluate this statement.

2.   When would you use the sole proprietorship form of ownership?

3.   Would you have articles of copartnership if you formed a partnership? Explain.

4.   Explain the two different types of partners.

5.   When would you use the partnership form of ownership?

6.   If you started a corporation, what instruments might you use to raise capital?

7.   Would you issue preferred or common stock?

8.   When would you use the corporation as a form of ownership?

9.   When would you use a joint venture?

10. What type of taxes must the various forms of ownership pay?

11. What is a Subchapter S corporation, and why is it important to some small businesses?

STUDENT PROJECTS

Find three businesses in your community—a sole proprietorship, a partnership, and a corporation.

1.   Ask each business why it has its form of business ownership.

2.   Ask the partnership what type of partners it has in the business.

3.   Ask the corporation from what state it obtained its charter.

4. Find out if the corporation uses Subchapter S.
5. Find out what types of securities the corporation has outstanding.
6. Find out if the partnership has articles of copartnership.

CASE A

Marie's Geothermal Energy Project

Marie Manor recently purchased a piece of land that has a hot water spring on it. One hundred gallons of water per minute flow from the well at a temperature of 165 F. Geological studies indicate a large underground reservoir of geothermal water. The temperature is estimated to be 260 F at 1000 foot depths and 390 F at 3000 foot depths.

Marie would like to use the geothermal water to generate electricity. She would like to drill four 1000-foot wells and one 3000-foot well at a total cost of $600,000. Once the wells were drilled and producing, she would place a closed loop freon system at each well to produce the electricity. The power-producing units operate much like the air conditioner in your home. Freon will be heated by the geothermal water, which causes the freon to expand and drive the generators. The freon is then cooled by cold water from an adjacent lake. The freon is next returned to be heated again. The total cost of the power-producing units is estimated to be $5.4 million. Marie has talked to officials at a large bank, and they have agreed to purchase the equipment and let her use it on a lease-purchase arrangement, but only when the wells are drilled and producing.

A customer for the electricity is assured because a federal law passed in 1980 requires local utility companies to purchase electricity generated by small producers (less than 80 megawatts a year). Marie's project would produce 5 megawatts of electricity per year. The law also establishes the price that must be paid for the electricity.

The project is particularly attractive from a financial point of view. There are a number of tax advantages passed by Congress to encourage alternate sources of energy. They are (1) the standard 8 percent investment tax credit, (2) an additional 15 percent investment tax credit for alternate energy, (3) a 15 percent depletion allowance every year the well is in operation, and (4) permission to deduct the lease-purchase cost every year. Projected income and expense figures indicate a 48 percent return on investment each year.

Marie is very enthusiastic about the project. However, she is about out of money after purchasing the land. She feels she can obtain investors for the $600,000 drilling costs by offering them 50 percent of the project. In fact, if she can obtain $75,000 from investors to drill the first well, the rest should be easy to obtain because the first well will prove the size and temperature of the underground reservoir.

Lately Marie has been thinking about what form of ownership would be best for the project. She has asked you to help her.

QUESTIONS

1. Would you recommend a sole proprietorship? Explain your answer.
2. Would you recommend a partnership? If you did, what kind would you recommend? Explain your answer.
3. Would you recommend a joint venture? Explain your answer.
4. Would you recommend a corporation? If you did, what kind of securities would you issue? Explain your answer.
5. If Marie were to select a corporation form of ownership, would you recommend that she use Subchapter S?

CASE B

A Cosmetic and Toiletry Business

Jean and Murray Kenedy are both 37 and have been married for 14 years. They have two adopted children, ages 10 and 12. Jean obtained her college degree in chemistry and has worked as a sales representative for a large chemical firm since leaving college. She is one of the company's best salespersons and has consistently earned above average in sales commissions. Murray obtained his college degree in business administration and is now the assistant plant manager in a medium-sized manufacturing plant that produces retail store shelves and counters.

Jean and Murray began talking about starting their own business even before they were married. The challenge of creating a business and making it grow appeals very much to them. Since the second year of their marriage, they have lived on Murray's salary and invested Jean's salary (after paying taxes on it) with the idea of obtaining enough money to start the business. They now have $215,000 and are ready to make their move into their own business.

They have investigated several ventures over the years and have changed their minds several times about what kind of business they wanted to create. About 3 years ago, Jean began to investigate the possibility of producing a limited line of cosmetics and toiletries. The couple is now convinced it offers them a good potential. Jean has formulated the following items to be their products:

Women's Products	Men's Products
Face cream	Hair tonic
Hair rinse	Shaving cream
Two perfumes	After-shave lotion
Hand cream	Men's cologne
Hair spray	
Shampoo	

Jean has attempted to make these products as allergy-safe as possible. These products appealed to both Jean and Murray because the manufacturing process is basically mixing and filling containers. The same general purpose machinery needed to produce any one of these products will also produce the rest. As a result, it is possible to produce all of them with a limited investment. Murray has leased a building that will fit their needs. He has also placed orders with manufacturers of the machinery they will need. His estimates show they will have $20,000 left to use as working capital after they have paid for everything required to produce the product.

Murray has turned in his resignation notice effective next week. Jean will keep her job as a safety factor until the business can get off the ground and produce a profit. The last month has been hectic for both of them trying to get everything lined up to get the business going. It has just occurred to them that they have never decided on the form of ownership they want for the business.

QUESTIONS

1. Would you select the sole proprietorship form of ownership? Explain your answer.
2. Would you select the partnership form of ownership? Explain your answer. If you did select this form of ownership, what type of partners would you use?
3. Would you select the corporation form of ownership? Explain your answer. If you did select the corporation form, would you issue bonds, preferred stock, or common stock or all three? Why?
4. Could things happen in the future that would cause a need for a change in the form of ownership? Explain your answer.
5. Could they be a Subchapter S corporation under IRS regulations? Could it be to their benefit to choose to do so?

SMALL BUSINESS ADMINISTRATION PUBLICATIONS

Free

Steps in Meeting Your Tax Obligations
Getting the Facts for Income Tax Reporting
Checklist for Going into Business
Incorporating a Small Business
Selecting the Legal Structure for Your Business

CHAPTER THREE
FRANCHISING

LEARNING GOALS

After reading this chapter, you will understand:

1. What franchising is.
2. That franchising occupies a significant place in the distribution of goods and services.
3. The advantages and disadvantages of franchising.
4. The various kinds of assistance franchisors make available to franchisees.
5. That there are retail, service, and wholesale franchised operations in which you may invest.
6. That franchising is growing in importance in international markets.
7. Why franchising offers an excellent opportunity for minority group members to become entrepreneurs.
8. The laws and regulations designed to protect the franchisee.
9. The factors one should evaluate before investing in a franchise.

KEY WORDS

Franchising	Franchise disclosure statement
Franchisor	Lease
Franchisee	Lessor
Product trade name franchise	Lessee
Business format franchise	Exclusive distributorship
International Franchise Association	Exclusive agency contract

SMALL BUSINESS PROFILE

McDonald's

In 1955, Ray Kroc observed the efficiency and the fine food served by the McDonald Brothers' drive-in restaurant in San Bernardino, California. Kroc studied their system, learned their operation, and, at age 52, bought the rights to use their name and franchise McDonald's. Success came quickly, attributed chiefly to the broad experience Kroc had gained from working in a variety of jobs over 30 years.

The McDonald's formula stresses the principles of quality, service, cleanliness, and value. To ensure uniformity of product and franchise image, McDonald's franchisees and managers learn the complete system of operation at Hamburger University in Elk Grove Village, a suburb of Chicago. Today McDonald's is a multibillion-dollar business, which has changed the eating-out habits of Americans and provided opportunities for success for many other independent business owners.

A Whopping Success Story

"There are only two things our customers have," James McLamore is fond of saying. "Time and money. And they don't like spending either of them." Taking that dictum to heart, McLamore and David R. Edgerton opened the first "Home of the Whopper" in Miami in 1954. It was typical of the times in some respects: it was a small building set in a large parking lot. But it was very different in one major way: it offered hamburgers, fries and drinks very quickly at extremely low prices. As the chain became known throughout Florida, the founders franchised the idea and eventually branched out across the Southeast.

In 1967, when Pillsbury Company gobbled up Burger King to add to its portfolio of diversified food businesses, the chain was composed of 35 company-owned and 239 franchised restaurants. Pillsbury acquired the chain for $18 million and expansion took off. Since the acquisition, Burger King has reported that sales have grown by an average of 36 percent annually.

As the chain grew and expanded, it acquired a male-dominated customer base. To encourage more customers, particularly families, in 1978 the chain began the "Magical Burger King" campaign in conjunction with "Operation Grand Slam." Burger King had long been known as an effective marketer, even when pitted against McDonald's with advertising budgets almost four times larger.

Other Burger King advertising campaigns have worked their ways into the American consciousness: from the memorable "Have it your way," to today's "Make it Special."

Making it special is exactly what Burger King intends to do in terms of building unit volume and profitability. And, through it all, McLamore's adage can still be heard on the lips of BK executives. They know that Americans still hate wasting their two most valuable possessions: time and money.

Source   Adapted from *A Century of Entrepreneurs* (San Mateo, Calif.: Federation of Independent Business Research and Education Foundation, 1981). Reprinted with the permission of the National Federation of Independent Business Research and Education Foundation. K. Farrell, "A Whopping Success Story," *Restaurant Business,* October 1981, p. 98.

Today, franchising is recognized as providing one of the best opportunities to small business owners for survival and growth. Franchising affords the small business owner the support services needed to compete with larger firms. The concept of franchising is also adaptable to many types of industries and services.

HISTORY OF FRANCHISING

Franchising has long been an effective form of distribution used primarily by manufacturers whose product lines were especially suited to exclusive or highly selective distribution. Historically, the concept of franchising in our country dates back to 1898, at which time it had its beginning in the automobile industry when an independent dealer was licensed to sell and service electric and steam automobiles. Until as late as the 1940s, franchise operations were primarily confined to automobile manufacturers, oil refineries, and soft drink companies. However, the early history of franchising is almost completely overshadowed by the dramatic upsurge of franchising in the United States in the relatively recent past. For example, about 90 percent of current franchisors have started their business since 1954. During the 1960s and 1970s, franchising has had its greatest impact in the United States. Franchising remains healthy and is a significant force in our economy, accounting for about 33 percent of all retail sales (see Fig. 3–1).

Many success stories are prominent in franchising. Certainly, one of the best-known franchises is Kentucky Fried Chicken, started by the late Harland Sanders.

Harland Sanders opened a small service station in Corbin, Kentucky, and also served meals to tourists at his family's dinner table in order to make ends meet during the depression of the 1930s. His reputation for food (especially his fried chicken) soon spread, and food preparation became the dominant business. Incidentally, he was made a Kentucky colonel in the 1930s in recognition of his contribution to the state's cuisine.

While catering for a banquet, he added an unusual combination of 11 herbs and spices to his special cooking processs, which sealed in the natural juices and flavor. In order to single out his fried chicken from "southern fried chicken," he designated his product "Kentucky Fried Chicken."

FIGURE 3–1
Franchising's share of the retail sales dollar (in percentages).
Source   U.S. Department of Commerce.

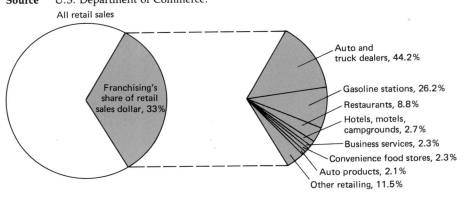

Kentucky fried chicken became his restaurant's specialty item. His restaurant grew to a capacity of 150 seats and prospered until the mid-1950s. Then a new interstate highway was planned that rerouted tourist traffic away from his restaurant. With this turn of events, he auctioned off his business at a loss, paid his debts, and began living on social security benefits.

Dissatisfied with retirement and having confidence in the quality of his fried chicken, the Colonel went into the chicken-franchising business. In 1955, at the age of 65, he took his first social security check, $105, and began traveling cross-country by car from restaurant to restaurant. He cooked his fried chicken, using his special recipe and utensils for the restaurant owner and employees. If their reaction was favorable, they entered into a handshake agreement that gave the Colonel a profit of a nickel for each chicken sold. The first franchise was opened in Salt Lake City, and by 1963 there were more than 600 Kentucky Fried Chicken franchised outlets. In 1964, Colonel Sanders sold his business to John Y. Brown and two associates. Colonel Sanders was retained as goodwill ambassador and media spokesperson, promoting Kentucky Fried Chicken through national advertising and personal appearances. He resigned his directorship in the company in 1970. He passed away in December 1980.

Kentucky Fried Chicken now has more than 5600 food outlets worldwide and annual sales of over $2 billion. This phenomenal growth has occurred from an investment of $105 and the vision of one person.

DEFINITION OF FRANCHISING

The International Franchising Association defines *franchising* as "a continuing relationship in which the franchisor provides a licensed privilege to do business, plus assistance in organizing, training, merchandising, and management in return for a consideration from the franchisee." Thus franchising is a method for the owner (**franchisor**) of a product, service, or method to obtain retail or wholesale distribution through licensed, affiliated dealers (**franchisees**). Frequently, the franchisor grants the franchisee the exclusive right to distribute the product, service, or method in a specific geographical area. In many ways, the franchising system of distribution is similar to a large chain-store operation in that all franchised outlets have an identifying trademark; standard symbols, equipment and storefronts; and standardized services or products, and they follow uniform business practices that are outlined in the franchise agreement.

A former president of the International Franchise Association described franchising as "a convenient and economical means for the filling of a drive or desire (for independence) with a minimum risk and investment and maximum opportunities for success through the utilization of a proven product or service and marketing method."[1]

TYPES OF FRANCHISE ARRANGEMENTS

There are two basic types of franchise arrangements—the product trade name franchise and the business format franchise. In the **product trade name franchise,** the manufacturer may franchise a number of retail dealers to sell the product. This is the traditional type of franchising, and this arrangement is common among automobile and truck dealers, in gasoline service stations, and in earth-moving equipment. Another type of product trade name franchise is that of the producer who franchises wholesalers to sell to retailers. This arrangement is most common in the soft drink industry. A national manufacturer of a syrup (Coca-Cola, Dr. Pepper, Pepsi-Cola) franchises wholesalers (independent bottlers) to serve retail markets.

Business format franchising is the newer type of franchising. Under this method, the franchisor establishes a fully integrated relationship with the franchisee. This relationship covers the total operations of the franchise, including the product or service, trademark, marketing strategy, quality control, and operating standards. A common type of business format franchise is the fast-food restaurant (McDonald's, Burger King).

ADVANTAGES OF FRANCHISING

A franchise operation offers some distinct advantages to the franchisee. Among the services the franchisor makes available to the franchisee are those that follow.

---

[1]*Franchise Opportunities Handbook* (Washington, D.C.: U.S. Department of Commerce, Bureau of Industrial Economics and Minority Business Development Agency, September 1982), p. xxvii.

Management Training

Earlier, we observed that over 90 percent of all business failures are attributable to inadequate management. Franchisors provide a wide range of management training. Franchise operators are given training in management skills and knowledge prior to opening as well as continued management counseling after the franchise is in operation. Management training covers all phases of franchise operation, and many training seminars are held at the franchisor's home office. New franchise owners receive thorough instruction in all prescribed methods of franchise operation, such as store management, accounting, sales, advertising, inventory control, and purchasing.

Some types of initial management training available to the new franchisee are presented here.

1. Holiday Inn provides a 3-week course at Holiday Inn University in Memphis, Tennessee.

2. Burger King operates regional training centers that provide extensive and detailed instruction in restaurant operation, equipment, and administration for franchisees or management or both. Burger King University in Miami, Florida, also offers ongoing and advanced training for franchisees in restaurant operations and administration.

3. Postal Instant Press (PIP), the world's largest while-you-wait printing operation, provides 2 weeks of intensive training at the PIP headquarters national training center. Training covers the use of all machines and equipment used, advertising, promotional aids, marketing, estimating, record keeping, inventory and cost control, counter procedures, sales, all phases of business management and procedures, in addition to communications, employee relations, and communication skills.

Preopening training is designed to instruct the franchisee in the professional and profitable operation of the business. Furthermore, training continues after the franchisee opens for business. Kentucky Fried Chicken, for example, provides assistance and training in operational activities of customer service, general restaurant management, quality control, and accounting methods. Immediately following the initial training, a PIP field coordinator spends one week assisting with the opening of the location. This is followed by a 3-day visit after 30 days of operation and another 3-day visit after 60 days of operation. After 90 days, a marketing specialist visits the owner. Quarterly visits are made thereafter.

The after-opening training may be conducted at the franchise location, or selected franchise personnel may attend a training session at a selected model store near the franchise location. Some franchisors bring franchisees together at regional meetings, where they may exchange views and opinions and receive management advice.

Franchisors recognize that management training and consultation provided franchise owners are a major reason for each franchisee's success.

A well-known name and product (or service) are advantages that are part of the franchising system of distribution.

Individuals with a minimum of business experience are given the opportunity to learn the management skills necessary for operating their own business successfully. And the success of the franchisor is reflected in the success of the franchisees.

Established Brand Name or Service

When franchisees are licensed, they acquire the right to use the nationally known brand name or trademark of the franchisor. The identification with an established name provides the franchisee with the distinct advantage of the drawing power of well-known products or services. Customers recognize a certain characteristic—the "Golden Arches" of McDonald's—and quickly identify that attribute as a symbol of courteous service, quality food, and cleanliness. These associations are important factors when consumers are selecting which firm to patronize.

Standardization of Products or Services

Because the franchise owner uses the brand name or trademark, the franchisor's national reputation depends to a large degree on the quality of his or her product or service provided by the dealer. To assure uniformity of goods or services nationwide, the franchisor assists the owner in maintaining his or her standard quality of performance. For example, Shakey's provides an operations manual to its parlor owners that details the following:

1. Pizza construction and ingredient specifications.
2. Other food products (salad, chicken, and potatoes).
3. Personnel (dress, hiring, training, managing).
4. Customer service.
5. Parlor maintenance and sanitation.
6. Equipment (purchase and maintenance).
7. Management and cost controls.
8. Use of Shakey's Incorporated trademarks and service marks.

Franchisees must adhere to the standard operating rules if the franchisor's goal of uniform product and services is to be achieved, and the national image is to be enhanced. The operations extend to all phases of a franchise's activity.

National Advertising

Association with a nationally known franchisor permits the franchise owner to benefit from the broader promotion of the product or service than would be possible on an individual basis. National advertising campaigns are financed by each franchisee's contribution of a specific percentage of monthly sales or a flat monthly rate to the franchisor. For example, Dunkin' Donuts and its franchisees agreed to increase their advertising contribution from 2 percent to 4 percent of sales. The additional sum allows national network television advertising to be undertaken as well as continuing the other advertising sources already employed. Another advantage is that the advertising is prepared by professionals, either advertising agencies or personnel on the staff of the franchisor.

To supplement national advertising, franchisors require local dealers to spend a minimum amount or percentage of sales on local advertising. For example, Taco Bell requires that each franchisee contribute 2.5 percent of gross sales to be applied to national advertising and an additional 2 percent of sales to be spent on company-approved local advertising and promotion.[2]

Financial Assistance

Becoming affiliated with a franchisor offers the franchisee several advantages in the area of financial assistance. In some instances, the franchisee may

[2] *Restaurant Business*, July 1, 1982, p. 114.

obtain partial financing from the franchisor. The following methods are illustrative of financing arrangements available.

1. An auto repair franchisor will arrange for financing of one half of the total requirement if the franchisee has good credit references.
2. A retail store selling high-quality domestic and imported cheese and sausages will finance up to $15,000 on equipment needs.
3. A general employment agency will finance up to 50 percent of the equity capital needed.

A second source of assistance by the franchisor is the counseling of franchisees on how to establish positive relationships with lending agencies and on how to seek long-term financing for the site and building through conventional loan sources. Because franchisees have access to the franchisor's business expertise, they are often able to obtain more favorable credit terms from lending agencies.

Other financial assistance may be provided in the form of short-term credit for the purchase of certain food and paper supplies if the franchisee elects to purchase these items from the franchising company. One major franchisor offers both short- and long-term financing arrangements to franchisees whose credit rating qualifies them. The advantages to this method of financing include a lower down payment than required by outside lending agencies, competitive interest rates, flexible repayment terms, and preparation of all necessary paperwork by the franchisor at no cost to the franchisee.

Substantiated Business Methods

A benefit of franchising is that the franchisee does not have to build the operation from the ground up. Instead, the franchisee is buying into a business firm that has established a record for success. The franchisee is able to capitalize on the combined knowledge and skills of the franchisor that are based on sound business management principles. Thus, the franchisee is able to avoid many of the common pitfalls of the independent small business owner.

Furthermore, the franchisee profits by capitalizing on the franchisor's developmental work in creating goodwill, building a consumer-accepted image, designing the physical facility and equipment, and providing proven products and services. The assistance received by franchisees in organizing and promoting the product, service, or method enables them to concentrate more attention on managing the business in the most efficient way. Reliance on substantiated methods of operation and experience of the franchisor enhances the franchisee's likelihood of success.

Chain Buying Power

Selling standardized products enables the franchisor to use centralized buying. Volume purchases enable the franchisor to obtain merchandise at lower prices. These lower prices can then be passed on to the franchisees when they purchase merchandise from the franchisor. This practice enables these quasi-chains to enjoy the buying power that chain stores enjoy.

Higher Success Rate

While owning a franchise is no guarantee of success, the success rate is higher than for other small, independent business owners. The Department of Commerce reports that since 1971 fewer than 5 percent of the franchised outlets have been discontinued each year. By contrast, the Small Business Administration reports that 65 percent of small businesses fail within the first five years of operation.

Favorable Income Potential

In general, the franchisee has a favorable income potential. Association with a company with a proven business system plus the owner's initiative can adequately reward the owner. For example, the average yearly sales for franchised outlets in 1982 was $1 million according to the Department of Commerce.

Standardized Control Systems

An important component of the franchisor's program of support services is assistance provided in the control over franchise operations. For example, the franchisor furnishes the franchisee with a standardized system of financial and inventory controls, such as standardized reporting procedures and forms. These financial controls are a valuable aid for the franchisee in the preparation of financial statements and tax returns. An inventory control system enables franchisees to maintain a more accurate count of merchandise available and merchandise needed. By using these operational controls, the franchisee is in a more favorable position to improve overall efficiency and effectiveness of the franchise.

Territorial Protection

Many franchises have a policy of assigning and protecting the territory of the franchise. Others do not. An area of a city, an entire city, or a larger territory may be designated for a franchise outlet. This procedure protects both franchisor and franchisee interests.

LIMITATIONS OF FRANCHISING

As with any business undertaking, there are limitations to the franchise distribution method that must be recognized. Some of these are now discussed.

Franchise Fees and Sharing of Profit

The initial financial requirements vary for the type of franchise and also within franchising companies. These variations depend on the size of operations that a franchisor desires to build. One franchisor's equity capital requirements range from $5 to $10,000. A national motel requires equity capital of $250,000 and a net worth of $1.5 million.

One franchisor's requirements include a dealership license fee, down payment on equipment, signs, furniture, and start-up operating capital. Operating capital expenditure covers supplies and inventory, wages and expenses while training key people, promotion and advertising of opening, franchise operating cash reserves, licenses and fees (health permits, business licenses), and other deposits such as insurance and utilities. Within this same franchise, the typical total investment depends on the size of the franchise operation. The investment for a smaller outlet is $115,500, and for a full-size outlet it is $208,500.

In addition, continuing fees (or profit sharing with the franchisor) must be paid to the franchisor for continuation of use of the franchising company's trademarks, service marks, trade names, and other items. This profit sharing is a stated percentage of monthly or annual sales or a flat annual fee. For example, one franchise agreement calls for the dealer to pay 5.5 percent of the monthly food sales for the life of the dealership to the franchisor. Other fees are also involved. To illustrate, a specific amount or percentage must be set aside for both national and local advertising. One franchise agreement requires the franchisee to spend a minimum of 3 percent of gross food sales on local advertising. Other fees are paid to the franchisor to cover continuing operational advisory services, such as purchase of the merchandise and financial management. Rental fees may be required if the franchisor owns the land on which the franchise is located.

Strict Adherence to Standardized Operations

Although franchisees own the business, they do not have the autonomy to run the firm as do independent business owners. The franchisor ordinarily exercises varying degrees of continuing control over the franchisee's operation in order to assure the quality and uniformity standards of products and services at each outlet. This control extends to the personnel of the franchising company, who usually have the right to visit and inspect each outlet to determine its compliance with company standards for operations and quality control. If the franchisee does not perform up to standard, this can result in loss of the franchise. For example, if the franchisee purchases and serves an inferior quality of food, this reflects on the image of the firm in the eye of the consumer and has the possibility of negatively affecting all franchises.

Restricted Freedom in Making Purchase Decisions

Under the terms of some franchise agreements, the franchisee must purchase certain merchandise (food or nonfood items) from the franchisor or from suppliers licensed by the franchisor. To the extent that this policy exists, the franchisee's independence in purchasing merchandise is limited. In some cases, this eliminates the competitive purchasing advantage a franchisee could have by using other suppliers who offer equal quality but at a lower cost.

Limited Product Line

The franchisor controls the products or services that may be sold through the outlet. The franchisee cannot introduce other products or services except as they are introduced by the franchisor or approved by the company.

A summary of the advantages and disadvantages of franchising is presented in Figure 3–2.

CODE OF ETHICS OF THE INTERNATIONAL FRANCHISE ASSOCIATION

The **International Franchise Association (IFA),** founded in 1960, is a nonprofit trade association that represents franchising companies in the United States and around the world. The purposes of the IFA are to serve as a spokesperson for franchising, provide services to member companies and those interested in franchising, set standards of business practice, serve as a medium for exchanging experience and expertise, and offer educational programs for top executives and managers.

The IFA has developed a Code of Ethics that is designed to enhance mutual trust and confidence between franchisor and franchisee and to set high standards of business ethics and conduct. Specifically, the Code of Ethics includes the following.

Code of Ethics—International Franchise Association

Each member company pledges:
1. *No member shall offer, sell or promote the sale of any franchise, product or service by means of any explicit or implied representation which is likely to have a tendency to deceive or mislead prospective purchasers of such franchise, product or service.*
2. *No member shall imitate the trademark, trade name, corporate name, slogan, or*

FIGURE 3-2

Advantages and limitations of franchising.

Advantages	Limitations
Management training	Franchise fees and sharing of profit
Established brand name or service	Strict adherence to standardized operations
Standardization of product or service	Restricted freedom in making purchase decisions
National advertising	Limited product line
Financial assistance	
Substantiated business methods	
Chain buying power	
Higher success rate	
Favorable income potential	
Standardized control systems	
Territorial protection	

> *other mark of identification of another business in any manner or form that would have the tendency or capacity to mislead or deceive.*
>
> 3. *The pyramid or chain distribution system is inimical to prospective investors and to the franchise system of distribution, and no member shall engage in any form of pyramid or chain distribution.*
> 4. *An advertisement, considered in its totality, shall be free from ambiguity and, in whatever form presented, must be considered in its entirety and as it would be read and understood by those to whom directed.*
> 5. *All advertisements shall comply, in letter and spirit, with all applicable rules, regulations, directives, guides and laws promulgated by any governmental body or agency having jurisdiction.*
> 6. *An advertisement containing or making reference, directly or indirectly, to performance records, figures or data respecting income or earnings of franchisees shall be factual, and, if necessary to avoid deception, accurately qualified as to geographical area and time periods covered.*
> 7. *An advertisement containing information or making reference to the investment requirements of a franchise shall be as detailed as necessary to avoid being misleading in any way and shall be specific with respect to whether the stated amount(s) is a partial or the full cost of the franchise, the items paid for by the stated amount(s), financing requirements and other related costs.*
> 8. *Full and accurate written disclosure of all information considered material to the franchise relationship shall be given to prospective franchisees a reasonable time prior to the execution of any binding document and members shall otherwise fully comply with Federal and state laws requiring advance disclosure of information to prospective franchisees.*
> 9. *All matters pertaining to the franchise relationship shall be contained in one or more written agreements, which shall clearly set forth the terms of the relationship and the respective rights and obligations of the parties.*
> 10. *A franchisor shall select and accept only those franchisees who, upon reasonable*

investigation, appear to possess the basic skills, education, personal qualities, and financial resources adequate to perform and fulfill the needs and requirements of the franchise. There shall be no discrimination based on race, color, religion, national origin or sex.

11. *The franchisor shall encourage and/or provide training designed to help franchisees improve their abilities to conduct their franchises.*

12. *A franchisor shall provide reasonable guidance and supervision over the business activities of franchisees for the purpose of safeguarding the public interest and of maintaining the integrity of the entire franchise system for the benefit of all parties having an interest in it.*

13. *Fairness shall characterize all dealings between a franchisor and its franchisees. To the extent reasonably appropriate under the circumstances, a franchisor shall give notice to its franchisee of any contractual breach and grant reasonable time to remedy default.*

14. *Franchisor should be conveniently accessible and responsive to communications from franchisees, and provide a mechanism by which ideas may be exchanged and areas of concern discussed for the purpose of improving mutual understanding and reaffirming mutuality of interest.*

15. *A franchisor shall make every effort to resolve complaints, grievances and disputes with its franchisees with good faith and good will through fair and reasonable direct communication and negotiation. Failing this, consideration should be given to mediation or arbitration.*[3]

FRANCHISE INFORMATION

An excellent source for information on hundreds of franchises is the *Franchise Opportunities Handbook*, published by the U.S. Department of Commerce. This guidebook provides a description of the operation, the number of franchises and the length of time the franchise has been in operation, how much equity capital is needed, the financial and managerial assistance available, and the training provided by the franchisor. Here is an example of the kind of information available on a particular franchise.[4]

INTERNATIONAL DAIRY QUEEN, INC.

P. O. Box 35286
Minneapolis, Minnesota 55435
B. V. Bloom, Director—New Store Development

Description of Operation: *International Dairy Queen, Inc., is engaged in developing, licensing and servicing a system of franchised retail stores which offer a selected menu of soft dairy products, hamburgers and beverages marketed under "Dairy Queen," "Brazier" and "Mr. Misty" trademarks.*

---

[3] *Franchise Opportunities Handbook* (Washington, D.C.: U.S. Department of Commerce, 1982), pp. xxxi and xxxii.

[4] From the *Franchise Opportunities Handbook* (Washington, D.C.: U.S. Department of Commerce, 1982), pp. 203–204.

Number of Franchisees: There are currently 4,780 "Dairy Queen" and "Dairy Queen/Brazier" stores located in all 50 states and 12 foreign countries.

In Business Since: The soft serve dairy product was first offered to the public in 1938 with the first "Dairy Queen" store being opened in 1940. In 1962 certain territorial operators formed International Dairy Queen, Inc., by contributing their respective "Dairy Queen" territorial franchise rights.

Equity Capital Needed: The franchise fees are $25,000 for plan "A." All prospective franchisees must meet certain financial requirements.

Financial Assistance Available: Qualified franchisees may purchase equipment on a conditional sales contract over a 5 year payment period with the required down payment.

Training Provided: International Dairy Queen, Inc.'s National Training Center in Minneapolis, Minnesota offers an intensive 2 week training course to all new and existing franchisees. The course covers sanitation, sales promotion, inventory control and basic functions of management. The company also offers new franchisees the services of a special opening team that assists operators in opening their new "Dairy Queen" or "Dairy Queen/Brazier" store.

Managerial Assistance Available: International Dairy Queen, Inc., maintains an operations specialty division in addition to regional and district managers, who provide continuing assistance involving store operation, product quality, customer convenience, product development, advertising, financial control, training, communication and incentives. A research and development department is engaged in developing new products, cooking methods and procedures. Sales promotion programs are conducted through newspapers, radio, television and billboards.

INTERNATIONAL FRANCHISING

Foreign markets are broadening the horizon for franchise expansion. The Department of Commerce reports that although there are rising costs and problems peculiar to specific nations, markets in many developed countries are showing the same characteristics as those that contributed to the growth of franchising in the United States. These characteristics are a rising demand for consumer goods and services, greater amounts of disposable income, expanding urbanization, increasing consumer mobility, and an economy that shifts emphasis from manufacturing to services.[5]

Another characteristic is population density. In the United States, population density averages 59 people per square mile. In Western Europe, the number increases to 339; in Great Britain, 539; and 798 in Japan. Singapore and Hong Kong support more than 10,000 inhabitants per square mile.[6]

For the period 1971 to 1980, the number of companies with franchises in foreign countries increased from 156 to 279, and the number of franchise units

---

[5]*Franchising in the Economy, 1981–1983* (Washington, D.C.: U.S. Department of Commerce, 1983), p. 5.

[6]Mary Timmins, "U.S. Ventures Abroad," *Restaurant Business,* November 1, 1982, p. 212.

increased from 3365 to 20,428. Canada is the dominant market for American franchisors, followed by Japan and the United Kingdom. Predominant franchises in foreign markets are nonfood retailing, automotive products and services, and many types of food franchises.[7]

McDonald's performance is a premier example of success in international franchising. The first unit outside the United States was opened in Canada in 1967, and the company now has 1185 international units in 29 countries throughout Western Europe, Japan and the Far East, Australia, New Zealand, Central and South America, and Canada. McDonald's has signed an agreement with the Yugoslavian government that will soon open Eastern Europe as well. Wendy's and Burger King have about 500 units in 21 countries between them, and Kentucky Fried Chicken has 1358 units in Canada and abroad. McDonald's strategy for marketing abroad, which has been followed by the competition, includes a variety of options for overseas development: company-owned units, joint ventures, territorial licenses, and individual franchises.[8]

Although opportunities abound, some problems faced by the franchising industry in foreign markets should be identified. They include

1. *Official limitations on royalty payments or licensing and trademark contracts. In some cases royalties on trademarks and brand names are taxable and payable by the franchisor whether he is domiciled in or out of that particular country.*

2. *Problems may exist in the protection of trademarks as no facility exists for their registration.*

3. *In some cases, franchising arrangements remain solely the concern of contracting parties, and there are no regulations to safeguard franchising agreements. Tie-in arrangements are discouraged and sometimes forbidden.*

4. *In some countries, a significant percentage of ownership share of the business activity is required by local nationals; in others, aliens cannot own real estate property; and in others, they cannot own retail businesses.*

5. *There are also import restrictions on equipment. This may impose a significant problem with respect to equipment or systems considered essential to the distinctiveness of the end product or the end service.*

6. *Wide economic variation as a result of inflation and currency valuation, exchange controls, and price ceilings on products pose problems affecting various types of franchising business categories.[9]*

Another problem may be the cultural differences of the various markets. For example, the fried chicken of Kentucky Fried Chicken (KFC) failed to gain acceptance in Germany, Hong Kong, and Brazil because people in these areas

---

[7]*Franchising in the Economy, 1981–1983,* p. 7

[8]Timmins, op. cit., pp. 212–213.

[9]*Franchising in the Economy, 1976–78* (Washington, D.C.: U.S. Department of Commerce, 1978), p. 7.

preferred chicken prepared by more traditional local methods. As a result, KFC developed a new marketing strategy that includes studies of the population; ethnic makeup; analysis of economic, social, political, labor, and business factors that will affect prospective consumers; investigation of laws and conditions affecting franchising; and a survey of available tools and materials.[10]

The United States is also the focus of franchising efforts by foreign investors. Among the foreign investors in the United States are Canada, the United Kingdom, Germany, Switzerland, Mexico, France, and Japan.

MINORITY-OWNED FRANCHISES

Two common problems to small investors, especially minority entrepreneurs, are the lack of managerial knowledge and skills and inadequate financing. The franchising distribution system has made it possible to overcome these obstacles in many situations because of the various services and assistance franchisors make available to franchisees, such as initial and continuing management training and financial advice and assistance. Thus, franchising is an avenue for minority group members to become entrepreneurs and to enhance the likelihood of success.

The greatest number of minority-owned franchises are owned by blacks, followed in order by persons with Spanish surnames, Orientals, and American Indians. According to the Department of Commerce, franchises most popular among minority entrepreneurs are automotive products and services, restaurants, food retailing other than convenience stores, and nonfood retailing.[11]

FRANCHISING AND THE LAW

The enthusiam for franchising opportunities must be tempered with a recognition of some of the risks and problems associated with this fast-growing field. A regulation enacted by the Federal Trade Commission seeks to put an end to some abuses by franchisors such as unsubstantiated profit claims and arbitrary terminations of franchises. Franchising has also become a focal point of regulation in many states.

Franchise Disclosure Statements

The Federal Trade Commission (FTC) requires franchisors in all states to provide a **franchise disclosure statement** to a prospective franchisee. Nine-

---

[10] Timmins, op. cit., p. 216.

[11] *Franchising in the Economy, 1981–83* (Washington, D.C.: U.S. Department of Commerce, 1983), p. 8.

teen states require franchisors to register their franchise offer with a state agency or provide disclosure statements similar to the FTC regulation to prospective franchisees.

The FTC disclosure statement makes available detailed information on 20 separate areas that may influence the decision to invest or not invest in the franchise. These areas are now described.

1. *Information identifying the franchisor and its affiliates and describing their business experience.*
2. *Information identifying and describing the business experience of each of the franchisor's officers, directors, and management personnel responsible for franchise services, training, and other aspects of the franchise program.*
3. *A description of the lawsuits in which the franchisor and its officers, directors, and management personnel have been involved.*
4. *Information about any previous bankruptcies in which the franchisor and its officers, directors, and management personnel have been involved.*
5. *Information about the initial franchise fee and other initial payments that are required to obtain the franchise.*
6. *A description of the continuing payments franchisees are required to make after the franchise opens.*
7. *Information about any restrictions on the quality of goods and services used in the franchise and where they may be purchased, including restrictions requiring purchases from the franchisor or its affiliates.*
8. *A description of any assistance available from the franchisor or its affiliates in financing the purchase of the franchise.*
9. *A description of restrictions on the goods or services franchisees are permitted to sell.*
10. *A description of any restrictions on the customers with whom franchisees may deal.*
11. *A description of any territorial protection that will be granted to the franchisee.*
12. *A description of the conditions under which the franchise may be repurchased or refused renewal by the franchisor, transferred to a third party by the franchisee, and terminated or modified by either party.*
13. *A description of the training programs provided to franchisees.*
14. *A description of the involvement of any celebrities or public figures in the franchise.*
15. *A description of any assistance in selecting a site for the franchise that will be provided by the franchisor.*
16. *Statistical information about the present number of franchises; the number of franchises projected for the future; and the number of franchises terminated, the number the franchisor has decided not to renew, and the number repurchased in the past.*
17. *The financial statements of the franchisors.*
18. *A description of the extent to which franchisees must personally participate in the operation of the franchise.*

19. *A complete statement of the basis for any earnings claims made to the franchisee, including the percentage of existing franchises that have actually achieved the results that are claimed.*
20. *A list of the names and addresses of other franchisees.*[12]

Legal Rights of Prospective Franchisee

The Federal Trade Commission regulation prescribes a number of legal rights to the prospective franchisee. They are

1. *The right to receive a disclosure statement at your first personal meeting with a representative of the franchisor to discuss the purchase of a franchise; but in no event less than 10 business days before you sign a franchise or related agreement or pay any money in connection with the purchase of a franchise.*
2. *The right to receive documentation stating the basis and assumptions for any earnings claims that are made at the time the claims are made; but in no event less than 10 business days before you sign a franchise or related agreement or pay any money in connection with the purchase of a franchise. If an earnings claim is made in advertising, you have the right to receive the required documentation at your first personal meeting with a representative of the franchisor.*
3. *The right to receive sample copies of the franchisor's standard franchise and related agreements at the same time as you receive the disclosure statement and the right to receive the final agreements you are to sign at least 5 business days before you sign them.*
4. *The right to receive any refunds promised by the franchisor, subject to any conditions or limitations on that right that have been disclosed by the franchisor.*
5. *The right not to be misled by oral or written representations made by the franchisor or its representatives that are inconsistent with the disclosures made in the disclosure statement.*[13]

A violation of the federal law could result in a civil penalty against the franchisor of up to $10,000 for each violation. If a prospective franchisee has been injured by a violation, the Federal Trade Commission may be able to provide a remedy for the injury suffered, such as compensation for any money lost or the setting aside of future contractual obligations.

However, your best protection as a prospective franchisee is to thoroughly investigate the franchisor, evaluate your own abilities, and to be aware of your legal rights.

---

[12]*Franchising Opportunities Handbook 1982* (Washington, D.C.: U.S. Department of Commerce, 1982), pp. xxxviii and xxix.

[13]*Franchising Opportunities Handbook, 1982* (Washington, D.C.: U.S. Department of Commerce, 1982), p. xxx.

SPECIAL INTEREST FEATURE

Franchise Analysis

One set of guidelines suggested for the prospective franchise is now provided. These 25 questions should be answered when evaluating the potential franchise.

CHECKLIST FOR EVALUATING A FRANCHISE

The Franchise

1. Did your lawyer approve the franchise contract you are considering after he studied it paragraph by paragraph?
2. Does the franchise call upon you to take any steps which are, according to your lawyer, unwise or illegal in your state, county or city?
3. Does the franchise give you an exclusive territory for the length of the franchise or can the franchisor sell a second or third franchise in your territory?
4. Is the franchisor connected in any way with any other franchise company handling similar merchandise or services?
5. If the answer to the last question is yes, what is your protection against this second franchisor organization?
6. Under what circumstances can you terminate the franchise contract and at what cost to you, if you decide for any reason at all that you wish to cancel it?
7. If you sell your franchise, will you be compensated for your good will, or will the good will you have built into the business be lost by you?

The Franchisor

8. How many years has the firm offering you a franchise been in operation?
9. Has it a reputation for honesty and fair dealing among the local firms holding its franchise?
10. Has the franchisor shown you any certified figures indicating exact net profits of one or more going firms that you personally checked yourself with the franchisee?
11. Will the firm assist you with:
    a. A management training program?
    b. An employee training program?
    c. A public relations program?
    d. Capital?
    e. Credit?
    f. Merchandising ideas?

12. Will the firm help you find a good location for your new business?

13. Is the franchising firm adequately financed so that it can carry out its stated plan of financial assistance and expansion?

14. Is the franchisor a one-person company or a corporation with an experienced management trained in depth (so that there would always be an experienced man at its head)?

15. Exactly what can the franchisor do for you which you cannot do for yourself?

16. Has the franchisor investigated you carefully enough to assure itself that you can successfully operate one of their franchises at a profit both to them and to you?

17. Does your state have a law regulating the sale of franchises, and has the franchisor complied with that law?

You—the Franchisee

18. How much equity capital will you have to purchase the franchise and operate it until your income equals your expenses? Where are you going to get it?

19. Are you prepared to give up some independence of action to secure the advantages offered by the franchise?

20. Do YOU really believe you have the innate ability, training, and experience to work smoothly and profitably with the franchisor, your employees, and your customers?

21. Are you ready to spend much or all of the remainder of your business life with this franchisor, offering his product or service to your public?

Your Market

22. Have you made any study to determine whether the product or service that you propose to sell under franchise has a market in your territory at the prices you will have to charge?

23. Will the population in the territory given you increase, remain static, or decrease over the next 5 years?

24. Will the product or service you are considering be in greater demand, about the same, or less demand 5 years from now than today?

25. What competition exists in your territory already for the product or service you contemplate selling?

    a. Nonfranchise firms?
    b. Franchise firms?

Source *Franchising Opportunities Handbook, 1982* (Washington, D.C.: U.S. Department of Commerce, 1982), pp. xxxii and xxxiii.

TYPES OF FRANCHISES

There are numerous types of franchise operations available for ownership to interested parties. The following list identifies many types of retailing, service, and wholesale operations. Information about specific franchises may be obtained from the franchisor. Addresses of many franchises are found in a U.S. Department of Commerce publication, *Franchise Opportunities Handbook*. The International Franchise Association (IFA) also furnishes information about IFA members. The address of the IFA is 1025 Connecticut Avenue, N.W., Washington, D.C. 20036.

Automotive products and services
Auto and trailer rentals
Beauty salons and supplies
Business aids and services
Campgrounds
Children's stores and furniture products
Clothing stores and shoe stores
Construction and remodeling materials and services
Cosmetics and toiletries
Dental centers
Drugstores
Educational products and services
Employment services
Equipment and rentals
Foods—donuts
Foods—grocery and specialty stores
Foods—ice cream, yogurt, candy, popcorn, and beverages
Foods—pancakes and waffles and pretzels
Foods—restaurants and drive-ins and carryouts
General merchandising stores

Health aids-services
Hearing aids
Home furnishings and furniture-retail-repair-services
Insurance
Laundries and dry cleaning services
Lawn and garden supplies and service
Maintenance, cleaning, and sanitation services and supplies
Motels and hotels
Optical products and services
Paint and decorating supplies
Pet shops
Printshops
Real estate
Recreation, entertainment, and travel services
Security systems
Soft drinks and water-bottling
Swimming pools
Tools and hardware
Vending
Water conditioning

ALTERNATE METHODS OF DISTRIBUTION

Manufacturers may utilize alternate methods for distributing their products and services. Two methods, leasing and exclusive distributorship, are now discussed.

Leasing

Small business owners may enter into a leasing agreement with the manufacturer. A **lease** is a contract between the property owner (**lessor**) and the tenant (**lessee**). The contract allows tenants the right of possession and use of the leased property, for which they pay the property owner rent. The lease specifies the rights of the parties to the lease.

As one example, in the distribution of gasoline and related products, oil companies frequently build stations and lease these stations to independent operators. The producer sells the station operator the brand name products as well as offering managerial assistance and guidance through periodic individual and group meetings with the company's distributors in a sales territory.

For use of the physical facilities, the operator must make a rental payment. This payment may be a specific amount or a flat fee plus a stated percentage of the gross or net income.

The lease arrangement enables the owner to avoid a large cash outlay required for purchasing a building. Hence, leasing may help the small business owner overcome some of the problems of obtaining financing.

Exclusive Distributorship

A somewhat different method of distribution from franchising is the **exclusive distributorship**. This method of distribution may be used for products that are purchased rather infrequently such as autos. In an exclusive distributorship, a manufacturer signs an **exclusive agency contract** with a distributor (wholesaler, retailer, agent). The agreement specifies that the manufacturer gives the distributor exclusive rights to sell the goods or services within a designated geographical area. In addition to restricting the sales territory, a manufacturer may provide the dealer with other services, such as sales training and cooperative advertising. In return, the dealer agrees to certain standards of the manufacturer, such as maintaining a satisfactory inventory level, charging the prices established by the manufacturer, or not stocking competitive products. This distribution arrangement gives manufacturers greater control over their product.

However, there are legal limits to this distribution arrangement. These restrictions are discussed in Chapter 22, "Government Control of Business."

OUTLOOK FOR FRANCHISING

Franchising will continue as a viable force in our economy and worldwide in the foreseeable future. Since 1970 franchisor sales have increased by 275 percent. However, some changes are foreseen in franchising. For example, although the sales of traditional types of franchising (product trade name) are expected to increase, the number of establishments is expected to decline owing mainly to the closing of auto and truck dealers and gasoline stations. However, business format franchising is expected to show strong growth in both sales and number of establishments.

The Department of Commerce projects that franchising will be broadened to include a variety of service industries, such as hairstyling salons, health and fitness centers, and franchises that concentrate on convenience and specialization (instant printing services and quick service oil and lubrication services for autos).

Professional services are likely to be the new wave in franchising. David Slater, former president of Mister Donut, has started Omnidentix Systems, a dental-care franchise. The company offers a dentist a complete operation in a shopping mall, including equipment, furnishings, and staff for a $50,000 license fee and $700 weekly management and advertising fee. Mr. Slater predicts: "Professional franchises are going to burgeon sensationally. Many shopping centers will have service courts; whole rows of walk-in lawyers, doctors, accountants, psychologists, plastic surgeons. You name it, it'll be there."[14]

Strong growth is seen for computers and computer services in many areas such as personal home computers, tax services, and computerized services to meet the needs of small business managers and professionals. Fast-food restaurants should continue strong as more Americans eat meals away from home.

The number of American franchisors planning to expand into foreign markets is likely to continue. Another trend that is developing is that foreign companies are beginning to operate franchises in other markets, especially the United States. Canadian and European franchisors have already established some franchises in the United States.

Another trend projected by the Department of Commerce is that the number of business format franchises being repurchased for company ownership will decrease whereas the number of company owned units being converted to franchisee-ownership will increase.

Thus, despite some problems, the general outlook for franchising is quite optimistic. Furthermore, new types of franchises, especially in the service industry, will create opportunities for individuals who desire to enter business for themselves but who prefer the type of support services the franchisor affords.

SUMMARY OF KEY POINTS

1. Franchising, as defined by the International Franchise Association, is "a continuing relationship in which the franchisor provides a licensed privilege to do business, plus assistance in organizing, training, merchandising, and management in return for a consideration from the franchisee."

2. Two basic types of franchise arrangements are product trade name franchise and business format franchise.

---

[14] *U.S. News & World Report*, December 6, 1982, p. 50

3. Specific advantages of franchising include (a) management training, (b) established brand name or service, (c) standardization of products or services, (d) national advertising, (e) financial assistance, (f) substantiated business methods, (g) chain-buying power, (h) higher success rate, (i) favorable income potential, (j) standardized control systems, and (k) territorial protection.

4. Limitations of franchising include (a) franchisee fees and sharing of profit, (b) strict adherence to standardized operations, (c) restricted freedom in making purchasing decisions, and (d) limited product line.

5. The IFA has adopted a Code of Ethics that is designed to strengthen the relationship that exists between franchisor and franchisee.

6. The *Franchise Opportunities Handbook* provides information and addresses on hundreds of franchisors.

7. Franchising has expanded to an increasingly important role in international markets.

8. Minority entrepreneurs may receive management and financial support through franchise ownership that will increase their chances of successful business ownership and operation.

9. The Federal Trade Commission has established regulations that require franchisors in all states to provide disclosure statements to prospective franchisees. The FTC has also outlined the legal rights of prospective franchisees.

10. Before entering into the franchise agreement, the prospective franchisee should carefully investigate the franchise, the franchisor, himself or herself (the franchisee), and the potential market.

11. There are many franchise opportunities available in a wide variety of interest areas for the prospective franchisee.

12. A leasing agreement is a contract between a property owner (lessor) and the tenant (lessee), and the lease specifies the rights of the parties to the lease.

13. In an exclusive distributorship, a manufacturer makes an agreement with a dealer (wholesaler, agent, retailer) specifying that the manufacturer will sell goods or services in a particular area only through a single dealer.

14. Franchising should continue to play a prominent role in the free enterprise economy in the 1980s and beyond.

DISCUSSION QUESTIONS

1. How does the International Franchise Association define franchising?
2. Explain the difference between a product trade name franchise and a business format franchise.

3. List the advantages of owning a franchised operation.

4. What are some of the limitations of franchising?

5. What type of information about franchisors does the *Franchise Opportunities Handbook* contain?

6. Discuss some problems likely to be encountered by the franchisor when expanding into international markets.

7. What is the purpose of the Code of Ethics for franchisors developed by the IFA?

8. Should the prospective franchisee make a thorough analysis of the franchisor before signing a franchise agreement? Why?

9. Discuss some of the legal issues involved in franchising.

10. What is an exclusive distributorship?

STUDENT PROJECTS

1. Review the classified ads of the local daily newspaper or the *Wall Street Journal*. From the section entitled "business opportunities," compile a list of the types and the number of franchise opportunities available as well as the investment needed.

2. Select a specific franchise, and write to obtain information about what it takes to start the franchise and the types of service the franchisor provides the franchisees.

3. Interview a franchisee, and have him or her explain the assistance provided by the franchisor.

CASE A

Wild Bill's

The televised expose of Wild Bill's Family Restaurant, Inc. in a fall 1978 episode of CBS "60 Minutes" is tinged with irony.

Although the broadcast brought the alleged fraud to the public's attention, it also triggered a breakdown in the current trial proceedings.

Prior to declaration of bankruptcy in 1978, Wild Bill's was a New Jersey corporation operating out of Fairfield, N.J.

The principals in the firm included: Gerald M. Cuthbertson, president; Allan G. Gorrin, executive vice president and director of marketing operations; John Klemans, controller and vice president for finance; Paul L. Gorrin, vice president of franchising; Richard Vickers Day, III, director of installation and construction; Samuel Bauman, independent accountant for the corporation; and Thomas P. DeVita, legal counsel.

All of the above were charged with 20 counts of wire and mail fraud, and conspiracy to commit fraud in interstate commerce on September 5, 1979 in *U.S. v. Gerald M. Cuthbertson, et al., U.S. District Court, District of New Jersey.* Included in the charges is the allegation that the company used false and fraudulent financial documents to induce people to invest in Wild Bill's Family Restaurant franchises.

The defendants claim the 60 Minutes broadcast was prejudicial to them and petitioned the court for release of the tapes and files of the TV show.

On July 23, 1980, the court directed CBS to turn over all material relating to the government's list of witnesses. CBS refused—citing its rights under the First Amendment—and a contempt of court order was issued.

As a result, the trial is being held in abeyance pending the outcome of a CBS petition to the Supreme Court. According to court sources, it is unlikely the proceedings in the Wild Bill's case will be resumed until after the first of next year.

Meanwhile, one defendant, Richard Vickers Day, III, has pleaded guilty to a conspiracy count.

Charges in the case center around claims that the defendants made false and misleading advertisements and representations contained in brochures to prospective investors and in telephone conversations and personal meetings that a Wild Bill's franchise (a) was a "guaranteed success," (b) meant purchase of a "total turnkey operation," and (c) had a "100 percent money-back guarantee."

Also cited in the indictment as false and misleading representations were Wild Bill's claims that:

- No company or franchised store had ever failed;
- All company and franchised stores were making substantial net profits;
- The sales figures of sample Wild Bill's franchises shown and reported to prospective franchisees represented actual sales figures at existing stores;
- Gross sales of at least $6000 per week would be expected from a Wild Bill's franchise;
- The cost of food would be at least as low as 38 percent of the gross sales at a Wild Bill's franchise;
- Average net profits of at least $47,000 per year would be expected from a franchise;
- Prior to choosing a franchise location, Wild Bill's would conduct extensive geographic, demographic and "psychographic" studies and surveys to ensure the profitability of each location selected by the company;
- Wild Bill's distinctive method of operation and unique concept utilized secret food recipes;
- Wild Bill's would establish a central commissary and warehouse which would purchase and provide large quantities of high-quality food at the lowest possible price and that the full benefit of this commissary operation was and would be passed on to the franchisee;

- If a franchisee was dissatisfied with his Wild Bill's franchise, he could readily exchange that franchise for another Wild Bill's franchise at another location.

Although the company claimed to have over 20 company and franchised locations operational—and profitable—and another 50 coming on line, it appears that there were closer to six locations operational and not necessarily profitable.

The company's officers were masters at playing at the great American dream of owning your own profitable business with little or no experience. Between mid-1976 and April 1978, they coaxed over $1 million in purportedly refundable deposits, and another $1 million-plus in unrefunded deposits and payments out of some 60 individuals, family groups and investment groups. Investors made deposits and payments to the company in amounts ranging from $5,000 to $60,000 each. While on occasion the defendants would pay refunds and honor buy-back guarantees to prevent the dissemination of adverse information to potential franchise purchasers, the defendants, for the most part, would not provide a franchise nor would they refund any of those deposits, according to the indictment.

It is alleged that the defendants attempted to conceal their fraudulent activities by burning Wild Bill's records and by instructing various store managers and employees to conceal actual sales figures and profits at Wild Bill's owned restaurants from prospective franchisees.

It is also alleged that the defendants on occasion would perform acts that were detrimental to Wild Bill's franchisees and would virtually abandon the franchisees. These acts listed in the indictment include: providing little training in the operation of a fast-food franchise; running the commissary as a profitable business arm of the company rather than as a low price food source for the franchisees; and refusing to pay the lawful debts of Wild Bill's for equipment and other goods and services which had been leased and sold to franchisees.

Complaints from franchisees about Wild Bill's began filtering into the New Jersey Bureau of Consumer Affairs in October 1977. At that time, a disgruntled franchisee contacted the bureau about failure to receive a refund of $50,000. The investor had appealed to the company and had received no action. A satisfactory mediation occurred through the company's attorney, Thomas DeVita, following the threat of a subpoena.

Complaints of contract violations—actual stores were not as represented in the sales brochure, deliveries did not arrive, site location and equipment were not as specified—were received by the bureau from four more franchisees. These complaints were eventually referred to the U.S. Attorney's office in the District of New Jersey.

The U.S. attorney is seeking criminal penalties against the defendants. Each of them faces a sentence of five years imprisonment and also a $5,000 fine on each of the 18 counts of mail fraud, wire fraud and conspiracy. In addition, each of the defendants faces a sentence of 10 years and a $10,000 fine on each of the two counts of inducing individuals to travel in interstate commerce to defraud them.

Source Denise Garbedian, Kevin Farrell and Pete Berlinski, "Franchise Fraud," *Restaurant Business* (November 1, 1980), pp. 153 & 158. Reprinted from *Restaurant Business* magazine—November 1, 1980.

QUESTION

What does this case suggest to the prospective franchisee?

CASE B

Midwest Restaurant

Fred Wilson was a labor union leader in a Midwest steel town, with 16 years of seniority on his job. He was well liked by his fellow workers, and found his dealings with management at the bargaining table interesting and challenging. But Fred did feel that he could go no farther in his job, and he and his wife talked often about a business of their own.

A newspaper advertisement of a drive-in restaurant franchise attracted Mrs. Wilson, and at her urging, Fred inquired about it. A meeting was arranged with a company representative, at which time the Wilsons were exposed to the company's management, sales territories, advertising policies, cost and profit projections, and financing arrangements. At the conclusion of the meeting, the Wilsons were convinced this was their golden opportunity.

The Wilsons did not have very much capital because Fred's salary had been invested in paying off the mortgage on their home as rapidly as possible, and they enjoyed the luxury of a fine automobile each year. However, the Wilson's credit was excellent, and they borrowed what they lacked from their local bank, setting up a rapid repayment schedule, just as they had done with their home. The projected income figures indicated to Fred that this was feasible.

Less than a month later, the former steel worker was listening to marketing experts, food technicians, and experienced accountants explain the franchise operation. The training period was brief, but quite thorough, and Fred decided that whatever he didn't quite understand at the moment he would learn as he went along. Filled with enthusiasm, Fred returned home, eager to enter into his new business.

In the initial few days of operation, a company representative helped him operate the business. Store traffic was excellent—Fred's enormous circle of friends began to patronize the establishment immediately, and the pleasure of being the "boss" masked the strain of the long hours in the new enterprise.

When the company's representative left, Fred and his wife both worked in the restaurant, and, although the traffic of the first few days slackened a bit, the Wilsons were still working a good 16-hour day. After the first 2 months, Fred and his wife felt that the strain on them was too great—Mrs. Wilson had not worked previously, and Fred was quite used to his comfortable 40-hour week. So the Wilsons made a decision to hire additional help to ease their burden.

Two new employees were hired and given a 2-day on-the-job training course by a franchisor company representative. By the end of the week, Fred was convinced that the new employees could handle the job, and he let them take over the evening shift.

After 2 weeks, it became apparent that this system wouldn't work—and the Wilsons split up the workday—Fred and one employee took one shift, and Mrs. Wilson and the other employee took the other shift. The system seemed practical—the customers wre being served properly, and all looked well . . . until the Wilsons looked at their accounts.

The additional cost of the help, on top of the financial obligations the Wilsons faced to repay their initial investment, was not leaving them very much. They were working very hard, and realizing less money than Fred had earned at his previous job. The only decision the Wilsons could make was to let the help go, and continue to do all the work themselves, on a 6-day week, 16 hours a day. By the time the sixth month had rolled by, Fred was searching earnestly for a buyer for his restaurant.

Source *Franchising: Instructor's Manual, Management Development Program,* prepared by the Small Business Administration.

QUESTIONS

1. Based on the supplied information, what do you feel was the principal reason for the Wilson's disenchantment with their franchise?

2. How compatible was Fred Wilson's background with the type of business he entered?

3. What financial arrangements could have been made to ease the Wilson's financial burden? Explain.

4. What would you suggest as a solution to the problem facing the Wilsons?

SMALL BUSINESS ADMINISTRATION PUBLICATIONS

Small Business Management Series (For Sale)

Franchise Index/Profile

ESTABLISHING THE FIRM

SECTION TWO

CHAPTER FOUR

BUY AN EXISTING FIRM OR START A NEW ONE

After reading this chapter, you will understand:

1. The advantages and disadvantages of buying an existing business.
2. There are advantages and disadvantages to starting a new business.
3. That if you plan to buy an existing business you will find you must analyze (a) why the owner wants to sell, (b) the physical condition of the business, (c) the market in which the business exists, (d) the financial condition of the business, and (e) legal aspects of the purchase in order to arrive at a true value of the business.
4. That you are buying future profit of the business and how you can capitalize this yearly profit to arrive at a guideline for a fair price.
5. That if you ever plan to start a new business, the feasibility study should include investigation of (a) the need for the business, (b) location, (c) market, (d) physical facilities, (e) operations and personnel, and (f) projected financial information.
6. Why you must spend time, effort, and money in investigating business opportunities to lessen the risk of business failure.

KEY WORDS

Physical facilities

Composition of population

Travel time

Market barriers

Customer attitudes

Customer attitude surveys

Financial condition

Legal aspects

Return on investment

Capitalization

Feasibility study

SMALL BUSINESS PROFILE

Roberto C. Ruiz
Maya Construction Company

Commercial development planning, bridge engineering, land use planning, and waterworks construction represent the general contracting and engineering projects undertaken by the two companies founded by Roberto Ruiz in Tucson, Arizona. Roberto Ruiz is a native of Mexico who moved to the U.S. with his family, assisting in their support while he completed high school. He earned a degree in civil engineering and after working for an engineering firm, resigned to open his own businesses, Maya Construction Company and Ruiz Engineering Corporation in 1977. The companies have won high praise for projects such as a complex corridor planning study and a roofing contract completed four months ahead of schedule for the Veterans Administration. Together, Maya and Ruiz now employ 103, and sales increased by more than 182 percent in one year to $4.7 million in 1982. Roberto Ruiz provides partial scholarships to 25 adults who are candidates for Associate in Administration degrees at Pima Community College. He has served for several years as an advisor to a program that trains and places minorities, as well as handicapped and economically disadvantaged individuals.

Source *There's No Business Like Small Business*, U.S. Small Business Administration, Washington, D.C. 1983.

The entrepreneur has many decisions to make once he or she decides to become engaged in a small business venture. One of the first—and one of the most important—decisions is whether to start a new business or buy an existing business. The answer to this question may vary in each case, and there are many factors to consider.

This chapter investigates the advantages and disadvantages of both buying an existing firm and starting a new one. In addition, the chapter provides an overview of the information needed to arrive at a realistic decision when buying an existing firm or starting a new one.

In some respects, information required for buying or starting a business and the methods of obtaining this information are a part of the entire field of small business management. Consequently, specific knowledge and methods of obtaining information are contained throughout the entire book. Therefore, this chapter serves as an overview and introduction to the knowledge necessary to perform adequate investigation for purchasing an existing business or starting a new one.

BUY AN EXISTING BUSINESS

There are both advantages and disadvantages to buying an existing business. If the small business entrepreneur decides to buy an existing business, then there are many things he or she must investigate and analyze about the business if he or she is to make a good purchase decision.

Advantages of
Buying an Existing Business

There are several factors that may make an existing business an attractive purchase.

1. It is a proven business, which reduces the risk and often makes it easier to finance.
2. The business often has well-established customer goodwill.
3. Lines of supply and credit have already been established.
4. Employees have already been hired and trained.
5. The physical facilities are sometimes available for rent rather than purchase, which reduces the amount of capital necessary to buy the business.
6. Sometimes it is difficult to find potential buyers for business firms because of lack of skills, lack of interest, or lack of capital. Consequently, one may find an existing business that is being sold at a very low price relative to the value of the business. This is often true of manufacturing firms, which are sometimes sold far below the replacement value of the building, machinery, and equipment.

A business that requires special skills.

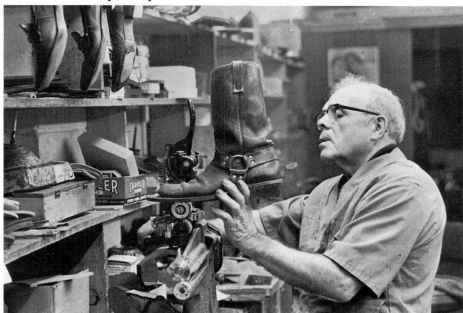

7. Usually, the methods of operation and systems have already been created, the "bugs" are worked out, and they are working.

Disadvantages of Buying an Existing Business

There are also several factors that may make an existing business unattractive as a purchase.

1. The business may be offered for sale because it is losing money. The buyer of an existing business must be very careful to determine the true reason why the business is being sold. The reason the seller gives may not be the real reason.
2. Customer, supplier, and creditor ill will, rather than goodwill, may have been established and carry over to the new owner.
3. The employees working in the firm may not be desirable employees, and it may be difficult to get rid of them because of unionization or other reasons. Also, firing undesirable employees often has an adverse effect on the morale of good employees in situations where they don't know what to expect when a new owner takes over the business.
4. It may not be the best location for the business.
5. The facilities may not be completely suited to the needs of the business. If remodeling is required, the cost may be excessive.
6. Innovations in the business may be difficult owing to present facilities. For example, the size of the building may prevent the addition of new lines of products that would help sales.
7. There may not be a business for sale of the type you are looking for in a given market, or it may cost an excessive amount of money to purchase one.

FACTORS TO INVESTIGATE AND ANALYZE

To arrive at a wise purchase decision, the small business entrepreneur must investigate various aspects of the existing business. The entrepreneur must analyze and evaluate (1) why the owner wants to sell, (2) the physical conditions of the business, (3) the market in which the business exists, (4) the financial condition of the business, and (5) legal aspects of the purchase, in order to arrive at (6) a true value of the business. (See Fig. 4–1.)

Why Does the Owner Want to Sell?

There can exist an almost endless list of reasons why a business is up for sale. Sometimes the reason the seller gives for selling the business is the real

FIGURE 4–1

Factors to investigate when buying an existing firm.

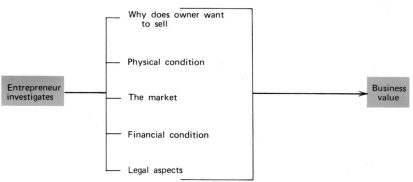

reason, and sometimes it is not. The owner may wish to sell because of such reasons as retirement, other business opportunity, or reduction of his business activities. On the other hand, the owner may wish to sell because the business is losing money; there is a continued trend of decreasing sales, new competition, and legal problems; or excessive effort is required for the level of profit being produced.

When the reasons for selling are factors that will ultimately mean the failure of the firm, the reason given for selling is usually not the real motivation. Few people would volunteer information that would automatically preclude anyone buying the business. For example, one individual looking for a small business to buy was offered a small grocery-gasoline store at a price that seemed very reasonable. An income statement provided by the owner indicated a very profitable business. However, a careful examination of sales and purchase records showed the firm to be making much less profit than claimed. In addition, talking to people in the nearby town revealed a new highway was being planned that would eliminate a large part of the store's business.

Rather than end up with a failing business and lost savings, any prospective buyer should expend considerable energy in evaluating the business.

Physical Condition of the Business

The **physical facilities condition** of the business is an important part of the total value of the business and the amount of capital that will be needed in the business.

The age and condition of such items as the building, equipment, and even inventory determine how much money must be spent in addition to the purchase price to get the business in proper operating condition. A buyer who must spend considerable money in remodeling a business should make sure that he or she can obtain the necessary funds when the business is purchased. The buyer must consider the cost of remodeling a part of the total cost of the business.

Old machinery and equipment may have to be replaced soon after the purchase, and the buyer must consider total cost and availability of funds for this before making the purchase. Inadequacy or obsolescence of inventory is also an expense and should be considered. In addition, if the buyer decides to purchase the business, a complete list of all inventory and equipment should be included in the purchase/sale agreement. There have been instances when a person agrees to buy a business at a specific price and then finds, on taking over the business, that the former owner has sold a large part of the inventory without replacing it. This reduction in inventory may represent a loss of thousands of dollars.

The prospective buyer must also evaluate the appearance of the business to determine if it provides an adequate image to customers. For example, a restaurant that is badly in need of paint does not produce an image of cleanliness to customers, and the cost of painting should be considered before purchasing the business.

Another consideration is that of adequacy of equipment. The manufacturing firm that has machinery and equipment that are not efficient and cause high labor costs may not be a good buy. In retail and service firms, the location of the business is an important factor to sales and should be evaluated during the purchasing decision.

The Market

To evaluate the market in which the business exists, the entrepreneur must determine (1) the composition of the population, (2) competition, and (3) attitudes of customers.

Composition of the Population

The first step in analysis of the **composition of the population** is to define the market in terms of where it exists. It may exist as the entire town, a large section of the town, or as a neighborhood. Studying maps, lists of customers, traffic patterns, and **travel times** (this is achieved by traveling major traffic arteries from the store at legal speed limits and marking the time it takes to reach various points on a map) help define the normal market area of the business.

Often looking for natural or psychological **barriers** helps define the **market** for a small business. Expressways, highways, and rivers with few crossings are examples of natural and psychological barriers. Figure 4–2 shows how highway and expressway locations in one town define the market for many small businesses in the area.

Once the market area has been defined, the composition of the population should be determined to help identify the number of potential customers in the market. The following information about the population of the market area should be collected and analyzed.

FIGURE 4–2

Market barriers in a city area.

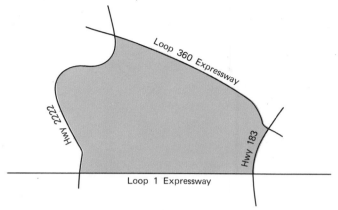

1. Characteristics of the population—such as income, education, unemployment, ethnic composition, average family size, and size of age groups.
2. The trend of size of the population over the past years.
3. Identify any significant changes in characteristics of the market area over the past 10 years.
4. Attempt to predict any future changes in size or characteristics of the market area.
5. Estimate the number of potential customers for the business from the population data collected.

   Some of this information can be found from census tracts in U.S. Bureau of Census publications (found in many public libraries). However, it may be out of date (the census is only taken every 10 years) in areas that are growing or changing.

   Sometimes, much of this data is available from local groups, such as city governments, local chambers of commerce, or other civic organizations. In other cases, little or none of the information is available and must be collected by statistical sample techniques (discussed in Chapter 16). Often, this information may be collected at the same time that customer attitude surveys are conducted.

Competition

The prospective buyer should measure competition of the business in the market area by obtaining the following information.

The correct market is vital to this ski rental shop.

1. How many direct competitors are there in the area (stores of the same type)?
2. How many indirect competitors are there in the area (stores that are different types, but handle some of the same merchandise)?
3. How many competitors have gone out of business in the past 5 years?
4. How many new competitors have entered the area in the past 5 years?
5. What is the volume of business of competition in the market area as compared to the store being investigated?
6. What are the pricing polices of the competition?
7. What customer services do competitors offer?
8. How much and how effective is the sales effort (including advertising and promotion) of the competition?
9. What is the appearance of the competition? Are their establishments attractive?
10. Identify and rank all competition as either strong or weak.

Most of this information concerning competition can be obtained by either direct observation or by talking to merchants and people in the marketing area. Many competitors will answer some questions themselves.

Customer Attitudes

The **attitude** of previous and current **customers** of the business is important to the prospective buyer. Goodwill of customers has value and definitely affects the purchase price of the business. A negative attitude, on the other hand, decreases the value of the business and should be studied to determine if the new owner can reverse these opinions.

The prospective buyer should perform a sample survey of people in the market area to obtain information about their attitudes toward the business. Often, this can be one of the most important types of information the buyer can obtain because it identifies actions that should be taken if the business is purchased. A discussion of the method of taking statistical **customer attitude surveys** is contained in Chapter 16. A sample customer attitude survey device is presented in Chapter 18.

Financial Condition of the Business

There are several financial areas of the business that should be investigated. Some of the questions that should be answered are

1. What has been the trend of profit over the past 10 years?
2. Has profit been consistent each year or are there wide fluctuations in profit?
3. What has been the trend of sales for past years?
4. Are assets valued realistically in the balance sheet? Significant amounts of intangible assets (goodwill, organization costs, etc.) and unrealistic depreciation may distort the true value of the assets.
5. Will there be sufficient funds after the purchase to meet current expenses and debt?
6. Are the expenses listed in the income statement realistic, or are there some that could be eliminated without harming the business?
7. Do you feel the profit record of the business is in line with the purchase price?

The prospective purchaser of the business should insist on at least the previous 5 years' (1) balance sheets, (2) income statements, (3) income tax returns, and (4) cash flow statements (accounting statement analysis is discussed in Chapter 11). Unfortunately, many small business firms do not maintain cash flow statements (Chapter 11) in spite of the fact that it is so important to a prospective buyer. However, cash flow statements can be almost always created from the records of the firm by an accountant if adequate records have been kept. The wise buyer will have this function performed by an accountant.

The wise buyer should also remember that the accounting statements provided by the seller may not be correct because of error or dishonesty. In addition, the income tax return is only a copy of the original and may not be accurate. The buyer (or preferably his or her accountant) should verify at the least the latest year of each different statement by examining sales, expenditures, and inventory records. The buyer should rely heavily on his or her accountant for the analysis of the **financial condition** of the business.

Legal Aspects

There can be many **legal aspects** to consider when a business is being investigated for possible purchase. Some of these are

1. The prospective buyer should investigate evidence of ownership of the business. It is wise to purchase title insurance because the title insurance company will conduct a complete search of legal records to make sure the buyer receives a clear title.

2. Is the business location zoned properly? Sometimes, businesses are in existence when zoning is created by the community, and they are allowed to continue in a nonconforming status. The nonconforming status prohibits additions to the business and can be a serious block to growth of the business.

3. Are there any liens or liabilities outstanding against the business that will be assumed by the new owner?

4. Does the business have the required licenses and permits, and will these be available in the future?

5. Are patents, trademarks, copyrights, and trade names protected under the law? Can an adequate defense of these be made if contested? (Defense of these must be made in court by the holder if contested.)

6. Does the firm have any exclusive dealerships, and do they pass on to the new owner? When do these agreements expire, and what are the terms of the agreements?

7. Does the firm have a union contract, and what does it specify?

8. Does the business have employment agreements with any other person or persons?

9. Obtain copies of all leases on buildings, equipment, and so forth, and study the terms of the leases.

10. Does the firm have any pending litigation against it?

11. Does the firm have any existing commitments?

12. Require the seller to sign an agreement that prohibits the seller from future competition with the buyer for a reasonable number of years.

The prospective buyer must obtain complete information about all legal aspects concerning the business because failure to do so can result in loss of thousands of dollars or even failure of the business.

VALUE OF THE BUSINESS

All the previous areas of investigation discussed make a definite contribution to the value of a business. However, they contribute to the value of the business in that they help determine the future profitability of the business. A prospective buyer, in reality, is buying the future profit of the firm. In a very real sense, future profit is the return on investment in money, time, and effort.

A fair **return on investment** is also dependent to some degree on the amount of risk sustained. For example, a government security (one of the safest investments available) may provide a 8 or 9 percent return on investment. To obtain a return of $20,000 per year, an investor would have to buy $400,000 worth of government securities having a 5 percent return ($20,000 ÷ 5%). If a buyer wishes to obtain the same $20,000 per year from an investment in a blue chip corporate bond (a higher risk than government securities but still considered a good risk) that returns an average of 10 percent per year, he or she would have to pay $200,000 ($20,000 ÷ 10%).

Investment in most small business firms is usually much more risky than either government securities or blue chip corporation bonds and stocks. The **capitalization** of the yearly profit of a firm usually varies between four and eight times the yearly profit figure (this would be from 12.5 percent to 25 percent return on investment). Consequently, a firm that was expected to produce a profit of $20,000 per year should reasonably expect to bring a price of between $80,000 and $160,000 depending on the degree of risk involved. Of course, price is established by the buyer and the seller, and what is paid often has no relationship to this capitalization guideline. However, a wise buyer will generally follow this guideline on future profit expectations in determining what price the buyer is willing to pay.

Many prospective buyers do not expend the time, effort, and money necessary to evaluate the purchase of a business adequately. This is definitely a mistake. It is far better to expend some time, effort, and money to make sure that the buyer is getting a fair deal than to take a chance that the purchase will turn out all right. If the prospective buyer does not perform an adequate analysis, the individual stands a strong chance of losing savings and being in debt for some period of time in the future. An analysis also helps the buyer operate the business more effectively once it is purchased because there is a considerable amount of information on which to base operating decisions. The buyer should be conservative and realistic in the analysis. In addition, the buyer should avoid being unrealistic about what can be done to improve the business.

START A NEW BUSINESS

Starting a new business also has advantages and disadvantages. Starting a new business also requires extensive investigation and analysis if the business is to have the best chance of success.

Advantages of Starting a New Business

Factors that may make it attractive to start a new business rather than purchase an existing business are these.

1. Location is many times one of the most critical decisions for a business firm. It can be the difference between success and failure in many businesses. Often the only way to obtain the best location is to start a new business.

2. Physical facilities can be constructerd to conform to the most efficient use for the business planned. Existing buildings seldom can be arranged to provide the most efficient work flow possible, particularly in manufacturing firms, without having wasted space.

3. Innovating in a new business is much easier than in an existing one because of physical limitations of the existing business.

4. All phases of the new business can be established by the owner without having to change something as when buying an existing business.

5. Existing businesses sometimes have ill will of some customers, suppliers, creditors, and employees. The existing business may also have an image (such as a price image) that the new owner does not want. Starting a new business allows the entrepreneur to establish whatever image is desired.

6. In many cases, there just are not any businesses of the type that fit the capabilities of an entrepreneur. Consequently, the only alternative left is to start one.

7. When purchasing an existing business, the buyer usually pays for the profitability of the firm. Sometimes a new firm can be established for less money and still realize the same profit.

Disadvantages of Starting a New Business

Factors that make it undesirable to start a new business rather than buy an existing business are:

1. There is a higher risk factor in starting a new business.

2. It often takes considerable time and expenditures of funds for a new business to build its customer patronage.

3. Funds are usually harder to obtain to start a new business than to buy an existing, successful firm.

4. It usually takes time to work out the "bugs" in a new business, both in facilities and procedures.

5. Lines of credit and supply must be established.

FIGURE 4–3
Factors to investigate when starting a new business.

6.   An existing business has sales, expenditures, and profit records to help project future profit. These must be estimated when starting a new business. This makes them much less accurate and dependable.

THE FEASIBILITY STUDY

Investigation and analysis of a new business is much more difficult and much less accurate than studying the purchase of an existing firm. Past records of the business operations are not available with which to make evaluations of the business. The **feasibility study** should include investigation of (1) the need for the business, (2) location, (3) market, (4) physical facilities, (5) operations and personnel, and (6) projected financial information. (See Fig. 4–3.)

SPECIAL INTEREST FEATURE

Checklist for Starting a New Business

	Check if answer is yes
ARE YOU THE TYPE?	
Have you rated your personal qualifications?	_____
Have you had some objective evaluators rate you?	_____
Have you carefully considered your weak points and taken steps to improve them or to find an associate whose strong points will compensate for them?	_____

WHAT BUSINESS SHOULD YOU CHOOSE?

Have you written a summary of your background and experience to help you in making this decision?

Have you considered your hobbies and what you would like to do?

Does anyone want the services you can perform?

Have you studied surveys and/or sought advice and counsel to find out what fields of business may be expected to expand?

Have you considered working for someone else to gain more experience?

WHAT ARE YOUR CHANCES FOR SUCCESS?

Are general business conditions good?

Are business conditions good in the city and neighborhood where you plan to locate?

Are current conditions good in the line of business you plan to start?

WHAT WILL BE YOUR RETURN ON INVESTMENT?

Do you know the typical return on investment in the line of business you plan to start?

Have you determined how much you will have to invest in your business?

Are you satisfied that the rate of return on the money you invest in the business will be greater than the rate you would probably receive if you invested the money elsewhere?

HOW MUCH MONEY WILL YOU NEED?

Have you filled out worksheets similar to those shown in Chapter 5 of this book?

In filling out the worksheets have you taken care not to overestimate income?

Have you obtained quoted prices for equipment and supplies you will need?

Do you know the costs of goods which must be in your inventory?

Have you estimated expenses only after checking rents, wage scales, utility, and other pertinent costs in the areas where you plan to locate? _____

Have you found what percentage of your estimated sales your projected inventory and each expense item is and compared each percentage with the typical percentage for your line of business? _____

Have you added an additional amount of money to your estimates to allow for unexpected contingencies? _____

WHERE CAN YOU GET THE MONEY?

Have you counted up how much money of your own you can put into the business? _____

Do you know how much credit you can get from your suppliers—the people you will buy from? _____

Do you know where you can borrow the rest of the money you need to start your business? _____

Have you selected a progressive bank with the credit services you may need? _____

Have you talked to a banker about your plans? _____

Does the banker have an interested, helpful attitude toward your problems? _____

SHOULD YOU SHARE OWNERSHIP WITH OTHERS?

If you need a partner with money or know-how that you don't have, do you know someone who will fit—someone you can get along with? _____

Do you know the good and bad points about going it alone, having a partner, and incorporating your business? _____

Have you talked to a lawyer about it? _____

WHERE SHOULD YOU LOCATE?

Have you studied the makeup of the population in the city or town where you plan to locate? _____

Do you know what kind of people will want to buy what you plan to sell? _____

Do people like that live in the area where you want to locate?   ———

Have you checked the number, type and size of competitors in the area?   ———

Does the area need another business like the one you plan to open?   ———

Are employees available?   ———

Have you checked and found adequate: utilities, parking facilities, police and fire protection, available housing, schools and other cultural and community activities?   ———

Do you consider costs of the location reasonable in terms of taxes and average rents?   ———

Is there sufficient opportunity for growth and expansion?   ———

Have you checked the relative merits of the various shopping areas within the city, including shopping centers?   ———

In selecting the actual site, have you compared it with others by using a score sheet similar to the one shown in Chapter 7?   ———

Have you had a lawyer check the lease and zoning?   ———

SHOULD YOU BUY A GOING BUSINESS?

Have you considered the advantages and disadvantages of buying a going business?   ———

Have you compared what it would cost to equip and stock a new business with the price asked for the business you are considering buying?   ———

HOW MUCH SHOULD YOU PAY FOR IT?

Have you estimated future sales and profits of the going business for the next few years?   ———

Are your estimated future profits satisfactory?   ———

Have you looked at past financial statements of the business to find the return on investment, sales, and profit trends?   ———

Have you verified the owner's claims about the business with reports from an independent accountant's analysis of the figures?   ———

Is the inventory you will purchase a good buy?   ———

Are equipment and fixtures fairly valued?   ———

**Check if
answer
is yes**

If you plan to buy the accounts receivable, are they worth the asking price?   _____

Have you been careful in your appraisal of the company's goodwill?   _____

Are you prepared to assume the company's liabilities, and are the creditors agreeable?   _____

Have you learned why the present owner wants to sell?   _____

Have you found out about the present owner's reputation with his or her employees and suppliers? _____

Have you consulted a lawyer to be sure that the title is good?   _____

Has your lawyer checked to find out if there is any lien against the assets you are buying?   _____

Has your lawyer drawn up an agreement covering all essential points including a seller's warranty for your protection against false statements?   _____

SHOULD YOU INVEST IN A FRANCHISE?

Have you considered how the advantages and disadvantages of franchising apply to you?   _____

Have you made a thorough search to find the right franchise opportunity?   _____

Have you evaluated the franchise?   _____

HAVE YOU WORKED OUT PLANS FOR BUYING?

Have you estimated what share of the market you think you can get?   _____

Do you know how much or how many of each item of merchandise you will buy to open your business? _____

Have you found suppliers who will sell what you need at a good price?   _____

Do you have a plan for finding out what your customers want?   _____

Have you set up a model stock assortment to follow in your buying?   _____

Have you worked out stock control plans to avoid overstocks, understocks, and out-of-stocks?   _____

Do you plan to buy most of your stock from a few suppliers rather than a little from many, so that those you buy from will want to help you succeed?   _____

HOW WILL YOU PRICE YOUR PRODUCTS AND SERVICES?

Have you decided upon your price ranges?   _____

Do you know how to figure what you should charge to cover your costs?   _____

Do you know what your competitors charge?   _____

WHAT SELLING METHODS WILL YOU USE?

Have you studied the selling and sales promotion methods of competitors?   _____

Have you studied why customers buy your type of product or service?   _____

Have you thought about why you like to buy from some salespeople whereas others turn you off?   _____

Have you decided what your methods of selling will be?   _____

Have you outlined your sales promotion policy?   _____

HOW WILL YOU SELECT AND TRAIN PERSONNEL?

If you need to hire someone to help you, do you know where to look?   _____

Do you know what kind of person you need?   _____

Have you written a job description for each person you will need?   _____

Do you know the prevailing wage scales?   _____

Do you have a plan for training new employees?   _____

Will you continue training through good supervision?   _____

WHAT OTHER MANAGEMENT PROBLEMS WILL YOU FACE?

Do you plan to sell for credit?   _____

If you do, do you have the extra capital necessary to carry accounts receivable?   _____

Have you made a policy for returned goods? _____

Have you planned how you will make deliveries? _____

Have you considered other policies that must be made in your
particular business? _____

Have you made a plan to guide yourself in making the best
use of your time and effort? _____

WHAT RECORDS WILL YOU KEEP?

Have you planned a system of records that will keep track of
your income and expenses, what you owe other people, and
what other people owe you? _____

Have you worked out a way to keep track of your inventory
so that you will always have enough on hand for your customers but not more than you can sell? _____

Have you planned on how to keep your payroll records and
take care of tax reports and payments? _____

Do you know what financial statements you should prepare? _____

Do you know how to use these financial statements? _____

Have you obtained standard operating ratios for your type of
business which you plan to use as guidelines? _____

Do you know an accountant who will help you with your records and financial statements? _____

WHAT LAWS WILL AFFECT YOU?

Have you checked with the proper authorities to find out
what, if any, licenses to do business are necessary? _____

Do you know what police and health regulations apply to
your business? _____

Will your operations be subject to interstate commerce regulations? If so, do you know to which ones? _____

Have you received advice from your lawyer regarding your
responsibilities under federal and state laws and local ordinances? _____

HOW WILL YOU HANDLE TAXES
AND INSURANCE?

Have you worked out a system for handling the withholding
tax for your employees? _____

Have you worked out a system for handling sales taxes? Excise taxes?   _____

Have you planned an adequate record system for the efficient preparation of income tax forms?   _____

Have you prepared a work sheet for meeting tax obligations?   _____

Have you talked with an insurance agent about what kinds of insurance you will need and how much it will cost?   _____

WILL YOU SET MEASURABLE GOALS FOR YOURSELF?

Have you set goals and subgoals for yourself?   _____

Have you specified dates when each goal is to be achieved?   _____

Are these realistic goals; that is, will they challenge you but at the same time not call for unreasonable accomplishments?   _____

Are the goals specific so that you can measure performance?   _____

Have you developed a business plan, using one of the SBA Aids to record your ideas, facts, and figures?   _____

Have you allowed for obstacles?   _____

WILL YOU KEEP UP TO DATE?

Have you made plans to keep up with improvements in your trade or industry?   _____

Have you prepared a business plan that will be amended as circumstances demand?   _____

Source   *Starting and Managing a Small Business of Your Own* (Washington, D.C.: Small Business Administration).

As mentioned earlier, methods and sources of collecting information concerning areas of the feasibility study are discussed in detail in many chapters of this book. The following discussion of the information needed in a feasibility study is intended to give an overview of some of the information an entrepreneur must analyze in order to arrive at a realistic evaluation of the proposed firm's chances of success. This information is also necessary for good planning and successful establishment of the business. It should also be noted that much of the information needed for a feasibility study of a new business is related to the information needed to evaluate the purchase of an existing firm.

Need for the Business

The entrepreneur should determine if there is a need for the business in the market area. If there is not sufficient demand, there will not be enough income for the firm to be profitable.

Usually, the most effective way to estimate how much income the business will receive is to perform a marketing research survey in the market area (Chapter 16). A survey device that asks people where they trade, why they trade there, how much they spend on the product or service, and other related questions will allow the entrepreneur to estimate potential sales for the new firm. The entrepreneur can evaluate each survey response to estimate if the firm can "take away" the business from the source potential customers are presently using. By projecting the total dollar volume of business from the sample survey to the total number of customers in the area, the entrepreneur can obtain an estimated sales volume for the proposed business. However, the entrepreneur should remember that the answer obtained is no better than the survey device, the sampling technique, the size of the sample, and the accuracy of the judgment used to estimate the amount of "take away" on each sample.

Also the entrepreneur can obtain the total number of inhabitants in the market area from census tract information or city government information and compare it to the national average of number of inhabitants per store shown in Figure 4–4. Using the total number of inhabitants in the market area, the national average number of inhabitants per store, and the number and quality of competitors in the area will provide an estimate of the need for the new business.

Location

Selection of the site for the business will usually require information that will include

1. Determining who your customers are and what causes them to buy the product or products or services or both you plan to offer. For example, if you were going to sell imprinted tee shirts, you would know that most of your customers would be below 35 years of age and generally buy this product on impulse. Consequently, the best location for your store would be in a high customer traffic area. A mall that was visited by a high percentage of young people would be an ideal site. Also, comparing the characteristics of your customers (age, education, income, etc.) with the distribution of these characteristics in city areas would show which would provide the most customers. Generally, retail, service, and whole-

FIGURE 4–4

National average of number of inhabitants per store by type of business, retail and service.

Kind of Business	Number of Inhabitants per Store
RETAIL	
Building Materials, Hardware, Garden Supply, and Mobile Home Dealers	
Building materials and supply stores	5,339
Hardware stores	8,008
Retail nurseries, lawn and garden supply stores	26,028
Mobile home dealers	20,823
General Merchandise Group Stores	
Department stores	26,029
Variety stores	9,465
Food Stores	
Grocery stores	1,073
Meat, fish stores	12,248
Fruit stores and vegetable markets	26,028
Candy, nut, and confectionery stores	16,018
Retail bakeries	10,959
Automotive Dealers	
Motor vehicle dealers, new and used cars	6,407
Motor vehicle dealers, used cars only	6,548
Auto and home supply stores	5,480
Gasoline Service Stations	921
Apparel and Accessory Stores	
Women's clothing	5,368
Men's and boy's clothing and furnishings stores	9,053
Family clothing stores	11,568
Shoe stores	7,712
Furniture, Home Furnishings, and Equipment Stores	
Furniture and home furnishings stores	3,107
Household appliance stores	10,411
Radio, television, and music stores	6,941
Eating and Drinking Places	
Eating places	823
Drinking places (alcoholic beverages)	1,964
Drug Stores and Proprietary Stores	4,004
Miscellaneous Retail Stores	
Liquor stores	4,957
Used merchandise stores	6,310
Automatic merchandising machine operators	16,017
Fuel and ice dealers	10,412

FIGURE 4–4
(Continued)

Kind of Business	Number of Inhabitants per Store
Florists	8,676
Cigar stores and stands	52,058
Sporting goods stores and bicycle shops	9,053
Bookstores	26,028
Stationery stores	34,705
Jewelry stores	8,329
Hobby, toy, and game shops	20,823
Camera and photographic supply stores	41,646
Gift, novelty, and souvenir stores	8,465
Luggage and leather goods stores	115,683
Sewing, needlework, and piece goods stores	11,568
SERVICE	
Hotels, Motels, Trailer Parks, Camps	
Hotels	14,873
Motels	4,658
Sporting and recreational camps	28,920
Trailering parks and campsites for transients	15,199
Personal Services	
Coin-operated laundries and dry cleaning	6,589
Photographic studios, portrait	6,948
Beauty shops	1,101
Barber shops	2,263
Shoe repair, shoeshine, and hat cleaning	16,141
Funeral service and crematories	9,963
Automotive Repair, Services, and Garages	
General automotive repair shops	2,896
Top and body repair shops	6,548
Automotive rental and leasing	19,869
Automobile parking	19,812
Miscellaneous Repair Services	
Radio and television repair shops	5,983
Reupholstery and furniture repair	8,499
Amusement and Recreation Services	
Motion picture production, distribution, services	24,326
Motion picture theaters	16,396
Billiard and pool establishments	35,594
Bowling alleys	24,643
Dental Laboratories	24,383
Legal Services	1,442

Source Computed from Bureau of Census publications.

sale businesses and manufacturers like to locate as near as is practical to their customers.

2. Determine who your potential competition are, how effective they are, and where they are located. A comparison of the areas that have the most customers with areas that have the most competition will provide insight into which is the best area for your new business.

3. Decide to build, buy an existing building, or rent based on the needs of the business, the amount of capital available, and the availability of adequate sites and structures.

4. A list of all available sites and their cost. Local realtors are a good source of this information. Location site is often a trade-off between desirability of site, cost, and available capital.

5. Identification of the major traffic arteries.

6. A traffic survey of automobiles and pedestrians (depending on the type of business) at the best sites.

7. Zoning information from the city on the various possible sites.

The Market

In many types of business, selection of a good location also depends to a large degree on the market. Some of the information that should be collected and analyzed includes the following.

1. Population size and characteristics (income, education, age groups, etc.).

2. Projections of population size and characteristic changes in future years.

3. Number, effectiveness, and characteristics of competition in the market.

4. A statistical customer survey. As discussed earlier, such a survey should be conducted in the selected market area to determine where and why people currently buy products or services the new business will offer.

Physical Facilities

If the decision is to build, rather than to rent or purchase, an existing building, the following information must be acquired.

1. Determine work flow and layout of equipment.

2. Determine building specifications and type of construction.

3. Establish amount of parking space needed based on number of employees and customers. Cities usually require a minimum number of parking spaces based on the type of business and size of the building.

4. Identify the type of and access to loading and unloading facilities needed by the business.

5. Based on the type of business, arrive at the type and cost of equipment needed.
6. Obtain city building requirements.
7. Design a floor plan for the business.

Operations and Personnel

Some of the information needed to arrive at operations and personnel planning includes the following.

1. Create job descriptions for all personnel needed in the business.
2. Draw up an organization chart showing lines of authority and responsibility.
3. Set a salary schedule for each job position based on current wage rates in the community.
4. Establish a work schedule showing hours and days worked for each position.
5. Establish a list of products to be carried with the amount of each that will be carried in initial inventory.
6. Determine sources of supply for all inventory items.
7. Determine if there will be any seasonal patterns of sales or if there will be seasonal items carried in inventory.
8. Establish price policies for all merchandise. Determine markups and obtain prices of competitors.
9. Create a plan for opening promotion and advertising.
10. Establish policies for amount and type of advertising to be conducted regularly after opening.

Projected Financial Information

Using the information gathered in the previous investigations creates the following financial information.

1. Create a projected budget for the first year of operation. Try to estimate all income and expense items as accurately as possible.
2. Create a projected balance sheet based on all assets you have determined the business will need plus all debts you plan to incur as a result of financing.
3. Create a projected cash flow statement for the first year's operation using income, expense, asset, and financing data.
4. If possible, draw a breakeven chart (see Fig. 4–5).

FIGURE 4–5
A breakeven chart.

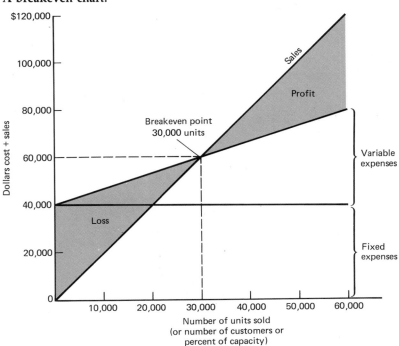

5. Determine your source of funds by contacting banks and other financial sources listed in Chapter 5.

The financial statements in Chapter 11 can be used as guides for the projected budget, projected balance sheet, and projected cash flow statement.

The breakeven chart is drawn by calculating sales revenue and costs at various levels. In the example, the number of units sold is multiplied by the selling price to determine the total dollars of revenue. Fixed costs are those costs that are sustained no matter how many units are sold. This figure would include such items as depreciation and insurance on plant and equipment. Variable costs increase as the number of units sold increases. They include such items as direct labor and raw material costs. The amount of these costs is computed at various levels of number of units sold. The breakeven point is the point at which the cost and sales lines cross.

As with the investigation of buying an existing business, the feasibility study for establishing a new business requires the expenditure of time, effort, and money. However, this expenditure of time, effort, and money greatly enhances the chances of success for the new firm. If a feasibility study is not made, the entrepreneur stands a very real risk that much more time, effort, and money will be lost as a result of failure of the business. Very few entrepreneurs perform adequate feasibility studies. If they did, the high failure rate of new business firms during the first year of operation would be reduced drastically. Most of the waste of business failure could be avoided.

SUMMARY OF KEY POINTS

1. The advantages of buying an existing business are (a) proven business, (b) established customer goodwill, (c) lines of supply and credit established, (d) employees hired and trained, (e) possibility of renting facilities, (f) possibility of being sold at low price because of lack of buyers, and (g) methods of operation and system in place.

2. The disadvantages of buying an existing business are (a) may be losing money; (b) customer, supplier, and creditor ill will; (c) employees may not be good employees and may have a union; (d) may not be best location; (e) facilities may not be adequate; (f) innovations may be difficult, and (g) may not be a business for sale that is suitable.

3. The factors to investigate in buying a new business are (a) why does the owner want to sell, (b) physical conditions, (c) the market, (d) financial condition, and (e) legal aspects.

4. The market analysis should include an analysis of the composition of the population, competition, and customer attitudes.

5. The value of the business usually should be computed by capitalizing the profit of the business. A general guideline is from four to eight times the yearly profit.

6. The advantages of starting a new business are (a) can select best location, (b) facilities are constructed to needs of business, (c) innovating is easier, (d) all phases of the business can be established by the owner, (e) there is no existing ill will, (f) it fits the capabilities of the owner, and (g) a new business may cost less for the same amount of profit.

7. The disadvantages of starting a new business are (a) higher risk factor, (b) time and funds needed to build customer patronage, (c) funds usually harder to obtain, (d) time to work out "bugs" in business, (e) lines of credit and supply must be established, and (f) lack of sales, expenditure, and profit records.

8. The feasibility study should include (a) need for business, (b) location, (c) market, (d) physical facilities, (e) operations and personnel, and (f) projected financial information.

9. A breakeven chart shows sales, fixed expenses, variable expenses, loss, and profit at various levels of units sold (can be number of customers or percent of capacity). Where the sales and cost lines cross is the breakeven point.

DISCUSSION QUESTIONS

1. Give three advantages and disadvantages of buying an existing business firm.

2. Why would an owner want to sell his or her small business?

3. What would be some factors of population in the market area you would want to investigate when deciding whether or not to buy an existing business firm?

4. What are some legal aspects to look for when buying an existing business?

5. How does a small business entrepreneur determine the value of an existing firm he or she plans to buy?

6. Give three advantages and disadvantages of starting a new business.

7. How should a person go about deciding whether or not to start a new business?

8. Why should a person spend time, money, and effort investigating the purchase of an existing business or the feasibility of starting a new business?

STUDENT PROJECT

Select a small business in your community, and do the following.

1. Ask the owner, if he or she were to sell the business, what price he or she would ask for it.

2. Ask questions to determine, in general, physical conditions of the business, the market, financial condition of the business, and legal aspects of the business.

3. Decide if you would purchase the business, and, if so, set a price that you believe is a fair one. Compare this price with the owner's price.

CASE A

The Seafood Restaurant

When Maria Adams graduated from college, she went to work in the accounting department of a large international corporation. After ten years she managed to amass $100,000, which she has in a money market account. Part of the $100,000 came from savings, but most came from an inheritance. Maria has decided that she does not like working in a large corporation and wants to go into business for herself. She has been looking at small business opportunities for the last six months.

Of all the businesses she has seen, the one she likes best is a seafood restaurant. It is located in a shopping center, the rent is $1800 per month, and there are still ten years to go on the long-term lease. The restaurant is popular, and the owner says he has consistently made between $40,000 and $50,000 profit each of the 5 years it has been open. The owner told Maria that he wants to sell it because he and his family want to move to a town in another state, where he and his wife grew up and where all their relatives live.

The owner offers a broad range of seafood products. Beer, wine, and mixed drinks account for about 20 percent of the sales. The restaurant employs 14 people. The owner has agreed to turn over all recipes and train Maria in all phases of the business operation.

The owner is also willing to sell the business for $120,000. He has told Maria he will take $100,000 as the initial payment and $10,000 each of the first 2 years with no interest. Maria likes the business, but is concerned about the price because she estimates the equipment and furnishings to be worth about $80,000. She feels she could open a new seafood restaurant for $40,000 less than what this one would cost her.

QUESTIONS

1. What do you think of the reasons the owner gave for selling the business?

2. What are some of the things Maria should investigate before deciding whether or not to buy the business?

3. If the owner has been making the profit he claims, do you consider $120,000 a fair price for the business?

4. If everything checks out as presented by the owner, would you recommend that Maria purchase the existing business, or should she start a new seafood restaurant?

CASE B

Susie Q

Susan Quintas has been interested in music for many years. She is 26 and unmarried and has $150,000 in municipal bonds inherited from one of her aunts. Susan tried a musical career as a pop singer (Susie Q) for three years after she graduated from the local college. Her singing career never amounted to much so she decided to try some other career. She would now like to start a stereo store selling medium- and high-quality stereo equipment.

Susan divided the town into five sections based on the location of physical and psychological barriers. She then created a customer questionnaire and hired several college students to conduct a survey. Her survey revealed that customers who bought the most stereo equipment were between the ages of 18 and 35, had incomes between $15,000 and $35,000, and had a high school or higher education. When medium- and high-quality stereo owners revealed where they had bought their stereo equipment, three stores (we will call them X, Y, and Z) accounted for about 72 percent of the sales. Customers listed equipment specifications as the first reason for their selection, with price a close second.

Susan has obtained information from census tracts, the city government, and the local chamber of commerce. She has broken this information down into the five areas of her survey.

Section	Median Income	Average Age	Average Years of Education	Competition	Characteristics of Section
1	$18,000	30	12	Firm X—Discount image	Fastest-growing
2	24,000	24	13	Firm Y—High price line	Old, established
3	40,000	38	14	Two minor stores	Old, established
4	12,000	30	13	Firm Z—Discount image	Old, becoming industrial
5	25,000	25	13	Three minor stores	New, growing

Firm Y is located in a shopping mall whereas X and Z are located in stores on major streets. A new shopping mall is being built in section five.

QUESTIONS

1. Which section of town would you pick in which to locate? Why?
2. Outline the steps Susan must go through to start her store.

SMALL BUSINESS ADMINISTRATION PUBLICATIONS

Free

What Is the Best Selling Price?
Attacking Business Decision Problems with Breakeven Analysis
Budgeting in a Small Business Firm
Simple Breakeven Analysis for Small Stores

Locating or Relocating Your Business
Checklist for Going into Business
Using a Traffic Study to Select a Retail Site
Thinking About Going into Business
Learning About Your Market
Setting Up a Pay System
Staffing Your Store
Incorporating a Small Business
Selecting the Legal Structure for Your Business
Marketing Research Procedures

For Sale

Starting and Managing a Small Business of Your Own
Buying and Selling a Small Business

CHAPTER FIVE
SOURCES OF FUNDS

LEARNING GOALS

After reading this chapter, you will understand:

1. The difference between short-term capital needs and long-term capital needs.

2. That equity capital comes from personal savings, partners, or sale of stock or from all three.

3. That commercial banks make several different types of loans—traditional bank loans, installment loans, discount accounts receivable, and discount installment contracts—and that they also have lines of credit for business firms.

4. That vendors and equipment manufacturers and distributors finance purchases for small business firms.

5. How factors and sales finance companies finance customer credit for small business firms.

6. That insurance companies and private investors make limited loans to small business.

7. How Small Business Investment Corporations provide funds to small businesses.

8. The many different types of financial assistance the Small Business Administration (SBA) provides small business firms.

9. Who is eligible for an SBA loan and how one goes about making application for such a loan.

10. What sources provide funds for different types of needs.

KEY WORDS

Equity capital

Debt capital

Commercial banks

Short-term loan

Traditional bank loan

Line of credit

Installment sales contract

Vendors

Equipment manufacturers and distributors

Factors

Sales finance company

Insurance company

Long-term loan

Private investor

Small Business Investment Corporation

Small Business Administration

SMALL BUSINESS PROFILE

Phyllis Griggs
Ahora Que, Inc.

Legend has it that the doughnut hole—though not the doughnut—is a product of American ingenuity; in 1847 a Maine sea Captain whose mother's doughnuts were always doughy in the middle suggested leaving a hole, and she did. Today, over $2 billion worth of doughnuts are sold in the U.S. annually, according to Phyllis Griggs, who took over a Mister Donut franchise in McAllen, Texas in 1973, with an investment of $26,000. In 1974, she opened a second Mister Donut in Edinburg. Because many of her clientele are Mexican-American, Mrs. Griggs gave her shop a local flavor; she produced a special "pan dulce" Mexican pastry similar to a sweet roll. Biscuits and sausage proved another successful innovation that many franchise holders nationwide have adopted. In 1975, the McAllen franchise was first in sales in the nation. Mrs. Griggs' Mr. Donut shops have sponsored numerous fiestas and special events. Sales totaled $1.4 million in 1982.

Source *There's No Business Like Small Business,* U.S. Small Business Administration, Washington, D.C. 1983.

The small business failure rate discussed in Chapter 1 indicates that many small business entrepreneurs make fatal mistakes when they start their business. It also indicates that one of the major causes of business failure is the lack of sufficient capital when the business is first started. The high failure rate of small businesses also makes it difficult to borrow funds to start a new firm. Knowing the correct amount of capital needed and the possible sources where these funds may be borrowed is extremely important to the small business entrepreneur.

AMOUNT OF CAPITAL, TIME, AND INTEREST RATE

Many small business entrepreneurs mistakenly feel that if they are able to rent a store, purchase equipment, and purchase the initial inventory, they have sufficient funds to start the business. These are major items requiring capital, but they are certainly not all that are required. There are many other costs that require a considerable amount of money. For example, most businesses are not immediately profitable, and the owners must sustain themselves and their families until the business can provide them a living. Also, they may have to finance customer credit until it begins to turn over and produce funds for the business. Figures 5–1 and 5–2 show work sheets that indicate the amount and type of capital that are usually needed by a new business. Please note that the entrepreneur must have funds to cover several months of expenses that recur each month. Most firms sustain greater cash payments than cash receipts during the first several months of operations.

In addition to the list in Figures 5–1 and 5–2, if the owner borrows money to start the business, the owner must also pay back the principal and interest of all loans. The amount of the payments of these loans is very important to the small business owner. It is not uncommon for a small business entrepreneur to establish a business that produces good profit but have it fail because of large monthly payments on loans. What normally would be sufficient profits are drained into repaying the loan.

The amount of the monthly payments is subject to three factors: (1) the total amount of money borrowed, (2) the time in which the loan must be repaid, and (3) the interest rate charged by the lender.

Amount

The more the small business entrepreneur must borrow, the greater the burden it becomes to repay. For example, if the following amounts are borrowed at 12 percent interest for 10 years, the payments will be:

Amount	Monthly Payment	Total Interest Paid
$ 10,000	$ 143.47	$ 7,216.40
25,000	358.68	18,041.60
50,000	717.35	36,082.00
100,000	1,434.71	72,165.20

Time

The length of time in which the loan must be repaid can be critical to the success of the business. For example, if a small business entrepreneur borrows $50,000 at 12 percent interest to start a business, the following amounts would have to be repaid depending on the length of repayment time.

Time to Repay	Monthly Payment	Total Interest Paid
5 years	$1,112.22	$16,733.20
10 years	717.36	36,083.20
15 years	600.08	58,014.40
20 years	550.54	82,129.60

Of course, this does not mean that the small business owner should always take as long to repay a loan as possible. The longer it takes to repay a loan, the more the borrower will pay in interest. For example, the 5-year loan just indicated would pay $16,733.20 in total interest whereas the 20-year loan would pay $82,129.60 in total interest.

FIGURE 5–1
Capital needs work sheet.

ESTIMATED MONTHLY EXPENSES

Item	Your estimate of monthly expenses based on sales of $_____ per year	Your estimate of how much cash you need to start your business (See Column 3.)	What to put in Column 2 (These figures are typical for one kind of business; you will have to decide how many months to allow for in your business.)
	Column 1	Column 2	Column 3
Salary of owner–manager	$	$	2 times column 1
All other salaries and wages			3 times column 1
Rent			3 times column 1
Advertising			3 times column 1
Delivery expense			3 times column 1
Supplies			3 times column 1
Telephone and telegraph			3 times column 1
Other utilities			3 times column 1
Insurance			Payment required by insurance company
Taxes, including social security			4 times column 1
Interest			3 times column 1
Maintenance			3 times column 1
Legal and other professional fees			3 times column 1
Miscellaneous			3 times column 1

FIGURE 5–1
(Continued)

STARTING COSTS YOU ONLY HAVE TO PAY ONCE

Fixtures and equipment		Fill in Figure 5–2 and put the total here
Decorating and remodeling		Talk it over with a contractor
Installation of fixtures and equipment		Talk to suppliers from whom you buy these
Starting inventory		Suppliers will probably help you estimate this
Deposits with public utilities		Find out from utilities companies
Legal and other professional fees		Lawyer, accountant, and so on
Licenses and permits		Find out from city offices what you have to have
Advertising and promotion for opening		Estimate what you'll use
Accounts receivable		What you need to buy more stock until credit customers pay
Cash		For unexpected expenses or losses, special purchases, etc.
Other		Make a separate list and enter total
Total estimated cash you need to start with	$	Add up all the numbers in column 2

Source *Checklist for Going into Business* (Washington, D.C.: Small Business Administration, 1973), p. 7.

FIGURE 5–2

Fixtures and equipment work sheet.

LIST OF FURNITURE, FIXTURES, AND EQUIPMENT

Leave out or add items to suit your business. Use separate sheets to list exactly what you need for each of the items below.	If you plan to pay cash in full, enter the full amount below and in the last column.	If you are going to pay by installments, fill out the columns below. Enter in the last column your downpayment plus at least one installment.			Estimate of the cash you need for furniture, fixtures, and equipment.
		Price	Downpayment	Amount of Each Installment	
Counters	$	$	$	$	$
Storage shelves, cabinets					
Display stands, shelves, tables					
Cash register					
Safe					
Window display fixtures					
Special lighting					
Outside sign					
Delivery equipment if needed					
Total furniture, fixtures, and equipment (Enter this figure also in Fig. 5–1 under "Starting Costs You Only Have to Pay Once.")					$

Source *Checklist for Going into Business* (Washington, D.C.: Small Business Administration, 1973), p. 12.

Interest Rate

Interest rates may fluctuate widely over a period of time and have a definite effect on how much an entrepreneur must pay for borrowed money. For example, if an entrepreneur borrows $50,000 to be repaid in 10 years at the following interest rates, the monthly payments and total amount of interest paid on the loan will be these.

Interest Rate	Monthly Payment	Total Interest Paid
10%	$660.75	$29,290.00
12%	717.35	36,082.00
14%	776.33	43,159.60
16%	837.57	50,508.40

FIGURE 5–3
Factors that increase loan payments.

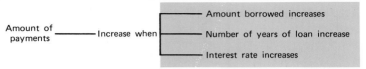

Of course, all three factors together determine the payment amount. For example, borrowing a smaller sum of money for a longer period of time than planned could still result in the same payment amount. (See Fig. 5–3.)

SOURCES OF EQUITY CAPITAL

Equity capital (ownership) may come from personal savings, from partners, or by selling stock in a corporation. The best and most common source of funds to start a business is from a person's own savings. As a general rule, most small business authorities suggest that the small business entrepreneur provide at least 50 percent of the starting funds in the form of equity capital. Usually, any amount under 50 percent requires a level of borrowing that creates payments that are extremely difficult, if not impossible, to meet.

If small business entrepreneurs do not have sufficient equity capital themselves, they may consider taking in partners or selling stock in a corporation. They may take in general or limited partners, but they must remember that they may have to give up some control over the businesses. If they incorporate and sell stock, they obtain the features of the corporation form of ownership (which may or may not be good for them), and they may have to give up some control of their businesses. In addition, if they decide to add partners or sell stock, they must be sure that there will be sufficient profits in the business to sustain themselves while providing funds for the equity investors.

SOURCES OF DEBT CAPITAL

Possible sources of **debt capital** (borrowed funds) for the small business entrepreneur are commercial banks, vendors, equipment manufacturers and distributors, factors, sales finance companies, insurance companies, private investors, Small Business Investment Corporations, and the Small Business Administration.

Commercial Banks

Commercial banks are primarily a source of **short-term loans**. In fact, they lend more short-term funds than any other type of financial institution.

FIGURE 5–4
Commercial banks' financial assistance to small business.

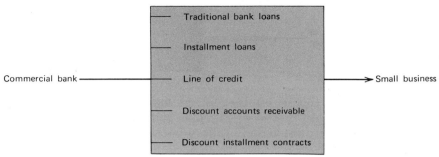

The bank receives both demand (checking accounts) and savings deposits from its customers and lends out a percentage of these deposits to businesses and individuals. Generally, 5 years is the maximum length of time of any loan a commercial bank makes and usually it doesn't exceed 3 years. However, banks do participate in loans with the Small Business Administration that are for longer periods of time.

As a rule, commercial banks usually do not lend funds for long-term fixed assets such as buildings and land. Often, they do lend money for the purchase of equipment and inventories and for financing customer credit.

The commercial bank may lend money in several ways—by traditional bank loans, installment loans, line of credit, discounting accounts receivables, and discounting installment sales contracts. (See Fig. 5–4.)

Traditional Bank Loan

The **traditional bank loan** may extend for a few days to finance such things as taking advantage of a cash discount. Also, it may extend for several months or years to finance various purchases or to provide working capital. Traditional bank loans are repaid when due and are not installment type loans.

Installment Loans

Installment loans are made to businesses by commercial banks usually to finance purchases of equipment and other fixed assets. Generally, they are for a year or more in time. For example, a business might borrow $9,000 for 3 years from a commercial bank to purchase a panel delivery truck. At 12 percent interest, the business would be required to pay the bank $298.93 per month for 3 years. The actual or true interest rate on this type of loan is almost always higher than the interest rate on the traditional bank loan for the same borrower.

Line of Credit

The **line of credit** is not a true type of business loan, but rather an established limit of credit a business may automatically borrow. All loans above an amount established by a bank must go to a committee made up of officers of the bank for approval. To avoid delay and save effort, a commercial bank's loan committee will usually establish a line of credit for a business firm. The business may then simply notify the bank that it is borrowing the money, and the money is automatically made available.

Discount Accounts Receivable

Another method by which commercial banks help businesses finance customer credit is called discount accounts receivable. The bank loans a business a percentage of the amount of its accounts receivable, and the business pledges its accounts receivable as collateral. For example, a business, to provide working capital, might take $10,000 worth of customers' 30-day accounts to the bank for discounting. The bank would make an estimate of the collectability of the accounts and lend a percentage of the total amount, for instance, $8,000. The business would receive cash immediately to use as working capital. As the business receives cash from customers on these accounts receivable, it turns them over to the bank until the entire loan plus interest is repaid. After the bank is repaid, the business retains any additional funds it collects. If it does not collect enough accounts to repay the bank, it must make up the difference.

Discount Installment Contracts

Commercial banks also assist businesses in their customer credit by discounting **installment sales contracts**. To illustrate, a customer makes a purchase of merchandise and signs an installment contract with a business. The business then takes the contract to a bank, where it receives money for the contract.

Most customer installment sales contracts contain an effective or true interest rate of between 21 and 24 percent. Banks usually will loan the business the full face value of the contract. The interest charged in the installment sales contract is then their fee for making the loan. The bank or business then collects the payments from the customer, which go to the bank to repay the loan. If the customer fails to repay the contract, the business must reimburse the commercial bank.

Prime Interest Rate and
Interest Rates to Small Business

The prime interest rate is the rate of interest the commercial bank currently charges its best customers. In other words, it is the lowest interest rate at which they will loan money. It varies considerably from small business customer to small business customer, but the average interest rate charged small businesses probably is about 2 percent above the prime rate. This interest rate applies to small businesses that have been in business a sufficient period of time to prove their profitability (ability to repay the loan). Because of the high failure rate of new small businesses, commercial banks usually will not lend money for a new venture unless the entrepreneur has "good" collateral that is about twice the amount of the loan to pledge against the loan.

FIGURE 5–5

Prime interest rate from 1973 to 1983.

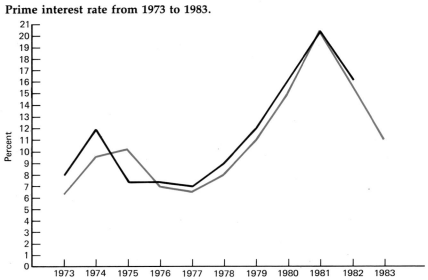

SPECIAL INTEREST FEATURE

High Interest Rates Cause Problems

Small businesses often must borrow money for various reasons. As demonstrated earlier, the interest rate determines to a large degree the amount of their payments. Relatively stable interest rates at reasonable levels are very important to most small businesses. If interest rates climb to very high rates, many of these businesses find it impossible to borrow funds and repay them. High interest rates and wide fluctuations in these rates have been a particularly troublesome problem for many small businesses in recent years. In fact, they probably have been the primary cause of many small business failures. Figure 5–5 shows how much the prime interest rate has fluctuated in recent years.

Applying for a Loan

Bankers generally look for three things when considering a loan application: (1) ability to repay the loan, (2) collateral, and (3) credit record. The small business entrepreneur should take along three recent financial statements when applying for a loan or a line of credit: (1) a balance sheet, (2) an income statement (a copy of the business's federal income tax statement may be substituted or added), and (3) a cash flow statement (see Chapter 11 for samples and a discussion of these statements). The entrepreneur should also

FIGURE 5–6
Sample financial statement presented to commercial bank.

BALANCE SHEET
December 31, 1982

Assets

Cash	$ 8,192	
Note receivable from sale of land	136,266	
Rent houses (2-current market value)	124,000	
Home	78,000	
Mineral rights (2 both leased)	50,000	
Personal property	40,000	
Total Assets		$436,458

Liabilities

Mortgages on rent houses	$101,800	
Mortgage on home	39,000	
Personal credit (automobile & personal)	2,500	
Total Liabilities		$143,300
Net Worth		$293,158

INCOME
1982

Salary	$ 53,460	
Interest income	17,831	
Cash from note receivable (principal)	6,500	
Income for 1982		$ 77,791

MONTHLY PAYMENTS

Rent houses		
Payments to mortgage company	$1,268	
Rental income	875	
Balance paid		$393
Home mortgage		418
Automobile and credit cards		400
Monthly payments		$1,211

take along a personal financial statement when applying for venture capital. Figure 5–6 is a financial statement used by one entrepreneur to obtain a $10,000 unsecured loan and a line of credit of $50,000.

Vendors

Vendors can be an important source of short-term credit for small business firms. Firms that sell inventories to a business usually will finance the purchase of these goods for short periods of time, usually from 30 to 90 days. For example, a drug wholesaler might sell merchandise to a drugstore on credit, with the store having 30 days to pay. For 30 days, the drugstore would then be selling merchandise for which it had not paid. At the end of the 30-day period, the drugstore would then take money that it had received from the sale of the merchandise and pay the amount owed the drug wholesaler.

Vendors also have needs for working capital, so it is a common practice for them to offer their business customers a cash discount. When they offer a cash discount, the terms of the purchase, such as "3/10 n/30," mean that the total amount of the purchase is due in 30 days; however, if the customer will pay the total amount of the purchase within 10 days, he or she is allowed to subtract 3 percent from the total amount. Business firms often find that they can borrow money from a commercial bank for 20 days to take advantage of this discount and the cost of the loan is less than the cash discount.

Equipment Manufacturers and Distributors

To encourage businesses to purchase their **equipment, manufacturers and distributors** often will finance the purchase. Usually, this loan exists in the form of an installment sales contract. The manufacturers or distributors may actually carry the note themselves or discount the installment sales contract with a financial institution. Machinery, equipment, display shelves, cash registers, and office equipment are some of the more common items financed by manufacturers and distributors.

Factors

Factors are financial firms that finance accounts receivable for business firms. They may either purchase or discount accounts receivable.

If they discount accounts receivable, they function exactly as the commercial bank example discussed previously. They will lend a certain amount of money based on their analysis of the collectability of the accounts, and the business turns them over to the factor until the original amount borrowed plus interest is repaid. All remaining collections are kept by the business firm. If the small business fails to collect the amount owed the factor (including interest), it must make up the difference.

When factors purchase accounts receivable, they make an analysis of the collectability of the accounts and pay the business firm a percentage of the total amount. The business firm (sometimes the factor) then collects the accounts and turns all collections over to the factor. It is very important to the factors that they judge the collectability of the accounts with considerable accuracy because the total they collect must cover what they loan and their expected profit. If they collect less, then they must suffer the loss.

Sales Finance Companies

Sales finance companies purchase installment sales contracts from business firms. The customer will sign an installment sales contract, after which the business firm sells the contract to the sales finance company. Usually, the business firm will receive the full face value of the contract, and the profit of the sales finance company is derived from the interest of the contract.

Sales finance companies also engage in what is known as "floor planning." Floor planning is common in the retail automobile trade and in retail sales of large appliances. To illustrate, the sales finance company finances the purchase of the dealer's stock of automobiles. In return for this financing, the dealer then pays the sales finance company interest on the loan until the car is sold. When the car is sold, the dealer then turns the contract over to the sales finance company and receives the full amount of the purchase. The sales finance company then collects principal and interest in monthly installment payments from the automobile purchaser. The automobile serves as collateral to the sales finance company until the loan is repaid.

Insurance Companies

Insurance companies make some **long-term loans** to small businesses for the purchase of fixed assets. Insurance companies collect premiums on their policies and then invest them in stocks, bonds, and business loans. Moreover, insurance companies are regulated by both state and federal agencies, and the type of loans they are able to make is controlled to some degree by government agencies in order to protect the policyholders. Insurance companies usually loan funds to small businesses that have high value collateral to pledge to ensure the repayment of the loan. Loans for shopping malls and apartments are common business loans made by insurance companies. Other than these types of loans, insurance companies provide a limited source of small business loans.

Private Investors

Private citizens who lend their savings are often a source of capital for small business. They usually lend their funds for a time period of 1 to 5 years. The **private investor** is generally an individual who is willing to risk his or her funds for a higher interest rate than he or she would be able to obtain from savings and loan associations or bonds. The interest rate private investors charge is usually above that of most financial institutions. It often is in the range charged by small loan companies that make consumer loans.

Small business owners should investigate private sources to make sure they are not dealing with someone who is associated with crime or usury or both.

Small Business Investment Corporations

Small Business Investment Corporations (SBIC) are privately owned financial corporations that are licensed, regulated, and promoted by the Small Business Administration, an agency of the federal government. SBICs may only loan or invest money in small businesses according to the SBA (Small Business Administration) definition of a small business. They themselves may obtain loans or guarantees of loans from the SBA to lend and invest in small businesses. An SBIC must have a minimum initial investment of at least $150,000. Often the investment exceeds more than $1 million. The SBIC may obtain loans or guarantees (the SBA guarantees the financial institution making the loan that the loan will be repaid) of loans that amount to twice the SBIC's paid-in capital and surplus with a $7.5 million maximum.

The SBIC then takes the funds it has invested and funds obtained through the SBA and either (1) makes loans that must exceed 5 years to small businesses or (2) invests in small businesses. SBICs often invest in small businesses but are prohibited from obtaining a controlling interest in the businesses. Many SBICs provide management consulting to the business firms to protect their investment.

In 1969 the SBA established a program of SBICs to aid minority enterprises. These are called MESBICs (Minority Enterprise Small Business Investment Corporations).

Small Business Administration

The **Small Business Administration** (SBA) was established as an agency in the Department of Commerce in 1953 to help promote small business. The SBA engages in various types of activities that assist small businesses, including financial assistance (other types of assistance will be discussed in Chapter 22).

The basic types of loans the SBA engages in are (1) direct and immediate participation loans, (2) loan guarantees, (3) pool loans, (4) economic opportunity loans, (5) development company loans, and (6) disaster loans. (See Fig. 5–7.)

Eligibility Requirements

The SBA makes loans only to small businesses. The SBA's definition of what is a small business differs according to type of business.[1] (See also Chapter 1.)

1. Manufacturing—number of employees may range up to 1500, depending on the industry.

2. Wholesaling—yearly sales not over $2 million to $22 million, depending on the industry.

---

[1] *SBA Business Loans* (Washington, D.C.: Small Business Administration, March 1978).

FIGURE 5–7
Types of Small Business Administration loans.

3. Services—yearly sales less than $2 million to $8 million, depending on the industry.
4. Retailing—yearly sales less than $2 million to $7.5 million, depending on the industry.
5. Construction—yearly receipts of less than $9.5 million for last three years.
6. Agriculture—yearly sales of less than $1 million.

(The SBA is currently considering a change in its definition of a small business.)

The SBA does not compete with financial institutions in making loans. If the applicant can obtain sufficient money at a private financial institution, federal law does not allow the SBA to make that person a loan. Before applying to the SBA, the applicant must seek private financing at a local bank or other lending institution. If the applicant lives in a city of more than 200,000 people, he or she must apply to two lending institutions before going to the SBA.

The SBA also specifies six general credit requirements.[2]

1. The applicant must be of good character.
2. The applicant must show ability to operate the business successfully.
3. The applicant must have enough capital so that, with an SBA loan, he or she can operate on a sound financial basis.

---

[2] Ibid.

4. The applicant must show the proposed loan to be of sound value or secured so as to assure repayment reasonably.

5. The applicant must show that the past earnings or future prospects indicate ability to repay the loan out of profit.

6. The applicant must be able to provide funds to have a reasonable amount at stake to withstand possible losses during early stages if the venture is a new business.

Ineligible Applicants

The SBA cannot make loans under certain circumstances.[3]

1. When funds are otherwise available at reasonable rates.

2. When the loan is to "(a) pay off a loan to a creditor or creditors of the applicant who are inadequately secured and in a position to sustain loss, (b) provide funds for distribution of payment to the principals of the applicant, or (c) replenish funds previously used for such purposes."

3. When the loan is for speculation in any kind of property.

4. When the applicant is a nonprofit organization.

5. When the applicant is a newspaper, magazine, or book publishing company.

6. When any of the gross income of the applicant is derived from gambling.

7. When the loan provides funds to lending institutions.

8. When the loan is used to purchase real property to be held for investment.

Direct and Immediate Participation Loans

The SBA can make a loan directly to the small business, or it can participate in loans with private financial institutions. When it is a participating loan, the SBA lends part of the funds, and the private financial institution puts up part of the loan. The maximum amount that can be loaned by the SBA in either type of loan is $150,000. The interest rate charged by the SBA is set by law, based on a formula that relates to the cost of money the government is currently borrowing. The current interest rate is 14.5 percent. Within certain limitations banks set the interest rate on their part of the loan. Direct and participating loans comprise a very small percentage of the total financing made possible by the SBA.

Loan Guarantees

The SBA is allowed by law to guarantee up to 90 percent of a loan to a financial institution, with a maximum of $350,000 ($500,000 in special situations). The lending institution lends all the money, but the SBA guarantees a

---

[3]Ibid.

specific percentage repayment. If the borrower defaults on the loan, the SBA then reimburses the lending institution the amount of the loan guarantee.

Guaranteed loans comprise a large percentage of the total financing by the SBA. The bank can charge any interest rate up to a rate maximum set by the SBA. At present a bank can charge a maximum rate of 2.75 percent over the prime rate charged by large New York banks if the loan is for 7 years or more. If the loan is for fewer than 7 years, the bank can charge a maximum of 2.25 percent over the prime rate. The SBA prefers guaranteed loans rather than direct or participation loans because this allows the SBA to make many times more money available to small businesses.

Pool Loans
Small businesses sometimes pool their purchasing power by forming corporations for the purpose of purchasing raw material, equipment, inventories, supplies, or research. For example, several small retail stores may form a corporation to purchase all or part of their inventory in order to obtain better prices from quantity purchases, such as in carload lots. The SBA is allowed to make loans to these corporations, the maximum being $250,000 multiplied by the number of small businesses in the pool.

Economic Opportunity Loans
The SBA makes economic opportunity loans to disadvantaged persons (1) whose total income is not sufficient for needs of the family and (2) who are unable to acquire financing through other lending institutions at reasonable terms. The maximum economic opportunity loan is $100,000 for up to 15 years. Economic opportunity loans historically have been high-risk loans with almost no collateral in an attempt to aid disadvantaged persons.

Development Company Loans
The SBA makes long-term loans to both state and local development companies, which they, in turn, lend to businesses for the purchase of land, buildings, machinery, and equipment.

State Development Companies   The SBA is able to lend a state development company an amount equal to all loans from other sources for as long as 20 years.

Local Development Companies   A local development company may be either a profit or a nonprofit corporation established to assist local economic growth. It must have at least 25 stockholders or members. The SBA is able to lend up to $350,000 for each small business the local development corporation assists.

Disaster Loans
The SBA is allowed by law to make low interest loans to small businesses that are damaged owing to some form of disaster, such as a hurricane or flood.

Disaster loans to small businesses are limited to $500,000 and may be for periods of up to 30 years.

Loan Application

Businesses that are in existence follow different steps from an entrepreneur trying to start a new business.[4]

For Established Businesses

1. Prepare a balance sheet (see Chapter 11) listing all assets and liabilities of the business (not personal items).
2. Prepare an income statement (see Chapter 11) for the previous full year and the current year to the date of the balance sheet.
3. Prepare a current personal financial statement of all owners (excluding stockholders who hold less than 20 percent of the stock).
4. Prepare a list of all collateral to be offered as security for the loan with present market value of each.
5. State the amount of the loan desired and the purposes for which it will be used.
6. Take all this material to a bank and apply for a loan. If the loan is refused, ask about a guaranteed loan or participation loan. If the bank is interested, have it contact the SBA. Remember, you must go to two banks before applying to the SBA if the city has more than 200,000 population.
7. If a guaranty or a participation loan is not available, write or visit the nearest SBA office.

Entrepreneurs Starting a New Business

1. Describe in detail the type of business you wish to start.
2. Describe your experience and management capabilities.
3. Prepare a statement of how much you or others have to invest in the business and how much you need to borrow.
4. Prepare a current financial statement listing all personal assets and liabilities.
5. Prepare a detailed projection of earnings for the first year of operation.
6. Prepare a list of all collateral to be offered as security and your estimate of the current market value of each.
7. Take all this material to a bank and apply for a loan. If the loan is declined, ask about a guaranty or participation loan. If the bank is interested, have it contact the SBA. You must go to two banks before going to SBA if the city has more than 200,000 population.

---

[4]Ibid.

8. If a guaranty or participation loan is not available, write or visit your nearest SBA office.

SOURCES OF FUNDS
BY TYPE OF CAPITAL NEED

A general picture of sources of capital for small business is shown in Figure 5–8. However, small business firms have various types of short-term and long-term needs. Short-term needs may include such items as working capital, customer credit, and inventories. Long-term needs include such items as land, buildings, machinery, fixtures, furniture, and equipment. Very few sources extend loans for all these needs. Most financial institutions specialize in lending money for only one or two areas of these needs. Figure 5–9 presents various sources of capital for small business listed by the general areas of needs for which they specialize in providing funds.

SUMMARY OF KEY POINTS

1. The total paid on loans increases when (a) the amount borrowed increases, (b) the number of years of the loan increases, and (c) the interest rate increases.

2. Equity capital may come from personal savings, from partners, or by selling stock in a corporation.

3. Possible sources of debt capital are commercial banks, vendors, equipment manufacturers and distributors, factors, sales finance companies,

FIGURE 5–8

Sources of capital for small business.

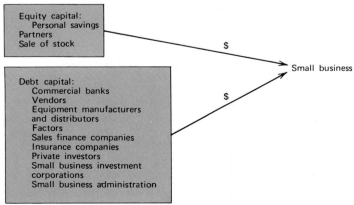

FIGURE 5–9
Sources of funds by type of capital needed.

SHORT-TERM CAPITAL

Working Capital (salaries and other expenses)	Customer Credit	Inventories
Commercial banks	Commercial banks	Commercial banks
	Factors	Vendors
	Sales finance companies	

LONG-TERM CAPITAL

Land and Buildings	Machinery, Fixtures, Furniture, and Equipment
Insurance companies	Commercial banks
Private investors	Equipment manufacturers and distributors
	Private investors

ALL TYPES OF CAPITAL NEEDS

Private Sources	Government Sources
Small Business Investment Corporations	Small Business Administration

insurance companies, private investors, Small Business Investment Corporations, and the Small Business Administration.

4. Commercial banks lend money by traditional bank loans, installment loans, line of credit, discounting accounts receivables, and discounting installment sales contracts.

5. The prime interest rate is the rate the commercial bank is currently charging its best customers. Loans to small business average about 2 percent above the prime rate.

6. A small business should provide (a) a balance sheet, (b) an income statement or a federal income tax return or both, and (c) a cash flow statement when applying for a loan.

7. Vendors that sell inventories usually will finance the purchase for 30 to 90 days.

8. Equipment manufacturers and distributors will often finance purchase of their equipment to small business.

9. Factors purchase or discount accounts receivable.

10. Sales finance companies purchase installment sales contracts and provide "floor planning" for many businesses.

11. Insurance companies are a source of funds for large buildings, shopping malls, and apartments.

12. Private investors sometimes lend money to small businesses, but their rate is usually higher than those of many other sources.

13. Small Business Investment Corporations borrow money from the Small Business Administration and either lend money to small businesses or invest in them.

14. The Small Business Administration makes six kinds of loans: (a) direct and immediate participation loans, (b) loan guarantees, (c) pool loans, (d) economic opportunity loans, (e) development company loans, and (f) disaster loans.

DISCUSSION QUESTIONS

1. What are some of the items for which a small business needs money?
2. Where may a small business obtain equity capital?
3. If you wanted to finance customer credit using a commercial bank, what types of loans might you ask for at the bank?
4. How do vendors help finance small businesses?
5. How do equipment manufacturers and distributors help finance small businesses?
6. How does a factor operate?
7. How does a sales finance company operate?
8. Where do insurance companies get money to lend, and what type of loans do they usually make to small businesses?
9. Why do private investors lend money to small businesses?
10. What is a small business investment corporation?
11. What types of loan does the Small Business Administration make?
12. If you were a small business owner, where would you look for funds to purchase machinery and equipment?

STUDENT PROJECT

Interview a small business owner and find out the following.

1. What were the sources of his or her starting capital? What percentage was equity capital and what percentage was debt capital?
2. Does he or she use any of the following financial sources? Are they used for short-term or long-term funds? What does he or she use them to finance?

   Commercial banks
   Vendors

Equipment manufacturers and distributors
Factors
Sales finance companies
Insurance companies
Private investors
Small business investment corporations
Small Business Administration

CASE A

Gene and Cindy's Auto Parts Store

Gene Tims and his wife, Cindy, have both held jobs that paid good salaries for 15 years. Gene has been the manager of an auto parts store, and Cindy is an accounting supervisor for a large electronics corporation. They have been very frugal and saved their money with the idea of starting their own business. They now have $210,000 in money market certificates.

Gene and Cindy want to open an auto parts store with a machine shop included. The location that they feel is the best for the store is on a major thoroughfare in a section of town that is growing rapidly. There are two auto parts stores in this section of town, but Gene and Cindy do not think they would offer any real competition. One store has only about $60,000 worth of inventory, and many customers have found that it often does not have what they are looking for. The other store is a block off the main street in a small shopping center. Most of the people who travel the main street do not even know it is there, and it has about the same amount of stock as the other store. Gene and Cindy feel a store in a good location with a large inventory would probably take over most of the business in the area.

The location they have selected is on the right side of the main street when people are traveling away from town. The price of the land is $75,000. The building Gene and Cindy want to build would be a sheet metal building with brick trim in the front. The front would also have large glass windows. The building itself will cost them $125,000. Counters, shelving, and equipment will cost $25,000. The couple plan to carry an extensive inventory, which will cost $120,000. They also feel it will take about 6 months to break even, and their working capital should be $20,000.

This means they will need an additional $155,000 to start their store. They have asked your advice on where they can obtain the funds for the business.

QUESTIONS

1. Examine all sources of small business financing, and determine which might give Gene and Cindy a loan and for what purpose.

2. What should they spend their $210,000 for, and where should they borrow the $155,000, and for what should it be spent?

CASE B

Marvin Matlock

Marvin Matlock has operated a restaurant in a town of 18,000 for the past 10 years. His restaurant is located at one of the off-ramps of a major highway, and his sign and building are visible for several hundred yards. He features "down home cooking" at reasonable prices with fast service. During the past 10 years he has been in business, Marvin has gone to considerable effort to make sure that the quality of his food stays constant and that the appearance of his establishment is always clean and neat. As a reward for his efforts, profits have always been good. The past 2 years the business has cleared about $40,000 per year.

Two weeks ago someone left a burner on under a skillet filled with grease. This resulted in a fire that completely destroyed the restaurant. Marvin had taken out fire insurance when he first started 10 years ago. The agent had asked Marvin on several occasions if he wanted to increase his insurance owing to increased costs, but Marvin had never done anything about the value of the policy.

The fire insurance policy paid Marvin $150,000. After checking with contractors and equipment dealers, Marvin finds that a new building will cost him $175,000, and equipment and furniture will cost another $60,000. Even with his savings and the insurance money, Marvin only has $180,000. It will take 5 months to get back into business. Marvin feels he must have at least $1500 a month to meet his personal needs. He has estimated that he needs about $65,000 more to get him back into business and provide enough money for working capital to get him going again.

Marvin lists his needs as follows:

Building	$175,000
Equipment	40,000
Furniture	20,000
Personal draw	7,500
Working capital and miscellaneous expenses	2,500
Total funds needed	$245,000
Funds on hand	− 180,000
Additional funds needed	$ 65,000

Marvin wants you to help him find the money.

QUESTIONS

1. Examine all sources of small business financing, and determine which might give Marvin a loan and for what purpose.

2. Which sources would you suggest Marvin borrow from, and how much should he borrow?

SMALL BUSINESS ADMINISTRATION PUBLICATIONS

Free

The ABC's of Borrowing

A Venture Capital Primer for Small Business

Sound Cash Management and Borrowing

Can You Lease or Buy Equipment?

Thinking About Going into Business?

For Sale

Capital Planning

Understanding Money Sources

Evaluating Money Sources

C H A P T E R   S I X

LOCATION ANALYSIS FOR THE SMALL BUSINESS

LEARNING GOALS

After reading this chapter, you will understand:

1. That location is of utmost concern for the small business owner.
2. That there are many factors that should be considered when evaluating the potential of a trading area.
3. That accessibility of the site is important to the success of the firm.
4. The difference between consumer, shopping, specialty, and impulse goods.
5. Why adequate parking is an important criterion in store location.
6. The differences between various sites: central business district, neighborhood locations, shopping centers and malls, string street locations, isolated locations, and retail affinity.
7. The importance of site economics.
8. That zoning laws are important to the small business owner.
9. Why a small business owner should conduct a traffic analysis of the proposed store location.

KEY WORDS

Trade area
Disposable personal income
Discretionary buying power
Convenience goods
Shopping goods
Specialty goods
Impulse goods
Shopping center

Community shopping center
Minimalls
Specialty centers
Fashion centers
String street location
Retail affinity
100 percent location
Traffic count

SMALL BUSINESS PROFILE

Tapping Unused Riches in the Slums

The English language is not exactly the forte of John Mariotta, founder of the Welbilt Electronic Die Corporation in New York City's notorious South Bronx. Born of Puerto Rican immigrants, he had little chance to polish his verbal skills. Still, his business has an annual sales volume of $12 million.

But this is a success story not so much about Welbilt's owner as about Welbilt's workers—ghetto youths and hard-core unemployed who learned a trade and discovered the work ethic.

Mariotta was 36 when in 1965 he set up Welbilt, his fourth attempt to go into business. Fred Neuberger, now vice president and part owner, was the needed extra ingredient, Mariotta says. An experienced sales engineer, Neuberger brought Welbilt its first big contract, for air filter assemblies for Bell helicopters.

Today, the Welbilt plant stands like a beacon in a sea of residential and industrial deterioration. While remaking society's castoffs into operators capable of running the latest in computerized metalworking machinery, it has become a respected supplier of precision parts and assemblies to the armed forces and the defense industry. The firm has won increasingly larger private and government contracts.

Teaching the unskilled was not a matter of choice, since getting machinists to commute to Welbilt was—and still is—impossible. Job hunters quickly lost interest when they found out where the factory was.

"How are you going to make machinists out of semi-illiterates?" parts buyers for the big corporations would ask him, Mariotta recalls. But he has done it, motivating his workers with the homilies of a Benjamin Franklin rather than the formulas of a Ph.D. in labor relations. Among the doubters that are now convinced are General Electric and TSARCOM (Troop Support and Aviation Readiness Command).

Mariotta still interviews every job applicant. "I tell them, 'You got to work hard. You got to learn.'"

Once he is convinced an applicant can be counted on, he hires on the spot. No effort is made to check references. "What do I care about the past?" he demands. A note of intensity colors his voice. "What if he did commit a crime? Today, right now, he wants to work. That's the only thing that counts."

Mariotta's unorthodox procedures stem from this conviction: Most people abhor idleness. But language and educational deficiencies, not to mention prejudice in hiring, bar some from decent opportunities, he contends.

"Everyone is saying, 'What are we going to do about the South Bronx?'" Mariotta growls. "Everyone is saying, 'You can't teach those so-and-so's anything. You can't get them to come to work on time.' Well, it's not so. I say to them, 'Maybe we have no education, maybe our manners aren't up to par, but this is where it's at between you and me: If you're willing to work, I'll increase your salary.'"

Chico is a good example, Mariotta says. "One morning, in walks Chico with a cigar box under one arm. He says he is working in a hotel, washing dishes. In Mexico he was a mechanic, but here no one will hire him because he doesn't speak English. I ask him what's in the box. He shows me a mike, a 4-inch caliper, two C-clamps and a 6-inch rule. They are all brand-new. I say to myself, if he spent half a week's pay to buy tools, he must really want to learn. So I put him on. When he came to the shop the next morning, he didn't even know how to turn the saw on. But day after day, we stood beside him at the bench till he learned."

The plant, which has never been struck, was organized by the Teamsters in 1974 after peaceful negotiations. "Our relations with the union are extremely cordial," Neuberger observes. "The attitude here is so good that the pilferage and vandalism that plague other industrial enterprises are nearly nonexistent."

Workers who have become supervisors have seen Mariotta fulfill his promises. A bonus arrangement instituted in 1980 pays $1,000 each to first-line supervisors for every $1 million the plant ships. The incentive plan, which added $10,000 to each supervisor's income last year, has also fostered interdepartmental cooperation, Mariotta says.

What the kids he recruited from the streets would have become had there been no Welbilt is a thought that stokes Mariotta's contempt for the nation's multibillion-dollar welfare system. "Everyplace in the U.S. where there is a South Bronx, we have more unused riches than all the Arab oil countries put together," he argues. "Our riches are in our people who want to work. Let the businessmen and the government put factories here where the people are, and you'll see how fast those billions will shrink."

Source   Gerson Goodman, "Tapping Unused Riches in the Slums," *Nation's Business*, February 1982, p. 41. Reprinted by permission of *Nation's Business* (February, 1982). Copyright 1982 by *Nation's Business*, Chamber of Commerce of the United States.

When anyone is launching a new business venture, especially retail firms, the analysis and choice of location have been singled out as two of the most crucial factors in determining the success of the firm. Owners of ongoing firms appreciate the importance of the site and its effect on the economic vitality of the firm. Site analysis is not a one-time activity. Instead, it is a continuous process, and owner–managers must select the management strategy that best meets the firm's specific requirements. For example, when a lease expires, should the owner renew the lease or relocate? If the owner has intentions of adding another store, the choice of site for the additional site is critical.

Most small business owners choose a location in their hometown or neighborhood. Frequently, the selection of a particular site is based on the availability of a vacant building or the site's proximity to the residence of the owner or owners.

Clearly, these convenience factors should not be the dominant reason for choosing a specific site without a thorough analysis of the overall potential for the site.

In the ensuing discussion, our attention is focused on retail, service, and manufacturing firms. Although the material emphasizes launching a new business, it can easily be adapted to the needs of the owner of the ongoing business who is contemplating relocation or expansion.

The major variables to be analyzed include trade area analysis, strategic factors in site selection analysis, accessibility of the site, parking, types of goods sold, site choices, site economics, zoning regulations, and traffic analysis.

TRADE AREA ANALYSIS

The **trade area** is the geographic area that provides a major portion of the continuing patronage necessary to support the individual business or a larger shopping district, such as a shopping center. The trade area can usually be divided into three zones of influence.

1. The *primary* trade area is the zone within which a business can serve consumers better than, or as well as, major competitors from the standpoint of convenience and accessibility, and it usually contributes about two thirds of the total traffic volume.

2. The *secondary* trade area is the area beyond the primary zone where a firm is still able to exert a reasonably strong pull but is at some disadvantage with respect to convenience and accessibility. This zone may generate 15 to 20 percent of all sales.

3. The *tertiary* trade area is often not definable in terms of geographical boundaries but consists of customers who patronize the store for reasons not related to proximity to residence. This zone often contributes 5 to 15 percent of total sales.[1]

The search for the business location involves finding the answers to three major questions regarding the trade area.

1. What town or city affords the greatest opportunity for the particular type of business under consideration?

2. What area within the chosen town or city demonstrates strong potential for survival and growth?

3. What specific site in the selected area best meets the requirements of the proposed business?

---

[1] William R. Davidson, Alton F. Doody, and Daniel J. Sweeney, *Retailing Management*, 4th ed. (New York: Ronald, 1975), pp. 491–492.

STRATEGIC FACTORS IN SITE SELECTION ANALYSIS

Analysis of the trade area should begin with an economic feasibility study that will aid in defining the potential of the area for the proposed business venture. The same factors should be evaluated in finding answers to the three major questions concerning the selection of the town or city, the area in the town or city, and the specific site. Strategic factors to be analyzed in studying market potential include population trends, income levels, occupational analysis and educational level, nature of the competition, site history, and community attitudes.

Population Trends

A study of the population enables the small business owner to create a profile of the people in the area. The profile will reveal significant characteristics of the population, such as the following.

1. What is the age distribution of the population?
2. Are young people able to find employment after graduation, or do most have to relocate to find employment?
3. Are the families chiefly younger families with children or older families?
4. How many persons or families are there in the area, and how has this changed over time?
5. How many families (or single persons) own their homes? How many rent?
6. What is the value of the homes? How much is the monthly rent?
7. How many one-person households and how many small or large families are there in the area?

To illustrate, an analysis of the population of a rapidly growing city was made to determine the area's potential for a fast-food franchise. The study revealed that the population had increased from 2800 in 1970 to 13,000 by 1980 and is projected to be 30,000 by 1990. The great influx of population consists of young married couples with children. Thus, the area has a strong potential for new home purchases and related furnishings as well as convenience goods, such as the fast-food franchise.

Income Level

A second important economic indicator is the income level in the trade area because it measures the total **disposable personal income of** residents as well as the income available for expenditure in the various retail categories: food, beverages, and tobacco; clothing; accessories and jewelry; personal care;

housing and household operations; medical care; personal business; transportation; and recreation. Disposable personal income is the amount of money that consumers have available to spend and is a measure of available purchasing power. As income levels rise, **discretionary buying power** rises. Discretionary buying power is that part of the income that is not required for the purchase of the basic necessities of life.

Estimating Purchasing Power

Purchasing power for a trade area can be estimated from several sources. One source is the Census Bureau, which publishes extensive data on characteristics of the population, such as income, education, housing, and occupation. Census Bureau data are available for various geographical designations. The standard metropolitan statistical area (SMSA) includes a county or counties containing a central city of at least 50,000 inhabitants plus contiguous counties that are socially and economically integrated with the central county. Census tracts are subdivisions of SMSAs. Each tract is divided into areas of 4000 to 5000 residents. Statistical information and a map of each tract are published. In urban areas, block statistics are available that contain housing and population characteristics of city blocks.

A second resource is the *Survey of Buying Power,* published by *Sales and Marketing Management* magazine. This annual survey reports data on individual and family purchasing power. A third source of data is information available from local sources, such as the chamber of commerce or trade associations. Finally, a market survey can be made to collect buying power data for the specific trade area. This technique is discussed in Chapter 16.

To illustrate the estimation of purchasing power, let us assume that a person is studying the possibility of establishing a furniture and appliance store in an area. A method of obtaining a general forecast of the trade area's purchasing power and ability to support a firm is presented in Figure 6–1. In

FIGURE 6–1

Estimation of purchasing power for a furniture and appliance store.

1.	Determine number of household (family) units in trade area (from census data or utility company).	1,600
2.	Multiply number of household (family) units by average household income (mean and median incomes available from census data).	$14,100
3.	Equals total purchasing power (total disposable income).	$22,560,000
4.	Multiply total purchasing power by percentage of disposable income spent for furniture and appliances (from census data or retail trade association).	$22,560,000
		× .05
5.	Equals total potential purchasing power for furniture and appliances.	=$1,128,000

this estimate, the percentage of disposable income for furniture is based on nationwide personal consumption expenditures. Local area percentage expenditures may reflect differences and should be noted. Likewise, higher income levels in an area represent greater potential for furniture and household equipment purchases. With the forecast in hand, the small business manager will be in a better position to judge the area's potential to support another furniture and appliance store.

Occupational Analysis and Educational Level

Income, occupation, and level of education are closely related. The occupational and educational survey should disclose the types of employment in the area as well as the percentage in each employment category. (See Fig. 6–2.) These data will reflect the stability of employment in the area. To illustrate, a high percentage of the work force employed in seasonal jobs would indicate a fluctuating employment picture for the area and thus involve more risk for a new or expanding firm.

The educational analysis will reveal significant data about the area also. Generally, a population with a higher educational level will have higher-level jobs and greater income. This fact indicates that consumers in this area have greater discretionary buying power to expend for nonstaple merchandise.

Analysis of the Competition

Analysis of the competitive situation in the trade area is one means of forecasting the chances of survival of the business. Evaluation of competitors should provide a conceptual view of the nature, location, size, quantity, and quality of competition in the trade area. The analysis will likely reveal trends in the local business environment. For example, the analysis will enable the

FIGURE 6–2

Percentage of employed persons in New York City on nonagricultural payrolls classified by industry division.

Industry Division	Percentage of Employed Persons
Government	15.2%
Services	28.5
Finance, insurance, real estate	14.4
Wholesale and retail trade	18.1
Transportation and utilities	7.3
Manufacturing	13.7
Construction	2.7
Mining	0.1

Source *Employment and Earnings*, vol. 30, no. 1 (Washington, D.C.: Bureau of Labor Statistics, U.S. Department of Labor, 1983), pp. 98–99.

small business owner to determine if other competitors are moving into the local area. The survey should also provide a perspective of the actions of established competitors; for example, are they expanding or maintaining the status quo or closing? If there are only a limited number of competitors, it does not necessarily suggest that an additional firm has a strong potential for success in the community. Instead, it may be an indicator that the local area cannot or will not support an additional firm of the proposed type.

Site History

The history of a site should at least be studied. If a site has an unfavorable history, one marked by a succession of failures, the owner should seek to ascertain the reasons for the failures. Many possibilities earlier identified include poor location, wrong type of business for the site, incompetent management, or unacceptable products or services. Past failures at a site do not mean that future occupants will fail. What site history does suggest to the prospective occupant is the need for capitalizing on the knowledge of causes of past failures and using this knowledge to advantage to avoid similar problems for the firm.

Community Attitudes

The prevailing community attitudes have a substantial influence on shaping the character and future of the town or city and, consequently, the small business. Positive attitudes encourage growth through aggressive programs and plans designed to stimulate the local economy. The development and implementation of plans to attract new businesses and to stimulate growth of existing firms reveal a positive business environment in the trade area. Specific plans may include a special tax break or availability of low interest loans for new businesses or renovating established businesses. Another program is the formation of community action groups for the purpose of promoting the patronage of businesses in the area. These cooperative efforts signify a healthy outlook toward businesses in the area.

ACCESSIBILITY OF THE SITE

Accessibility is an integral part of site analysis. Accessibility refers to the ease and safety that consumers experience when entering and leaving a site. For many types of businesses, such as apparel shops, accessibility is one of the most prominent factors in site selection.

In site selection, careful analysis must be made to identify any factors that could impede pedestrian and vehicle movement to and from the site. These limitations must be weighed in relation to the specific area chosen: central business district, shopping centers, or locations along heavily traveled streets and highways.

Traffic congestion often discourages shoppers from patronizing a particular store, especially in downtown business districts. Another major consideration is how easily and safely autos can enter and exit from a particular site. If the entrance or exit poses a hazard to the driver, getting onto or off the parking lot may keep customers away from a shopping center or a drive-in type of business. Furthermore, a site with only limited access or located at an intersection may discourage shoppers.

Likewise, accessibility must be analyzed for pedestrian traffic flow. Owners need to identify potential hazards to pedestrian traffic. The presence of sidewalks and easy entrance are positive access factors. Because pedestrians desire to avoid congestion just as the vehicle operator does, ease of entry and exit is vital. If customers have to follow a circuitous route, such as climbing stairs to a site, chances are very strong that this will be a strong disincentive for shopping.

Another matter is the accessibility of the site by public transportation (bus, streetcar, subway). Convenient public transportation to and from residential areas is an inducement to customers to patronize a business.

Studying the traffic pattern and traffic arteries allows small business owners to determine the accessibility of their specific location. They can develop a time travel map detailing peak periods of traffic that assist them in deciding on their hours of operation.

Inaccessibility is frequently a prime reason for business failure. To illustrate, a restaurant was opened in a small shopping center located near a larger shopping mall. Luncheon business was good, but the lack of traffic for the evening meal spelled the failure of the restaurant. The restaurant was located down a dark street between a park and a lower middle-class neighborhood. In order to reach the restaurant, customers had to pass many other restaurants. Nine months after its opening, the restaurant closed its doors. And a second food establishment was also unsuccessful at the same site for the same reason—inaccessibility.

In analyzing the accessibility of a site, small business owners must consider traffic interruption factors. These factors disrupt free-flowing traffic and can adversely affect a site's potential. The following six negative factors should be considered when evaluating site accessibility.

1. Dead spots where a shopper loses interest in going farther.
2. Driveways and other physical breaks in the sidewalk.
3. Cross traffic, either vehicular or pedestrian.
4. Areas that are identified with hazard, noise, odor, unsightliness, or other pedestrian-inhibiting qualities.
5. Businesses that generate traffic in the form of trucks, public vehicles, private automobiles, or pedestrians who are not shoppers and that tend, therefore, to create congestion.
6. Businesses whose customers' average parking time is extremely long.[2]

---

[2] Richard L. Nelson, *The Selection of Retail Locations* (New York: F. W. Dodge Corporation, 1958), p. 346.

PARKING

In our highly mobile society, even with energy shortages and higher fuel costs, consumers still rely on the automobile as the primary form of transportation to complete their shopping. In addition to accessibility, the adequacy of parking facilities is often a key factor in the success of the firm. For shops located downtown, especially in the larger metropolitan areas, lack of adequate parking is a major problem. Consumers become frustrated if they have to search for a parking space. In some cases, store owners park their cars in the spaces in front of their own business. The result of this practice is discouraged shoppers who take their patronage elsewhere.

Merchants in downtown areas have taken positive actions to confront the parking issue. Old buildings have been razed and replaced by parking lots and garages. A common action is for merchants to make arrangements with parking lots or parking garages whereby customers are given free or reduced price parking while shopping. An advantage of shopping centers is the capacity to provide adequate customer parking.

There are no uniform standards for determining parking adequacy for retail and service establishments. The Urban Land Institute surveyed the parking space needs of shopping centers and discovered that 5.5 spaces per 1000 square feet of gross leasable area has proved satisfactory for meeting the demand for most shopping periods during a year. A factor in parking space requirements is the type of tenant. A supermarket requires five times more parking space than a furniture store of equal size.[3]

A list of the basic considerations for use in determining parking requirements should include the following.

1. Type of neighborhood in which the site is located.
2. Frequency and length of store visit by shoppers.
3. Number of customers who use public transportation to visit the store.
4. Volume of walk-in traffic.
5. Variation or fluctuation in business on daily, weekly, and seasonal pattern.
6. Extent of competition.

TYPES OF GOODS SOLD

In the choice of a location, a retailer's decision in particular is strongly influenced by the type of goods sold. Retailers sell consumer goods (goods purchased by the ultimate consumer for personal use). Consumer goods can

---

[3]J. Ross McKeever and Nathaniel Griffin et al., *Shopping Center Development Handbook* (Washington, D.C.: Urban Land Institute, 1977), pp. 95, 97.

be classified into four categories: convenience, shopping, specialty, and impulse.

Convenience Goods

Convenience goods are those that the customer needs immediately and are usually purchased from a source that is most convenient to the shopper. These goods are sold through many outlets, and generally the price per unit is low. These goods are advertised nationwide, the frequency of purchase is high, and consumers give little thought either to the purchase of these items or where they are purchased. Types of convenience goods include gum, candy, and soft drinks.

Shopping Goods

Consumers spend a great amount of time and effort and do a considerable amount of comparison before purchasing a shopping good.

Shopping goods are sold through a selected number of outlets. The per unit cost is usually substantial, so customers normally make both quality and cost comparisons. These items are purchased infrequently and have a relatively long life expectancy. It also takes a concerted effort to sell these goods. Shopping goods include refrigerators, ranges, TVs, stereos, autos, and furniture.

Specialty Goods

Specialty goods refer to items that have a special quality or characteristic. Price is not a factor in the purchase of specialty goods, and they are sold through only a restricted number of outlets. An attribute of specialty goods is that customers will go out of their way to purchase them. Some examples of specialty goods are specific brands, exotic perfumes, jewelry, cameras, and special types of foods.

Impulse Goods

Impulse goods are "spur-of-the-moment" purchases. Impulse items usually have a low or moderate price per unit and appeal to personal taste, and they are distinguished from necessity goods. Impulse goods are placed in store locations that have heavy customer traffic and afford high visibility, as at checkout counters.

SITE CHOICES

In the smaller town, the choice of a site may be limited to the availability of a structure or a site. In larger areas, multiple sites are usually available, and the selection of the site is made more complex. There are several kinds of locations available, each having its own advantages and disadvantages. The site choices include (1) central business districts, (2) neighborhood locations, (3) shopping centers and malls, (4) string street locations, (5) isolated locations, and (6) retail affinity.

Central Business Districts

The central business district has been the traditional center of a town's or city's shopping area because of the early development of this section of town and the convergence of the transportation systems in the central area. A business locating in a central business area has the advantage of being able to draw customers from the entire trading area. Another advantage is that small businesses capitalize on the drawing power of the larger downtown stores, such as major department stores. In addition, the large number of employees of companies and financial institutions located in the central city represent a huge potential market. Stores that sell convenience, shopping, specialty, and impulse goods find the central business district a suitable location.

However, certain drawbacks are associated with the central business district. One disadvantage is that this location usually has higher operating costs

Revitalized downtown areas encourage lunchtime strolling and shopping in a pleasant environment.

and higher rental rates. Furthermore, competition is usually very keen in the downtown area. With increased traffic congestion, downtown locations have had increasing difficulty in attracting customers. To counteract these problems, some cities have initiated programs to revitalize the downtown business areas to make them more appealing. Building renovations and the creation of pedestrian walkways are part of the plan to breathe new life into central cities.

Neighborhood Shopping Areas

Within most cities are found clusters of several stores scattered throughout the residential areas. Ordinarily, these stores are convenience type stores. Stores located in neighborhood shopping areas include drugstores, hardware stores, grocery stores, and small variety stores. Service establishments (barber, beauty shops, dry cleaners) also find neighborhood locations attractive.

Neighborhood shopping area stores depend largely on the patronage of people who live in the area immediately surrounding the location. Compared to downtown locations, neighborhood stores have lower operating costs and lower rental rates. A distinct advantage of neighborhood locations is the opportunity afforded the owner–manager to enjoy direct, personal contact with customers. Through personalized attention, such as knowing customers by name, the small business manager is able to promote repeat patronage for the store.

Shopping Centers and Malls

The period following World War II ushered in major changes in the United States. A major change was the movement away from the inner city to the suburbs as the population became more mobile. The relocation of large segments of the population was instrumental in the rise of the planned, surburban shopping centers. A **shopping center** is "a group of architecturally unified, commercial establishments built on a site which is planned, developed, owned, and managed as an operating unit related in its location, size, and type of shops to the trade area that the unit serves. The unit provides on-site parking in definite relationship to the types and total size of the stores."[4] A discussion of planned centers follows.

Convenience Centers

Convenience centers are usually located along a heavily traveled street. They may consist of from 5 to 10 outlets for convenience goods and personal services. The major tenant is normally a convenience store, such as 7-Eleven. Other tenants may include a dry cleaner, a laundromat, and a beauty and barber shop.

---

[4]J. Ross McKeever and Nathaniel Griffin et al., op. cit., p. 1

Neighborhood Shopping Centers

Neighborhood shopping centers usually serve a population of from 2500 to 40,000 living within a driving time of 6 to 10 minutes. The firms in the center offer convenience goods (food, drugs, sundries) and personal services (barber and beauty shops, dry cleaning). A supermarket or drugstore or both comprise the chief tenants in the center and are responsible for pulling most of the traffic into the center. These centers may have from 10 to 25 tenants.

Community Shopping Centers

The trading area of the **community shopping center** usually overlaps with other trading areas, and the population served ranges from 40,000 to 150,000. In addition to convenience goods and personal service shops, these centers have many shops that offer shopping goods. Thus, community centers offer shoppers a greater assortment of merchandise—with a greater range of prices, clothing sizes, styles—than the neighborhood centers. This enables shoppers to make price and quality comparisons. The major store in this center may be a junior department store, a variety store, a supermarket, or a discount store. The number of tenants may range from 25 to 50.

Regional Shopping Centers

Regional centers cater to a trade area that has 150,000 or more people, and the area may extend from 10 to 15 miles or more in all directions. The trading area of the center depends on the location of competitors as well as on travel time needed to reach the center (usually 20 to 40 minutes of driving time). Regional centers have one or more full-line department stores as the anchor store or stores serving as the prime customer draw. This type of center offers a wide range and depth of shopping goods, apparel, furniture, general merchandise, and home furnishings. Other features of the center that attract customers are community rooms, theaters, medical clinics, banks, and postal services. In addition to major department stores, regional centers may have as many as 200 small specialty shops.

Many shopping centers have enclosed, weather-controlled malls. These centers provide the added advantages of making it convenient and pleasant for customers to shop at all times because a consumer can complete all shopping under one common roof. These centers have other features, such as fountains and landscaped interiors that add to their attractiveness.

Shopping center locations are advantageous in that occupants of a center can pool their advertising efforts and take advantage of group sales promotions. Further, shopping centers offer ample parking close to the stores and shops and have modern, attractive interiors and exteriors.

An enlargement of the regional center is the superregional center. This center may include three to six department stores and a unique location within the largest trade area of the city. One example of such a center is the creation of "downtown malls" in the attempt to generate new life into the central city.

A number of variations have occurred in conventional shopping centers that are discussed in the following sections.

Minimall

The **minimall** is designed for customer convenience. The major tenants are a junior department store; a food, drug, or variety store; and a number of specialty and service outlets. In addition to offering convenience of location for goods and services, the center is designed to reduce energy consumption and lessen the distance traveled to reach the center.

Small Regional Mall

The small regional mall is a scaled-down version of the regional center. The tenants are similar to tenants of the larger mall and can serve the needs of smaller markets. This mall may be desirable for the small business owner who desires having an outlet in a smaller center.

Specialty or Theme Centers

Specialty centers cater to unusual market segments. The theme center can be adapted to historical buildings. An example is Ghiradelli Square in San Francisco. This complex consists of eight buildings originally used for manufacturing chocolate and spices. The buildings have been renovated and converted into many small, specialty shops and restaurants.

Fashion Centers

Fashion centers, more suited for high-income areas, consist of apparel shops, boutiques, and handcraft shops that sell high-quality and high-priced specialty goods. These centers usually draw customers from a wide trade area because of their offering of specialty merchandise.

String Street Locations

When a group of retail outlets develop in an unplanned fashion along a heavily traveled street or highway, the result is referred to as a "**string street location.**" Each outlet must be able to stand on its own and attract its own customers. Drive-in grocery stores, furniture stores, auto dealerships, auto parts houses, and fast-food restaurants are common types of retailers found in string street locations. Small service firms that cater to the immediate needs of passing traffic also find such a site suitable.

Isolated Locations

When a single retailer or service firm chooses to locate in urban areas or along heavily traveled streets or highways, the choice is referred to as an isolated location. As no other retailers are in the area, the business must be able to attract its own customers. A fruit and vegetable stand or a pottery store is an example of the type of retailers who may choose an isolated location. Merchandise is usually lower priced, there is usually ample parking, and rent and other operating costs are lower in these locations.

Retail Affinity

Many types of stores have a strong **retail affinity** to one another because they sell similar or complementary merchandise. Locating near competition makes it easier for shoppers to do comparison shopping. Hence, competing stores have more customer-pulling power than they would have individually. For example, department stores often locate near each other, as do antique shops and theaters. In evaluating whether to locate near establishments that sell similar or complementary merchandise, the store owner should consider several factors, such as how many competitors there are in the trade area, the buying power of prospective customers, and the size and financial strength of competitors.

In shopping centers, the grouping of certain kinds of stores has been found to be desirable.

- Men's stores—shoes, clothing and haberdashery, sporting goods—tend to swell each other's volume.
- Similarly, women's apparel, shoes, and millinery, and children's clothes and toys—the soft lines—prosper in proximity to one another.
- Food products do well when grouped together—groceries, meat and fish markets, delicatessens, bakeries, doughnut shops, and confectioners.
- Stores that sell personal services and conveniences naturally go together, but in shopping centers they should be as close as possible to the parking area.[5]

Other examples of retail affinity include the following.

1. Men's and women's clothing stores and variety stores frequently locate near department stores.
2. Restaurants, barber shops, candy, and tobacco stores are commonly located near theatres.
3. Florists usually are grouped with shoe stores and women's clothing stores.
4. Paint, home furnishings, and furniture stores are generally located near each other.
5. Drugstores and tobacco stores may be found in any of the preceding groupings.

---

[5]J. Ross McKeever and Nathaniel Griffin et al., op. cit., p. 72.

6. Jewelry stores, however, have no strong affinity for other types of retail establishments.

Studies of specific sites show that one side of the street is preferable for retail stores. This is especially true in sections of the country that have long, hot summers. More people tend to walk on the cooler side of the street, and it permits more effective window use for displays. Corner locations are beneficial in that they provide more window display space as well as being accessible to two distinct flows of traffic.

SPECIAL INTEREST FEATURE

Site Analysis

The extensive number of questions that follow should prove extremely useful in studying various site alternatives. This analysis will enable the entrepreneur to develop a locational profile of the trade area, accessibility, competition, and cost.

POTENTIAL OF THE TRADING AREA

1. How big is the trading area? _____ Sq. mi.
2. What is the customer potential within 5 miles? _____ Customers. Within 30 minutes travel time? _____ Customers.
3. What is the density of population? _____ People per sq. mi.
4. Is there adequate transportation? _____ Yes. _____ No.
5. What is the income level of the trading area? $_____ Per capita.
6. Is the local employment pattern good? _____ % People unemployed.
7. What is the general makeup of the community? _____ Residential. _____ Old. _____ Growing.
8. What are the trends in population and income? _____ Up. _____ Down.
9. Is new construction on the increase? _____ Yes. _____ No.
10. Are school enrollments up? _____ Yes. _____ No.
11. Are retail sales on the increase? _____ Yes. _____ No.
12. Have average business improvements been made recently? _____ Yes. _____ No.
13. Is there a high vacancy rate for business property? _____ Yes. _____ No.
14. Have shopping patterns changed drastically in recent years? _____ Yes. _____ No.

15. Are customers moving to or away from the potential location? _____ To. _____ From.

16. What are the present zoning restrictions? _____
_____

CAN CUSTOMERS GET TO THE LOCATION?

1. Is the area served by adequate public transportation? _____ Yes. _____ No.

2. How broad an area does the transportation service encompasss? _____ Sq. mi.

3. Is the area generally attractive to shoppers? _____Yes. _____ No.

4. Can it be easily reached by automobile? _____ Yes. _____ No.

5. Is public parking adequate and relatively inexpensive? _____ Yes. _____ No.

6. How many spaces in the available, nearby parking space are taken up by all-day parkers? _____ Many. _____ Few.

7. If located on a highway, is the location easily accessible from the main traffic flow? _____ Yes. _____ No.

8. What are restrictions on signs and store identification? _____
_____

9. If on a limited-access road, how close is the nearest interchange? _____ Miles.

10. Is the location accessible to delivery trucks? _____ Yes. _____ No.

11. Is the traffic speed too fast to encourage entrance by automobile? _____ Yes. _____ No.

12. Are the customers who drive past the location on their way to work or on shopping trips? _____ On way to work. _____ On shopping trip.

13. Will nearby stores help you? Are the other stores in the shopping center, neighborhood, or highway location of a nature that will attract customers who will also become patrons of your store? _____ Yes. _____ No.

14. What are the prospects for changes in traffic flow in the near future? _____ Slight. _____ Likely.

15. Will anticipated changes improve or damage the location? _____ Improve. _____ Damage.

16. Are zoning changes planned which would affect accessibility of the location? _____ Yes. _____ No.

JUDGING THE COMPETITION

1. Are there other businesses of the same kind and if so, how many, between the prospective location and the most highly populated area? _____ Stores.

2. Is this spot the most convenient store location in the area? _____ Yes. _____ No.

3. How many other stores of the same kind are in this trading area? _____ Stores.

4. How many of them will compete with you for customers? _____ Stores.

5. Do they have better parking facilities? _____ Yes. _____ No.

6. Do they offer the same type of merchandise? _____ Yes. _____ No.

7. Do you consider them more aggressive or less aggressive than your own operation will be? _____ More. _____ Less.

8. What other competing stores are planned in the near future? _____
   _____

9. Are other potential sites which are closer to the majority of customers likely to be developed in the near future? _____ Yes. _____ No.

10. Are your major competitors well-known, well-advertised stores? _____ Yes. _____ No.

11. Is there actually a need for another store of this kind in the area? _____ Yes. _____ No.

12. How well are the demands for this product being met? _____ Good. _____ Fair. _____ Poor.

13. If there are empty stores or vacant lots near the location, what is planned for them? A competitor store? _____ Yes. _____ No.

CAN THE LOCATION ATTRACT NEW BUSINESS?

1. Is the location in an attractive business district? _____ Yes. _____ No.

2. Are there numerous stores which will draw potential customers for you into the area? _____ Yes. _____ No.

3. Is the location near well-known and well-advertised stores? _____ Yes. _____ No.

4. Is this location the most attractive one in the area? _____ Yes. _____ No.

5. Is the location on the side of the street with the biggest customer traffic? _____ Yes. _____ No.

6.   Is the potential location nearer to the general parking area than locations of competing firms? _____ Yes. _____ No.

7.   Is the location in the center of or in the fringe of the shopping district? _____ Center. _____ Fringe.

8.   Is it near common meeting places for people, such as public offices? _____ Yes. _____ No.

9.   Are most of the people passing the store prospective customers? _____ Yes. _____ No.

10.   Are the people who pass usually in a hurry or are they taking time to shop? _____ In a hurry. _____ Out shopping.

COST OF THE LOCATION

1.   What will your rent be? $_____ per month.

2.   Who will pay the utility costs? _____ You. _____ Others.

3.   Who pays additional costs such as taxes, public services, and costs of improvements? _____ You. _____ Others.

4.   What are the possibilities for eventual expansion? _____ Good. _____ Poor.

5.   Are good employees available? _____ Yes. _____ No.

6.   Will potential income justify your costs? _____ Yes. _____ No.

Source   *Starting and Managing a Small Retail Hardware Store,* Starting and Managing Series, vol. 10 (Washington, D.C.: Small Business Administration), pp. 17–20.

SITE ECONOMICS

For each type of business, there is an optimum location, commonly referred to as the "**100 percent location**." Thus, location analysis may reveal an optimum site in terms of accessibility, trade area, and the other factors previously mentioned, but the occupancy cost is excessive. In that case, another site with lower occupancy costs may be the only alternative. Occupancy may be on an ownership or lease or rental basis, with leasing or renting the most common practice.

Store owners must analyze their store's unique requirements to evaluate the economic feasibility of the site relative to occupancy cost. For example, the optimum location for a drugstore in a central business district is a corner site, and the owner pays a premium for this location. The checklist presented in Figure 6–3 serves as a guideline for analyzing the economics of a site.

When renting, small business owners must evaluate the rent-paying capacity of the site. Certain businesses can sustain high-rent areas such as convenience goods stores, drugstores, and apparel shops. Other stores, such as

FIGURE 6–3
Cost and return analysis—building sites (building existing on property).

	Rating			
	Excellent	Good	Fair	Poor
Site				
Area—square feet				
Sale price or rental				
Real estate tax rate (if building to be purchased)				
Other annual assessments and costs				
Total annual taxes (or rent) and other costs				
Estimated volume expectancy				
Ratio of total costs to volume expectancy				
Stability of tax or rental costs in area				
Trend in expansion of schools and other tax-supported improvements in area				
Cost of razing, additions, or other remodeling				
Cost of cleaning and other improvement				
Cost of heating				
Cost of light and other utilities				
Other				

Source Richard L. Nelson, *The Selection of Retail Locations* (New York: F. W. Dodge Corporation, 1958), p. 346.

furniture and furnishings, should locate in a low-rent site. Some characteristics of stores appropriate for high- and low-rent areas are shown in Figure 6–4.

ZONING REGULATIONS

In the search for a site for the business, the owner–manager must be aware of the zoning regulations in the area under consideration. Zoning refers to the division of a city or county into districts in order to control the location and the use of buildings, land, and construction. The three broad categories of zoning include residential, business or commercial, and industrial although there may be subcategories within the major classification. In cities or counties, a governing body, either a zoning commission or a city or county planning commission, establishes zoning regulations that define the purpose for which land or buildings are to be used. This commission can also bring action to prevent or restrain the construction or remodeling of a building or the use of a building or land that violates the city or county zoning regulations.

A basic aim of zoning laws is to ensure a degree of consistency in the types

FIGURE 6–4

Characteristics of stores appropriate for high- and low-rent sites.

HIGH RENT AREA

1. High value of merchandise in proportion to bulk.
2. Window display highly important.
3. High rate of turnover.
4. Low gross margin per item.
5. Impulse or convenience goods sold.
6. Appeal to transient trade.
7. Relatively little advertising.
8. Price and convenience stressed.
9. Low overhead.

LOW RENT AREA

1. Low value of merchandise in proportion to bulk.
2. Large amount of floor space for interior display.
3. Low rate of turnover.
4. High gross margin per item.
5. Shopping lines sold in addition.
6. Established clientele.
7. Much advertising.
8. Uses features of various kinds to attract customers.
9. High overhead.

Source Small Business Administration, *Small Business Location and Layout* (Washington, D.C.: U.S. Government Printing Office, 1965), p. 18.

and uses of buildings in a given area. The owner–manager must be aware that zoning laws affect not only the type of business that may be permitted to be established in an area but may also determine the kind of building that may be constructed as well as its height and size.

For example, an individual purchased a home in an area zoned residential with the expectation of starting a small beauty parlor business in the home. She applied to the zoning commission for a change in zoning category that would have permitted the overlapping of commercial and residential zones areas. Her application was denied on the basis of objections from the neighbors as well as on the basis of traffic and parking problems that would have been caused.

This case directs a word of caution to small business owners about the prospective site. They must ascertain that the intended business will not violate the zoning laws of an area. Hence, a site may be a good location, but city or county zoning regulations may prohibit locating there. Thorough investigation into zoning laws is an essential part of the site selection process. A zoning map of the city and surrounding territory can be useful in determining location and boundaries of zoning categories in a city or county.

Although it may be possible to get a site rezoned, the small business owner should not purchase a site until the site's classification has been changed. Too often, a site is purchased with no asurance, only hope, that it can be rezoned. Purchasing on the expectation that it may be rezoned is at best a risky business venture and fatal to the business if a reclassification cannot be obtained.

TRAFFIC ANALYSIS

Traffic flow is a basic factor in location analysis for many types of businesses. A traffic study is a valuable tool in location analysis for at least two reasons. First, the **traffic count** can measure the amount of pedestrian and vehicle traffic passing a site that represents potential customers. Second, the study serves as one measure for comparing the relative desirability of sites under consideration.

Pedestrian Traffic Count

To make a pedestrian traffic study, the owners must decide (1) who is to be counted, (2) when the count will take place, and (3) where the count should be made. The purpose of this study is to establish the number of potential customers moving by the proposed site during the hours the business will be open.

Prior to taking the count, the small business owners should decide who is to be counted in order to give the count more reliability. A heavy volume of traffic is of little or no value if it does not represent potential customers. For example, a ladies' apparel shop owner would be more interested in the number of women passing the site whereas the drugstore owner would be interested in total traffic volume.

Another criterion for counting should possibly be the age categories of pedestrians. Pedestrians should also be classified according to their purpose in passing the site. Employees rushing to work or rushing home are not potential customers for shopping goods. The in-between hours are the best hours to study traffic for some store owners. For example, the best time for an owner of a downtown store to make a study is between the hours of 10 and 5. However, shopping center traffic is heavier during the afternoon and evening hours.

Other considerations in determining traffic flow are the season as well as the month, week, and day. Traffic normally is much heavier before holidays and during the latter part of the week.

When a day with normal traffic flow has been selected, it is a good policy to divide the day into half-hour and hour intervals. This enables traffic to be counted and recorded for each half-hour interval that the store is open for business.

Another factor in pedestrian traffic counting is to establish where the count will be made. Will all traffic passing near the site or just the traffic passing in front of the site be counted? Care must also be taken not to count people twice, as when customers enter and leave a store.

Thus, the pedestrian traffic study can provide data as to the sales potential for the site. If the following information is known, based on either past experience of the retailer or from a trade association, a reasonable estimate of sales volume can be forecast.

1. Characteristics of individuals who are most likely to be store customers (from pedestrian interviews).

2. Number of such individuals passing the site during store hours (from traffic counts).

3. Proportion of passersby who will enter the store (from pedestrian interviews).

4. Proportion of those entering who will become purchasers (from pedestrian interviews).

5. Amount of average transaction (from past experience, trade association, and trade publications).[6]

Automobile Traffic Count

The sales potential of many convenience type firms and service firms depends on the quantity and composition of automobile traffic. The technique used to ascertain the who, when, and where pedestrian traffic analysis may be used also to establish auto traffic flow and potential. Data on traffic flow along major streets are available from city and state government agencies or outdoor advertising companies. However, the traffic analysis should be conducted with emphasis on any unique requirements of the company.

Auto traffic may be classified on the basis of the kind of trip taken: work trip, planned shopping trip, or pleasure trip. For example, along heavily traveled arteries, a dry cleaning establishment finds the location on the workbound side of the street favorable whereas the drive-in grocery more effectively utilizes the homeward-bound side. Location analysis shows that a good retail location for the planned shopping trip is on the right-hand side of the main street going into a shopping district and next to streets carrying traffic into, out of, or across town. Motels, restaurants, and service stations attract pleasure-trip traffic by locating along heavily traveled highways with easy exit and access.

Analysis of pedestrian and auto traffic makes it possible for small business owners to develop a time-travel map. This map allows a picture of the quality and quantity of traffic flow during normal shopping hours to be developed and is one major element in evaluating whether a site will generate a sufficient sales volume for profitable operation.

---

[6]James R. Lowry, *Using a Traffic Study to Select a Retail Site*, U.S. Small Business Administration Management Aid, No. 2.021 (Washington, D.C.: U.S. Government Printing Office, 1980).

Traffic analysis is more significant in location evaluation for some types of outlets than for others when considered on the basis of the type of consumer goods sold. Outlets distributing convenience goods must rely on the quantity of pedestrian and auto traffic as the most important measure. Drive-in stores that sell convenience goods are more attractive to consumers if they are located close to their residence.

Shopping goods outlets depend more on quality than quantity because people who visit these stores usually make a deliberate effort to shop there. Specialty goods outlets are usually able to locate in a more out of the way site because customers seek them out. Hence, traffic analysis is not as essential for specialty outlets as it is for convenience and shopping goods stores.

LOCATION ANALYSIS FOR SMALL WHOLESALERS

Wholesalers are intermediaries. Their sales are usually made to retailers or to other wholesalers. Small wholesalers usually serve a local market, such as the wholesale grocer supplying merchandise to grocery stores in the immediate town or making deliveries to nearby towns.

Briefly stated, the small wholesaler has to consider many of the same location factors we have outlined earlier for retailing and service establishments. However, they must be evaluated in light of the wholesaler's unique requirements.

For example, the small wholesaler must consider the trading area's potential when evaluating sites. In most towns or cities, there is a wholesaling district that must be determined as far as its suitability and accessibility. Recently, some wholesalers have begun to locate on the edge of towns to provide more flexibility.

LOCATION ANALYSIS FOR SMALL MANUFACTURERS

As with retailing and service establishments, the choice of locating the new small manufacturing firm or relocating the established firm is one of the keys to success. A major cause of the manufacturing operation's moving from a position of marginal profitability to a healthy profit position is frequently attributed to choice of site. In the search for the most suitable location, many factors must be considered and evaluated. Among the common factors are the general area and the site, markets and raw materials, labor supply, transportation, community attitudes, and community services and facilities.

General Area and Specific Site

In selecting an area for locating the manufacturing operation, the small owner should identify specific needs, such as immediate land requirements as well as planned expansion, type of plant, and labor supply. With these data, the search to find the general area that meets the specific needs can progress. Once a general area has been selected, the next phase consists of determining the availability and suitability of a site to meet the firm's needs, such as the proper terrain required for the plant's foundation.

Markets and Raw Materials

A manufacturer frequently has to choose between locating the plant close to the source of the raw materials or near customers. If a firm manufactures products whose raw materials are more costly to ship than the finished goods, the owner will usually locate near the source of raw materials. If the small firm depends primarily on the local customers or manufactures a product that is perishable, however, it may be more advantageous to locate near customers so that they can have convenient access to the finished goods.

Transportation

The importance of rail, water, highway, or air transportation is usually determined by the weight, size, and price of the product. When the firm produces goods that sell for a relatively low price and the cost of shipping is high relative to the cost, such as concrete, transportation costs are significant, and the firm will usually compete only in the local market. Conversely, if the shipping cost is low relative to selling price, as for electronic parts, transportation costs are not as significant, and the manufacturer will distribute goods in a broad market. Another factor to be considered in choosing the transportation system is the speed with which customers demand delivery. Thus, the relative importance of the various transportation systems depends on the kind of business to be served. Furthermore, the manufacturer must try to evaluate not only current transportation needs but future needs as well.

Labor Supply and Wages

One of the more important considerations in plant location is the availability of an adequate labor supply. A small electronics manufacturer that requires highly technical personnel pays much greater attention to availability of that type of labor than does the operation that requires unskilled labor almost exclusively. If the firm employs chiefly unskilled labor, the prevailing wage rates and the extent of unionization of employees in an area may be critical. Should other factors outweigh the availability of labor in an area, the owner should determine if the site will offer enough amenities to attract employees.

Community Attitudes

In site selection, the manufacturer should determine if the people in the community favor the firm's locating in the area. Some cities permit only "clean" manufacturing operations in the community, that is, those firms that do not pollute the environment, such as electronics firms. A community that is anxious to attract the new facility often makes special tax concessions, such as exempting the firm from taxes for a specific period of time. However, there is no assurance that this advantage will endure because it can be changed by local governments.

Community Services and Facilities

The types of community facilities that are available or will be supplied by the city may become a strategic factor in site selection. Frequently cited service and facility requirements are housing, education, recreation, hospitals, police and fire protection, adequacy of power supply, and ability to provide utilities to the firm.

The factors just mentioned plus a number of other considerations are presented in Figure 6–5. By assigning a point value to each item to be considered,

FIGURE 6–5

Factors to be evaluated in selecting a location for the small manufacturing operation.

Factors	Quality of Each Factor 1 (lowest) to 10 (highest)	Importance of Each Factor 1 (least important) to 5 (most important)
1. Accessibility to market and customers served.	_____	_____
2. Quantity and quality of labor supply available (short- and long-term).	_____	_____
3. Adequate supply of raw materials.	_____	_____
4. Tax burden of business in the community.	_____	_____
5. Community attitudes toward business.	_____	_____
6. Availability of transportation systems.	_____	_____
7. Suitable climate.	_____	_____
8. Community services and facilities (housing, schools, police and fire protection, hospitals).	_____	_____
9. Adequacy of utilities (gas, water, electrical).	_____	_____
10. Evaluation of site chosen in relation to site chosen by competitors.	_____	_____
11. Potential of site for expansion and growth.	_____	_____

the small manufacturer can be in a stronger position to evaluate location alternatives.

SUMMARY OF KEY POINTS

1. Major factors to analyze in site analysis are trade area and its potential, accessibility of the site, parking, site choices, site economics, zoning regulations, and traffic analysis.
2. Small business owners should evaluate three categories of the trade area and its potential: the town or city, the specific area of the town or city, and the specific site.
3. A retail location is dependent in part on the type of goods sold: convenience, shopping, specialty, and impulse goods.
4. The small business owner must include as a part of location analysis the accessibility of the potential site to auto and pedestrian traffic.
5. Adequate parking is a major factor in analysis of site potential.
6. The small business owners may choose a location from a number of alternatives: central business district, neighborhood location, shopping centers and malls, string street locations, isolated locations, and retail affinity.
7. Site economics involves the analysis of the economic feasibility of the potential site.
8. Zoning regulations govern the location and use of buildings, land, and construction.
9. To aid in establishing sales potential, the small business owner should conduct a traffic analysis of pedestrian and auto traffic.

DISCUSSION QUESTIONS

1. Discuss some of the factors that should be considered in analyzing the trading area for a small retail store.
2. Explain why accessibility of site is a major criterion for locating the small business.
3. Identify the four types of consumer goods.
4. What are some of the chief factors to consider when evaluating the parking facilities of a proposed site?
5. Explain the advantages and disadvantages of the central business district.
6. What is site economics? Why is it important to the small business owner?
7. What is the role that zoning plays in site selection?
8. Discuss the factors to consider in making a pedestrian and automobile traffic count.

9.   Identify and briefly discuss the factors that should be evaluated by a small manufacturer in choosing a location for the factory.

STUDENT PROJECTS

1.   Select a line of merchandise as reported in *Sales and Marketing Management* magazine. Lines of merchandise reported are groceries and other foods, health and beauty aids, women's and girl's clothing, footwear, major household appliances, and furniture and sleep equipment. Choose these data for a specific city (or the city in which you live if it is reported in the magazine). Then find the population for the city selected and the effective buying income for that city. Use this information to make an estimate of the area's purchasing power for the potential of the line of merchandise selected.

2.   Consult Bureau of the Census data, and determine the percentage of people employed in each industry for your city, county, state or all three.

3.   Assume you have been asked to serve as a consultant to a group of individuals who are going to open a florist shop. What factors would you identify as most important for the florist business when you advise these people?

CASE A

A & A Sales and Repair Company

Robert Anderson owns and operates as a sole proprietor the A & A Sales and Repair Company. Twelve employees work for Mr. Anderson, and the firm sells and repairs household appliances.

Over the 25 years that the firm has been in operation, it has earned an excellent reputation for quality work and fast, efficient service. Consequently, the firm has developed a large number of repeat customers.

All employees are well-trained technicians who have been with the firm for at least 6 years, but most have been with the firm 11 years or more. However, none of the employees have managerial experience. Mr. Anderson's two sons, 18-year-old Raymond and 17-year-old Wallace have expressed no interest in staying in the business.

At this time in the life of the firm, Mr. Anderson, who is 49 years old, faces some challenging problems. However, whatever the outcome, Mr. Anderson knows that he definitely desires to remain an entrepreneur. With that conviction, he must chart the direction for himself and the firm. Some of the major considerations include the following.

1.   He can stay in the present location or move to a new location in an outlying business district. The present location is situated in a declining area of the central city. In addition, a new highway system is to be

constructed soon, which will cause a major reduction in the automobile and pedestrian traffic flow past the firm.

2. Whether the choice is to remain at the present location or move, modifications will be needed in the firm's physical facilities, such as more working and storage space and more equipment repair facilities. Mr. Anderson has the financial reserves needed to make the changes at the present location but would need to borrow the funds for making the move. The current building and location are worth $65,000. A new location will mean an investment of approximately $200,000.

3. Should the firm continue to sell and repair appliances or concentrate on expanding the repair service for individuals and warranty repair for sellers of appliances, such as department stores? The retail sales growth potential is minimal owing to the decline in this section of the city.

4. If repair service is expanded, Mr. Anderson will need additional management assistance to supervise the expanded repair department. This addition would benefit the firm because the actual management would not depend completely on Mr. Anderson. A related problem will be where this manager should come from because no current personnel have management experience or training.

As Mr. Anderson evaluates the situation, he concludes that there are four alternatives available to him.

1. The business can remain in the present location and continue to sell and repair home appliances as it has done for the past 25 years.

2. The business can be relocated to a more desirable location in an area outside the center of the city.

3. The business can retain its present location but concentrate on appliance repairs and establish pickup stations in outlying areas near shopping centers.

4. He can sell the present business and reinvest in a new busines venture.

QUESTION

Evaluate each of these alternatives, and make a recommendation that you feel is the most advantageous for Mr. Anderson and his firm.

CASE B

Weston Animal Clinic

When Dr. Alice Weston graduated from the State University with a Doctor of Veterinary Medicine degree, she joined the Taylor Animal Clinic, which was owned and operated by Dr. Samuel Taylor. Two years later, when Dr. Taylor retired, Dr. Weston bought the clinic and changed its name to Weston Animal Clinic. Now she operates it as a sole proprietor.

The Weston Animal Clinic is located in a small town near a large lake. The area is a popular recreational area for boating, camping, and fishing. The nearest veterinarians are located about 30 miles away. The clinic serves a population of some 10,000 people in the lake area, where most of the people reside at the southern end of the lake. There are also many weekend visitors and summer residents who come to the area to enjoy the camping and water sports.

Most of the animals treated at the clinic are small animals (pets). The relatively few large farm animals that are treated must be cared for away from the clinic because of the lack of space.

During the past two years the clinic's revenue has grown, with net income before taxes as a percent of gross revenue being 46 percent and 53 percent, respectively, for each of the two years.

Dr. Weston prefers to make this area her permanent residence. Her objectives for the business are to expand the veterinary practice and at some future time add a partner.

Dr. Weston currently is considering expanding the clinical facilities. This may necessitate relocation. The specific reasons for expansion are the increased demands to treat larger animals and the increased demand for kennels for smaller animals for boarding and medical treatment. If the clinic is expanded, this would provide additional work for the anticipated partner. One factor that hinders the expansion objective is the space in the current building.

Three choices are available to Dr. Weston.

1. The building in which Dr. Weston is located contains three separate businesses: a florist, a dentist, and the clinic. The clinic has an area of 1100 square feet, 800 of which are used for the clinic and the remaining 300 used for kennels. Dr. Weston has a 2-year lease for $200 a month. There is the possibility the building could be purchased and remodeled. However, the construction of the building is not of the quality that would warrant a long-term investment, and it is set on a small lot that would not allow adequate expansion.

2. A second choice is to try to locate an existing building that is more suitable. A concern with this choice would be the need for remodeling to convert the building into a functional animal clinic.

3. A third alternative is the purchase of property that has some acreage and building a new veterinary clinic. Dr. Weston estimates that a facility of 2500 square feet would be large enough initially for the clinic and kennels for the small animals and also for a small outside barn with fenced area for housing larger farm animals. The space required for the clinic, including office space and treatment rooms, is 1200 square feet, and the kennel

space requirements are 1300 square feet. This alternative would provide space needed for future expansion. This option would cost approximately $65,000 for the land, clinic, and barn. Monthly payments would be $700 compared to the current monthly lease of $200.

Some property with acreage that is available is located just outside the city limits. The property is close to a small shopping center that has a convenience store, post office, and hardware store. A medical clinic is being planned for the area. The town is expected to grow as it becomes more popular as a resort area.

QUESTION

Analyze each of Dr. Weston's choices, and recommend the most suitable site for the stated objectives of the business.

SMALL BUSINESS ADMINISTRATION PUBLICATIONS

Management Aids (Free)

Locating or Relocating Your Business

Business Plan for Small Manufacturers

Factors in Considering a Shopping Center Location

Using a Traffic Study to Select a Retail Site

Business Plan for Small Service Firms

Store Location "Little Things" Mean a Lot

Association Services for Small Business

Small Business Management Series (For Sale)

Management Audit for Small Manufacturers

Management Audit for Small Retailers

Small Store Planning for Growth

Starting and Managing Series (For Sale)

Buying and Selling a Small Business

CHAPTER SEVEN

PHYSICAL FACILITIES OF THE SMALL BUSINESS

After reading this chapter, you will understand:

1. That there are a number of issues involved in choosing between occupying a new facility or an existing structure.
2. What factors should be considered in the decision to buy or lease a facility.
3. That the space and construction requirements for each type of business must be determined.
4. That there are a number of factors that should be analyzed pertaining to the architectural style and interior features of the building.
5. The importance of store layout.
6. The difference between process layout and product layout in a factory.
7. The difference between a merchandising service establishment and a processing type service establishment.

KEY WORDS

Layout
Grid layout
Free-flow layout
Process layout
Product layout

Merchandising service
   establishment
Processing type service
   establishment

SMALL BUSINESS PROFILE

Six Who Succeeded: The Candlemaker

Among those of little faith were bankers, landlords and even her father, who pronounced her project hopeless. Cheerfully unfazed, Joyce Lund, 42, took an idea generated in the kitchen of her suburban Seattle home and turned it, by means of grit and womanpower, into a $5 million-a-year business. Now Lund's Lites is one of the biggest makers of decorative candles in the U.S. Among its inventive products: Baby Boo Bears—a pair of matching pink and blue bear candles for nurseries.

It all began in the fall of 1971 when Lund needed some extra cash to buy Christmas presents for her six children. She had made candles before but had always given them away as gifts. Then a friend who dropped by one morning offered a suggestion: Why not sell some of her homemade candles?

So, melting wax on her kitchen stove, Lund started turning out candles like, well, hotcakes. She set up a display shelf in her living room and spread the word. Recalls Lund: "People started coming to the house in droves. They were buying candles as fast as I could make them."

Lund and her husband Howard, an air traffic controller, took to turning out candles through the night, napping in alternating two-hour shifts. Lund called friends and relatives and asked them to work for her. Some helped make candles; others sold them, holding Tupperware-style parties in other people's homes. "Everyone says you're not supposed to hire friends or relatives or untrained housewives," she says, "but I did it from the beginning and still do."

In early 1973, she moved the business from her home to a small warehouse. Recalls Lund: "The owners demanded that we sign a month-to-month lease. They thought we were a bunch of kooky, bored housewives who wouldn't last a year." Bankers evidently thought so too. When Lund sought her first loan, for a mere $500, her husband had to cosign.

In 1978, Lund's Lites moved into the 20,000-square-foot factory where Lund and her employees recently celebrated her being named Pacific Northwest Woman Entrepreneur of the Year. Today the company sells candles in 30 states. Lund won't reveal her net worth but avers: "I thought millionaires were supposed to have chauffeurs and maids. I don't."

Source Marlys Harris, "Six Who Succeeded—The Candlemaker," *Money*, vol. 11, no. 12 (December, 1982), p. 70. Reprinted from the December, 1982 issue of *Money* magazine by special permission, © 1982, Time, Inc.

The design, appearance, and unique features of a business's building are seen as assets in attracting customers. Franchisors certainly realize the prominent role of the physical facility in customer recognition. Their goal is for consumers to associate quality goods and services when they see a particular physical facility. This is one of the main reasons why they stress uniformity of building design for their franchised outlets.

Planning the physical facility should be a high priority item for the small business owner. The building should be carefully studied from the standpoint of establishing its suitability for effectively serving customers or for manufacturing a product.

In the preceding chapter, criteria for site analysis were presented. In this chapter, we examine some of the considerations in evaluating the physical facility requirements of the small business.

THE PHYSICAL FACILITY

The small business owner is confronted with several alternatives in selecting an appropriate physical plant. These decisions include (1) whether to construct a structure or occupy an existing structure and (2) whether to lease (or rent) or purchase the facility.

Construct a New Facility

The ideal situation for small business owners is to determine the building requirements and design the facility from the ground up. The advantage of this approach is that modern features can be incorporated into the building plans. The exterior design as well as the interior and layout can be arranged to suit the special needs of the small business owner. In addition, the physical location can be chosen.

Occupy an Existing Facility

Most small business owners occupy buildings that are already constructed. In evaluating the existing building or space in a shopping center, small business owners must not only determine if the location is suitable but also if the available building will meet their requirements or can be remodeled to meet the required specifications.

To illustrate, since the energy shortages beginning in the early 1970s, some 56,000 gasoline service stations have closed. Many of these stations have been sold to franchisees and other small business owners and have been converted into adequate facilities for various types of businesses. The net result is that the cost of remodeling the building is considerably less than constructing a new building and the remodeling process is faster than constructing a new facility.

A typical conversion can take as little as 45 days and cost from $10,000 to $65,000. It is less if the project is done by the owner–manager. One Houston couple turned an old Texaco station into an exotic plant boutique for $500. In addition, many facilities have good locations with large, paved parking lots and utilities in place and sometimes even landscaping.[1]

Fast-food operations have been especially successful in converting service stations into satisfactory facilities. Service stations have also been converted into dry cleaning plants, printshops, used-car lots, muffler shops, bookstores, doughnut bakeries, pawn shops, and various types of repair shops.

Buy or Lease

After the decision has been made to locate the business in an existing structure or build a new one, the choice of renting or buying the building must be made.

In smaller towns or in areas where real estate values are not too high, small business owners may own their building. Another alternative is to lease the facility, either on a stated dollar rental fee per month or year or on the basis of paying rent as a percentage of the firm's annual sales or gross profit.

When choosing between leasing and buying, small business owners should weigh the following advantages and disadvantages.

Advantages of Buying

When owner–managers buy their building, they have the option to maintain it in the way they desire. They do not have to obtain permission from the building's owner if they wish to modernize the structure in any way. Furthermore, by owning the building, small business owners do not have to be concerned about being evicted as long as the business is solvent. Another advantage of ownership is that if the property appreciates in value, the small business owner reaps the benefit. Still another advantage is that building depreciation is an expense of business operations for income tax purposes, as are taxes and any mortgage interest payments.

Disadvantages of Buying

On the other side of the coin are the negative factors of ownership. Property may decline in value if a business district declines. A large initial capital outlay is required if the building is purchased plus the cost of regular interest and mortgage payments. Additionally, ownership limits the mobility of the owner. If owners want to relocate, they must dispose of the owned building in some manner. In addition, there are substantial costs involved in taxes and maintenance and repairs that may limit the amount of working capital for other ongoing business operations.

Advantages of Leasing

Leasing offers several advantages to small business owners. By leasing, the owners do not have to make a large initial cash outlay as they would if they purchased a building. Hence, more funds are available for current operations.

---

[1]Peter Mohr, "Life After Death Along Gasoline Alley," *Fortune*, November 1979, pp. 86, 88.

Leasing also increases the mobility of owners if they decide to move when the lease expires. By leasing, they do not suffer the financial loss if the building declines in value. For income tax purposes, rent is also an expense of doing business. Moreover, the lease agreement may stipulate that the building owner pay for all or part of any renovation desired by the building occupant.

Disadvantages of Leasing

One disadvantage of leasing is that the building owner may elect not to renew the lease, forcing the small business owner to relocate. The owner's permission must be secured to make building modifications, and such permission may not be given. Some leases contain restrictions or provisions as to what actions the small business manager can take with regard to the building. For example, one small business owner leased a building. After signing the lease, the small business owner read the fine print of the contract and discovered that the lease prohibited the display of any type of store sign on the property. In order to advertise, the manager had to rent a portable sign trailer and park it off the property in order to display the store name.

SPACE REQUIREMENTS

Determining the space requirements of the small business is a critical factor. Yet it is also one of the more difficult needs to gauge because the owner must project the firm's needs into an uncertain future. Each business has varying space requirements depending on the nature of the business. A carpet store with displays of rolls of carpeting has much greater space requirements than a small gift shop.

If the projected space needs are underestimated, a new building or an addition to the existing structure becomes necessary, resulting in increased cost to the owner and inconvenience to both customer and owner. Overestimating space needs results in inefficient use of the building and increased costs of operation until the volume of business matches the available space.

The initial size of the facility should be adequate to meet current needs but should also provide for a kind of construction that can easily and economically be expanded when growth of the firm justifies it. For example, in selecting a building for locating a men's specialty shop, initial spatial requirements must be established for the retail selling area as well as storage area. But the existing structure also needs to be evaluated in terms of its flexibility for modification. For example, are there existing walls that can be easily removed if future growth requires more selling and display area?

CONSTRUCTION REQUIREMENTS

The building should be functional for the specific type of business as well as attractive in appearance. The small business owner must be aware of the zoning regulations governing building design codes and fire codes for the particular site. Specifically, owners must know the exact requirements in order to comply with local building codes. Specific questions to be answered in regard to construction requirements are as follows.

1. What type of exterior and interior walls are required?
2. What type of roofing is required?
3. What is the type of insulation to be used for the roof and walls?
4. What type of structural frame meets the building code?
5. Is the architectural design appropriate for the business district?
6. What type of flooring is required?
7. How many entrances are needed?

Before making a final decision, the small business entrepreneur would be well advised to seek professional advice, as from a builder or architect, in analyzing the space and construction requirements.

ARCHITECTURAL STYLE OF BUILDING

For many firms, particularly retail and many types of service firms, the architectural style is critical in creating a favorable image in the mind of the consumer. Often a distinctive exterior can give the owner–manager a competitive edge. The factors discussed in the following sections are representative of architectural features that should be analyzed.

Storefront

Small business owners should choose building materials and a storefront design that are consistent with the store image the store owner is trying to create. The type of building materials used for the storefront may be dictated by the funds available. More expensive materials, such as brick or fieldstone, or less expensive materials, such as aluminum, wood, or special types of structural glass, may be used. Remodeling the storefront of the older building can project a modern refreshing appearance or a historical look.

Display Windows

"Window shopping" is a favorite pastime for many Americans. Small business owners should use this knowledge of shopping habits to their advantage as they plan their show window displays. (See Fig. 7–1.) Attractive show windows not only are used to display merchandise but also to project the

FIGURE 7–1

A checklist for window displays.

MERCHANDISE SELECTED

1. Is the merchandise timely?
2. Is it representative of the stock assortment?
3. Are the articles harmonious—in type, color, texture, use?
4. Are the price lines of the merchandise suited to the interests of passersby?
5. Is the quantity on display suitable (that is, neither overcrowded nor sparse)?

SETTING

1. Are glass, floor, props, and merchandise clean?
2. Is the lighting adequate (so that reflection from the street is avoided)?
3. Are spotlights used to highlight certain parts of the display?
4. Is every piece of merchandise carefully draped, pinned, or arranged?
5. Is the background suitable, enhancing the merchandise?
6. Are the props well suited to the merchandise?
7. Are window cards used, and are they neat and well placed?
8. Is the entire composition balanced?
9. Does the composition suggest rhythm and movement?

SELLING POWER

1. Does the window present a readily recognized central theme?
2. Does the window exhibit power to stop passersby through the dramatic use of light, color, size, motion, composition, and/or item selection?
3. Does the window arouse a desire to buy (as measured by shoppers entering the store)?

Source John Wingate and Seymour Helfant, *Small Store Planning for Growth*, Small Business Management Series no. 33 (Washington, D.C.: Small Business Administration, 1977), p. 77.

store image. Show window merchandise displays may catch the casual shopper's eye, creating a desire to purchase the merchandise.

Much thought and attention should go into planning how the display window can be used most effectively. For example, show windows should be designed that are appropriate for the merchandise sold. Displays for rings, watches, and other jewelry items that are of small size need to be set up between waist and eye level whereas larger items, such as shoes or luggage, can be displayed much lower (below waist level).

Many retail outlets have a recessed storefront. This arrangement permits people to window-shop in a more relaxed atmosphere out of the mainstream of pedestrian traffic.

Store Entrances and Exits

Store entrances and exits establish how smoothly customer traffic flows in and out of the business. Obstacles that impede the smooth flow of traffic may drive customers to competitors. Obstacles that may discourage customers are doors that are difficult to open, poor location of doors, doors that are too narrow, no provision for entry for the handicapped or elderly (such as steps leading up to the entrance), or poor condition of the walkway leading to the store entrance.

To facilitate customer traffic, the small business facility should have an adequate number of properly located entrances and exits. Steps that may be taken to accomplish this objective are the installation of doors that open automatically, removal of obstacles to permit ease of entry by all (including the handicapped or elderly), and clearly marking and lighting entrances and exits. Awnings placed over the store entrance may provide an added measure of shopper convenience.

Outside Signs

Properly placed signs guide the customer to the store just as a lighthouse guides a ship. Shoppers become frustrated when they are looking for a specific store and are not able to find it because a sign does not clearly mark its location. The small business owner should be aware of some of the common problems encountered with respect to outside signs. These include improperly designed signs, signs placed in a poor position, signs that are the wrong size, signs that are illegible (faded out), signs that are in poor condition, or signs that are of a poor color.

BUILDING INTERIOR FEATURES

Shoppers tend to have favorable attitudes toward shopping in stores where the interior is both appealing and inviting. The small business owner should pay special attention to those features that help to create a favorable shopping environment: floors, walls and ceilings, lighting and fixtures, color scheme, and year-round climate control.

Flooring

Flooring should be sturdy enough to handle traffic as well as the weight of materials that will move over it. In a factory, a painted concrete floor may be satisfactory. For a retailing firm, flooring should have a type of covering that matches the decor of the store and also be safe and comfortable for the customer. This may include various kinds of tile, hardwood, carpet, linoleum, or terrazzo. The condition of the flooring should be considered also. Some questions need to be answered regarding flooring. How difficult is it to maintain the floor? Is the floor covering unsuitable or dangerous (e.g., does it become slick if it gets damp)? Is the floor covering an unsuitable color or of poor material? Does the flooring add to the noise or reduce the noise in the store? Is the flooring durable? What is its cost?

Walls and Ceiling

Like flooring, the walls and ceiling are an essential part of the store's overall appearance. Walls should be of sufficient strength to support the requirements of the building, such as holding up shelving as well as matching the color scheme of the store. Partitions are useful in that these movable walls allow for variety in the arrangement of the store. Likewise, the ceiling requirements must be analyzed. Will it be plaster or acoustical tile? By the use of a suspended acoustical tile ceiling, some flexibility in ceiling height can be obtained. Lowering the ceiling can also reduce the cost of operation, as with lower heating and cooling costs. Inclusion of fireproof partitions can also help to reduce insurance costs. Use of the proper type of paint on the interior walls and partitions helps to reduce maintenance costs.

Lighting and Fixtures

Adequate lighting aids the shopper. Lighting requirements must be analyzed for each type of store. A proper lighting system enhances the environment of the store. Equally important, proper lighting enables the customer to see merchandise clearly and makes selection of desired items easier. Insufficient lighting can cause customers to shy away from a store. Glaring or obscure lights are examples of this problem. In the factory, lighting must be adequate for workers to perform their job efficiently. Lights should be bright but not glaring.

A lighting system must be designed that is energy-efficient. It must also be a flexible system so that it can be increased at some future time if the need arises. Moreover, it must have the proper appearance, be maintained easily and inexpensively, and be sturdy in construction.

Color Scheme

Colors can be used to advantage to give the store specific appeal. Paint manufacturers suggest that different colors can create certain visual effects. For example, certain colors can be used to make a building appear larger. Painting the rear walls a darker color creates the illusion of making a long, narrow building seem wider.

The owner should use colors wisely in the selling space and in fixtures. It is best to avoid using bright shades of color. Though they are attention getters, they may overpower the merchandise. Loud colors and strong color contrasts should be used only in the proper environment, as in a store specializing in youth-oriented apparel.

Soft pastel shades lend themselves to overall store decor whereas darker colors can be used for accents. The color scheme should enhance the merchandise displayed. Blue, green, gray, and black are best used with displays of more expensive merchandise. Low-priced bargain merchandise displays use bright shades of yellow, orange, and red with white to make them stand out. Colors can also be used to brighten a store or factory and make it more appealing to customers and more conducive to promoting employee efficiency. Certain colors reflect light. Hence, they help to reduce lighting needs and save electrical energy.

Climate Control

Year-round temperature control is a necessary feature for the comfort of customers and employees. Care must be taken to see that the climate-control equipment selected or in place in the building should be energy-efficient because utility costs continue to rise and are an important factor in the efficient operation of the business.

Other Facility Requirements

In most instances, there will be other specifications for the individual business. Consequently, the small business owner must determine if the existing facility is adequate in terms of meeting current needs and if it is adaptable for expansion and renovation if future growth dictates it. A prior determination of this type of information can result in substantial cost-savings if future expansion or building changes are mandated.

Facility requirements that should be evaluated are now enumerated.

Adequacy of electrical wiring, gas pipes, and plumbing.

Absence of structural obstacles (columns and posts that will not interfere with store operations).

Adequacy of restroom facilities and rest area equipment and water fountains.

Adequacy of shelves and display cases.

Adequate transportation for personnel, freight, and merchandise (elevator, escalator, conveyors).

Security system (burglar alarm, window bars).

Fire Department requirements (fire extinguishers, sprinkler system).

Location, size, and type of loading docks.

Availability of protective covering at loading docks.

Adequate waste disposal facilities.

STORE OR FACTORY LAYOUT

The layout design in the retail store, service firm, and manufacturing facility is a critical factor in the overall efficient operation of the firm. Manufacturing and service firms will be discussed later in the chapter. In the retail establishment, **layout** means "the arrangement of selling and nonselling departments, aisles, fixtures, displays, and equipment in the proper relationship to each other and to the fixed elements of the building structure."[2]

Considerable attention should be given to planning the store layout. The goals of retail store layout are to attract customers and serve them efficiently and also to aid in the efficient operation of the business. The attainment of these goals is facilitated by the use of climate control, lights, and color scheme, and by the ease with which the premises can be maintained and made secure (store security is discussed in detail in Chapter 14). In selecting the appropriate store configuration, owners should evaluate a number of factors that will now be discussed.

Type of Merchandise

In the development of a store layout, the type of merchandise should be considered. For the retailer, the store's success is dependent almost entirely on selling. Properly designed store layout makes the products easily accessible. The layout of the selling floor should be planned with customer convenience uppermost in importance. Related merchandise should be displayed in close proximity to ensure ease of shopping. For example, shirts, slacks, ties, shoes, and belts should be located in adjacent areas.

If it is feasible, merchandise should be displayed openly for customer examination. For some types of merchandise, such as jewelry and cameras, open displays are not practical. Items likely to be purchased on impulse need to be displayed near the store's entrance or where there is heavy customer traffic. Figure 7–2 presents a classification of goods as well as a suggested location of merchandise in the small retail store.

Size of Store

A well-planned layout enables the owner to utilize the total area of the store efficiently. The space requirements for inventory, office, washroom, and selling and display area must be established. Selling is the most important activity in the retail outlet and must be given major space allocation. Although the nonselling activities should not be oversized and thus occupy valuable selling space, they should be allocated sufficient space in order to ensure that all work can be completed in an orderly manner.

Customer Traffic

In planning the store arrangement, the owner should give thought to how many customers will be in the store at the peak hours and how readily these

---

[2]William R. Davidson, A. Doody, and D. Sweeney, *Retailing Management*, 4th ed. (New York: Ronald, 1975), p. 523.

FIGURE 7–2

Classification and arrangement of merchandise in small retail stores.

I. IMPULSE GOODS	**II. CONVENIENCE GOODS**
Bought	**Bought**
As a result of attractive "visual merchandising" displays	With frequency and in small quantities
Should Be Placed	**Should Be Placed**
Near entrance in small store—on main aisle in larger stores	In easily accessible feature locations along main aisle
III. NECESSITIES OR STAPLE GOODS	**IV. UTILITY GOODS**
Bought	**Bought**
Because of an actual need	For home use—brooms, dust pans, etc.
Should Usually Be Placed	**Should Be Placed**
To the rear of one-level stores—on upper floor of multilevel stores (not an infallible rule)	As impulse items up front or along main aisle

V. LUXURY AND MAJOR EXPENSE ITEMS

Bought

After careful planning and considerable "shopping around"

Should Be Placed

At some distance from entrance

Source *Small Business Location and Layout*, Administrative Management Course Program, Topic 13 (Washington, D.C.: Small Business Administration, 1965), p. 34.

customers can be served. Fast, efficient service is especially important in retail and service establishments. Locating cash registers convenient to the selling area reduces the time a salesclerk must spend walking to and from the sales floor; hence, customer service is improved. More customer traffic can be accommodated if self-service fixtures (display cases, counters) are situated for customer convenience. By using a counter with several tiers, one can use vertical space efficiently. Stock areas should be located as near the selling area as practical to reduce the amount of time a salesclerk must be away from the selling area getting additional stock. In a shoe store, for example, the shoe stock is ordinarily located on shelves immediately behind the displayed stock. Because only a limited stock can be displayed, the salesclerk ordinarily must go to the stockroom to obtain the size and style of shoe desired. The salesperson merely steps through a curtained opening, selects the shoes requested, and is back on the sales floor in a very short time. By considering these factors, the small business owner will be able to serve his or her customers more efficiently at peak hours of business and, in turn, increase store sales.

Display Fixtures

Fixtures are an integral part of effective layout design. A useful guide to the small business entrepreneur for deciding on the kind of display fixtures needed is a realization that the most practical and economical fixtures permit merchandise to be displayed in proper arrangement for each line of merchandise with maximum exposure and minimum amount of distractions.

Other factors that should be considered in determining store layout are building construction, fire and security protection measures, the number of employees and facilities, and service to customers (restrooms and fitting rooms). A checklist for evaluating the interior arrangement and display of a retail store is the subject of the special interest feature in this chapter.

INTERIOR STORE LAYOUT

The store layout should make merchandise accessible. In considering the layout plan, the retailer should use the plan that facilitates consumer shopping. An essential consideration in store layout is for the store area that contributes most to sales to be located in the front quarter of the store near the entrance and checkout counter. As much as two thirds of the store's annual

The interior layout of this small basket store is designed to make merchandise easily accessible to shoppers.

FIGURE 7–3
Grid layout of a retail store.

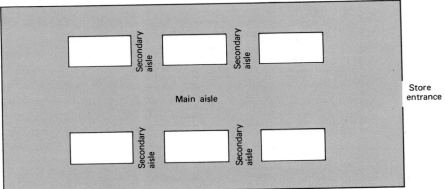

sales may be made in the front quarter of the store. In the retail firm, the grid and the free-flow layout are two basic designs.

Grid Layout

The **grid layout** is a rectangular store arrangement that features a main aisle and secondary aisles that are located at right angles to the main aisle (see Fig. 7–3). The main aisles carry a large share of the traffic and provide the best location for convenience goods, impulse items, and seasonal merchandise. Shopping goods may be displayed on the secondary aisles, and specialty goods may be placed in less traveled areas of the store.

SPECIAL INTEREST FEATURE

Checklist for Interior Arrangement and Display

LAYOUT	YES	NO
1. Are your fixtures low enough and signs so placed that the customer can get a bird's-eye view of the store and tell in what direction to go for wanted goods?	___	___
2. Do your aisle and counter arrangements tend to stimulate a circular traffic flow through the store?	___	___
3. Do your fixtures (and their arrangement), signs, lettering, and colors all create a coordinated and unified effect?	___	___

4. Before any supplier's fixtures are accepted, do you make sure they conform in color and design to what you already have?   ____ ____

5. Do you limit the use of hanging signs to special sale events?   ____ ____

6. Are your counters and aisle tables not overcrowded with merchandise?   ____ ____

7. Are your ledges and cashier-wrapping stations kept free of boxes, unneeded wrapping materials, personal effects, and odds and ends?   ____ ____

8. Do you keep trash bins out of sight?   ____ ____

MERCHANDISE EMPHASIS

1. Do your signs referring to specific goods tell the customer something significant about them rather than simply naming the products and their prices?   ____ ____

2. For your advertised goods, do you have prominent signs, including tear sheets at entrances, to inform and guide customers to their exact location in the store?   ____ ____

3. Do you prominently display both advertised and nonadvertised specials at the ends of counters as well as at the point of sale?   ____ ____

4. Are both your national and private brands highlighted in your arrangement and window display?   ____ ____

5. Wherever feasible, do you give the more colorful merchandise in your stock preference in display?   ____ ____

6. In the case of apparel and home furnishings, do the items that reflect your store's fashion sense or fashion leadership get special display attention at all times?   ____ ____

7. In locating merchandise in your store, do you always consider the productivity of space—vertical as well as horizontal?   ____ ____

8. Is your self-service merchandise arranged so as to attract customers and assist them in selection by the means indicated below:

    (a) Is each category grouped under a separate sign?   ____ ____
    (b) Is the merchandise in each category arranged according to its most significant characteristic—weather, color, style, size, or price?   ____ ____
    (c) In apparel categories, is the merchandise arranged

	YES	NO

by price lines or zones to assist the customer in making a selection quickly? _____ _____

(d) Is horizontal space usually devoted to different items and styles within a category (vertical space being used for different sizes—smallest at the top, largest at the bottom)? _____ _____

(e) Are impulse items interspersed with demand items and not placed across the aisle from them, where many customers will not see them? _____ _____

Source   John W. Wingate and Seymour Helfant, *Small Store Planning for Growth* (Washington, D.C.: Small Business Administration, 1977), pp. 100–101.

An advantage of the grid layout is that it is conducive to low building costs and is easily adapted to situations where structured columns are numerous and close together. Other advantages of this layout plan are that total floor space requirements are minimized because aisles are of consistent width, and a greater amount of merchandise can be displayed in a given amount of space because of the regularity of the arrangement; it is easier to use a standardized type of display fixture throughout resulting in fixture economies; and it is easier for customers to become familiar with the regularity of the features of the grid layout.[3]

Free-Flow Layout

Store owners using the **free-flow layout** recognize that customers normally travel to their right when they enter a store. Under this plan, the store layout may be circular, octagonal, or U-shaped. Unlike the grid layout, the free-flow design has no uniform pattern of arrangement. This plan has considerable flexibility because display counters can be added, removed, or rearranged without disrupting the overall layout pattern. Another advantage of this plan is that it makes it possible for customers to move easily from one display area or department to another. As a result, customers are given greater exposure to merchandise, which may result in increased sales.

The grid layout is less expensive to design and probably better suited to the needs of the small business owner. However, some owners use a free-flow layout in an attempt to create a distinct store personality.

---

[3]Ibid., p. 525.

MANUFACTURING
FACILITY LAYOUT

Layout in the plant refers to the efficient arrangement of the manufacturing facilities and employees. In the plant layout, attention is centered on how the equipment is to be set up as well as the location and space requirements of support services, such as maintenance, receiving and shipping, and storage. Some of the benefits of good factory layout are listed as follows.

1. Lower cost of manufacturing.
2. More efficient use of floor space.
3. Reduced manufacturing bottlenecks.
4. More effective control.
5. Better quality of products.
6. Better service to customer.
7. Minimized material handling.
8. Less time needed to manufacture goods.

Types of Manufacturing Layout Plans

There are two basic patterns of layout used in manufacturing operations. These are the process layout and the product layout.

Process Layout

Process layout, shown in Figure 7–4, is usually found in plants where many different kinds of products are produced or are produced for customer

FIGURE 7–4

Process layout of a small manufacturer producing wooden products (chairs and desks).

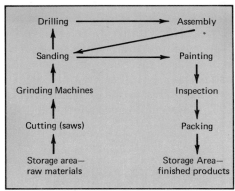

specifications. It is often called job order production and is characteristic of many small plants.

Process layout means that similar equipment is located in one area or department of the plant. Hence, all lathes or drills would be in one area. In this arrangement, all work of a specific kind is sent to the specific department or area. All lathe work required in the factory would be sent to the lathe machine area.

The advantages of the process layout are these.

- Superior control of intricate processes.
- Greater utilization of machinery.
- Lower capital investment in equipment.
- Increased flexibility; readily adaptable to frequent rearrangement of operational sequence.
- Steadier operation; production can be maintained better during absenteeism. Machine breakdowns are not serious because work may be routed to other machines.
- Improved service; maintenance requirements of equipment can be grouped for specialized service.
- Lower unit cost; more economical where volume of work is too small to justify a production line.
- Best suited for items requiring a flexible sequence of operations.
- Reduced equipment; fewer duplicate machines necessary to meet production requirements.
- Production stimulated; more incentive to workers to increase production through incentive plans.[4]

Product Layout

Manufacturing facilities that use a **product layout** ordinarily mass-produce goods. (See Figure 7–5.) Product layout has all equipment needed to produce a specific product arranged in sequence as on an assembly line. This equipment is used only for producing the one product. Raw materials enter the manufacturing sequence and as each stage of the operation is completed, the material moves to the next stage until all stages have been completed and the product "rolls off the assembly line." Thus, there may be a considerable amount of duplication of kinds of machinery in the manufacturing operation.

Product layout is usually too sophisticated and expensive a system for the small business, but it is adaptable to the requirements of the larger, mass-production industries. This system is especially suitable for automated manufacturing processes.

---

[4]Raymond Newton, *Principles of Plant Layout for Small Plants*, Technical Aids for Small Manufacturers (Washington, D.C.: Small Business Administration, 1971), p. 3.

FIGURE 7–5

Floor diagram of product layout in small factory.

Storage raw materials	**Product A** Saws	Drills	Sanding machines	Assembly	Painting		Storage finished product
Storage raw materials	**Product B** Lathes	Milling	Sanding machines	Assembly	Varnishing		Storage finished product
Storage raw materials	**Product C** Saws	Lathe	Heat treating	Plating	Assembly	Painting	Storage finished product

Advantages of product layout include these.

- Simplifies controls and reduces cost accounting.
- Reduces materials-handling costs.
- Provides smoother flow of materials.
- Reduces floor space required for goods in process.
- Cuts production time.
- Reduces investment in work in process.
- Develops efficient labor through job specialization.
- Provides better overall supervision and reduces paper work.
- Reduces floor space required per unit produced.[5]

SERVICE ESTABLISHMENT LAYOUT

The layout for the service establishment is determined primarily by whether it is a merchandising or a processing establishment.

Merchandising service establishments include barber shops, beauty shops, and motels. Layouts in these establishments must center on customer convenience and attractive physical appearance of the facility.

Processing type service establishments include tailor shops, laundries, and printshops. These businesses have their processing operations separated from where customers' orders are taken. A small printshop, for example, takes customer orders in front, and the printing equipment is in the back of

---

[5] Ibid.

the building. The separation of work area and service area makes for more efficiency in work performance.

ASSISTANCE IN PLANNING THE LAYOUT

The small business owner should seek as much assistance as possible in determining the most efficient layout of the business. Many sources are available to provide this assistance. Retail trade associations provide planning services to their members. Manufacturers of store equipment and fixtures will also provide assistance. Other valuable resources are contractors, financial advisers, architects, interior designers, business suppliers, and government agencies, especially the Small Business Administration. Much of this service is offered free or at a minimal cost. Carefully thought-out plans can avoid unnecessary waste and expense later in relation to store or plant layout.

SUMMARY OF KEY POINTS

1. The small business owner must choose whether to construct a new facility or occupy an existing facility and whether to buy or lease (or rent) the facility.

2. The size and type of building must be analyzed in terms of current and future needs.

3. Factors to be evaluated in regard to building exterior are architectural style, storefront, display windows, entrances and exits, recessed front, and outside signs.

4. Building interior analysis should include flooring, walls and ceiling, lights and fixtures, color scheme, and climate control plus any special features required by the individual firm.

5. To design the proper store layout, the owner–manager should consider the type of merchandise, size of store, customer traffic, and display fixtures.

6. The two types of store layout for retail firms are grid and free-flow.

7. Manufacturing facilities may be organized on a process layout or product layout basis.

8. Service firm layout depends on whether it is a merchandising service establishment or a processing type of service establishment.

9. The small business owner can receive assistance in planning store layout from numerous sources, including retail trade associations, equipment manufacturers, contractors, financial advisors, architects, business suppliers, and government agencies such as the SBA.

DISCUSSION QUESTIONS

1. What decisions does the small business owner have to make when choosing a physical facility?
2. What factors should be evaluated when deciding whether to buy or lease a facility?
3. Identify some of the issues that need to be studied when determining the size and type of facility desired.
4. List and explain the important features of exterior architectural design.
5. Briefly discuss the interior building features that should be evaluated by the small business owner.
6. What is the meaning of layout?
7. What items need to be considered when determining a retail store layout?
8. What is the difference between a grid layout and a free-flow layout?
9. Explain the difference between process and product layout of a factory.
10. Discuss the difference between a merchandising service establishment and a processing service establishment.

STUDENT PROJECTS

1. Select a small retail store, and evaluate the store's interior and exterior features.
   a. Building exterior
      (1) Type of building architecture
      (2) Storefront
      (3) Display windows
      (4) Entrances
      (5) Outside store signs
   b. Building interior
      (1) Flooring
      (2) Walls
      (3) Ceiling
      (4) Lights and fixtures
      (5) Color schemes
      (6) Climate control
2. Draw the floor plan of the layout of the store, and describe the layout plan.
3. Assume you are asked to serve as a consultant to a group of people who are interested in starting a retail apparel shop. Would you advise them to buy or lease the physical facility?

CASE A

Harry and Evelyn's Restaurant

By the time Harry and Evelyn Williams retired from their civil service jobs, they had decided that they wanted to remain active and start a new business venture. Evelyn loved to cook and had collected an extensive assortment of exotic recipes. Harry and Evelyn felt that this interest in cooking led them logically to decide to enter the restaurant business.

After some searching for a suitable site, they finally located an older building in the downtown area, which they could lease for 10 years. The building needed repair and renovation for a restaurant business. And though the three-story building was larger than what they actually needed, Harry decided that the upper two floors could be used for storage.

The building had no parking lot, and the street on which it was located was away from the main auto and pedestrian traffic flow. Nevertheless, Harry and Evelyn felt they could appeal to a sufficient amount of walk-in traffic of downtown office workers to support the location. They expected that, by serving quality food, they could rely on word-of-mouth advertising to promote the business. With this knowledge of the situation, they signed a lease for the building.

The building had to be renovated to meet the requirements of the restaurant. The renovation cost more than Harry had budgeted, but they both wanted the building to be attractive and have a special appeal. The hardwood floors were refinished, and fancy Tiffany lamps were hung over each table.

Because the renovation had cost more than planned, Harry could not afford new kitchen equipment but instead opted for used kitchen equipment. Harry found a restaurant owner in another area of the city who was going out of business and who was willing to sell him used kitchen equipment, such as a freezer, stove, broiler, sinks, and so on.

With the kitchen furnished, the next step was to develop the menu. Evelyn created a menu that featured many of her favorite recipes, which contained special ingredients. Lunch prices averaged about $6.00. Harry and Evelyn realized this was probably high for a lunch, but they reasoned that the quality of the food would outweigh the cost factor.

As opening day drew close, Harry and Evelyn realized that the preparation of the building and the equipment had cost substantially more than they had planned. As a result, little savings were left to hire professional waiters. Instead, they employed some friends of their grandson. Though these employees would work for a small hourly wage and tips, they had no experience waiting on tables.

When the restaurant opened, lunch crowds were large, and for a while it seemed that Harry and Evelyn had made the right choice. However, some problems became apparent. The combination of the untrained waiters plus the length of time it took to prepare Evelyn's special food items made service slow. Customers were kept waiting too long for lunch. Also, the price of the meals discouraged many customers from returning, so that after heavy customer traffic during the opening, the number of customers began to drop off. And when the motor on the used freezer stopped running and all the food needed for Evelyn's special menu items spoiled, they could not afford another freezer. In addition, because this was an older building, it was poorly insulated. This fact plus the rising utility costs further strained their financial resources.

With this turn of events, in addition to all the bills coming due for the renovation and inventory purchases, Harry and Evelyn decided they should try to get out of their lease. They couldn't. Within six months of the opening, they filed for bankruptcy.

QUESTIONS

1. With regard to the physical facilities, what are some specific problems Harry and Evelyn failed to recognize?
2. What were other problems they failed to anticipate?
3. Where could they have gotten assistance on physical facility planning?
4. What advice would you give Harry and Evelyn if you had been their adviser before they opened their restaurant?

CASE B

House's Jewelry Store (A)

House's Jewelry Store is a small, single unit retail jewelry store located in the downtown shopping area of a city of 10,000 population. The business opened in 1959 in a smaller store but moved to its present location in 1969. The location has been good, and rental payments are relatively low. There is one other competitor in the downtown area.

Floor space is 3000 square feet. One fourth of the floor space is allocated to repair facilities, clerical space, and storage areas. The remaining floor space is divided into four areas. Diamonds, expensive gemstones, and wedding sets comprise one fourth of the selling area. Watches, gold necklaces and bracelets, gold-filled jewelry, and other assorted pieces occupy about one fourth of the selling floor. Gift items, pottery and china, silver and pewter serving pieces, and stemware utilize another one fourth of this space. The remaining floor space is aisle space.

In addition to the owner and his wife, three full-time employees and one part-time employee work in the store. Each person performs a wide range of duties in the store. The watch repair department is a leased-out service department designed to increase sales by attracting additional customers to the store. The store's downtown competitor has no in-store watch repair service. All watches brought in for repair are sent out of town.

During the past two years, the Houses have been evaluating whether to move the business to a new shopping center located at the edge of the city. Population shifts, the movement of other retailers, the deterioration of the downtown area, and the favorable atmosphere at the shopping center area have been the factors that have made them decide to move.

There is a suitable location in the new center. The Houses want their new store to have an efficient, well-planned layout.

Specifically, they want the following to be incorporated into their design layout.

1.   A workshop area located in the store rather than behind the store as is the case with the present location. This would allow the owner to have closer contact with actual store operations.

2.   Pieces of jewelry that have a similar function, such as watches, bracelets, and chains, should be placed in close proximity to each other. This arrangement will facilitate customer shopping.

3.   Use track lighting to enable displays to be mobile and to add to the flexibility of the layout.

4.   All display cases should be lined with materials of a related color scheme to allow jewelry to be accentuated by reflection of light on its surface.

The proposed store layout is now shown.

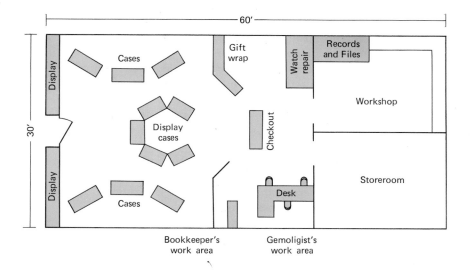

Proposed Layout:
    Area (30 feet by 60 feet)
    Space allocation
        Space should be divided into departments.
        Dropped ceilings over certain areas will enhance different items.
        Wall space should be used for display.
Layout spaces
    Record room (6 feet by 8 feet) for security files
    Workshop (10 feet by 20 feet) for jewelry repair and casting
    Watch repair room (6 feet by 8 feet)
    Checkout stand placed at back of store
    Gift-wrapping area
    Desk and working area for bookkeeper
    Desk and diamond salon for owner (desk—L-shaped with 3 chairs)

QUESTION

Evaluate the store layout as to its suitability for the new jewelry store.

SMALL BUSINESS ADMINISTRATION PUBLICATIONS

Management Aids (Free)

Stock Control for Small Store
Reducing Shoplifting Losses

MANAGEMENT CONTROL

SECTION THREE

CHAPTER EIGHT

MANAGEMENT AND EMPLOYEE RELATIONS IN THE SMALL BUSINESS

After reading this chapter, you will understand:

1. What management is.
2. That the small firm has a number of objectives.
3. The functions of the small business manager.
4. What employee relations are vitally important in the small firm.
5. The importance of the internal organizational environment of the small business.
6. The needs of the individual.
7. What employee morale is as well as what the indicators of low employee morale are.
8. Some of the problems of employee discipline.
9. The guidelines for making communication effective.

KEY WORDS

Manager

Planning

Organizing

Staffing

Organization chart

Directing

Control

Time Management

Employee relations

Internal organization environment

Motivation

Morale

Autocratic leader

Free-rein leader

Participative leader

Progressive discipline

SMALL BUSINESS PROFILE

Frederick G. Luber
Super Steel Products Corp.
Milwaukee, Wisconsin

In 1966, Fred Luber and two associates acquired Super Steel, a small metal fabricator with 18 employees and annual sales of $200,000. Focusing on innovative technology, the company expanded into new and more productive methods of metal technology, such as computer aided design, computer assisted manufacturing, and robotics. It increased employment as high as 360 employees and sales to $3.5 million. Its customers range from very small firms to very large corporations, and it has been a subcontractor in the Federal procurement marketplace. The company has taken an innovative approach to its personnel policies, instituting the first employee stock ownership trust in the city of Milwaukee. Frederick Luber is an active advocate of small business concerns outside of Super Steel. He has spoken on behalf of "research parks" in Madison and Milwaukee. He has served as chairman of the Milwaukee Private Industry Council and was director of a venture capital fund owned by Competitive Wisconsin, which he cofounded in 1980.

Source   *There's No Business Like Small Business*, Washington, D.C.: Small Business Administration, 1983.

The ability of small businesses to retain their strategic position in our economy and to compete effectively with larger business firms rests primarily on the shoulders of the owner–managers. Small business firms that have survived and demonstrated growth have been led by owner–managers who not only recognized and capitalized on the opportunities available to them, but in countless situations the owner–managers created the opportunities that contributed to their success. Thus, the leadership provided by competent managers is paramount for strengthening the firm's position in the business community.

THE MANAGER IN THE SMALL BUSINESS

A **manager** supervises the work activities of employees in order to see to it that they accomplish their specific tasks. Thus, in a large company, managerial activities are distinct from the "doing" activities of employees. However, this separation is not so definite in the small firm, where owner–managers ordinarily work side by side with employees. Nevertheless, owner–managers must give highest priority to their management responsibilities and not devote their major energies to nonmanagement activities.

THE MANAGEMENT FUNCTIONS

The owner–manager's responsibilities involve coordinating the firm's total resources—human, physical, and financial—so that the goals of the company can be achieved. Managers complete these responsibilities by performing the functions of management: planning, organizing and staffing, directing, and controlling.

Planning, Goal Setting, and Decision Making

The management function of planning represents one of the most challenging and important aspects of managerial work because it involves considerable analysis and thought. **Planning** is the process of setting objectives and then choosing the course of action the firm will follow to reach these objectives. Planning must be considered a continuous process because the firm operates in a dynamic environment. The initial phase of the planning process requires owner–managers to develop objectives that outline the expected goals of the firm. To formulate objectives clearly, owner–managers should put them in writing. It is essential that the owners give careful consideration to develop objectives and continuously monitor them because the small business operates in an environment that is constantly changing. Changes in the environment may present obstacles to goals initially set. As a result, managers must continually evaluate objectives and make modifications when the situation demands it, as when external market conditions change.

Objectives reflect concern and attention for the various parties at interest to the firm: ownership (sole proprietorship, partnership, corporation, stockholders), employees, customers, and the community at large. Representative objectives that recognize the various constituencies of the firm may be as follows.

To ownership: It shall be the goal of the owner and manager of this company to attempt to maximize profits.

To employees: To pay a fair, competitive wage or salary and afford employees with opportunities for training and development that will allow them to utilize and expand their talents.

To customers: To provide products and services of the highest quality at the lowest prices possible.

To community: To use all available safeguards to protect and improve the environment in the area in which the business operates.

Objectives also provide the guidelines for setting policies and procedures. Policies are more detailed than objectives and serve as a guide for the decisions and actions necessary for reaching objectives. Policies are developed to provide guides for action in the basic functional areas of the firm, such as sales, production, finance, and personnel. For example, a store will establish a policy that specifies its check-cashing policy: "Checks cashed for the amount of purchase only provided that proper identification is given and the check is properly completed."

Procedures detail the exact actions or steps for accomplishing a certain activity. Procedures usually specify how a policy should be carried out. For example, the following procedure outlines the steps to be followed when a customer presents a credit card for payment for gasoline purchases.

1. Check card to determine that it is honored in this location and has not expired.
2. Set imprinter for amount of sale, insert card, insert invoice, and imprint the invoice.
3. Check hard copy to see that all information has been printed.
4. Fill in all appropriate information such as number of gallons, price per gallon, vehicle license number, and initials of person filling out the card.
5. Get signature of cardholder and give tissue copy to cardholder, ring up sales on gas sale key, and put hard copy into cash register.

Rules are specific guides that define action that should or should not be taken in regard to a situation. For example, the rule of a small grocery store states: "Do not smoke or eat while waiting on customers."

Planning also involves the dual time dimensions of long-range and short-range planning. The long-range plans focus attention on the overall direction of the company whereas short-range plans designate the specific measures necessary to reach long-range goals. Most small business managers spend the greater portion of their time and energies on short-range, day-to-day planning, usually the result of daily job pressures. However, immediate pressure should not preclude managers from concentrating their time and energies on long-range plans.

Decision Making

The manager is continually called on to make decisions, and the quality of these decisions defines the level of success enjoyed by the firm. Decision making permeates every activity of the company. Objectives, policies, procedures, and rules provide the manager with the bases needed for making many decisions. The four phases of the decision making process are these: (1) define the problem, (2) develop alternatives, (3) evaluate alternatives, and (4) implement the plan of action. Each of these steps is discussed in the following sections. (See Fig. 8–1.)

Define the Problem

The first phase of decision making begins with an evaluation of the current status of the small business. The owner–manager's attention is focused on

FIGURE 8–1

The four steps in the decision-making cycle.

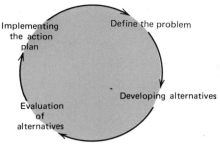

identifying problems and analyzing if there are problems. If a problem exists, the manager must state specifically what is wrong or what area of the company should be producing better results.

It is paramount to define the problem area correctly because if the problem is diagnosed incorrectly, the solution will fail, no matter how well thought out and applied it may be. For example, the owner of a ladies' apparel shop saw sales of the firm level off during the preceding year. The owner knew that if she was to survive and remain competitive, sales would have to increase by an annual rate of at least 5 percent for the next three years. The manager was confronted with developing suitable alternatives that would reverse the trend of lagging sales.

Developing Alternatives

After the manager has defined the specific problem area, he or she must develop and analyze various alternative courses of action that will yield positive results. The experienced manager realizes that in most situations more than one alternative can be developed that will lead to desired outcomes. For example, possible alternatives to be considered for increasing sales of the apparel shop include the following.

1. Increase advertising expenditures.
2. Use a wider variety of advertising media.
3. Plan more sales promotion activities to coincide with special dates or events in the local community.
4. Add new lines or brands of merchandise.
5. Expand customer services.
6. Provide sales personnel with additional training in personal selling techniques.
7. Make special incentives available to sales personnel.
8. Relocate the apparel shop, such as moving to a shopping center.

Evaluate Alternatives

After preparing a rather complete list of alternatives, the owner should evaluate each in terms of its advantages and disadvantages. The owner–manager should consider the following when studying the feasibility of each alternative.

1. Will this alternative provide a satisfactory solution to the problem?
2. If this alternative is adopted, will it likely prevent the problem from redeveloping in the future?

For the owner–manager of the apparel shop, the alternatives that did not appear to be feasible for implementation at the present time were set aside for consideration at a later date. In this case, adding more lines or brands of merchandise and relocation were eliminated from the list of alternatives because financial resources were not available.

Implement the Plan of Action

The completion of the evaluation of the alternatives should indicate which alternative or combination of alternatives seems to be the most appropriate course of action to achieve a solution to the problem. In many situations, instead of choosing a single course of action, the manager may incorporate several alternatives into the final plan of action. In the drive to increase sales, the owner–manager chose to increase the amount expended for advertising and to begin advertising selectively on television to promote special sales. Another part of the plan of action was to give additional training in selling techniques to the sales personnel. The net effect of these actions has been to increase sales by 6 percent the first year.

Organizing and Staffing

Organizing is the management function of coordinating the human, financial, and physical resources of the firm so that they follow the course needed to reach the firm's objectives specified in the planning phase. Included in the organizing function are the following related activities: identifying jobs to be performed, staffing, defining authority and responsibility, and establishing authority relationships.

Identification of Jobs

The initial activity that the manager must be concerned with in performing the organizing function is to identify the jobs that must be performed for the firm to realize its goals. The organizing function also involves the concept of division of work to provide for greater efficiency in task performance. Insofar as is possible in the small firm, it is desirable to divide the jobs and group them into logical units, such as a department, usually on the basis of similarity. Thus, each department is accountable for a specific phase of the operation. For example, all sales functions would be grouped together in the sales department and all record-keeping activities would be grouped together in the office administration department.

Staffing

Once the tasks have been identified, the need is to match personnel to jobs. The goal of *staffing* is to see that employees are selected and placed in tasks for which they are qualified. This activity is discussed more completely in Chapter 9.

Define Authority and Responsibility

How much authority and responsibility each employee has should be clearly defined. Even in the small firm, it is preferable that this information be in writing. Authority is the right of persons to take action and make the necessary decisions for completing the tasks assigned to them. Responsibility is the obligation employees have to perform the tasks assigned to them to the best of their ability.

In the small business, the owner–manager has complete and final authority and responsibility. As often happens, however, owner–managers find that they do not have time to devote to every detail in the company. Effective managers realize that one of the most practical methods of running a successful company is to delegate some authority to their employees. Delegation of authority enables employees to make decisions in areas where they are qualified. It also allows the manager to devote extra time to more important matters. Delegation encourages key employees to take initiative. In addition, employees can have authority delegated to them to keep the company running if the owner–manager must be away from the business. When authority is delegated, employees are responsible for performing the tasks satisfactorily.

One small manufacturer recognized the necessity for establishing the formal organization. He divided the firm into three departments: production, sales, and administrative.

He then designated the responsibilities for each department manager. The production manager was given authority and responsibility for manufacturing, packing, and shipping. The sales manager's authority and responsibility included advertising, attracting new customers, and customer service. The administrative department manager's authority and responsibility were for accounting, purchasing, and personnel activities.

After working with department managers, both individually and as a team, the owner–manager was able to establish the job procedures and to avoid the overlapping of authority and responsibility between departments. All these procedures were then written down. Thus, managers had specific information on what decisions they could make and which actions needed approval by the owner. The owner also designated the production manager to be in charge during the owner's absence.

FIGURE 8–2
Organization chart of a small retail store.

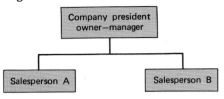

Determining Authority-Responsibility Relationships

The authority and responsibility relationships among personnel must be clearly defined to avoid confusion and overlapping authority. The **organization chart** is useful in this regard for representing graphically the authority and responsibility relationships among people in the various departments as well as for delineating the channels of formal communication. Usually, the organization chart is quite simple in the small business because of the relatively small size of the company. For example, Figure 8–2 depicts the organization structure of a small store with the owner–manager and two employees. However, as the firm grows, additional employees are hired, and an assistant manager may be added. The revisions would then be reflected as shown in Figure 8–3.

Directing

Directing involves the owner–manager with employees on a daily, face-to-face basis. Directing includes the activities of leadership, communication, and motivation. The quality of the face-to-face supervision that the owner–manager has with employees is a major factor in determining the success of the firm. A more detailed discussion of this topic is presented later in this chapter in the section entitled "Employee Relations in the Small Business."

FIGURE 8–3
Revised organization chart of a small retail store showing addition of employees.

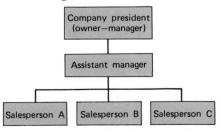

FIGURE 8–4
The control cycle.

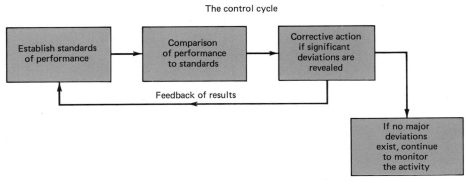

The control cycle

Feedback of results

Controlling

The planning function involves setting specific objectives in all critical phases of the company's operation. The purpose of the **control** function is to provide owner–managers with the information necessary to determine if current operations conform to established plans.

The control function is the process of signaling what is happening in the business currently and providing managers with continual feedback on the progress of the company toward achieving specific objectives. Without a control system in place in the small business, the owners have no way of gauging the results the firm is achieving. If feedback from control measures indicates that plans are not being achieved, the owner must identify the causes of the failure and develop specific actions to overcome them. The three basic stages of the control process are discussed as follows and are shown in Figure 8–4.

Establish Standards of Performance

Standards are the performance levels expected if the firm's goals are to be realized. Standards must support the overall goals of the firm. Furthermore, standards of individual performance must be set realistically if employees are to be able to achieve them.

Types of standards that are used in the functional areas of the firm are included in Figure 8–5.

Comparison of Performance to Standards

If standards are to serve a worthwhile purpose, they must be compared with actual performance levels of employees. This will enable the owner to determine if employees are operating at an acceptable performance level so that objectives can be achieved. Control standards that have been clearly defined

FIGURE 8–5

Standards used in functional areas to gauge performance.

Production	Personnel Management
Quality	Labor relations
Quantity	Labor turnover
Cost	Labor absenteeism
Machine	Safety
Individual job performance	

Marketing	Finance and Accounting
Sales volume	Capital expenditures
Sales expense	Inventories
Advertising expenditures	Flow of capital
Individual salesperson's performance	Liquidity

can more easily be compared to actual performance, for example, the sales quota expected for each salesperson. Performance may be checked at various times—hourly, daily, weekly, monthly—depending on the specific circumstances in order to determine if any variations are occurring.

Corrective Action

If the comparison of standards and performance reveals no significant deviations, the owner only needs to continue to check the activity. However, if major variations are revealed, steps must be taken to correct the deviation and improve future performance. Specific actions that may be needed may include additional training or reevaluating the standards and adjusting them to a more realistic level.

SPECIAL INTEREST FEATURE

What Makes An Organization Successful

Let's take a look at specific characteristics of those organizations that have been most successful and the techniques and programs that they've used to develop their organization teams.

First, there must be a nucleus of organization personnel, including a few people at the top, that have committed themselves to one type of philosophy and set of goals so that over a period of time the nucleus will grow and build the philosophy into the team structure of the total organization. (Unfortunately, over the past few decades, there has been a tendency for the nucleus to shrink, rather than grow. Recently, however, for a period of about a year, there has been evidence that the trend is being reversed for the better.)

Just as we recognize the character of an individual, so can we identify a character of a successful business or industrial organization. Let us consider a few of these characteristics.

- Housekeeping is good; work places are in order.
- It is evident that people know what they are doing.
- Responsibilities are delegated.
- Workers are diligent and skillful; little idle time is evident.
- Product and customer consideration is evidence of individual personal commitment.
- Respect for fellow workers is evident.
- A pleasant atmosphere prevails.

As we observe a little more carefully and talk to a few people we find the following:

- They take pride in what they are accomplishing, both individually and as a team.
- They know the present performance levels and goals, both personally and as a group.
- They know where to get information and help.
- They are interested in what they are doing, even simple tasks, because they know why it is necessary.

If the above are the characteristics that are desirable to develop within an organization, let's review a list of the techniques and programs that have proven successful in bringing the above about.

- All plans and actions are structured on the premise that it is essential for all individuals in the organization to know where the organization is going, and at any time to know where it has progressed to, whether it is on schedule, ahead of schedule, or behind schedule.
- Key people must be leaders, not bosses.
- Responsibilities and authority are delegated to the lowest point in the organization where the specific action will take place, where its quantity and quality can best be evaluated.
- Opportunity for constant personal growth through training and experience in the current job environment with advancement available to those who have a high-level record of past performance. This opportunity must exist throughout all levels of the organization. There must be no barriers. Because all job opportunities are clearly identified by measurable standards and objectives, strong emphasis can be placed on personal accountability for a job well done.

- Because of the principle of acceptance of accountability, wide freedom of group-determined action is possible with a very low risk factor.

Source   George F. Crosby, "Getting Back to Basics on Productivity," *Administrative Management*, vol. 42, no. 4 (November, 1981), p. 33. Excerpted from Office Administration and Automation, © 1981 by Geyer-McAllister Publ, Inc., N.Y.

Time Management

Managers in all sizes of firms can realize substantial improvement in their own performance and in their company's performance through more efficient use of their time. The small business owners are certainly no exception. In fact, with the many pressures and decisions facing the owners, efficient use of time is a matter of utmost importance. **Time management** is a systematic analysis of how the owner, as well as all other employees of the firm, uses time in performing job activities. Analysis of time use can reveal to owners the type of activities on which they are spending their time and consequently help them devote their time to more critical, high-priority items. High-priority items can then be identified for the owner, other managers, and each employee. In this way, items of less importance can be delegated to other persons, for whom these activities become high-priority items on that level.

One method of evaluating whether managers are using their time properly is through an analysis of their skill and use of delegation of authority. If managers respond with many "yes" answers, it is suggested that they take an in-depth look at their performance and restructure their activities so that they delegate more authority. Typical questions that are useful in making this analysis are listed as follows.

		Yes	No
1.	Is your pile of unfinished work increasing?	_____	_____
2.	Do you find that daily operations are so time-consuming that you have little time left for planning and other important matters?	_____	_____
3.	Do you feel you have to have close control of every detail to have the job done right?	_____	_____
4.	Do you frequently find yourself bogged down, trying to cope with the morass of small details?	_____	_____
5.	Do you frequently have to postpone long-range projects?	_____	_____
6.	Is a good part of your working day spent on tasks your subordinates could do?	_____	_____

		Yes	No
7.	Do you lack confidence and respect for your subordinates' abilities to shoulder more responsibilities?	_____	_____
8.	Do your subordinates defer all decisions on problems to you?	_____	_____
9.	After delegating a project, do you breathe down the subordinate's neck?	_____	_____
10.	Do you feel that you're abdicating your role as a manager if you have to ask your subordinates' assistance in order to complete your projects?[1]	_____	_____

EMPLOYEE RELATIONS IN THE SMALL BUSINESS

Of the many issues that confront the small owner–manager, one of the more challenging is found in the area of employee relations. Small business managers often possess a high level of technical skills, for example, being a highly productive salesperson, or having the ability to work with "things," such as machine shop equipment, computers, or accounting procedures. However, for a person in a role of owner–manager, one of the most valuable skills is human relations, or the ability to work effectively with people to achieve individual and company goals.

In our text, the term **employee relations** refers to the daily interpersonal relationships that exist between small business managers and employees. The quality of interpersonal relationships determines the type of **internal organization environment** or climate that exists in the firm. The internal organization environment is shaped by the following factors in the workplace.

1. Social factors (group interaction, superior-subordinate relationships).
2. Physical factors (working conditions, lighting, layout, equipment).
3. Economic factors (salary, wages, fringe benefits).

The perception that employees have of these factors influences, either directly or indirectly, their attitudes and resulting behavior toward the company's objectives, policies, working conditions, superiors, subordinates, and peers and also their expectations about their job and their level of productivity.

Many small firms have at least a few employees on the payroll, and a

---

[1]Questions adapted from "Delegate Your Way to Success," *Computer Decisions*, March 1981, p. 164.

Employee teamwork is an essential ingredient for the small business.

primary goal of managers is to have employees work together as a team rather than as individuals. Teamwork stresses mutual understanding and cooperation for goal achievement at both the individual and company level.

In this section, we will explore some of the prominent "employee relations" issues. This discussion should provide an owner–manager with a framework for understanding employee behavior. This need for broad understanding of what causes employees to act and react as they do is very real for the small firm owner–manager because there is usually a small number of employees, and cooperation and support among all employees are essential for goals to be accomplished.

THE INDIVIDUAL IN THE ORGANIZATION

Because employees spend a substantial portion of their lives at work, owners should realize that the workplace has a profound impact on the lives of individuals. Modern managers recognize that individuals are unique, each with his or her own values, feelings, interests, physical makeup, needs, and emotions. Each person's behavior in the place of work is shaped by a combination of many factors, including physiological makeup, previous work experience, needs, wants, goals, and influences of cultural background (family, peers, and race).

Employee Needs

Each person has a unique set of needs. In our discussion, needs are defined as all the things people must have in order to survive as well as the things they want. Thus, all human behavior is directed toward need satisfaction. Consequently, managers must be aware of what employees demand from a job in order to understand more clearly why they behave the way they do (motivation). **Motivation** is the inner drive that ignites behavioral actions to satisfy needs. Employees may be motivated either positively or negatively. Positive motivation occurs when employees strive toward a goal, such as putting forth extra effort on the job to gain a promotion, recognition, or a salary increase. Negative motivation results from such reasons as fear of failure or frustration and causes an employee's motivation to be aimed toward protection of self. Negative motivation may result in an employee's rejecting new work methods or a promotion, becoming apathetic, fighting the system, or leaving the company.

When owners more fully comprehend employee needs, it leads to more constructive employer-employee relations because owners then understand *why* employees behave as they do. In addition, knowledge of the needs of employees is beneficial to owners because they can use this information to build an organization environment that offers opportunities for these needs to be satisfied. Where employees are provided opportunities to fulfill their needs, they usually respond with more favorable attitudes toward the organization and their work assignments.

Figure 8–6 presents a diagram of the need satisfaction process. For example, an employee has the desire to be promoted (need identification). In order to satisfy this need, the employee undertakes the actions that he or she feels will result in the job promotion (motivation to act). When the employer recognizes the employee's outstanding performance and rewards him or her with a promotion, the need is satisfied (satisfaction of needs).

FIGURE 8–6

The need satisfaction process.

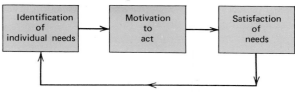

The need satisfaction process is continuous within individuals. When one need is satisfied, it no longer serves as a motivator. Instead, other needs are recognized by the individual, and the new needs become the basis for an individual's motivation to act.

Kinds of Human Needs

Though not everyone has exactly the same kinds of needs, there does exist a generally common set of needs among people. Furthermore, the intensity of the needs may vary among persons. Owner–managers should develop empathy with employees. By being empathetic, managers can view and evaluate a situation or problem from the perspective of the employee. By empathizing with employees, owner–managers will be in a more favorable position to understand employee needs, which in turn aids them in becoming more effective managers.

The needs included in our discussion are physiological, security and safety, affiliation, power, achievement, and ego needs.

Physiological Needs

Everyone has physiological needs. These are the basic needs that an individual must have in order to survive—food, oxygen, water, shelter. The owner–manager of the firm provides employees with a wage or salary that is adequate for their obtaining the resources necessary to satisfy these basic maintenance needs.

Security and Safety Needs

Each person has a need to feel safe and secure from anything that might harm him or her in all phases of the person's life, including the workplace. Safety and security needs can be provided for in various ways. Safety needs may be satisfied when the owner–manager attempts to provide employees with safe working conditions, as by purchasing equipment with special safety features and maintaining a physical environment that is not harmful to people's health.

Security needs may be fulfilled by offering job security, health insurance, pension plans, and other means of offsetting an employee's economic insecurity.

Affiliation Need

The affiliation need is demonstrated by our desire to interact with others. Affiliation needs include the need for belonging, for acceptance by co-workers, and giving and receiving attention. Americans are often described as a "nation of joiners." Most people are members of several groups simultaneously—social clubs, civic organizations, religious groups, and, of course, work groups. Group memberships enable individuals to satisfy their belonging and acceptance needs. Employee belonging and acceptance needs can be satisfied on the job when individuals are accepted as members of the work group. Owner–managers can provide employees with opportunities to satisfy the affiliation need through a variety of activities—company picnics and the design of jobs that permits interaction among the employees.

Power Need

Power is the capacity to influence or control. An individual expresses this power need when he or she seeks to be dominant over, or control the use of, physical objects and the actions of others. In an organization, power may be acquired in a number of ways, as described below.

Formal power—gained from formal authority or position in the firm.

Reward power—based on an individual's ability to administer and control rewards, such as pay increases and promotions, of others.

Expert power—derived from an individual's special knowledge, experience, expertise, or skill. The employee who is the most skilled machine operator may be approached by other employees and managers for technical assistance. Because of this expertise, he or she has power.

Coercive power—based on the leader's ability to administer and control punishment (such as withholding a promotion or denying a pay increase) to others because they failed to comply with the leader's directives.

Charismatic power—based on an individual's possession of personal characteristics that make him or her attractive to others. The group decides that personal characteristics are important and grant this person power over them.

Achievement Need

The achievement need tends to be characteristic of people who have a strong desire to accomplish a task through their own efforts. David McClelland identified the characteristics of the people who have a strong achievement need. These characteristics are the following.

1. They like situations in which they take personal responsibility for finding solutions.
2. They tend to set moderate achievement goals and to take "calculated risks."
3. They want concrete feedback on how well they are doing.[2]

According to McClelland, an individual who is likely to have a strong achievement need is the entrepreneur. Where employees have a high need for achievement, the owner–manager should provide them with tasks that allow them to assume greater responsibility and initiative.

---

[2]D. C. McClelland, "Business Drive and National Achievement," *Harvard Business Review*, vol. 40, no. 4 (July–August 1962), pp. 104–105.

Ego Needs

Ego needs include self-esteem (self-confidence, independence) and personal reputation (recognition and status). As people mature, they develop a need to be independent, both on and off the job. On the job, employees express the independence need through a desire to have some control over their work and freedom from close supervision. In this way, employees can demonstrate their maturity.

People have a need for recognition. Employees can have this need satisfied by being given recognition for their contribution to the company, such as special recognition as salesperson of the month or a cash award for a suggestion. Recognition also increases one's status.

Status is the relative social ranking a person has compared with others in the group. Status may be either formal or informal. Formal status refers to the rank of people as specified by the authority structure of the organization. Sources of formal status include job title, occupation, and organization level. Informal status refers to the social rank given people because of feelings toward them. Informal sources of status include such personal factors as seniority, work schedule, age, education, and expertise.

The visible status symbols that identify one's rank in the social position include size and location of office, type of office equipment (desk, chair, typewriter), job title, and number of windows in an office.

ORGANIZATIONAL CHANGE

Managers need to realize that all decisions they make and actions they undertake will affect employee needs. One positive step in building strong employer-employee relations is to assess the impact that proposed actions and decisions will have on employees prior to taking the action and to ascertain what steps should be taken to lessen an adverse impact.

One common problem deals with changes in the company that affect operations and personnel of the firm. Change may be reflected in methods or procedures of work, such as a change to automated facilities, a change in personnel, or a move by the company to a new location. Change has a definite impact on individuals and should be undertaken so as to encounter as few obstacles as possible.

Change is a fact of an organization's life and is desirable if the firm is to remain abreast or move ahead of the competition. Yet the major barrier to change is resistance. The owner–manager resists change on the grounds that the business has been successful. Therefore, why is there a need to change? Employees resist change because they fear the unknown and desire to maintain the status quo in which they feel secure. Employee relations can be adversely affected if employees feel they are being pressured or manipulated into making changes. Employee resistance to change may be evidenced by more hostility or aggressiveness on the job. They may resort to sabotage in the work area, absenteeism and tardiness may increase, or they may develop apathetic attitudes toward their work.

Resistance to change can be reduced but not totally eliminated. Managers should recognize the importance of communicating clear and complete information about the change. They should also get the employees who will be affected by the change involved by encouraging them to contribute their suggestions on how to implement the change. Participation of employees is the type of constructive action that can aid in reducing their resistance to change.

EMPLOYEE MORALE

The organizational environment has a major impact on employee morale. **Morale** is defined as the mental attitude of individuals and work groups toward their work environment (job, company). In this context, employee morale may be described as being either high or low. Morale is a mental attitude, a feeling that employees have, and it is difficult to measure. In fact, morale cannot be measured directly as can the number of dollars of profit earned during the business year. Instead, indirect techniques are used to measure the attitudes of employees and provide a reading of employee morale.

For example, one technique of measuring employee attitudes is an objective survey. This survey technique asks employees to check how they feel about particular items in the company. Questions may be the true-false variety, multiple choice, or on a scale ranging from completely satisfied to completely dissatisfied. Figure 8–7 presents one method of collecting data on employee morale.

Descriptive surveys are another method of collecting morale data. Employees are requested to supply written answers to questions. Regardless of the method employed, morale surveys can profitably be used regularly to identify the strengths and weaknesses of the company.

INDICATORS OF EMPLOYEE MORALE

There are indicators, or warning signals, that alert the owners to the realization that employee morale is low. Some of the indicators that the small business owners should be aware of are shown in Figure 8–8.

Any of these negative morale indicators will adversely affect the small firm. Considerable amounts of time and money, ranging to thousands of dollars, are involved in employee selection and placement. Employees who are properly placed in a job tend to have higher morale. Poor selection and placement

FIGURE 8–7

Employee morale survey.

Listed below are 16 statements. Please check each of the statements according to how you feel toward them—completely agree, somewhat agree, somewhat disagree, completely disagree.

	Completely Agree	Somewhat Agree	Somewhat Disagree	Completely Disagree
1. I am given the opportunity to participate in decisions that affect me.				
2. Communication within the company provides me with adequate information on current and future plans.				
3. My superior does not exert excessive pressure to meet work deadlines.				
4. My job performance is evaluated fairly and constructively.				
5. I am allowed considerable freedom in the performance of my job.				
6. I have assurance of job security as long as I perform at a satisfactory level.				
7. There are opportunities for promotion and advancement.				
8. My pay is competitive.				
9. Physical working conditions are satisfactory.				
10. I am doing a job that is interesting and challenging.				
11. I am treated fairly in the handling of my grievances and in being disciplined.				
12. I derive personal satisfaction from doing my job well—I have a feeling of pride in the job I am doing.				
13. I am given recognition for doing a good job.				
14. Superiors and subordinates work together as a team.				
15. Standards of performance set for my job are realistic.				
16. Fringe benefits are at least equal to benefits in other companies.				

FIGURE 8–8

Indicators of low employee morale.

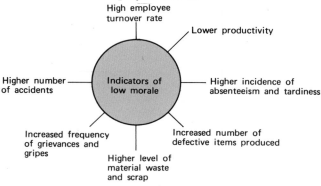

procedures lead to frustration and low morale. Eventually, employees will leave the firm or be low producers. Firms that have a high turnover rate of employees experience increased costs of operations. New employees must be selected and placed. While they are being trained, their productivity is below standard, and chances for error or waste of material are greater. Where the firm is experiencing a high turnover rate, the manager's real concern should be to uncover the reasons why and take steps to correct them.

If absenteeism increases, the small business will be understaffed. In the retail or service establishment, it will be difficult to provide the customer assistance needed, especially during peak business hours. This may result in driving customers away to competitors or at least creating inconvenience for the customers. In the small manufacturing firm, the absence of a machine operator means a machine must be idled, thus reducing the firm's output. Or, if the machine must be operated, it will likely have to be operated by a marginally qualified worker. The result will be lower productivity and increased number of defective products.

If accidents increase, not only must the personal injury be a matter of real concern but also the effect that the accidents have on the company. A valuable worker is lost for a period of time, productivity suffers, and the cost of employee accident insurance increases.

The negative effect of low morale should be an area of major concern for small business managers. Consequently, they should attempt to maintain up-to-date information relating to the state of employee morale and strive to improve the overall state of employee morale in the concern.

If these indicators begin to surface, small business managers should recognize that they are merely *symptoms*. The critical task is to establish the *cause*. Why is turnover increasing? Why is productivity suffering? Why are accidents increasing? Only by ascertaining the *cause* of these problems will it be possible to take constructive steps to correct them.

LEADERSHIP STYLE AND MORALE

The owner–manager's leadership style is another important factor in determining employee morale. A leadership style that has a positive impact on employee morale is one that creates a positive environment by providing employees with the opportunity to satisfy their goals and needs while at the same time allowing the firm to realize the attainment of its objectives.

Basically, there are three styles of leadership of which the small business manager should be cognizant. These are the autocratic, free-rein, and participative styles.

Clearly, small business managers should recognize that no one of these leadership styles is applicable to all situations. Leadership style, of necessity, varies from situation to situation. However, managers who create an organizational environment that encourages employees to participate discover that it can be an important avenue for developing positive employee morale.

Autocratic Leadership

Autocratic leaders strive for maximum control of the firm. They delegate little or no authority and provide few outlets for employee creativity. Close supervision is the practice, and pressure is applied to obtain greater employee productivity. Because formal communications flow primarily downward from managers to employees, there is little opportunity for the exchange of information and ideas. Employees are usually reprimanded for mistakes. Autocratic leadership usually has a negative impact on employee morale, especially if employees have strong needs for independence and participation.

Free-Rein Leadership

Free-rein managers believe that the best leadership style is one in which there is minimal contact with employees. These managers frequently manage by abdication, not delegation. They spend much time away from the business. Instead of delegating authority to employees, however, these managers offer little or no direction for operations during their absence. Employee morale usually declines when managers follow this leadership style.

Participative Leadership

Participative leaders encourage employees to share in making decisions that affect them. By encouraging participation, the leader desires to get employees ego-involved in their work and in the company. The leader strives to build an organizational environment that recognizes the importance of the individual. The participative leader encourages two-way communication.

Participative leaders also strive to tap the creative talents of their employees. A basic ingredient of the participative leader's philosophy is that employ-

FIGURE 8–9

Company guidelines for employees.

PROHIBITED ACTS

1.   Disorderly conduct: reporting to work under the influence of liquor or consuming intoxicants on company premises or while on company business.
2.   Conclusive evidence of dishonesty.
3.   Obtaining employment by using false or misleading information.
4.   Continued violation of safety practices.
5.   Selling or soliciting in the company.
6.   Gambling.
7.   Excessive tardiness or absenteeism without reason.
8.   Refusal to work as directed (insubordination).
9.   Willful destruction of company property.

ees are more likely to support ideas and actions that they have had a part in creating.

EMPLOYEE DISCIPLINE

When employees work together, conflict will occasionally develop. If managers fail to cope with conflict and discipline situations constructively, the result can be a lowering of employee morale. Employees lose respect for managers who cannot tolerate mistakes, who are too lax and apply discipline only under the most severe circumstances, or apply discipline inconsistently.

One suggested way to reduce the number of instances where discipline is required is to inform employees of the company rules and regulations. For example, many firms specify employee actions that are prohibited and that, if engaged in, will result in disciplinary action being taken. It is important, however, that employees perceive the rules as being fair and related to their job performance. A typical set of guidelines is shown in Figure 8–9.

Some factors involved in discipline or areas where discipline problems arise include (1) absenteeism, (2) tardiness, (3) rule violations, (4) insubordination, (5) failure to carry out orders, (6) errors in work, (7) deviation from established procedures.

Frequently, these problems arise because of lack of knowledge, poor understanding, poor attitudes, lack of interest, or carelessness.

Progressive Discipline

Progressive discipline is one approach that applies a minimum of discipline to a first offense but that increases the degree of discipline for subsequent violations of rules or policies. Progressive discipline actions may include the following sequence:

Step One: Oral warning.

Step Two: Written warning stating the consequences of future violations.

Step Three: Disciplinary layoff or demotion.

Step Four: Discharge.

The "hot stove rule" has been recommended as a series of steps to make discipline more effective. It uses the analogy of touching the hot stove and administering discipline. The sequence should include

1. A forewarning—all are warned by the heat generated not to touch the stove.
2. Immediate action—touching the stove results in being immediately burned.
3. A consistent rule—each time the stove is touched, you are burned.
4. Impersonal administration—all who touch the stove are burned.[3]

Positive Discipline

The most effective discipline is positive discipline, that which corrects or strengthens an individual. It is also the most difficult type of discipline to apply. Disciplining should be conducted in private, away from the noise of the job and certainly not in front of fellow employees. When disciplining, managers should concentrate on the mistake rather than on the person. It is essential that managers listen carefully to the employee's view as to what occurred in order to get the full facts and clarify any misunderstanding. The manager should explain not only that something is being done incorrectly but also explain why employees should be doing it another way. A further step is to work out an equitable solution that is fair to both employer and employee.

Some guidelines that will enable the owner to establish a climate of positive discipline are suggested as follows.

1. There must be rules and standards that are communicated clearly and administered fairly.
2. Rules and standards must be reasonable.
3. Rules should be communicated so that they are known and understood by all employees.
4. While a rule or a standard is in force, employees are expected to adhere to it.
5. Even though rules exist, people should know that if a personal problem or a unique situation makes the rule exceptionally harsh, the rule may be modified, or an exception may be granted.

---

[3]Burt Scanlon and J. Bernard Keys, *Management and Organization Behavior* (New York: Wiley, 1979), p. 382.

6. There should be no favorites, and privileges should be granted only when they can also be granted to other employees in similar situations. This means that it must be possible to explain to other employees who request a similar privilege with less justification why the privilege cannot be extended to them in their particular situation.

7. Employees must be aware that they can and should voice dissatisfaction with any rules or standards they consider unreasonable as well as with working conditions they feel are hazardous.

8. Employees should understand the consequences of breaking a rule without permission.

9. There should be an appeals procedure when an employee feels you have made an unfair decision.

10. Employees should be consulted when rules are set.

11. There should be recognition for good performance, reliability, and loyalty.[4]

COMMUNICATION AND EMPLOYEE MORALE

A communication system that allows employees to be informed about company actions is a strong factor in creating high employee morale. An effective two-way communication system provides employees with the opportunity to be involved in company matters. It provides managers with insight into employee attitudes toward the company.

In many small businesses, most communication is exchanged on a face-to-face basis because the manager has direct, personal contact with employees. The manager plans the work, gives instructions, and evaluates jobs to see that they are done properly. Other forms of communication are nonpersonal and may be written or visual (posters, for example).

The manager must realize that effective communication does not just occur. Instead, it involves a conscious effort on the part of the manager to build a communication system. Some specific guides for effective communication are included here.

1. The manager must be a good listener—listening to ideas and suggestions as well as complaints.

2. Employees should be kept informed of matters that affect them, such as changes in policies or procedures.

3. Two-way communication should be encouraged.

---

[4]"Employee Relations and Personnel Policies," *Business Basics*, no. 1023 (Washington, D.C.: Small Business Administration, 1980), pp. 15–17.

4. Subordinates should be allowed to participate in discussions of decisions that will affect them before the final decision is reached.

5. Create a climate of trust and confidence by reporting facts honestly to employees.

6. The communication messages should be accurate, definite, simple, and suitable for the occasion.

7. The communication messages should not contain any hidden messages.

STRENGTHENING EMPLOYEE RELATIONS

Small business managers should recognize the uniqueness of their firms. They can contribute greatly to improving employee relations by being aware of the specific suggestions listed here.

1. Improve your own general understanding of human behavior.

2. Accept the fact that others do not always see things as you do.

3. In any differences of opinion, consider the possibility that you may not have the right answer.

4. Show your employees that you are interested in them and that you want their ideas on how conditions can be improved.

5. Treat your employees as individuals; never deal with them impersonally.

6. Respect differences of opinion.

7. Insofar as possible, give explanations for management actions.

8. Provide information and guidance on matters affecting employees' security.

9. Make reasonable efforts to keep jobs interesting.

10. Encourage promotion from within.

11. Express appreciation publicly for jobs well done.

12. Offer criticism privately in the form of constructive suggestions for improvement.

13. Train supervisors to be concerned about the people they supervise in the same way as they would be about merchandise or materials or equipment.

14. Keep your staff up-to-date on matters that affect them.

15. Quell false rumors and provide correct information.

16. Be fair![5]

---

[5] Martin M. Bruce, *Human Relations in Small Business* (Washington, D.C.: Small Business Administration, 1969), pp. 14–15.

SUMMARY OF KEY POINTS

1. A manager supervises the work activities of employees in order to see to it that they accomplish their specific tasks. The owner frequently works side by side with employees in the daily operations.

2. The management functions of the owner–manager include planning, goal setting, and decision making; organizing and staffing; directing; and controlling.

3. Planning is the process of setting objectives and then choosing the course of action the firm will follow to reach the objectives.

4. Decision making involves the four phases of defining the problem, developing alternatives, evaluating alternatives, and implementing the plan of action.

5. The function of organizing involves coordinating the firm's resources so that they follow the course needed to reach the firm's objectives.

6. The activities involved in the organizing function are (1) identification of the jobs to be performed, (2) staffing, (3) defining the authority and responsibility of each employee, and (4) determining authority-responsibility relationships.

7. The directing function is the face-to-face leadership provided by the owner–manager.

8. Control is the function of determining if efforts conform to plans and objectives.

9. Time management is the systematic analysis of how owners and employees use their time in performing their activities.

10. Employee relations refer to the daily, interpersonal relationships that exist between small business owners and employees.

11. Each employee is unique and has a unique set of needs.

12. Employees have physiological needs, security and safety needs, affiliation needs, power needs, achievement needs, and ego needs.

13. All organizations face changing internal and external conditions. A major problem of change is overcoming or reducing employee and owner resistance to change.

14. Employee morale is the mental attitude that employees have toward the owner–manager, the firm, their job, and their fellow employees.

15. Indicators of low morale include higher rates of turnover, absenteeism, and tardiness; lower productivity; more grievances and gripes; higher incidence of accidents; and increased spoilage and waste of materials.

16. The three basic styles of leadership are autocratic, free-rein, and participative styles. The style that is appropriate depends on the requirements of the situation.

17. Employee discipline is necessary to maintain order in the firm. The owner should specify guidelines that govern employee conduct.

18. Communication is essential for keeping employees informed and can be an influential factor in creating high morale.

DISCUSSION QUESTIONS

1. What are the management functions of the small business manager?
2. Explain the difference between technical skills and human relations skills.
3. Define the term *employee relations*.
4. Explain what is meant by the "internal organization environment."
5. Identify some specific needs of employees.
6. What is the difference between motivation and morale?
7. Name several indicators of low employee morale.
8. Why is it difficult to discipline employees? What are some actions that can be taken to make discipline positive?
9. Explain the difference between autocratic, free-rein, and participative leadership styles.
10. What are some suggestions for improving communication?

STUDENT PROJECTS

Interview a small business manager and obtain the following data.

1. What are the objectives of the business? Are the objectives written down?
2. Does the firm have an organization chart? If so, obtain a copy of the chart.
3. Are morale surveys conducted in the firm? If so, how often?
4. Does the firm have written rules and regulations? If it does, what are they?

CASE A

The Apparel Shop

Harry Wilson, office manager, and Robert Ellison, manager of the men's department, were leaving The Apparel Shop on their way to lunch. As they approached the front door, they observed Daniel Masters, the owner and president of the firm, in conversation with Norma Jackson, manager of the jewelry department. Mr. Masters was trying to end the conversation, and he appeared anxious to leave. Finally, in a voice expressing some impatience, he told her he had to leave, but added, "Drop by my office anytime. The door is always open."

Daniel Masters took control of the store a year ago when his father unexpectedly died of a heart attack. Daniel has had a difficult time adjusting to his role as president. He worked in the store while in high school and college, and his father taught him all the technical operations of the different departments.

As Harry and Robert were eating their lunch, they discussed the situation at The Apparel Shop. Both agreed that Daniel knew all phases of store operations, but one of the main problems was getting Daniel to listen to ideas or suggestions. Harry remarked, "I have been with the store for about 2 years. During the year that I worked for Daniel's father, he gave me a great deal of freedom in the office operations. He let me make a lot of changes after we had discussed them. He was easy to talk to and encouraged ideas."

Robert agreed and added, "Daniel is just the opposite. We don't have a chance to discuss ideas or problems with him. And we are strongly discouraged from making our own decisions. Everything has to be decided by Daniel. And I have stopped dropping in that 'open door.' Just last week I made an appointment to discuss our new lines of merchandise that we have been handling for the past month."

Robert continued by describing his meeting with Daniel. When Robert walked in, Daniel was on the telephone, and he motioned for Robert to sit down. When he hung up, he rushed out of the office without a word to Robert to talk to his secretary. He returned, wrote some notes on his desk pad, and turned to Robert and said, "Well, what's your problem today?"

Robert reminded him that they were to discuss the merchandise lines as well as sales figures, customer relations, and salespersons. When Robert mentioned the salespersons, Daniel interrupted him to comment about the shortage of salespersons in the women's department. Then the conversation was interrupted by another phone call. Finally, the discussion returned to the purpose of the meeting, but as they were looking at the sales figures, Daniel interrupted again, commenting on how he felt one of the salespersons' performance had begun to decline.

Robert was ready to give up on that session when they were interrupted by another phone call. Daniel was clearly angry when he ended the telephone conversation. He said, "Trouble in the jewelry department again. Norma is always asking for assistance. But I believe we have your problems worked out, Robert, haven't we? Norma is coming up now. But when you have a chance, drop back, and let's take a close look at all phases of your department, especially the new merchandise lines we have added."

As Robert got up to leave, Daniel commented, "Thanks for coming, *Harry.* Come back anytime. You know my door is always open."

QUESTIONS

1. What leadership style best describes Daniel?
2. What is likely to happen to the general state of employee motivation and morale if Daniel continues to manage in the manner described earlier?

3. What is wrong with the way that Daniel acts in meetings with his employees?

4. What does an "open door" policy really mean?

5. What could you recommend that would improve employee meetings as described earlier? Role-play the situation.

CASE B

Wood Manufacturing Company

Samuel Jackson is the supervisor of the bending and press department of a small manufacturing company known for its quality products. Forty of the company's 220 employees work in this department. The products of the company include tubular and plate heat exchangers, pressure vessels, absorption towers, and equipment for dairy and chemical plants.

Six months ago, Andrew was hired as a punch press operator. He is 24, single, has received training at a technical training school, and has three years' experience. He is ambitious and plans to work for a higher degree by attending evening classes.

The work of the punch press operators is such that workers must cooperate in performing tasks of similar nature, and the contribution of particular members is difficult to measure. The company has a group incentive plan under which production workers are paid a bonus for production above standard. Data of production standards and the bonus rate are arrived at by members of the industrial engineering department with consultation between management and employees. The bonus is available only to direct production workers (machine operators). Tool setters are not eligible and receive a flat, hourly wage. The group of which Andrew is a member usually receives a bonus of between 35 and 40 percent over their basic wage.

Matthew has been with the company 7 years and is employed as a die setter in the punch press department. His job is to set dies to the press for stamping or forming metal sheets as required. For each item, different sets of tooling are required. Thus, to change production from one item to another means tools must be set and machines adjusted. This is Matthew's job. He is conscientious, loyal to the company, and particularly methodical in his approach to his task. He is somewhat slow but does his job well. At times the punch press operators became irritated with Matthew because they felt that his slowness kept them from making a bonus.

To speed up the process, Andrew began setting the tools of his machine himself about three months ago. Matthew accused Andrew of trying to take his job away. Andrew assured Matthew that he was only trying to help him. Andrew felt that while they had to wait, the group members were losing money. He did not feel Matthew would mind because all tool setters were paid a flat hourly wage.

This situation caused resentment to build between Andrew and Matthew.

Samuel, the supervisor, was unaware of the conflict between the two. Samuel did notice that Andrew did adjust his machine and set a die occasionally, but he did not object because this helped to get the work out on schedule, and Andrew did the work correctly.

One day, near the end of work when both men were tired, Matthew openly accused Andrew of trying to steal his job, and a quarrel developed between them. Andrew told Matthew he was too slow and could not do his work properly and that he should be replaced. Matthew became enraged and moved closer to Andrew. Assuming that Matthew was going to strike him, Andrew punched him, knocking him to the floor. A scuffle followed until Samuel came running to the scene and broke it up. He then reported the incident to the personnel manager, Roy.

The company policy prohibits fighting on company premises.

QUESTIONS

1. What disciplinary action should be taken by Roy, the personnel manager?

2. What effect will this situation have on employee morale if it is not handled properly?

SMALL BUSINESS ADMINISTRATION PUBLICATIONS

Management Aids (Free)

Profit by Your Wholesaler's Services
The Equipment Replacement Decision
Planning and Goal Setting for Small Business
Management Checklist for a Family Business

Small Business Management Series (For Sale)

Small Store Planning for Growth

Starting and Managing Series (For Sale)

Managing for Profit

Business Basics (For Sale)

Retail Merchandise Management

CHAPTER NINE
PERSONNEL MANAGEMENT IN THE SMALL BUSINESS

LEARNING GOALS

After reading this chapter, you will understand:

1. The purpose of job analysis, job description, and job specification.
2. That employees may be recruited from many sources.
3. The procedures involved in the hiring process.
4. The necessity and significance of employee orientation.
5. The various types of training that employees may receive both within and outside the company.
6. The role of counseling in the small business.
7. The variety of payment plans that small business managers may use.
8. Some federal laws that may affect the operations of the small business.
9. What employee fringe benefits are.
10. Why employee safety is a critical concern of the small business owner.

KEY WORDS

Job analysis

Job description

Job specification

Application blank

On-the-job training

Apprenticeship training

Counseling

Performance appraisal

Management by objectives

Job evaluation

Fair Labor Standards Act of 1938

Fringe benefits

Worker compensation

Civil Rights Act of 1964

Equal Employment Opportunity Act of 1972

Bona fide occupational qualification

SMALL BUSINESS PROFILE

Six Who Succeeded: The Employment Agent

If now is a hard time to start a business, so too was April 1974. But it was good enough for Ruth Clark. Despite a recession and a prime rate rising toward a then inconceivable 11%, Clark took $3,900 of her savings and started Clark Unlimited Personnel. Says she: "I'm the type who turns every negative into a positive."

The clients of Clark's Manhattan firm are corporations that need workers mainly to fill temporary clerical and secretarial positions. Annual revenues top $2 million. Perhaps equally gratifying to Clark, 40: "We keep 1,500 to 2,000 people a year employed." About 70% of them are black. Says she: "I provide good service for everyone, but I'm very happy that I've done well for my own people."

Clark went into business for herself after working for several years in a similar New York City placement firm. The first few months were decidedly hand to mouth. When she couldn't get a bank loan, Clark turned to factoring houses, which lend to high-risk businesses on the basis of the money that is owed to them by customers. Such lenders command premium interest rates —in Clark's case, 21% on the $12,000 she borrowed.

She concentrated her sales pitches on blue-chip New York City companies that were eager to do business with minority-owned firms. Among her clients today are Chase Manhattan Bank, Bankers Trust, Irving Trust and the three major broadcasting networks. Says she: "I never aim for the middle. I go straight for the top." Born and raised in Harlem, Clark, a divorced woman, now lives in a $1 million co-op in the same Sutton Place building as designer Calvin Klein.

Source   Marlys Harris, "Six Who Succeeded—The Employment Agent," *Money*, vol. 11, no. 12 (December, 1982), p. 65. Reprinted from the December 1982 issue of *Money* magazine by special permission, © 1982, Time, Inc.

In the small business, one of an owner's primary concerns is attracting the best available talent because employees are the key asset of the company. The owners who surround themselves with competent employees realize that this is one of the most effective ways of staying competitive because these employees are more efficient and their performance levels are higher.

In larger firms, personnel management specialists are delegated the authority and assigned the responsibility to perform all personnel functions. However, small business owners often do not employ a full-time personnel manager because of limited financial resources. Instead, owners may take personal charge of the personnel activity or delegate the assignment to an employee who performs these functions in conjunction with another job assignment.

Although there may not be a full-time personnel manager, this in no way lessens the critical nature of this function. Rather, it should signal to owners the necessity for intensifying the time and energy to be expended on this vital function so that the objectives of the personnel function may be achieved.

The goal of owners is to ensure that competent people are hired and placed in job assignments that match their unique qualifications. Specific personnel management activities include (1) assessing job requirements, (2) employee recruitment, (3) establishing selection procedures, and (4) providing for employee training and development.

ASSESSING JOB REQUIREMENTS

The process of selecting competent personnel for each position can be accomplished more efficiently through a systematic definition of the requirements of each task and the skills, knowledge, and other qualifications that employees must possess to perform each task satisfactorily. Identifying the requirements of tasks and the qualifications of employees encompasses three phases: conducting a job analysis, developing a job description, and preparing a job specification.

Job Analysis

The job analysis forms the foundation for developing the job description and job specification. The **job analysis** is a systematic investigation to collect all pertinent information about each task. From the job analysis, the skills, knowledge, and abilities that employees need to perform a task effectively and efficiently plus the duties, responsibilities, and requirements of each task are identified. The job analysis should provide the following information for each task.

1. Job title.
2. Department in which the job is located.
3. Line of supervision.
4. Description of job, including major and minor duties.
5. Relation to other jobs (promotion opportunities, transfer possibilities, experience required, normal sources of employees).
6. Unique job characteristics (location, physical setting).
7. Supervision (type given and received).
8. Types of material and equipment used.
9. Qualifications
   a. Experience requirements.
   b. Education requirements.

        c.   Mental requirements.

        d.   Manual dexterity requirements.

        e.   Physical requirements (walking, climbing, standing, kneeling, lifting, talking, etc.).

10.   Working conditions (inside, outside, hot, cold, dry, wet, noisy, dirty, etc.).

11.   Hazards (mechanical, high places, electrical hazards, toxic conditions, working alone, working around others).

Job Description

The job description is developed from facts revealed in the job analysis. The **job description** is a written record that defines the major and minor duties of each task. It also contains a description of the responsibilities of each task, such as care for equipment and materials, safety and health of others, and contact with the public. The description further defines the various task requirements, such as physical activities, working conditions, and any hazards associated with the performance of a task. It should also designate the approximate time that the employee should devote to each activity. The job description focuses on the what, why, where, and how tasks are to be performed.

Small business owners can collect information from a number of sources that will be particularly helpful in preparing the job description. Obviously, one source is the employees themselves. When an individual is writing a new job description, a government publication, the *Dictionary of Occupational Titles,* can be extremely useful. It contains 20,000 actual job descriptions.

Job Specification

Whereas the job description describes the job, the **job specification** describes the person. It details the qualities, knowledge, skills, and abilities an individual needs to perform a task satisfactorily. Included in the job specification is the identification of the worker characteristics (planning, directing others, making decisions), experience, education, and skills needed to perform the tasks described in the job description. The job specification provides a gauge to measure how well an applicant matches the job opening. For example, a specification for a salesperson should define any special aptitude or technical knowledge needed to sell a product or service. Figure 9–1 outlines the job description and specification of a credit manager and bookkeeper in a small business.

RECRUITMENT OF EMPLOYEES

Personnel qualifications for the various jobs in the small business are defined in the job specification. To translate job specifications into action, small busi-

FIGURE 9–1
The job description and job specification.

Job Title:	Credit Manager and Bookkeeper
Report to:	Store Manager
Job Summary:	In charge of the credit and bookkeeping functions of the business; control over the firm's assets and expenditures; and acts as assistant to the store manager.
Job Description:	Processes credit applications: analyzes financial status and payment record of customers; checks references and credit bureau to determine credit responsibility.
	Sends collection notices to past-due accounts through mail, telephone calls, or personal visits.
	Checks the accuracy and completeness of price, stock classifications, and delivery information.
	Prepares bank deposit, listing checks and cash, and takes deposit to bank.
	Does all bookkeeping and prepares balance sheet and profit and loss statements of store.
	Sells merchandise during rush hours of the store.

Job Specification:	Education:	A minimum of a high school education is required.
	Experience:	Some prior bookkeeping and/or credit and collection experience is desirable.
	Skills:	Ability to keep a set of books and prepare balance sheet and profit and loss statements.

Job Duties	Approximate Time Spent on Each Assignment (percent)
Bookkeeping	40%
Credit and collection	20
Selling on retail floor	20
Inventories and stock control	10
Miscellaneous functions	10

ness owners must recruit those individuals whose qualifications match the job requirements. Owners should explore many sources of prospective employees. The discussion that follows, though not exhaustive, represents some of the major sources for recruiting employees.

Current Employees

Whenever possible, current employees should be given first priority for job openings within the company that offer opportunities for promotion. Furthermore, a policy of advancement from within will have a positive impact on employee morale. In addition, present employees may be able to recommend friends or relatives who are qualified for the vacancy.

Media Advertising

Advertising is an often used technique to attract prospective employees. Job vacancies may be publicized in the newspaper classified section or broadcast over a local radio station or television station. Job announcements in newspapers in nearby cities and in trade association magazines may also produce job applicants.

In-store Advertising

Many owner–managers use in-store advertising to call attention to job openings. "Help wanted" signs are placed in the store window, or the vacancy may be announced on the store's marquee or on a portable sign trailer located in front of the store.

Drop-in Applicants

Occasionally, individuals will stop and inquire if any jobs are open even though no vacancy has been advertised. Even if a job is not open at the time, the owners should take down some information about the interested parties, such as name and phone number and the type of position wanted, or they may be asked to fill out an application blank so they can be contacted if a vacancy occurs.

Vocational-Technical Schools

Area schools provide a large pool of highly trained individuals. Many high school programs offer excellent training in vocational and technical skills, and community colleges have outstanding technical training programs. In addition, private technical training schools, such as business colleges or electronics schools, train many qualified candidates.

Former Military Personnel

Persons retired from military service may possess technical skills and knowledge that can fill the firm's employment needs. These personnel may also have extensive management experience.

Colleges and Universities

Placement offices at colleges and universities maintain an active file of candidates who possess a wide range of qualifications. The owner–manager should consider this source, especially if the firm needs an employee who has received specialized training such as in accounting. In addition, the owner–manager should not overlook contacting teachers for recommendations of possible employees.

Public Employment Agencies

Public employment agencies, such as state and federal government agencies, offer their services in helping to locate and place employees. State employment agencies, for example, maintain employment offices at strategic locations throughout the state, and each office has direct contact with all other offices. They have on file an up-to-date listing of potential employees who possess a wide range of skills. Unskilled, skilled, technical, and professional employees may be recruited through these agencies. An advantage of public employment agencies is that their services are provided at no cost to users.

Private Employment Agencies

Private employment agencies maintain an extensive listing of applicants who possess skills necessary for performing a variety of tasks. Private employment agencies charge a fee for their placement services, which must be paid by either the applicant or the employer.

Labor Unions

Some firms may consider labor unions as possible sources of personnel. Unions can be especially helpful in supplying workers for certain types of occupations, such as carpenters or brickmasons.

Former Employees

Employees who may have voluntarily quit for personal or health reasons may be rehired at a later date. For example, someone who moved to another city and later returned to the local area may be reemployed.

Part-Time Employees

For many types of business, sales fluctuate sharply upward as a particular holiday season approaches, such as Christmas or Easter. This upturn in business activity often puts pressure on the regular work force to provide all customers with personalized service. Hence, the owner–manager can effectively employ part-time employees to fill in during the rush season. Part-time employees can also work odd-hour shifts, such as in the evenings or on Saturdays.

Other firms have need of extra help certain times of the day or week, but business activity is not sufficient to justify hiring a full-time employee. For example, a small retail store in a shopping center found its peak business hours were from 2 P.M. to 9 P.M. and its peak days were Friday and Saturday. The manager was able to hire two part-time employees to help meet the needs of the peak hours and days. A small hardware store owner and his wife operate their store by themselves. When peak business periods develop or when the owners want to get away for a vacation, they employ their neighbor, a retired military officer, to manage the store.

A vast supply of part-time employees is usually available. Possible sources include students, both high school and college, retired persons who desire only a few hours of employment a day or week, or a person whose health permits only a limited amount of work each day or week.

SPECIAL INTEREST FEATURE

Luring Talent to the Small Business

In talks with owners and managers of small or medium-sized restaurants or chains, I always hear the same complaint: We can't compete for excellence. With large foodservice corporations offering recruits a pretty package of impressive starting salaries, fringe benefits and retirement programs, officers of small firms frequently despair. They fear they cannot match the allure. One manager told me that his company couldn't even afford adequate advertising exposure. The feeling is that inevitably small firms have to settle for second best.

This need not be true today. Twenty years ago, perhaps. Then, employees were interested primarily in a good salary and job security. Priorities are different now.

In a recent survey, management trainees rated informality and attention to accomplishment as two of the most important qualities of a working place. Other job attributes they sought were: flexibility, independence, community involvement, results orientation and personal interest. All are clearly strengths of the small business.

Recognizing the unique advantages the small firm has to offer will help you develop a positive, and rewarding, recruiting effort.

PROMINENCE

One of the most serious complaints of the 20th century worker is a feeling of anonymity. In large corporations, people can go to work each day, perform a task that has little meaning or satisfaction in itself, receive neither praise nor criticism, and return home no more fulfilled or enlightened than when they left. They feel alienated from their job, their peers and their superiors, and in a very real sense, they feel lost.

Young recruits show marked preference for a chance to make significant professional contributions. They rate job fulfillment high above job security.

After all, since very few people voluntarily stay in their first jobs for their entire working life, the importance of job security to the young employee is comparatively small.

In the small company, each person's job generally encompasses more responsibilities than the same position in a large organization. Moreover, the competent employee can expect his or her responsibilities to increase faster than they would along the career path typical of a large corporation.

The managerial hierarchy of a small firm is narrower and much less complicated than that of a large one—simply because there are fewer people working there. The employee has fewer steps to take on his or her way up, and the steps are larger and more significant. Positions of greater importance and more meaningful work are far more within reach of the employee in a small firm than of his counterpart in a large one.

Because each member of a small company has to pull more weight than the job description might imply, the experience gained is invaluable. The employee of a small firm sees, firsthand, almost all phases of the business and participates in many of them. This varied work is not only more interesting than a single, limited task; it is also more useful to the employees. They learn the whole business.

A small company is just that: a company of people who meet regularly and share in each other's professional and, sometimes, social lives. Often, small businesses have many community ties. Employees feel part of a definite group of people, not an amorphous monolith.

The small business owner or manager has no reason to feel he or she is recruiting from a position of weakness. Even if you cannot permit yourself widespread advertising exposure, even if the "big boys" are offering what sound like dream packages, remember the undeniable benefits that only a small business can offer. Show your recruits that their needs can be well married to your opportunities—and look forward to a flock of new top talent.

Source James L. Hayes, "Luring Talent to the Small Business," *Restaurant Business*, vol. 79, no. 10 (August 1, 1980), p. 82.

THE EMPLOYEE SELECTION PROCESS

The purpose of the selection process is to obtain as much information about an individual as possible relative to skills, knowledge, and attitudes to determine if that person is suited to and qualified for the type of work available. Small business managers can prevent unpleasant situations from developing if they do not short-circuit the selection process. In most instances, it is equally as poor a decision to hire someone who is overqualified as one who is underqualified for a position.

What can happen when highly qualified persons are hired and their skills are not utilized is shown in the following situation. Jean, an ambitious law school graduate, took a position 2 years ago as an assistant to the president of a small public relations firm. After a period of job orientation, she was told she would be assigned to handle clients of the firm.

Instead of handling legal matters, Jean was assigned secretarial-receptionist responsibilities. She scheduled the president's luncheons, arranged his tennis matches, and spent much of her time on the job reading novels. As a result of her job skills' being underutilized, she became so bored and frustrated that she quit.

The underqualified person will likely become frustrated because of the lack of skill or knowledge, job performance will likely be substandard, and the person will usually quit or have to be replaced or retrained because he or she is not producing at a satisfactory level. Hiring overqualified or underqualified persons results in undesirable consequences for both the individual and the company.

The hiring process involves a number of activities, all of which are designed to elicit pertinent data about job candidates. These activities include the application blank, personal interviews, and employee testing.

The Application Blank

An **application blank,** as shown in Figure 9–2, provides managers with a written record of an applicant's qualifications and enables them to compare and evaluate applicants. Generally requested information on the application form is the name, address, telephone number, kind of work desired, social security number, marital status, work experience, education, and job references. The application form is completed by the job candidate. By having the potential employee complete the form, managers can evaluate how well the candidate organizes and presents these data.

The completed application form is a useful reference for the manager or the person designated by the manager when conducting the personal interview. Some restrictions on the information requested on the application form are discussed in a later section, "The Civil Rights Act of 1964 and the Equal Employment Opportunity Act of 1972."

Personal Interviews

An extensively used selection technique is the personal interview. During the interview, the manager has the opportunity to learn more about the applicant through face-to-face contact. A requirement of the interview session is that the prospective employee be made to feel at ease because the applicant is likely to be a bit edgy. Putting the applicant at ease may be accomplished by adopting an informal approach at the interview to help break the tension. After the preliminaries, the interview should be guided but not dominated by the manager. It is especially important to let the candidate speak freely, answering as well as asking questions about areas of concern. By using the application blank as a reference, the manager will be able to guide the discus-

FIGURE 9–2
Application for employment.

EMPLOYMENT APPLICATION
(An Equal Opportunity Employer)

Date _____

Name _____ Social Security Number _____
       Last   First   Middle Initial

Address _____ Telephone Number _____
         Street   City   State   Zip Code

Military Service   Rank
Branch _____ From _____ to _____ Achieved _____
Special Schools or Training in Military _____

_____

If Related to an Employee of This Firm, State Name: _____

Person to Notify in Case of Emergency _____
                                         Name   Telephone

List Equipment and Office Machines You Are Qualified to Operate: _____

_____

EMPLOYMENT RECORD
(List most recent employment first)

Name and Address of Company	Position & Duties	Dates Employed	Salary	Reason for Leaving

EDUCATION

Schools Attended	Dates Attended	Major Subject Studied	Degree or Certificate

REFERENCES

Name	Address	Telephone	Occupation

sion and obtain in-depth information about the applicant's background. The personal interview also affords the opportunity for the manager to observe the applicant's personal appearance.

The manager should check the references listed by the applicant. A telephone call to a former employer (immediate supervisor where possible), teacher, or personal reference provides a quick means of validating the accuracy of the data supplied on the application form and in the interview. Another means of obtaining references is by letter, but it takes much longer to get the desired information this way. Some factors to evaluate in checking references are inflated salary figures, incorrect dates of employment, false claims on the amount of education and experience, and claiming a higher level of job responsibility than actually held.

A note of caution is appropriate with regard to reference checks. Some firms do not give information about former employees because of the risk that former employees may claim an unfavorable reference spoiled their chance for a better position. Such action may result in a former employee's bringing legal action against a former employer.

Though most small business managers are busy with the many activities of the firm, they should not neglect the job interview because it is an integral part of the selection process.

Employment Tests

Some owners use tests advantageously as part of the selection process. However, the role of the employment test is to serve as an aid to owners in making employee selection more efficient. Tests should not be the sole criteria for selection. Some types of tests that are used are aptitude, achievement, intelligence, and personality tests.

Aptitude Test

Aptitude tests measure mechanical and clerical aptitude, manual dexterity, or other potential talents a person has for learning a new job.

Achievement Test

The achievement test seeks to measure the skill proficiency that a person has for a specific job. Some of the more familiar achievement tests, also referred to as performance tests, measure a person's skill level in typing, shorthand, or operation of office machines.

Intelligence Test

Intelligence tests measure general mental ability, such as verbal ability (ability to learn, associate, and understand words). It may also measure specific abilities such as reasoning or visualizing.

Personality Test

Personality tests are often used to aid in selecting managers or salespersons. These jobs require skills in interpersonal relations. Hence, the manager may find this test useful as a guide in evaluating applicants on this trait.

Provisions of the Civil Rights Act of 1964, discussed later in this chapter, will note restrictions on the use of employment tests.

Physical Examination

Some firms require employees to have a physical examination as part of the selection process to determine if they meet the health standards required before a health permit will be issued for specific types of businesses, such as food handling, or if they can meet the physical requirements of specific tasks. Can they work in dusty areas or damp working conditions, or do they have the physical strength to lift and move heavy materials? A physical exam requirement is a sound policy for a number of reasons. If the company carries health insurance for employees, the premiums paid for the insurance increase greatly if employees who are hired are in poor health and cannot meet the physical demands of the job. The exam also should reveal any injury the potential employee may have suffered on a previous job. This action protects the current employer from being held liable for injuries suffered elsewhere.

EMPLOYEE ORIENTATION

When the decision has been reached to employ an individual, attention should turn to orienting the new employee thoroughly into the company and into the specific work area. This orientation procedure markedly reduces the normal apprehension of new employees, especially during the first few days on the job. New employees should be introduced to other employees and made to feel welcome, receive an explanation of how this job fits into the overall company operations, and be informed again of the conditions of employment, method of pay, deductions, and work and break schedules.

Employee Manual

Small business owners should consider the value of an employee manual or handbook as a vehicle for communicating vital information about the company to the employees. The handbook explains among other things what the company expects of employees; policies on pay, working conditions, and benefits; and company philosophy toward customers.

Handbooks may range from a few typewritten pages to a printed booklet. In addition to its being useful for orienting new employees, older employees find it beneficial as a reference. Even though most small businesses do not have an employee handbook, its value should not be overlooked as a means of reinforcing communication and promoting positive employer-employee

FIGURE 9–3
Topics of the employee manual.

Welcome Message to Employees	Use of Telephones
History of Company	Prohibited Acts
Introduction to Company's Products and Services	Absence from Work and Reporting Absences
Your Future with the Company	Pay Policies
Hours of Work	Accrued Vacation Pay for Terminated Employees
Holidays	
Insurance	Loss of Time due to Death in Immediate Family
Hospitalization and Surgical Benefits	
	Overtime Pay
Group Life Insurance	Shift Pay Differential
Jury Duty	Pay Period
Military Leave	Profit Sharing Plan
Parking Facilities	Bonuses
Personal Appearance and Work Habits	Suggestion System and Awards
Cleanliness	Retirement Plan
Dress	Training Program
Leaving the Plant Premises During Work Hours	Safety and Accident Prevention
	Disciplinary Procedures
Personal Debts	Termination of Employment
Personal Work	Vacations

relations. Figure 9–3, which presents the table of contents of a small manufacturer's employee handbook, illustrates the wide range of topics of interest to employees.

EMPLOYEE TRAINING AND DEVELOPMENT

Whether the new employees have had prior experience or this is their first formal job, some type of training must be given. Some of the purposes of employee training are (1) to improve employee job performance, (2) to develop employees for new responsibilities, (3) to prepare employees for a promotion, (4) to reduce accidents, and (5) to instruct employees in the operation of new equipment.

Training should not be considered a one-time event but rather a continuous process. Training seeks to upgrade employee knowledge and skills in order to keep them abreast of changes occurring in the competitive business environment and give them the preparation required for advancement to more challenging opportunities. The overall effect of a continuous training program is mutual benefit for both the employees and the company.

In the small business, the owner–manager has the responsibility for developing and conducting the training program. The kind of training given depends largely on the kind of work being performed. Some types of training available to employees are discussed here.

On-the-Job Training

On-the-job training (OJT) is the most practical and most often used training technique in the small business. Depending on the complexity of the task and experience level of employees, training may vary from a few hours to several full days.

This training is given by the manager or a designated employee and involves three phases. First, the job is demonstrated to the employees, and each step of the process is thoroughly explained. The demonstration should be done slowly, instructions should be given clearly, and the trainees should be asked questions to determine if they understand the process. Second, the trainees perform the task by applying what they have learned in step one. In the third step, the work is inspected, and immediate feedback of the job performance is given to the trainees. This technique provides for reinforcing correct performance or correcting improper job techniques at the beginning by showing what was wrong.

On-the-job training is used to provide continuous training to employees in order to keep their job skills current or prepare them for a promotion.

Most of the training given salespersons in the small store is on-the-job training given by either the store owner–manager or another experienced salesperson. This training can be supplemented by "role playing," a technique that helps salespersons to identify with customers. In this approach, one person assumes the role of the customer and the other, the salesperson. Role playing permits salespersons to view the sale through the eyes of the customer. After one or more role-playing sessions, the roles may be reversed. This type of training can be conducted on the sales floor during slow times of the business day.

Apprenticeship Training

Apprenticeship training is a formal type of training that combines both formal classroom learning and on-the-job experience. This kind of training program is provided mainly in the skilled trades—plumbers, electricians, meat cutters, bakers. The length of time spent in apprenticeship varies from 2 years to 4 or 5 years, depending on the kind of skill being learned.

Job Rotation

Particularly in the small business, it is beneficial if each employee has a thorough understanding of the different functions performed in the firm. In this way, if one employee is absent, another employee can fill in. One way to

Apprenticeship training in this machine shop combines formal classroom learning with on-the-job experience.

accomplish this objective is by rotating employees from job to job for a few hours a day, a few days, or several weeks, depending on the difficulty of the task. Job rotation should best be done during the slack periods of the business day or season.

Job rotation is also one means of combating the problem of monotony and boredom on the job and boosting morale because a person encounters a variety of work experiences.

Group Training

The conference method is one means of achieving group training. A particular advantage of this technique is that participants in the training session have the opportunity to express their viewpoints and share experiences while listening and learning from the contributions that others make in discussing common problems or expressing opinions.

Some group training aimed at increasing the salespersons' knowledge of merchandise and services may be accomplished in sales meetings. These meetings may focus on a discussion of new products, additional services, a special sale, or a change in store policies. These group meetings can be conducted before the start of the business day or during slow periods during the day. When group training is used, care should be taken to see that there are specific goals to be accomplished so that valuable employee time is not wasted.

Training Off Company Premises

Sources outside the company may be a valuable training resource. Some of these sources are now given.

University and Community College Courses

Some small businesses pay for all or part of the cost for some of their employees to continue their education at the university and community college level. The employee may attend on-campus classes in the evening, early morning, or late afternoon and still be available for employment either all day or a major portion of the workday. Often this type of training is specialized training such as in engineering, accounting, or computer technology.

Extension Courses and Correspondence Courses

Colleges and universities offer a number of extension courses. Regular faculty members go to a particular locale where there is a demand for a course. They usually teach the course in the evening so that it does not interfere with the work schedule of employees.

Correspondence courses enable a person to receive high school or college credit or learn other skills by completing prescribed lessons in his or her own home. A wide range of courses are offered through correspondence, as in accounting or business law.

Business Suppliers

Business suppliers may serve particular training needs. For example, suppliers frequently provide specific training in technical operations of new computer equipment or instruct employees in the procedures of a new accounting or record-keeping system.

Training Films

Training films are available from private sources, trade associations, and the Small Business Administration. Films are available to serve a variety of training needs, such as group training, job procedures, communication, and leadership.

Training Guidelines for the Small Business

In setting criteria for training in the small firm, owner–managers will be aided in determining their training needs by evaluating the following questions.

1. What are the objectives of the training?
2. What do employees need to learn?
3. How much will the training program cost?
4. What type of training should be offered?
5. What method or methods of instruction should be used?
6. What kind of physical facilities will be needed?
7. How long will the training period be?
8. Will training be conducted during or after working hours?
9. Who will conduct the training?
10. Will special equipment be required (such as audiovisual)?
11. Which employees should be selected to attend the training sessions?
12. What type of feedback will be given employees?
13. How will the effectiveness of the program be measured?
14. What is the applicability of the training to the specific needs of the firm?
15. How should the program be publicized?

COUNSELING EMPLOYEES

Counseling serves as a vital link in interpersonal communication between the owners and employees. Counseling may be conducted formally, as in the performance appraisal. Counseling may also be done on an informal continuous basis. This type of counseling occurs when employees require information and feedback concerning the approach to be used in coping with day-to-day situations. Counseling serves at least four purposes.

1. To give instructions (to explain new job procedures).
2. To gain employee cooperation (to explain changes in company policies, work assignments, and work schedules in order to get employees to support these changes).
3. To obtain information (to deal with employee grievances, one must gather information as to the nature of the complaints).
4. To give advice (employees may request advice on personal matters). In this situation, the best posture is for the owner–manager to be a good listener and offer advice sparingly.

Counseling in the Probationary Period

Many companies have a probationary period for new employees. The length of time for the probationary period varies, depending on the time it takes to learn the task. During the probationary period, the owners can gauge the performance level of the new employees and their capacity for learning. If this is needed, owners can offer guidance and constructive feedback to assist new employees in greater understanding of the task and how to improve performance. During this time, employees have the opportunity to form their opinion of the company.

At the end of a specified time, preferably at the end of the first week, new employees should be interviewed. This counseling session serves a number of purposes.

1. Employees can raise questions about company rules or policies about which they are not clear.
2. Employees can offer their impressions of the job.
3. Employees can identify types of assistance or instructions they need.

Throughout the probationary period, periodic counseling should be given to evaluate employees' performance. In addition to the immediate supervisor, fellow employees are valuable resources for counseling. This counseling process enables owners to ascertain if new employees, the job, and the company are compatible at the end of the probationary period. If they are, the firm has potentially good employees. If they are not compatible, separation should be as painless as possible.

Guidelines for Effective Employee Counseling

Some specific guidelines for formal counseling that the owners should find helpful are enumerated here.

1. Have a purpose for the counseling interview.
2. The counseling interview should be conducted in private.
3. Use the "we" viewpoint instead of "I" to gain the cooperation of the counselee.
4. Such questions as who, what, where, why, when, and how can be used effectively.
5. Listen without interrupting.
6. Conclude each interview with a positive emphasis.

PERFORMANCE APPRAISAL

Performance appraisal is a form of counseling and coaching of employees. **Performance appraisal** is the process by which owners gather information about each employee's performance effectiveness. Owners have the responsibility of maintaining up-to-date information on employee performance and communicating this information to them.

The performance appraisal process is a control function. Consequently, performance appraisal includes (1) establishing standards, (2) recording performance, (3) reviewing performance in accordance with standards, and (4) taking corrective action where and when necessary. A sample appraisal form is shown in Figure 9–4 that is appropriate to the requirements of the small firm.

In a real sense, employee performance in the small firm is evaluated daily by owners who work with employees. However, it is a sound business practice to have regular periods scheduled for performance review, such as once or twice a year. Where it is possible and company size permits, employees should be evaluated by the immediate supervisor and the owner. Periodic evaluations enable owners to chart the progress of employees and suggest areas that need improvement.

Employees should be evaluated on factors relating to the type of work performed. Areas commonly evaluated are skill, responsibility, effort, and attitude.

Purposes of Performance Appraisal

The success of the performance appraisal and follow-up counseling depends on whether employees comprehend the purposes of the evaluation. Performance appraisal serves a number of important functions.

1. Evaluation of performance over a specified time.
2. Motivation of employees by providing them with relevant feedback of job performance.
3. Evaluation of potential for growth and development of each employee, such as the potential for promotion to a position of more authority and responsibility.
4. Provide data for decisions concerning the distribution of rewards for outstanding performance, such as merit increases.
5. Provide information for decisions concerning transfers and terminations.
6. Evaluation of effectiveness of training programs and training needs.
7. An effective method for communicating the goals of management.

The results of the appraisal should be communicated to each employee. Because most people are apprehensive about any type of evaluation, the

FIGURE 9–4

A performance appraisal rating form.

EMPLOYEE RATING SCALE

Name _____ Date _____

Dept. _____ Job _____

Rated by _____

INSTRUCTIONS

This Rating Scale is an aid to measuring—with a reasonable degree of accuracy and uniformity—the abilities of one of your employees and his skill in his present job. It will help you to appraise his present performance as compared with previous performance in the same job; and it may indicate promotion possibilities. Because the rating requires your appraisal of the employee's actual performance, snap judgment must be replaced by careful analysis. The following instructions may be helpful.

1. Disregard your general impression and concentrate on a single factor at a time.
2. Read all four specifications for each factor before determining which one most nearly fits the employee.
3. In rating an employee, make your judgment on instances occurring frequently in his daily routine. Don't be swayed by isolated incidents that aren't typical of his work.
4. Don't let personal feelings govern your rating. Make it carefully so that it represents your fair, objective opinion.

	Factor	1	2	3	4
a.	Quality of work	Poor; often does unacceptable work; is careless, requires constant supervision.	Fair; needs supervision and frequent checking.	Generally good; makes only occasional mistakes; requires little supervision.	Excellent; work is A-1 most of time; makes very few mistakes; needs supervision only very occasionally.
b.	Quantity of work	Very slow; almost never does complete job in time assigned for it.	Erratic; sometimes fast and efficient, other times slow and unskillful.	Steady worker, does job consistently, and occasionally does more.	Exceptionally fast; does work quickly and well; does extra work to stay busy.
c.	Flexibility	Does not adapt readily to new situations; most of the time, instructions must be repeated frequently.	Adequate; requires thorough, complete instruction before taking on new duties or new type of work.	Quick; learns new assignment in short time if given some instruction.	Very adaptable; fast learner, quickly meeting needs of new situation or assignment.
d.	Job knowledge	Limited knowledge of job; shows little desire to improve.	Passable knowledge of job; needs frequent instruction and continuing supervision.	Well informed about job; rarely needs instruction or assistance.	Full knowledge of job; able to proceed alone on almost all work.
e.	Responsibility	Irresponsible in attendance; seldom carries out orders without being prodded.	Some absences; occasionally needs reminder to do work assigned.	Attendance record good; reliable in work.	Excellent attendance record; most reliable in doing work assigned; can always be depended on.
f.	Housekeeping and safety	Never cleans working area; is reckless in behavior.	From time to time, cleans work area; is occasionally negligent about safety.	Keeps work area clean; is careful about safety.	Keeps work area spotless; is unusually careful about safety.
g.	Attitude	Uncooperative; often complains; is a disruptive influence among other employees.	Some cooperation, but is often indifferent both to fellow workers and to quality of own work.	Usually cooperative; attentive to work; gets along well with others.	Exceptionally cooperative; very interested in work; always helpful to others and considerate of them.

Source *Personnel Management*, Administrative Management Course Program, Topic 6 (Washington, D.C.: Small Business Administration, 1965), p. 35.

owners should take care to put the employees at ease at the beginning of the performance feedback session. Furthermore, emphasis should not single out negative performance factors, but positive accomplishments should also be underscored. If the evaluation process reveals that worker performance is below standard, steps are taken to improve performance in the future, such as giving the employee additional training. If standards have been met or exceeded, the employees should be commended and rewarded.

MANAGEMENT BY OBJECTIVES—
A RESULTS-ORIENTED APPRAISAL

Traditional performance evaluation systems have been criticized because they deal with subjective matters such as evaluating personal traits rather than measuring specific results. A results-oriented approach to appraisal, **management by objectives** (MBO), has been developed. The purpose of MBO is to focus attention on results achieved by employees and move away from emphasis on subjective criteria. The MBO program involves the following procedures.

1. Each employee states his or her objectives in specific and measurable terms. A salesperson's objectives could be stated as "increasing sales by 10 percent this year." A production supervisor could state an objective of "reducing material waste by 5 percent this quarter." Expressing the objective in specific, measurable terms enables all concerned (managers and employees) to understand clearly what is expected.

2. Goals are submitted (preferably in writing) by each employee and the manager. The expectations of each employee are mutually agreed upon by the owner–manager and employee. The goals that are set must be attainable and consistent with the goals of the firm. Unrealistic expectations serve only to frustrate employees. A key element of the MBO process is participation in goal setting that creates a climate that encourages open, two-way communication.

3. At regular intervals, progress toward reaching the goals is determined. When progress is not in accordance with the goals, corrective action is required, incorporating new data and disregarding irrelevant data.

4. At the end of the period, the objectives must be the basis for performance evaluation. The employee is evaluated in terms of results achieved. If a goal is not realized, corrective action is proposed that can be taken so that this expectation can be accomplished in the future. Then new goals are set for the next evaluation period as the entire MBO process is repeated.

Management by objectives is a complex system. If MBO is to be used as the basis for conducting appraisals, the system must be thoroughly understood by managers and employees alike. Furthermore, MBO requires that objectives be clearly and correctly stated because employees will be evaluated on the results achieved.

EMPLOYEE COMPENSATION

The objectives of a compensation plan are to motivate employees to perform at higher levels of performance and to attract and keep employees in the company. If the plan is to reach these objectives, it must be perceived as equitable. Equity is based on employee perception of fairness. Employees compare their economic rewards with others who perform essentially the same kind of task either in the company or in competitor firms. Equity is evaluated in terms of the effort put into a task and the rewards received for that effort. If the rewards are perceived as equitable, employees will likely stay with the firm and be a productive member of the firm. However, if employees perceive rewards as inequitable, they will tend to react negatively, as by lowering the rate of output. Economic rewards are distributed as hourly wages or salaries (a specific amount paid at regular intervals such as weekly or monthly).

To establish equity of rewards, the small owners should use a **job evaluation.** This is a systematic and orderly process for determining the correct rate of pay for each job in relation to other jobs.

Employee Compensation Plans

In addition to equity, compensation plans that are easy to understand and to administer are ideally suited to the small business. Some of the compensation plans commonly used by small business owners are now discussed.

Straight Salary
One very popular payment method in small businesses is salary. Employees receive a fixed amount each pay period, and the plan is quite easy to understand and to administer.

Hourly Wage
Employees may be paid a specific rate for each hour worked. This method of payment can be used to reward employees where it is difficult to measure employee output or where the employee has no control over the work output. This plan is also quite easy to understand and to administer.

Piece Rate
Piece rate is an incentive pay plan that rewards employees for the number of acceptable units produced. This incentive pay plan is especially suited to manufacturing operations. Piece rates may be paid on the basis of individual employee output or group output.

Straight Commission
A straight commission plan is well suited to sales positions. It provides a built-in incentive because earnings are proportionate to the amount of sales. This plan is often used with big ticket merchandise, such as appliances or autos.

Combination Plans

The combination plan is another method for rewarding salespersons. It provides a base salary plus a commission on sales. Advantages of combination plans are that they provide for both economic security and as an incentive for generating higher levels of sales.

Bonus Plan

A bonus plan is suited for managers. This plan compensates managers above their base salary and is tied to company profits. These payments are made to the managers who have a significant effect on profits.

FAIR LABOR STANDARDS ACT OF 1938 AND WAGES

Generally known as the Wage and Hour Law, the **Fair Labor Standards Act** applies to most private employers and federal agencies. The basic provision requires employers to pay a minimum wage to employees. The law also sets regulations governing the maximum number of hours employees can work (40) without receiving overtime pay. Employees must be paid at least time and one half of their regular rate for all hours of overtime.

The law also contains an equal pay provision that prohibits wage differentials based on sex, between men and women employed in the same establishment, on jobs that require equal skill, effort, and responsibility and that are performed under similar working conditions.

The child labor provisions stipulate that the minimum legal age for employing minors (outside of agriculture) is 14, but the employment must be outside of regular school hours for a limited number of hours and not in a hazardous job. At age 16, a youth may be employed for an unlimited number of hours in any nonhazardous job. At age 18, youth may be employed in any job for unlimited hours.

All employees of a business are subject to the law's provisions if they

1. Are engaged in interstate commerce.
2. Produce goods for interstate commerce.
3. Are in an activity closely related or directly essential to interstate commerce.
4. Are beyond a certain size (measured by dollar volume of business) and have at least two employees covered under the interstate commerce criteria.

The law has been interpreted liberally, and today few small businesses are entirely outside the coverage of the law. However, there are exemptions from the minimum wage or overtime provisions of the law. Owners should carefully check the exact terms of the exemption before applying them to their employees. Some examples of exemptions are presented here.

1. Retail sales and service establishment employees are exempt if the firm has an annual gross volume of sales of less than $362,500.

2. Executive, administrative, and professional employees and outside salespersons are exempt from both the minimum wage and overtime provisions.

3. Employees of certain seasonal amusement or recreational facilities are exempt from both the minimum wage and overtime provision.

4. Employees of motion picture theaters are exempt from the overtime provisions only.

Small business owners should contact the Wage and Hour Division of the United States Department of Labor to determine if the law affects their employees.

The law requires employers to maintain specific records covering the following topics, and these required records must be maintained for 3 years.

Personal information, including the employees' name, home address, and birth date if under 19.

Sex and occupation.

Hour and day when workweek begins.

Regular hourly pay rate for any week when overtime is worked.

Hours worked each workday and total hours worked each workweek.

Total daily or weekly straight-time earnings.

Total overtime pay for the workweek.

Deductions or additions to wages.

Total wages paid each pay period.

Date of payment and pay period covered.

EMPLOYEE BENEFITS

Employee benefits or "**fringe benefits**" have increased substantially both in type and cost. For example, the U.S. Chamber of Commerce surveys a cross section of firms concerning type and extent of fringe benefits provided. The chamber's survey indicates that employee benefits now exceed 37 percent of payroll costs.

Wages and salaries are classified as "direct" compensation. Fringe benefits are identified as "indirect" payments. A broad range of fringe benefits are common in larger firms. However, few small businesses can afford the extensive benefit package of larger firms. The small firms that offer some fringe benefits have found this is a positive feature in attracting and keeping employees.

Many items are categorized as fringe benefits. Some are required by law; others are offered as a result of agreement between employer and employee.

FIGURE 9–5

Types of fringe benefits.

Legally required payments (old age, survivors, disability and health insurance)
Pension plan
Insurance plan (life insurance, health insurance, accident insurance)
Discounts on goods and services purchased by employees from the company
Employee meals furnished by company
Paid rest periods, lunch periods, wash-up time, travel time, etc.
Paid vacations
Paid holidays
Payment for jury duty, National Guard, or Military Reserve duty
Profit-sharing payment
Bonuses (Christmas, year end)
Employee education
Worker's compensation
Unemployment compensation

Benefits vary among firms. The small firms that offer benefits commonly provide such benefits as major medical plans, life insurance, and pension plans. A listing of types of fringe benefits is shown in Figure 9–5.

One type of fringe benefit is paid holidays. The company's policy should indicate the days that are holidays. Frequently, holidays allowed are New Year's Day, Memorial Day, Independence Day, Labor Day, Thanksgiving Day, and Christmas Day. Vacation time varies, but usually 1 or 2 weeks are given after a year's employment. After 5 or 10 years, vacations may increase to 3 weeks. Sick leave benefits are also important to the employees. A policy of many firms is to allow employees to earn from one-half day to one full day of sick leave per month.

As with wages and salaries, it is an essential policy to observe the pattern of employee benefits in the local community and follow this pattern in setting guidelines for the firm's fringe benefit package.

EMPLOYEE SAFETY

The Bureau of Labor Statistics (BLS) estimates that 41 million employee work-days were lost because of disabling injuries in 1980 alone. And office workers, though working in relatively safe conditions, nevertheless face job hazards. The BLS estimates that some 40,000 disabling injuries occur in offices annually and $100 million in medical and indemnity expenses from injury alone is lost by businesses annually.

Employee safety should be of utmost concern for all managers. One key to successful accident prevention in the small firm is employee motivation to observe work rules that make the job as safe as possible. Employee safety is of primary concern because of the costs that both employer and employee incur when a job-related injury keeps the employee off the job. For the employee, there is the waste of a productive human asset, the suffering, the medical expense, and the financial loss that may result in the loss of future earnings potential if the employee is unable to return to the same task. For the employer, lost-time accidents result in higher costs of operation. Productivity is lowered if a less qualified employee must be hired as a replacement while the injured employee recovers or if the business tries to operate without a replacement during the recovery period.

No business is immune from accidents. In the small business, the best managerial strategy in regard to safety is one that emphasizes accident prevention. Employee safety should be continuously emphasized as part of the company's training program and education process. Reminders in the form of posters or notices of the need for safety should be placed in conspicuous places around the company. Employees should be encouraged to wear protective clothing or goggles, and should be given the reasons why the protection is necessary. Training films on safety may be beneficial for emphasizing certain aspects of safety. A safety campaign can be used and recognition given to employees or departments that have the longest period without an accident. Periodic checks should be made of employee work habits. When unsafe acts are discovered, they should be explained to the employee so they can be corrected. If unsafe working conditions are discovered, steps should be taken to correct them. The Occupational Safety and Health Act of 1970, discussed in Chapter 22, is a major law enacted to assure every working person has a safe and healthful working environment.

Workers' Compensation

Many states require employers, regardless of size of the firm, to provide **workers' compensation** benefits in the form of insurance. Employers purchase insurance, and the rates they pay are based on the hazards of the industry. Where accident and injury may be expected more often, rates are higher. Hence, by reducing the accident and injury rate, a single firm can reduce its insurance premium costs. Workers' compensation provides for financial reimbursement or payment for medical expenses or both. Payment is made to employees for any physical loss or disease resulting from working conditions.

THE CIVIL RIGHTS ACT OF 1964 AND THE EQUAL EMPLOYMENT OPPORTUNITY ACT OF 1972

The **Civil Rights Act of 1964** and the **Equal Employment Opportunity Act of 1972** apply to employers engaged in industry affecting interstate commerce who have 15 or more employees for each working day in each of 20 or more calendar weeks in the current or preceding year. These acts stipulate that an employer cannot discriminate in hiring, firing, promotion, or any other terms and conditions of employment, including fringe benefits, on the basis of race, color, religion, sex, or national origin. There are a restricted number of instances where the employer can discriminate on the basis of religion, sex, or national origin. These distinctions are allowed when it can be shown that any of these factors is a **bona fide occupational qualification** or "BFOQ." For example, employees of a religious organization are not subject to the ban on religious discrimination. The law also makes an exception regarding occupations for which sex is a BFOQ, such as acting, modeling, and attending washrooms. Under these acts, race and color can never be a BFOQ for any job. Likewise, it is unlawful to advertise jobs separately as for "help wanted—male" and "help wanted—female."

Employers covered by the act must refrain from requesting information on the employment application form that violates either federal or state fair employment practice laws or the right to privacy. For example, the following questions are almost always illegal.

1. Are you married? Single? Divorced?
2. Have you ever been arrested?
3. How old are you?
4. How much do you weigh? How tall are you?
5. Will you attach a picture of yourself to your application form?
6. What is your ethnic origin, religious affiliation, sex, and race?

Some state laws conflict with the federal Civil Rights Act. For example, some states have restrictions on the hours women can work or how much weight they are permitted to lift. The federal law prevails, prohibiting such discrimination in those firms subject to the act. Thus, small business owners must determine if their firm is subject to state or federal law and then abide by the proper regulations.

The laws also place restrictions on the use of tests for hiring and promotion. Employment tests must be shown to be specifically related to the specific job involved and must be designed so as not to discriminate against a specific group on the basis of race, color, religion, sex, or national origin. As a result, many firms no longer use employment tests.

SUMMARY OF KEY POINTS

1. Personnel management activities include assessing job requirements, employment recruitment, establishing hiring procedures, and providing for employee training and development.

2. In order to assess job requirements properly, the owner–managers must conduct a job analysis and then develop a job description and job specification from the results of the job analysis.

3. Employee recruitment is the process of locating persons whose skills and knowledges and abilities match the requirements of the job. Employees may be recruited from many sources.

4. In selecting employees, the owner–managers attempt to collect pertinent data about candidates from such sources as the application blank, personal interviews, and employment tests.

5. There are a variety of employment tests that may aid the owner–managers in the employee selection process. Some of these tests are aptitude, achievement, intelligence, and personality tests. Some firms require a physical examination for all new employees.

6. A thorough orientation into the company will assist employees in adjusting to the new work environment. An employee handbook is an effective vehicle for communicating information about company policies, procedures, and rules.

7. Small business managers should afford opportunities for training and development to employees. Types of training programs that are feasible for small business operations include on-the-job training, apprenticeship training, job rotation, group training, training provided by suppliers of goods and services, training films, and various types of community college, and university courses.

8. Counseling provides small business owners with the opportunity to work more closely with employees and to play a supportive role with their employees.

9. Performance appraisal is a control function in which the owner–managers obtain information about each employee's performance, communicate this information to the employee, and provide avenues for improvement in the situations that demand it.

10. A requisite of employee compensation plans is that they be perceived as being equitable by employees. Compensation plans used by small business owners include straight salary, hourly wage, piece rate, straight commission plan, combination salary and commission plan, and bonus plan.

11. The Fair Labor Standards Act of 1938 requires employers to pay a minimum wage to employees and establishes the number of hours employees can work without receiving overtime.

12. Fringe benefits offered by small business owners may be a positive factor in attracting and keeping employees in the firm.

13. Many states require all businesses to provide worker compensation as a form of insurance to reimburse employees for job related illness or injury.

14. Employee safety should be of utmost concern in the small business. The Occupational Safety and Health Act of 1970 was enacted to require employers to provide employees with a workplace from hazards that are likely to cause injury or death to employees.

15. The Civil Rights Act of 1964 and the Equal Employment Opportunity Act of 1972 governs hiring, firing, promotion, and fringe benefit practices of some small businesses. The acts stipulate that employers shall not discriminate in hiring practices on the basis of sex, national origin, race, color, or religion. The acts also specify limitations on employment tests.

DISCUSSION QUESTIONS

1. Distinguish between job analysis, job description, and job specification.
2. Explain the significance of employee orientation.
3. Identify and explain the different types of training programs given in the small business.
4. What sources outside the firm are available to provide employee training?
5. Make a list of questions a small business owner should ask when planning a training program.
6. What are the purposes of counseling?
7. Explain the difference between the types of compensation plans used by small business owners.
8. What is the significance of the Fair Labor Standards Act of 1938 to the small business owner?
9. What effect does the Civil Rights Act of 1964 have on the hiring practices of the small business owner?

STUDENT PROJECTS

1. Interview a small business manager, and request a copy of his or her firm's employment application form.
2. If the owner has a personnel handbook, examine it, and make a list of the major topics it contains.

CASE A

Fred Howard, the New Manager

Robert Camp has been the manager of a small coffee-shop for over 2 years. The owner of the shop is satisfied with his performance. However, Robert has found another job and is leaving in 2 weeks.

About a month ago a manager trainee, Fred Howard, was hired to work with Robert and be his replacement. Fred, a conscientious worker, received his B.B.A. degree several months ago. He received excellent performance ratings from Robert.

Fred has observed several situations within the coffee-shop that concern him. He has observed that Robert is very reluctant to exercise authority over employees except when things get completely out of control. This has led to the situation where the head cook has assumed many of Robert's managerial duties and much of his authority. At times this has caused much dissension among the other cooks and the waitresses. The head cook also has considerable influence in other matters such as work schedules, raises, transfers, and so on.

The result has been that the head cook is the boss much of the time. Several other cooks have quit or requested transfers because of the head cook's dominance over them. The waitresses have been more successful in resisting the head cook's authority. However, there is considerable conflict between the cooks and waitresses. Many times the two groups have had shouting matches over a mistake on a customer's order. Sometimes the hostility is so apparent that the customers have mentioned it to Robert.

Fred has also noticed the high turnover of dining room attendants. Several times an attendant has quit in the middle of a workday. The attendants perform tasks that are designed to help both the waitresses and the cooks. Sometimes, especially during rush hours, the waitresses and cooks will compete for the services of the dining room attendants. This has furthered the split between the waitresses and cooks and left the attendants in a very undesirable position.

In three days Fred will assume the position of coffee-shop manager.

QUESTIONS

1. What should be Fred's first actions?
2. How should the head cook be dealt with?
3. How should Fred attempt to "recapture" Robert's lost authority?
4. What should be the job description of: head cook, waitresses, dining room attendants?

CASE B

TLC Industries

TLC Industries is a small manufacturer of cosmetic prosthetic devices employing a total of 50 people in the plant and office. It manufactures very specialized products, and orders are received from orthopedic physicians around the world.

The organizational structure shows that the president, who owns 51 percent of the company stock, also serves as the general manager. The office staff consists of a sales manager, office manager, and one clerical employee.

Edward Green, the sales manager, has a business administration degree and has worked for the firm for 2 years. His job consists of taking orders by phone and by mail, writing specification sheets, routing orders to the plant, and checking on the progress of the orders. Edward has become very knowledgeable concerning all plant operations and is respected by all employees in the plant. He has been led to believe by the president that he would be promoted to general manager in the near future.

Sally White, the office manager, is the president's stepdaughter and has been with the company 3 years. Sally has a college degree in business. Her job involves serving as personal secretary to the president, maintaining all files, preparing the payroll checks, and performing other related clerical duties.

The plant supervisor, Tom Brown, has been with the company since it was founded 30 years ago. He knows all aspects of plant operations and is respected by plant employees.

This year the president reorganized the plant to try to help reduce his own work load. The reorganization made Tom, the plant supervisor, and Sally, the office manager, general managers of the company with sizable salary increases. This change generated resentment among plant workers because they knew Sally had no knowledge or experience in plant operations. Tom resented Sally because she now had equal authority with him in matters of plant operation.

Edward resented the move because he had been overlooked for promotion. Sally was now his superior and earning much more money than he. In fact, Edward still considered Sally an overpaid secretary.

QUESTIONS

1. Identify some of the problems that resulted from the change in the organization structure.
2. What are some factors that caused the resentment toward Sally by Tom and Edward?
3. Promotions in this company appear to be made on what basis?
4. What kinds of problems can this type of promotion policy create?
5. Edward was passed over for promotion. What are his alternatives for actions he can take?
6. Do you think effective communication exists in this company?

SMALL BUSINESS ADMINISTRATION PUBLICATIONS

Management Aids (Free)

Checklist for Developing a Training Program
Pointers for Using Temporary-Help Services

Setting Up a Pay System
Staffing Your Store
Managing Employee Benefits

Small Business Management Series
(For Sale)

An Employee Suggestion System for Small Companies

Business Basics (For Sale)

Job Analysis, Job Specifications, and Job Descriptions
Recruiting and Selecting Employees
Training and Developing Employees
Employee Relations and Personnel Policies

CHAPTER TEN

FINANCIAL RECORD KEEPING AND CASH CONTROL

LEARNING GOALS

After reading this chapter, you will understand:

1. That financial record keeping is vital to the successful small business and that it should be custom-built for the business.
2. The accounting equation and how it is the basis for double entry book-keeping.
3. How debits and credits are used to record increases and decreases in assets, liabilities, capital, income, and expenses.
4. The difference between the cash and accrual methods of accounting.
5. How the Sales Journal is a record of daily income to the business and the Disbursement Journal is a record of expenditures of funds by the business.
6. How a firm keeps a record of credit purchases by individual customers and how it bills them for the amount they owe.
7. That the books in a small business may be kept by a public accountant, a full-time or part-time employee, a free-lance bookkeeper, or the owner.
8. How a change fund operates for a business that handles many cash transactions.
9. How a Sales and Cash Receipts form works and why it is important to the small business.

KEY WORDS

Financial control	Capital
Accounting equation	Cash accounting
Liabilities	Accrual accounting
Assets	Sales Journal
Income	Disbursement Journal
Expenses	Accounts Receivable
Debit	Change fund
Credit	Sales and Cash Receipts Record

SMALL BUSINESS PROFILE

Alice Elizabeth Nolan: Natural Motion by Liz, Inc.

Having grown up with her grandfather in a rural South Carolina setting, Alice Elizabeth Nolan was no stranger to the country. But she also knew what Washington, D.C.'s city people wanted: they wanted what she wanted—to look elegant, tailored, to look and feel good. She began her business career as a partner in a small beauty shop at Georgia Avenue and Jefferson Streets Northwest. In 1976, she bought out her partner and began thinking of expansion. She named her new shop "Natural Motion," employed three shampoo attendants and installed refurbished furniture to save in initial costs. Since then, the single salon has become a three-salon business, with locations in Rockville, Maryland and Herndon, Virginia, in addition to the D.C. shop. The business Liz Nolan started with the help of three attendants now employs 60 to 80 hair stylists, male and female, serving 350 persons a day. Gross sales in 1982 reached nearly $900,000. Mrs. Nolan's community activities included fund-raising fashion shows for the Child Development Center of Washington's Howard University.

Source *There's No Business Like Small Business*, U.S. Small Business Administration, Washington, D.C. 1983.

It is not unusual for a small business firm to have adequate sales and still fail because of inadequate financial control. **Financial control** is vital to the success of a small business firm. Good financial records must be constantly maintained in a business if it is to have effective financial control.

Good record keeping does not mean that a complex accounting system is required for every business. In fact, record keeping should be as simple as possible and still get the accounting job done. To illustrate, a small, one-chair barber shop used an old cash register, a drawer in the cash register stand, a loose-leaf notebook, and a checkbook to maintain its financial records. The owner would "ring up" each receipt of cash on the cash register during the day. At the end of each day, he would compare his cash register tape against the amount of cash in the register and record it in a loose-leaf notebook. Every time he purchased supplies or paid a bill in cash, he would put the receipt in the drawer. He also kept check stubs of every bill he paid by check in the drawer. At the end of each week, he would add up daily cash sales records, all expense receipts, and all check stubs for the week. He would then subtract the expense items from the cash sales total to determine the amount of his net cash gain for the week. At the end of the year, he divided his expense receipts and canceled checks into categories of expenses, figured depreciation on his equipment, and totaled his cash sales book. From these records he prepared his income tax return. It was a very simple system, but it fulfilled his accounting needs.

Larger firms, on the other hand, often require rather complex accounting systems with many different types of journals, ledgers, and report forms. In addition, many small business firms and almost all large firms perform their record keeping functions on computers (most small firms should be using computers). However, no matter whether it is a simple or complex system, hand- or computer-based, the accounting system depends on the same general concept—recording changes in the basic accounting equation.

THE ACCOUNTING EQUATION

The basic **accounting equation** is assets = liabilities + capital (net worth) or assets − **liabilities** = capital. For a simple illustration of the equation, imagine that all your possessions consisted of an automobile valued at $600, personal property (clothing, etc.) worth $800, and $200 in a bank checking account. Your total **assets** would be $1600. Now imagine your only debt was $400 in payments on your automobile. Using the accounting equation, you would find you were worth $1200.

$$
\begin{array}{ccccc}
\text{Assets} & = & \text{Liabilities} & + & \text{Capital (net worth)} \\
\$1600 & = & \$400 & + & \$1200
\end{array}
$$

If you then earned $100, the accounting equation would change as follows.

$$
\begin{array}{ccccc}
\text{Assets} & = & \text{Liabilities} & + & \text{Capital} \\
\$1600 & = & \$400 & + & \$1200 \\
+\ 100 & & & & +\ 100 \\
\hline
\$1700 & = & \$400 & + & \$1300
\end{array}
$$

If you made a $75 payment on your automobile, the accounting equation would change as follows.

$$
\begin{array}{ccccc}
\text{Assets} & = & \text{Liabilities} & + & \text{Capital} \\
\$1700 & = & \$400 & + & \$1300 \\
-\ 75 & & -\ 75 & & \\
\hline
\$1625 & = & \$325 & + & \$1300
\end{array}
$$

If you then spent $25 for a night on the town, your equation would be

$$
\begin{array}{ccccc}
\text{Assets} & = & \text{Liabilities} & + & \text{Capital} \\
\$1625 & = & \$325 & + & \$1300 \\
-\ 25 & & & & -\ 25 \\
\hline
\$1600 & = & \$325 & + & \$1275
\end{array}
$$

Recording the effect of every change in the accounting equation is the basis for the foundation of bookkeeping, which is called double entry bookkeeping.

Every financial transaction should leave the accounting equation in balance. Therefore, each time there is a transaction, there must be (1) equal minuses and pluses on one side of the equation or (2) the same amount of minuses and pluses on both sides of the equal sign. For example, purchasing a shirt for $10 gives the results under assets of adding $10 to personal property and reducing cash by the same amount. Also, receiving an asset, such as cash, means increasing an asset on one side of the equal sign and capital on the other side.

The entire process of bookkeeping and accounting, no matter how simple or complex the system, is based on this concept of keeping the accounting equation in balance by the process of double entry bookkeeping.

In order to keep records of what is earned by the business and what is paid out by the business, the categories of **income** and **expenses** are used rather than adjusting the capital section for each transaction. For example, suppose you bought fruit for $20 from a farmer and sold it to customers for $100. The difference between all income and all expenses could then be adjusted to the capital account. This difference would also be equal to the difference in cash.

	Income		Expenses		Cash
Sales of fruit	$100				+$100
Purchase of fruit			$20		− 20
	$100	−	$20	=	$ 80

The $80 increase in cash would be equal to an $80 increase in capital when adjusted to the capital account. Your basic accounting equation would then appear as follows:

Assets	=	Liabilities	+	Capital
$1600	=	$325	+	$1275
+ 80				+ 80
$1680	=	$325	+	$1355

Accounting language uses the terms **"debit"** and **"credit"** to describe increases or decreases in the categories of the accounting equation (assets, liabilities, and capital) and income and expenses. Figure 10–1 shows debits and credits relative to increases and decreases in these categories. Figure 10–1 also shows what type of balance the account usually carries at any given time. Notice that increases in income have the same effect as *increases* in the **capital** category and that increases of expenses have the same effect as *decreases* in the capital category.

In double entry bookkeeping, for every debit there must be an equal amount of credits and vice versa. For example, imagine you sold your car for

FIGURE 10-1
Accounting categories and debit and credit entries.

Category	A Transaction Increasing the Amount	A Transaction Decreasing the Amount	Usual Balance Carried in the Category
Asset	Debit	Credit	Debit
Liability	Credit	Debit	Credit
Capital	Credit	Debit	Credit
Income	Credit	Debit	Credit
Expense	Debit	Credit	Debit

$700 cash and paid off the note. The entity in a journal would appear as follows:

		Debit	Credit
Sale received in cash	(asset)	$700	
Automobile sold	(asset)		$600
Income			$100
Note payable paid off	(liability)	$325	
Paid in cash	(asset)		$325

Your income could be transferred into your capital account at a later date by the following entry.

	Debit	Credit
Income	$100	
Capital		$100

The income account would then have both the same debit and credit entry, which would result in a zero balance in the account. Your accounting equation would then appear as follows.

	Assets	=	Liabilities	+	Capital
	$1680	=	$325	+	$1355
Sold automobile	− 600				
Received cash	+ 700				
Paid note			− 325		
With cash	− 325				
Made profit					+ 100
	$1455	=	0	+	$1455

CASH OR ACCRUAL ACCOUNTING

A small business may use either a cash or an accrual method of accounting. The Internal Revenue Service allows many firms to select either method, but once selected, the firm must stay with the method unless they receive special permission from the IRS.

Cash Method

Using the **cash** method, a business records all monetary transactions, both income and expenses, as they occur. For example, a small business might pay its property taxes for the previous year in January. If January 1 is the start of the firm's fiscal year, then the deduction cannot be counted until the year it is paid even though the tax expense was incurred during the previous year. (See Fig. 10–2.)

The cash method is usually the easiest method in terms of keeping accounting records. However, it sometimes distorts the financial picture of the business when applied to a specific period of time. Because it is easier to use and understand, the cash method is the better method for most small businesses.

Accrual Method

The business that uses the **accrual** method records income and expenses at the time they are earned or incurred regardless of when the monetary transaction occurs. For example, the small business in the previous example would

FIGURE 10–2

Cash versus accrual accounting method.

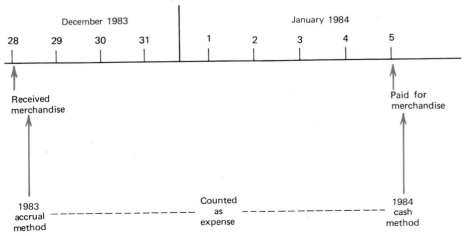

record the property tax expense during the year it was incurred regardless of when it paid the tax. (See Fig. 10–2.)

The Internal Revenue Service requires the accrual method in businesses where inventories play an important part in creating income. This means that many retail stores must adopt this method. The accrual method is more complex in terms of accounting records and statements. However, it is usually a more accurate picture of the financial state of the firm over a specific period of time.

BASIC BOOKS OF RECORD

Although some very small stores can manage to keep adequate accounting records with very few books, such as our barber example, most small stores need at least two basic books of record. These are the (1) Sales Journal and (2) Disbursement Journal.

Sales Journal

Basically, the **Sales Journal** is a record of daily income to the business. Figure 10–3 presents a simple Sales Journal for a small business that operates on a cash rather than accrual basis. Additional columns may be added to the example when additional information is desired by the small business owner. Many days of income can be shown on very few pages. In the example, the business owner found it desirable to break the sales down by product group. If the owner felt a more extensive breakdown of sales were not needed, all retail sales could have been combined into one column (it is best to have wholesale sales separate for state sales tax information). Having the separate column for sales tax is desirable because all the business owner has to do when it is time to remit sales tax collections to the state is total the column for the period.

Sales information usually comes from sales tickets made out during the day or from cash register tapes.

All income and expenditures should go through the firm's bank account. Consequently, the column entitled "Total Cash Received from Sales" is also the amount that is deposited in the bank each day. This column can be of value when reconciling the bank statement.

Firms that operate on the accrual basis and finance their own accounts must use different columns. Figure 10–4 illustrates a simple Sales Journal for these firms.

The entry for April 30 in Figure 10–4 shows the business had $890 in total sales. Of this amount, $570 ($890 − $320) was in the form of cash sales, and $320 was in customer credit sales. The business collected $210 from customer credit accounts, the cash register was short $8 owing to change errors, and the business deposited $772 in the bank.

By totaling the separate columns for a specific period of time, the business

FIGURE 10-3
Sales Journal.

Date	Description or Account	Total Cash Received from Sales	Sales Tax	Retail Sales			Commercial Sales
				Product Group A	Product Group B	Other Products	
		Dr.	Cr.	Cr.	Cr.	Cr.	Cr.
Apr. 1	Daily sales	$ 433.50	$13.50	$100.00	$ 90.00	$ 80.00	$150.00
2	Daily sales	455.50	15.50	120.00	100.00	90.00	130.00
3	Daily sales	515.00	15.00	100.00	100.00	100.00	200.00
4	Daily sales	505.50	15.50	120.00	140.00	50.00	180.00
5	Daily sales	547.00	17.00	130.00	150.00	60.00	190.00
	Total for week	$2,456.50	$76.50	$570.00 (A)*	$580.00 (B)*	$380.00 (C)*	$850.00 (D)*

*Letters under the totals indicate where they belong in the income statement and will be discussed in Chapter 11.

FIGURE 10-4
Sales Journal of firm on the accrual basis and financing its own credit.

Date 19—	Description and/or Account	Total Sales	Credit Sales	Collected on Account	Misc. Income & Expense Items		Cash Deposited in Bank
					Income	Expense	
		Cr.	Dr.	Cr.	Cr.	Dr.	Dr.
4/30	Daily summary	$890.00	$320.00	$210.00			$772.00
	Cash short					$8.00	
5/1	Daily summary	940.00	290.00	180.00			832.00
	Cash over				$2.00		

is able to derive information for its financial statements (financial statements are discussed in Chapter 11). For example, by totaling its sales column, it knows the total amount of sales for the period to be used in the income statement.

Errors are easily detected in the Sales and Cash Receipts Journal by adding the total of all credit columns and all debit columns. If the two totals are not the same, then there is an error in the entries. Totaling of debit and credit columns for all daily entries pinpoints the error because daily entries must also balance.

Disbursement Journal

The **Disbursement Journal** is a record of expenditures of funds by the business. (Some small business owners attempt to keep their personal and business funds together, but this is a serious error and causes many problems.) With only one exception, all expenditures of the firm should be paid by check. The one exception is the petty cash fund. The petty cash fund is maintained to pay in cash for items of very small value (usually less than one dollar). However, a check should be processed through this journal to establish and replenish the petty cash fund. Records of expenditures from the petty cash fund should also be maintained by the business for tax and control purposes.

Figure 10–5 shows a simple Disbursement Journal. (Additional columns may also be added to the Disbursement Journal if needed by the small business.) Daily entries in the Disbursement Journal must balance in terms of debits and credits. The total of the columns must also balance in terms of debits and credits. Errors are easily recognized by checking debit and credit totals in the columns.

At the end of specific periods of time (the end of every month is recommended), totals of the columns in the Disbursement Journal may be used to derive various items for accounting statements. Also, combining information from both the Sales Journal and the Disbursement Journal provides valuable information for the business. For example, the total of "Total Cash Received from Sales" or "Cash Deposited in Banks" and the total of the "Amount of Check" column is an excellent device for checking bank statements.

Accounts Receivable

Most retail small businesses no longer carry 30-day charge accounts (discussed in detail in Chapter 20) because of the money required and the cost and time involved in keeping records and collecting accounts. Instead, they accept bank credit cards for sales that are essentially the same as a cash sale. However, some businesses still carry 30-day charge accounts. Those firms that do must keep records of each customer's charges and payments. Figure 10–6 shows a simple **Accounts Receivable** card that can be maintained on each customer.

The firms may keep these on cards that are easily reproduced on a copier

FIGURE 10-5
Disbursement Journal.

Date	Payee or Account	Check No.	Amount of Check Cr.	Product Group A Dr.	Product Group B Dr.	Other Products Dr.	Commercial Products Dr.	Office Supplies Dr.	Gross Salaries and Wages Dr.	FICA Cr.	Income Tax Cr.	Utilities Dr.	Other Expenses Dr.	Nonexpense Payments Dr.
Apr. 1	Smith Wholesale	101	$ 100.00	$100.00										
1	Alford Supply	102	120.00		$120.00									
2	Jones Supply Co.	103	150.00			$150.00								
2	Johnson Products	104	100.00				$100.00							
2	Austin Office Sup.	105	30.00					$30.00						
2	Austin Utilities	106	200.00									$200.00		
3	Trust Insurance Co.	107	50.00										$ 50.00	
3	S.B.A. on note ($20.00 interest)	108	220.00										20.00	$200.00
4	Texas International (airline ticket)	109	140.00										140.00	
4	Petty cash fund	110	25.00										25.00	
5	Weekly payroll	111	420.00						$500.00	$30.00	$50.00			
5	State of Texas (sales tax)	112	76.50											76.50
5	Payroll taxes paid to IRS	113	60.00										60.00	
5	FICA & income tax deduction paid to IRS	114	80.00											80.00
	Total for week		$1,771.50	$100.00 (E)*	$120.00 (F)*	$150.00 (G)*	$100.00 (H)*	$30.00 (I)*	$500.00	$30.00	$50.00	$200.00 (K)*	$295.00 (L)*	$356.50 (M)*

*Letters below the totals indicate where they belong in the income statement, which will be discussed in Chapter 11.

FIGURE 10–6
Accounts Receivable card.

<table>
<tr><td colspan="5" align="center">Mr. & Mrs. Joe Paul Jackson
3232 Blue Herron Road
Santa Monica, Cal. 90401</td></tr>
<tr><th>Date</th><th>Item</th><th>Charge</th><th>Payment</th><th>Balance</th></tr>
<tr><td>1/20</td><td>Hardware</td><td>$28.50</td><td></td><td>$28.50</td></tr>
<tr><td>2/5</td><td></td><td></td><td>$28.50</td><td>0</td></tr>
<tr><td></td><td></td><td></td><td></td><td></td></tr>
</table>

and put in a window envelope and mailed to the customer on the billing day. They may also be maintained on a computer, and the computer can print out monthly statements to send customers (the computer can also print the mailing labels).

MAINTAINING THE BOOKS

Small businesses can have books set up to meet their needs by a public accountant. The accountant will investigate the requirements and build a bookkeeping system that will provide the owner with financial information needed. Also, there are firms that have established general bookkeeping systems and have created copyrighted books and forms for small business owners in many types of businesses to use in maintaining their financial records. These are available at most office supply firms.

Small business owners also have several choices as to how the day-to-day bookkeeping will be performed. They may use (1) a public accountant, (2) a full-time or part-time employee, or (3) a free-lance bookkeeper; or (4) they may keep the books themselves.

Public accountants are available for a wide range of accounting services, such as complete bookkeeping services, auditing, periodic preparation of accounting statements, and preparation of income tax returns.

The firm may use a full-time employee, who is properly trained, to maintain the books. When the bookkeeping function is not a full-time job, the bookkeeper may be used part of the time for keeping the books and part of the time for other functions, such as selling.

Some firms use part-time people, such as homemakers, who wish to work a few hours a day and have the training to keep a set of books. Retired persons also are sometimes employed on a part-time basis to maintain the books.

Some people, who are trained in bookkeeping, keep books for several firms on a fee basis. Such an individual usually contracts with firms that require only a few hours a week of his or her time to keep their books. Use of these individuals is often less expensive than the use of public accountants.

Small business owners may wish to maintain their own books if they have the ability to perform the function or are willing to learn the process. This method of bookkeeping has an advantage in that small business owners are constantly exposed to their financial records. As a result, they are probably more aware of their financial status than if someone else kept the books. However, it also has a disadvantage in that it takes time, and they may neglect other important functions.

CASH CONTROL

Daily cash control is important to a small business that handles volumes of cash, particularly retail stores. The function of cash control is to compare and balance what is actually received in cash to what should have been received.

Having less cash on hand at the end of the day than should have been received may be the result of (1) recording or ringing up an amount larger than the sale, (2) money taken from the register without being recorded, or (3) giving a customer too much change.

Having more cash on hand at the end of the day than should have been received may result from (1) not recording or ringing up a sale, (2) not ringing up or recording the full amount of a sale, or (3) not giving a customer enough change.

No matter what the cause of the overage or shortage of cash, it should be detected and steps taken to help prevent any future errors. Of course, any firm handling large volumes of cash transactions will have some small amount of human error that cannot be totally eliminated.

In addition, cash control is vital to preventing employee theft. No one likes to think that their employees would steal from the business, but the fact is that billions of dollars are lost each year to employee theft. In fact, many authorities feel employee theft exceeds losses from both shoplifting and burglary.

SPECIAL INTEREST FEATURE

Financial Control and Computers

Greatly reduced cost and capabilities of computers, particularly microcomputers, have made them feasible for almost all small businesses. They can greatly increase the efficiency of small businesses in many areas, such as inventory control, theft control, and word processing. Two of the more important functions that may be performed with computers are cash control and accounting.

Cash control can be achieved by tying the cash register to the computer.

The inventory control function and cash control function can then be performed by the computer from input into the cash register at the time of sale. As the inventory change is made, the computer records the selling price and totals the sales at the end of the day and reports how much should be in the cash register. Even if a cash register is not tied to the computer, it is possible to run the total inventory sold during the day from records in the computer and compare them to the total amount of cash from the register.

There are many software packages (computer programs) small businesses may use to perform their accounting functions. Examples of some of these software packages for microcomputers and some of the more important things they do for the small business are listed below.

ACCOUNTS RECEIVABLE SYSTEM

Maintains on a continuing basis all customer accounts.

Calculates and records interest charged on the accounts.

Calculates and prints statements to be sent to the computers.

PAYROLL SYSTEM

Calculates withholding items from each employee's wages.

Calculates payroll taxes to be paid by the business.

Calculates amount of paycheck for each employee and prints checks.

Prints payroll journals.

Calculates and prints W-2 forms at the end of the year.

ACCOUNTS PAYABLE

Maintains accounts payable records.

Reports complete vendor listing, cash requirements, and so forth.

Calculates and prints checks.

GENERAL LEDGER

(This takes the place of the Sales and Disbursement Journals.)

Posts to all accounts (cash, sales, supplies, etc.).

Posts checks to accounts.

Calculates and prints income statements.

Calculates and prints trial balances.

Calculates and prints balance sheets.

Change Fund

Most retail stores must have currency and coins on hand at the start of business each day in order to make change. A small business should determine what amount of change is needed for each cash register based on past history. This should include a specific number of tens, fives, ones, halves, quarters, nickels, and pennies.

This change should be available in each cash register at the start of the day's business. The same amount should be deducted from the total cash in the register at the end of the day and kept for the next day. All other cash should be placed in the night depository of the bank. The **change fund** should be left in a safe overnight if possible and, if not, in the cash register itself. Some businesses that handle excessively large amounts of cash for change and open after the bank opens, place all cash in the bank at night and write a check for the next day's funds, which are obtained before the store opens.

Sales and Cash Receipts Balance

A **Sales and Cash Receipts form,** as shown in Figure 10–7, should be completed at the end of business each day.

FIGURE 10–7

Sales and cash receipts.

Date 5/1/84

TOTAL SALES

1. Cash sales	$650.00
2. Credit sales	290.00
3. Total sales	$940.00

CASH RECEIPTS

4. Cash sales	$650.00
5. Collections on accounts receivable	180.00
6. Total cash to be accounted for	$830.00

CASH ON HAND

7. Cash in register or till:		
Coins	$ 30.00	
Bills	609.00	
Checks	268.00	
Total cash in register or till		$907.00
8. Less change fund		75.00
9. Total cash deposit		$832.00
10. Cash short		$
11. Cash over		$ 2.00

All sales during the day should be recorded on either a cash register, if used, or some other record, such as a sales slip, if a register is not used. There should also be some method of identifying cash and credit sales. Credit tickets, which are posted to customer accounts, are usually used to identify credit sales and then subtracted from total sales on the cash register to arrive at the amount of cash sales.

Cash that is received from customers on their credit accounts should be recorded separately. In addition, any withdrawals from the register should be recorded with full information and placed in the register or cash till.

The small business firm that is able to identify cash sales, credit sales, cash received on customer credit accounts, and cash withdrawals from the business has the information necessary to complete the Sales and Cash Receipt form at the end of the business day. Completion of this form identifies errors and the amount of the error. The Sales and Cash Receipts form may also be combined with inventory control techniques (discussed in Chapter 13) to aid in the control of mistakes, shoplifting, and employee theft.

Financial record keeping, as discussed in this chapter, is vital to the day-to-day operations of the small business firm. It must be performed adequately if the small business is to realize the full benefits of accounting analysis, which is presented in the next chapter.

SUMMARY OF KEY POINTS

1. Record keeping systems should be custom-designed for each business, and they do not have to be complicated for most small businesses.
2. The accounting equation is stated thus: Assets = Liabilities + Capital (net worth).
3. The bookkeeping system is based on the concept of keeping the accounting equation in balance by the process of double entry bookkeeping.
4. The cash method of accounting means that transactions are recorded when there is a cash transaction. The accrual method records income and expenses at the time they are earned or incurred regardless of when the monetary transaction occurs.
5. The basic books of record are the Sales Journal and the Disbursement Journal.
6. The Sales Journal is a record of daily income to the business.
7. The Disbursement Journal is a record of all expenditures (except for petty cash items) made by the business.
8. If the small business grants 30-day charge accounts, it must record charges, payments, and balances on accounts receivable cards or in its computer.
9. If the bookkeeping system is maintained by hand rather than by com-

puter, the small business may use (a) a public accountant, (b) a full-time or part-time employee, or (c) a free-lance bookkeeper; or (d) it may keep the books itself.

10. The function of cash control is to compare and balance what is actually received in cash to what should have been received.

11. Cash control is vital to preventing employee theft.

12. Most retail stores must have currency and coins on hand each day to make change for customers.

13. A Sales and Cash Receipts form should be completed at the end of each business day.

DISCUSSION QUESTIONS

1. Does every small business firm need the same type of accounting system?

2. What is the relationship between double entry bookkeeping and the accounting equation?

3. What is the relationship between income, expenses, and capital?

4. What is a Sales Journal, and how do you find errors in its entries?

5. What is a Disbursement Journal, and how do you find errors in its entries?

6. Which is the lowest cost method of keeping books? Give one advantage and one disadvantage of this method.

7. Why is cash control important?

8. How does the change fund operate?

9. How does the Sales and Cash Receipts Record function?

10. What is the difference between cash and accrual methods of accounting?

STUDENT PROJECT

Visit a small retail establishment, and find out the following information.

1. What type of bookkeeping system does the business use?

2. Who keeps the books, and are they audited?

3. What method does the business use for cash control? Does it use a daily Cash and Sales Receipt Form? If so, compare it to the one in the textbook, and try to obtain a copy to show the class.

4. Does the business use the cash or the accrual accounting method? What is its reason for using this method?

CASE A

Davis Shoe Store

Sandra Davis owns a shoe store that is located in the central business district in a small town. Davis Shoe Store sells medium-priced shoes for men, women, and children. Sandra carries 30-day charge accounts for some customers who have traded with her for a long time. There is only one cash register, and it starts each day with a $75 change fund. The store has one full-time clerk in addition to Sandra. Sandra keeps her own accounting records, but does have a CPA prepare her federal income tax return each year. Sandra's store uses the accrual method of accounting.

On January 15 the store had the following transactions.

1. The cash register tape recorded $342 in sales for the day.
2. Customer charge tickets showed $80 in credit sales for the day (these are rung up on the cash register along with cash sales).
3. Checks and cash totaling $70 were received from customers on their charge accounts.
4. The following checks were issued by the store:

Check No.	To	For	Amount
524	Acme Shoe Corporation	Shoes	$125
525	City Utilities	Utilities	150
526	Sam Robertson	Weekly payroll	161 (total earned $200, withheld income tax $25, FICA $14)
527	First City Bank	Loan payment	280 (interest $100, principal $180)

5. There was $406 in the cash register in cash and checks at the end of the day.

QUESTIONS*

1. Set up a Sales Journal similar to the one in Figure 10–4 and a Disbursement Journal similar to the one in Figure 10–5, and record the day's transactions in them.
2. Set up and complete a Sales and Cash Receipt form for the day.
3. Do you think Sandra would have been better off to use the cash method rather than the accrual method of accounting?

*Forms are provided in the Student Study Guide for this case.

4. Do you think Sandra should keep her own books? Should she keep them on a computer?

CASE B

Pete's Parts (A)

Peter Wagner worked for a wholesale automobile parts warehouse for 16 years before he decided to open an automobile parts store that would sell retail to individuals and wholesale to service stations, garages, and other businesses that bought automobile parts. Pete found a building for rent on a busy street and remodeled it to fit what he felt was a good layout for a parts store. The store has been open for a week. Business has been good, and Pete feels he is making a profit.

All retail sales are for cash only, but he does carry 30-day accounts for his wholesale customers. Pete employs three people—one full-time and two part-time employees.

Pete's experience with the wholesale automobile parts warehouse did not include an exposure to accounting, and Pete feels he does not have the knowledge to set up his books and keep them.

You have been hired to establish Pete's bookkeeping system and train one of the employees to operate it. A study of Pete's records reveals the following transactions for the first week.

Cash Received for the First Week

Day	Total Cash Received from Retail Sales	Sales Tax	Total Cash Received from Wholesale Sales*
May 1	$126	$ 6	$40
2	105	5	20
3	147	7	50
4	126	6	60
5	168	8	80
6	210	10	20

*Sales tax is not collected in this state on wholesale sales.

Checkbook Entries for the First Week

May 1	U.S. Post Office	(stamps)	$ 15
2	Sam's Office Products	(office supplies)	$ 25
3	World Parts Suppliers, Inc.	(parts)	$200
4	Menton Insurance Agency	(insurance payment)	$ 60
5	Jones Supply Co.	(parts)	$ 40
6	Week's payroll (Gross salaries, $200—FICA withheld, $13—Income tax withheld, $30)		$157
7	First State Bank (payment on loan: Principal $50—interest $2)		$ 52

After talking to Pete, you feel he needs the following columns in his Disbursement Journal: Parts, Utilities, Office Supplies, Gross Salaries, FICA Withheld, Income Tax Withheld, Miscellaneous Expenses, and Nonexpense Items.

Jim's Service Station started trading with Pete the first day he was open. He bought parts on credit the following days: 5/1, $10; 5/2, $15; 5/4, $10. He came in 5/5 and paid his entire bill for the week.

You feel Pete should operate on the cash accounting basis and have his sales broken down only into retail and wholesale sales.

QUESTIONS

1. Set up a Sales Journal similar to the one in Figure 10–3, and record the week's sales.

2. Set up a Disbursement Journal similar to the one in Figure 10–5, and record the week's transactions.

3. Set up an accounts receivable card for Jim's Service Station, and record the week's charges and payment.
   (Note: Forms are provided in the Student Study Guide.)
   (Save a copy of your journals for use in Chapter 11.)

SMALL BUSINESS ADMINISTRATION PUBLICATIONS

Free

Accounting Services for Small Service Firms
Keeping Records in Small Business
Can You Use a Minicomputer?
Computers for Small Business—Service Bureau or Time Sharing
Recordkeeping Systems—Small Store and Service Trade

For Sale

Financial Recordkeeping for Small Stores

CHAPTER ELEVEN

ACCOUNTING STATEMENTS AND ANALYSIS

LEARNING GOALS

After reading this chapter, you will understand:

1. That a balance sheet is a measure of the basic accounting equation: Assets = Liabilities + Capital.

2. That the balance sheet is an estimate of value of the business for one moment in time.

3. The various uses of the balance sheet by small business owners and other groups.

4. That the income statement measures profit or loss over a period of time by subtracting all expenses from all income of the business.

5. The various uses of the income statement by small business owners, investors, creditors, and governmental agencies.

6. That the budget is an estimate of next year's income statement and is a major planning and control device for the small business.

7. Why the cash flow statement is important to the small business owner and the investor.

8. How to create a monthly income and cash flow statement from the information in the Sales and Disbursement Journals.

9. Various accounting ratios and how they act as guidelines to the small business owner.

KEY WORDS

Balance sheet	Budget
Assets	Cash flow statement
Liabilities	Ratio
Capital	Current ratio
Income statement	Acid test ratio
Expenses	Debt to net worth ratio
Cost of goods sold	Rate of return on assets
Cost of goods manufactured	Inventory turnover

SMALL BUSINESS PROFILE

Joyce Prince & Billie Brown: The Frog Pond, Inc.

Forest creatures appliqued on aprons, patchwork crib quilts, and handmade placemats were such a hit at Galloway School's children's carnival in 1971 that their creators, Billie Brown and Joyce Prince, decided not to quit. Investing about $700 in fabric, the two mothers of young children began sewing at home, selling at first to friends and relatives, and through a Hendersonville, North Carolina gift shop owned by Brown's mother. The growing business, named The Frog Pond after a pond near the Galloway School, estimated sales after one full year of operation at $50,000. Gradually, the work force grew to 36 in the manufacturing location and 70 home workers. Hand-held scissors have given way to a saw that cuts through scores of layers of fabric. Within its first five years, the Frog Pond's "Ben and Blair" children's line was selected to appear in the Neiman-Marcus Christmas catalog, and the labels now appear in high quality stores coast-to-coast. Sales in 1982 exceeded $3.6 million.

Source   *There's No Business Like Small Business,* U.S. Small Business Administration, Washington, D.C. 1983

Accounting statements are very important to the small business firm because they provide a basis for planning and control in the business. The principal accounting statements are the balance sheet, the income statement, the budget, and the cash flow statement.

BALANCE SHEET

The **balance sheet** provides a measure of the value of the business at one moment in time. Balance sheets should be prepared periodically for the small business firm. Usually, small businesses have accountants prepare a balance sheet at the end of their fiscal year (January 1 and July 1 are the most common). (See Fig. 11–1.)

Components of the Balance Sheet

The balance sheet is a measure of the basic accounting equation.

$$\text{Assets} = \text{Liabilities} + \text{Capital}$$

Assets
Assets are usually divided into three categories in the balance sheet—current assets, fixed assets, and intangible assets.

FIGURE 11–1
Balance sheet.

DOVE WHOLESALE PAINT COMPANY
Balance Sheet
January 1, 1984

ASSETS

Current Assets

Cash		$ 9,000	
Accounts receivable	$10,000		
Allowance for bad debts	500	9,500	
Merchandise		24,000	
Supplies		2,000	
General Motors stock		3,500	
Total current assets			$ 48,000

Fixed Assets

Land		$12,000	
Building	130,000		
Depreciation allowance	40,000	90,000	
Equipment	60,000		
Depreciation allowance	15,000	45,000	
Delivery truck	4,000		
Depreciation allowance	1,000	3,000	
Note receivable from Acme Products due 1/1/87		2,000	
Total fixed assets			152,000

Intangible Assets

Organizational costs		$ 1,000	
Total intangible assets			1,000
Total Assets			$201,000

LIABILITIES

Current Liabilities

Accounts payable		$18,000	
Income tax payable		1,500	
FICA tax payable		500	
Total current liabilities			$ 20,000

Long-term Liabilities:

Mortgage payable		$25,000	
Note payable to bank 6/1/88		5,000	
Total long-term liabilities			30,000

CAPITAL

Carl Dove, capital			151,000
Total liabilities and capital			$201,000

Current Assets   Current assets are assets that can be easily and quickly converted into liquid assets (cash). Current assets include such items as cash, accounts receivable, notes receivable that are due in less than a year's time, raw materials inventory, finished goods inventory, supplies, and stocks and bonds of other corporations that are traded regularly on the securities market. Generally, most current assets are used up or change in amounts on hand over relatively short periods of time.

Fixed Assets   Fixed assets are items of property that are not used up over short periods of time. They usually are not easily converted into cash, and they often are depreciated over long periods of time. Fixed assets (sometimes called plant assets) include such items as land, buildings, machinery, equipment, automobiles, trucks, and notes receivable that are due in excess of one year's time.

Intangible Assets   Intangible assets are items that have value to the business but do not exist as tangible property. Some intangible assets that are sometimes listed in the balance sheet are goodwill (the reputation of the business), patents, copyrights, and organizational costs (cost of establishing a form of ownership).

Liabilities
Liabilities are debts of the business. Liabilities are broken down in the balance sheet into current liabilities and long-term liabilities.

Current Liabilities   Current liabilities consist of debts that are due in less than one year's time. Current liabilities include such items of debt as accounts payable, notes payable within a year, and cash that is paid to governmental agencies on a regular basis (e.g., income taxes withheld from employee salaries and paid to the government every 3 months).

Long-term Liabilities   Long-term liabilities are debts that are due in more than a year's time from the date of the balance sheet. Long-term liabilities include such items as notes payable that are due in excess of one year's time, mortgages, and bonds payable.

Capital
Capital is a measure of the value of the business to the owner or owners. It is a measure of all assets minus all liabilities. The result is the net worth of the business.

Characteristics of the Balance Sheet

The balance sheet is both an estimate of the value of the business and an estimate for only one moment in time.

Estimate

Except for cash, almost all other assets listed in the balance sheet are estimates. All accounts receivable cannot be collected, and an estimated amount is subtracted for bad debts. Prices of inventories change from time to time, and their value is not always certain. All fixed assets are estimates. Buildings, machinery, equipment, automobiles, and trucks are listed at cost, and depreciation is estimated and deducted each year. To illustrate, many firms have depreciated buildings and machinery over several years and carry them on their books at scrap value; yet they still have considerable market value. Intangible assets, such as goodwill and patents, are very subjective judgments and are extremely difficult to value because they are intangible.

Liabilities are accurate in the balance sheet because they are specific debts the business owes. By subtracting accurate liabilities from estimated assets, one obtains an estimated capital section of the balance sheet. The only real way to determine the exact value of a business would be to sell it.

Moment in Time

Theoretically, the balance sheet measures the value of the business at one moment in time and represents only that moment in time. Assets, such as machinery, are used up a little each day. Consequently, the estimated value of machinery, on the balance sheet, is an estimate for the day the balance sheet is prepared. In addition, raw materials are constantly being used up and regularly being replaced. Therefore, the value of inventory is an estimate only for the day of the balance sheet date. Liabilities are continually being incurred and paid by the business; consequently, liabilities on the balance sheet represent only that day's amount. Because assets and liabilities change from day to day, capital changes from day to day and is estimated for that day only on the balance sheet.

Uses of the Balance Sheet

Because balance sheets are prepared periodically, they present measures of changes in the business. By looking at balance sheets of several years, one can recognize growth or decline in various phases of the company's financial position. The balance sheet also reveals the company's ability to meet both short-term and long-term debt. By computing ratios from balance sheet data, the firm is able to recognize weaknesses or strengths in its financial position. Balance sheets are also important to creditors who make loans to the business because they reveal the firm's potential for repayment of debts.

INCOME STATEMENT

The **income statement** is a measure of how the business has performed over a specific period of time—usually a year. It measures all income less all expenses to arrive at the amount of profit or loss generated by the business for the period. The income statement is also called the expense and revenue summary, profit and loss statement, and income and expense statement.

Components of the Income Statement

The main components of the income statement are income and expenses.

Income

All income that flows into the firm is listed in this section. There are several items that may come under the heading of income, such as revenue from sales, interest earned, and dividends earned.

Expenses

Expenses in the income statement are usually broken down into Cost of Goods Sold (in retail and wholesale firms), Cost of Goods Manufactured (in manufacturing firms), Operating Expenses, General Expenses, and Other Expenses.

Cost of Goods Sold **Cost of Goods Sold** in wholesale and retail firms is comprised of the beginning inventory for the period plus all purchases for the period minus the inventory at the end of the period (see Fig. 11–2).

Cost of Goods Manufactured **Cost of Goods Manufactured** in manufacturing operations is comprised of all direct labor, raw materials, and factory overhead (depreciation on building and machinery, supplies, foremen salaries, etc.) that have gone into the manufacturing process during the year (see Fig. 11–3).

Operating Expenses Operating expenses are expenses that contribute directly to the sale of goods. Some of the items commonly included under Operating Expenses are advertising, insurance, truck depreciation, salespersons' salaries and commissions, entertainment, and travel.

FIGURE 11–2

Cost of Goods Sold section of the income statement for a retail firm.

Cost of Goods Sold	
Beginning merchandise inventory 1/1/84	$ 50,000
Purchases for the year	150,000
Merchandise available for sale	200,000
Less	
Ending inventory 12/31/84	40,000
Total cost of merchandise sold	160,000

FIGURE 11–3

Cost of Goods Manufactured section of the income statement for a manufacturing company.

Cost of Goods Manufactured	
Direct labor	$120,000
Raw materials	80,000
Factory overhead	90,000
Total cost of goods manufactured	$290,000

General Expenses Items usually presented under General Expenses are those that are indirect costs incurred in the administration of the business. Some of the expenses commonly included under this category are office expenses, postage, telephones, payroll taxes, and utilities.

Other Expenses The category Other Expenses usually contains all other items that do not seem to fit into the other expenses categories, items such as interest expense and bad checks expense.

Characteristics of the Income Statement

The income statement is an estimate of profit or loss, and it measures profit or loss over a period of time.

Estimate

The income statement, shown in Figure 11–4, presents several items of expenses that exist in the form of depreciation. Building, equipment, and truck depreciations for the year appear as operating expenses. If any expense items are an estimate, then the total expenses figure for the firm is an estimate. Income for the firm is accurate, but when the total of all expenses is an estimate, then the profit or loss figure is an estimate.

Measures Profit over a Period of Time

The income statement deducts all expenses from all income for a specific period of time to arrive at the firm's profit or loss for that period. The income statement usually is prepared once a year at the end of the fiscal period; however, it may be prepared for shorter periods. Some business firms feel they gain better control of their business by preparing their income statements monthly.

FIGURE 11–4

Income statement.

DOVE WHOLESALE PAINT COMPANY			
Income Statement for 1984			
Revenue from Sales			$430,000
Cost of Goods Sold			
Beginning inventory 1/1/84	$ 30,000		
Purchases	264,000		
Merchandise available for sale	294,000		
Less ending inventory 12/31/84	24,000		
Total cost of goods sold			270,000
Gross Profit on Sales			$160,000
Operating Expenses			
Advertising	$ 20,000		
Insurance	6,000		
Depreciation expenses			
Building	4,000		
Equipment	6,000		
Truck	1,000		
Sales personnel	35,000		
Entertainment	2,000		
Travel	1,000		
Total operating expenses		$75,000	
General Expenses			
Office expense	$ 12,000		
Postage	800		
Telephone	1,200		
Payroll taxes	3,000		
Utilities	4,000		
Total general expenses		21,000	
Other Expenses			
Interest expense	$ 3,000		
Bad check expense	1,000		
Total other expenses		4,000	
Total Expenses			$100,000
Net Income			$ 60,000

SPECIAL INTEREST FEATURE

Depreciation and Profit

As a general rule, firms should write off depreciable items as fast as the Internal Revenue Service (IRS) will allow. A simple illustration of the benefits could be illustrated by the following example. Suppose a firm saved $1000 the first year it depreciated the asset and invested it in a money market fund paying 10 percent interest. The business would earn $100 the first year in interest on the amount saved on its taxes. Of course, it will save less in later years by accelerating depreciation, but it will have earned more interest in the early years to reinvest. Inflation would also be a factor in that the firm can realize today's purchasing power.

Firms may manipulate their depreciation in various ways to show different levels of profit. An example is the rates currently allowed by IRS the first year on real estate (houses, buildings, etc.), which are (1) straight line for 15 years, (2) any straight line in excess of 15 years elected by the taxpayer, or (3) accelerated cost recovery system (ACRS) of 12 percent of the cost for the first year. (Once a method of depreciation is elected, the firm cannot change it without permission from the IRS.) A firm that purchased a new building for $200,000 could show the following depreciation expense for the first year.

Depreciation Method	Years Depreciated	First Year Depreciation
Straight line	30	$ 6,667
Straight line	15	13,334
ACRS	15	24,000

This firm could show a profit that could deviate by as much as $17,333 depending on which of the three methods the firm selects. People investing in or loaning a business money should realize that the income statement is an estimate, and they should check such items as the method of depreciation very carefully.

Uses of the Income Statement

The small business firm uses its income statement to analyze the success of operations of the business over a specific period of time. Investments, purchases of assets, and distribution of profit are just a few of the decisions that rely on the information provided in the income statement.

The income statement is also used by other groups. Federal income tax returns of the business could not be properly prepared without the income statement. Other government agencies, including various state and local taxing agencies, require income statements from the business for their use. Creditors and investors consider the income statement very valuable, and few would be willing to loan or invest money without its availability for their analysis.

BUDGET

In reality, the **budget** is the estimate of next year's income statement. It is a major planning and control device for the small business firm (see Fig. 11–5).

Components of the Budget

The budget is comprised of (1) income, (2) cost of goods sold or cost of goods manufactured, (3) controllable expenses, and (4) uncontrollable expenses.

FIGURE 11–5
Budget.

DOVE WHOLESALE PAINT COMPANY
Budgeted Income Statement for 1984

(All figures are estimates)		
Expected Sales Revenue		$450,000
Expected Cost of Goods Sold		275,000
Estimated Gross Margin		$175,000
Controllable Expenses		
Advertising	$25,000	
Sales personnel	37,000	
Entertainment	1,500	
Travel	2,500	
Total controllable expenses		66,000
Margin for Uncontrollable Expenses and Income		$109,000
Uncontrollable Expenses		
Insurance	$ 6,000	
Depreciation expenses		
Building	4,000	
Equipment	6,000	
Truck	1,000	
Office expense	12,000	
Postage	900	
Telephones	1,300	
Payroll taxes	3,600	
Utilities	4,200	
Interest expense	3,000	
Total uncontrollable expenses		42,000
Estimated Net Income Before Federal Income Taxes		$ 67,000

Income

Expected sales revenue is forecast by the business and is the basis for almost all the budget. The number of units forecast to be sold during the next year determines the cost of goods sold or manufactured, controllable expenses, and, to some extent, uncontrollable expenses.

Cost of Goods Sold—
Cost of Goods Manufactured

The Cost of Goods Sold section in retail and wholesale firms is estimated usually on the basis of past experiences in markup on the total volume of expected sales. For example, the income statement in Figure 11–4 shows the firm's cost of goods sold is usually about 60 percent of sales. Therefore, with expected sales of $450,000 in its budget, it can expect about 60 percent or $275,000 to be the Cost of Goods Sold figure in the budget.

The Cost of Goods Manufactured section in manufacturing firms is estimated by taking the total number of units estimated to be manufactured for the next year and multiplying by the standard per unit labor and raw material cost. For example, if it requires $1.40 in direct labor and $1.60 of raw materials to produce one unit, it would cost $300,000 of direct labor and raw materials to produce 100,000 units. Factory overhead is usually applied on a past experience basis, usually as a percentage of the total direct labor cost. To illustrate, if factory overhead has usually been about 60 percent of direct labor costs, then 60 percent of the forecasted direct labor expense would be used as the forecasted factory overhead expense.

Controllable and
Uncontrollable Expenses

Instead of Operating Expenses, General Expenses, and Other Expenses shown in the income statement, the budget uses controllable and uncontrollable expense categories.

Controllable expenses are those expenses that the firm has some control over. Advertising, number of sales personnel, entertainment, and travel may be controlled by the firm.

Uncontrollable expenses are expenses that are relatively fixed if the business is operating in a normal business manner. Insurance, all depreciation, office expenses, postage, telephones, payroll taxes, utilities, and interest are expenses that occur as a result of normal business activity (see Fig. 11–5).

Characteristics of the Budget

The characteristics of the budget are the same as the income statement because it contains the same items and estimates profit or loss over a future period. Whereas the income statement contains many items that are accurate and some that are estimates, all figures in the budget are estimates because they are amounts forecast for a future period of time. The budget also covers a period of time, usually the coming year. However, some firms do have budgets for shorter periods of time. They forecast the budget for the next year and then break it down into months or quarters.

Uses of the Budget

The budget is one of the most important accounting tools small business owners have at their disposal. It helps control the business, and it aids them in making decisions that concern the business.

The budget is a valuable controlling device in that it is a standard against which to measure current performance of the business. The business has expenses on a continuing basis, and the manager can compare these against those projected in the budget. If the current expenditures deviate from the budgeted amount, the manager knows something is wrong and may then investigate to discover the problem and correct it.

The budget also tells the manager what funds are available for different expenditures. The expected profit figure will allow the manager to estimate how much profit can be taken out of the business and how much will be left for purchases of fixed assets, such as machinery.

The budget is also an excellent device for forecasting future financial needs. For example, the manager knows of financial needs months in advance. As a result, he or she is able to arrange for the money in advance rather than waiting until the need arises.

CASH FLOW STATEMENT

The **cash flow statement** is a measure of changes in cash the business has on hand from month to month. It records or projects all cash receipts less all cash disbursements. A business may use the cash flow statement as a record of what has occurred to cash or as a projection into the future to determine future needs for cash or as both (see Fig. 11–6).

Components of the Cash Flow Statement

The cash flow statement takes the amount of cash on hand at the beginning of the month, adds all cash receipts to the balance, and subtracts all cash disbursements to arrive at the amount of cash on hand at the end of the month.

Cash Receipts
Cash receipts include all funds that are received in the form of cash. It usually includes such items as cash sales and cash received in payment of accounts receivable. It does not include sales in the form of credit.

Cash Disbursements
This category contains all expenses, purchases, and payments made in cash. It does not include depreciation or amounts for any items purchased on

FIGURE 11–6
Cash flow statement.

DOVE WHOLESALE PAINT COMPANY Projected Cash Flow			
	January	February	March
Beginning Cash Balance	$ 9,000	$11,850	$19,825
Cash Receipts			
Cash sales	$22,000	$23,000	$23,000
Cash from accounts receivable	8,000	14,000	16,000
Total cash received for month	$30,000	$37,000	$39,000
Cash Disbursements:			
Cash payments on accounts payable	$18,000	$20,000	$20,000
Advertising	2,500	2,500	2,500
Insurance	500	500	500
Sales salaries and commissions	3,000	3,000	3,000
Entertainment	150	125	125
Travel	200	100	100
Office expenses	1,000	1,000	1,000
Postage	100	100	100
Telephone	100	100	100
Utilities	350	350	350
Interest expense	250	250	250
Payroll taxes	0	0	900
Total cash disbursed for month	$26,150	$28,025	$28,925
Cash Increase or Decrease from Operations	$ 3,850	$ 8,975	$10,075
Mortgage Payment	$ 1,000	$ 1,000	$ 1,000
Net Change in Cash Position	$ 2,850	$ 7,975	$ 9,075
Cash Balance Carried into Next Month	$11,850	$19,825	$28,900

credit. The cash disbursement category often includes such items as advertising, payments to vendors for purchases, insurance premiums, salaries, travel, utilities, office expenses, and long-term debt payments. Such items as payroll taxes, which are incurred monthly but are only paid quarterly, are not recorded until they are actually paid.

Characteristics of the Cash Flow Statement

The cash flow statement is accurate when it is a record of past receipts and disbursements and an estimate when it is projected for future months. The cash flow statement is usually calculated on a monthly basis for an entire year.

Uses of the Cash Flow Statement

The projected cash flow statement is important to small business owners because it identifies future problems with cash. The cash flow statement will warn them months in advance when there will be a cash shortage and tell them how much so that they are able to plan in advance. By knowing in advance, they can often obtain debt funds at the best interest rate available to them. If it shows surplus funds will be available that are not needed in the business, it allows them to make arrangements for use of the funds in other investments.

For an investor, it is one of the most important accounting statements he or she can use. It is possible for a business to show a loss on the income statement and still be an attractive investment. For instance, it is quite common for entrepreneurs to build apartments, take accelerated depreciation on them, show a loss on the income statement for several years, and still have increases in cash each month even after making the mortgage payment. By doing this, the entrepreneur usually keeps the apartments until they are depreciated to the point where he or she is showing a profit. The entrepreneur then sells them and pays only a capital gains tax on the difference between what is received for the apartments and what is shown on the books after depreciation. Since the capital gains tax is paid on only 40 percent of the gains, the entrepreneur has gained considerably in the total profit derived from the apartments.

COMBINED MONTHLY INCOME AND CASH FLOW STATEMENT

The authors recommend to small businesses that they post their Sales and Disbursement Journals to a combined Income and Cash Flow Statement each month. When the columns in their Sales and Disbursement Journals are totaled each month, the business should carry each column total to the statement shown in Figure 11–7. The Sales Journal (Fig. 10–3) and the Disbursement Journal (Fig. 10–5) in Chapter 10 are keyed to the various items that appear in Figure 11–7.

By posting to the Income and Cash Flow Statement, the small businesses are able to see how well they are doing each month. They do not have to wait until the end of the year, when it may be too late to correct anything that might be going astray.

RATIOS

Accounting **ratios** are calculated on various items that appear in the accounting statements of a business firm. They are important to the firm in that they

FIGURE 11–7
Monthly income and cash flow statement.

CASH FLOW AND INCOME STATEMENT[a]

Sales			
Retail			
Ⓐ Product group A		$ 570.00	
Ⓑ Product group B		580.00	
Ⓒ Other products		380.00	
Total retail sales		1,530.00	
Ⓓ Commercial		850.00	
Total Sales			$2,380.00
Cost of Goods Purchased			
Retail			
Ⓔ Product group A		$ 100.00	
Ⓕ Product group B		120.00	
Ⓖ Other products		150.00	
Total retail purchases		$ 370.00	
Ⓗ Commercial		100.00	
Total Cost of Goods Purchased			470.00
Sales Less Cost of Goods Purchased			$1,910.00
Expenses			
Ⓘ Office supplies		$ 30.00	
Ⓙ Salaries and wages		500.00	
Ⓚ Utilities		200.00	
Ⓛ Insurance		50.00	
Ⓛ Interest on note		20.00	
Ⓛ Travel		140.00	
Ⓛ Payroll taxes		60.00	
Ⓛ Other expenses		25.00	
Total Expenses			$1,025.00
Net Cash Increase			$ 885.00

Cash Flow		Income	
Net cash increase	$885.00	Net cash increase	$885.00
Ⓜ Less principal paid on debt	200.00	Add any decreases in inventory level	160.00
Cash flow for the period	$685.00	Deduct any increases in inventory level	
		Less depreciation for period	230.00
		Net taxable income	$815.00

[a]Letters indicate column totals from the Sales Journal (Fig. 10–3) and the Disbursement Journal (Fig. 10–5).

provide measures of performance against a guideline to let the business know if it is operating as planned. (All sample calculations shown in the following sections are based on data in the accounting statements shown in Figures 11–1 and 11–4.)

Current Ratio

The **current ratio** is a measure of the firm's ability to meet current debt. It measures the relationship between current assets and current liabilities.

$$\frac{\text{Current Assets}}{\text{Current Liabilities}} = \text{Current Ratio}$$

$$\frac{\$48,000}{\$20,000} = 2.4$$

Acid Test Ratio

The **acid test ratio** is sometimes called the "quick ratio." It measures the firm's ability to meet current debt by measuring the relationship between its liquid assets (cash plus other current assets that are quickly converted into cash) and current debt. It is a more specific measure of the firm's ability to meet debt than the current ratio.

$$\frac{\text{Cash} + \text{Accounts Receivable} + \text{Marketable Securities}}{\text{Current Liabilities}} = \text{Acid Test Ratio}$$

$$\frac{\$9000 + \$9500 + \$3500}{\$20,000} = 1.1$$

Debt to Net Worth Ratio

The **debt to net worth ratio** measures creditor contributions relative to owner contributions. It is a measure of the firm's ability to meet creditor and owner obligations in case of liquidation of the firm. It is also a measure of whether the firm is overextended in terms of debt.

$$\frac{\text{Total Liabilities}}{\substack{\text{Tangible Net Worth} \\ \text{(Net Worth} - \text{Intangible Assets)}}} = \text{Debt to Net Worth Ratio}$$

$$\frac{\$\ 20,000 + \$30,000}{\$151,000 - \$\ 1,000} = 0.33$$

Rate of Return on Assets

The **rate of return on assets** ratio is a measure of profitability of the firm. It indicates the amount of assets necessary to produce the current level of profit.

$$\frac{\text{Profit}}{\text{Total Tangible Assets}} = \text{Rate of Return on Assets}$$
$$\text{(Total Assets} - \text{Intangible Assets)}$$

$$\frac{\$60,000}{\$201,000 - \$1,000} = 0.3$$

Inventory Turnover

The inventory turnover is a ratio that measures how often inventory is sold and replaced. The **inventory turnover** ratio indicates the adequacy of the amount of inventory on hand relative to the amount of sales. Inventory turnover is usually calculated in terms of how many times it completely turns over each year.

$$\frac{\text{Cost of Goods Sold}}{\text{Average Amount of Inventory for the Year}} = \text{Inventory Turnover}$$
$$\text{(Beginning Inventory} + \text{Ending Inventory divided by Two)}$$

$$\frac{\$270,000}{\dfrac{\$30,000 + \$24,000}{2}} = 10$$

A small business firm should strive to maintain each of its ratio measures near some optimum point. To illustrate, if the optimum point for a specific business for its acid test ratio was 1.5, then any figure much below this would indicate the business is not maintaining enough liquid assets in relation to its current debt. The firm could expect to have problems in meeting its debts during the year. On the other hand, if the figure is much above 1.5, the business is maintaining too many liquid assets that could be invested elsewhere for additional profit.

An optimum ratio figure differs not only by type of ratio but also by type of business. For example, one would not expect the same inventory turnover figure for a jewelry store as for a supermarket. Small business owners often establish optimum ratio figures based on experience in their business. Also, they should compare their firm's ratio analysis with industry averages that are published in sources such as the *Almanac of Business and Industrial Financial Ratios*. Many trade organizations also publish financial ratios for their industry.

In conclusion, the authors have found that one of the most common weaknesses of small businesses is their accounting system and analysis. Many activities of the small business firm cannot be fully effective without adequate accounting practices and analysis, for example, inventory control, which is discussed in Chapter 13.

SUMMARY OF KEY POINTS

1. The components of a balance sheet may be shown as Assets = Liabilities + Capital, and this is also the basic accounting equation.

2. The balance sheet is an estimate of the value of the business at one moment in time.

3. The balance sheet measures changes in the business, reveals the company's ability to meet debt, and can be used to compute ratios.

4. The income statement is a measure of income less expense, which equals profitability.

5. The income statement is an estimate and measure of profit over a period of time.

6. The method of depreciation selected can change the profit for the period.

7. The income statement measures the success of the business for the period and is required by the IRS and other groups.

8. The budget is an estimate of next year's income statement, which measures estimated income less controllable and uncontrollable expenses.

9. The budget is important because it is next year's plan and is a controlling and decision-making device.

10. The cash flow statement is a record of all cash receipts and disbursements.

11. The projected cash flow statement is important in that it warns of future cash problems. Past cash flow statements are extremely important to investors.

12. Ratios are important to businesses because they provide measures of performance against a guideline to let the business know if it is operating as planned.

DISCUSSION QUESTIONS

1. What is the balance sheet, and what are some of its components?
2. Why is a balance sheet an estimate for one moment in time?
3. If you were a small business owner, how would you use the balance sheet?
4. What is an income statement, and what items are contained in the income statement?
5. Why is the income statement an estimate, and why does it measure profit or loss over a period of time?
6. Can the small business owner do without some form of income statement? Explain.
7. Why is the budget like the income statement?
8. Why is the budget important to the small business?
9. What is a cash flow statement?
10. Why is a cash flow statement important to the small business and the investor?
11. Why would a small business owner compute ratios?

STUDENT PROJECTS

1. Prepare a balance sheet for yourself, listing all assets and liabilities to arrive at your net worth.
2. Keep a record of all income and expenditures for a week's period, and from this record prepare an income statement and a cash flow statement.
3. Prepare a budget for the next week.

CASE A

The West Bookstore

Richard West owns and operates a bookstore in a shopping mall on the west side of a large city. At a recent small business clinic sponsored by a local college and the Small Business Administration, Richard learned that financial ratios are valuable tools in evaluating and controlling a small business. Richard knows very little about ratios and has asked your help. The following are copies of his latest income statement and balance sheet.

THE WEST BOOKSTORE
Income Statement for Year Ending 12/31/84

Sales		$230,000
Cost of Goods Sold		
Beginning inventory 1/1/84	$120,000	
Purchases	110,000	
Merchandise available for sale	$230,000	
Less ending inventory 12/31/84	130,000	
Total cost of goods sold		100,000
Gross Profit on Sales		$130,000
Operating Expenses		
Advertising	$ 8,000	
Rent	22,000	
Depreciation on furniture and fixtures	6,000	
Salaries and wages	15,000	
Insurance	4,000	
Total operating expenses	$55,000	
General Expenses		
Postage	$ 600	
Telephone	1,200	
Payroll taxes	1,500	
Utilities	5,700	
Total general expenses	$ 9,000	
Total Expenses		$ 64,000
Net Income Before Taxes		$ 66,000

THE WEST BOOKSTORE
Balance Sheet

Assets

Current Assets		
Cash	$ 20,000	
Merchandise	130,000	
Supplies	1,000	
ABC Company Stock	40,000	
Total current assets		$191,000
Fixed Assets		
Furniture and Fixtures	$ 40,000	
Total fixed assets		40,000
Intangible Assets		
Organizational Costs	$ 1,000	
Total intangible assets		1,000
Total Assets		$232,000

Liabilities

Current Liabilities

Accounts payable	$ 20,000	
Income tax payable	5,000	
FICA tax payable	3,000	
Total current liabilities		$ 28,000

Long-term Liabilities

Note payable to bank 6/1/89	$ 60,000	
Total long-term liabilities		60,000

Capital

Richard West, capital		144,000
Total Liabilities and Capital		$232,000

QUESTIONS

1. Compute the following ratios for Richard.

   Current ratio

   Acid test ratio

   Debt to net worth ratio

   Rate of return on assets

   Inventory turnover

2. Tell Richard how he can use these ratios.

CASE B

Pete's Parts (B)

See Pete's Parts (A) (Case B in Chapter 10) for background information. After setting up Peter Wagner's Sales and Disbursement Journal, you decided he should have a monthly Income and Cash Flow Statement. To illustrate how it is done, you plan to create a sample statement keyed to his journals.

Pete's inventory system involves reordering all items that he sold from stock each day. He has ordered replacements for everything he sold the first week. However, only $240 worth of parts (at cost) have come in, and he still requires $200 worth of parts (at cost) that have not come in to restock his inventory completely. This means he currently has a decrease of $200 in inventory. Depreciation for the first week amounted to $50.

QUESTIONS*

1. Set up a monthly Income and Cash Flow Statement similar to the one in Figure 11–7.

2. Post the Sales and Disbursement Journals to your Income and Cash Flow Statement. (It will be a weekly statement in this case.)

SMALL BUSINESS ADMINISTRATION PUBLICATIONS

Free

Basic Budgets for Profit Planning
Cash Flow in a Small Plant
Accounting Services for Small Service Firms
Analyze Your Records to Reduce Costs
Budgeting in a Small Business Firm
Keeping Records in Small Business

For Sale

Cost Accounting for Small Manufacturers
Ratio Analysis for Small Business
Financial Recordkeeping for Small Stores

---

*Forms are provided in the Student Study Guide.

MERCHANDISE CONTROL, INSURANCE, AND COMPUTERS

SECTION FOUR

CHAPTER TWELVE

PURCHASING IN THE SMALL BUSINESS

LEARNING GOALS

After reading this chapter, you will understand:

1. The role of purchasing in the small business.
2. The goals of purchasing.
3. Why policies and procedures must be established so that the purchasing function may be successfully completed.
4. The considerations in the make or buy decision.
5. The factors included in vendor analysis.
6. When title to merchandise passes from seller to buyer.
7. What consignment purchasing is and how it affects the small business owner.
8. The importance of purchase discounts to the small business owner as well as the different types of purchase discounts.

KEY WORDS

Purchasing	F.O.B. buyer
Value analysis	Consignment purchasing
Lead time	Cash discount
Safety factor	Quantity discount
Title	Trade discount
F.O.B. seller	Seasonal discount

SMALL BUSINESS PROFILE

Furniture That's a Smash Hit

It was a most memorable party. The hangover is gone, but today, nearly eight years later, the remedy survives as a testimonial to entrepreneurship.

Steve Robertson, 26 at the time, recollects it was a "boisterous, very boisterous" party. In fact, by evening's end, Randall Ward's apartment was devoid of usable furniture. Tables, chairs—all had been smashed during the revelry.

The party's host, 28-year-old Ward, had had a disillusioning day. Some months earlier he had given up a boring sales job with a New York textile firm to start his own building business in Raleigh, N.C. The business went broke. A party, a spirited celebration of failure, seemed apropos.

Robertson, like Ward, was a graduate of North Carolina State, but the two hadn't known each other at school. Filled with wanderlust, Robertson had spent the years after college sailing the South Pacific. He returned to the U.S. to apply for an Australian work visa so he could teach sailing in Australia. While in Raleigh, scratching for pocket money, he worked for Ward one day—the final day.

The morning after, viewing the wreckage, Robertson worried about his new friend's lack of furniture. He came up with the throbbing idea: fashion primitive but sturdy chairs and tables from the wooden packing crates he had brought back from Australia.

"When friends saw the crate furniture, they thought we had something," Robertson recalls. "They told us to try to market it. Since Randall and I were out of work, that weekend we took the newly made pieces down to a local flea market."

That was in 1974. When asked what total sales now run annually, neither man gets specific. They hint, however, that the figure is close to $10 million.

At the flea market the entrepreneurs took deposits along with the orders and used the money to buy lumber and tools. "That first year," recalls Robertson, "we each put in 80 hours a week. We'd take orders and sell pieces at the flea market on weekends, build the furniture during the day and then deliver it at night." Only the original pieces came from packing crates. This End Up Furniture Company now uses kiln-dried southern yellow pine, cut in its own sawmill.

After a year Robertson phoned his sister and brother-in-law—Libby and Stewart Brown—to ask whether they'd like to open a store in Richmond as a side venture to Brown's stockbrokerage job.

They did, and 12 months later, with five stores scattered throughout Virginia, Brown left the stock and bond business to devote full time to This End Up furniture.

Today's 45 stores are spread along the East Coast from New York to Atlanta. Ward foresees 12 more opening this year, including several in the

Midwest and Southwest. The stores just take orders; they do not stock furniture. Delivery time is four to six weeks.

More than 35 pieces—from couches (weighing 180 pounds and containing 200 board feet) to small end tables—are made in the company's two Raleigh plants. All the wood is stained the same color, but the upholstery on couches and chairs makes use of 30 fabrics.

The furniture is ideal for cottages and recreation rooms, explain Robertson and Ward, adding that an entire living room—eight pieces—can be purchased for under $1,000.

According to Robertson, This End Up Furniture Company has dozens of competitors now making similar furniture. "One of the smartest things we did in the beginning was to patent our designs," he says. The company has been to court several times to fight infringements on its products.

Robertson and Ward each own half of the manufacturing portion of the company. All but nine stores in the retail operation are owned by the Browns.

Boisterous parties are over for Robertson, now 33, and Ward, 36, but they remain bachelors and run the company in a relaxed, almost casual manner. They try not to be workaholics. The 85 plant employees, who punch no clocks and work no set hours, follow their example.

"We pay them well for what they produce, and as long as we get the orders out, they can work or not work as they please," according to Robertson and Ward.

The young men contend the key to their success, in both sales and production, is to be "honest with your employes and your customers." It's a philosophy that keeps paying off for This End Up Furniture Company.

"Every week we do more business than we did the entire first year," says Robertson.

Source Del Marth, "Furniture That's a Smash Hit," *Nation's Business*, vol. 70, no. 4 (April 1982), p. 70. Reprinted by permission from Nations Business, (1982). Copyright (1982) by Nations Business, Chamber of Commerce of the United States.

Purchasing is a major cost of operation in the small business. In manufacturing establishments, 57 cents of each sales dollar goes to pay for purchases of materials and services according to the Department of Commerce. Thus, efficient performance of the purchasing function is mandatory for achieving higher levels of profitability in the small business.

Small manufacturers plan for purchasing the proper type of raw materials that can be processed into finished goods for sale. Small wholesalers base their purchase decisions on projected demand from retailers and service firm operators. Small retailers analyze consumer buying habits, and purchase decisions regarding finished goods are shaped by the expectation of consumer demand. Service firm owners' purchases of special parts and standard items are planned with the objective of having available the parts and materials they require to perform their specific services.

Purchase activities must be coordinated with all other operations of the firm. In the small business, one person or a small department should be given the authority and responsibility for coordinating the purchasing function. Centralizing the purchasing function affords greater efficiency and uniformity in completing this activity. In addition, the central purchasing authority enables better vendor relations to be established. If problems arise, the vendor can negotiate with the purchasing representative of the firm. In the small firm, the owner or an assistant designated as the purchasing manager has the authority and responsibility for coordinating the purchasing activity.

GOALS OF PURCHASING

Small firms consistently outdistance their competitors. Ordinarily, this competitive edge is not accidental or attributable to luck but is achieved in part by the quality of purchasing decisions made by the firm's owner or purchasing manager. Effective purchasing is one of the most promising avenues for achieving growth in the small firm.

The purchasing process encompasses a number of interdependent activities as the following definition indicates. **Purchasing** is the process of buying the right quality of materials, products, and supplies in the appropriate quantity at the best price and at the proper time from the right vendor. (See Fig. 12–1.) This statement outlines the objectives of sound purchasing in the small business.

FIGURE 12–1
The purchasing process.

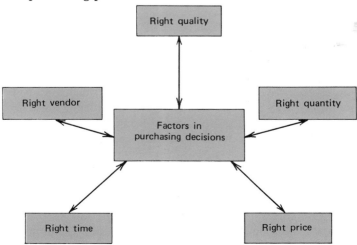

FIGURE 12–2
Factors to be evaluated in value analysis.

What is the precise function of the item?
Can the item be eliminated?
If the item is not standard, can a standard item be substituted?
Are there any similar items used by the company that can be substituted?
Can the item be redesigned to allow greater tolerances?
Will a design change permit the item to be made from a lower-cost process or a
  lower-cost material?
Could the item be produced within the firm at less cost?
Are the finishing requirements greater than necessary?
If different sizes of the item are stocked, can some of these be combined to reduce
  inventory and take advantage of quantity buying?

Source J. H. Westing, I. V. Fine, and Gary J. Zenz, *Purchasing Management* (New York: Wiley,
1976), p. 238.

Quality

Quality is related to the suitability of the raw materials or product for the
intended purpose. The raw materials purchased by the manufacturer should
be of the best quality needed to meet the manufacturer's specifications at the
lowest possible price. Quality requirements can be ascertained through so-
called **value analysis**. Value analysis is the systematic study of a component
or a product to determine whether any changes in parts or function can be
made that will provide the same "value" to users at less cost or greater
"value" at the same cost.

Quality specifications can be in the form of shape, strength, size, color,
flexibility, appearance, or any other essential features. Conducting a value
analysis often results in eliminating a part, substituting one part for another,
or changing the design or material requirement of the part. The list shown in
Figure 12–2 indicates factors to be considered in value analysis.

Quantity

A second objective of purchasing is to buy the proper quantity of materials or
products. If the small retailer or wholesaler purchases too large a stock of
merchandise, the result may be an unusually high proportion of funds tied up
in inventory. There is the added danger of spoilage or obsolescence of merchandise as well as the added cost for additional storage space if needed.
Conversely, small quantity purchases result in frequent reordering, and the
possibility exists of the product's not being in stock when it is requested by
the consumer. Furthermore, frequent reordering of small quantities may result in higher per unit costs whereas substantial savings in the form of discounts may result from quantity purchases.

The small manufacturer must be assured that an adequate stock of raw materials will be available to minimize or eliminate any disruptions in production activity. The manufacturer can use the guidelines in the following list to aid in assessing the quantity of material to be purchased.

1. How much material will be used in production.
2. How much material may be lost through damage or defects.
3. How much material is in inventory when the order is placed.
4. The average inventory carried.[1]

Price

The right price is not necessarily the lowest purchase price because the lowest price may not meet the quality requirements or may not receive the best service from the supplier. As discussed in value analysis, the best price is the lowest price at which merchandise can be purchased that is consistent with the quality specifications required. Consequently, the aim of the small business owner is to secure the highest value of merchandise that meets the specific requirements at the lowest purchase price.

Time

The decision of when to purchase materials or services is crucial. In anticipating future demand, small business owners must determine the "lead time" for delivery of materials or services so that they will be available when demand exists. **Lead time** is the elapsed time between the issuance of a requisition and the delivery of the required goods or services. Buyer and supplier actions must be coordinated with regard to the timing of the purchase order and the capacity to delivery materials or services when needed. For example, if the small retailer orders too far in advance of the selling season, operating capital is tied up in inventory. Orders placed with insufficient lead time often result in the delivery of merchandise after the selling season has peaked. Consequently, the small retailer will have a large unsold inventory that must be disposed of at cost or at a loss.

Manufacturers plan their purchase of raw materials so that these materials are available at the time they are needed in the manufacturing process in order to convert raw materials into finished goods. Manufacturers produce goods for stock in anticipation of ultimate demand for them. Or, they manufacture them to specific customer requirements. Whichever situation exists, they must be able to deliver according to the date promised. Wholesalers plan their merchandise needs to allow sufficient lead time to ensure delivery of goods when they are needed. By planning purchases with sufficient lead

---

[1] "Purchasing for Manufacturing Firms," *Business Basics*, no. 1015 (Washington, D. C.: Small Business Administration, 1980), p. 6.

A trade show, such as this office supply trade show, gives the small business owner the opportunity to interact with and evaluate many vendors.

time, the wholesaler will be able to make delivery of merchandise to retailers or operators of service firms as the need arises. In turn, retailers or service establishment operators then have merchandise in stock when consumer demand arises.

The person in charge of purchasing also tries to avoid the two problems of excessive inventory and stockouts. These problems are the result of poor planning and incorrect application of the "safety factor." The **safety factor** is the volume decided upon to be kept in inventory to meet contingencies in the company. This inventory level is a judgmental decision based on the knowledge of the firm's operations, suppliers' abilities, industry conditions, and the general economic situation.[2] Procedures for inventory control are discussed in Chapter 13.

Vendor

Selection of the vendor is a critical part of sound purchasing. Vendors should be selected who can provide the quality and quantity at the price and time specified by the small business owner. After they are selected, vendors should be evaluated to make sure that they continue to provide the type of

[2] Clifton M. Smith, "Policy and Procedure Manuals," in *Aljian's Purchasing Handbook*, 4th ed., Paul V. Farrell, ed. (New York: McGraw-Hill, 1982), pp. 3–31.

service that the firm requires. The best purchasing strategy can be defeated by selection of an inadequate vendor. A more detailed discussion of vendor analysis is presented later in this chapter.

PURCHASING POLICIES

If the purchasing objectives specified earlier are to be realized, policies must be created that will clearly establish the guidelines that company personnel are to follow. Policies should address representative issues such as the following.

1.   The person who has authority to make purchases.
2.   The number of vendors to be contacted to assure adequate competition.
3.   The person who has authority for selecting vendors.
4.   The person who has authority to contact, conduct, and conclude all purchasing negotiations for goods and services.
5.   Specifications of the company's bid policy.
6.   Contacts with vendors by others in the company should be conducted with the knowledge and prior approval of the purchasing representative.
7.   Purchasing has the full authority to question the quality and type of materials requested for the purpose of protecting the overall interests of the company.
8.   Development of new sources of supply.
9.   Purchasing from customers of the firm (reciprocal buying).
10.   Handling of legal questions.
11.   Type of information that should be considered confidential.

The following statement is an example of a policy regarding vendor selection.

Purchasing is charged with, and must not delegate to others, the overall responsibility for selecting vendors. It is recognized that there are occasions when other groups concerned with design and production problems will recommend or request specific sources for material. In such instances, Purchasing must determine that such source direction has the approval of the manager involved. Upon ascertaining the reasonableness of the proposed source, Purchasing will proceed to handle this purchase as any other purchase.[3]

---

[3]William E. Dollar, *Purchasing Management and Inventory Control for Small Business*, Small Business Management Series, no. 41 (Washington, D. C.: U. S. Small Business Administration, 1980), p. 7.

THE PURCHASING PROCEDURE

The purchasing procedure spells out in detail the actions that are required to complete the purchasing function. The purchasing procedure must correlate with the goals and policies of purchasing stated earlier in order to achieve the desired results. The purchasing procedure shown in Figure 12–3 outlines a basic format of activities that are necessary for completing the purchasing cycle.

FIGURE 12–3

The purchasing procedure.

Issuance of purchase requisition

Evaluation and selection of vendors

Determination of price

Purchase order

Follow-up action with supplier on purchase order

Merchandise receiving action

Completion of purchase records and payment of invoice

Issuance of Purchase Requisition

When a department requires specific materials or supplies, a purchase requisition is issued. This requisition serves as the basis for action by the person in charge of purchasing. The purchase requisition contains a description of the materials or supplies wanted, the quantity required, the date the materials should be available, the place they are to be delivered, and who is making the request. The purchase requisition should be a standard form used throughout the company. In order to make sure that the appropriate quality and quantity are ordered, the purchaser must specify on the requisition an accurate and complete description of the materials and supplies needed.

Evaluation and Selection of Vendors

Decisions concerning the source of supply from whom to secure prices is the next phase of the purchasing procedure. For some special materials, there may be only a single supplier. However, in most instances, there will be a number of vendors. In this situation, the vendor selection process consists of narrowing the choices to a relatively few suppliers. The number of vendors from whom prices should be obtained, wherever possible, is spelled out in the policy statement. The extent of investigation of suppliers will depend on whether the purchase is a routine or nonroutine purchase. Factors to be considered in vendor selection are examined later in this chapter.

Determination of Price

Prices may be determined from several sources. One method is to determine them from current catalogs of manufacturers containing price quotations. A second method is through price negotiation between buyer and seller. A third method is through competitive bidding. This latter method involves considerable time to secure price quotations and usually is not used by the purchasing manager of the small business.

The Purchase Order

The purchase order is the legal order that requests the vendor to supply the materials or services to the firm. The purchase order should be in writing, should be filled out completely, and should clearly and precisely cover the purchase quantities, type of product or service, price, delivery, and any other terms of the agreement between supplier and the firm, and it should be signed by the authorized company official. This will aid in preventing misunderstanding from developing between buyer and supplier. The importance of the purchase order as a legal document must be underscored. It represents the supplier's authorization to ship and charge for the goods or services in the order and the purchaser's obligation to reimburse the supplier for the value of the goods or services ordered. The purchase order should be a preprinted form similar to the one shown in Figure 12–4.

FIGURE 12–4

The purchase order of a small business.

TRAVIS TILE SALES
3811 Airport Blvd.
AUSTIN, TEXAS 78768

478-8705

PURCHASE ORDER

Show this Purchase Order Number on all correspondence, invoices, shipping papers and packages. **N° 1064**

TO

_____

_____

_____

DATE OF ORDER	REQ. NO.

SHIP TO

WHEN SHIP	SHIP VIA	F.O.B. POINT	TERMS

	QTY. ORDERED	QTY. RECEIVED	STOCK NUMBER/DESCRIPTION	UNIT PRICE	TOTAL
1					
2					
3					
4					
5					
6					
7					
8					
9					
10					
11					
12					
13					
14					
15					
16					
17					
18					
19					
20					

1. Please send_____copies of your invoice.
2. Order is to be entered in accordance with prices, delivery and specifications shown above.
3. Notify us immediately if you are unable to ship as specified.

Authorized by _____

FORM F462 Available from GRAYARC CO., INC., Brooklyn, NY 11232   ORIGINAL

Follow-up Action with Supplier on the Purchase Order

An effective control technique is the follow-up of the purchase order with the vendor. This action will confirm that the order has been received and that the vendor will be able to meet the delivery date. The procedure described as follows is used by a small machine-tool manufacturer.

Purchase orders are prepared in quadruplicate. Two copies, the official copy and an acknowledgment copy, are sent to the vendor (both white). A pink copy is placed in a loose-leaf folder in chronological sequence. The fourth copy (blue) is filed alphabetically by vendor in an unfilled order file. The file of pink copies is checked weekly, and if the acknowledgment copy has not been received after the lapse of a short period of time, a reminder is sent to the supplier.

When the acknowledgment copy is received, it is filed in a loose-leaf folder of unfilled orders which are arranged chronologically. At this time the pink copy of the purchase order is removed from the folder and permanently filed as a record of purchase orders placed. At regular intervals the folder of acknowledgment copies is reviewed and, if the buyer thinks it necessary, past due orders are followed up by further communication with the supplier.[4]

Merchandise Receiving Action

When the seller's invoice is received, it should be compared with the purchase order. When materials are received, the quantity, terms, prices, and description of the material should be carefully inspected to assure that they conform to the original purchase order. This control technique enables the purchaser to determine if the materials supplied match the buyer's order. If discrepancies are found, the buyer should promptly call this fact to the seller's attention and return the invoice for corrections. If material is rejected, the buyer must obtain an authorization from the seller for return and replacement. Whenever errors occur or material must be returned and replaced, the date on the invoice should be changed to allow the purchaser to take advantage of any purchase discounts.

Completion of Purchase Records and Payment of Invoice

When the purchase cycle is completed, the information should be placed in the "completed order" file and the check issued for payment of the invoice. Purchasing records should be maintained as an additional control technique in the purchasing process because it provides an indicator of vendor capability to satisfy the requirements of the small business. In addition, the length of

---

[4]J. H. Westing, I. V. Fine, and Gary J. Zenz, *Purchasing Management*, 4th ed. (New York: Wiley, 1976), p. 53.

time that purchasing records must be kept to meet legal requirements should also be ascertained.

Through all phases of the purchasing procedure, developing a supportive relationship with the vendor should be a primary concern of the small business owner. A healthy link between the small business owner and the vendor is essential in ensuring current and future success in attaining the goals of purchasing.

SPECIAL INTEREST FEATURE

Evaluating the Efficiency of the Purchasing Function

The following factors will serve as a useful guide for evaluating the efficiency of the purchasing function in the small business.

1. Do you or your designated representative have final authority and responsibility for purchasing?
2. Do you have established policies governing the purchasing activity to ensure efficiency in all phases of the purchasing operation?
3. Do you have clearly established purchasing procedures?
4. Do you have reputable vendors from whom you make your purchases?
5. Is competition among vendors encouraged, and are purchases competitive whenever possible?
6. Do you strive to maintain good relationships with vendors?
7. Do you attempt to develop new and better sources of supply?
8. Are materials and supplies being purchased at lowest prices consistent with quality requirements?
9. Do purchase records clearly show previous prices and suppliers so that you do not have to estimate prices when reordering?
10. Do you have a reliable but simplified method of pricing small orders to keep the cost of such orders lower than the value of the materials?
11. Are purchases made against written requisitions to guard against overbuying or unnecessary buying?
12. Are alternative sources of supply for critical materials maintained as a safeguard in emergency situations?
13. Do you have a follow-up system on orders with vendors to ensure timely delivery?
14. Have specifications of items you purchase been standardized where possible in order to obtain the advantages and economy of volume buying?
15. Are delivery receipts processed promptly so that you do not lose cash discounts because of delays?

MAKE OR BUY DECISION

An issue that confronts small manufacturers is the decision of whether to make product components or complete products or buy them from suppliers. In the small firm, owner–managers should seek out the advice of others rather than rely solely on their own judgment or intuition to make this decision. Value analysis is also useful for determining whether it is more economical to make or to buy. The factors of quality, quantity, price, time, and suppliers enter into this decision as well.

The small manufacturer evaluates three alternatives: purchase the complete product or component, purchase some parts and make others, or make all components. As a general guide, growth companies should buy parts because they can more profitably use their funds to expand product lines. Companies in highly competitive industries may find it more efficient to make as many of their components as possible in order to reduce operating costs.

Many considerations enter into the make or buy decision. Some of the specific concerns are included in Figure 12–5.

VENDOR ANALYSIS

Vendor analysis is one of the most important evaluations performed by the small business managers. Vendors that are selected should be those best able to serve the demands for quality, quantity, service, price, time, and place. The vendor has a strong influence on the firm's competitive position and marketing strategy. There are many factors to consider in vendor analysis. The factors described in the following sections are suggestive of some of the major items that small business owners should incorporate into their evaluation of vendors.

Dependability and Reliability

One factor to consider in vendor analysis is the dependability and reliability of the vendors. For example, is the quality of the product supplied by the vendor consistent? Another question to be answered is, Does the vendor have the capability of supplying merchandise in the quantity required whether it be in large or small lots? Further, it is essential that the supplier's operation be stable so that an uninterrupted flow of goods or services can be maintained.

Services of the Vendor

The owner must judge the type of service the vendor is capable of providing. One concern is how the supplier services repair and replacement of defective or unsatisfactory materials. The technical capability of the supplier is a vital issue for many situations. For example, if technical equipment is purchased

FIGURE 12–5

Factors to evaluate in a make or buy decision.

Decision to Buy	Decision to Make
1. Is the supplier reliable?	1. Can present equipment be used, or will new equipment have to be leased or purchased?
2. Can suppliers produce the quality standards needed for component?	2. Do current employees have the skill and knowledge necessary to produce the component?
3. Can the supplier guarantee quality of the product?	3. Can the desired quality standards be produced by the firm?
4. Can components be delivered on schedule?	4. Will the required quantities be large enough to justify setup costs and personnel training needed to produce the part?
5. What are all costs per unit involved in buying the component (such as packaging, freight, shipping, handling, and receiving costs) vs. making?	5. What are all costs involved in production (labor, material, overhead)?
6. What is the likelihood of suppliers being unable or unwilling to supply you owing to a strike or fire or demands of a more important customer?	6. What is the demand for the part (stable or seasonal)?
7. What is the seasonal demand for the product?	7. How many suppliers are available? (If there are too few, extra risks are incurred.)

by the small manufacturer, what type of services does the vendor provide in relation to installation and servicing of the equipment after installation? Or can the supplier provide assistance in advising the purchaser in technical aspects of the purchase? Other services that the vendor may offer are creative problem solving and offering suggestions on how materials may be more efficiently utilized.

Number of Vendors

Another factor in the evaluation process is the determination of whether a single vendor can best meet the needs of the small firm or whether several suppliers should be utilized. Certain problems may arise if the firm utilizes a single vendor. To illustrate, the vendor may encounter financial difficulties or

FIGURE 12–6
Advantages of concentrating purchases with a limited number of suppliers.

1. Receive more individualized attention and assistance from suppliers who know you are giving them most of your business.

2. Maintain a smaller inventory investment.

3. Purchases of larger quantities that may result in larger purchase discounts.

4. Simplifies credit problems.

5. Become known in local community as seller of certain brand or line of merchandise, if buying for resale.

6. Maintain a fixed standard for products, if buying materials to be used in making other goods.

Source Wendel O. Metcalf, *Starting and Managing a Small Business of Your Own* (Washington, D.C.: Small Business Administration).

unanticipated catastrophic events may occur, such as a fire or labor problem, making it impossible to deliver the materials on the date promised. A further consideration is that the single supplier may be unable to supply the small firm's needs at peak sales periods adequately. In addition, the single supplier may lack the motivation to provide goods or services because he or she has no competition. Ordinarily, small business owners will find it advantageous to spread their purchases over a limited number of vendors and strive to develop a close, harmonious relationship with them. This policy offers the best assurance of maintaining the level of service and supply of merchandise necessary to carry on business activity because suppliers seek to maintain or increase their share of business. Figure 12–6 lists the advantages of purchasing from a small, select group of vendors.

Vendor's Location

The geographical location of the vendor is crucial for a variety of reasons. One, transportation costs can substantially increase the cost of the product if the supplier is located some distance from the buyer. Second, correlated with this consideration is the time involved in shipping materials to their destination. Third, the greater distance materials have to be shipped increases the chances for transportation services to be interrupted owing to strikes or other unforeseen occurrences. Fourth, delivery over longer distances may require higher levels of safety stock if delivery is unreliable. Where the small firm can find a local supplier to supply its needs adequately, it may be advantageous because the local supplier is usually able to provide quick and reliable delivery of merchandise. A result of purchasing from a local supplier is that it enables the owner to demonstrate his or her support for the local business community because those purchase dollars stay in the local community. An outgrowth of this local purchasing is the creation of goodwill toward the small business

The ability to deliver merchandise when and where it is needed is a critical factor in choosing a vendor.

owner by area residents. Because the local suppliers are more accessible, they are able to provide quick price quotations and to handle any problems that may develop.

Terms of Sale

Small business owners should analyze the terms of sale offered by vendors because these may vary considerably. For example, one vendor offers cash discounts if payments are made within the regular credit period whereas another vendor makes no such allowance. Cash discounts make a significant difference in costs of goods. Another criterion in vendor selection is the length of the credit period offered by the vendor. One vendor may offer a 30-day credit period whereas another may extend credit for 60 or even 90 days.

Vendor's Sales Representatives

The quality of the sales representatives of the vendor should be carefully analyzed. Small business managers frequently rely on the vendor's sales representatives to provide them with prompt and accurate price quotations, to follow through on their orders, to expedite delivery, and to handle complaints in a satisfactory manner. Small business managers also expect sales

FIGURE 12–7
"F.O.B." seller.

representatives to be knowledgeable about the company and the products they are selling as well as to make regular sales calls. Furthermore, sales representatives can provide information about possible sources of supply of noncompeting products or services.

Vendor representatives perform an inventory function for many small retailers. In cases when the vendor's representatives visit regularly and are considered dependable, the owner will have them check inventory items and recommend how much stock should be purchased.

Other considerations that should be analyzed are the ethical standards of the supplier, the financial strength, the labor-management relations, and management capability of the supplier.

TRANSFER OF TITLE

When the purchase transaction occurs, the time and place where **title** to the merchandise passes must be established in order to determine legal ownership. Although some transactions may be very simple, the usual transaction is more involved as was indicated in the discussion of purchasing procedures earlier in this chapter. The question of when title passes is ordinarily answered by the designation "free on board" (f.o.b.) seller or buyer.

"F.O.B." Seller

The designation **"f.o.b." seller** means that title to goods passes as soon as the seller delivers the merchandise to the shipper (airline, truckline, bus, or railway system). Under the terms of this arrangement, the buyer pays for the shipping costs and is responsible for all activities relating to the movement of goods, such as providing insurance protection against damage or loss during shipment. Figure 12–7 depicts when title passes under "f.o.b." seller.

The responsibility of the seller and the buyer under "f.o.b." seller are listed as follows.

F.O.B. (named point of origin)

A. Seller must
    1. Place goods on or in cars or vehicles.
    2. Secure receipted bill of lading from carrier.
    3. Be responsible for loss and damage until goods have been placed in

FIGURE 12–8
"F.O.B." buyer.

or on cars or vehicles at point of origin and clean bill of lading has been furnished by carrier.

B. Buyer must
  1. Provide for the movement of goods after they are on board.
  2. Pay all transportation charges to destination.
  3. Be responsible for loss or damage or for filing claims with carrier for loss or damage to shipment while in transit.
  4. Pay any demurrage and storage charges.

C. Title passes to buyer when shipment is turned over to carrier.[5]

"F.O.B." Buyer

Transactions designated as **"f.o.b." buyer** indicate that the title of goods does not pass until the merchandise is delivered to the buyer's place of business. Under the terms of this arrangement, the seller pays for shipping charges to the buyer's firm. In addition, the responsibility for insurance protection of goods in transit remains with the seller. Figure 12–8 illustrates when title passes under the "f.o.b." buyer agreement.

By mutual agreement, the buyer and seller may select any other intermediate points for delivery of goods where title would then pass.

The responsibilities of the seller and the buyer under "f.o.b." buyer are listed as follows.

F.O.B. (named destination)

A. Seller must
  1. Place goods on or in cars or vehicles.
  2. Secure receipted bill of lading from carrier.
  3. *Pay all transportation charges until goods have arrived at destination.*
  4. *Be responsible for loss or damage or for filing claims with carrier for loss or damage to shipment while in transit.*

B. Buyer must
  1. Provide for any movement of the goods after arrival at named destination.
  2. Be responsible for any loss and damage incurred after arrival of goods at named destination.

---

[5]J. H. Westing, I. V. Fine, and Gary J. Zenz, op. cit., p. 307.

3. Pay any demurrage and storage charges.

C. Title remains with seller until the shipment is delivered to buyer.[6]

CONSIGNMENT PURCHASING

Consignment purchasing is a stockless purchasing system. Under consignment purchasing, the vendor's merchandise is usually displayed in the small owner's establishment, and the vendor is responsible for maintaining the merchandise display. Ownership of the inventory resides with the vendor until the materials are used or sold. Consignment purchasing has certain advantages to the small business owner. While merchandise is available for resale and sale on the premises, the owner's funds are not tied up in inventory. The problem of obsolescence of merchandise is reduced for the small business owner because unsold or unused merchandise is reclaimed by the vendor. The consigned merchandise may attract customers to the store and may result in additional purchases of regular merchandise as well.

For example, a rack jobber often consigns merchandise to retail firms. The rack jobber places his or her own display rack of merchandise in the store. Rack jobbers regularly check the merchandise rack to see that there is an adequate stock of goods and that they are priced and displayed properly. Title does not pass, and payment for the merchandise is not made until the products are sold or are used by the small business manager.

The small business owner must have a complete understanding with the vendor regarding the status of the consigned goods. The following factors should normally be included, and the consignment agreement should be in writing.

1. Listing of items to be consigned, prices, quantities, and maximum and minimum levels.

2. Duration of consignment agreement, which should not exceed a year's period.

3. Title of consigned inventory remains with the vendor until withdrawn from stock.

4. Designation of insurance responsibility.

5. Policy on rejects—seller responsible for defects; buyer to be responsible for any missing or damaged materials resulting from buyer's negligence.

6. Termination provisions.

7. Provisions for disposition of any unused consigned inventory at the end of the consignment agreement.[7]

---

[6] Ibid., p. 308.

[7] Caleb L. Johnson, "Inventory Management," in *Aljian's Purchasing Handbook*, 4th ed., Paul V. Farrell, ed. (New York: McGraw-Hill, 1982), pp. 12–35, 12–36.

FIGURE 12–9

Types of purchase discounts.

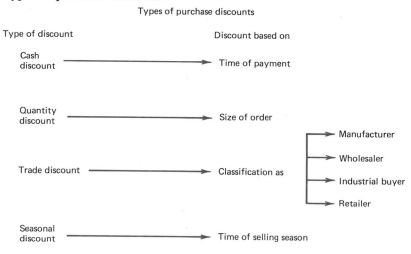

Types of purchase discounts

Type of discount	Discount based on
Cash discount	Time of payment
Quantity discount	Size of order
Trade discount	Classification as — Manufacturer / Wholesaler / Industrial buyer / Retailer
Seasonal discount	Time of selling season

PURCHASE DISCOUNTS

Small business owners should carefully evaluate all opportunities to reduce their cost of operation and take advantage of these situations in order to improve the firm's overall operating efficiency. One such avenue of profit improvement is through taking the various purchase discounts that may be available because discounts represent a reduction in price of the purchased material from vendors. A high priority item to be evaluated in deciding whether to take the discount is to weigh the cost of money at prevailing interest rates versus the amount of the discount allowed.

Thus, the decision of whether the discount should be taken becomes a financial decision. As interest rates rise and the cash position of the buyer becomes tight, the small business owner should try for longer terms of payment—60 days or more—unless discounts of at least 2 percent are offered.[8]

Principal types of discounts offered to small business owners are the following: cash, trade, quantity, and seasonal. (See Fig. 12–9.)

Cash Discounts

Vendors offer **cash discounts** to small business owners as an incentive for prompt payment of merchandise. Cash discounts reduce the purchase price, thus making funds available for other uses in the company. The most common cash discount is stated as "2/10, net 30." These discount terms mean that

---

[8]Myron E. Frye, "Price Considerations," in *Aljian's Purchasing Handbook,* 4th ed., Paul V. Farrell, ed. (New York: McGraw-Hill, 1982), pp. 10–9.

the vendor extends credit to the small business owner for the amount of the purchase for a period of 30 days. The total bill is payable at the end of 30 days. However, if the bill is paid within 10 days of the invoice date, the owner-manager is given a 2 percent discount on the net purchase price. Hence, if the purchase order is substantial, sizable cash savings can result, and these funds become available for other uses.

Many other discount terms are available from suppliers, such as "1/10, net 30"; "2/10, net 60"; and "2/10, EOM." The "2/10, EOM" means that a 2 percent discount can be taken if the owner pays the bill by the tenth of the month following the purchase. For merchandise purchased in September, the owner–manager would be able to take the 2 percent discount if the bill were paid by October 10.

Another way of evaluating the value of the cash discounts is to calculate them on the basis of annual rates. To illustrate, the "2/10, net 30" cash discount is equivalent to earning an interest rate of approximately 36 percent on the amount involved in the transaction because there are 18 periods of 20 days each in a year that might be anticipated if the owner receives merchandise shipments regularly throughout the year. Other examples of the range of discounts available on an annual basis are shown here.

1% 10 days—net 30 days = 18% per annum
2% 10 days—net 60 days = 14% per annum
2% 30 days—net 60 days = 24% per annum
3% 10 days—net 30 days = 54% per annum

Quantity Discounts

Quantity discounts are made available on the basis that it is more economical to process and ship fewer orders of greater size than many smaller orders. However, the small business owner must compare the carrying costs of a larger inventory with the quantity discount savings. Larger inventories may result in other problems, such as spoilage or obsolescence.

Two types of quantity discounts are found in business practice. One plan is the noncumulative quantity discount. Under the terms of this plan, quantity discounts are granted if a larger volume of merchandise is purchased in a single order. To illustrate, a supplier may put forward the following schedule.

Size of Order	Percent Discount on Order
Under a dozen	0%
1–2 dozen	2
3–4 dozen	4
5–6 dozen	6

The second plan is a cumulative quantity discount. This discount plan calls for the supplier to allow the purchaser a discount if purchases exceed a specified quantity or dollar amount over a predetermined time period. The time span may be a month, but a yearly basis is more common. For example, a manufacturer may permit a 3 percent discount if a small business firm's purchases total $5000 for a year.

Trade Discounts

Manufacturers in some lines of trade may establish a system that allows discounts off the list price or suggested retail price on the basis of their trade classification, that is, wholesaler or industrial buyer. These discounts are called **trade discounts**, and to qualify for them, a firm must perform some of the marketing functions for the manufacturer. These discounts are available to the purchaser regardless of the size of the order.

A manufacturer that sells to both wholesalers and industrial buyers may allow different percentage discounts to each based on the marketing functions performed for the manufacturer. Wholesalers store goods and sell to small users in the area and would be allowed a higher discount than the industrial buyer who purchases directly from the manufacturer. For example, the manufacturer may grant the wholesaler a 40 percent discount off the list price and the industrial buyer a 25 percent discount.

It is helpful to point out that trade discounts are often tied to catalog or price lists. Many suppliers publish comprehensive and costly catalogs at infrequent time periods. The wholesaler or manufacturer can use the same catalog or price list for different types of customers. For example, a manufacturer might publish a list price of a specific item at $10, then allow the wholesaler to take a 30 percent discount, the retailer a 20 percent discount, and the consumer a 10 percent discount. The discounts are often used to allow a business to adjust prices in a catalog or price list without having to reprint the entire catalog or price list. For example, an item might sell to wholesalers for $10 with a 20 percent discount. If the firm wishes to reduce the price for clearance, it may offer a 20 percent, 10 percent chain discount. Or if the firm wishes to increase the price, it may only offer a 10 percent discount on the item.

In other situations, suppliers may provide for a string of chain discounts available to the various classes of firms in the selling chain. In addition, a firm may qualify for more than one discount on a purchase depending on the services performed. Each additional level for which the firm qualifies is applied to the previous net amount. For example, a wholesaler may be offered a chain discount of 30, 20, and 10. Thus, the wholesaler would receive a discount off the manufacturer's list price of 30 percent less an additional 20 percent less an additional 10 percent. The chain discount allowed is calculated in the following manner.

Manufacturer's list price	$100
Less 30%	$ 30
	$ 70
Less 20%	$ 14
	$ 56
Less 10%	$ 5.60
Net price paid by wholesaler	$ 50.40

Seasonal Discount

Seasonal discounts are offered by suppliers during off-seasons. Before buying at lower prices, the small business owner should consider all aspects of the purchase, including disadvantages such as style change, overbuying, high inventory costs, spoilage, theft, and technical obsolescence.

SUMMARY OF KEY POINTS

1. Goals of purchasing include buying the right quality in the right quantity from a reputable supplier at the best price and at the right time to meet demand.

2. Purchasing policies must be created that will guide company personnel in the purchasing activities.

3. Purchasing procedures detail the specific actions necessary to complete the purchasing function. Procedures include request for materials or supplies, description of materials or supplies required, selection of potential vendors, determining price, the purchase order, follow-up on the purchase order, checking invoices, and maintenance of records and files.

4. One decision that must be made by the small business owner is the decision of whether to make components or complete products or buy them from suppliers.

5. Vendor analysis requires determining the best source of supply. Factors to be evaluated include dependability and reliability, services offered, number of vendors, vendor's location, terms of sale, and vendor's sales representatives.

6. The point at which title to goods passes must be established in the purchase transaction. When title passes may be determined by "f.o.b." seller or "f.o.b." buyer.

7. Consignment purchasing is a stockless purchasing system.

8. Types of discounts available in the purchasing process are cash discounts, quantity discounts, trade discounts, and seasonal discounts.

DISCUSSION QUESTIONS

1. What are the goals of purchasing?
2. Identify some of the areas for which purchasing policies should be set.
3. How would you explain the purchasing procedure to a small business owner?
4. What factors should the small business owner evaluate when choosing suppliers of materials and services?
5. Is it better for the small business manufacturer to make or buy the necessary components for a product? Explain.
6. Explain the importance of time in the purchase decision.
7. What is the significance of "f.o.b." seller and "f.o.b." buyer?
8. What is a consignment purchase?
9. Distinguish between a trade discount and a quantity discount.
10. Explain what is meant by the term, "1/10, net 30."

STUDENT PROJECTS

Interview one or several small business owners, and seek to obtain the following information from them.

1. What are some of the factors they consider most important when choosing vendors?
2. Do they handle goods on consignment? If so, what kinds of goods?
3. What is their opinion of purchase discounts?
4. What kinds of services do sales representatives provide?

CASE A

Arden's Gift Shops (A)

Mrs. Jean White is the manager of Arden's Gift Shops. Arden's Shops consist of the main gift shop and three smaller gift shops plus a warehouse, which are located in a tourist attraction complex owned by Philip Arden. The nature of the business is highly seasonal.

Not all shops carry the same merchandise. Anywhere from 6000 to 10,000 items may be carried in stock. The items range in price from less than $1 to higher prices for turquoise jewelry.

In addition to being the manager for 18 years, Mrs. White has also been the buyer for merchandise for all the shops for 16 years. She has been assisted in managing and purchasing for the last 2 years by Mrs. Barbara Adams. Mr. Arden oversees the operation of the tourist operation but leaves managing the shops and warehouse to Mrs. White. She and Mrs. Adams maintain close control over the operation, and both are very competent personnel.

In the firm, there is no standard inventory level set. For example, there is no determination of the number of different items to be stocked nor of the quantity levels for the particular items that are stocked. Consequently, there is no set time to order or reorder. All inventory and purchasing inventory are kept in the heads of the two buyers rather than being put into formalized policies and procedures. Purchasing decisions are based on the buyer's intuition.

It should be noted that the gift shop has always managed to show a profit.

QUESTION

What problems are indicated in the gift shop operation with regard to purchasing procedures?

CASE B

Wilson Manufacturing Company

Jim Wilson is the owner and president of Wilson Manufacturing Company. The company manufactures various types of pressure gauges. The firm was founded by his parents, and Jim literally "grew up" in the business. When his parents retired from active involvement in the business, Jim bought the business from them.

Since the company opened for business 35 years ago, the materials needed to manufacture the pressure gauges (such as dials and brass and steel cases) have been purchased from a single vendor, Harry Reeser. Harry has always been able to supply materials on schedule and fill rush orders promptly when the occasion demanded. Over the years, a healthy business relationship built on trust and dependability has been created between the Wilsons and Harry. Harry is five years from retirement.

While Jim is quite satisfied with Harry's reputation and performance as a supplier, he has received catalogs and sales visits from other suppliers of gauge parts that offer prices 8 to 10 percent lower than Harry's. Jim realizes that he is caught in a dilemma. On the one hand, he recognizes the sound business relationship that has been built up over 35 years between the Wilsons and Harry Reeser. On the other hand, he realizes that a savings of 8 to 10 percent could be put to work in other critical areas of the firm.

QUESTIONS

1. How do the goals of purchasing relate to Jim Wilson's situation?
2. What factors should Jim consider in evaluating whether to stay with Harry as the single supplier or switch to a new supplier?

SMALL BUSINESS ADMINISTRATION PUBLICATIONS

Management Aids (Free)

Business Plan for Small Manufacturers
Can You Lease or Buy Equipment?
Stock Control for Small Stores
Selling Products on Consignment

Small Business Management Series (For Sale)

Purchasing Management and Inventory Control for Small Business

Starting and Managing Series (For Sale)

U.S. Government Purchasing and Sales Directory

Business Basics

Retailing Buying Function
Inventory Management—Wholesale/Retail
Purchasing for Manufacturing Firms

CHAPTER THIRTEEN
INVENTORY CONTROL

LEARNING GOALS

After reading this chapter, you will understand:

1. That inventory control is important to small business because it reduces costs while aiding customer relations.
2. How keeping a record of customer requests for items not in stock aids in inventory control.
3. How the basic perpetual inventory system works and how some firms use specialized forms of perpetual inventory control.
4. How visual, periodic, and partial inventory control systems operate.
5. The importance of the two basic methods of physical inventory counts.
6. How to identify and clear slow-moving items in inventory.
7. The value of shelf space analysis and how it is performed.

KEY WORDS

Inventory

Perpetual inventory system

Bin tags

Sales ticket

Stub control

Floor sample control

Punched card control

Visual control

Periodic inventory system

Partial control system

Physical inventory count

Shelf space analysis

SMALL BUSINESS PROFILE

C. Vincent Phillips: Alkon Corporation

In "state-of-the-art" cement mixing, an operator selects the type of concrete and the amount to be mixed and starts the system. With that, a batch control system weighs out each of the various ingredients, checks the actual weight for accuracy, and loads the materials onto a truck with no further human intervention. Alkon Corporation's "Compu/Key" system also documents the weight, prepares a delivery ticket, manages inventory and communicates with other computers to receive orders or carry out other transactions. In 1970, concrete batch weighing systems were large, unreliable, and had to be custom designed and manufactured for each installation. C. Vincent Phillips formed Alkon Corporation that year, and introduced the first small, accurate, totally electronic system. In 1976, the microprocessor chip allowed a drastic reduction in the system's complexity. Today, the company holds a significant share of its market, with $4.4 million in sales in 1982. With future growth limited in the specialized Compu/Key market, Alkon is diversifying into a more broadly applicable product line of inventory control systems.

Source *There's No Business Like Small Business*, U.S. Small Business Administration, Washington, D.C. 1983

Retail and wholesale firms carry merchandise for resale, manufacturing firms carry raw materials and finished goods inventories, and service firms carry parts and supplies. All of these firms incur expenses that are a result of their **inventory.** How much inventory they carry and how well they control it is very important to their business.

COST OF INVENTORY

The major costs of inventory are from (1) storage facilities, (2) spoilage and obsolescence, (3) insurance, (4) handling, and (5) interest.

Storage Facilities

The larger the size of the inventory, the larger storage facilities must be to accommodate the merchandise. Land, building, or rental costs or all three are major expenditures for the small business. The requirements of storage also may vary in cost. For example, construction and maintenance of a sheet metal shed is much less expensive than construction and maintenance of cold storage facilities.

**The inventory in this store
is highly perishable.**

Spoilage and Obsolescence

Some inventories are perishable, and larger inventories of these items usually result in some losses from spoilage. Other goods are subject to obsolescence owing to fashion changes, for instance, clothing. Inventory items may also suffer from obsolescence because better products are introduced on the market, and the greater the amount of the item in stock, the greater the loss.

Insurance

Various types of insurance should be carried to provide coverage on the inventory, primarily fire and theft. Larger amounts of inventory mean higher insurance costs because premiums are based, in part, on the dollar value of the inventory.

Handling

Generally, the more inventory a small business carries, the more often it must be handled. This handling is an expense to the business in terms of costs of manpower, equipment, and damaged goods.

Interest

Inventory also requires an investment of funds. If the firm borrows money to maintain an inventory, it must pay interest on the borrowed funds. Even if

FIGURE 13–1
Good inventory control reduces costs and aids customer relations.

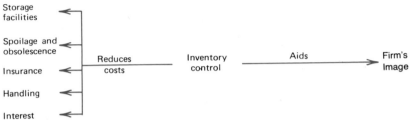

the business does not borrow funds, it is still considered an expense because it would be able to use the funds it has invested in inventory for other uses. Even putting the funds into a savings account would earn the firm money that it will not receive if it is tied up in inventory.

All these are costs that the business firm must sustain in order to maintain an adequate inventory. However, if the firm carries too much inventory, it will significantly increase these costs. In addition, if the firm does not perform good inventory control, it can sustain additional losses in these costs. (See Fig. 13–1.) For instance, one small retail appliance store discovered that it had several thousand dollars' worth of appliances that had been covered with other merchandise in a crowded storeroom for several years. The appliances were out of style and had to be sold at a large loss.

Poor inventory control encourages employee theft and prevents the business from recognizing shoplifting problems or even knowing how much is being lost to theft. Inadequate records of inventory cause problems in insurance claims in losses resulting from burglary. The small business that does not practice good inventory control may lose money it does not even know it is losing.

One example of how much a firm can lose without knowing about it is the case of a large store handling hardware and do-it-yourself items. The firm did not have an adequate inventory control system in its three stores in one city. It was notified by the police that three of its employees were caught in a police fencing operation run to trap thieves. The employees, it was later discovered, had stolen more than $100,000 of merchandise during the past year. The store had no idea it had lost any merchandise until the police uncovered the loss.

INVENTORY AND CUSTOMER RELATIONS

A small business must carry sufficient amounts of inventory in order to maintain good customer relations. Customers who go into a retail store several times and are told the store is out of a product soon develop a feeling that they won't be able to find what they want if they return. They will soon trade elsewhere. The service firm that makes customers wait for service while the business obtains parts or supplies will suffer the same fate from its customers. The wholesaler who is often out of products retailers order will find that these merchants will soon patronize other wholesalers. Customers of manufacturers who experience too many delayed delivery dates will also shift purchases to other manufacturers.

The idea, then, is to balance inventory costs and customer relations. The firm must maintain as small an inventory as possible to reduce costs, yet maintain an inventory that is adequate to satisfy customer needs. Good inventory control is the key.

REQUESTS FOR ITEMS NOT IN STOCK

As a part of their inventory control system, small business firms should keep a record of all requests for merchandise that they do not have in stock. Inadequate reorder points can be easily spotted through this type of record. If a specific item that is regularly carried in inventory appears more than once over a reasonable period of time on the report, the firm should consider setting the reorder point higher. If an item that the firm does not stock appears more than once over a reasonable period of time, the business should consider adding the item to inventory.

INVENTORY CONTROL SYSTEMS

A business firm may utilize three basic types of inventory control systems: (1) perpetual inventory systems, (2) visual systems, and (3) periodic and partial control systems.

Perpetual Inventory Systems

A basic **perpetual inventory system** is used by many types of small business firms, including manufacturers, wholesalers, retailers, and service establishments. In addition, specialized perpetual inventory systems are used by different types of businesses, particularly retail operations.

Basic Perpetual Inventory System

A basic perpetual inventory card is shown in Figure 13–2. Variations of this basic card are used by many small businesses. Some manufacturers, wholesalers, and service firms use **bin tags** that carry the same information as this card but are in the form of a tag. These tags are attached to the storage bin or shelf, and receipts and withdrawals of the item are noted on the tags when

FIGURE 13–2

Perpetual inventory card (grocery wholesaler).

Item Green Giant English Peas - 303 Can				
Reorder Point 100 cs		Order Amount 400 cs		Stock Control # CV-1604

In		Out		Balance
Date	Amount	Date	Amount	
				80
3/21	400			480
		4/1	60	420
		4/4	40	380

they are made. Retailers use several variations of the basic perpetual inventory system, which will be discussed later in this chapter.

The perpetual inventory card carries such general information as the name of the item, stock number, and reorder point. Every time additions to the inventory of this item are received from vendors, the number is recorded and added to the balance. Every time some of the items are issued or sold, the withdrawal is recorded and subtracted from the balance.

If the perpetual inventory method is used, a look at the balance at any time will reveal the amount of inventory on hand for this item. According to need, other information may be recorded on the card, such as price, amount ordered but not received, specifications, location in stockroom, and what department uses the inventory item.

Firms that have a relatively small number of items and a small number of transactions per day are ideal for perpetual inventory systems using these in-out-balance cards. It does not take a person too long to record about 50 purchases a day. However, in small stores that have a large variety of items or a large number of purchases each day or both, it takes a considerable amount of time to post the daily purchases to perpetual inventory cards. For example, the small drive-in grocery would find it very time-consuming to make a record of each item purchased and post them all to perpetual inventory cards.

Many firms with a wide range of inventory items and many additions and withdrawals each day have gone to computer-based inventory control. The same basic system is used in computer systems as is used in a manual operation. Instead of using perpetual inventory cards, the firm's personnel feed data on receipts and withdrawals of specific items into the computer, and a balance is retained in the computer's memory banks. Many of these firms tie their cash registers into their computer systems. As each sale is recorded on the cash register, it is also fed into the computer inventory control records.

The price of microcomputers has dropped during the past few years to such an extent that it is now feasible for almost all small businesses to perform their inventory control function on a computer.

Specialized Perpetual Inventory Systems in Retail Stores

Retail stores often use specialized systems for collecting and transferring information into their perpetual inventory systems. Some of the more common methods are (1) sales ticket control, (2) stub control, (3) floor sample control, and (4) punched card control.

Sales Ticket Control   **Sales tickets** are one method of collecting perpetual inventory sales information. Sales tickets are completed each time merchandise is sold, listing such information as department, number of items sold, type of item sold, unit price, tax, and total price. This ticket is then used for posting to the card or computer perpetual inventory system. The sales ticket is also useful in accounting control, such as cash control and sales taxes payable (see Fig. 13–3).

A good method for using sales tickets is to have a locked box with a slit in the top, and each time a sale is made, the clerk puts the ticket in the box. At the end of the day, the box is opened, and the total of the sales tickets is used as a check against the amount of cash in the register and the cash register tape. The sales tickets are then posted individually on perpetual inventory cards. When the inventory is checked against the perpetual inventory cards, any shortages are identified, and the manager immediately knows he or she has a theft problem.

Another method of using sales tickets for perpetual inventory control is common in some retail firms, such as automobile parts stores. A basic inventory is established on a yearly basis, and all items of the desired inventory are placed in stock. When a sale is made, a sales ticket is completed listing the part, its code number, and the number of units sold. Each day all items that appear on sales tickets are reordered to bring the inventory back to its original level. If the inventory on hand plus all items on order differs from the basic inventory, it is a warning signal to the manager that he or she has a theft or recording problem.

Stub Control   **Stub control** of perpetual inventory consists of attaching a two or more part stub to each item that is offered for sale. (See Fig. 13–4.) All the stub parts have such information as the department number, vendor code, types of merchandise, and any other coded information of value to the

FIGURE 13–3
A very simple sales ticket sold by most office supply firms.

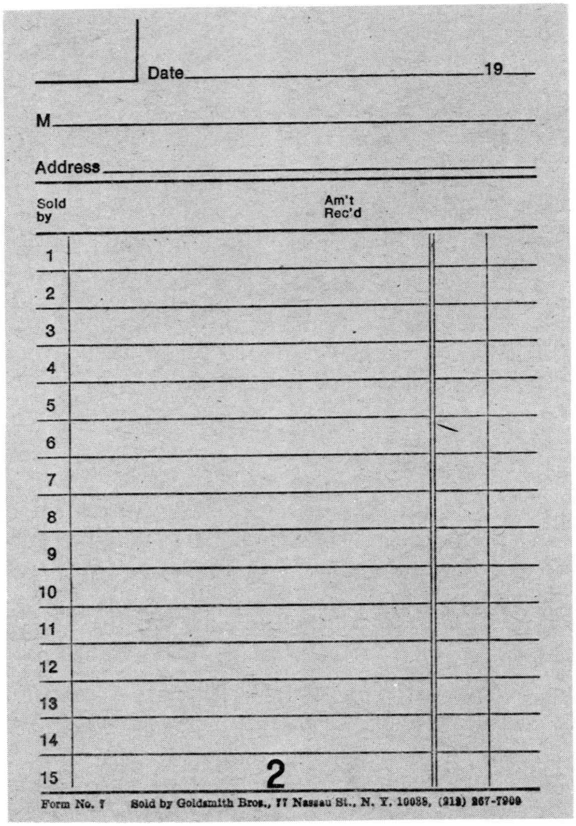
Date ______ 19__
M ______
Address ______
Sold by
Am't Rec'd

1			
2			
3			
4			
5			
6			
7			
8			
9			
10			
11			
12			
13			
14			
15	2		

Form No. 7 Sold by Goldsmith Bros., 77 Nassau St., N. Y. 10038, (212) 267-7900

inventory and accounting systems of the store. When the merchandise is sold, one part of the stub is removed and placed in a collection container. The removed stub is then used to post to the perpetual inventory system and in accounting control procedures. If the customer returns the merchandise, the stub remaining on the merchandise is used to restock the merchandise and correct accounting records.

Floor Sample Control **Floor sample control** is common to appliance and furniture type operations that place one of each item in stock (floor samples) in the showroom area and then fill customer orders from inventory. One method is to have small pads with consecutive numbers printed on each page. The pads may be numbered from 1 to 100, and the total number of merchandise items that are received in stock is attached to the floor sample. For example, an appliance store may receive 25 units of a specific model of

FIGURE 13–4

Sales stub inventory control.

refrigerator. Numbers 26 through 100 are removed from a printed pad and the numbers 1 through 25 are attached to the floor sample. Each time a clerk completes a sale, he or she removes a number. Consequently, sales personnel are able to look at the remaining numbers on the pad and know immediately how many are left in stock.

Punched Card Control   A **punched card control** system uses two or more part tags or standard computer punched cards attached to the merchandise for sale. When an item of merchandise is sold, a part of the tag or punched card is removed from the item and placed in a collection container. The tags or standard computer cards are fed into a special ticket-converting machine or automatic card sorter for sorting into categories. The cards are then fed into specialized tabulating equipment or a computer to record inventory and accounting control information.

Visual Control Systems

Many small firms feel they are unable to maintain a perpetual inventory system for various reasons—high volume of small-volume items, large stock of small-value items, lack of funds to pay personnel to maintain a perpetual system, or an unfounded belief that computer systems are excessively complicated and expensive (or all of these).

The small business manager often is very familiar with inventory and knows approximately how much should be on hand at any given time. A daily visual examination allows the manager to estimate how much should be ordered.

Visual control is probably the most common method of stock control in small business firms and is the least effective. Visual control works better for firms that have stable sales, large numbers of each item in stock, merchandise that can be obtained quickly from vendors, and merchandise that is segregated on shelves or in bins. Inability to determine shortages of items is a major disadvantage of the visual control system.

For example, one small business located near a school was losing several thousand dollars each year owing to shoplifting and never realized the extent of the problem until one of the authors set up an inventory control system for the business. Shortages in inventory revealed by the inventory control system indicated the extent of the problem. By installing several shoplifting prevention techniques, the firm was able to significantly increase its profit level.

Periodic and Partial Control Systems

Small business firms that feel they are unable to maintain perpetual systems because of inventory volume, size, or cost or all three may elect a **periodic inventory system** or **partial control system** in conjunction with the visual system.

The periodic control system involves recording purchases and inventory levels at reorder times. For example, a sporting goods merchant would record the amount of baseballs on hand. When he or she feels it is time to reorder, the number purchased and the number remaining in stock are recorded. This record tells the merchant what normal turnover period is for each item and gives the merchant some approximation of how many items are on hand based on this normal turnover. It also has a major weakness of not identifying shortages.

A closely related system involves taking a complete inventory count of the business and then at the end of some period (such as 3 months) taking the entire physical inventory count again. The difference between the first and the second inventory count is computed, and all purchases for the period are added to the balance. All items that have the same percentage markup are then put in a category (such as 20 percent markup items into one group and 30 percent markup items into another group). By taking the cost of all the items and applying the markup for each group, the firm can come somewhat close to what its sales should have been for the period. If the sales total for the period differs significantly from the projected sales figure, the firm then knows it probably has a theft problem.

In order to help identify shortages, but still not use a perpetual inventory system for all merchandise, some small business managers use a partial perpetual inventory system. They may keep perpetual inventory records on more expensive items or items of merchandise more prone to theft. Other low-value merchandise is maintained by visual or periodic inventory control.

Some small business managers attempt to identify shortages by keeping a perpetual inventory on part of their merchandise on a rotating basis. For example, one drug retailer takes a physical inventory count on one part of total stock, such as gift items. He then keeps a record of all gift item sales and purchases for a month's period. At the end of the month, the drug retailer then takes another physical inventory count. By adding purchases to starting inventory and deducting the ending inventory, he knows how many gifts should have been sold during the month. By applying markup on gifts and comparing the total to sale of gifts, he is able to identify shortages from employee or shoplifting theft. The revolving perpetual inventory also allows the drug retailer to (1) identify reorder points more accurately, (2) establish optimum order size more accurately, (3) spot slow-moving items, (4) institute greater control over items more susceptible to theft, and (5) identify sections of the store that have greatest losses of merchandise.

PHYSICAL INVENTORY COUNT

Every small business should perform a periodic inventory count. Even if the firm has a perpetual inventory system that is designed to provide inventory information on a continuous basis, it should still perform a **physical inven-**

An employee making a physical inventory count.

tory count to identify mistakes and shortages. There are two basic methods of performing inventory counts.

One method is to perform it on all inventory at regular intervals, at least once a year. Retailers often run special sales to reduce their inventory just before inventory time. They then bring employees in on an overtime basis when the store is normally closed to perform the inventory count. This method provides the most accurate income statement if prepared at the same time as the inventory count. The count is also checked against the perpetual inventory at this time.

One very efficient method is to have the firm's computer (microcomputers will perform this function) print out a complete list of all items in stock with the number that should be in stock listed and a space for what is counted in stock. One person calls out the item and the number in stock, and another person marks the number actually in stock on the list. The number that should be in stock is next to the number that is actually in stock, and any deviation is instantly noted.

SPECIAL INTEREST FEATURE

Microcomputer Inventory Control

The importance of inventory control to maintaining good customer relations and decreasing costs (which increases profit) has been discussed at length in this chapter. One of the more important functions of good inventory control is theft control. Without sufficient information about inventory, it is almost impossible to detect and pinpoint theft problems.

The number of items gone from inventory, sales amounts, and cash received must balance. If they do not balance, then there is an error or a theft problem. The business must investigate and determine which is the case. An inexpensive microcomputer can perform the inventory control function quickly and efficiently. It can also provide valuable information and reports that are usually too time-consuming and expensive when the inventory control function is performed by hand.

The normal software package (program) for inventory control costs between $200 and $1000. Some of the many functions it will perform are these.

1. Posts sales transactions and prints reports for inventory sales performance by product, by class of product, by salesperson, and so on. It provides information about the contribution of profit by each item or group of items.

2. Creates and prints purchase orders. Lists open purchase orders and suggests items that should be ordered.

3. Lists the complete inventory with amount, price, code, and other related information.

4. Keeps a perpetual inventory record.
5. Keeps a record of and prints a report that contains a complete list of all vendors.
6. Prints work sheets that contain a complete list of all inventory with number of items and a space for the physical inventory count.

Another method is to perform a count of a few items each week on a continuous basis. These continuous inventory counts provide an ongoing check against the perpetual inventory system. This method sometimes allows the identification of mistakes and shortages sooner than the periodic count.

SLOW-MOVING ITEMS

Items in inventory tend to turn over at widely different rates whether they are raw materials or finished goods inventory of manufacturers, merchandise of wholesalers, parts and supplies of service establishments, or goods of the retailer. The slower the turnover of items in inventory, generally, the greater the chance of loss owing to spoilage or obsolescence. A good inventory system is necessary to keep this loss at a minimum by identifying slow-moving items. Once the slow-moving items are identified, there are various means that a small business manager may employ to deal with them.

One possibility is to eliminate the item from inventory. An analysis should be made to determine the amount that this item contributes to profit each year, relative to the cost of keeping it in stock. Many items that are slow movers cannot be eliminated from stock. The firm's customers may expect them to carry the item, and it may affect customer relations and patronage if eliminated.

The most common method of dealing with slow-moving items is markdown. Markdown of merchandise is not only a method of clearing slow-moving merchandise but is also a good promotional technique. In fact, many retail stores offer markdowns on a wide range of merchandise at one time in order to maximize the promotional effect. Almost all retail stores engage in markdown sales, which are attempts to build customer patronage and store image as well as clear slow-moving items from inventory.

Markdowns may be the result of various factors. The firm may buy too many of the item in expectation of greater sales volume than is actually realized. They may price the item too high in relation to competitors. They may order too many as a result of poor inventory control. The sales personnel may be pushing the sale of another similar item and cause this other item to be slow in sales. Even the weather may have an effect on how fast a product sells, such as an unusually dry season's effect on umbrella sales.

Many times it is advisable to sell a particularly slow item below cost in order to clear it out of inventory. The cost of storage plus lost sales from not having a faster moving item in its place may make sale of the item at a price below cost desirable. For example, one men's clothing store kept a style of men's sports shirts in stock for 3 years after they had gone out of style. Even reducing the shirts to one fifth their original cost would not move them. The owner finally gave them to a charity in order to clear them from the shelf to have the space for more fashionable shirts.

SHELF SPACE ANALYSIS

Up to now, we have talked in terms of slow-moving items and have generally ignored profitability of products. As a simple illustration, a firm may sell 10 watches in a month at a gross profit of $2 each and still make more money on them than by selling 100 toys at a 10¢ gross profit per unit. Another factor that has not been taken into consideration is the amount of store space required to sell a specific item. The store just mentioned might be able to sell watches and rings in the same space it would require just to sell the toy.

A retail store has just so much space it may use to sell products. The firm must also pay for its selling area in the form of rent, depreciation, utilities, and so forth. Consequently, maintaining every square inch of selling space is a cost to the firm.

A technique called **shelf space analysis** is a means of measuring the profitability of each item in terms of turnover, profit per item, and amount of selling space required to sell the product.

To perform shelf space analysis, the firm must first measure each item it sells in terms of the amount of shelf space (in square inches) it occupies in the selling area. The average number of items it sells per month is then computed using beginning inventory plus all purchases for the year minus ending inventory and dividing by 12. Seasonal goods should be computed over the number of months they are actually carried in the selling area. Other seasonal goods may be carried in the same space during the other seasons. Examples are the following two items.

	Watches	Beach Balls
Beginning inventory	30	100
Purchases for year	50	1150
	80	1250
Less ending inventory	20	50
Total sold for year	60	1200
Divided by months in stock	5 (12 months)	300 (4 months)

The average cost of a unit plus markup is then computed to determine the average gross profit per unit sold. The average number of items sold per month times the per unit gross profit gives the gross profit per month.

	Watches	Beach Balls
Cost per unit	$20	$0.50
Times markup percentage	×50%	×40%
Equals gross profit per unit	$10	$0.20
Times units sold per month	×5	×300
Equals gross profit per month	$50	$60

The amount of shelf space required for each item is then computed and divided into the average monthly gross profit to determine the amount of gross profit per square inch of shelf space each item produces. The linear inches of the front of the shelf space can be used in place of square inches when it produces just as good an analysis, such as when the depth of all shelves are the same.

	Watches	Beach Balls
Shelf space occupied	15 by 20 inches	40 by 60 inches
Total shelf space occupied	300 square inches	2400 square inches
Gross profit per square inch of shelf space per month	$50 ÷ 300 = $.167 *or* 16.7¢	$60 ÷ 2400 = $.025 *or* 2.5¢

It is obvious in our example that watches are more profitable in terms of gross profit produced relative to selling area required.

This is a fairly simple process, but a more complex formula may be used that includes such items as storage cost, investment cost, spoilage and obsolescence costs, and frequency of stocking the items on the shelves. (See Fig. 13–5.)

It would appear that shelf space analysis would be a large undertaking for a store with a large number of inventory items, such as a drug or grocery retailer. The best method of achieving shelf space analysis in this type of store is to take a few items each week until the entire inventory analysis is completed. After the initial analysis is completed, it is necessary to perform the analysis on items that are added or on items that have undergone some drastic change in price, volume, or shelf space required.

Retailers are able to carry just so many goods on their shelves; however, at

FIGURE 13–5

Shelf space analysis.

Cost of item per unit	×	Percentage markup	=	Gross profit per unit
Gross profit per unit	×	Number of units sold during period	=	Total gross profit for period
Total gross profit	÷	Shelf space occupied in square inches	=	Gross profit per square inch for the period

the same time, they are continually offered new products to stock and sell. In this case, shelf space analysis is a method of measuring the profitability of different products and knowing which to eliminate. New products can be analyzed on the basis of cost, markup, shelf space required, and estimated volume of sales. As pointed out before, there are some items that a merchant is not able to eliminate because the customer expects the merchant to carry them. For example, a drugstore manager would probably carry tobacco products even if they were among the lowest gross profit items per square inch of shelf space. Walk-in trade for tobacco products increases other sales, and customers expect the store to stock them.

From this chapter, it should be obvious that the small business manager must maintain good inventory control techniques in order to maximize profit.

SUMMARY OF KEY POINTS

1. The major costs of inventory are from (a) store facilities, (b) spoilage and obsolescence, (c) insurance, (d) handling, and (e) interest.

2. A firm must maintain as small an inventory as possible to reduce costs, yet maintain an inventory that is adequate to satisfy customer needs.

3. A list should be kept that records all items requested by customers that are not in stock in order to evaluate reorder points and identify new items that should be carried in stock.

4. The basic perpetual inventory system records additions, withdrawals, and the balance on a continual basis.

5. Sales ticket control consists of the clerk's filling out a sales ticket for each sale, which is then posted to the perpetual inventory system at the end of each day.

6. Stub control consists of attaching a two or more part stub to the merchandise. One part of the stub is removed at the time of sale and used to post to the perpetual inventory control system.

7. Floor sample control is maintained by placing pads with numbers on them on the floor sample. One number is removed from the floor sample at the time of sale.

8. Punched card control is used when punched computer cards are attached to the merchandise and are removed at the time of sale for posting to inventory control records.

9. Visual control consists of viewing the inventory each day and reordering what looks low.

10. Periodic and partial control systems consist of taking inventory and adding purchases to see what should have been sold.

11. A physical inventory count should be taken on a periodic basis (at least once a year) to identify shortages.

12. The inventory control system should identify slow-moving items, which can be cleared from inventory in markdown sales.

13. Shelf space analysis measures the profitability of each inch of space of each product.

DISCUSSION QUESTIONS

1. Why is inventory control important from the standpoint of costs? From the standpoint of customer relations?

2. Why is the basic perpetual inventory control system called perpetual?

3. Which inventory control system is the most efficient? Why?

4. Briefly explain how the following work.
   a. Sales ticket control.
   b. Stub control.
   c. Floor sample control.
   d. Punched card control.

5. Which types of inventory control systems have failure to identify shortages as their major weakness?

6. What are the two basic methods of physical inventory counts?

7. What are some of the reasons for having markdowns of items in inventory?

8. Is there a good side to markdowns? Explain.

9. Why is shelf space analysis valuable?

10. What does shelf space analysis attempt to discover?

STUDENT PROJECT

Visit an area with a high concentration of retail stores such as a shopping center or mall. Select three small retail stores, and attempt to discover what types of inventory control system they use.

CASE A

Karen Kay Perfumes

Karen Kay last year leased space in a new shopping mall and opened a shop named Karen Kay Perfumes. She stocked her store with several brands of perfume, one top line of cosmetics, and a limited line of higher priced toiletries. The shop has a total of 60 different items offered for sale.

Sales have been good since she opened her shop, but she does not seem to be making as much profit as she feels she should, considering her volume of sales. In addition, she has had some complaints because a few customers were unable to purchase a particular item they wanted. Most of the time it was because Karen was out of the item in stock, and a few times because it was in stock, but she overlooked it and thought she was out.

Karen has exclusive distributorships for two brands of very expensive perfumes. She wants to get rid of one brand so that she will have room to add another perfume she feels has a very high profit potential. However, she is not sure which is the more profitable of the two brands she now carries. The following is some information she has gathered about the two brands:

	Brand X	Brand Y
Total yearly bottle sales	144	420
Cost per bottle	$15	$10
Markup percentage	100%	100%
Shelf space occupied	15 by 10 inches	20 by 10 inches

The difference in shelf space used for the two perfumes is the result of Brand Y's requiring Karen to exhibit its perfume in a special display device on the shelf.

QUESTIONS

1. Does Karen need some type of inventory control? Explain.
2. What type of inventory control system would you suggest?
3. If she uses a perpetual inventory system, what kind would you suggest?
4. Would you suggest a physical inventory count and, if so, what type?
5. Perform a shelf space analysis on Brands X and Y. Which should Karen eliminate?
6. How would you suggest she dispose of current stock of the brand you have chosen to eliminate?

CASE B

Martha's Office Supply

Martha Molina owns and manages a rather large office supply firm (the inventory does not include office furniture). The store handles around 300 different products and makes several hundred sales transactions each day. The firm is moderately profitable, but is not making as much money as Martha thinks it should, considering the volume of business.

Each time the clerk makes a sale, the clerk fills in a two-page form that gives the items that were sold and their price. One page is given to the customer, and the other is retained. At the end of the day, Martha totals all the sales tickets and checks the total against the amount of money in the cash register. It usually is the same amount, but sometimes there is a two- or three-dollar deviation.

Martha checks the shelves each day and notes on a pad the items she wants to reorder because the stock on the shelf looks low. There have been times when an item that was ordered came in, and Martha discovered she already had a box or two in the storeroom. In addition, she has had some customers ask for a product that she usually carries in stock and discovers she does not have any on hand.

Martha knows she needs some sort of inventory control system but is not sure what type of system she needs. She has asked you for advice.

QUESTIONS

1. If Martha maintains an inventory control system manually, what kind of inventory control system will you recommend to Martha?
2. Would you recommend a computer control system? If you do, what would be your reasons?
3. What would lead you to believe that she has an inventory problem?
4. What other recommendations might you make to Martha?
5. Do you think shelf space analysis would be beneficial to Martha? Explain.

SMALL BUSINESS ADMINISTRATION PUBLICATIONS

Free

Keeping Records in Small Business
Stock Control for Small Stores
Inventory Management

For Sale

Purchasing Management and Inventory Control for Small Business
Inventory Management—Manufacturing/Service
Inventory and Scheduling Techniques

CHAPTER FOURTEEN
RISK, INSURANCE, AND THEFT

LEARNING GOALS

After reading this chapter, you will understand:

1. That all small businesses face risks on a daily basis.
2. That small businesses control risk by (a) avoiding the risk, (b) reducing the risk, (c) assuming the risk, and (d) shifting the risk.
3. Small businesses often need fire, theft, liability, loss of earning power, surety, automobile, and life insurance.
4. The difference between the three basic types of life insurance—whole life, endowment, and term.
5. The various benefits a business may derive from life insurance and the relative cost of each type.
6. That there are different types of people who are shoplifters.
7. The different methods you may use to discourage shoplifting.
8. That employee theft is a major problem in business, that there are different methods employees use to steal, and that there are various ways to discourage employee theft.
9. How to discourage burglary.

KEY WORDS

Risk	Surety insurance
Subcontracting	Automobile insurance
Hedging	Life insurance
Fire insurance	Shoplifting
Theft insurance	Employee theft
Liability insurance	Burglary
Loss of earning power	Burglar alarm systems

SMALL BUSINESS PROFILE

Marolyn Schwartz: I.M. Cookie Company

The Fleet-Footed Monster Cookie

Specially delivered chocolate-chip cookies the size of a pizza are turning up at management meetings, office birthday parties and all manner of other places. They are the brainchild of New Yorker Marolyn Schwartz.

Schwartz, 31, a former executive in the rock-and-roll music business, first baked the huge cookies for friends when she found herself at home with an infant daughter and time on her hands. Several friends commented that the cookie, which is 13 inches across, cuts like a pizza and serves more than 20, would be a perfect snack for meetings. The cookies were always a hit. "I use only natural ingredients, and each cookie contains a whole pound of chocolate chips," Schwartz says.

Last summer, Schwartz turned her baking into a business, the I.M. Cookie Company, using her daughter's initials. She launched a delivery service and ran a small ad in *New York* magazine, featuring the service's name, The Cookie Courier.

As orders came in and volume increased, Schwartz worked harder and longer. "I had started mixing all the cookies by hand with a wooden spoon, and I resisted using any machines because I kept telling myself, 'That must be my magic.'"

Her husband, Jerome, an accountant whose father is a baker, finally talked her into buying a mechanical mixer. "I realized that if the business was to succeed, I would have to make the changes growth demanded," says Schwartz, who was delighted to find that the machine-mixed cookies tasted just as good.

Orders continued to increase. "Even with some help, Christmas was a round-the-clock operation, and I was afraid my oven would give out from constant use," she says.

In January she moved the operation from her Manhattan residence to a small store nearby on Ninth Avenue. With a $5,000 loan from friends and relatives, she equipped it with commercial mixers and ovens. "That was a good move," she says, "because Valentine's Day was busier than Christmas."

Her staff now totals six, and her line of cookies has expanded to chocolate with chocolate chips, peanut butter chip, oatmeal, a giant brownie and others. Schwartz also makes fruit muffins and sells an assortment of gift packages of small cookies.

The large cookies come in colored wrappings with ribbons and greetings. They are packed for shipping according to the distance. The Cookie Courier has filled orders for members of Congress and Hollywood stars and has even shipped a cookie to London—for $80. A cookie costs $24 in New York, where delivery is by cab, and $25 to $35 if delivered elsewhere in the U.S.

"I love my work," says Schwartz, who says she is always tempted to sample her products. "We grossed $125,000 in the first six months of 1982, and I expect sales to double in the second half of the year."

Source   "The Fleet-Footed Monster Cookie," *Nation's Business*, 1982. Reprinted by permission from Nation's Business, August, 1982. Copyright 1982 by Nation's Business, Chamber of Commerce of the United States.

Small business owners face risk on a continuing basis. **Risk** to small business owners exists in many forms. Every time they purchase merchandise, they take a risk that it will not sell. They face a risk every time the delivery driver drives the company truck. This list is almost endless. Many of the risks to which the small business is exposed are major risks that could result in failure of the business.

RISK CONTROL

Small business owners must control risks if their businesses are to survive and prosper. There are four basic methods by which they are able to deal with risks: (1) avoid the risk, (2) reduce the risk, (3) assume the risk, and (4) shift the risk (see Fig. 14–1).

Avoid the Risk

Sometimes it is possible for a small business to avoid risks, particularly high-level risks. A small business owner may avoid risks by substitution, screening, or elimination or all three.

Substitution
A small business may avoid risk by substituting high-risk materials and processes with low-risk materials and processes. For example, a manufacturer

FIGURE 14–1
Risk control in small business.

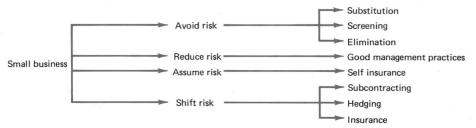

using a highly explosive chemical in the manufacturing process may find it is possible to substitute a chemical that is safer and achieves the same results.

Screening

The small business owner may avoid risk by screening out high-risk items. To illustrate, a small business should not extend credit to everyone; rather, it should screen out high-risk individuals to aid in helping reduce bad debt losses.

Elimination

Sometimes the small business is able to avoid risk by elimination of high-level risks. The firm that requires employees to wear eye goggles when operating a grinder is eliminating one chance of injury to the employee.

Reduce the Risk

Many risks the small business faces may be greatly reduced with good management practices. To illustrate, periodic inspections and training often contribute greatly to reducing risk of injury to customers and employees. Good hiring procedures help reduce the risk of employee theft.

Even when risks are shifted to others, as in the case of insurance, good management practices can still reduce the risks and lower the cost of insurance to the business.

Assume the Risk

Some small businesses assume certain risks because it is either impossible to avoid the risk or too costly to shift the risk to someone else. Often some types of insurance cost too much to justify the protection. For example, shoplifting insurance premiums are often too expensive for the purpose they serve. The small business may elect not to carry this insurance, but rather to institute as many deterrents to shoplifting as are practical. There are many risks that the small business must face on a continuing basis. Often the only thing the business can do is practice good management in order to reduce the risk as much as possible.

To illustrate, a small women's clothing store must purchase clothing several months in advance of its being sold. It is often very difficult to determine what fashions will be so far in advance. If the store purchases the wrong style of clothing, it may lose a considerable amount of money. To reduce the risk it must take, the store needs to evaluate continually its customers' tastes, study the market, and find out what authorities in the fashion field are predicting.

Shift the Risk

The small business owner may shift many risks to other persons by subcontracting, hedging, and insurance.

Subcontracting

A small business may be willing to perform certain functions, but may feel other functions are too high a risk for the capabilities of the business. To illustrate, a small contracting firm may feel that it has the ability to perform adequately all construction activities on a new building except the electrical work. To avoid the risk of failure on electrical work and still get the contract, the small business may bid on the contract and **subcontract** the electrical work to another firm for a specified price.

Hedging

Small business firms that deal in goods traded on the commodity market often shift the risk of price fluctuations by **hedging.** For example, a cattle feedlot may buy and sell cattle futures in the commodity market in order to avoid price fluctuations that could ruin the company.

Making Investments Today That Will Pay off later

Insurance

The most ~~common~~ *popular* method of shifting risk in small businesses is by purchasing insurance. For premium payments, insurance companies are willing to insure a business against a wide range of risks.

The small business may shift the entire risk or a part of the risk. It usually depends on the probability of the risks occurring and the cost of shifting the risk.

TYPES OF INSURANCE FOR SMALL BUSINESS

The principal types of insurance used by small businesses are fire, theft, liability, loss of earning power, surety, automobile, and life (see Fig. 14–2).

FIGURE 14–2
Types of risks shifted to insurance companies.

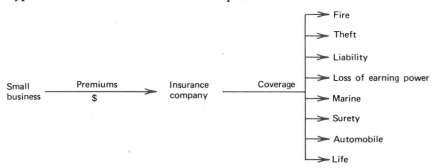

Fire

Fire insurance policies insure the small business from loss due to fire and lightning. Both the building and its contents may be insured in a policy. In addition, a small business may obtain insurance against all the loss or part of the loss. Most small businesses carry fire insurance against part of the loss due to the difference in cost. For example, a small business may have 90 percent coverage, in which case, the insurance company pays for 90 percent of the loss and the small business pays for the other 10 percent of the loss.

Additional riders may be purchased to accompany the fire insurance policy. For an additional premium, the small business firm may purchase insurance against explosion, riot, windstorm, hail, aircraft and vehicle-caused damage, and smoke damage.

There is a growing concern among fire fighters in the United States over the rapidly increasing number of arson fires. Mentally ill persons who set fires have always been a problem; however, most of the increase is believed to be due to property owners themselves. For example, the owner of one small store who was floundering financially was sentenced by a jury to 2 years in prison when fire fighters discovered the fire in his store was due to a cup full of gasoline with a candle in it. In addition to accidental fires, the small business person may face a risk of having the firm's property damaged by the acts of adjoining property owners. Also, the fire insurance premium of the small business is determined by the statistics of fires in its city, which may result in higher premiums.

Theft

The small business firm may purchase **theft insurance** for all types of thefts. It may be protected against loss from theft by persons outside (burglary and robbery) and inside (employee theft) the business. Small businesses with employees who handle money often insure against embezzlement of funds by bonding these employees.

Liability

Owners of small business firms may be liable for (1) their own acts, (2) acts of their employees while at work, (3) conditions within the business, or (4) products they manufacture or sell, or all of these. If an individual is injured while on the firm's premises, the business is liable for damages if the injury is the result of neglect. For example, if a customer fell and was seriously injured because of a broken step, the business would be liable. Also, the business would be liable for damages if an employee who was driving the delivery truck ran a stop light and injured the occupant of another automobile.

Good management practices are important to keeping down liability claims and premiums. For example, one firm did not check the driving record of employees it hired that were to drive on company business. One employee had a very bad driving record and, while driving himself and another employee, passed in a no passing zone. A head-on collision killed the passenger, and a very large judgment against the business resulted because it had failed to check the driving record of the driver.

Liability insurance is one of the most important forms of insurance for the small business to carry. Injuries to individuals often result in very large damages being awarded by the courts against the business. To illustrate, an accident that caused the death of a person, such as the delivery employee's running the red light, would usually amount to very large sums, often in excess of $100,000. Very few small businesses are able to sustain this type of loss. In addition, unlimited liability for the general partner and the sole proprietor may not only result in business failure but may also put them personally in debt for long periods of time.

There are many types of coverage by liability insurance. Some of the forms of liability coverage are damages resulting from elevator operations, druggists' mistakes, physicians' malpractice, and contractor accidents.

Insurance to protect against product liability is very important to most retailers and manufacturers. For example, it was claimed that a fire had been started by a defective television set in a building. Both the manufacturer and the retailer who sold the set were involved in an expensive damage suit. A doctor, hospital, and manufacturer were sued because a patient claimed that failure of a certain piece of equipment caused permanent damages to a patient. This suit is still in litigation 8 years later. Even if litigation is resolved in favor of the retailer or manufacturer, or both, they can incur considerable expense in legal fees. Insurance companies usually provide legal representation to clients who carry their liability insurance.

It is also important that the small business purchase sufficient amounts of liability insurance. The small business may have a $50,000 liability policy against losses, but this does not limit the amount of the judgment that may be obtained against the business in court. If the same business were to sustain a $100,000 judgment, then the insurance company would pay only $50,000, and the small business would be required to pay the rest.

Loss of Earning Power

The small business firm may sustain losses not only to physical aspects of the business but also to its ability to earn income. Loss of income may be very damaging and can result in failure of the business in some cases. For example, a fire might cause the business to cease operations for several months, but the need for income to the owner still exists and may not be covered by the fire insurance policy. Also, the owner of a business might sustain an injury that would prevent him or her from working in the business, resulting in the loss of income.

Insurance covering **loss of earning power** may be purchased for many different occurrences. The owner may purchase disability insurance, which provides against loss from disability. He or she may also purchase insurance against loss of income due to the business's not operating as a result of property damages. Loss of income may prevent the owner from meeting debt payments.

Surety Insurance

Some types of small business firms obtain bonding, **surety insurance,** to assure their customers of their ability to complete contracts. To illustrate, a small business contracting company may bond itself against losses to customers arising from its failure to complete contracts. If it fails to complete a contract, the bonding company will hire some other business to complete the terms of the contract. It is common in some industries that a business must bond itself or find it very difficult to obtain business, as in the construction industry.

Automobile Insurance

Automobile insurance is in reality another form of property and liability insurance. There are several types of property insurance available covering the automobile, such as collision, theft, fire, glass breakage, and damages from malicious mischief. Automobile liability insurance covers other peoples' property, other automobiles, persons in other vehicles, and persons in the insured automobile.

Property type automobile insurance often has a deductible clause. For example, a small business may carry $100 deductible on collision. If the car is damaged in an accident, the owner must pay the first $100, and the insurance company pays anything above $100 of the damages.

Small businesses may feel that it is not economical to carry property type insurance on their automobiles and trucks after they are several years old. However, a small business should carry liability on its vehicles regardless of age. Liability claims may be so expensive that they ruin a business. In fact, many states require businesses and individuals to carry liability insurance to protect other people.

Cost of Protection

Insurance premiums differ by coverage, type of business, and location. However, adequate coverage is a significant expense for most small businesses. One small fast-food hamburger restaurant currently spends $2700 in premiums each year just for property and liability insurance (including $300,000 personal injury liability). A feed and seed ranch store is spending $3500 a year in premiums. To most small businesses, this is a major expense; however, when you consider the protection it provides against loss, it is well worth the cost. Businesses face many losses that could easily bankrupt them.

Life Insurance

Many people feel that **life insurance** is for individuals and is not important to business firms. This is not true, particularly in the case of small business firms. If a general partner or sole proprietor dies, the form of ownership ceases to exist, and the sale or transition usually results in some loss. Even if it is a corporation, the death of a principal officer often creates some problems and losses. In many partnerships, the firm may carry life insurance on the partners as a means of the other partners' having the funds with which to buy out the partner in order to create a new partnership.

Some of the benefits derived from life insurance by a small business are these.

1. Ensures that immediate funds are available to meet taxes, debts, and other expenses.
2. Provides an income for the heirs of the small business person and does not drain cash from the business.
3. Allows for a more equitable distribution of the property values to the heirs.
4. Enables the executor, administrator, or trustee to dispose of the business to best advantage if the family is not taking over.
5. Puts the heirs on a sound financial footing if they are assuming direction of the business.
6. Stabilizes the credit of the business.
7. Helps maintain good employee relations by removing uncertainties and hazards.[1]

It is not at all unusual for a person to build a very profitable business and then have it sold at less than it is worth at his or her death. When the businessperson dies, the estate must pay estate taxes. Often the businessperson has considerable assets but not large sums of cash. In order to pay the estate taxes, the heirs often must sell the business to raise the cash. The time that is allowed to raise the cash is often not sufficient to get the best price for the business. Rush sales usually result in a low price.

There are all types of attachments that can be added to life insurance policies, such as a rider that provides for insurance premiums to be waived in case of disability of the person paying the premium. However, there are only three basic categories of life insurance policies: whole life, endowment, and term.

---

[1] *Business Life Insurance*, Management Aid, no. 222 (Washington, D.C.: Small Business Administration, 1975).

Whole Life

Whole life insurance insures an individual for the remainder of his or her life as long as premium payments are maintained. Usually, premium payments continue until the person dies or reaches 100 years of age. However, there are exceptions in that the person may pay the entire premium at one time or compact the payments into a limited time, such as 20 years. The amount of the premiums is based on the age of the insured when the policy is first taken out. An individual, at 25 years of age, would expect to pay premiums for many more years than a person 50 years of age. The younger the individual, the lower the cost of premiums. When the insured dies, the heirs are paid the face value of the policy.

Whole life insurance also has a cash or loan value. The policyholder may obtain cash or a loan on the policy after it has been in effect for a specified length of time, usually 3 years. The longer premiums are paid, the greater the cash or loan value. If the policyholder takes out a loan, the amount of the loan is subtracted from the face value if he or she dies before it is repaid. Often interest rates on policy loans are lower than the market rate. Many owners of small businesses have found insurance policy loans to be a cheap source of debt capital.

Endowment

Endowment insurance policies insure the individual for a specific period of time. If he or she dies during that period of time, the heirs are paid the face value of the policy. However, if the individual does not die, he or she is paid the face value of the policy at the end of the specified period. Premiums are usually paid for the entire period of coverage. Although it is not common, the insured may also elect to pay one lump sum payment, or compact the premiums into a shorter period of time than the coverage.

Endowment insurance premiums are also based on the age of the insured when the policy is purchased and the time period of the policy. Endowment insurance also has a cash or loan value. For most small businesspersons, endowment insurance is not the best type of life insurance to obtain because of the cost of premiums.

Term

Term life insurance insures an individual for a specific period of time and then terminates. The term policy may be for any length of time, but the most common period is 5 years. The insured pays premiums on a regular basis for 5 years, and if he or she dies within the 5-year period, the insurance company pays the full face amount to the heirs. The cost of premiums is based on life expectancy for the individual's age during the 5-year period. Term life insurance does not have a cash or loan value.

Another type of term life insurance is decreasing term. This type of insurance is popular with homeowners. If they borrow a specific amount of money to purchase a home, say $30,000 for 25 years, then they take out a decreasing term insurance policy on the life of the main provider in the family. The term

FIGURE 14–3

Annual premiums for various types of insurance.

Type of Insurance (no special riders)	Yearly Premium per $1000 at Age 25
Whole life	$11.44
Endowment with maturity at age 65	20.00
5-year term	3.49
25-year decreasing term	2.51

policy would be valued at $30,000 and decrease in the same proportion as the home loan over the 25-year period. Small business owners sometimes find decreasing term insurance very attractive to protect payment of their loans on land and buildings.

Term insurance is the best type of life insurance for most small businesses because of the lower cost of premiums.

Cost of Life Insurance

The cost of life insurance varies by type of insurance, company, age, and riders added to the policy. As an illustration of the differences between types of insurance, one large insurance company charges the yearly premiums shown in Figure 14–3 for each $1000 of the face value of the policy for a person 25 years of age.

SHOPLIFTING

Authorities report that business crime in the United States is currently amounting to more than $50 billion each year. This amounts to about $220 for each man, woman, and child in the United States. **Shoplifting** accounts for a large part of this loss. Shoplifting is a major problem for retail stores. Department stores continually try to control shoplifting and still estimate they lose between 1 and 2 percent of their total sales to shoplifting. Small business retail firms that do not make a continuing effort to control shoplifting undoubtedly lose much more to shoplifters.

Shoplifting is not only a burden to the business firm, but it is also a cost to every consumer. Losses due to shoplifting are a cost of business, and retail stores pass this cost on to their customers in the form of higher prices. In addition, they must pass on to the consumer the more than $14 billion per year they spend trying to control various types of theft. Many small businesses that close their doors each year report they were forced to do so as a result of employee and customer theft.

Types of Shoplifters

There are several different types of shoplifters; in fact, most are amateurs rather than professionals. Some of the types of shoplifters are (1) juveniles, (2) housewives, (3) psychologically sick persons, (4) vagrants, (5) addicts, and (6) professionals.

Juveniles account for more than half of all shoplifting. Almost all juvenile shoplifting occurs, not because of need of the goods, but from dares or for "kicks." The problem has become so bad around large high schools that some merchants will not allow more than a few students in their store at a time.

Women comprise the largest number of adult shoplifters. Most of the women who are caught shoplifting are married women. The reason is probably because women traditionally have done a major part of the shopping for their families. Most of these women shoplift on impulse and, if caught early, will stop before it becomes a regular pattern of behavior.

Some individuals shoplift for psychological reasons. The more common name for this group is *kleptomaniacs*. The value of the goods is seldom any motivation for this group. Their motivation is the act of stealing. These individuals are in dire need of psychological therapy. If being caught results in their receiving psychiatric attention, the merchant has done them a service.

Vagrants and habitual drunkards shoplift because of a real need. They usually steal for food, drink, and clothing. This group is usually the easiest to detect because of appearance and clumsiness.

Narcotic addicts must have large sums of money daily to support their habit. Some of these individuals obtain money by shoplifting items and selling them for money. Of all the shoplifters, this group is usually the most dangerous for the merchant to apprehend.

The professional engages in shoplifting strictly for the money obtained by "fencing" stolen goods. This individual is also the most adept at shoplifting and is usually difficult to detect. The professional shoplifter is also adept at picking the easiest stores from which to steal. As a result, the store owner who does not practice good shoplifting prevention techniques is more likely to be the target of the professional shoplifter than the store owner who does practice good prevention techniques. The professional shoplifter may also be a member of a crime organization. These shoplifters usually have a ready market for their stolen goods and, often, an organization that helps them out with bail and attorneys when they are arrested.

Prevention of Shoplifting

Often merchants may have a serious shoplifting problem and not even know the problem exists. Consequently, one of the most important aspects of shoplifting control is to recognize it as a problem and also know the extent of the problem. This can best be achieved by adequate records and a good inventory control system. The merchant who keeps good records of sales, purchases, and inventory will recognize if merchandise is getting out of the store without anyone's paying for it. By this method, the merchant is able to determine the extent of losses due to shoplifting and employee theft.

There are many things a merchant can do to help prevent shoplifting, but the most effective is a sales force trained in shoplifting detection. Another major weapon for discouraging shoplifting is a consistent policy of prosecuting all shoplifters. Persons caught shoplifting usually have some type of "heartrending story" and claim it is their first time. Most of the time it is not true, and even if it is, letting them get by with it usually encourages them to do it again. Stores that have a reputation for apprehending and prosecuting shoplifters are usually shunned by professionals and, to some extent, by many amateurs.

Some other practices that can help reduce shoplifting losses are these.

1. Post signs around the store saying that shoplifters are prosecuted by the store. One store posted the number of shoplifters it had caught and prosecuted as of that date and found it to be very effective.

2. Keep small expensive items in an enclosed display case and near where a clerk can see it at all times.

3. Have clerks keep a watchful eye on rest rooms and fitting rooms.

4. Keep unused checkout lanes closed.

5. If possible, post a guard at the exit door. Keep the number of exits as few as possible.

6. Have an adequate number of salespeople at all times. Part-time help can be valuable in rush periods.

7. Large convex mirrors placed around the store and two-way mirrors are good devices for reducing shoplifting.

8. Large stores often find that two-way radios, closed circuit television, and store detectives are helpful.

Mirrors help deter shoplifting.

To inhibit the amateur shoplifter, a store owner may find that simple devices and techniques may be of help in reducing shoplifting. To illustrate, one of the authors assisted a small store that had an extremely bad shoplifting and employee theft problem. The store was in such bad shape financially that the author obtained an old home movie camera, installed a small red bulb in the front of it, wired the bulb so that it could be plugged into an electrical socket, mounted the camera in a prominent place, and placed a sign below it that said the store was electronically surveyed to prevent shoplifting. This simple device proved to be so effective in frightening amateur shoplifters that the night after the second day it was installed, someone fired a rifle shot through a door window into the camera.

One of the more effective means of preventing shoplifting is being used by many clothing stores. A 1-by-3-inch tag imbedded with a simple microwave transmitter the size of a pencil point is attached to the items of clothing. The tag can only be removed by the cashier with special shears. Anyone leaving the store without having the tag removed sets off an alarm from a hidden receiver. Cashiers must be very conscientious in removing the tags. One woman sued a clothing store when the clerk forgot to remove a tag and the alarm sounded as she left the store. She was detained by store personnel until the mistake was discovered.

One form of shoplifting is what is called "ticket switching." Some shoplifters change price tags or exchange them with a cheaper item. Some methods of preventing ticket switching are as follows.

1. Hide an extra price tag on the merchandise.
2. Place hard-to-break strings on tags.
3. Use gummed labels that tear apart when removed.
4. Use rubber stamps or machines to mark tags; do not use pencils.
5. Use special type staples when attaching price tags so clerks will know if a tag has been removed and restapled.

Merchants must be very careful in apprehending shoplifters so that they do not leave themselves open to lawsuits for false arrest. In some states they must wait until the shoplifter is out of the store to detain and have him or her arrested. The shoplifter may claim that he or she intended to pay for the merchandise, and it is up to the merchant to prove otherwise. There have been cases where the item was concealed under the person's clothing and the individual maintained successfully in court that he or she was still going to pay for the item before leaving. Also, sometimes a shoplifter will have a confederate and pass the merchandise on to the other person before leaving the store. Fortunately, many states have adopted new legislation aimed at protecting the merchant from so much risk of suits for false arrest. These new laws often have "willful concealment" clauses, which permit the merchant to move on the shoplifter before the shoplifter leaves the premises. Every small business person should check the law in his or her state. In addition, local police departments are usually able to provide valuable advice on shoplifting prevention and prosecution.

EMPLOYEE THEFT

Everyone likes to think his or her employees are honest, particularly small business owners, because they are usually close to their employees. Unfortunately, **employee theft** is widespread and accounts for business losses in the billions of dollars each year. Most authorities claim that employee theft accounts for more losses than either shoplifting or burglary.

As was the case with shoplifting, many small business owners don't even know they have a problem with employee theft. For example, one small grocery store recorded an almost unbelievable theft record by having $59,000 cost of goods sold and sales of only $56,000 for one year. The owner was convinced employee theft was not a factor. It turned out that two nephews had pocketed several thousand dollars while working the cash registers during the year. In another case, an employer found that his trusted employee had been systematically pocketing $100 a week for several years. One of the most important factors in stopping employee theft is keeping adequate records of sales, purchases, and inventory to determine if a problem exists and, if it does, the extent of the problem.

Employee thefts may occur by several different methods. Many times employees will carry merchandise out of the business in pockets, in lunch boxes, or hidden somewhere on their person. Employees sometimes leave merchandise in trash boxes carried out of the business. They return at night and recover the merchandise.

SPECIAL INTEREST FEATURE

Lie Detectors

Two very controversial devices that are sometimes used to help prevent employee theft are the polygraph and the voice stress analyzer. The polygraph measures heartbeat, respiration, and skin response with the theory that a lie will cause a marked change in the pattern of these body functions. The voice stress analyzer measures the human voice for "microtremors" that may indicate stress when a person is not telling the truth.

No authority claims either machine is 100 percent accurate. Tests over the years indicate the polygraph to be somewhere between 85 percent and 90 percent accurate. The new voice stress analyzer differs in reliability according to which expert you are talking to. Some experts claim it is no better than a flip of a coin. Others claim it is at least as accurate as the polygraph and probably higher. Some people question the potential ethical misuse of the voice stress analyzer by pointing out that it can be administered without the knowledge of the subject (it is illegal in some states).

A growing number of firms use these devices to screen applicants for employment and to control employee theft. Some persons question the use of the devices. They point out that they are not 100 percent accurate, are sometimes run by incompetent operators, have been used by unethical persons to learn personal matters not related to the job, and are a crutch for the business that does not have adequate financial and inventory control systems. In addition, fear of the devices or the questions or both has caused completely honest persons who would make excellent employees to withdraw their applications for employment. Others feel that if these devices are used correctly, it is ethical to use them and that they are an effective and valuable aid in controlling a serious problem, employee theft.

One person found 14 watches in a box behind a large discount house when he was collecting boxes to store some of his personal belongings. When he returned them to the store, the owner was completely unaware any watches were missing. A restaurant owner found several top-quality steaks wrapped in a plastic bag when searching the garbage for knives, forks, and spoons. Employee theft may also take the form of salespeople's charging friends or accomplices lower prices or not charging for all the goods they purchase.

Some stores sell damaged goods to employees. Employees have been known to remove a part from a piece of merchandise, buy it at a greatly reduced price, and then restore the part when they get it home.

Cash thefts by employees also may occur in different ways. Clerks may not register all sales and pocket the cash. Some shortchange customers and pocket the extra cash. This practice is particularly bad in that the business may also lose customers. Some employee theft occurs in the form of embezzlement through manipulation of accounting books and checks.

Most employee theft is done by people who would never think of committing any other type of crime and do not consider themselves to be dishonest. They rationalize their theft in various ways with the most common excuse being that the business is not paying them what they are really worth and it is a way of supplementing their salary. This is why some small business persons are completely taken by surprise when they discover an employee, who they thought was incapable of stealing, stealing from the business.

The best way to prevent employee theft is be aware that a problem exists. Good accounting records, good cash control procedures, and having a good inventory control system are the keys to controlling theft. Without these a small business can go bankrupt and never even know the primary reason was theft.

The following is a list of things a business should do to help prevent employee theft.

1. Let your employees know you expect honesty and will not tolerate thefts.

2. Inspect all employee packages leaving the premises.

3. Keep all doors, except customer exit doors, locked, and make someone responsible for the key.

4. Keep trash from accumulating in the store, and inspect it at *irregular* intervals to make sure no merchandise is going out of the store in this way.

5. Watch the loading-unloading area. Collusion between drivers and employees sometimes occurs. Spot-check incoming merchandise to make sure you receive all of it. Do not let drivers load their own trucks from stock.

6. If at all possible, assign clerks to one register only. Check the register tape against the amount of cash at the end of the employee's time on the register. If trading stamps are given, check these against the tape and cash to spot missing stamps or cash.

7. Have your books audited regularly by a competent accountant.

8. Watch cashiers to make sure they are ringing up all sales and ringing them up at the correct price.

9. Above all, check out each employee hired in an attempt to determine his or her honesty and character.

10. Many of the devices used to detect shoplifting may also be used to identify employee theft, such as two-way mirrors, closed circuit television, and convex mirrors.

11. Have persons not known to the employees periodically buy an item in the business, and have them watch to make sure the correct amount is rung up on the cash register.

BURGLARY

Burglary is also a problem for small businesses. More than 80 percent of all burglaries are never solved. This is a crime that is committed mostly at night. Apprehension of burglars should be left to the police because the thief often can be a very dangerous person.

Although small business owners should never try to apprehend a burglar, they can perform many functions that will lessen the likelihood of loss due to a burglary. The following are some of the things they may do.

1. Install good locks and sturdy doors.

2. Install a burglar alarm system. Silent alarms direct to the police are very effective.

3. Maintain adequate indoor and outdoor lighting.

4. Use steel gratings over windows when possible.

5. Keep show window advertising in a manner where the inside of the store can still be seen from the outside.

6. Don't leave more cash than is absolutely necessary for starting the next day's business in the store. Take all other funds to bank night depositories.

7. Have a good safe if change must be kept overnight in the store.

8. Change the locks on your doors on a periodic basis. Control the keys with records of what employees have what keys. If keys are lost, have the lock or locks changed immediately.

9. Ask the local police to inspect your store to point out things you might change to protect your store from burglary.

10. Post signs that state that no money is kept on the premises overnight.

11. Check the possibility of an armored car service if large amounts of funds are used in the business.

12. Check the feasibility of using a guard dog. Even a pet dog that barks can often scare off a would-be burglar.

Burglar Alarm Systems

There are about eight basic systems used in **burglar alarm systems.** These are

Electromechanical. Electromechanical devices are simple alarm systems that rely on something activating an electrical circuit. For example, windows and doors can be equipped so that a spring and plunger will function to make contact if they are opened, thereby setting off the alarm.

Pressure. Pressure devices are often used under mats and carpeting. Any pressure on them closes the circuit and the alarm sounds.

Taut wire. Taut wire detectors consist of wire strung along a fence or wall so that anyone climbing them will disturb them. They are often used on roofs. Any change in the tension of the wire will set off the alarm.

Photoelectric. Photoelectric devices use a beam of light that is transmitted for a distance to a receiver. If the beam is broken, the alarm is sounded. For best protection, infrared or ultraviolet light is used.

Motion detection. Motion detection alarms may be either radio frequency or ultrasonic wave transmissions. The first method uses a set radio frequency, which is transmitted to a receiver. Any disturbance in the wave patterns sets off the alarm.

Ultrasonic involves transmitting specific ultrasonic waves to a receiver. The alarm sounds when the waves are disturbed.

Capacitance alarms. Capacitance alarms are proximity alarms used to protect metal containers such as safes. They may also be used on door knobs. An electromagnetic field is set up on an ungrounded metal object by using two oscillator circuits, which are set in balance. Whenever these circuits are disturbed, the alarm sounds.

Sonic systems. Sonic alarms consist of microphones connected to a receiver, which sets off the alarm when noise is detected in the area. They are usually set above normal noise to avoid false alarms.

Vibration detectors. Vibration alarms consist of special type microphones attached to an object. If the object is disturbed, the vibrations are picked up by the microphone and sent to the receiver, which sounds the alarm.

Cost of System

Burglar alarm systems range from simple systems to very sophisticated systems. They may be alarms that are sounded at the business, or they may be silent alarms that are activated only at a police station. Their cost may range from a few hundred dollars to several thousand dollars. Most small businesses should have some form of burglar alarm system. It can save them in insurance premiums and losses from burglary. The firm's resources and individual situation determine which system is best for them.

This chapter has discussed many risks the small business firm faces in its operations; however, these risks should not discourage the prospective small business entrepreneur. Good management practices allow the small business owner to control these risks and operate a profitable business.

SUMMARY OF KEY POINTS

1. Small businesses may avoid risk by substitution, elimination, and screening.
2. Small businesses may reduce risk by good management practices.
3. Small businesses may assume risk by self-insurance.
4. Small businesses may shift the risk by subcontracting, hedging, and insurance.
5. Fire insurance insures the business from loss due to fire and lightning.
6. Theft insurance provides protection from burglary, robbery, and embezzlement.
7. Liability insurance insures a business against liability due to its own acts, acts of employees while at work, conditions within the business, or products the business manufactures or sells or all of these.
8. Loss of income may be shifted to insurance companies.
9. Surety insurance bonds small businesses to insure their ability to complete contracts.
10. Automobile insurance provides protection for various losses due to damage or liability.
11. The three basic types of life insurance are whole life, endowment, and term.
12. Types of shoplifters are juveniles, housewives, psychologically sick persons, vagrants, addicts, and professionals.

13. There are many methods of reducing shoplifting.

14. Employee theft is a serious problem, but there are methods of controlling it.

15. Burglar alarm systems and other methods of protecting the facilities can greatly reduce the chances of burglary.

DISCUSSION QUESTIONS

1. Give an example of each of the following methods of controlling risk in a small business.
   a. Avoid the risk,
   b. Reduce the risk,
   c. Assume the risk,
   d. Shift the risk.

2. Why is liability insurance so important to small businesses, and what types of liability may a small business be protected against?

3. If a small business burns to the ground and the owner has 100 percent fire insurance coverage, is he or she completely covered against all types of loss? Explain.

4. What is surety insurance?

5. What is the basic difference between coverage of whole life, endowment, and term insurance?

6. What is the difference between cash and loan value of the three basic types of life insurance?

7. Identify the following shoplifters.
   a. The most common,
   b. The most common of adult women,
   c. The one who needs therapy,
   d. The easiest to detect,
   e. The hardest to detect,
   f. Usually, the most dangerous.

8. Give three ways that a drugstore could help prevent shoplifting.

9. What is ticket switching, and how can it be discouraged?

10. Why is employee theft a problem in small businesses?

STUDENT PROJECT

Visit a small business that is a retail store, and find out the following information:

1. What types of insurance does the business carry? Do you personally feel the insurance coverage is sufficient? Explain.
2. Is shoplifting a problem for the store?
3. What methods of shoplifting prevention does the store use?
4. Are employee theft and burglary a problem for the store?
5. Does the store do anything to prevent employee theft and burglary?
6. Could you make recommendations that would help the business prevent the different types of theft?

CASE A

The Groove Shop

Bob Bishop has just opened a record store in a neighborhood shopping center near the local high school. His grand opening promotion seemed to be very successful and brought many people into the store. Bob has hired one full-time clerk and two part-time clerks to help him sell. Bob tries to ring up most of the sales himself, but the other clerks ring up sales at various times.

Bob is 30 years old and has worked at several types of employment since he graduated from college. His most recent job was managing a record store in another town. When he had saved enough money, he realized a lifelong dream of opening his own business.

The Groove Shop sells a wide range of music on LPs, 45s, and tapes. The store also stocks blank tapes, a limited line of cartridges and styli, record cleaning products, and other stereo-related products.

Bob felt the record store he had managed had a degree of shoplifting, and he suspected some employee theft. Bob would like your help in controlling all types of theft problems in this store and would like you to make recommendations about controlling risk.

QUESTIONS

1. Tell Bob how he might control risk in the business.
2. Do you think Bob should carry life insurance and, if so, what types?
3. What types of other insurance should Bob carry?
4. Do you think shoplifting will be a problem? Explain.
5. What are some of the ways Bob can control shoplifting in this type of business?
6. What are some of the ways he can control employee theft? Would you recommend lie detector tests?
7. Help Bob determine some ways to prevent burglary.

CASE B

Pretty Pets

Eric Oram is getting ready to open his new pet store, which he has named Pretty Pets. The building is completed; and all shelves, equipment, fish tanks, furniture, and inventory are being installed and stocked; and the store should be ready for opening in about 10 days. Eric owns the store building and everything inside it. However, he does have a $75,000 Small Business Administration loan, which has a first lien against his store and everything in it. Eric has hired one full-time employee and one part-time employee. Eric has been so busy he has not thought about insurance or theft until today.

He is stocking a wide range of tropical fish, some birds, hamsters, white mice, fish and pet medicine, pet toys, grooming products, fish and pet foods, and other miscellaneous products normally associated with a pet store. The building has a front and back door with large windows in the front.

The store will have a panel truck, which will be used to pick up tropical fish at the local airport when they arrive and to pick up and deliver pets that the store grooms. The part-time employee will drive the truck most of the time.

The layout of the store follows.

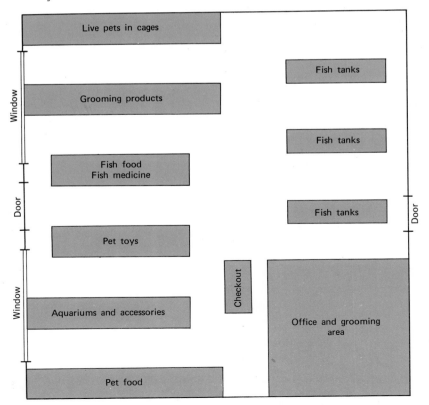

QUESTIONS

1. What kinds of insurance does Eric need? Explain.
2. Do you think Eric should expect shoplifting problems? Explain.
3. What can Eric do to minimize shoplifting?
4. What can Eric do to minimize employee theft?
5. What can Eric do to minimize the chances of burglary?

SMALL BUSINESS ADMINISTRATION PUBLICATIONS

Free

Insurance Checklist for Small Business
Preventing Retail Theft
Reducing Shoplifting Losses
Preventing Burglary and Robbery Loss
Preventing Embezzlement
Preventing Employee Pilferage

For Sale

Insurance and Risk Management for Small Business
Risk Management and Insurance

CHAPTER FIFTEEN

COMPUTERS IN THE SMALL BUSINESS

After reading this chapter, you will understand:

1. Some of the advantages derived from utilization of a computer system in the small business.
2. Some of the factors to be analyzed when conducting a feasibility study of computer use in the small firm.
3. The advantages of buying, leasing, and renting a computer.
4. The components of the computer system.
5. The functions performed by the computer.
6. The distinction between a computer service center and a time-sharing center.
7. The feasibility of minicomputers and microcomputers in a small business.
8. A number of the applications of computers in the small business.

KEY WORDS

Feasibility study	Output
Computer hardware	Flowchart
Computer software	Source documents
Input	Computer service center
Central processing unit	Time-sharing center
Computer program	Turnaround time
Batch processing	Minicomputer
On-line processing	Microcomputer

SMALL BUSINESS PROFILE

Steven P. Jobs and Stephen G. Wozniak: Trailblazers for the Personal Computer Industry

The founding of Apple Computer is as much the story about chemistry between people as it is about technology. Many talented, enthusiastic individuals began microcomputer companies in the seventies, but none have sparked the kind of human/technology formula that Steve Jobs and Steve Wozniak did.

Jobs had been working in video design at Atari and Wozniak had been designing calculators at Hewlett-Packard when they started going to meetings of the Homebrew Computer Club. Together they designed a single-board computer hooked up to a TV and a keyboard. Immediately all their friends wanted one, so the two devised a way to make and sell a limited number in the form of blank printed circuit boards.

To their surprise, a local computer store ordered 50 units but wanted them completely assembled. First, Jobs and Wozniak had to convince two parts distributors to give them $25,000 worth of parts on 30-day credit. "Paying it back in 29 days," Jobs recounts, "started our attention to cash flow." What they created for the Byte Shop turned out to be both the first single-board computer and the first product shipped using 16k RAM chips.

With Jobs and Wozniak working on their mainstay, the Apple II, the burgeoning company needed venture capital and business management skills. A. C. (Mike) Markula was hired to help write a comprehensive business plan. "We always tried to hire people who were better at certain things than we are," Jobs says. "The key is a balance of chemistries."

One hallmark of Apple Computer is that the founders, both talented engineers, did not try to retain total ownership and control; they gave stock to every employee they hired. "We would rather have 50% of something than 100% of nothing," Jobs observes. Today chairman of the board, Jobs expects the company to ship its millionth unit within the next year, when Apple will also probably join the Fortune 500. Wozniak, however, has gone off in a new direction: he recently organized the US Festival, the first of several rock concerts billed as a union of technology and music for the eighties.

As to where the company is going, Jobs notes, "We still haven't got to the point where we can give a computer to somebody and they can learn to use it in a short time." He wants to make a machine so human oriented that anyone could learn to use it within a half hour. Further down the road, he hopes, will be "a computer the size of a book."

To these ends, Apple has maintained a "loan to own" program. All employees, from janitor to top executive, can borrow a complete Apple system for one year, after which they own it. Apple's philosophy is that better products will come about if people feel that computers have been designed to meet their particular needs. After all, that's the human/technology formula that made Apple Computer in the first place.

Advances in computer technology are occurring rapidly. New computers are smaller in size yet more powerful, more efficient, and less expensive than many of the earlier, larger, and more expensive models. Consequently, small business owners are confronted with the decision of whether to invest in a computer or retain their current manual system of operation.

COMPUTERS IN THE SMALL BUSINESS

When conducting an analysis of their unique circumstances, small business owners may conclude that a computer system is not feasible for the size and scope of their operation. In many cases, this analysis is correct. However, small businesses are among the chief beneficiaries of the tremendous progress made in computer technology. The greater versatility of today's computer has significantly expanded the applications of the computer so that they are virtually unlimited. And new applications are on the drawing boards. Thus a small computer system is well within the realm of reality for millions of small business operators.

There are substantial data available to support this view. One study has found that 2.5 million businesses with less than $10 million annual sales can cost-effectively use computers. The same study estimates that 25 percent of these firms have already installed computers and that by 1990 the percentage will rise to 77 percent. Nearly 4 million small business computers are projected to be sold during the 1980s, and more than 75 percent will cost less than $10,000. This study further estimates that during the 1980s small businesses will spend $35 billllion on computer hardware and software systems and another $17 billion on applications software.[1]

In the small business, detailed information is mandatory for continuous monitoring of the company's performance. We have observed earlier that a common problem that contributes to business failure is lack of vital information, such as inadequate records in the areas of inventory control and credit control. One purpose of a computerized system is to provide owners with detailed, current, and accurate information that will aid them in more efficiently managing their operations.

Small business owners are deriving significant benefits from computer

---

[1] Willie Schatz, "New Conquests for the Computer," *Nation's Business,* June 1982, pp. 67–68.

usage. Small computers now provide them with the same type of operating and accounting information that formally was available only to users of large computer systems. Some illustrations are noted as follows.

1. A small automotive parts warehouse installed a computer system to handle inventory. In 6 months, the inventory was reduced by $30,000 with no loss in effective delivery of auto parts to dealers.

2. An accountant who prepares about 1500 tax returns annually switched from a computer service center costing $18,000 annually to his own microcomputer for a one-time cost of $11,000. The system paid for itself in one year.

3. A small marine construction company owner purchased a microcomputer. The first application of the system was to handle cash disbursements. He was able to complete one week's clerical work in one day.[2]

4. A supplier of petroleum products to cab fleets, bus companies, and airlines computer system enables the company to bill customers daily whereas billing was formerly done on a weekly basis when manual billing was used. Likewise, accounts receivable schedules are produced daily instead of monthly, accurate inventory reports are maintained, and labor costs for payroll and general ledger tasks have been reduced.[3]

Advantages of Computers

The preceding few from countless illustrations point to distinct advantages that can be derived when a computer system is installed. The following representative list of advantages suggests how performance in the small business may be improved with the introduction of a computer system.

1. *Timely information.* Information can be made available on a more timely basis because of the rapid speed with which data can be processed. Computerized statements and invoices can be prepared and sent within the specified time. Preparation of many required reports, such as those mandated by governmental agencies, is facilitated.

2. *Cost reduction.* Manual systems replaced with computerized systems result in lower costs of operation. The computerized system enables operations to be streamlined with a corresponding reduction in paper shuffling, thus increasing the overall efficiency and effectiveness of the firm.

3. *Improved Customer Service.* Customer relations are improved through more efficient handling of customer accounts, such as more accessible records and ability to complete transactions more quickly.

---

[2]Bill Langenes, "Personal Computers in Business: An Emerging Competitive Edge," *Apple,* vol. 1, no. 2 (n.d.), pp. 4 and 5.

[3]Robert L. Sample, "Mini's: Moving Beyond the Small Business User," *Administrative Management,* September 1981, p. 60.

4. *More Efficient Utilization of Human Resources.* Employees are freed from many dull and routine record-keeping activities and concentrate their attention and effort on more productive and demanding tasks.

5. *Better Management Decisions.* Owners can be supplied with more data and newer kinds of data that provide them with a stronger foundation on which to base their decisions.

6. *Accurate Information.* Many of the routine transactions can be performed by the computer, and a reduction in ''human errors'' is realized.

7. *Better Control over Operations.* More comprehensive information is available, and, as a result, internal control over the firm's operations is improved. For example, inventory control is more efficient because current and complete information concerning shipments and inventory levels is available.

IMPACT OF THE COMPUTER ON PERSONNEL

The introduction of any type of change in a firm should be thoroughly studied with respect to the impact the change will have on the employees. People generally oppose change for many reasons. As we observed in Chapter 8, employees will often resist change even when it is designed for their own best interests in the long run. It may take time for the computerized system to be accepted by employees even though the system offers the promise of many advantages. To minimize the impact of the computer, positive actions (such as those suggested earlier) should be taken in order to introduce the change in an orderly, well-planned approach. Employees must be encouraged to participate in the development of the change from early on and to cooperate in the implementation by stressing the benefits of the system to themselves and to the company. This approach is designed to lessen the impact on employee morale and reduce resistance to the new system in order to ensure its success.

FEASIBILITY OF COMPUTERS IN THE SMALL BUSINESS

Before small business owners conclude whether a computer is desirable, a comprehensive evaluation should be undertaken to include the overall objectives, the computing needs of the firm, and the specific information requirements that the owners need in order to perform the managerial functions more accurately. This analysis should identify the benefits versus the costs of the system.

A feasibility study should be conducted regarding the computer's feasibility in the small business. A **feasibility study** is a survey of the current information requirements of the firm, the areas of the company that would benefit the most from a computerized system, an evaluation of the possible computer systems that would meet the firm's requirements, the anticipated cost savings of the system, and a recommendation of the preferred system.

Because the small business owner's knowledge is limited, specialized advice should be sought before any decision on computer utilization and acquisition is reached. Sales representatives of the various computer systems are available to explain the advantages and uniqueness of their system. However, the small business owners should realize that the sales representatives' views are biased in favor of the system they represent. Although the cost of acquiring the services of outside advice may be considered high in the short term, the expert knowledge and advice of a consultant may offer the small business owner an alternative that is more cost effective in the long run in regard to identifying needs and selecting a system that will meet those needs.

Some specific concerns to be analyzed in the feasibility study are suggested here.

1. Analysis of the current operations of the company, its goals, and objectives.
2. Determination of the desirability of using a computer to achieve information processing goals. Current operations may be revised that may eliminate the need for the computer.
3. Determination of the cost-benefit relationship of the computer. Will the costs be offset by the benefits? Will the computer system increase the firm's output capability, as by producing more statements and letters, faster processing of orders, reducing errors in billing?
4. Evaluation of renting, purchasing, leasing, or combination plans of computer acquisition and the costs of each option. The relative advantages and disadvantages of each option are presented in Figure 15–1.
5. Determination of the effects of the system on the personnel. Will a higher level of motivation result? Will greater employee productivity be achieved?
6. Determination of the costs of training personnel to use the computer.
7. Determination of the specific output needs of the firm.
8. Determination of the weaknesses or inadequacies of the current information processing method.
9. Study of the desired overall information flow in the company.

COMPONENTS OF THE COMPUTER SYSTEM

Information processing systems consist of two chief elements: computer hardware and computer software. **Computer hardware** is the computer and the peripheral equipment. A peripheral is any external input or output device

FIGURE 15–1

A list of the advantages and disadvantages of the four methods of equipment acquisition.

Methods	Advantages	Disadvantages
Rent	1. Helpful to user who is uncertain as to proper equipment application. 2. Normally psychologically more acceptable to management. 3. High flexibility. 4. If an organization does not have past experience with computers, this may be the safest method. 5. Maintenance charges included in rental payments. 6. Allows a favorable working relationship with the vendor. 7. No long-term commitment. 8. Avoids technological obsolescence.	1. Over approximately five years, this is the most expensive method. 2. Rental payments increase by some factor less than one if usage exceeds a specified number of hours per month, assuming prime shift contract.
Purchase	1. The more mature users no longer need to depend on the security of renting. 2. Stabilization of computer industry means that changes in technology are not as disruptive as they once were. 3. Lower costs for an organization with a fairly stable growth pattern that will keep the equipment relatively longer than a growth company (i.e., not subject to operational obsolescence). 4. Investment credit offers certain tax advantages. 5. All other advantages accruing to ownership.	1. Organization has all the responsibilities and risk of ownership. 2. Usually if equipment is purchased, separate arrangements must be made for maintenance. 3. In a growth company there is a high probability of being locked into a computer configuration that fails to meet the changing requirements of the system. 4. Must pay taxes and insurance on equipment. 5. If the organization has better alternative investment opportunities, it would be more profitable for it to use the funds for these alternatives. 6. Ties up capital, thereby impinging upon cash flow. 7. Increased risk of technological obsolescence. 8. Low resale value.
Lease	1. In long run, can save 10 to 20 percent over the rental method. 2. Tax benefits. 3. Conservation of working capital because of low monthly payments. 4. Allows users to select their equipment, have it purchased, and then have it leased to them.	1. Lessee is obligated to pay a contracted charge if lease is terminated before end of lease period. 2. Little support and consulting service. 3. Lessee loses a great deal of negotiating leverage. 4. For maintenance, the lessee must depend upon a service contract from the vendor, not from the leasing company.
Combination	1. Optimizes the best of other methods. 2. Flexible.	1. More recordkeeping. 2. Might have to deal with several vendors in case of breakdown.

Source John G. Burch, Jr., Felix R. Strater, and Gary Grudnitski, *Information Systems: Theory and Practice*, 3d ed. (New York: Wiley, 1983), p. 417. © 1983. Reprinted by permission.

FIGURE 15–2

Components of the computer information processing system.

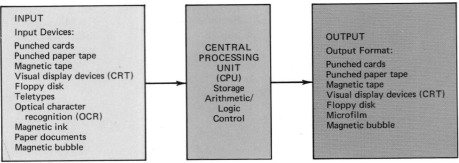

that communicates with the computer, such as printers, plotters, light pens, and disk drives. **Computer software** refers to the languages, programs, and instructions used to communicate with the computer and direct its operation. A significant application software package is VisiCalc,® developed by Visi-Corp. VisiCalc® is referred to as an electronic work sheet for budget and financial planning. When a single number in a table of calculations is changed, VisiCalc® automatically computes the effect on all the other figures in the table. For example, a manager can develop a financial model and evaluate the effect of various changes, such as increases in advertising expenditures, on the level of profitability of the firm.

The components of the computer system include (1) input, (2) central processing unit, and (3) output. (See Fig. 15–2.)

Input

Input data are converted from the form they are recorded in, such as punched cards or paper documents, and entered into the computer to be processed by means of various input devices. Input devices include card readers, tape readers, tape drives, disk drives, optical character recognition (OCR) readers, magnetic ink character recognition (MICR) readers, and typewriter keyboard terminals.

Central Processing Unit

Input data are transmitted electronically to the **central processing unit (CPU).** The CPU contains the storage, control, and arithmetic/logic sections of the computer. The computer processes the data according to the **computer program**—the detailed set of instructions that outlines the specific sequence of operations the computer is to perform.

These programs are written in a "computer language." Though there are many software packages available, specific computers will accept commands only from certain languages. The more common languages applicable for small computers include the following.

1. BASIC (beginner's all-purpose symbolic instruction code—the most popular computer language).
2. COBOL (common business-oriented language).
3. PASCAL (named for the French mathematician and philosopher).
4. FORTRAN (formula translation).
5. LOGO.

Batch processing is a widely used technique of information processing. Data are accumulated for a specific period of time and at the end of the time period are processed by the computer. Payroll and inventory data are two examples of common uses of batch processing.

On-line processing enables data to be processed as they are collected through direct access to a central computer. This processing system is used when output is needed continuously, as in a manufacturing operation.

Storage

The primary storage unit is the computer's filing system and holds the processed data in the computer's memory bank until they are needed, as when periodic reports (income statements and balance sheets) are prepared. Random access memory (RAM) refers to any memory into which the user can enter or access data. The size of memory needed is an important factor because as the memory size is increased, the cost of the computer increases. Memory is measured in kilobytes (K's) and megabytes (M's) and is expandable for many computers. A byte is a unit of primary storage that represents and stores exactly one character of data (alphabetic, numerical, and special characters). A byte consists of 8 bits or 16 bits (the smallest unit of storing data). One K contains a thousand bytes, and one M contains a million bytes.

Control

The control unit oversees all operations of the computer. It coordinates and controls the operations to ensure that the instructions contained in the computer program are performed correctly. The control unit gives the computer the capability to execute in an orderly manner the instructions contained in the program and to direct and coordinate the entering and removing of data from storage. The control unit also directs the arithmetic calculations of the computer and controls both the input and output of data.

Arithmetic/Logic Unit

The arithmetic/logic unit performs the arithmetic and logic functions contained in the program at high rates of speed. The arithmetic section performs the basic math functions of addition, subtraction, multiplication, and division. The logic unit performs the decision-making function by making arithmetic comparisons of data.

Output

The final product is the **output** data that have been processed, the "computer output." Output must be processed and presented to the owner in an understandable and usable format. Output provides the computer user with the information needed for decision making and action taking. Output may be produced in many different formats, as shown in Figure 15–2.

COMPUTER OPERATIONS INVOLVED IN PROCESSING INFORMATION

Though there are many sophisticated applications of the computer, a primary purpose of the computer in the small business is to increase the efficiency and effectiveness of record keeping and improve overall control of operations. The computer processes data rapidly through a step-by-step sequence of specific operations, following the principles of manual procedures.

For example, when the payroll clerk manually prepares a payroll check, the clerk identifies the employee and determines how many hours the employee has worked during the pay period from a time card or sheet. Then the payroll clerk determines the employee's hourly wage, multiplies the number of hours worked by the hourly wage, and records the gross wage information in the company records. Any deductions, such as for withholding tax, social security, or insurance, are made from the gross wage. A check is then prepared for the net amount. This process is repeated for each employee check.

A **flowchart** outlines the activities needed to solve a problem by the computer. From the flowchart, the computer program is written. Specific operations performed by the computer that facilitate processing of raw data into usable information are briefly discussed in the following sections.

Originating

All information for data processing systems originate by being recorded on various business forms, called **source documents.** Source documents include sales orders, payroll time cards, and purchase order orders.

Recording and Verifying

Data must be recorded and converted into a usable format for processing. Data may be recorded on punched cards, magnetized tape, "floppy disks," punched paper tape, optical character recognition (OCR), cathode ray tube (CRT), or point-of-sale (POS) terminal. Accuracy of data must be verified. For example, when data are keypunched onto cards, errors may occur in the transfer of data. To ensure accuracy of the data from the source document to the punched card, a machine called the verifier checks or "verifies" the punched cards for accuracy.

Classifying and Coding

After data are recorded in usable form and verified for accuracy, they have to be classified in specific categories that are meaningful to the user. Common forms of classification are grouping merchandise according to product line, sales data according to geographical territory, sales by type of customers, or sales by size of orders. Data must also be coded. Coding refers to the process of converting data to some symbolic form such as a numeric, alphabetic, or number-alphabet (alphanumeric) combination.

Sorting

Sorting arranges data in a desired order or logical sequence to facilitate information processing. For example, all transactions may be sorted into an account-number sequence, such as the sorting of all check transactions numerically. Inventory may be arranged by product code.

Calculating

The process of performing the arithmetic or logic operations or both is *calculating*. For example, computations may be performed to derive a customer's bill or an employee's pay. Calculating converts data into final form so that data may be summarized.

Summarizing and Preparing Reports

Data are summarized to emphasize main points of interest. Summarizing presents the processed data in usable form for decision making by the owner.

Communicating

If an owner–manager is to be able to use the information, it must be presented clearly, concisely, and promptly either in report form or on a visual display device, such as a cathode ray tube (CRT). This enables the owner to use data effectively for decision making.

Storage and Retrieval

Data are stored so that retrieval is expedited. Retrieval is the operation of searching out and gaining access to the specific data desired. The computer makes rapid retrieval possible from the computer's memory bank.

COMPUTER SERVICE CENTERS
AND TIME-SHARING CENTERS

If small business owners elect not to install a computer system, the advantages of computerized information processing may be realized by using the services of firms that process information, either **computer service centers** or **time-sharing centers.**

Computer Service Centers

A computer service center's purpose is to process data of the small business and produce the required reports. In this system, data (checks, sales slips, etc.) are delivered to the service center, where they are processed and output is generated in the form of the specific report required by the small business owner. The computer service center is able to furnish a single report or many reports, for example, transaction records (sales register, payroll register) and statements (balance sheet, income statement) depending on the needs of the small firm owner. Fees charged by the computer center include the cost of writing a specific program for processing the firm's data and the charge for information processing. If the small business can use a standard or "canned" program, the costs are substantially less than for a custom design program package. If a canned program is used, record-keeping and reporting systems of the small business must be designed to conform to the standardized programming package. The cost for using a standardized package is based on the computer time required to generate the needed reports.

This may be the information system best suited to the needs of many small businesses. For example, a firm experiencing rather stable growth may achieve greater operational efficiency through a service center.

Time-Sharing Centers

Some small businesses need computerized assistance for a limited number of information-processing needs that does not justify the acquisition of a computer. A method that accommodates this need is the "time-sharing center." Through time sharing, many individual small business users lease computer time and concurrently share the information-processing capability of a larger computer. Individual small businesses are linked to the larger computer by a remote terminal installed in the business. In addition to the installation charge, there are monthly charges and the transaction fees that are usually based on the processing time used. Data to be processed are transmitted from the in-house terminal via regular or leased telephone lines to the central computer, where information is processed and printed out on the remote terminal in the small business. **Turnaround time** is the time it takes for the data to be processed and returned to the user.

Time sharing may be a feasible first step in moving from a manual to a computerized system, or it may satisfy the firm's requirements entirely. This method results in greater productivity because employees are freed to concentrate their efforts on more demanding activities.

Some factors that should be considered in evaluating the computer service center and the time-sharing center are listed as follows.

1. The type of services offered.
2. The length of turnaround time.
3. The cost of services. Are rates competitive?
4. Experience of the service firm's employees.
5. Type of computer hardware and software available.
6. Reputation of the firm.
7. Reliability of the firm.

Finally, the checklist shown in Figure 15–3 offers some guidelines in deciding if the small business requires the services of a computer service center or time sharing center.

If the total is 100 or more, the small business owner would probably benefit from using a computer service center or time-sharing center. Even if the total is less than 100, the owner may be able to benefit. However, no simple test

FIGURE 15–3
Do you need EDP?

How Many of These Do You Have Each Month?		Give Yourself These Points	Your Points
Number of checks written	_____	10 points for each 100	_____
Number of employees (including salespersons)	_____	1 point per employee	_____
Number of customers' accounts receivable	_____	10 points for each 100	_____
Number of invoices you prepare	_____	10 points for each 100	_____
Number of purchases or purchase orders	_____	10 points for each 100	_____
Number of different items you carry in inventory	_____	10 points for each 1000	_____
Do you have very large items in inventory, such as trucks?	_____	10 points if answer is yes	_____
Do you need help in keeping track of your inventory?	_____	10 points if answer is yes	_____

Source Victor Vurpillat, *Computers for Small Business,* Management Aid no. 2.019 (Washington, D.C.: Small Business Administration, 1982), p. 3.

such as this can make the decision for the owner—each situation must be evaluated on its own merits and unique requirements.

MINICOMPUTERS AND MICROCOMPUTERS

Advances in computer technology continue to make computer acquisition a feasible alternative to all levels of businesses. Ownership of smaller-sized, less expensive computers with a vast array of processing capability is possible today by thousands of small businesses that previously had not the resources to afford a computer or time sharing. The minicomputers and microcomputers have found widespread acceptance in the small business community.

Minicomputers were introduced in the 1960s and offered an information-processing system smaller and less costly than the large mainframe systems of the day. Minis were the original small computers. Minis are small, general purpose computers with the capacity to service a wide range of data-processing needs, such as financial planning, processing accounts receivable and accounts payable, and auditing. Though minis were less expensive than the larger systems, they still represented a substantial investment for the small business operator. In the computer world today, superminicomputers are being developed that rival the mainframe computer systems in both price and performance.

Computer accessibility was broadened tremendously as a result of the technological advancements made in integrated circuitry. This event was instrumental in enabling computer researchers to develop **microcomputers** or personal computers. Micros, the smallest and least expensive computers, are often referred to as "computers on a chip." The miniature integrated circuitry containing the central processing unit of the microcomputer, called the **microprocessor,** is printed on a silicon chip. Many micros are general purpose computers whereas others are dedicated to the performance of specific tasks.

Micros can perform an extensive range of processing tasks and display the results. The small, desk-top micros can be programmed for word processing, writing purchase orders, locating slow-moving inventory items, performing repetitious calculations (such as mortgage payments), alphabetically sorting a mailing list, and on and on. As technology makes smaller computers available, more will become portable and more mobile.

An illustration of the mobility of the microcomputer is shown in the resourcefulness of a public accountant in southern California who uses a mobile computer setup in her accounting practice. The computer sits on a specially built stand in the backseat of her automobile. She provides accounting services for clients who do not need and cannot afford their own computer system or a full-time accountant. This mobile accounting service has resulted in a number of benefits to both her clients and herself. First, clients retain their source documents in their firm rather than having them taken to the accountant's office for processing. Secondly, the turnaround time in providing accounting information to clients has been reduced by at least 50 percent. And the public accountant has been able to expand her customer base because of the time saved in servicing each client.[4]

Though microcomputers are called personal computers, the majority are used in business and professional applications. International Data Corporation reports that 54 percent are used in business and professional applications, and this percentage is expected to rise to 59 percent in 1988. Doctors, dentists, lawyers, and other professionals who conduct their own business can use a microcomputer for processing patient history or preparing legal documents.

Numerous firms are engaged in the manufacture of computer hardware. Some 140 firms that produce small business computer systems and software packages are listed by *Modern Office Procedures* magazine. Among the leading manufacturers of minis and micros are Tandy Corporation (Radio Shack), Apple Computer, Atari, Commodore International, IBM, Wang Laboratories, Digital Equipment Corporation, Data General Corporation, Texas Instruments, Hewlett-Packard Company, Honeywell, NCR Corporation, and Burroughs Corporation. Microcomputers and software packages are now available through many retail computer centers and software stores throughout the nation.

CRITERIA FOR SELECTING A MINICOMPUTER OR MICROCOMPUTER

The decision to incorporate a computer into the firm's operations should be guided by a well-planned strategy. Because there is such an extensive assortment of hardware and software to choose from, the initial decision must focus on specifying what the exact information-processing needs of the small business are. Care must be taken to make sure that a decision to acquire a computer is based on the correct reasons. Once the information needs have been firmly established, users should select the software that will match the information needs *before* selecting the computer hardware. This action is recommended by computer manufacturers as well.

The critical evaluation of the firm's needs should enable the small business owner to choose the computer information system that will match current as well as future needs. A number of criteria to analyze before making the final computer decision are presented in the following sections.

Quality of Software

One factor to be considered in software analysis is the number of ready-to-run programs that are available. Among other software criteria are price, the

---

[4]Victoria Jackson, "The Backseat Computer Service," *Modern Office Procedures*, August 1982, p. 80.

languages that are available (BASIC, COBOL, etc.), availability of the appropriate software packages (accounts receivable, accounts payable, payroll, etc.), software available from more than one source, software compatibility with the system, and system security to prevent unauthorized access to programs.

Hardware Capacity

Several factors need to be investigated concerning the computer hardware. Included in this evaluation are the expansion potential of the system, memory capacity, ease of using the system, ability to interface with other systems, speed and quality of the printer, quality of video display (size, color, readability), system security, and any unique requirements for the hardware, such as special wiring or air conditioning (most do not require these, but they should be investigated).

Vendor Qualifications

The reputation of the vendor is a vital concern in the selection of the computer. Items that should be evaluated concerning the vendor include the vendor's knowledge of the industry, the type of professional assistance offered the small business owner in selecting the computer system, financial stability of the vendor, application experience, size of the firm, installation support, responsiveness to the needs of customers, length of time in the computer business, and the extensiveness of the line of computer hardware and software in stock. After the sale, does the vendor have a staff of technically qualified customer service representatives available to support and assist the owner in adapting the system to the specific company requirements?

Training and Continuing Education

Training in computer use and application and continuing education are essential because there is often some "mystery" surrounding the computer. Among the critical training and education factors to be analyzed are the provision for "hands on" experience, availability of professional seminars designed to expand applications of the computer, provision for on-site training for all company personnel, continuing technical assistance and support, and availability and quality of the manuals for the computer user.

Maintenance and Support

The analysis of maintenance and support factors should include the delivery of products, installation support, ongoing support, a clarification of the service agreements available to the computer user, provision of on-site service and maintenance, cost of service agreement, location of service facilities, speed of responding to requests for service when the computer is down, and the availability of a backup system when the computer is down.

Cost of Hardware and Software

The cost of the hardware and software should be carefully screened with the realization that the lowest price is not necessarily a sign of the best hardware and software to purchase. Factors that may be considered in cost are the availability of a lease or rental plan, designation of the equipment included in the base purchase price, and any discounts offered by the vendor.

SPECIAL INTEREST FEATURE

Computer Security

With the number of businesses and individuals using minis and personal computers rapidly expanding, a serious security problem also is spreading. Many users of computerized systems simply cannot afford the security devices and the EDP-audit techniques available to large computer installations. Several effective measures are available, without the high cost, to increase the security of small business and personal computers.

SENSIBLE PROCEDURES

The majority of large corporations and major financial institutions take the necessary steps to achieve a high level of security, using techniques such as security software, encryption and backup computer facilities. These procedures are for the most part not a cost-justified answer for the personal computer owner or user. However, with common sense and practical knowledge, minis and micros can be as secure as the huge mainframes at the large companies.

Basically, there are three major types of security hazards for the small or personal-type computer: environmental disasters, accidental errors and deliberate criminal schemes. It is vital to protect computers against these hazards.

The following suggested business security checklist will afford a measure of protection against accidental errors and deliberate schemes.

1. Is your computer and peripheral equipment in a safe and secure location?
2. Is your computer and peripheral equipment protected against fire, natural disaster, water damage, temperature and humidity changes, electrical power surges and electrical power losses?
3. Do you have and use backup procedures?
4. Do you have a tested contingency plan?
5. Do you have the exact insurance coverage for your computer equipment?
6. Are your employees bonded?
7. Do you have separation of duties with respect to the data-processing function?

8. Are programs fully tested before implementation?

9. Is the computer area restricted to a limited number of employees?

10. Is the computer area locked at night?

11. Is a log of computer job runs maintained and reviewed?

12. Are passwords and/or other security procedures used?

13. Does your computer system provide verification of input?

14. Is the documentation sufficient to maintain and operate the computer system?

15. Are the changes to the software reviewed by someone other than the programmer?

Source Lawrence Beitman, "A Practical Guide to Small Business Computer Security," *The Office*, August 1982, p. 86. Reprinted by permission.

COMPUTER APPLICATIONS IN THE SMALL FIRM

The problems and operations to which a computer system can be applied is a *computer application.* The number of computer applications has increased significantly as new software packages have been created for small business computer systems. And new applications continue to be added. A few representative computer applications are described now, followed by a listing of other appropriate applications for the small business.

Payroll Preparation

Payroll preparation, one of the basic uses of the computer, is frequently the first application because of the amount of computation this activity requires. Input data are time cards, and output data are the payroll checks.

Accounts Receivable

The computer application of accounts receivable is to provide current information to the owner to help keep the amount owed the company under control. Typical input data are invoices, payment vouchers, and credit memos indicating adjustments in customer accounts. Output data are individual customer records, monthly statements, and management reports, such as showing delinquent accounts and the length of time amounts have been owed by customers.

Accurate processing of accounts receivable is important because they represent money to the firm. Additionally, accuracy is important to keep customer goodwill because inaccurate records are a source of irritation to customers.

Accounts Payable

Input data include the accounts payable records of the charges and payments and accounts payable checks. This application assists the owner–manager in determining correct charges before payment is authorized by comparing the purchase order and invoice. The accounts payable application helps the owner to take advantage of any cash discounts. Additionally, the information provided helps to keep costs under control.

Inventory Control

A large share of the firm's assets are tied up in inventory. Control over inventory enables the small business owner to protect the business against two key problems: not enough inventory resulting in lost sales or too much inventory resulting in excessive carrying costs and possibly spoilage and loss due to theft. Many types of computer technology, including punched cards, are available for use in inventory control that monitors changes made in inventory.

For example, a manufacturer using punched cards could follow this procedure. Items issued from inventory for use in production have punched cards attached that contain information relating to the individual items. These cards are removed when the parts are taken out of inventory by the inventory clerk, who records the date and number of the project on which the part is to be used.

All cards are collected at the end of the workday and taken to data processing, where they are keypunched and batch processed perhaps once a week. The output is an inventory control report showing all parts used listed by part number. This management report provides inventory control information such as which items need to be reordered and which are moving rapidly.

Many other basic computer applications are possible, including those shown in the following listing.

Financial statement preparation	Quality control
Monthly sales analysis	Writing sales orders
Credit screening	Billing of customers
Cash reconciliation	Production scheduling
Ratio analysis	Personal search
Scheduling loan payments	Job costing
Financial statement analysis	Statistical analysis
Lease or buy analysis	Mailing lists
Lead time for purchasing	Form letters
Make or buy decision	Real estate calculations

SUMMARY OF KEY POINTS

1. Advances in computer technology that have resulted in small, powerful computers have made the computer a feasible alternative for information processing in millions of small businesses.

2. Firms that utilize computers realize a number of advantages, including timely information, cost reduction, improved customer service, more efficient utilization of human resources, better management decisions, accurate information, and better control over operations.

3. Because the introduction of the computer into the firm represents a significant change, the impact of the change on personnel should be explored and adequate preparation made to make sure that employees will understand the reasons for the change as well as the benefits to be gained from using the computer.

4. Before the owner–manager decides whether a computer is appropriate for the small firm, a feasibility study should be undertaken to analyze the needs of the business thoroughly.

5. One alternative to be evaluated by small business owners is whether to buy, rent, or lease a computer.

6. The components of the computer system are input, central processing unit (CPU), and output. The central processing unit contains the computer's storage, control, and arithmetic/logic unit.

7. Computer operations involved in the processing of data include originating, recording and verifying, classification and coding, sorting, calculating, summarizing and preparing reports, communicating, and storage and retrieval.

8. For the firm that chooses not to install a computer, the advantages of computer information processing may be obtained through the use of services provided by computer service centers and time-sharing centers.

9. The minicomputers and microcomputers are suitable computers for filling the needs of the small business owners.

10. A number of criteria should be carefully evaluated before a decision is made to acquire a computer.

11. A wide range of applications can facilitate the processing of information in the small business, thus giving the manager access to greater amounts of information needed for decision making.

DISCUSSION QUESTIONS

1. Explain some of the advantages of computers to the small business owner.

2. Discuss how a computer service center serves the small business owner.

3. Explain how company personnel can complicate the introduction of a computer into the small business.

4. Why should the small business owner conduct a feasibility study before deciding whether to use a computer system?

5. What are some advantages of leasing a computer?

6. What is a microcomputer?

7. Identify the components of the computer hardware system.

8. Explain the difference between computer hardware and software.

9. What are some factors that should be evaluated in choosing a manufacturer or distributor of a computer?

10. List some of the possible applications of computers for the small business.

STUDENT PROJECTS

1. Report on the content of an article from a magazine or newspaper that describes a computer application in small business.

2. Visit a retail computer store, and prepare a report on the kinds of computers that are available for a small business. If possible, collect some literature, and bring it to class.

3. Assume you received a telephone call this morning from Josephine, who owns a small ladies apparel shop. How would you answer her question, "How can a computer help my business?"

4. Have a small business owner who uses a computer in the firm's operation explain why the decision was made to use the computer in the firm.

CASE A

Page Office Supply Company

Page Office Supply Company was founded in September 1945 by Nick Page's father, Gene A. Page. Nick took control of the firm in 1975, when his father retired. Nick has worked in the firm since high school days, so he has a thorough understanding of the firm's operations. Page Office Supply is a distributor of office supplies to retail office supply stores and larger business firms, educational institutions, and hospitals in the area. Sales volume has increased to $3.5 million annually and is projected to continue at a steady pace in the future.

In order to maintain an adequate inventory level to meet sales, Page's purchasing system requires that approximately 4000 office supply items be evaluated for reordering each week. Sales and accounting records are maintained by two women, both of whom have had long service with the firm. They post sales all day on two rather out-of-date bookkeeping machines.

The sales staff consists of 2 in-house salespersons and 10 outside field sales representatives. Last year, the salespersons generated over 75,000 sales invoices. In order to maintain their clientele, the company must provide customers with the quick response to their orders that they expect, such as overnight delivery of many items.

One of the long-service women employees will be retiring in two months. Nick is faced with the decision of replacing her. If he follows one plan, he will have to hire two or more employees to replace her in order to meet the growing sales volume and the corresponding record-keeping requirements. Or he will have to change the entire record-keeping system of the firm.

Nick finds the second alternative very appealing although he realizes that, before making a final decision, he will have to conduct a rather thorough analysis of the firm's needs in order to justify the implementation of a new system. He wants to see his firm continue to grow, and he ponders whether this goal will be enhanced if a changeover to a computer system is implemented.

QUESTIONS

1. What advantages could accrue to Page Office Supply Company with the changeover to a computerized system?
2. What would be some of the possible applications of a computer system in a firm of this type?
3. What possible cost savings could result from the addition of a computerized system instead of maintaining the present system?
4. Should Nick Page install a computer?

CASE B

Arden's Gift Shops (B)

Arden's Gift Shops (Part A, Chapter 12) maintains an extensive variety of gift item merchandise sold through a larger main gift shop and three smaller gift shops. Each retail gift shop sells a differing and wide range of products, typical of the souvenirs found at tourist attractions.

One of the main problems that the operation has encountered has been in control of inventory. All purchases of the thousands of items bought are recorded manually as are all withdrawals from inventory. This recording process is extremely time-consuming.

Another problem has developed around the fact that the managers of the individual gift shops do not have formal, continuous means for providing input to the buyers concerning sales and inventory levels of specific merchandise. Neither is there a standard inventory as to the number of items or the quantity of a particular item to be stocked.

There is a warehouse in which inventory is stored. However, all purchases and disbursements are made through the main gift shop account rather than through a warehouse account.

A physical inventory is taken at the end of the firm's fiscal year, September 30. This inventory is completely manual and requires many hours to accomplish. Even though the firm is profitable, Mr. Arden is considering the feasibility of installing a computerized system to improve overall operational control and efficiency.

QUESTIONS

1. What are some points to consider in determining the feasibility of a computer for the firm?
2. What types of computer applications would be appropriate in this business?
3. Would you recommend a computer system for this gift shop operation?

SMALL BUSINESS MANAGEMENT PUBLICATIONS

Management Aids (Free)

Can You Use a Minicomputer?

Computers for Small Business—Service Bureau or Time Sharing

MARKETING THE PRODUCT OR SERVICE

SECTION FIVE

CHAPTER SIXTEEN

MARKETING, MARKETING RESEARCH, AND INTERNATIONAL MARKETING IN THE SMALL BUSINESS

LEARNING GOALS

After reading this chapter, you will understand:

1. The meaning of the term *marketing*.
2. The eight functions of marketing.
3. The marketing concept.
4. The "marketing mix" of a firm.
5. Why marketing policies are essential for a small firm.
6. The significance of marketing research for the small business.
7. The sequence of activities in the marketing research process.
8. The types of marketing research data available to the small business manager.
9. The difference between observation, interview, and experimentation methods of collecting data.
10. The relationship of sampling to marketing research.
11. A technique for conducting a sample survey.
12. The role of small business in international marketing.

KEY WORDS

Marketing

Marketing functions

Marketing concept

Market segment

Marketing mix

Brand

Manufacturer's brand

Private brand

Channel of distribution

Marketing research

Universe

Sample

Domestic International Sales Corporation (DISC)

Export Trading Company Act

Licensing

Joint venture

SMALL BUSINESS PROFILE

Creating a Camera Is No Snap

You tend to think of creators of new technology as scientific or mechanical types who perhaps were physics majors or tinkered with gadgets in garages in their youth. Not Jerry C. Nims.

Nims, 47, may carry the same 192 pounds on his 6-foot-1 frame that he did when he played varsity halfback at San Francisco State University, but his mind-set is far different. In college days he focused on people-oriented theory—he got a B.A. for completing an interdisciplinary course of philosophy, sociology, psychology and semantics. Today he focuses on product-oriented practicality.

Jerry Nims is co-creator with Allen K.W. Lo, 45, of the Nimslo three-dimensional camera. More, Nims is chairman and chief executive officer of Atlanta-based Nimslo International Ltd., whose sales, just beginning, topped $30 million in 1982. Nims predicts they will be six times that this year.

Time will tell whether the camera is a fad or a true success in the marketplace. But events have already shown Jerry Nims to be a true success at innovation, raising capital and, incidentally, amassing personal wealth—all on an international basis.

The four-lens camera, which weighs 12 ounces, works with standard 35 mm. color negative film. Shooting half frames, it produces a thin photo that, unlike much 3-D of the past, gives you the impression of depth without your wearing special glasses. Nimslo processes the film—standard price is $15.50 for the 18 pictures a 36-frame roll makes. The camera lists retail at $269.95.

San Francisco-born Jerry Nims dreamed of such a camera while working out of Japan for Asahi, the conglomerate, as a commissioned packager and marketer abroad of new publishing concepts. (Example: "sight and sound" children's books that came with recordings.) Asahi's materials included 3-D pictures, which Nims felt were not good enough—"2½D," he says—and required a bulky camera and laborious film processing.

What was Nims doing in that line of work, and in Japan? He had thought about a career in psychology, but he had helped pay for his education by working part-time as a salesman, had found himself good at it and had shifted his sights to business. Single, traveling footloose around the world on the cheap, he stopped off in Japan, which had charmed him when he visited it as a serviceman. Asahi had an opening, and he talked his way in.

After eight years with Asahi, Nims quit in 1970, determined to invent his dream camera. He settled in Atlanta—he had married an Atlanta girl he met on a business trip—and asked Lo, who was working on 3-D design for Asahi, to join him. Lo, an ethnic Chinese from Vietnam with a degree in structural engineering, agreed. Living "below the poverty line" in quarters supplied free by his father-in-law and paying Lo a small salary out of savings, Nims rented two rooms in a modest section. He "filled them with everything ever written about 3-D,'' he says, adding: ''For four months Allen and I would go there early every morning and read all day.''

Finally, they were ready to try making a camera. They chose a trial-and-error method—drawing a picture of what they wanted, making something that looked like it and seeing whether it worked. Because rents and labor were bargains in Hong Kong, they moved there. Plenty of error cropped up amid the trial, but in 1972 they were back in Atlanta with a camera, though it still needed further development.

Nims had gotten to Hong Kong on $200,000 raised from private investors, an average of $10,000 per investor. ''I must have knocked on 50 doors before I heard a yes,'' he says. ''I would call on someone who might be willing to invest and, when he turned me down, ask for leads.'' Now, with his 3-D camera more than just an idea, Nims raised another $1.8 million the same way.

But frustration lay ahead. There were six more years of trial and error. ''Many times,'' Nims says, ''I felt like surrendering.'' He did not, and one day the camera was ready.

Nims went looking for money so that he could get into production. He found it in England—$23.4 million from British institutions. Then, in 1980, the Olsen Group, Norwegians who own the Timex watch company, bought a major interest in Nimslo. They paid ''in the eight figures,'' Nims says guardedly. He became wealthy, and those Georgia investors—attorneys, doctors, a former governor—got as much as 20 times their money. In 1981, British institutions put another $46 million into the company.

Nimslo cameras, produced in Tokyo, Japan, and at Timex plants in Little Rock, Ark., and Dundee, Scotland, went on sale last March in Florida and are now sold in 40 states.

Jerry Nims, a Baptist minister's son who in off-hours is active in refugee relief work, says faith helped him through the trying times. He took a biblical verse as the ''text for my life.'' The verse, Matthew 24:13, reads: ''But he that shall endure to the end, the same shall be saved.''

Source Henry Altman, ''Creating a Camera Is No Snap,'' *Nation's Business*, January 1983, p. 40. Reprinted by permission from Nation's Business, January, 1983. Copyright 1983 by Nation's Business, Chamber of Commerce of the United States.

For all types of small businesses, the development of the marketing strategy for the distribution of products or services must be a high-priority item. Unfortunately, many small business owners believe that the only requirement for a successful venture is to open the doors of the business and wait for the large throngs of customers who will rush to patronize the firm. What they fail to recognize is that the distribution of goods and services is a complicated undertaking involving both internal and external factors. The astute small business owner realizes that the distribution of goods and services in the dynamic, competitive environment is a highly complex, demanding task. In this chapter, we will explore some of the essential features of the small firm's marketing strategy.

MARKETING IN THE SMALL BUSINESS

Today the importance of marketing is increasing as our economy has shifted from a production-oriented philosophy to one emphasizing marketing and consumerism. **Marketing** is defined as "the performance of business activities that direct the flow of goods and services from the producer to the consumer or user"[1] to satisfy their specific needs. This definition stresses that marketing is a process that involves critical planning and decision making, encompassing many functions that must be accomplished if the firm is to attain its objectives. Thus, if small business managers are to develop a vigorous marketing plan for their firm, they must recognize that their firm is part of a larger, total system and as such the firm is subject to influences of both the external and internal environment. Factors in the external environment include economic conditions, characteristics of the population, social and cultural forces, technology, competition, and political and legal forces. Some of the internal environmental factors included are the firm's financial, production, and personnel resources as well as the location and physical layout. Small business managers should take note of the fact that the firm's success is dependent on their ability to plan, organize, direct, and control the marketing system in relation to the external and internal environment.

Marketing Functions

An understanding of marketing is not complete without an explanation of the activities involved in the marketing process. The activities are the **marketing functions**—buying and selling; transportation and storage; risk taking, standardization and grading, and financing; and market information. These marketing functions are described in the following paragraphs. (See Fig. 16–1.)

Buying and Selling
Buying and selling comprise the exchange process. The "buying" function involves the anticipation of customer demand and searching for and evaluating the materials and services that will satisfy these needs. Success in selling is directly related to buying. In addition to making sales, the "selling" function includes a determination of potential customers of the firm and using a combination of sales promotion techniques to stimulate demand for goods and services.

---

[1]Committee on Definitions, *Marketing Definitions* (Chicago: American Marketing Association, 1960), p. 15.

FIGURE 16–1
The functions of marketing.

Transportation and Storage

Transportation and storage involve the movement and handling of goods.
The "transportation" function makes efficient, long-distance movement of
goods possible. The small manufacturer may locate a factory in an area in
order to take advantage of any special attributes of that area (natural resources, labor supply) and then ship the manufactured goods to widely dis-
persed markets. Small retail, service, and wholesale firms depend on transportation systems to handle the goods and services necessary for use in the
business operation or for sale to their customers. Obviously, not all products
are sold at the time they are manufactured. Thus, the "storage" function must
be provided by wholesalers and others in order to have goods available at the
time and place they are needed.

Risk Taking, Standardization
and Grading, and Financing

The "risk-taking" function is inherent in all business operations. Risk taking
is involved in storage because goods may spoil, be stolen, or destroyed as the
result of a fire or storm. Customer preferences may change, leaving the small
business owner with large stocks of goods that cannot be sold. Though some
risk can be shifted through insurance coverage, the most effective means of
dealing with risk is sound management planning and decisions. The "standardization and grading" functions are important in that they facilitate buying and selling, such as enabling consumers to make comparisons of products. Standardization establishes the specifications for products that can be
manufactured uniformly, such as size in clothing. Grading is used to classify
products that cannot be produced uniformly in color, weight, or size such as
fruit or eggs. "Financing" is an essential marketing function. Small retailers

ordinarily do not have sufficient funds to pay cash for merchandise shipments, so the wholesaler may grant credit for a period until the funds are
available. Likewise, small business owners may grant credit to customers, as
by the 30-day charge account or a revolving charge plan.

Market Information

The "market information" function involves providing current data about
consumer preferences, such as clothing style changes, in order to plan for
future needs. More coverage of this topic is given later in the chapter when
we discuss "marketing research in the small firm."

THE MARKETING CONCEPT

Modern marketing programs of the small business embody the philosophy of
the **"marketing concept."** The marketing concept stresses that the objectives
of the business are twofold. First, the needs of potential customers must be
identified, and, second, all the resources of the firm must be used to offer the
goods and services that will satisfy consumer needs while earning a profit for
the firm. The owner must ensure that the firm stays on target and that all
efforts are directed to achieving the goals of satisfying the customer and
earning a profit. In order to accomplish these objectives, the business must
develop marketing policies that provide the basis for the decisions required
for maximization of customer satisfaction and profitability. Small business
managers should incorporate the following basic guidelines into planning the
marketing program for the firm.

1. Identify potential changes taking place in the firm's market that could
    materially affect the business.
2. Identify the firm's target customers.
3. Maintain an inventory of merchandise that appeals to the customers'
    needs in terms of price, quality, and selection.
4. Integrate all marketing functions and related activities to maintain the
    company's profit position.

MARKETING STRATEGY

To develop an effective marketing program, the owner–managers must de-
vise the marketing strategy of the firm. Marketing strategy consists of two
elements: the market segment and the marketing mix.

Market Segment

The **market segment** is the firm's target market. The target market is comprised of a fairly homogeneous group of customers to whom owners wish to

appeal. For example, consumer markets may be segmented on the basis of age, sex, urban-suburban-rural population, income, or geographical area.

Marketing Mix

The second phase of the marketing strategy is to choose the proper **marketing mix** to realize the goals of customer satisfaction and profitability of the firm. The marketing mix consists of four variables that owners integrate to serve the needs of their market segment. These four variables are (1) products and services, (2) promotional strategy, (3) physical distribution, and (4) pricing. Each of the variables in the marketing mix is discussed in the following sections.

Products and Services

The decision on products and services includes planning and developing the right products and services to be offered by the company that will satisfy the needs of the target market. Marketing policies must be set that will serve as the guidelines for the following: the product lines to be carried (by the wholesaler and retailer) or produced by the manufacturer, whether to add or drop products or services, and streamlining the product lines so that costs can be maintained at competitive levels.

The sale of products and services is often facilitated by brand names because customers have knowledge of products and request them by the brand identification. A **brand** is a "name, term, sign, symbol, or design or combination of them which is intended to identify the goods or services of one seller or group of sellers and to differentiate them from those of competitors."[2]

In establishing a product or service line, small business owners should have a brand policy to determine if national brands or distributor brands will be stocked. A **manufacturer's brand** or national brand is owned by a manufacturer (producer) and is advertised and sold in all, or nearly all, sections of the country. **Private brands** or "distributor's brands" or "dealer's brands" are owned by an intermediary such as a wholesaler or retailer and are usually advertised and sold in a more limited geographical area, such as a region or a state. However, many private brands (Sears, Safeway, Penney's) are also sold nationwide. The advantage of selling private brands is that the selling price is lower and profits usually higher than for the national brands.

The decision as to whether to stock and sell national or private brands is important for the owner because brand names of products sold by small retailers are directly linked to the demand for the product. For the owner, the general guideline to follow should be to stock and sell the better-known national brands promoted by national firms that have a good reputation for the quality of their products. The small business owner should find that the well-known national brands offer several advantages. They usually sell faster,

---

[2]Committee on Definitions, *Marketing Definitions* (Chicago: American Marketing Association, 1960), pp. 9–10.

and the owner is able to capitalize on the popular brand names when advertising.

Promotional Strategy

Promotional strategy informs customers about the firm's products and services by means of advertising, personal selling, and sales promotion. Promotional policies set the guidelines for the advertising program: what types of media to use, how often to advertise, how much to spend.

Promotional strategy policies also should set guidelines for special sales or promotional events. (See Chapter 19 for a more detailed discussion of promotional strategy.)

Physical Distribution

Manufacturers and intermediaries, such as wholesalers, must choose the proper channel of distribution for their products and services. The **channel of distribution** is the route that goods and services follow to the final user of the product. One criterion for selecting the channel of distribution is whether goods are consumer or industrial goods. *Consumer goods* are products that are bought by the ultimate consumer for personal or household use whereas *industrial goods* are goods used in making other products.

Figure 16–2 illustrates the alternate channels that the small manufacturer of consumer goods may use for the distribution of products. The channels available are these.

1. Manufacturer—Consumer.
2. Manufacturer—Retailer—Consumer.
3. Manufacturer—Agents or Brokers—Retailer—Consumer.
4. Manufacturer—Wholesaler—Retailer—Consumer.
5. Manufacturer—Agents or Brokers—Wholesaler—Retailer—Consumer.

FIGURE 16–2
Channels of distribution for consumer goods.

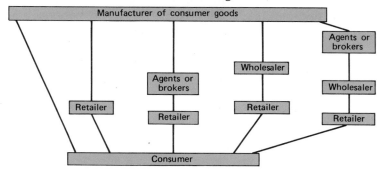

FIGURE 16–3
Channels of distribution of industrial goods.

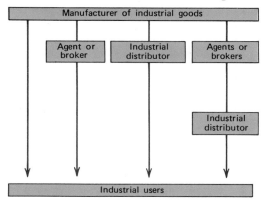

Manufacturers of industrial goods have available four basic channels for distributing their products, as shown in Figure 16–3.

These four channels are

1. Manufacturer—Industrial Users.
2. Manufacturer—Agent or Broker—Industrial Users.
3. Manufacturer—Industrial Distributor—Industrial Users.
4. Manufacturer—Agents or Brokers—Industrial Distributor—Industrial Users.

Pricing Strategy

Customers must be charged a fair price for the products or services that will also produce a fair profit for the company. Pricing policies should give guidance in several areas. They must be set in accordance with the potential market to which the firm seeks to cater. Pricing should also reflect the pricing strategy of competitors. Other pricing decisions must include consideration of whether to adopt specific prices such as odd-even and whether to use varying prices or a one-price policy as well as quantity discounts. (See Chapter 17.)

MARKETING RESEARCH IN THE SMALL BUSINESS

A vitally important requirement of small business owners is the availability of accurate and up-to-date information on which they can base their marketing decisions. For years, marketing research has been recognized by managers of large- and medium-sized firms as the basic tool for collecting the information needed for decision making. Small business owner–managers, however, have almost completely neglected the practical application of marketing research for their firms.

Because of limited financial resources and expertise, some small business entrepreneurs have relied on "hunch" or intuition rather than marketing research techniques in their efforts to maximize customer satisfaction profitably. Managers offer products and services they "feel" will satisfy customers, seldom receiving feedback from customers as to the success of their efforts. As a result, many small business owners have instituted practices that are objectionable to customers. However, the small business owner may never realize that a problem exists.

Many small business owners feel they are doing an outstanding job. However, they are unaware of serious problems confronting them in the area of customer relations. To illustrate, an owner–manager of an automobile dealership in a relatively small community had a stated policy toward customers "to present a high-volume, low-price dealership that has a reputation for good service." However, a random survey of customers reported they felt his prices were too high. Two thirds of the customers who had used his service department were dissatisfied with the service and indicated they would no longer do business with him.

It is also possible for the small firm to be located in an area where a large part of the population is unaware of its existence. For example, one small appliance store had been in business for six months in a town of 12,000 population. A random survey of people in the community indicated that 55 percent had never heard of the firm.

Cases such as these are common and stress the use and value that marketing research can have for the small firm. For example, in the second illustration just given, the appliance store manager was able to use the information to advantage. By changing its advertising policy and installing adequate store signs, the firm was able to make people aware of its location and its products and services. As a result, its sales were substantially increased.

Purposes of Marketing Research

Marketing research is the process of collecting, recording, and analyzing data pertaining to the target market to which the firm caters. These data include identifying (1) the market potential, such as size and income level of possible customers; (2) changes in consumer interests, tastes, and habits; (3) competitor's practices; and (4) economic trends in the market area.

Small business owners can benefit greatly by using marketing research techniques to survey customers' attitudes and opinions. Specifically, this marketing research survey can provide the small business owner with the means to accomplish the following.

1. To determine if the firm is obtaining a reasonable share of the market.
2. To decide if it is carrying a product brand and offering customer services best suited to the demands of its specific market segment.

3. To determine if the price range of the firm's merchandise is compatible with the demands of the market.

4. To uncover facets of the business that customers find objectionable.

5. To identify what customers like about the business so these features may be continued and reinforced.

Marketing research, then, enables the small business owner to base many decisions on facts, instead of relying on hunches.

The Marketing Research Process

The marketing research process should be carefully planned. In order to make the marketing research survey more meaningful, the entire marketing research process should be systematically thought through. The framework of the marketing research process involves a sequence of activities as shown in Figure 16–4.

Defining the Problem

The initial step in the marketing research process is to determine if a problem exists that warrants study. If a problem exists that requires the use of marketing research techniques, it is important that it be properly defined. Correct identification of the problem enables the small business owners to specify what issues are involved in the research, what types of information need to be collected, and what the development of alternative solutions is. The first step is especially critical. The expenditure of extra time, effort, and money at this initial step to identify the problem correctly frequently results in substantial savings of time, effort, and money on the overall project.

Determining Relevant Information

Once the types of information that are needed are identified, it is possible to determine what data are already available from both internal company records and external sources. If the available information does not appear to be sufficient to provide answers to the problem, then the decision must be made as to what additional information must be collected.

Planning the Research Design

After identifying what additional information is needed, market researchers develop a research design that sets out in detail the plan that will enable them

FIGURE 16–4

The marketing research process.

to gather the needed data. For example, if data are to be collected from interviews with customers, then a survey questionnaire must be designed, and the number of people to be interviewed must be decided. In preparing the questionnaire, one must take care to see that it does not contain biased or prejudicial questions.

Conducting the Research

The first three steps in the marketing research process involve a considerable amount of planning. However, a properly planned marketing research project expedites the data collection. A number of methods may be used to collect the data, such as interviews, observations, or experimentation. The methods used are determined by the research design and the information already available.

Analysis of the Data

When the data are collected, they should be presented in a format that allows small business owners to analyze the results more easily. For example, data can be tabulated and presented in a table, chart, graph, or map format. After the marketing research process is completed and the data have been analyzed, small business owners are in a better position to make a decision and take action. The quality of the decision should be strengthened because owners have support on which to base their decisions rather than mere intuition, hunch, or rule of thumb.

SOURCES OF ASSISTANCE FOR MARKETING RESEARCH

There are many sources of assistance readily available to small business managers to aid in the collection and analysis of market research data. One source for developing a market research effort can be drawn from the firm's own personnel resources. However, this alternative is not practical for most small businesses because they do not have the personnel who possess the specialized skills. A second source of assistance may be provided by various trade associations and business suppliers. A third alternative is the Small Business Institute (SBI). The SBI is a program sponsored jointly by the SBA and participating colleges and universities. In this program, college students undertake and complete research projects in coordination with the needs of small business owners. (See Chapter 22.) A fourth alternative consists of hiring a professional marketing research consultant, but the cost of this option may be prohibitive for most small firms.

In deciding which source to utilize, owners should weigh such factors as the following.

1.   The availability in the firm of personnel with research expertise.
2.   The availability of the required data.

3. The cost of the project and funds available in the firm.
4. The complexity and size of the problem to be studied.
5. The importance of the problem to the firm's survival and growth.

Sources of Marketing Research Data

When it has been established that data must be collected to complete the study, the source from which to gather the desired information must be determined. Sources of marketing information may be collected from internal company records and external sources.

Internal Company Records

The records of the firm should be the initial area of investigation. Company records reveal a picture of the company's performance. Analysis of sales records discloses the number of units of each product sold, the products that were the best-sellers, whether the best-selling products were in the high-priced or lower-priced lines, the amount of the average purchase of consumers, the salesperson who had the best performance record in selling, and the distribution of customers from various sections of the trading area. Other pertinent data that may be ascertained from internal records include the amount of credit granted, how much merchandise was returned, and the number and ages of employees.

External Sources of Data

An extensive array of data already in published form is available from external sources. A representative sampling of the sources of data is presented here.

Government Sources   Federal, state, and local government agencies publish numerous resource materials that contain marketing information.

The federal government publications include those published by the U.S. Bureau of the Census. These census publications contain data on population, housing, agriculture, business manufacturers, and so forth.

Other government agencies, including the Small Business Administration, Departments of Labor and Commerce, and the Federal Reserve Board, publish reports and pamphlets covering many subject areas, many specifically directed to the small business. Government agencies also publish special reports relating to specific industries, trades, geographic areas, and marketing operations. Retail trade and wholesale trade are examples of subjects of these publications.

State and local governments also publish vast quantities of data pertaining to specific geographic areas, such as industrial growth.

Trade Associations   A trade association is an organization that represents a particular type of business or industry, such as a restaurant association, builders' association, or hardware association. Association membership is voluntary, and the main purpose of an association is to further the best interests of the members. Trade associations offer many services and often develop statistical data and marketing research programs that assist membership in the following ways.

1. Accounting services (publishing comparative ratios).

2. Advertising and marketing services (conducting studies or providing methods of merchandising).

3. Aid to disadvantaged (encouraging minority group entrepreneur programs).

4. Consumerism (publish a code of ethics that includes requirements for consumer protection).

5. Ecology and environmental programs (conduct research to improve methods of waste disposal and to eliminate pollution).

6. Education (sponsor short courses, clinics, seminars and workshops for industry).

7. Employer-employee relations (conduct surveys concerning members' employees—wages, work schedules, fringe benefits).

8. Government relations (inform members about federal, state, and local legislative actions).

9. Publishing (public magazines, trade journals, newsletters, digests of laws, directories of suppliers and buyers).

10. Publicity and public relations (provide members with news stories that they can use in their own community).

11. Research, standardization, and statistics (regularly gather and distribute data on orders, sales, production, construction, inventories, operating ratios, profits).[3]

Local Business Sources   The chamber of commerce is often able to provide information on local business conditions at no cost to the firm. Likewise, the telephone company, utility companies, banks, and local newspapers can provide market research information.

Bureaus of business research at colleges or universities provide data covering a wide range of topics, such as employment, market surveys, and economic conditions of the area.

Periodicals and Newspapers   Many business magazines and newspapers contain a wealth of information that may be beneficial to the data collector. Trade journals such as *Advertising Age*, business magazines such as *Business Week* and *Forbes*, and business newspapers such as *The Wall Street Journal* are invaluable sources of marketing information and current business trends.

---

[3] James P. Low, "Association Services for Small Business," Management Aid no. 7.002 (Washington, D.C.: U.S. Government Printing Office, 1982).

METHODS OF COLLECTING
MARKET RESEARCH DATA

There are three widely used methods of gathering information. These methods are observation, interview, and experimentation.

Observation Method

The observation technique involves direct observation for collecting marketing data. For example, observers may count the number of pedestrians or autos passing a site in order to determine if there is enough potential traffic to locate a store in that area. An observer, perhaps posing as a customer or a store employee, may record the comments of customers regarding the store, layout, or service. In this way, positive steps could be taken to improve service or rearrange displays or add signs to make it easier for customers to complete their shopping.

The major disadvantage of the observation method is that only a limited number of observations are possible because of time and cost factors. Thus, this method is not feasible for collecting much of the information needed for decision making by the owner-manager.

Mechanical observation is accomplished by automatic counters that are used to make traffic studies.

Interview Method

Interviewing is the most widely used method for gathering external data. This technique consists of interviewing a small number of people selected from a larger group. There are three basic interview techniques employed to ask respondents for their opinions in collecting external data: personal interviews, mail surveys, and telephone surveys. The interview method that is best is the one that yields the information needed with the highest degree of accuracy in the least amount of time at the lowest cost.

SPECIAL INTEREST FEATURE

Conduct Consumer Research with Careful, Cautious Eye

Asking people what they like or dislike, what they will buy or not buy is not always accurate. Consumer research can be misleading if you are not careful, as the following case histories reveal.

1. In a survey, a large group of people were asked, "Do you borrow money from a personal loan company?" Every single person answered, "No." But all names of the people interviewed were taken from the records of a personal loan company. All had recently borrowed money.

2. In a survey, people were asked whether they had a library card. Nearly half the people who said they had a library card, did not have one.

3. Consumers were asked whether they preferred to drink the "light" version of a particular beer, or the "regular" type. A ratio of three to one stated their preference for "light." But where both types were available, "regular" was outselling "light" by a nine to one margin.

4. Housewives told interviewers that a new household appliance was "a very good and useful item." When it was demonstrated, they asked, "When can we get one?" The product was then introduced in leading stores, backed by a strong television campaign. Sales results were pitiful.

5. Members of a club were asked what type products they would like to buy from their club. Club members recommended very fashionable and very expensive items. The club produced a lovely catalog featuring them. A big bust.

6. It was something almost all American consumers agreed upon. The need for a wide-mouthed catsup bottle. So it was developed and marketed. When was the last time you saw one?

Source   Andrew J. Byrne, "Conduct Consumer Research with Careful, Cautious Eye," *Direct Marketing*, vol. 45, no. 8 (December 1982), p. 56. Copyright *Direct Marketing* magazine.

Personal Interviews

A major advantage of the personal interview is the likelihood of obtaining a higher percentage of responses when individuals are asked face-to-face for their opinions. A disadvantage of this technique is the high cost of collecting the data. Two types of personal interviews that may be conducted are the *store interview* and the *home interview*.

Store Interview   In the store interview technique, interviewers question a small number of customers at the point of sale or as they leave the store. Only a few, short questions should be asked to avoid irritating the respondent. Typical questions may include these: "How often do you patronize this store?" "Why do you shop at this store?" "Why did you purchase a specific product or brand of product?"

Home Interview   Although the home interview method can produce very positive results, it is also the most expensive interview technique. In-home interviews enable researchers to collect a broad range of data about consumer attitudes, socioeconomic status, size of family, and other personal data. The personal nature of the interview is a positive feature. However, the success of the method depends largely on the effectiveness of the interviewers. If they lack motivation or are not properly trained, they may record incorrect data, ask the wrong questions, or offend the consumer. There is also the disadvan-

**Interviewing shoppers is an important
method of collecting market research data.**

tage that some prospective interviewees may refuse to participate in the survey.

For the results of home interviews to provide valid information, a representative number of homes must be included because it is impossible to survey every home in an area. Marketing research depends, then, on *sampling*. A sampling technique will be discussed later in this chapter that is practical for use by the small business owner.

Mail Survey

A second interview technique is the mail survey. Advantages of questionnaires are that they can be mailed to a large number of potential respondents and represent a less expensive method of data collection than personal interviews. However, care must be taken in the design of the questionnaire so that questions are clearly stated, easy to answer, and not biased.

Disadvantages of the mail survey are that the mailing list may not be accurate and respondents may be slow in returning the questionnaire.

A low response rate has been a significant problem for users of mail questionnaires. Frequently, the response rate was below 25 percent, which made users suspect that those who responded were different from the remainder of the population. However, most well-run general population surveys today get a 50 percent or greater return.[4]

Telephone Survey

Telephone surveys are an inexpensive means for collecting data as compared to personal interviews because one interviewer can interview many respondents. This technique is timely because interviewees are requested to answer questions immediately, thus providing instant feedback.

One disadvantage of the telephone survey technique is that interviewees can easily terminate the interview by merely hanging up. Furthermore, not all homes have telephones or listed numbers.

A Telephone Survey Technique   A practical method of conducting a telephone survey is outlined. This procedure has been used extensively by the authors, and the results have been very satisfactory.

Step 1. The first stage is to determine the number of telephone exchanges in the trading area served by the firm.

Step 2. The second step is to determine the total number of telephones in each exchange of the trade area. Information for steps 1 and 2 can be obtained with the assistance of telephone company personnel.

Step 3. The third step involves selecting the telephone directory page numbers to be used to locate the actual telephone numbers to be dialed. If 100 telephone contacts are desired and if there are four telephone exchanges in the firm's trading area, then 25 pages must be selected. Random numbers selected must fall within the maximum number of pages in the directory. To illustrate, the Austin, Texas, telephone directory has 508 pages of listing of residential phones. Random numbers must be between 1 and 508. A table of random numbers was used to generate the following 25 random numbers. These numbers specify the page numbers to be used for the telephone survey.

1. 345	**6.** 199	**11.** 117	**16.** 354	**21.** 501
2. 423	**7.** 048	**12.** 435	**17.** 139	**22.** 163
3. 062	**8.** 164	**13.** 322	**18.** 341	**23.** 481
4. 356	**9.** 174	**14.** 046	**19.** 014	**24.** 167
5. 279	**10.** 136	**15.** 202	**20.** 004	**25.** 085

Step 4. On the pages selected, the first telephone number for each exchange prefix previously identified should be dialed. Thus, from each page, four numbers (one from each exchange) should be contacted. No business firms should be included in this survey. If a number is dialed and there is no

---

[4]Harper Boyd, Ralph Westfall, and Stanley Stasch, *Marketing Research*, 5th ed. (Homewood, Ill.: Irwin, 1981), p. 121.

answer, the next number with the same exchange prefix should be called until there is an answer for that prefix. If a selected page does not have any or all of the telephone exchanges, then either the next page can be used or the random numbers table can be used to select another page.

If there is more than one telephone exchange in the trade area, calls should be allocated according to the percentage of telephones in each exchange. This should account for the population density in the trade area. For example, suppose 100 people are to be called and there are two exchanges in the trade area and one exchange has 60 percent of the phones. Then, 60 percent of the calls should be made to that exchange, and the remaining 40 percent, to the second exchange.

Based on actual usage of this sampling technique, we find that the number of calls necessary to provide satisfactory results will range from 60 to 100, with 100 calls preferred.

Experimentation Method

The small business owner can use experimentation to gather some types of important market research data. Experimentation may take different forms. For example, the retailer may use different promotional strategies to determine which is more effective. Or the store may experiment staying open longer hours to ascertain if sales sufficiently increase to justify the longer hours of operation. Another possibility for experimenting is the handling of different lines of merchandise to discover which has the greatest customer appeal. This method usually has limited application for gathering specific marketing data, and it can be costly and time consuming.

Sampling

The total of every person or every household in a city or trade area that is to be surveyed is called the **universe**. However, it is not feasible, both in terms of time and money, to make a complete survey. Instead, marketing researchers rely on sampling. A **sample** is the part of the total population (the universe) that is included in the survey. If the sample is to provide valid data, it is mandatory that the people who are included in the sample be representative of the universe because the results that are obtained from the sample are used to make generalizations about the total population.

A representative sample can be obtained by use of random sampling. A random sample is designed so that every person in the universe has an equal and known chance of being selected. To illustrate, if there are 2000 people living in the market area and a random sample of 100 is to be taken, then the chances of being included in the survey are 100 in 2000. Because the sampling process is random, with each person having an equal chance of being selected, those surveyed should be representative of a cross section of the area's total population. The sample results can then be used to draw conclusions about the characteristics of the total population.

A Sampling Technique for the Small Business

The survey technique outlined in the following list presents a method of obtaining as random a sample as possible within practical limitations. This technique has been designed to meet the specific needs of the small business owner.

1. Draw equally spaced horizontal and vertical lines on a map of the market area. Spacing of the lines should usually range from ¼ to 1 inch depending on the size of the map. Usually more than 100 squares should result from the intersections of the lines. These resulting squares should then be numbered consecutively, eliminating all squares that are business districts and unoccupied land areas.

2. Determine the percentage of the market to be surveyed. Though statistical methods may be used, a more realistic approach for small business firms is to take into consideration cost, time, and size of the market to arrive at a sample size on a judgment basis. For this type of sample, 100 households is often an optimum size sample. It is usually a large enough sample to provide sufficiently accurate data without being too expensive and time-consuming.

3. On small pieces of paper place numbers from one to the largest number appearing on the consecutively numbered map. From a table of random numbers or the slips of paper, select the numbered squares that are to be used in the sample, in a quantity equal to the size of the sample. Mark these areas on the numbered map.

4. The members of the research team should be "clean-cut" and courteous. The team should inform customers interviewed that the survey is being performed to measure customer opinion as part of the firm's continuing efforts to serve the community better.

5. A standardized pattern for selecting households to survey should be established—such as the first house in the selected area or the most northeastern house. If an interview cannot be conducted at this house— no one at home, refusal to answer the questions, and so on—the interviewer should then proceed to the next house until a survey has been performed in the randomly selected area.

Survey Questionnaire

The sample survey questionnaire shown in Figure 16–5 has been used successfully in making surveys of men's clothing stores. However, it can easily be modified to meet the survey requirements for a wide range of business firms.

Analysis of the Survey Data

From the data collected, a "customer buying profile" can be developed that measures the firm's potential share of the market, suitability of brands to the market, and acceptability of product prices.

To determine the firm's potential share of the market, each response must be analyzed on a judgment basis to measure what part of the customer's total yearly expenditure for each item the firm should be receiving. The total of all item expenditure estimates is a measure of how much the customer would be expected to spend in the store after considering brand preference, price preference, and reason for purchasing at different stores. A total of all dollar estimates on all the surveys divided by the total number of surveys yields an average per household expenditure the firm should expect to receive. This average expenditure per household multiplied by the total number of households in the market area will produce the total amount of sales potential for the firm. This figure should then be compared to total yearly sales to determine if there is an excessive deviation. If the difference is large, the causes should be uncovered.

The profile also measures the distribution of consumer preference for different product brands as well as price ranges in the firm's market area. An analysis of the firm's competition and market helps determine which brands and price lines offer the greatest sales potential for the store.

INTERNATIONAL MARKETING AND THE SMALL BUSINESS

The growth of worldwide markets has opened business opportunities for small business owners in international markets. It has frequently been assumed that only big businesses are capable of operating in international markets. However, a recent survey of manufacturers revealed that small firms (those with 250 or fewer employees) had greater export sales in terms of gross sales than did the larger firms (those with over 250 employees). Although exporting is the main avenue open for small business firms to enter international markets, there are other means of entry, such as through licensing, joint ventures, and overseas manufacturing. Of course, many small businesses are already involved in international marketing by selling imported merchandise, purchasing imports through an importer or wholesaler.

To encourage small businesses to become active in international trade, **Domestic International Sales Corporations (DISCs)** were created under the 1971 Revenue Act. The law allows manufacturers to set up a separate DISC that pays no tax on an export income up to $100,000 and can defer taxes indefinitely on 50 percent of the income above that amount. Although many large manufacturers have taken advantage of these tax benefits, most small business owners feel that creating and operating a DISC is too complicated and expensive. The White House Commission on Small Business that met in

FIGURE 16–5

Customer profile.

1. Will you please give us some information about yourself?

   a. Age _____   d. Occupation _____

   b. Sex _____   e. Income _____

   c. Highest educational   f. Marital status   Single ____

      level achieved _____   Married __

                                                         Other ____

   g. Number of females in household over age 16 _____

   h. Number of females in household under age 16 _____

   i. Number of males in household over age 16 _____

   j. Number of males in household under age 16 _____

   k. Area of residence

2. Answer the following for all purchases of apparel made by this household for males over 16 years of age in the average year. FILL IN THE NUMBER bought in each price range.

   a. Suits $50–80 _____ , $80–100 _____ , $100–120 _____ , $120–150 _____ ,
      Other _____ , None _____ .
      Where purchased? _____
      Why there? _____
      What brand? _____

   b. Sport coats $30–50 _____ , $50–70 _____ , $70–90 _____ , $90–110 _____ ,
      Other _____ , None _____ .
      Where purchased? _____
      Why there? _____
      What brand? _____

1980 recommended that small companies be given a direct tax advantage for marketing their products abroad without having to set up a separate DISC.

Pros and Cons of International Marketing

The potential for exporting is increasing because many countries around the world are realizing substantial economic and social development. The rise in the standard of living among the people of these developing nations creates demands for new products and services. Exporting has distinct advantages. One, the firm can increase its profits by expanding its sales territory. Two, the diversity of markets served may help to reduce the impact of an economic

FIGURE 16–5
(Continued)

---

c. Slacks $10–15 _____ , $15–20 _____ , $20–25 _____ , $25–30 _____ ,
$30–35 _____ , $35–40 _____ , Other _____ , None _____ .
Where purchased? _____
Why there? _____
What brand? _____

d. Shirts $5–10 _____ , $10–15 _____ , $15–20 _____ , $20–25 _____ ,
Other _____ , None _____ .
Where purchased? _____
Why there? _____
What brand? _____

e. Shoes $10–20 _____ , $20–25 _____ , $25–30 _____ , $30–35 _____ ,
$35–40 _____ , $40–50 _____ , Other _____ , None _____ .
Where purchased? _____
Why there? _____
What brand? _____

f. Approximately how much is your total annual expenditure for undergarments, socks, ties, belts?
$5–15 _____ , $15–30 _____ , $30–45 _____ , Other _____ .

Check the three most important reasons in order of importance for your selection of a clothing store.

Size of store: large _____   Quality _____
                small _____   Merchandise
Convenience _____   selection _____
Adequate parking _____   Price _____
Other_____
                            (please fill in)

---

downturn in one country if the economy is on the upswing in other markets. Three, there is a favorable tax advantage allowed exporters by the U.S. government. Four, because many products have a seasonal domestic market, it may be possible to sell merchandise to other countries in the off-season.

However, there are some negatives in the exporting picture. For example, the entry into a foreign market requires that the small owners conform to the laws, social customs, and special regulations of the host country. Small business owners have sometimes been reluctant to enter world markets because of these complications encountered in international marketing. In the earlier chapter entitled franchising, we noted some potential problem areas of international franchising. Other factors that must be weighed in international marketing include the following.

1. Different market requirements that may require different product design, dimensions, packaging, or other standards.
2. Uncertainties and differences in laws, regulations, and business practices.
3. Differences in marketing distribution methods.
4. Unfamiliarity with local competition.
5. Difficulties and cost of maintaining effective communication, especially in foreign languages.
6. Special considerations governing payments, credit, currency relationships, duties, product warranties, and so on.
7. Physical and procedural problems and costs associated with export handling, such as packing and traffic.[5]

Checklist for Evaluating Exporting

The following checklist should enable small business owners to obtain a better perspective of the potential for exporting for their firm.

1. What domestic forces are likely to make exporting more attractive in the future?
2. At what level of commitment can the company most profitably enter exporting?
3. If exporting is undertaken, what strains would be created on the company, and how can they be met?
4. What domestic sales and profit opportunities exist? What costs, risks and returns can be expected?
5. What features of the product currently being sold in the United States provide a competitive edge in overseas markets?
6. Is the market being sought likely to be a country or a group of buyers?
7. What kind of buyers is this product likely to appeal to? How can they be identified?
8. What are the consequences of product modification for the company?[6]

Selling in International Markets

We have stated that exporting is the most common means of access to world markets. A number of distributors are available to assist the small owner in selling in international markets. Exporters, usually producers of raw materials or manufacturers of finished goods, ordinarily select to distribute their goods

---

[5] Eugene Lang, "Venturing Into the World," *Enterprise*, September 1978, p. 13.

[6] *Export Marketing for Smaller Firms*, 4th ed. (Washington, D.C.: Small Business Administration 1979), p. 9.

through indirect export agencies, such as export management companies. Indirect export agencies are professional export companies that assume the responsibility of shipping and selling goods in foreign markets. They receive a commission for their selling efforts.

A second alternative is to sell products to firms that buy for export. These "buyers for export" purchase merchandise from the firm for resale overseas. Most buyers for export specialize in specific merchandise categories, such as department store merchandise.

A third export opportunity is to sell directly through a foreign selling agent, distributor, retail store, or customers. Shipping goods remains the responsibility of the exporting firm.

In 1982 the **Export Trading Company Act** was passed. This act makes exporting practical for small and medium sized firms. Prior to the act, U.S. businesses had been constrained in setting up joint exporting operations for fear of antitrust prosecution. Under this act, companies can form export trading companies and consequently pool a full range of export services. Thus, the act permits manufacturers to join with banks, ocean shipping companies, advertising agencies, distributors, and others to complete the distribution process necessary to handle a product from a U.S. factory to foreign consumer.[7]

Such a firm has been established in the upper Midwest with the merger of MITCO International, a trade promotion firm and MANTRA, an export-management company. The new company, MITCO International, Inc., provides four major kinds of services to clients in the region: finding markets in the United States for importers; marketing products abroad; helping firms obtain service contracts, such as contracts for the design and construction of sewage treatment plants and dams; and helping clients with countertrade arrangements, under which U.S. firms receive payment abroad in merchandise rather than cash.[8]

EVALUATING THE FOREIGN MARKET

When evaluating a foreign market, small business owners should conduct a market research. This research will provide indicators of potential product demand and market share. In effect, this market research activity affords the same data as a domestic market research study. Specifically, the market research should be centered around discovering answers to the following questions.

1. How large is the market for my type of product?

---

[7] Richard L. McIllheny, "Starting an Export Trading Company," *Enterprise*, December 1982–January 1983, p. 19.

[8] Bob Gatty, "Putting More Wind in Yankee Traders' Sails," *Nation's Business*, January 1983, p. 63.

2.   What types of customers are in the market?

3.   Where are the customers located? (urban or rural)

4.   How much of my type of product is being sold in the foreign market?

5.   What share of this market is each of my competitors getting?

6.   What are the selling prices for my competitors' merchandise and what is the best way to price my products?

7.   What kind of and how much advertising do my competitors offer?

8.   How do my products compare with competitors in terms of style, price, advertising, and services?

9.   Is the country an agricultural or an industrial nation?

10. What is the income level of the population?

11. What is the educational level of the population?

12. Are products made in the United States allowed in the country?

Sources of Assistance for the Small Exporter

A wide range of services is available from both public and private sources to assist the small exporter in evaluating foreign markets. For example, the Bureau of International Commerce of the U.S. Department of Commerce is specifically responsible for promoting overseas trade and helps small businesses in the following ways.

1.   How to find overseas buyers and learn about specific, current opportunities for selling, exhibiting, and promoting their products abroad.

2.   How to keep abreast of important marketing, economic, government, and other developments abroad.

3.   How to exhibit their products overseas and meet foreign buyers through sponsorship of trade missions, trade exhibitions, trade fair exhibits, and other specialized events.

Other sources of assistance are the 43 field offices of the U.S. Department of Commerce, the Bureau of East-West Trade, international banks, and freight forwarders. Still other sources include industry trade organizations, local, U.S. and foreign chambers of commerce, export management companies, air freight carriers, and international consulting firms.

ALTERNATIVE FORMS OF INTERNATIONAL MARKETING

Though exporting is the predominant means of entry into international markets, small business owners may want to consider other forms. These other forms of entry are licensing and joint ventures. These two methods may be the only means available of gaining entry into some countries because of national interest.

Licensing

Under the **licensing** arrangement, a foreign manufacturer is authorized to produce the products of the domestic company. The production process and the patents remain under the control of the domestic firm. An advantage of this method is that entry can be gained into a foreign market with a minimum of investment while the company maintains control of the product. However, the licensing agreement must clearly stipulate the responsibilities of the licensee to manufacture the goods according to the quality standards. A disadvantage of the licensing agreement is that the domestic firm may be creating a competitor because the licensee may operate independently after the licensing agreement expires.

Joint Venture

Another form of entry into the international market by small business owners is the **joint venture**. This arrangement is similar to licensing except that the domestic firm acquires an equity interest in the foreign firm. Share of ownership may be any percentage basis. An advantage of the joint venture is that the equity ownership gives the domestic firm some control in the decision making and operation of the firm.

SUMMARY OF KEY POINTS

1. Marketing is defined as the "performance of business activities that direct the flow of goods and services from the producer to the consumer or user" to satisfy their specific needs.

2. The marketing functions are buying and selling; transportation and storage; risk taking, standardization and grading, and financing; and market information.

3. The marketing concept stresses the twofold objective of business: to satisfy the needs of customers and earn a profit for the firm.

4. Marketing strategy consists of two elements: the market segment and the marketing mix.

5. The marketing mix consists of the four variables of products and services, promotional strategy, physical distribution, and pricing. The small business owner must select the proper combination of these variables to achieve the dual goals of customer satisfaction and profitability.

6. Marketing research is designed to make sufficient, accurate, and current

information available to the small business owners on which they can base their marketing decisions.

7. The marketing research process consists of defining the problem, determining relevant information, planning the research design, conducting the research, and analyzing the data.

8. Marketing research data are available from the internal records of the company and external sources.

9. Market research data may be collected by means of observation, interviews, and experimentation.

10. Opportunities for small business owners are growing in international markets.

11. The small business owners must select the method of distributing goods in the foreign markets.

12. The small business owners should conduct a market research study to establish the potential of the foreign market.

13. There are many sources of assistance to aid the small business owners as they evaluate the potential of foreign markets.

DISCUSSION QUESTIONS

1. What is the definition of *marketing* as it relates to the small business owner?

2. What should the "marketing concept" mean to the small business owner?

3. What is the "marketing mix" of the small business?

4. Why should a firm have marketing policies? What are some examples of marketing policies?

5. Why is marketing research so essential to the small firm owner?

6. List the steps in the marketing research process.

7. Identify three sources of assistance to the small business owners when they are conducting marketing research.

8. What is the difference between the observation method and the experimentation method of collecting market research data?

9. Identify different types of interviews that may be used to collect marketing research information.

10. Discuss the role of small business in international marketing.

STUDENT PROJECT

Use the customer survey in Figure 16–5, and interview several people. Develop a "customer buying profile" for a store.

CASE A

Dieter's Delight

Dieter's Delight is a new, low calorie frozen dessert. The frozen dessert is labeled a "dieter's delight" because each 1-ounce serving contains about one third of the calories of an equivalent serving of regular ice cream. The frozen dessert is promoted as tasting and looking more like real ice cream than any other product available. Dieter's Delight is the answer to everybody's dream of being able to enjoy the "ice-cream taste" whenever he or she desires to do so while limiting his or her calorie intake.

Dieter's Delight is a franchise operation. Bob and Martha Cox purchased the franchise rights for a city of some 300,000 population. In addition to the frozen dessert served in sundaes, cones, shakes, and floats, they serve cold beverages. They have opened one shop in a new shopping center in the southwestern section of the city and have plans to open another shop in the northwestern area. Both areas are demonstrating major growth patterns. The center in which the Coxes' shop is located has a number of spaces for lease, but the vacancies are slowly being leased. The magnet stores in the center are a supermarket, variety store, and drugstore. A new health center that caters to both male and female patrons will open in two weeks. In addition, there are three established health centers located in other centers within 1.5 miles of Dieter's Delight.

Bob and Martha opened the shop 16 months ago. Although in-store sales have slowly been increasing, Bob and Martha have been analyzing various marketing strategies for expanding the business, such as considering the possibility of adding other products.

QUESTIONS

1. What should be the target market for Dieter's Delight?
2. Propose several marketing strategies that will allow Bob and Martha to increase their sales.

CASE B

House's Jewelry Store (B)

One of the concerns of Mr. House was to determine the image his store projected in the community as well as the share of the market he obtained.

In order to accomplish this task, he employed two students from the state university in the city to design and conduct a market survey.

A questionnaire was designed, and a telephone survey of 100 people was conducted. Every twentieth name in the local phone book was called, and, if there was no answer, the next number was called.

The questionnaire followed the pattern of questions now given.

1. My name is (interviewer's name). We are conducting a survey on jewelry stores. Will you please tell me which store you would go to in order to buy jewelry? (name of store)

2. Why do you prefer (name of store)?

3. On a scale of 1 to 5 (with 1 the most important and 5 the least important) how would you rate these items for (name of store)?
   a. Convenience (2.7).
   b. Extra services provided (gift wrapping, layaway, credit) (2.9).
   c. Quality of merchandise (1.5).
   d. Price (1.8).
   e. Selection (1.9).
   f. Expertise of sales staff (1.8).
   g. Watch repair work (1.9).

Seventy-six percent of those surveyed were women; and 24 percent, men. Of those responding, 41 percent shopped at House's Jewelry, 31 percent shopped at the other local jewelry store, and 28 percent shopped out of town.

The numbers in parentheses above are the average score for the responses to each question. The lower the average, the more important the item.

QUESTIONS

1. Evaluate this market research technique (telephone interview).

2. Are there additional questions that should be asked to assist Mr. House in obtaining the information he needs?

3. What are some other techniques that might have been used to develop the same or additional information?

4. Do you see any errors in the research method used?

SMALL BUSINESS ADMINISTRATION PUBLICATIONS

Management Aids (Free)

Finding a New Product for Your Company

Tips on Getting More for Your Marketing Dollar

Marketing Checklist for Small Retailers

Learning About Your Market

Association Services for Small Business

Market Overseas with U.S. Government Help

Small Business Management Series (For Sale)

Practical Business Use of Government Statistics
Decision Points in Developing New Products

Nonseries Publications (For Sale)

Export Marketing for Smaller Firms
Managing for Profit

Business Basics

Marketing Strategy

CHAPTER SEVENTEEN
PRICING

After reading this chapter, you will understand:

1. How and why a small business promotes a price image to customers.
2. The relationship between price and volume of business.
3. That there are other factors that can offset price.
4. That retail establishments use one or more methods of setting price— markup on cost, markup as a percentage of selling price, suggested retail price, follow-the-market pricing, competitive pricing, and pricing for clearance.
5. How manufacturers set their price, using direct labor, raw materials, manufacturing overhead, and nonmanufacturing overhead costs, plus a margin for profit.
6. That wholesalers add all their costs to their cost of goods plus a profit to set their price.
7. That service firms usually set their price by charging an hourly fee plus list price for parts.
8. Why bidding is a difficult pricing activity for small business firms.
9. How a small business can use a bid, cost, variance system to measure profit on each job, set bidding prices, and see how far from the estimates its actual costs are.

KEY WORDS

Prices	Suggested retail prices
Price image	Follow-the-market pricing
Discount prices	Competitive pricing
Volume of business	Pricing for clearance
Markup	Bid, cost, variance system
Standard markup	Bidding
Flexible markup	

SMALL BUSINESS PROFILE

Suzanne Hershfield: Organica Jeunesse

What started as a hobby for Suzanne Hershfield as she was growing up in Paris is now a rapidly expanding cosmetics business.

"I got interested in chemistry when I took my first lab course at the age of 14," she says. She soon started making shampoo at home for her long, reddish-blond hair.

Although her intention at that time was to become a pharmacologist, she couldn't resist entering a competition for a scholarship to study English language and literature at the University of London. As one of eight winners, Hershfield spent two years in London with a retired chemist and his family.

There, with books, equipment and guidance available to her, she started making skin cleanser and other products for herself and soon for some friends, whom she charged only for the materials.

Hershfield continued her cosmetics experiments while she completed three English degrees in the United States. By the time she received her doctorate from Syracuse University, she was married and the mother of a son and two daughters. "In Syracuse I didn't have access to a lab, so I tested my products for stability by leaving one batch in a snowbank over the winter and putting another batch in the sauna at the gym for a few weeks."

Her childhood familiarity with herbs and other natural ingredients for skin care led her to use them almost exclusively in her products. The Food and Drug Administration pronounced the compounds "good enough to eat" when, at friends' urging, she took the first steps toward marketing her cosmetics. Sold mostly by Hershfield's enthusiastic friends, Produits Organica by Suzanne went on the market in 1975. Sales for the year were $1,500.

Hershfield says she knew then it was time to move out of her kitchen, where she mixed the moisturizers and cleansers in her blender and sterilized jars in the dishwasher. So she scouted around Walnut Creek, Calif., where she lived, and in 1976 contracted with a laboratory to make her products. That year sales rose to $8,800.

In 1979 the Commerce Department carried an article praising her products in one of its publications that was distributed abroad. Orders came in from many countries.

With a mother's concern for her children, Hershfield began experimenting with products for preteen skin care. "There wasn't a product on the market mild enough for prepubescent skin yet strong enough to dry up minor acne eruptions," she says. Her children and their friends were the first users of Organica Jeunesse products, which are now sold at Macy's in New York and several stores in San Francisco and will soon be on the market in other cities. Mail orders from individuals still make up the major part of her business.

With the addition of the teen line, Hershfield says she expects to sell about

$30,000 worth of cosmetics per month and is now considering going public. "I just put on the market something anybody could make," she says.

Source "Back to Nature and Forward in Beauty," *Nation's Business,* October, 1981. Reprinted by permission from Nation's Business, October, 1981. Copyright by Nation's Business, Chamber of Commerce of the United States.

Pricing of products and services is one of the more important decisions a small business owner-manager must make. **Prices** that are established set the firm's **price image** to the consuming public and to a large extent determine the volume of business the firm receives. Various types of small business firms have different pricing practices.

PRICE IMAGE

Any small business firm must determine what segment of the market the business is going to operate in. It must then determine who its customers are (demographics, etc., that describe customers) and what they want. This establishes the image the firm must present to its customers. The firm should never do anything to damage this image. Its advertising, pricing, and so on, should always be pointed toward maintaining this image.

To a great extent, what the customer perceives as reality is more important to the small business than what reality is. Most customers are unable to judge accurately the quality of most products they purchase. Consequently, what they perceive as quality in products is what is important to the small business. For example, aspirin is a chemical compound that must be marketed in a certain state of purity to meet federal government standards. Consequently, all brands of aspirin tablets are, for all purposes, the same. If customers realized this, they would probably purchase the lowest priced aspirin they could find. However, the largest selling aspirin for many years is also one of the highest priced aspirins. It would seem customers of this product perceive the brand to have a higher quality, which is not a reality. Advertising tends to continue this false perception of the product.

It is possible for a small business to build in its customers' minds a perception that may or may not be reality. For example, a small drive-in grocery must maintain higher prices than the supermarket. It is impossible for it to be price competitive. By offering items whose price the customer is familiar with (bread, milk, etc.) at competitive prices, it can somewhat build an image in many customers' minds that its prices are not as high as they really are. The customer still realizes there is some difference but thinks there is a narrower gap than there really is. An automobile parts house can do the same thing. It can offer items that the customers buy more often (spark plugs, oil filters, oil, etc.) at cost or slightly above cost. When customers see that prices on these items are competitive or below the discount house price, they tend to perceive the price image of the firm in the same light. The firm can have the same price markup or slightly higher on other products, and the customer will tend to see them as low prices. For instance, do you know, even within 50 cents, the price of a master cylinder repair kit for your car? This image building may not work for all customers, but it does for a large part of them.

Some of the images a small business actively tries to promote with prices are discount prices, high-quality products, or exclusiveness.

Discount Prices

It would be rare, if at all possible, to find a business that intentionally attempts to represent to the public that it handles low-quality goods. However, many firms attempt to convey to the public the idea that they offer quality products at **discount prices.** The discount house is an outstanding example. Discount houses attempt to maintain a pricing policy that holds prices at a low level in order to create an image of offering discount prices to the consumer. Most small businesses that stress discount prices are attempting to offer a low markup in order to build their volume of business.

Many manufacturers also attempt to build a price image on their products. Often they strive to convince the consumer that their product is of good quality and offered at "popular" prices. For instance, Black and Decker, a

A storefront that promotes a discount price image.

manufacturer of tools, has long maintained a reputation of quality for its line of tools. In recent years, it has used this image, along with low price, to achieve an image of good quality at low prices. By creating this image, the company is obviously attempting to use price as a means of increasing sales of its products.

High Quality

In direct contrast to the discount image is the firm that attempts to create an image of high quality and uses pricing decisions to reinforce this image. These small business retailers, manufacturers, and service firms are relying more on higher per-unit profit than on volume. In fact, some firms use price to establish an image of high quality even when the quality is not high. In addition, some firms achieve high volume because of their higher price (this is the exception rather than the rule). To illustrate, the manufacturer of a perfumed shaving lotion had the option of offering its product at a low price because of the basic cost of producing the product. The final decision involved a choice between $.50 a bottle and over $3.00 a bottle. The firm selected the higher price in an attempt to establish a high-quality image. A large part of the per-unit cost of the after-shave was added on in the form of expensive packaging and advertising. This firm enjoyed a large volume of sales, probably many times higher than if it had decided on the lower selling price.

A store window that promotes a quality image.

Exclusiveness

Exclusive stores often try to maintain a high price image to promote the idea of exclusiveness (high quality usually accompanies the exclusive image in the mind of the customer). These firms are attempting to stress per-unit profit rather than volume of sales. To illustrate, high-fashion designers often price their creations in terms of hundreds and thousands of dollars. Their customers buy their creations because of the image of exclusiveness. Even though other firms copy their designs and reproduce them in the same, equal, or even better cloth, the customer of the high-fashion designer will still pay many times more for the original. Another example is Neiman-Marcus (a Dallas-based exclusive retail store), which uses its annual catalog offering expensive items such as his-and-her airplanes to build its image of exclusiveness.

PRICE VERSUS VOLUME

As a general principle, price does not move with **volume of business.** Most often, as price increases on a product, volume tends to decrease. Conversely, as price decreases, volume tends to increase. The shaving lotion example, mentioned earlier, is one of the rare exceptions (See Fig. 17–1.)

As a result, most small business firms are faced with the decision to (1) offer low prices and strive to obtain volume, (2) offer high prices and make more per-unit profit on fewer sales, or (3) set prices somewhere in between and obtain volume somewhere in between. It is often a difficult decision and usually a qualified guess as to which is the more profitable. To illustrate, suppose a manufacturer is considering three different prices for his or her product and each price will produce the following amount of sales:

Price		$ 15.00 each	$ 16.00 each	$ 17.00 each
Volume		40,000 units	35,000 units	25,000 units
Total sales		$600,000	$560,000	$425,000
Cost	$13 each	520,000	455,000	325,000
Profit		$ 80,000	$105,000	$100,000

It might appear that a small business would be able to experiment with price in order to determine its most profitable selling price. However, there are some problems with experimenting with prices. First, the firm may not have the financial ability to sustain fluctuations in business. Also, the firm presents one price image with one price and another price image with another price. This changing of price and price image will damage customer relations to some extent, possibly enough to ruin the firm. Consequently, the small business entrepreneur must perform an analysis of his or her market and make an estimate of the effect on profit of various pricing policies. Small

FIGURE 17–1

Inverse changes in price and volume of goods sold.

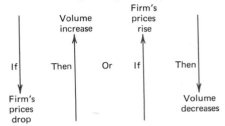

business owners should then stay with such a pricing decision until they find evidence that another pricing policy is more profitable.

OTHER FACTORS THAT OFFSET PRICE

Price is important to most customers, but it is not the only thing that is important to them. As previously discussed, high quality and exclusiveness are able to offset and even negate price considerations. In addition, service, selection, and convenience are factors that offset price considerations to some extent.

Service

Many customers find different types of customer services important and are willing to pay higher prices, within reason, for these extra services. Some customers want credit and purchase from stores that offer credit even though the price they pay is usually higher. Customers of some small businesses, for example, drugstores, often pay higher prices in order to have merchandise delivered to them. In addition, some customers are willing to pay a slightly higher price for products such as appliances in order to be sure of after-purchase repair and service.

Selection

Being sure of finding what they want at a store is important enough for some customers that they are willing to pay slightly higher prices. For example, some people may want specific merchandise and feel they could pay a little less for it at a discount house. However, they may go to another store because they are not certain the discount store sells it, and they are sure the higher-priced store will have the product. More than one store has built its patronage on this concept. One large do-it-yourself and building materials store has such a large selection of merchandise that a person is almost sure of finding what he or she needs at this store. The prices are a little higher on most products than at many other stores that do not have the same degree of selection. Many people patronize this store for the extensive selection of merchandise. They may be justified in their patronage because, if they have to go to several stores to find what they want, the cost of transportation can more than make up for the difference in price.

Convenience

Many people are willing to pay higher prices for goods and services because of convenience. For example, the small drive-in grocery almost always charges higher prices than the supermarket, but it is able to stay in business because of the convenience it offers customers on small purchases. Convenience is particularly important to consumers when small amounts of money are involved and becomes less important as the money amount of the purchase increases.

RETAIL PRICING

Retail firms use several methods in pricing their merchandise. Each firm may use one method or a combination of more than one method. The most common methods of pricing in retail establishments are (1) markup on cost, (2) markup as a percentage of selling price, (3) suggested retail price, (4) follow-the-market pricing, (5) competitive pricing, and (6) pricing for clearance. (See Fig. 17–2.)

Markup on Cost

Markup on cost by retailers is achieved by taking the cost of the merchandise (which includes incoming freight) from the vendor and adding a percentage of the cost to the amount.

Cost	$4.00		Cost	$4.00
Markup percentage	40%		Markup amount	1.60
Markup amount	$1.60		Selling price	$5.60

In our example, the 40 percent markup of $1.60 is designed to cover all selling costs (sales personnel salaries, advertising, etc.) and overhead costs (rent, utilities, etc.), and provide a profit. For instance, the retail store may figure 20 percent for selling costs, 14 percent for overhead costs, and 6 percent for profit.

A retail store should calculate all its selling and overhead costs on at least a yearly basis and compare them to total Cost of Goods Sold (see the income

FIGURE 17–2

Retail pricing practices.

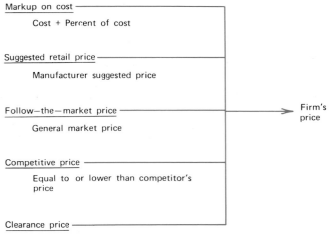

statement in Chapter 11) to arrive at what percentage these costs are. In our preceding example, if total selling costs were $79,200, overhead costs were $50,400, Cost of Goods Sold was $360,000, and sales were $504,000, then the percentages would be these.

Cost of Goods Sold	$360,000		Sales	$504,000
Selling costs	79,200		Cost	−489,600
Overhead costs	50,400		Profit	$ 14,400
Total cost	$489,600			

Selling cost percentage:

$$\frac{\$79,200}{\$360,000} = 22\%$$

Overhead cost percentage:

$$\frac{\$50,400}{\$360,000} = 14\%$$

Profit percentage:

$$\frac{\$14,400}{\$360,000} = 4\%$$

It is obvious the firm is not realizing as much profit as had been planned because of an increase in selling costs. The firm must then raise the selling percentage or decrease its selling costs (which may result in lower sales) or accept a lower profit than planned or use some combination of the three. Competition and other market factors would probably dictate the decision.

The small business owner should be careful in determining what markup to add to the cost of goods. If the store has been in business for a time, then the firm's records will reveal how much selling and overhead costs have been, historically, in proportion to the cost of goods. If it is a new business, the small business owner should attempt to identify and estimate as accurately as possible every cost he or she expects to incur. Mistakes or overlooking a cost can be very costly to the firm because any increases will reduce profit. Good financial records are very valuable to the small business firm.

Markup on cost of goods can be used by the small business as a standard markup or as a flexible markup.

Standard Markup

A small business firm may elect to mark up all merchandise on one **standard markup** percentage. This policy usually is adopted by retail stores that have products that are alike or closely related. Many retail stores that are franchised operations, handle products in the same price range, or have little competition often are able to use a standard markup.

The standard markup is easy to administer in daily operations; however, a retail store may find it difficult to maintain in the face of varying degrees of competition on different merchandise.

Flexible Markup

Flexible markup is used to adjust price when there is a change in competition or market demand. Increases in competition or decreases in market demand usually require a retail firm to lower its markup in order to maintain a satisfactory volume of sales.

Flexible markup is also used when there is wide variation in types and prices of products. For example, a department store may vary its markup from department to department in order to allow for the vast difference in products handled. If the department store were to attempt to adopt a standard markup for all products in the store, it would find that its volume of sales of some products would be very low.

Markup as a Percentage of Selling Price

Some small businesses like to tie their markup to their expenses by taking expenses as a percentage of their total sales. For example, a small business might take all its expenses (other than cost of the goods sold) from last year's income statement and find it was $50,000. It could then derive its total sales for the same period and find it was $200,000. Its expenses as a percentage of sales then would be calculated as follows:

$$\frac{\text{Expenses}}{\text{Sales}} \quad \frac{\$\ 50,000}{200,000} = 25\%$$

After analyzing its market and competition, the firm might feel 10 percent of sales would be a reasonable profit. This would mean that 35 percent of each item's selling price would be markup. Knowing the cost of each item sold ($8 in this example), it would then be able to compute its selling price on each item as follows:

Selling price	100%
Markup	-35% of selling price
Cost of item	65% of selling price

$$\frac{\text{Cost of item in dollars}}{\text{Cost of item as a \% of selling price}} \quad \frac{\$8.00}{65\%} = \$12.30$$

Using this method, the firm can easily derive expenses and total sales from its income statement each year and compute the ratio of expenses to total sales. Its profit markup can be adjusted as the business desires after taking into consideration competition and the market. If its volume of sales increases faster than its expenses, it may want to pass on the savings to customers in an attempt to capture more of the market, or it may want to increase its advertising for the same purpose. Its profit as a percent of sales would remain the same; however, it would increase its total income because sales volume would increase.

Suggested Retail Price

Many manufacturers print **suggested retail prices** on their products, supply catalogs with suggested retail prices, or give suggested retail prices on invoices. Some wholesalers also provide suggested retail prices to retail stores. For example, some wholesale grocers provide inventory lists to their customers that have both the wholesale price and a suggested retail price.

It is very common for small business firms to follow these suggested retail prices. It allows the small business owner to avoid the pricing decision. Many small business owners feel uncertain about the adequacy of their pricing decisions or do not want to go to the trouble of checking prices of other merchants.

The suggested retail price is easy to use. However, it may create a price image the small business owner does not want. In addition, it does not take into consideration competition, which varies to some degree by locale and type of business.

Some stores, such as retail automobile parts stores, use the manufacturer's suggested retail price as a base and then sell to the customer at a lower price, which is often the manufacturer's suggested wholesale price. Often the retailer lists both prices on the sales ticket to build an image in the customer's mind that he or she is getting a very good price on his or her purchase.

Follow-the-Market Pricing

Some small business firms do not attempt to lead in competitive pricing and simply follow the usual or average price of other firms. They achieve **follow-the-market pricing** by attempting to stay close in price to other firms. In fact, in small towns, it is not unusual for the owners of the same types of stores to agree to prices (this is actually a violation of antitrust legislation, which is not usually enforced in the case of small businesses because of the large number of them). For example, in the past, it had been standard practice in many small towns for the owners of gasoline service stations to meet and determine what prices will be in their stations. They often set categories of prices for major brands located on highways, major brands located in residential areas, and independents.

Competitive Pricing

Some firms strive to set prices on part or all of their products that are lower than most other firms. These stores often run competitive shopping lists on their competition. For example, a supermarket sends an employee to other supermarkets to record prices on various items of merchandise. From these lists, the supermarket then adjusts its prices in order to be highly competitive.

Competitive pricing can take the form of special prices for selected items for a specific period of time. For example, supermarkets run special price ads in newspapers each week trying to attract customers. It is fairly common for firms to get into price confrontations on specials for the same item. One store will offer a low price, and its competitor will then offer a lower price. Some firms make a practice of guaranteeing they will meet or beat any advertised price of their competitors. The extreme of this occurred when one automobile dealer offered to beat any advertised price on an oil-and-filter change on a specific make of car. Its competitor then advertised it would change the oil and filter on the same make of car for 1¢, which meant the original dealer would have to do it for free to beat their price.

Many retail stores adopt one of the previous pricing methods discussed, but, in addition, are often forced to adjust prices on some products to a more competitive price.

Pricing for Clearance

Pricing for clearance is common in retail firms. A large number of retail firms regularly reduce prices, sometimes below cost, to clear slow-moving items from their stock. In addition, many retail stores have loss leaders in which they sell merchandise at cost or below cost in order to attract customers for other products (this is a common practice of supermarkets). (A discussion of reduced pricing in order to clear slow-moving stock is contained in Chapter 13.)

Manufacturers sometimes find they have large stocks of a product on hand, and they offer the product at a reduced price to wholesalers and retailers so they can run specials on these products.

MANUFACTURERS' PRICING

Manufacturers usually base their product price on cost plus profit. The specific categories they use are direct labor, raw materials, manufacturing

FIGURE 17–3

Formula for manufacturers' pricing.

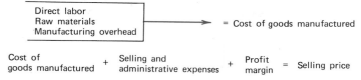

overhead, nonmanufacturing overhead (selling and administrative costs), and profit. (See Fig. 17–3.)

Some manufacturers take one additional step. They use the previously mentioned categories to determine their cost and then add on their profit plus the usual markup added on by the retailer. This then becomes their suggested retail price. They then sell the merchandise to retailers at a discount from suggested retail price. For example, it is common practice for textbook publishers to sell books to bookstores for 80 percent of suggested retail price. This 80 percent covers their cost and profit markup. If the bookstore uses the suggested retail price, 80 percent of sales price covers the cost of the book, and 20 percent of sales price must cover all other expenses plus a profit for the store.

As in other types of businesses, manufacturers must take competition into consideration when pricing their products. They also must make a decision about volume relative to price. In order to obtain sufficient volume, they must balance price, advertising, and quality of their products in terms of market conditions, which include competition.

Manufacturers who have produced their products over a period of time are able to determine their labor costs by the number of products each work station is able to complete in a day's time. The number of products divided into the labor cost for each work station and totaled for the entire process provides per-unit labor costs. The total of all raw materials used in the production of one unit of product plus waste allowances provides per-unit raw material costs. Past records of expenditures for supervisor salaries, plant depreciation, machinery depreciation, supplies, plant utilities, and other factory-related costs provide a basis for arriving at manufacturing overhead. Office salaries, sales salaries, advertising, travel, office depreciation, office utilities, and administrative salaries are among the items that comprise nonmanufacturing overhead. All these costs plus a margin for profit, adjusted for market conditions and competition, provide the necessary information for the manufacturers to set their price.

Manufacturers who are producing a new product do not have historical records to provide this information. Consequently, they must estimate these costs and data in order to arrive at a price for their product. Manufacturers of a new type of product also face an important question about price. Should they price the product high until competition arises to recover as much devel-

FIGURE 17–4
Wholesaler pricing practices.

Cost of goods from manufacturer	+	All costs	+	Profit	=	Price

opment cost as fast as possible, or should they set the price low to discourage competition from entering the field as long as possible?

WHOLESALER PRICING

Wholesalers generally base their price on cost of goods (which includes freight required to bring the product from the manufacturer to the wholesaler) plus a markup, which covers all other costs plus a profit. Wholesalers must take into consideration all costs when arriving at a markup, including such items as building rent or depreciation, warehouse salaries, office salaries, administrative salaries, selling salaries, delivery costs, utilities, and equipment depreciation. (See Fig. 17–4.)

Wholesalers must also pay close attention to competition and market conditions when setting price.

Many wholesalers print catalogs that contain both product listings and prices and provide them to retail customers. From time to time, they issue loose-leaf pages that notify the retailer of changes in price. However, the price they charge the retailer for products is, to some degree, inflexible for a period of time because it requires some time before they are able to notify customers of changes. This inflexibility means the price decisions must be sufficient to provide a profit while maintaining an effective competitive position.

SERVICE FIRMS' PRICING

Service firms generally charge an hourly fee for the number of hours spent in providing service. Some even charge one amount for the main service person and another rate for a helper. This is common practice in the plumbing trade. This hourly fee includes not only service salaries but also overhead, all other costs (except parts), and a margin for profit.

Some firms charge by the actual number of hours spent in repair. Others charge a standard number of hours the job should have required regardless of the time spent. For example, most automobile repair shops usually charge the customer so much per hour of labor. They may charge $30 per hour. However, they do not charge for the actual time spent in repair but, rather, consult a standard rate manual for how long it should take to complete the job. For example, the rate manual may list replacing a water pump at 2 hours. In this case, the customer would be charged for 2 hours times $30 or $60 in labor costs. In addition, parts are charged to the customer at list. As a general rule

FIGURE 17–5
Service firms' pricing practices.

Actual time or standard time	×	Hourly rate	+	List price of parts	=	Price

of thumb, list is roughly twice the cost of the part to the automobile repair shop. (See Fig. 17–5.)

The automobile repair shop usually pays the mechanic a fee that is a part of the total labor cost. In our example, the automobile repair shop might pay the mechanic 50 percent of all labor costs or $30 of the labor costs on the water pump repair job. The owner of the shop then keeps $30 for the labor costs plus the markup on the parts to cover his or her overhead (equipment, building, utilities, office expenses, supplies, etc.).

When price is based on a standard rate manual, the efficient mechanic who can complete the work in less time receives more per hour than the mechanic who is not as efficient and takes as much as, or more time than, the manual allows. In this way, the customer is neither rewarded nor penalized for the speed of the mechanic.

Service firms that use actual hours or standard rate manuals usually adapt their price to meet competition by adjusting the dollar amount charged per actual or standard hour. To illustrate by using our automobile repair shop example, the shop might drop its labor cost from $30 to $25 per hour to meet new competition that is reducing its volume.

SPECIAL INTEREST FEATURE

Bidding

Bidding is probably one of the most difficult pricing activities in which a business can engage. Many times the firm has not produced a specific product or service exactly like the one on which it is bidding. For example, a construction firm may bid on construction of an apartment complex. Even though it has constructed other apartment complexes, there are usually problems unique to each job, such as site preparations, foundations, or new construction designed by the architect. It is often very difficult to figure the exact cost of each problem and technique before it is performed.

On the other hand, the firm that is bidding a job must be fairly accurate in its bidding. If the job costs more than expected, the firm sustains the loss. Conversely, if the firm bids too high, it probably will not get the job.

Another aspect of bidding is the costs to bid on a contract, which may range from a few hours of one person's time to the million or more dollars it sometimes costs aircraft manufacturers to design and build a mockup for a bid to the government. Consequently, a firm must be efficient enough in bidding to be assured that it has a reasonable chance to obtain contracts.

Another problem a firm faces in bidding on contracts that extend over long periods of time, sometimes in terms of several years, is continuing inflation of costs. Bidding usually requires a specific price. The firm that bids may find that costs have increased because of inflation to the point that fulfilling the contract costs more than the price it is receiving. However, it is becoming increasingly common to find contracts that contain some form of escalator clause as a hedge against inflation.

There are even cases when a small business might bid at cost or even below cost. If business activity is slow, the firm might consider a very low bid to keep its personnel and resources active. A bid to cover fixed costs and part of the variable costs might be the most profitable short-run action to take until business increases again.

BID, COST, VARIANCE SYSTEM

Any job order shop (one that does not produce to stock but only to customer orders) that bids or prices based on estimated costs should maintain a simple **bid, cost, variance system** as shown in Figure 17–6. It allows the firm to learn just exactly how much it is making on each job. In addition, it allows the firm to see how accurate its bids are and over a period of time makes the **bidding** of the firm much more accurate by showing how much variance there is from bid price to actual cost for direct labor, raw materials, manufacturing overhead, selling and administrative overhead, and profit.

Direct Labor

The amount of time each operation should take to complete the work is estimated and multiplied by the hourly rate paid the workers at each work station. For example, Figure 17–6 shows it is estimated that it will take the welder 2.4 hours to complete the task. Because the welder is paid $6.00 per hour, it is estimated that it will cost $14.40 to weld the job. However, it only took the welder 2 hours to complete the job, and the actual cost was only $12.00. Thus, the business saved $2.40 on this job.

Raw Materials

All raw materials that are needed to finish this job are estimated. Some firms call suppliers to check current prices at this point. Some items that are used in the job are difficult to assign to any one job, such as nuts and bolts. The welding rods used in Figure 17–6 are considered a supply rather than a raw material. These items are taken into account in manufacturing overhead.

In Figure 17–6 the cost of strip steel is estimated to be $210, but the firm

FIGURE 17–6

Bid, cost, variance sheet.

JOB # 106	BID			ACTUAL COST			VARIANCE
Direct labor	Hours	Rate	Amount	Hours	Rate	Amount	Amount
Cleaning	.5	$4.50	$2.25	.5	$4.50	$2.25	$ 0
Cutting	.8	5.00	4.00	.6	5.00	3.00	−1.00
Welding	2.4	6.00	14.40	2.0	6.00	12.00	−2.40
Painting	1.1	4.50	4.95	1.0	4.50	4.50	− .45
Total direct labor			$25.60			$21.75	−$3.85
Raw materials							
Steel ¼ × 2 × 8 ft. strip			$210.00			$205.00	$−5.00
¼ × 4 × 8 ft. angle			300.00			320.00	+20.00
Paint 4 gal.			30.00			30.00	0
Total raw materials			$540.00			$555.00	+$15.00
Manufacturing overhead							
Direct labor × overhead ratio _____ × .55			$14.08			$11.96	$2.12
Total manufacturing cost			$579.68			$588.71	+$9.03
Selling & administrative overhead Total mfg. × Total S&A cost overhead ratio _____ × .20			$115.94			$117.74	+$1.80
Total cost of goods manufactured			$695.62			$706.45	$10.83
Profit markup 10%			$69.56		Price $765.18		
Bid price			$765.18		Cost $706.45 Profit $ 58.73		−$10.83

was only charged $205, giving a savings of $5. On the other hand, angle steel had gone up, and it cost the firm $20 more than the estimate.

Manufacturing Overhead

A common shortfall of small business is to fail to apply overhead on a realistic basis in pricing. To illustrate, one small business bid $6800 on a city government job. Later it found city engineers had estimated the job at $8200, and the second lowest bid was $10,200. The owner of the business had been estimating his cost of direct labor and raw materials and then applying a 60 percent markup to cover overhead and profit. An analysis of past income statements showed that overhead costs were running 120 percent of each dollar spent in direct labor. The entire markup of 60 percent did not even cover his overhead much less profit. Needless to say, he lost money on the job.

Manufacturing overhead is computed by taking the total direct labor cost and multiplying it times the manufacturing overhead ratio. The manufacturing overhead ratio is determined by taking the manufacturing overhead cost from the income statement for the last year and dividing it by the total direct labor costs for the same period. Manufacturing overhead is comprised of such items as supervisors' salaries, machinery depreciation, supplies, utilities assigned to the factory, cost of the factory space in rent or depreciation, and insurance for the factory space and equipment.

In our example, the total of last year's manufacturing overhead was $264,000 whereas the total direct labor expense for the same period was $480,000. The calculation of the manufacturing overhead ratio would be:

$$\frac{\text{Manufacturing overhead cost}}{\text{Total direct labor cost}} \quad \frac{\$264,000}{\$480,000} = 0.55$$

Multiplying the job labor cost in Figure 17–6 of $25.60 by the overhead ratio gives $14.08 for estimated manufacturing overhead. Notice that the actual direct labor hours are also multiplied by the manufacturing overhead ratio. The labor cost savings are also reflected in a manufacturing overhead savings of $2.12.

Selling and Administrative Overhead

The selling and administrative (S&A) overhead cost is calculated by muliplying total manufacturing cost by the S&A overhead ratio. The S&A overhead ratio is calculated by taking all selling expenses and administrative expenses from the income statement and dividing them by the total cost of goods manufactured for the same period. Selling and administrative overhead is comprised of all expenses other than direct labor, raw materials, and manufacturing overhead. In Figure 17–6, the total selling and administrative expenses for the year were $280,000. The S&A overhead ratio should be

$$\frac{\text{Selling and administrative costs}}{\text{Total costs of goods manufactured}} \quad \frac{\$\ 280,000}{\$1,400,000} = 0.2$$

In Figure 17–6, multiplying the estimated total manufacturing cost of $579.68 by the selling and administrative overhead ratio of 0.2 gives an estimated S&A overhead of $115.94. The actual manufacturing cost is also multiplied by this ratio to give the actual S&A overhead cost.

Profit Markup

The profit markup is a somewhat arbitrary percentage assigned by the small business. Of course, competition must often be a prime factor in setting the profit markup percentage. Our example in Figure 17–6 shows the firm wants to have a profit equal to 10 percent of total costs. Unfortunately, the small business missed its projected profit by $10.83 primarily as a result of estimating the angle steel price too low.

As with other forms of pricing, effective bidding is dependent on good records and careful analysis of costs. The small business firm that approaches pricing on a hunch or halfway basis usually doesn't stay in business very long.

SUMMARY OF KEY POINTS

1. A small business must determine its segment in the market and then maintain a pricing policy that is consistent with the image that is required.
2. Pricing helps promote an image of discounting, high quality, or exclusiveness.
3. Usually, the level of prices goes converse to the volume of business.
4. Service, selection, and convenience are factors that may offset price.
5. Retail pricing may consist of markup on cost, markup as a percentage of selling price, suggested retail price, follow-the-market pricing, competitive pricing, and pricing for clearance.
6. Markup on cost may be performed as a standard markup or as a flexible markup.
7. Manufacturers usually base their prices on direct labor, raw materials, manufacturing overhead, nonmanufacturing overhead, and profit.
8. Wholesalers usually base their price on the cost of goods plus a markup that covers all other costs plus a profit.

9. Service firms compute their price by taking actual time spent or a standard time times the hourly rate plus list price of parts used.

10. Bidding is probably one of the most difficult pricing activities, and it must be fairly accurate if the firm is to make a profit.

11. A bid, cost, variance system should be used to calculate the bid price, record the actual cost, and measure the difference between the two.

DISCUSSION QUESTIONS

1. Name one type of small business that would use price to promote the following images—discount prices, high quality, and exclusiveness.

2. Explain the relationship between price and volume of business.

3. Is price the only factor that causes patronage of small business firms?

4. If you were to establish a neighborhood drugstore with delivery service, what type of pricing policy would you use? Explain your reasons.

5. What are some of the factors involved in the method manufacturers use to price their products?

6. What method of pricing is used by most wholesalers to set their prices?

7. If you set up an automobile repair shop, how would you set your prices?

8. Why is bidding one of the most difficult pricing activities in which a small business can engage?

9. If you owned a job shop manufacturing operation, would you use the bid, cost, variance system for bidding and recording actual costs? Explain how you would use it.

STUDENT PROJECTS

1. Attempt to identify retail stores (one each) that use price to create
   a. A discount image.
   b. A high quality image.
   c. An exclusive image.

2. Identify a retail store that attempts to offset price considerations by using service, selection, or convenience.

3. Attempt to identify a retail store (one each) that you feel uses the following pricing methods.
   a. Markup on cost.
   b. Suggested retail prices on some items.
   c. Follow-the-market pricing.
   d. Competitive pricing.
   e. Pricing for clearance.

4.   Identify a service firm that uses a standard rate manual.
5.   Identify a business that bids for jobs.

CASE A

The Bat and Ball

The Bat and Ball is a sporting goods store owned by Jim Matson. The store is located in a town of 50,000 population and has only one competitor, which is a smaller store. The Bat and Ball offers a complete line of sporting goods and also has a gun repair shop that does enough business to keep a skilled repair worker busy on a full-time basis.

In addition to its regular retail sales, the Bat and Ball bids on athletic equipment purchased by the local college. Jim Matson computes all the bids the store makes to the college. Jim includes the cost of the merchandise plus his usual markup in figuring the bids. Jim is concerned because the other sporting goods store usually gets the college purchase by bidding lower than he does.

Jim has decided that he is going to review all his policies and practices and revise any that need changing. As you have completed a course in small business management, he has asked for your help, particularly with his pricing policies.

QUESTIONS

1.   What method or methods would you advise Jim to use on pricing his merchandise for regular retail sales?
2.   What method of pricing would you establish for Jim in regards to the gun repair shop?
3.   Would you advise any changes in his method of bidding on the college purchases?
4.   What pricing image would you attempt to establish with your pricing recommendations?

CASE B

Jan's Sandwich and Ice-Cream Shop

One month ago, Jan Sokol quit her job with a large corporation and bought out a sandwich and ice-cream shop that had been in operation for two years in a neighborhood shopping center. The shop had been just breaking even during the two years it was open before she bought it. The previous owner had not advertised, and Jan felt the shop could be profitable with good promotion techniques. She was able to buy the business at a very good price because it had not been profitable.

The shop offers a good selection of various types of sandwiches, including hamburgers. It also carries a local ice cream that is considered by many to be the best ice cream sold in the city. Jan has improved the appearance of the shop and extended the hours that it is open. She has also distributed handbills in her market area with special price coupons on several items.

In Jan's market area there are three nationally franchised fast-food places, one chicken-oriented and two that are primarily hamburger-oriented. There is only one ice-cream store in the area, and it also is a nationally franchised store. Jan made a survey of her competitors' prices and found that her ice-cream prices were sightly lower than those of the ice-cream store and found, too, that she was 20¢ to 30¢ lower on items the other three franchised food places sold that she also sold.

Jan is now wondering about her prices. She has asked your help in setting a pricing policy for her store.

QUESTIONS

1. Consider the retail pricing practices, and determine what should be Jan's overall pricing policy.

2. What should be her pricing policy for sandwiches? For ice cream?

SMALL BUSINESS ADMINISTRATION PUBLICATIONS

Free

What is the Best Selling Price?
Profit Pricing and Costing for Services
A Pricing Checklist for Small Retailers

CHAPTER EIGHTEEN
CONSUMER BEHAVIOR AND PERSONAL SELLING

After reading this chapter, you will understand:

1. The importance of consumer buying behavior to the small business.
2. That people buy to satisfy different needs.
3. The phases of the purchase-decision process.
4. The buying motives that influence customer purchases.
5. The significance of the business image of the firm.
6. Why community relations are critical for the small business.
7. Some techniques for strengthening customer relations in the firm.
8. The importance of personal selling activities to the success of the small business.
9. The two different types of salespersons.
10. The importance of sales training.
11. The phases of the personal selling process.

KEY WORDS

Primary needs
Secondary needs
Primary buying motive
Selective buying motive
Rational buying motives
Emotional buying motives
Patronage motives
Word-of-mouth advertising

Personal selling
Service salesperson
Order takers
Creative salespersons
Order getters
Suggestion selling
AICDC principle

SMALL BUSINESS PROFILE

Revealing Victoria's Secret

For many a man, the idea of shopping in a lingerie boutique holds about as much appeal as spilling a drink in his lap; at best, it's awkward.

Roy Raymond, 35, of San Francisco, knows the feeling well; he used to experience it every time he went to buy lingerie for his wife. Says he: "I'd find myself wanting to say, 'It's O.K.; we've been married for six years.'"

Convinced that other men shared his feelings, Raymond came up with a solution: He launched his own company, Victoria's Secret, to sell sensual and exclusive designer lingerie in an atmosphere that would set men at ease. He personally chose his saleswomen for their ability to relate to both men and women so that everyone would feel comfortable. Apparently he hit on the right formula: Half the boutique customers are men.

Raymond no longer participates in the hiring of saleswomen, but he insists that they be knowledgeable about the products so that they can coax male customers through the process of selecting garments, even when they are unsure of the size to buy.

In 1978, his first full year of business, he grossed $300,000. Sales have more than doubled every year since then, and in 1982 Victoria's Secret will generate more than $7.4 million in sales from its 60,000 mail-order customers nationwide and its four boutiques in the San Francisco Bay area.

"I never thought I would fail," Raymond says, "but neither did I expect to be this successful."

The idea for Victoria's Secret began at a party with Raymond, his wife, Gaye, and other couples. His male friends shared his feelings about shopping for lingerie. "The marketing side of me recognized an opportunity," he recalls.

With start-up capital of $120,000—his sources included a second mortgage and loans from a bank and his parents—Raymond opened a boutique that offered lacy lingerie in a Victorian setting of soft lighting, dark wood paneling and plump velvet furniture.

Translating the romantic image into mail order, which began simultaneously with the first boutique, proved challenging.

"Intimate apparel is extremely personal, so marketing it required a special touch," he says. Raymond wanted a four-color catalog. And he wanted the garments shown on real models.

The financial risk was substantial: His first catalog cost more than $40,000 to produce. But the gamble paid off. Victoria's Secret gained instant recognition in an already competitive field. The catalog's early editions are collectors' items.

As for the name, Victoria's Secret, Raymond wanted to project an image of subdued elegance. "My wife and I considered a number of possibilities, but none seemed as well suited." Customers regularly write to "Victoria," and some even send poems. All get a response—signed "Victoria."

Mail orders account for about half of Raymond's business; the rest comes from boutique sales. Gaye Raymond is director of store operations.

Roy Raymond was a natural for pairing entrepreneurial spirit with marketing talent. A native of Connecticut, Raymond, when he was 13, earned enough money from mowing lawns to start his own enterprise, printing invitations and business and greeting cards. By the time he entered high school, he had five youngsters working for him on commission. "That's when I discovered how much I enjoyed operating my own business," he says.

He attended Tufts University, where he earned a B.S. in motivational psychology, and then Stanford University, where he got an M.B.A. in marketing. He worked for two firms, including a California winery, developing markets for new products. "The skills I learned were easily applied to the Victoria's Secret venture," he says.

From the beginning, Raymond has incorporated marketing and sales techniques to encourage customer satisfaction. Merchandise is shipped within three days after orders are received, for example. "These things cost a little more, but they generate a lot of reorders," Raymond says.

Raymond considers Victoria's Secret "play." It's a good thing, too, because he devotes six days a week, 14 hours a day to his business. He spends Sunday with his wife and 3-year-old son.

Has success changed his life-style? "Not a bit," says Raymond, who lives in a modest San Francisco home. Eventually he would like to buy a ski chalet near Lake Tahoe. For the time being, however, he puts his profits back into Victoria's Secret.

Next month, Raymond will open a boutique in Walnut Creek; he plans only one more. He has received more than 150 offers to franchise Victoria's Secret nationwide but has turned them all down. "I want to keep the operation small so that it will stay personal," he says. "Besides, if it got much bigger, it wouldn't be as much fun."

Source   Tony Velocci, "Revealing Victoria's Secret," *Nation's Business,* July 1982, p. 76. Reprinted by permission from Nation's Business, July, 1982. Copyright 1982 by Nation's Business, Chamber of Commerce of the United States.

An area of special interest for the small business owner is finding answers to such questions as the following: "Why do customers buy one product and not another?" "Why do consumers prefer a specific brand or service?" "Why do customers patronize one store and not another?"

It is essential for small business owners to be sensitive to these questions as they try to understand the purchasing motivation of consumers. Knowledge of consumer buying behavior will enable the small business manager to plan the offering of products and services more effectively and have them available when they are requested. In today's highly competitive business environment, small business owners who anticipate consumer demands more accurately than their competitors have a distinct advantage. However, small business owners cannot afford to become complacent because consumer buying behavior is a dynamic process that demands their full attention. For example, changes in the standard of living of the population will be reflected in changes in consumer buying patterns.

In this chapter, the initial discussion of consumer buying behavior will be followed by another critical activity in the small business: personal selling.

CONSUMER MOTIVATION

The fundamental answer to the question of why people buy is that they are motivated to purchase products or services because they satisfy a need. An understanding of the motivational forces is critical for the small business firm, and the following discussion identifies some of the motivational forces behind consumer buying behavior.

Satisfaction of Primary Needs

In chapter 8, we stated that motivation is the force that arises within an individual, stimulating the person to take action to satisfy an aroused need or reach a goal. Thus, only when the need is aroused or awakened will it serve as an energizer for action.

One set of needs that people are motivated to satisfy is physiological, safety, and security—the **primary or basic needs.** Purchases of food, clothing, and shelter are motivated by the physiological desire for survival. Other purchases are made to satisfy safety and security needs. For example, safety features may be added to the home, such as covering a slippery patio floor with outdoor carpeting. The concern for security may result in the homeowner's having a burglar alarm, burglar bars, and a smoke alarm installed. Though these purchases may satisfy the basic needs, they do not answer the question of why one product or service is selected in lieu of another.

Satisfaction of Secondary Needs

However, there are other needs that serve as a major influence of buyer behavior. These are the **secondary or higher order needs.** Consumers make purchases that will satisfy their primary needs and also their secondary needs, such as recognition, peer approval, and status. When a person buys an automobile, the basic need for transportation is satisfied. However, the brand, model, color, style and price of the automobile satisfy higher order needs as well. For example, a particular auto purchase can serve as a status symbol or a means of self-expression.

Thus, no single motive influences purchasing behavior. Instead, consumer buying behavior is stimulated by the desire to satisfy a combination of primary and secondary needs. Consequently, no simple answer exists to the question of why people make the purchases they do.

THE PURCHASING PROCESS

The actual purchasing process focuses on all the forces that influence the consumer in making the choice. In the preceding section, we centered our attention on the *why* of buying. Next we turn our attention to the purchasing process that influences *how, when,* and *where* the purchase will be completed. The purchase decision process includes the phases of recognition of a need, evaluation of alternatives, purchase decision, and postpurchase behavior.

Recognition of a Need

Whatever the product or service, consumer buying behavior is first awakened by the recognition of an unsatisfied need. The need awareness may be the result of a change in life-style, family composition, dissatisfaction with a current product, or countless other factors. The consumer's becoming aware of the existence of the need that influences him or her to purchase a certain kind or a general class of product or service is classed as a **primary buying motive.** For example, the carpeting in the family living room may be badly worn. Thus, the consumer becomes aware of the need to take some action to replace the carpet now or at a later date.

Evaluation of Purchase Alternatives

When the consumer recognizes the need for new floor covering (primary buying motive), the next action is to evaluate the possible alternatives for satisfying the need. If the consumer decides to recarpet, the search for and evaluation of alternatives that determine the specific floor covering that will be purchased is known as the **selective buying motive.** Before the actual purchase is made, the consumer will evaluate many alternatives, such as color, kind of material, weight, style, price, guarantee, and reliability of the seller.

Rational Buying Motives

The consumer is influenced by other motives before making the final choice. One set of motives is the **rational buying motives.** A rational decision to buy involves a considerable amount of conscious thought and deliberation before the purchase is made. The consumer tries to evaluate all positive and negative features of the product or service. The consumer researches the products by gathering information from many sources, such as the *Consumer Reports Magazine.* Some of the factors that would influence a rational purchase decision are economy, dependability, and convenience in use of the product or service.

Emotional Buying Motives

Another set of motives that influence the purchase is **emotional buying motives.** Unlike rational purchases, emotional purchases involve little or no deliberation prior to the purchase. These are purchases characterized by impulse, by spur-of-the-moment action. Some motives that influence this type of purchase are a desire for social acceptance, emulation, and esteem.

Patronage Motives

Customers usually identify features about particular places of business that have strong appeal for them. These features are **patronage motives,** the factors that influence customers to return repeatedly to the same store to make their purchases. These motives influence *where* consumers will shop. The small business owners should seek to capitalize on these assets in order to build stronger patronage for the firm. Some representative patronage motives are discussed in the following sections.

Sales Personnel   One factor that influences consumer opinion, especially about retail or service establishments, is the quality of the salespersons. Sales-

Consumers may be motivated to purchase designer items in order to gain social acceptance or esteem.

persons who are courteous and friendly and who volunteer assistance to customers do much to help create a positive store image. Customers frequently remark that they patronize a particular store because they enjoy the kind of service accorded them by the salespersons. Conversely, indifferent or discourteous salespersons are often the reasons many customers begin patronizing the firm's competitors. The importance of building and maintaining positive customer relationships should be constantly emphasized in the sales training program.

Customer Service   Customers may be attracted to a store because of the product-related services it provides. Service after the sale is especially important as products become more complex. Often shoppers are willing to pay more for an item because of the quality service that the store provides. Consumer-oriented services are frequently cited as significant patronage motives also. These may include layaway, delivery, product return policies, check cashing, receiving of payment for utility bills, selling of car license plates, or serving as a postal substation.

Convenience of Location   A convenient location is a prime reason for the growth of shopping centers and the drive-in type of store. Customers want to avoid traffic congestion and shop where parking is available.

Merchandise Selection   The variety and the breadth of assortment of merchandise are important patronage motives. When a store stocks a wide selection of merchandise, consumers can find much of the merchandise they want at one place.

Price and Quality   Customers expect to receive a dollar's worth of value for each dollar expended. A policy that encourages repeat purchases is to charge a fair price for the quality of merchandise offered for sale.

The Purchase Decision

After the consumer has searched for information and evaluated the alternatives, the culmination of the evaluation process is the actual purchase decision. In reality, it is difficult to separate the search and evaluation processes from the actual purchase because they are both closely related. Because there are always the elements of uncertainty and risk in any purchase, consumers often seek to take steps to strengthen their purchases, by buying brand-name products.

Postpurchase Behavior

After making a purchase, most consumers reevaluate their decision and wonder if they made the correct choice. They remember the positive characteristics of the product they did not select, especially if the purchase represented a substantial expenditure, such as an auto or major appliance. Each purchasing experience provides feedback that results in learning. Thus, each purchase experience has considerable influence in shaping the next purchase decision. Many consumers seek reinforcement for their choice by reading additional literature or talking with others about their purchase. The small business owner can use this knowledge of consumer behavior advantageously to build repeat business for the firm. One method of accomplishing this is to follow up with customers after the sale is made in regard to their satisfaction with the product or service and to provide other postpurchase information.

THE IMAGE OF THE FIRM

Small business owners strive to create a unique personality or image for their firm. By electing to sell fashion merchandise, the retailer tries to create an atmosphere of exclusiveness. Another retailer builds an image emphasizing economy. In developing the image for a firm, almost everything the manager does reflects on the store image because the store and the owner are viewed as one and the same by most people in the general public.

A firm's image is partly created by the physical appearance of the store, the attitudes and appearance of employees, and its advertising. However, one factor that plays a critical role in creating a unique image is the reputation of the owner. Customers generally have a high regard for owners who have built a reputation for honesty and fairness, for selling quality merchandise, and for providing effective service over the years. Small business owners know that one method of enhancing their image is by emphasizing customer satisfaction as a major goal of the firm. The following statement of a small retail firm stresses this goal.

Thank You

The merchandise purchased by you from this store was selected because of its unusual Quality and Style—we hope it will live up to your expectations. If for any reason it does not you will confer a favor upon us by reporting same to the Management so that we may serve you BETTER.

Customer Relations

An essential feature of creating a favorable image is the action of the store owner in building positive customer relations. The customer–owner relationship is largely determined by the role that the owner plays in the community activities and the day-to-day interactions with customers.

Community Relations

If small business owners are community-relations-conscious and sincerely want to do something about it, they can invest a part of their time in various community-relations programs. It is important to recognize that the little things that the owner does in community relations are the most important. The small business owner should help formulate community policies and make sure that the activities of the business conform to them.

One means of strengthening community relations is through keeping informed about what the public thinks of the firm. By getting feedback from a cross section of people in the community, the owner–manager can develop a picture of public opinion. With this information, he or she must take action to capitalize on the strong points and must strive to overcome any weaknesses.

The firm that views community relations as something to turn to only in time of trouble is actually creating more problems. Good community relations cannot be created in a sporadic fashion. Rather, they must be conscientiously and actively developed on a continuous basis. Community relations are similar to a bank account. They are built up so that they are there when they are needed. The more the owner deposits, the more there is that can be drawn upon.[1]

The small business owner would be wise to consider what is best for the public at large as well as the firm when major decisions are made. In the long run, the interest of the community at large and the interest of the firm are inseparable. This interdependency is emphasized in the statement taken from the back of a sales ticket of a small grocery store.

We are your friends and neighbors. The money you spend in our store stays in our town and helps support your schools, roads, churches, and other local enterprises. This is our way of saying THANK YOU—CALL AGAIN.

Investment of the owner's time is more productive if he or she actively participates in a few activities rather than offering lukewarm participation in all activities. The owner can also encourage employees to become involved in community activities to broaden the involvement in community relations. There are many avenues for becoming involved in community relations, examples of which are now shown.

1. Membership in a civic club (Lions, Rotarians, Kiwanis, etc.).
2. Membership in the local chamber of commerce.
3. Supporting of town activities, such as the July 4 parade, or special events, such as water shows or art festivals, by contributing time or money or both.
4. Sponsorship of a Little League team (buying uniforms or equipment) or coaching a team.
5. Contributing use of equipment, such as a truck, during the town's annual cleanup day.

---

[1]"Profitable Community Relations," *Small Business Management Series*, no. 27 (Washington, D.C.: Small Business Administration), p. 32.

6. Selling tickets to local events.

7. Supporting programs that will promote civic progress, such as bond elections, for new schools or utility improvements.

Customer Relations in the Firm

The most important consideration in bringing about positive in-store customer relations is that the customer comes first. Store owners must express through their actions and attitudes that they need the customer more than the customer needs the small business. Simply stated, without customers there is no business! Some of the actions that may be engaged in that will promote healthy customer relations are presented in the following discussion.

1. Store owners should empathize with their customers. They should look at their firm objectively as the customers view it and ask themselves, "Do I like what I see?" and "Would I feel comfortable if I were a customer in this store?"

2. Positive customer relations are fostered by the fairness and honesty of the small business owner. These actions will result in strengthening the owner's reputation as a person of high integrity.

3. Customers should be treated courteously and attentively. Salespersons must be alert to the needs of customers and provide fast, courteous assistance.

4. The advertising in the store should be truthful. False, misleading, or exaggerated claims must be avoided.

5. Customer complaints settled in ways that are satisfying to customers is another means of enhancing customer relations. Small businesses, in particular, often depend heavily on **"word-of-mouth advertising."** This type of advertising can be very beneficial or harmful to the firm. A satisfied customer frequently recommends the business to friends and relatives. A dissatisfied customer can start an epidemic of ill will by telling friends and relatives unpleasant things that can severely injure the firm if the issue causing the problem is not solved. For example, the Direct Selling Foundation reports that customers with complaints will tell an average of 9 to 10 other people about their gripes. And a business can retain as many as 95 percent of its unhappy customers by resolving the problems quickly.

6. A firm that is attractive and well kept can be beneficial in creating goodwill. The condition of the physical facility is an expression of the owner's pride in the firm.

Finally, we must reemphasize that customer relations encompass the total system of the firm's operations. This suggests that a program must be consciously developed to strengthen both community and customer relations. It does not happen accidentally.

Customer Store Evaluation

The small business owner needs to be aware of the customer opinions of the firm. These data can be collected by using the "Customer Store Evaluation" questionnaire shown in Figure 18–1.

This questionnaire is designed to identify customers' perceptions of the many facets of the firm—store management, employees, and policies. The small business owner can measure the total responses to each question in order to arrive at an overall picture of the perceptions of the firm. Visual observation of each completed questionnaire serves to highlight favorable and unfavorable attitudes toward the firm. The owner can then use this information to take any necessary actions to increase customer goodwill and enhance the image of the firm.

PERSONAL SELLING

Sufficient mention has been made to underscore the importance of the salesperson's role in developing patronage motives as well as in creating positive customer relations. **Personal selling** is the process of personally informing customers about a product or service through personal communication for the purpose of making a sale. Personal selling may be carried out on a face-to-face

A salesperson in this computer store must know the company products and services in order to provide the best assistance possible to customers.

FIGURE 18–1

Customer store evaluation.

CUSTOMER STORE EVALUATION

Name of firm: _____ Town: _____

1. Have you ever traded with this firm? _____ Yes _____ No. If your answer is no, please state why _____

2. If your answer is yes, do you still trade with this firm? _____ Yes _____ No. If your answer is no, please state your reason for no longer trading with this firm

_____

3. If you have ever traded with this firm, please rank the firm in comparison to other men's clothing firms by placing an X in the appropriate column.

	Very high	Above average	Average	Below average	Very low
Convenience of location					
Quality of goods or services					
Variety of choice of goods or services					
Quantity of goods or services					
Appearance of establishment					
Neatness					
Cleanliness					
Spaciousness					
Uniformity of appearance					
Number of hours a day the business is open					
Number of days in week the business is open					
Management's knowledge of product or service					
Availability of latest fashion or style					
Speed of service					
Prestige of business					

basis or by means of the telephone. Personal selling is especially vital for the small firm. In fact, customers of small firms usually expect personal service. Because many large retailers have gone to more self-service, the small business owner has an opportunity to fill this vacuum by providing personal services and may even gain a competitive edge in the process.

The goal of personal selling is to meet the consumers' needs by offering the proper mix of goods and services at the time, place, and price requested. When this goal is realized, the result is a satisfied customer, and there is the distinct likelihood that a long-term relationship between the firm and the customer will be established. In the remainder of this chapter, we will explore many facets of personal selling.

FIGURE 18–1
(Continued)

	Very high	Above average	Average	Below average	Very low
Adequacy of merchandise displays					
Customer services					
Liberal credit policy					
Layaway					
Delivery					
Product guaranty					
After guaranty repairs					
Product return policies					
Purchase bonuses (trading stamps, etc.)					
Satisfies customer complaints					
Parking facilities available					
Quality of advertising					
Dependability of business					
Employees					
Knowledge of product or service					
Attitude: (1) friendly					
(2) helpful					
Appearance					
Adequacy of price of goods or service					
Acceptability of sales pressure					
Adequacy of traffic movement					
Street					
Sidewalk in front of store					
Inside store					

TYPES OF SALESPERSONS

In developing salespersons, the small business owners must identify the type of salespersons that they need to sell the products or services. Most salespersons in small firms are classified as either service (order takers) or creative (order getters).

Service Salespersons (Order Takers)

Service salespersons, or **order takers,** assist the customer in completing a sale. In this sales situation, a customer has already made a decision to buy and has a good idea of what product or service to buy. The service function of the order taker is to provide the customer with the information needed to make the buying decision. For example, if a customer .wants to buy new clothing, the salesperson's service selling activities center around showing the customer various styles, fabrics, colors; providing assistance in measuring for size; making arrangements for alterations if necessary; writing up the sales ticket; and informing the customer when the purchase can be picked up or delivered.

Creative Salespersons (Order Getters)

The selling function of the **creative salesperson,** or **order getter,** is significantly more challenging. In creative selling, the potential customer does not have a purchase in mind. The order getter's selling activity is to recognize potential customers and to arouse their need for merchandise or services by providing them with necessary information. The creative salesperson tries to convert the customer's neutral attitude to a positive desire for a product or service.

Suggestion selling offers possibilities for the creative salesperson. In this sales situation, the salesperson tries to build upon the customer's initial need by suggesting additional or better quality products or services. For example, the salesperson could suggest a blouse to go with the purchase of a skirt. Or the salesperson may suggest that the consumer purchase a higher-priced, better-quality item rather than the one initially considered.

SELECTION OF SALES PERSONNEL

The owner–manager or some designated person has the authority and responsibility for selecting the sales personnel. As a means of making the selection process more efficient, the position requirements must be clearly defined. Position descriptions are a necessary aid for selecting the person who has the qualities required for the service or creative sales position.

The *Dictionary of Occupational Titles* (4th ed., Department of Labor, 1977) suggests some of the duties of a general sales position. This information is an extremely useful guide for small business managers as they develop the specific job requirements in order to match people with jobs. The job description for a retail and wholesale salesperson taken from this source follows.

Salesperson (ret. tr.; whole. tr.)
Sells merchandise to individuals in store or showroom, utilizing knowledge of products sold. Greets customer on sales floor and ascertains make, type, and quality of merchandise desired. Displays merchandise, suggests selections that meet customer's needs, and emphasizes selling points of article, such as quality and utility. Prepares sales slip or sales contract. Receives payment or obtains credit authorization. Places new merchandise on display. May wrap merchandise for customer. May take inventory of

FIGURE 18–2
Ways to drive customers away.

Employees are slow in greeting customers.

Employees appear indifferent and make customers wait unnecessarily.

Personal appearance of employees is not neat.

Salespeople lack knowledge of the store's merchandise.

Customers complain of employees' lack of interest in their problems.

Mistakes that employees make are increasing.

Qualified employees leave for jobs with the store's competitors.

Source Bruce Goodpasture, "Danger Signals in Small Store," *Small Marketers Aids, no. 141* (Washington, D.C.: Small Business Administration, 1978).

stock. May requisition merchandise from stockroom. May visit customer's home by appointment to sell merchandise on shop-at-home basis. Classifications are made according to products sold as SALESPERSON, AUTOMOBILE ACCESSORIES (ret. tr.; whole. tr.); SALESPERSON, BOOKS (ret. tr.); SALESPERSON, SURGICAL APPLIANCES (ret. tr.).

The total employment process for selecting salespersons is the same as the employment process discussed in chapter 9.

TRAINING THE SALES PERSONNEL

An effective training program for sales personnel follows and reinforces the employment selection process. Even though the small firm normally has only a few salespeople, the owner should understand the contribution that sales training offers to the success of the firm.

One area of performance that is frequently weak is personal selling. The owner should be concerned about the warning signals noted in Figure 18–2 that reflect the type of attitudes and actions that threaten to drive customers to competitors' firms. Thus, one of the concrete steps that can be taken to prevent the development of poor attitudes is to give proper sales training.

In developing the sales staff, the small business owner recognizes that salespeople need at least three basic skills to make personal selling effective.

1. Salespeople must be skilled at learning the needs of the customer.

2. They must have a thorough knowledge of the merchandise and service offered by the retailer.

3. They must have the ability to convince customers that the merchandise and services offered by their store can satisfy the customer's needs better than that of their competitors.[2]

---

[2] Bert Rosenbloom, "Improving Personal Selling," *Management Aid,* no. 4.014 (Washington, D.C.: Small Business Administration, 1980), p. 4.

The training and development process should begin immediately when the employee is hired. Starting training immediately has the advantages of reaching a reasonable level of employee productivity in the shortest possible time, avoids unnecessary expenses and lost sales, and takes advantage of the new employee's natural interest in the job and willingness to learn about it.[3]

Training is a continuous process during the employee's tenure with the firm. Experienced salespersons may need training to learn how to sell a new product line or service or to improve their selling techniques. Whatever the reason, there are a variety of training methods that can be used as we discussed in Chapter 9. Regardless of the method used, employees will derive the greatest benefit from training if the training cycle, outlined here, is followed step by step.

1. Analyze learning needs—what knowledge and skills do your people need for their work that they do not already possess?

2. Develop a training plan (in conjunction with the learner) that lays out what has to be done so that the learner will acquire the knowledge and skills that have been decided upon in the needs analysis.

3. Evaluate results—determine what has been learned and what remains to be learned and whether the results of that learning are indeed the ability to do the work better.

4. Follow up to see that additional learning takes place where needed and that the learning actually brings better work performance.[4]

Focus of Training

The ultimate goal of personal selling is the satisfaction of consumer needs. The salesperson can more effectively work to attain this goal when given training that concentrates on the critical areas of product and service information, company information, customer information, and self-awareness. (See Fig. 18–3.)

Product and Service Information

Knowledge of the attributes of the products and services one is selling is essential. Product information includes a broad range of knowledge, including the types, sizes, varieties, special features, and physical and operating characteristics of the products; the quality of the product; the uses of the product; and warranties of the product. Product information requires some knowledge of the competitive products in order to emphasize the line that the salesperson is selling. Frustration occurs when the salesperson cannot ade-

---

[3] "Managing Retail Salespeople," *Business Basics*, no. 1019 (Washington, D.C.: Small Business Administration, 1980), p. 19.

[4] "Training and Developing Employees," *Business Basics*, no. 1022 (Washington, D.C.: Small Business Administration, 1980), p. 2.

FIGURE 18–3

Focus of training for salespersons.

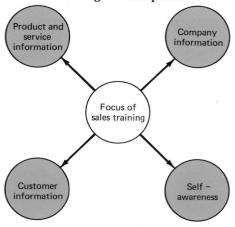

quately explain the features of the product or service. Training for developing product and service knowledge may be general or specific. General knowledge may suffice if the salesperson engages in selling a wide range of merchandise or services. Specific knowledge is required when salespersons are selling technical equipment, such as personal computers.

Company Information

A portion of the training program should be devoted to informing the employee about the company. Employees who are familiar with the firm's operations can represent it more effectively to the public and have a better understanding of their role in the firm. Company information focuses on such topics as history of the company; objectives; organizational structure; departmental structure; policies on customer services, sales, advertising, and personnel; rules and regulations on work schedules, uniforms, use of equipment, and credit and collections; delivery; and pricing. Much of this information is found in the employee manual. (See Chapter 9.)

Customer Information

The discussion of consumer buying behavior is intended to help the salespeople do a more effective selling job by providing them with information about consumer needs, interests, characteristics, and purchasing behavior. One of the most important qualities that is stressed for the salesperson is the need for empathy. The empathetic salesperson closely identifies with the consumer. Consequently, he or she gives more personal attention to understanding the customer's problems and feelings and tailors the sales approach to products or services that will satisfy customer's needs. In turn, this sales approach helps build customer loyalty. One of the surest ways of developing empathy is by learning to be a good listener.

Evaluating one's skills and personal qualities (physical appearance, personality, tact) allows each person to assess himself or herself. Through greater self-awareness, the salesperson is able to realize the type of image he or she projects and to identify areas that demand improvement. The old cliché "Good salespersons are born, not made" fails to account for the significant benefits derived from sales training. For example, a shy person can become a successful salesperson by becoming aware of the situation and making a concerted effort to work to overcome the shyness. The person with an outgoing personality can improve his or her skills in customer relations through training. The point of the matter is that greater self-awareness will not of itself make one a better salesperson. What makes a successful salesperson is the desire to change and to improve.

THE PERSONAL SELLING PROCESS

Personal selling is the most widely used technique for marketing goods and services. Therefore, salespersons must be well grounded in all phases of the selling process. Likewise the owner of the small firm must be familiar with the personal selling process and ensure that this information is made a part of the sales training program.

In the preceding section, we discussed the types of information that should be included in the presale preparation of salespersons. The personal selling process includes the activities involved in the completion of the sales transaction. Not all sales situations require equal emphasis on each of the phases in the selling process. For example, the service salesperson would ordinarily concentrate on the last five phases of the selling process whereas the creative salesperson would emphasize all phases.

We will examine each of the seven phases of the personal selling process in turn: prospecting, preapproach, sales approach, sales presentation, dealing with objections, closing the sale, and sales follow-up. (See Fig. 18–4.)

Prospecting

Prospecting is the process of developing a list of potential customers. The name of potential customers may be obtained from an almost endless number of sources, as from the company's sales records; present customers who can offer possible leads; newspaper announcements of births, graduations, mar-

FIGURE 18–4

Seven phases of the personal selling process.

riages, or relocation; the telephone directory; personal acquaintances; or current customers who may be considering purchasing a new model of a product. When the salesperson has developed a list, he or she subjects it to an evaluation to determine likely candidates for making a purchase.

Preapproach

In the preapproach or preparation phase, the salesperson attempts to gain as much knowledge of potential customers as possible in order to plan how and when to approach them. The salesperson must be aware of the customers' needs and the products and services the firm offers that will satisfy those needs. The more prepared the salesperson is in terms of awareness of the needs of customers, the more effective will be the sales presentation.

Sales Approach

The proper sales approach is critical because this is the initial opportunity for the salesperson to make a positive impression on the potential customer of himself or herself and of the product or service being sold and also to create sufficient interest so that the customer will listen to the sales presentation. Selling in the small business is often conducive to the creation of a favorable initial impression because of the opportunity to develop a warm, personal, and sincere relationship. Salespersons who can learn to know their customers and greet them by name and demonstrate that they consider the needs of the customers of utmost importance will greatly improve their chances of success.

Sales Presentation

The salesperson must make an effective sales presentation in order to attract and hold the prospect's attention. The sales presentation is reinforced by demonstrating the product or explaining the service or allowing the customer to participate in a trial of the product in order to appreciate it fully, for example, test driving a new automobile or trying on new clothing. The salesperson should not dominate the sales presentation but should listen and allow the customer to ask questions. Some specific procedures that may be included in the sales presentation are listed here.

1. Make strong, persuasive points about merchandise or service early in the presentation—there may be no second chance.
2. Work on "selling benefits"—the value should be established before discussing price.
3. Give the customer complete attention.
4. Never confuse the customer with too wide an assortment.
5. Whenever possible, try to show the item in use.

6. Whenever possible, involve the customer.
7. As a sales presentation progresses, be more specific and more emphatic.
8. Listen to make the customer feel important.
9. Look for polite ways to make the customer feel at ease.
10. Demonstrate enthusiasm and a sense of satisfaction about your job.[5]

SPECIAL INTEREST FEATURE

Powerful Sales Persuaders

One formula for the sales presentation is suggested by the "**AICDC principle of selling.**"

The "A" is to remind you that you have the prospect's attention. *Obviously, it's the first order of business. No attention, no sale because the selling message doesn't get through. The prospect's senses must be* actively *involved.*

The "I" is for interest. *Attention must be maintained. The stimulus must be prolonged and pleasurable. The interest must be long enough to engage the prospect in the actual presentation.*

The "C" is for conviction. *The customer must sense that what the salesperson claims is true. He must be convinced of the rightness of your proposition.*

The "D" is for desire. *Desire is a natural result of the senses being pleasantly stimulated and the feeling that something good is in the offing.*

The last "C" is for close. *This is the payoff. It's the point where the salesperson's skill in appealing to the prospect's senses is measured and rewarded. The prospect is moved because he is stimulated to move!*

Source Douglas J. Christopher, "Powerful Sales Persuaders," *Salesman's Opportunity*, vol. 120, no. 6 (November 1982), p. 28. Copyright 1982, Salesmakers Syndicate Services, 22 Bittersweet Trail, Wilton, CT. 06897-3934. Reprinted from *Salesman's Opportunity* magazine, 6 N. Michigan Avenue, Chicago, IL 60602.

Dealing with Objections

Dealing with objections in a satisfactory manner is probably the most difficult step in the personal selling process. Whereas salespersons should anticipate some objections, they should not raise them. Instead, objections should be handled as they arise. Customer objections may include these: "The price is too high; the merchandise is the wrong color; it is not the kind of material I

---

[5]C. Winston Borgen, *Learning Experiences in Retailing* (Pacific Palisades, Calif.: Goodyear Publishing Company, 1976), pp. 296–298.

want; or, I have an older model at home with which I am satisfied." Some common methods of handling objections are shown now.

1. Use the "yes-but" technique. (Turn the customer's attention to other factors. The key here is not to contradict.)
2. Ask questions of the customer.
3. Use the turn-it-around principle. (Give the customer confidence in his or her own thinking and a feeling the observation is his or her own.)
4. Select another feature for emphasis. (Turn customer attention from the objection point to another point with more appeal.)
5. Direct denial. (Handle very carefully so no offense is taken by the customer.)[6]

Closing the Sale

Salespersons should be prepared to close a sale at any time during the presentation or while handling objections. In closing the sale, the salesperson tries to find the appropriate time to get the customer to act—to buy the product or service. Among the reasons a salesperson fails to close a sale is that he or she pushes the customer to make a decision before the latter is ready or that the salesperson demonstrates a feeling of superiority over the customer. A number of closing techniques are offered now.

1. Use the principle of positive suggestion, and assume the sale is made. If the customer does not stop the salesperson, the sale has been completed.
2. Offering an added incentive may help in prompting customer action. If the customer appears to be hesitant about the purchase, the salesperson may offer an extra incentive to buy, such as cash discount or free delivery.
3. A good closing technique is to summarize the main benefits of the product or service. Emphasize those benefits that match the customer's buying motives.
4. Asking for the order is an obvious but often overlooked closing technique. Many customers respond favorably to this sales technique.

Sales Follow-up

A supportive step that aids in developing goodwill and repeat sales is a follow-up after the sale by the salesperson. This may be accomplished by a

---

[6]Ibid., p. 299.

telephone call or by a short, courteous personal note thanking the customer for the purchase and offering to be of assistance to the customer any time in the future. Follow-ups are usually provided on larger purchases, such as major household appliances.

EVALUATING SALES PERSONNEL

The performance evaluation of the salesperson should be designed not only to gauge past performance but also to reinforce future job performance and provide opportunities for self-development. Performance evaluation should be applied in a systematic manner in order to benefit both employer and employee. Performance may be evaluated by using a rating scale similar to the one presented in Chapter 9. Another appraisal technique is "Management by Objectives." The reader is referred to Chapter 9, where performance evaluation was discussed in some detail. The Guide for Improving a Salesperson's Performance shown in Figure 18–5 can be extremely useful for counseling the salesperson in the areas of planning, measuring, and correcting performance.

SUMMARY OF KEY POINTS

1. Consumer buying behavior is a dynamic process.
2. Consumers are motivated to make purchases to satisfy both primary and secondary needs.
3. The purchasing process consists of the following phases: recognize a need, evaluate purchase alternatives, the purchase decision, and post-purchase behavior.
4. The buying motives that influence the consumer are primary, selective, rational, emotional, and patronage.
5. Patronage motives are the features that cause a person to continue to buy from a specific firm.
6. Small business managers attempt to create a unique image for their firm.
7. The small business manager can strengthen customer relations with the firm by involvement in community activities and through in-store actions.
8. The Customer Store Evaluation (see Fig. 18–1) offers insight into the consumers' perception of the business.
9. Personal selling is of critical importance for the small business.
10. There are basically two types of salespersons: service (order takers) and creative (order getters).

FIGURE 18–5
Guide for improving a salesperson's performance.

One goal of measuring a salesperson's performance is to help him/her improve. The three steps in bringing about improvement, when, and if, it is needed are: planning, measuring, and correcting.

PLANNING

- Get the salesperson's agreement about what he/she is to attain or exceed for the next year.
  1. Total profit contribution in dollars.
  2. Profit contribution in dollars for:
     Each major product line.
     Each major market (by industry or geographical area).
     Each of 10–20 target accounts (for significant new and additional business).
- Get the salesperson's agreement about expenses within which he/she is to stay for the next year:
  1. Total sales expense budget in dollars.
  2. Budget in dollars for: travel, customer entertainment, telephone, and other expenses.
- Have the salesperson plan the number of calls he/she will make to accounts and prospects during the next year.

MEASURING

- Review at least monthly the salesperson's record for:
  1. Year-to-date progress toward 12-month profit contribution goals.
  2. Year-to-date budget compliance.

CORRECTING

Meet with salesperson if his/her record shows that he/she is 10 percent or more off target. Review with him/her the number of calls he/she has made on each significant account plus what he/she feels are his/her accomplishments and problems. In addition, you may need to do some of the following to help him/her improve performance:

- Give salesperson more day-to-day help and direction.
- Accompany salesperson on calls to provide coaching.
- Conduct regular sales meetings on subjects which salespersons want covered.
- Increase sales promotion activities.
- Transfer accounts to other salespersons if there is insufficient effort or progress.
- Establish tighter control over price variances allowed.
- Increase or reduce selling prices.
- Add new products or services.
- Increase salesperson's financial incentive.
- Transfer, replace, or discharge salesperson.

Source Raymond Loen, *Measuring Salesforce Performance,* Management Aid no. 4.003 (Washington, D.C.: Small Business Administration, n.d.), p. 4.

11. Selection and training of salespersons are areas that must be emphasized even in the small business that has only a few employees.

12. There are seven phases in the personal selling process.

DISCUSSION QUESTIONS

1. Why should small business managers analyze consumer behavior?
2. Why do people buy?
3. Explain the difference between a primary and a selective buying motive.
4. Identify several rational buying motives and emotional buying motives.
5. What are patronage motives?
6. Identify some of the factors that encourage buying from a particular firm.
7. Why is personal selling so important, especially to the small retailer?
8. What areas of knowledge should be stressed in a sales training program?
9. Identify the steps in making a sale.
10. Explain the difference between a service and a creative salesperson.

STUDENT PROJECTS

1. Select two stores that sell comparable merchandise. Use the Customer Store Evaluation found in Figure 18–1 for evaluating one store where you regularly shop and a store where you shop infrequently. How do the two stores compare based on the evaluation?

2. Recall a recent purchase you have made. Reconstruct the process you followed in making that purchase.

3. Concerning your own shopping habits, what factors do you consider most influential in your choice of a store to patronize?

4. Develop a model of what you would consider to be the "ideal" retail store. What factors would you include in your description of this "ideal" firm?

5. In your opinion, what are the requirements for being an effective salesperson?

6. Identify as many examples as you can of small business involvement in the local community that strengthen the small business firm's image in the community.

CASE A

Nothing But Lookers

Stan Clark and Wilbur Fiddler, two shoe clerks in the National Shoe Store in the Plaza Shopping Center, were totaling up their sales for the day. As usual, Stan had a pretty good day compared to Wilbur's mediocre one.

"Stan, you must be made of luck. I just can't understand it," said Wilbur. "You get all the customers, and all I get is 'lookers.'"

"Do you really think it's luck, Wilbur?" asked Stan.

"What else would it be? It isn't as if I bit off customers' heads or something," replied Wilbur firmly.

"Oh, I think you are very courteous and helpful to customers," said Stan tactfully.

"Well, then, what is the matter?" implored Wilbur.

Stan hesitated, then said, "I'm not sure I can answer that, Wilbur. But maybe you don't help potential sales along as well as you could."

"Help them along? What more can I do than show them the shoes, tell them about the quality, and see that they fit?" asked Wilbur.

"Oh, there's a good deal more than that," suggested Stan. "You have to work to find out what they really want, then help them satisfy those wants."

"I guess I'm going to have to study your methods. I sure would like to improve my sales volume," Wilbur said sincerely.

"I'll be glad to help any way I can," Stan replied.

That night Wilbur thought things over. Maybe there was something he was doing wrong. He would listen when Stan approached prospects and see what he said in answer to their questions. Then Wilbur had an idea. Maybe Stan would also listen to his sales technique when Stan wasn't busy with customers himself and help Wilbur locate anything he was doing wrong.

When Wilbur presented the idea to Stan next morning, Stan said he'd do his best to help. The first time that Wilbur had a customer, Stan took his dusting cloth to the display behind the fitting lounge so he could hear Wilbur.

Wilbur began, "Good morning! May I help you?"

The lady customer returned his smile and said, "Why yes, do you have those smart little 'T' strap pumps in anything but black? And in size 6 double 'A'?"

Wilbur shook his head and said, "I'm awfully sorry but we're all out of those in other colors. That was last season's fashion, you know. But we have lots of the blacks in your size. Would you like to try them on?"

Rather regretfully the lady said, "No, I guess not."

"Can't I show you something else?" Wilbur put in eagerly.

Thoughtfully the lady said, "Well, I guess if you have something in beige, something like that only in the newer style. What I wanted was something to wear . . . ."

Happily, Wilbur interrupted, "Beige. Yes, we've got something in beige. Just came in. Let me get your size and please have a seat over there."

Thinking he was on the way to the sale, Wilbur dashed off for the shoes. The lady started for the seat, saw a display, and stopped to examine a dressy pair of black pumps.

Wilbur came back hurriedly with the shoes and the box. He pulled one shoe out of the box and held it up proudly. "How about this one?"

The lady reached for the shoe and said, "Well, I don't know. I had thought something a little dressier."

"These are very practical and comfortable," said Wilbur. "Let's try them for size."

"It looks so big!" the lady said as soon as one was on.

Wilbur laughed good-naturedly, then said, "Oh, come on now, they're only size 6. This one probably just looks big next to the black one you're wearing."

"No, these won't do at all. I'm sorry," she said firmly.

"We've got a dressy little linen shoe in beige trimmed with black," said Wilbur hopefully.

"Wouldn't linen be hard to keep clean?" asked the lady.

"Gosh, I don't know," said Wilbur. "Maybe not."

"No, I wouldn't want linen," said the lady. "I was just looking, anyway."

Source   *Why Customers Buy, Instructor's Manual, Management Development Program* (Washington, D.C.: Small Business Administration, 1967).

QUESTIONS

1. If you were Stan, what would you tell Wilbur he could do to improve his sales technique?

2. What questions might Wilbur have asked the customer to develop what she wanted more fully?

3. How do you think Stan would have handled the same customer?

CASE B

The Leather Jacket

Alice Shoemaker was anxious to buy her husband, Fred, an especially nice Christmas gift in recognition of his promotion to general manager at Ace Manufacturing Company. After considering several gift possibilities, Alice decided that a leather jacket would be a most appropriate gift.

While shopping for the jacket, she was shown a number of leather jackets in several stores. However, she particularly liked the style of one jacket she had seen at the University Shop, one of the better shops in the city. She purchased this jacket for the price of $225.

When Fred opened his gift Christmas day, he was delighted. He immediately tried on the jacket, but, to his dismay, it was too small even though it was labeled his size, medium.

After discussing the jacket and what to do about it, Alice and Fred decided that they would return it and get their money back. The store has a policy of "Satisfaction Guaranteed or Your Money Back."

When Alice returned the jacket to the University Shop, she was greeted by the salesperson who had sold her the jacket. Alice explained that the jacket was too small and rather than an exchange, she would like her money refunded. She had the sales ticket in hand.

However, the salesperson refused to give her a refund and even became somewhat hostile. Seeing she was getting nowhere with the clerk, Alice asked to talk to the store owner. After discussing the matter with the store owner for a few minutes, Alice could see that he was beginning to lose his composure. His face became flushed, and it appeared to Alice that he was becoming quite angry over her request for a cash refund.

Finally, though begrudgingly, he gave Alice her money back. After he had finished counting out the refund, he remarked to Alice in a sarcastic tone of voice, "The only reason you want your money back is so that you can return next week and purchase the jacket for $65 less when we have our annual inventory sale." Without further comment, Alice walked out of the University Shop.

QUESTIONS

1. How does the purchase decision process relate to the purchase of the leather jacket by Alice?

2. What buying motives were influential in Alice's purchase of the jacket?

3. Discuss the store owner's actions and that of the clerk in terms of patronage motives.

4. What effect can negative word-of-mouth advertising have from a dissatisfied customer on the store owner's image in the community?

SMALL BUSINESS ADMINISTRATION PUBLICATIONS

Management Aids (Free)

Measuring Sales Force Performance

Is the Independent Sales Agent for You?

Developing New Accounts

Improving Personal Selling in Small Retail Stores

Small Business Management Series (For Sale)

Training Salesmen to Serve Industrial Markets

Business Basics (For Sale)

Managing Retail Salespeople
Recruiting and Selecting Employees
Training and Developing Employees

CHAPTER NINETEEN

PROMOTIONAL STRATEGY IN THE SMALL BUSINESS

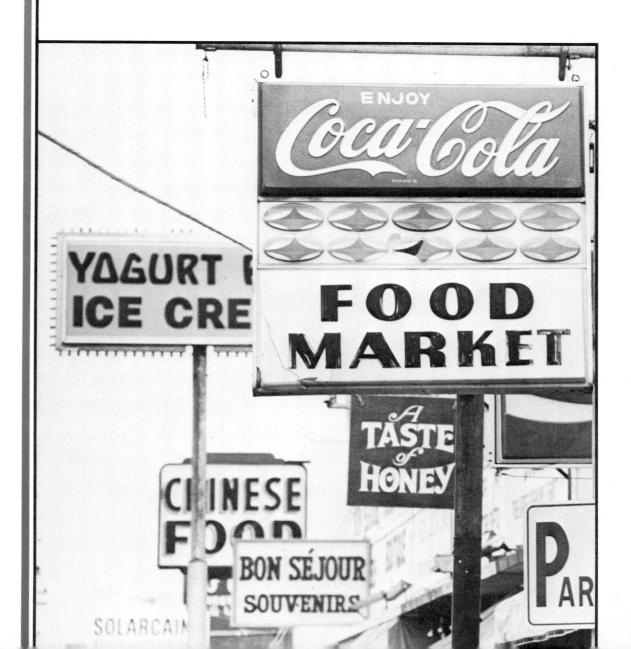

LEARNING GOALS

After reading this chapter, you will understand:

1. The purposes of advertising in the small business.
2. The difference between promotional advertising and institutional advertising.
3. The limitations of advertising.
4. The advertising media used by the small business manager.
5. The overall ingredients that go into the advertising program of the small business.
6. Two methods of preparing the advertising budget for the small firm.
7. The characteristics of a good advertisement.
8. The difference between advertising and sales promotion.
9. Some of the commonly used sales promotion techniques utilized by small business owners.

KEY WORDS

Promotional strategy	AIDCA principle
Advertising	Specialty advertising
Advertising copy	Percentage of sales method
Advertising medium	Unit of sales method
Advertising media	Cooperative advertising
Promotional advertising	Sales promotion
Institutional advertising	Impulse purchases
Publicity	Point-of-purchase display

SMALL BUSINESS PROFILE

In Their 20s and Making Millions

Most people keep their vocations and avocations in separate compartments of their lives. Not Robert Keith Vicino, an advertising executive and hot-air ballooning enthusiast. The result: a business idea that has, well, taken off.

"Like other balloonists, I helped support my hobby by carrying advertising on my balloon," says Vicino, who in 1976 was owner of Ad Art, a Hartford agency. "I found that people remembered the balloon but not the company that was advertising." So he and Ann Wawer, a sales representative, came up with the idea of making giant balloons in the shape of familiar consumer products.

"A giant bottle or beer can is hard to forget," he says.

For advertising they chose cold-air balloons, which are safer and cheaper than their levitating cousins. Nevertheless, the first effort—a 40-foot-high balloon shaped like a whisky bottle—was costly beyond all expectations. After some $2,500 and 500 hours of sewing vinyl-coated nylon, the job was completed—but they had charged the client, a distilling company, only $250.

Vicino and Wawer decided to make a new start in more ways than one. They took what was left of their savings, moved to San Diego and got married.

They were still figuring out what to do with their lives when they heard from Heublein, the Connecticut liquor firm. "We had approached Heublein with our balloon idea when we were living in Hartford," says Wawer. "It took them several months to decide to go with it."

Heublein ordered one balloon in the shape of a Club Cocktail can. With that order in hand, they incorporated as Robert Keith & Company in 1978. Subcontractors did the production this time around. Heublein then requested five more balloons in the shape of José Cuervo tequila bottles—three and four stories high.

Vicino, 28, is the artist; Wawer, 26, is corporate secretary and treasurer and takes care of the business—often creatively. "At first I would stay home and answer the phone, 'Robert Keith & Company; please hold.' Clients thought we were a big company!"

They have since attracted many major advertisers with their larger-than-life inflatable displays. Among them are PepsiCo, Miller Brewing, Atari, R. J. Reynolds and United Artists.

Cost of the inflatables ranges from $200 to $400 per linear foot. This is about 20 to 30 percent more than the cost of conventional signs, but the company says its clients get 200 to 300 percent more visibility with inflatables.

The company has developed a three-dimensional billboard, which uses an inflatable addition that sticks out into space as much as 15 feet. One such billboard features a 12-foot killer whale leaping from it to advertise the Miami Seaquarium. A huge jetliner appears to fly through a Canadian billboard promoting Pacific Western Airlines. Like the balloons, the inflatable portions of the billboards stay filled with the help of small electric fans. And like the inflatables, the billboards are a success.

"Our growth rate has been incredible," says Wawer. "The company has grown 300 to 400 percent a year, and we expect to have $6 million in sales this year." Says Vicino, "I told my father I'd be a millionaire by the time I was 25, but it took me till I was 27."

Last summer Wawer received an award for her outstanding work as a young entrepreneur from Junior Achievement, a business-sponsored non-profit organization that promotes economic education and free enterprise.

Vicino has developed some new designs, among them the Portaboard—an inflatable, portable billboard on which a company could mount its own display.

One idea that may soon spring from the drawing board is the "moon ball," a balloon that when fastened parachute-style to the back, allows the wearer to experience something similar to the near weightlessness of the moon. A moon ball could, for example, allow a 175-pound person to spring 60 feet into the air. Wawer and Vicino are now working on a model with a mechanism to assist takeoff and control steering; they hope to introduce the moon ball at a nearby amusement park within the next few months and perhaps go national next spring. "The moon balls will make a million or two," says Vicino. "You have to think big."

Source   Mary Tuthill, "In Their 20s and Making Millions," *Nation's Business*, December 1981, p. 64. Reprinted by permission from Nation's Business, December, 1981. Copyright 1981 by Nation's Business, Chamber of Commerce of the United States.

Ralph Waldo Emerson said, "If a man write a better book, preach a better sermon, or make a better mousetrap than his neighbor, though he builds his house in the woods, the world will make a beaten path to his door." This statement embodies the assumption that a new or improved product or service is all that is necessary to generate sales for the firm. However, small business owners who sit back and wait for customers to beat a path to their business to purchase their products or services will likely fall victim to their competitors. Though the products or services form one of the major variables of the marketing mix, consumers will not buy them unless they know of their existence and believe that they will satisfy their wants and needs. Promotional strategy is the means of accomplishing this goal.

Promotional strategy is the means that small business owners use to communicate information about the firm and its products and services to potential customers with the objective of influencing customers to purchase the products or services that will satisfy their wants and needs. The promotional methods utilized by small business owners to communicate this information are advertising and sales promotion (both are discussed in this chapter) and personal selling (discussed in the preceding chapter).

THE ROLE AND
PURPOSES OF ADVERTISING

Though small business owners may not feel that they can afford the expense of advertising their goods and services because of limited financial resources, such an attitude will significantly lessen the firm's likelihood for success. In fact, advertising should be considered an investment rather than an expense. Owners should realize the value of advertising and that advertising on a regular basis will materially increase the possibility for growth of the firm. Sales are the lifeblood of the small business because they are the means by which income is generated. In the highly competitive business environment, a well-planned advertising strategy is one of the most effective means of increasing sales.

Personal selling was described as the personal communication between the customer and the salesperson. On the other hand, **advertising** is any type of sales presentation that is nonpersonal and is paid for by an identified sponsor. The advertising message, called the **advertising copy,** contains the written or spoken words of the ad or both. Owners may choose to place advertising messages in a single source **(advertising medium)** or in more than one source **(advertising media).**

Advertising has many purposes, depending on the nature of the business and products and services promoted. For example, a manufacturer's advertising is designed to stimulate interest and increase sales in the line of merchandise. A retailer's advertising is intended to stimulate consumer awareness and to increase sales.

In this section, we examine the role and purposes of advertising, focusing our attention on small retailers and small service establishment operators. However, wholesalers, manufacturers, and other types of small businesses can modify these goals to their specific requirements.

The two general objectives of advertising are promotional and institutional. Each of these is discussed in turn.

PROMOTIONAL ADVERTISING

The objective of **promotional advertising** is to inform and remind the target market of the firm about its goods and services. Some of the specific goals of promotional advertising are discussed in the following sections. The greater amount of advertising dollars is spent for promotional advertising.

Increasing Sales

A major purpose of all advertising is to create an action-response by the consumer that will result in sales of a product or use of a service. Such advertising is designed to bring about an immediate increase in sales. The small business owners may emphasize specific appeals in their advertising messages, such as encouraging the immediate purchase of a product or a reduced charge for a specific service if used by a specific date. For example, a chimney sweep service offers a $5 reduction of the normal service charge if the service is used between November 1 and November 15.

Creating Awareness of a Company's Products or Services

The advertising message of the firm can be geared to create increased customer awareness or interest in the firm's products or services. This advertising message offers potential customers the following kinds of product and service information.

1. The types of products or services sold.
2. The benefits to be gained from the use of company products or services.
3. How products can be used.
4. The prices of products or services.
5. Where company products or services may be obtained.[1]

Attracting New Customers

Small business managers should not be complacent with their current volume of business and patronage. They may feel they have all the customers they can adequately serve and consequently see no purpose in advertising to attract new customers. However, the National Retail Merchants Association estimates that the small business would have to close its doors at the end of 3 or 4 years if it stopped advertising. This association reports that a store annually loses between 20 and 25 percent of its customers. Each year the market composition changes as people move in and out of the trading area. For example, the Bureau of the Census estimates that about 18 percent of the nation's population changes its place of residence annually. And customer tastes and shopping habits change. The younger generation has different demands from the older generation it replaces. In order to maintain the status quo, small business owners advertise to keep the firm's name before the public in order to attract new customers.

To increase patronage, small firm owners should identify their market segment and develop their advertising strategy for this market. Markets may be segmented in many ways, as by age or by ethnic or geographical grouping. Thus, if the target market is teenagers, small business owners should discover such characteristics as where they live, their radio and television listening and viewing habits, and their income in order to direct advertising efforts at this specific market.

---

[1] Adapted from Harry D. Wolfe, *Measuring Advertising Results*, Studies in Business Policy, no. 102 (New York: National Industrial Conference Board, 1962), pp. 10–11.

Promotion of a Special Offer or Special Sale

Advertising may promote a special event or a special sale. To illustrate, a pizza parlor advertises a special price on its pizza to help celebrate the pizza parlor's birthday. By purchasing one size of pizza at the regular price, the customer will receive the next smaller size of the same kind of pizza free. The ad also specifies how long the special price is good. Ads can be used to promote special sales, such as the 1-cent sale. Buy one item at the regular price and get a second for only 1-cent more. A men's store ad promotes a "1-day-only" sale of its famous name brand suits at a specially reduced price.

Small business owners may find it useful to develop a promotion calendar to note opportunities for special events.

Special Dates	**Special Promotions**
Valentine's Day	Sidewalk sales
St. Patrick's Day	Presummer, summer, spring, fall
Easter	fashion parades
Mother's Day	Anniversary sale
Father's Day	Renovation sale
Labor Day	
Thanksgiving	
Christmas	

Promoting Greater Uses of Product

Advertising may be used to inform customers of additional uses for a product or service. One of the premier examples is baking soda. Today this product is widely advertised as having many uses in addition to its original one as a baking ingredient, such as a deodorizer for the refrigerator, a cleansing agent, or a toothpaste. Some advertising is designed to increase the length of the buying season for a product. Antifreeze is advertised for its use as an engine coolant for summer driving as well as a protection against radiator freeze-up in the winter. This type of advertising may also suggest increasing the number of items purchased at one time or replacing the products more frequently.

Introducing New Products or Services

Not only do customers change but so do the products or services that a store offers for sale. Many old products are replaced by new ones. Advertising helps to inform customers of the availability of new merchandise. In addition

Advertising and sales promotion aid in making consumers aware of new products and services. An effective sales promotion technique is allowing consumers to sample a new product.

the small business may also begin offering new services that are announced in the firm's advertising.

Institutional Advertising

Institutional advertising is aimed at providing the general public with information about the company. Institutional advertising's purposes are to create goodwill toward the company, to build consumer confidence in the company, and to create or strengthen the image of the firm in the community. Through institutional advertising, the small business manager seeks to improve the firm's public relations stature by demonstrating that the owner is a concerned, active, socially responsible member of the community. For example, with the energy shortage, one firm advertised in a local newspaper a message reminding consumers and business firms alike of the critical need to employ energy conservation measures. The ad also contained suggestions on how energy might be conserved.

The small firm may also direct some of its advertising emphasis toward public service announcements. For example, announcements may be made informing the public of activities that are going to take place in the community. Announcements about special community events, such as an arts and crafts show or activities of local civic organizations, may be sponsored by a particular firm. This type of advertising aids in fostering good public relations and strengthening the ties of the business to the community.

The company may also benefit from the publicity it receives. **Publicity** is not the same as advertising, however. Publicity is a news item about a company reported by the media because the information has some apparent news value. A firm may donate time, money, or merchandise to a civic project that is reported by the various media. Unlike advertising, publicity is not paid for by the firm.

Limitations of Advertising

Although advertising is a powerful tool to aid the small business owner, its limitations must also be recognized. For example, advertising cannot force people to buy things they do not want. Another limitation of advertising is that, if a firm advertises extensively but offers poor service or inferior products, no amount of advertising will overcome these deficiencies. Many customers visit a store in response to an ad. However, if they are ignored or treated discourteously by sales personnel during their visit, the outcome will be dissatisfied customers who are unlikely to return to the store. If the small business manager charges higher prices than competitors for similar merchandise, advertising will not aid in selling the overpriced merchandise indefinitely. A further limitation of advertising is that it usually does not produce dramatic results immediately. Rather, the manager should follow an advertising strategy of advertising in several media and consistently in at least one medium. Furthermore, advertising effectiveness will be severely reduced if it contains false or misleading statements. Not only is this illegal but it also seriously damages the firm's image in the community. Additionally, advertising's value will be diminished if it is poorly timed or improperly prepared. In summary, the owner–manager should recognize these advertising limitations.

1. Advertising will not overcome discourteous treatment of customers by salespersons.
2. Advertising will not sell inferior products or services more than once.
3. Misleading or untruthful advertising will result in a loss of customer confidence in the firm.
4. A single advertisement will not bring about a sustained increase in sales and store traffic.

ADVERTISING MEDIA

One of the many decisions facing small business managers is deciding which advertising medium or media best serve their type of business. No one formula is available to provide the answer. Advertising media that are appropriate for the needs of the small business are discussed as follows.

Newspapers

Newspapers are the single most important advertising medium for the small business manager. Nationwide, about 30 percent of all advertising dollars is spent for newspaper ads. An advantage of newspapers is that circulation covers a selected geographical territory (a section of a city, a single town, a number of adjoining towns, or a number of adjacent counties). In addition, newspaper advertising provides broad coverage in the trade area. Ads reach people in all economic classes. Newspaper ads are flexible and timely because they can be changed frequently. Newspapers have short closing times. "Closing times" refers to the deadlines prior to publication by which advertising copy must be submitted. For daily newspapers, this period seldom exceeds 24 hours, thus giving the advertiser the opportunity to make last-minute changes. Closing dates for Sunday supplements, however, are generally much longer, usually ranging from 4 to 6 weeks.[2] When compared with other media, advertising costs in newspapers are relatively low. This is significant for the small business manager who has a limited budget for advertising. Newspapers serve as a guide for shoppers who are looking for information about products or services. The ads inform them what is available, where it is being sold, when, and at what price. Managers should study the feasibility of using the newspaper coverage that matches their goals. If they are concentrating on a trading area of a specific section of town, they may advertise in a newspaper that has a circulation limited to one section of town, such as the *Southside News*.

A disadvantage of newspaper advertising is that its coverage is not selective. If the firm caters to a specific market segment, much of the newspaper ad coverage will be wasted. Another disadvantage to consider is that many ads are presented together in one newspaper, and a single ad may be missed. Most newspapers are read or scanned hurriedly and kept for a short time, which means the life of the ad is of short duration. Small business managers should analyze their firm's target market to determine whether newspaper advertising should extend to the larger audience or be limited to a more select audience. The Special Interest Feature presents a checklist for a promotional ad in a newspaper.

---

[2] James Engel, Martin Warshaw, and Thomas Kinnear, *Promotional Strategy*, 4th ed. (Homewood, Ill.: Irwin, 1979), p. 273.

SPECIAL INTEREST FEATURE

Checklist for Promotional Advertising in a Newspaper

*Merchandise	Does the ad offer merchandise having wide appeal, special features, price appeal, and timeliness?
Medium	Is a newspaper the best medium for the ad, or would another—direct mail, radio, television, or other—be more appropriate?
Location	Is the ad situated in the best spot (in both section and page location)?
Size	Is the ad large enough to do the job expected of it? Does it omit important details, or is it overcrowded with nonessential information?
*Headline	Does the headline express the major single idea about the merchandise advertised? The headline should usually be an informative statement and not simply a label.
Illustration	Does the illustration (if one is used) express the idea the headline conveys?
*Merchandise information	Does the copy give the basic facts about the goods, or does it leave out information that would be important to the reader? ("The more you tell, the more you sell.")
Layout	Does the arrangement of the parts of the ad and the use of white space make the ad easy to read? Does it stimulate the reader to look at all the contents of the ad?
Human interest	Does the ad—through illustration, headline, and copy—appeal to customers' wants and wishes?
*"You" attitude	Is the ad written and presented from the customer's point of view (with the customer's interests clearly in mind), or from the store's?
*Believability	To the objective, nonpartisan reader, does the ad ring true, or does it perhaps sound exaggerated or somewhat phony?
Typeface	Does the ad use a distinctive typeface—different from those of competitors?
*Spur to action	Does the ad stimulate prompt action through devices such as use of a coupon, statement of limited quantities, announcement of a specific time period for the promotion or impending event?

Sponsor identification Does the ad use a specially prepared signature cut that is always associated with the store and that identifies it at a glance? Also, does it always include the following institutional details: store location, hours open, telephone number, location of advertised goods, and whether phone and mail orders are accepted?

*The seven items starred are of chief importance to the smaller store.

Source John W. Wingate and Seymour Helfant, *Small Planning for Growth*, 2d ed. (Washington, D.C.: Small Business Administration, 1977), p. 69.

Newspaper ads must meet certain criteria if they are to be effective. One set of guidelines for newspaper ads is the **AIDCA principle.** This principle outlines the basic requirements of a good newspaper ad.

1. *Attention* Causes the customer to stop and read the copy.
2. *Interest* Brings about a sense of curiosity.
3. *Desire* Increases the urge to acquire.
4. *Conviction* Substantiates that a decision to buy would be a good judgment.
5. *Action* Actually moves the consumer to going out to buy.[3]

Radio

Nationwide, 99.9 percent of all households have radios, and most autos also have radios. Thus, radio provides the small business owner a medium for reaching nearly all listeners in the local trade area as often as necessary. Radio advertising is advantageous in that it makes it possible for advertisers to select the market they wish to receive their message. Radio ads can be aired to a particular market segment in a trade area because radio stations plan their programming to appeal to specific groups of listeners, such as listeners to certain types of music or talk shows. Other advantages of radio advertising are its flexibility and timeliness. Commercials can be prepared in the morning and aired the same afternoon. Certain times are better for reaching a large market, such as before, during, or after sporting events. Radio ads can also be presented frequently and at different times of the day or night if the small business manager chooses.

Radio ads are sold in 10-, 30-, and 60-second spot announcements. Ad costs vary according to the time of day and size of the listening audience.

[3]C. Winston Borgen, *Learning Experiences in Retailing* (Pacific Palisades, Calif.: Goodyear Publishing Company, 1976), p. 259.

Most expensive rates are usually for the prime time periods from 6 A.M. to 10 A.M. and 3 P.M. to 7 P.M. on weekdays.

Other factors influencing cost are (1) how often the business advertises in a given week; (2) how many consecutive weeks the ads run; (3) whether spots are scheduled on a run-of-the-station basis, that is, aired at times the station selects, or in more costly fixed time slots; and (4) any combination packages of time amounts, slots, and frequencies.

Rates for a station are available from the station itself and are also quoted in the *Standard Rate and Data Service,* an industry survey of the costs of various media. For example, a spot announcement rate taken from this publication for a small radio station is shown as follows along with its time rates.

Time Rates		
AAA:	Monday through Friday	6 to 10 A.M. and 3 to 7 P.M.
AA:	Monday through Friday	10 A.M. to 3 P.M.
	Saturday	6 A.M. to 7 P.M.
A:	Monday through Saturday	7 P.M. to midnight
	Sunday	6 A.M. to midnight

Cost for Each Spot Announcement, 1 Minute[a]		
	6 times per week	12 times per week	18 times per week
AAA	$30	$28	$26
AA	26	24	22
A	18	14	12

Source *Spot Radio Rates and Data* (Skokie, Ill.: Standard Rate and Data Services, Inc.), vol. 64, no. 10 (October 1, 1982).

[a] Twenty-second and 30-second ads cost 80 percent of 1 minute; 10-second ads cost 50 percent of 1 minute.

There are some disadvantages to radio advertising. Obviously, radio advertising will not reach a person who is not listening. Frequently, radios are turned on while people are busily engaged in other activities, and they may not be paying attention to the advertising message. In addition, radio permits only a spoken message to describe a product or service, radio ads must be brief because of the time limit, and radio ads must be broadcast repeatedly in order to reach the target market.

Television

Television is being used with increased frequency by small business managers. One reason for the growth is that advertising rates have been lowered, enabling more small business managers to fit this medium into their advertising budget. Television is an important medium for reaching large markets. Census data indicate that nationwide there are television sets in 96 percent of the households, and in the average home a television set is turned on over 6 hours a day. Consequently, in a local market area, the likelihood of a firm's ad's being seen and heard is quite high. Television ads offer a threefold advantage: (1) products or services can be advertised, (2) they can be demonstrated, and (3) the advertising message can be presented simultaneously with the demonstration.

Television time is sold in 10-, 20-, 30-, and 60-second spots. The 30-second spot is most popular with small business owners. Spot announcements enable the advertiser to select the time, audience, and program for the commercial ad. The ad message can vary because it can be presented over different stations. As with radio advertising, the time and makeup of the viewing audience should be considered for the television ad. For example, a toy store can effectively present its ad during the Saturday morning time period when cartoons are to be televised and there is a large children's viewing audience.

There are some disadvantages to television ads. Television ads are projected onto the screen for a short time and may be missed by the prospective customer. Also, most trade areas are exposed to more than a single TV station, meaning only a part of the total viewing audience will be exposed to the ad. And the viewing audience usually does something else during commercials, especially when they are aired during station breaks.

In evaluating radio and television station advertising, the small business manager should consider using small stations or stations in small towns. Advertising rates on these stations are lower and frequently are more effective in reaching a particular market segment.

Handbills

Handbills are one of the most inexpensive methods of advertising if properly managed. The cost of producing handbills is low. They are usually reproduced by either mimeograph or multilith methods. The small business manager is able to control the distribution of the handbills because they are distributed by store employees or others (school children) in a small selected area. Handbills may be distributed door to door in selected neighborhoods, placed under the windshield wiper blade of cars parked in a shopping center lot, handed out to customers in the store, inserted in their shopping bag by cashiers as they check out, or laid out on a store counter where they can be picked up by the customers. (See Fig. 19–1.)

A disadvantage is that many customers consider handbills a nuisance and react negatively when they find handbills on their car or at their front door, and many are thrown away without every being read. In addition, individuals who distribute the handbills should be reliable.

Direct Mail Advertising

Circulars, letters, folders, postcards, and leaflets stuffed into monthly bills are types of direct mail advertising. An advantage of direct mail advertising is

FIGURE 19–1
The handbill is an inexpensive means of advertising.

that advertisers can select the specific audience whom they wish to receive their message. The tone of the message should be personal.

One main consideration for direct mailing is that the mailing list be accurate and current. Usually the small business manager can compile an effective mailing list from charge account records and sales slips. Lists can also be compiled from city directories, obtained from government agencies such as licensing bureaus, or bought or rented from firms that specialize in compiling and selling or renting mailing lists. Fees are charged for each name or for each thousand names.

Mailings may be made on a regular basis, such as a weekly mailing of a grocery store circular. Or they may be used for a one-time announcement, such as a change in store name, hours, personnel, or ownership. Also, a series of mailings may be sent to promote the sale of a single offer. Other uses of direct mail ads are shown in Figure 19–2.

Store Signs

Store signs and other outdoor signs such as billboards and portable trailers are one of the most useful direct forms of visual advertising available to the small business owner.

Store signs are street advertising. Effective signs must be noticeable and readable. They are important because they provide in an easily recognizable form information about the business and its products and services, give direc-

FIGURE 19–2

Uses of direct mail advertising for manufacturers, retailers, and service businesses.

To solicit mail-order or phone-order business.

To presell prospects before a salesperson's call—to soften up the buyer by acquainting him or her with your company and your products.

To announce new models, new designs, new lines, new items, or changes in your products, services, or equipment.

To notify your customers of price increases or decreases.

To substitute for a salesperson's call on a regular customer.

To follow up on salespersons' calls to prospects.

To welcome new customers.

To help regain lost customers.

To increase the full-line selling of your salespeople.

To thank all customers for their business at least once a year.

To create an image for your business.

To remind customers and prospects of seasonal or periodic needs.

To make the most of special events such as feature sales.

To take advantage of printed advertising materials supplied by manufacturers.

Source Harvey R. Cook, *Selecting Advertising Media* (Washington, D.C.: Small Business Administration, 1969).

tions to the business, and help build the image of the business. Specific advantages of store signs are these.

1. Signs are oriented to your trade area.
2. Signs are always on the job repeating your message to potential customers.
3. Nearly everyone reads signs.
4. Signs are inexpensive.
5. Signs are available to every shop owner.
6. Signs are easy to use.[4]

Transportation Advertising

The company name may be painted and displayed on the sides of the firm's delivery vehicle. Another form of transportation advertising is to display an advertising message on a mode of public transportation—taxicabs, buses, commuter trains. Posters may be displayed on the sides of buses or on the backs of taxicabs, or rotating signs may be displayed on top of taxis. This type of advertising is relatively inexpensive, and the advertising area to be covered can be controlled.

Magazines

Magazine advertising can be used by the small business owner if it is used selectively. National magazines, which have high circulation and charge advertising rates that far exceed the advertising budget of the small firm, are impractical. However, magazines published in the local area, which have smaller circulation and lower advertising rates, permit the small business owner to consider them as a medium for ads. There are a variety of types of local magazines that can adequately serve the needs of the small business manager.

City and Community Magazines

City and community magazines do not differ greatly from national magazines. The content of these magazines relates to the local area. Some of them are privately owned; others are sponsored and published by local groups, such as the chamber of commerce.

Visitor Magazines

These magazines emphasize places to go and things to do in the local area. Ordinarily, these magazines are placed in hotels and motels and are directed toward the tourist or convention visitor.

---

[4]Karen Claus and R. J. Klaus, *Signs in Your Business,* Management Aid, no. 4.016 (Washington, D.C.: Small Business Administration, 1982).

Publications of Special Interest Groups

Each locality has specific groups, such as women's clubs and fraternal orders. Frequently, these associations publish a magazine, either on a regular basis throughout the year or annually. If magazines are sent to a specific segment of the market to which the firm caters, the small business owner may wisely use this source as an effective vehicle for conveying advertising messages.

The advantage of advertising in a magazine is that the ads have a longer life expectancy than newspaper ads since magazines are kept longer and read in a more leisurely fashion. Disadvantages of magazine advertising are the fact that ads must be placed well in advance of the time of actual publication of the magazine and the higher cost for ad space compared to the newspaper.

Specialty Advertising

Advertisers may get their advertising message into the consumers' hands and keep their advertising message before consumers by using **specialty advertising.** Small business owners have their name and message printed on a wide range of useful items and distribute them free to their customers. Owners use these specialty advertising tokens for expressing appreciation of past patronage. Ball-point pens, pencils, rulers, key rings, coin purses, book matches, calendars, thermometers, and ashtrays are a few examples of specialty advertising.

Directories

Small business owners commonly use the *Yellow Pages* of the local telephone directory for their ads. These ads have long life, usually a year, as well as wide circulation. Another benefit is that the telephone company extensively advertises the *Yellow Pages*, making potential customers aware of the value of looking in the *Yellow Pages* for specific firms. In addition to the *Yellow Pages*, other industry and trade groups frequently publish directories identifying their membership and their business products or services.

Other Advertising Media

Other media are used by the small business owners. Business cards are an effective advertisement for many owners. Other owners develop an advertisement on film or slides and show it regularly in movie theaters.

THE ADVERTISING PROGRAM OF THE SMALL FIRM

An advertising program requires deliberate, systematic planning. A wide range of decisions must be made in regard to the advertising program, such

Some advertising decisions of the small business owner.

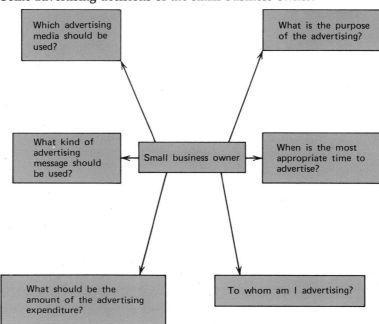

as purposes of the advertisement, media to be used, and the advertising message. (See Fig. 19–3.) Because each firm is unique, these decisions must be based on the needs of the firm. Several guidelines are offered that should prove beneficial for owners in planning their firm's advertising campaign.

Analysis of Firm and Customers

An initial concern of small business owners should be to analyze their own strengths and weaknesses as well as identify their potential market. In this way, a coordinated advertising program can be developed and implemented.

The evaluation of the firm should reveal how well it compares to competitors—what unique services or products are offered that are not provided by competitors. Another facet is the quality of merchandise carried in the store. Other factors include identifying customer services offered, location of store, and selling techniques used.

An effective advertising program necessitates the identification of the market segment the firm is attempting to reach. Another significant need relating to the composition of the customer market is to forecast changes that are anticipated. Especially pertinent is the determination of whether the market size is expected to increase or decrease, whether incomes continue upward, and so forth.

Sales Objective

The purpose of planning management is to project the short-term and long-term growth of the firm. To illustrate, the small business manager may establish a goal to increase sales by 6 percent a year over the next five years. Advertising must be planned and coordinated to aid in achieving this goal. In setting the projected goal, the owner must evaluate the trading area to establish the feasibility of the sales objective. As noted previously, if the objective is to attract 10 percent more customers but the market potential is not there, no amount of advertising will make the goal attainable. The small business owner should plan the sales objectives for the year on a month-by-month basis. As each month passes, the manager will be able to gauge the sales performance and compare the sales forecast with actual results. In this way, the manager will be able to evaluate how well the advertising program is progressing.

Schedule of Advertising

Deciding when and what is the appropriate time to advertise in order to reach the desired audience is necessary to maximize the advertising dollar expenditure. For a small retailer, advertising can be planned to coincide with the heaviest shopping days. Friday and Saturday are traditionally heavy shopping days for grocery stores. Consequently, many grocery store owners plan their food ads to appear in Thursday papers. Other advertising should be scheduled to coincide with payroll days in the trading area. The small business owner must also consider what is to be advertised when deciding on the schedule of advertising, such as the introduction of new merchandise or end-of-the season closeout items.

The Advertisement

There are a number of desirable qualities in an ad that assist in making it more effective in achieving the intended results. For example, consider the following.

1. *Make your ads easily recognizable.* Try to give your own copy a consistent personality and style.
2. *Use a simple layout.* In printed media, your layout should carry the eye through the message easily and in proper sequence, from art and headline to copy and price and to signature.

3. *Use dominant illustrations.* Featured merchandise should be shown in the dominant illustrations. Pictures emphasizing the product in use are good.

4. *Get the main benefit to the reader or viewer.* Prospective customers want to know, "What's in it for me?" Emphasize the main reason why readers or listeners should buy the advertised item.

5. *Give complete information.* Give all essential information about the item such as: the manufacturer, model, various sizes, and colors. Your description should have a warm, sincere, and enthusiastic tone.

6. *State price or range of prices.* Don't be afraid to quote a high price. If the price is low, support it with statements that create belief, such as clearances or special purchases.

7. *Specify branded merchandise.* If the advertised merchandise is a known brand, say so. Take advantage of advertising allowances and the preselling that the manufacturer has done. As one small marketer says, "Cooperative advertising is one of the most valuable types of programs available to me from my suppliers."

8. *Be sure to include store name and address.* Check every ad or commercial to be certain you have included store name, address, telephone number, and store hours.[5]

THE ADVERTISING BUDGET OF THE SMALL BUSINESS

One goal of small owner–managers is to realize a maximum return of sales from each dollar expended for advertising. One means for getting more results for each advertising dollar is to feature nationally advertised products in the ads. Millions of dollars are spent each year by manufacturers to promote their products and services nationwide. Incorporating brand names and symbols into advertising enables small owner–managers to capitalize on the pulling power that well-known products and services have.

In the preparation of the ad budget, the amount that should be budgeted depends on a number of factors.

1. Stores in less favorable locations or managers opening a new store or expanding a present store may require more advertising.

2. The intensity of competition increases advertising requirements.

3. The greater the number of special sale dates, the greater the need for an increased advertising budget.

---

[5] Charles T. Lipscomb, Jr., "Checklist for Successful Retail Advertising," *Small Marketers' Aids* (Washington, D.C.: Small Business Administration, 1973).

4. The larger the competing firm or the more it spends for advertising, the more you may need to spend for advertising.

Methods of Preparing an Advertising Budget

There are several alternatives for preparing the ad budget. Two alternatives that may be considered are the *percentage of sales* and the *unit of sales* methods.

Percentage of Sales Method

Owners most often use the **percentage of sales** method for establishing an ad budget. This method bases the ad budget on a percentage of sales and maintains the ad budget in a consistent relationship to sales volume. Guidelines are available from a variety of sources for setting percentages for specific types of businesses. Sources include trade magazines and associations, the Internal Revenue Service, census data, and financial reporting services such as Dun and Bradstreet and the Robert Morris Association. Table 1 presented in this chapter, taken from the Bank of America's *Small Business Reporter*, is another example of data for preparing the ad budget by a percentage of sales method. These figures are guidelines and should be adjusted for local business conditions and for noting any special circumstances such as suggested earlier.

The sales period used to serve as the base for preparing the ad budget may be past sales, projected sales, or a combination of past and projected sales.

Unit of Sales Method

The **unit of sales** method requires that owner–managers set aside a definite amount of funds for each unit of the product that is sold. The advertising budget is based on the number of anticipated units to be sold rather than sales dollars. Thus, if the firm plans to sell 1000 units and it takes $2 worth of advertising to move the product, $2000 will have to be spent for advertising this product. This method is suited for specialty goods, such as automobiles. It is not very useful for style merchandise.[6]

Cooperative Advertising

One plan for extending each advertising dollar is through **cooperative advertising.** Cooperative advertising is the plan by which the cost of advertising is shared by manufacturers of nationally known brand-name products and the retailer who advertises and sells the products in the local trade area. The advantage of this type of advertising is that it allows retailers to reduce their share of the advertising expenditure.

---

[6]Stuart Henderson Britt, *Plan Your Advertising Budget,* Management Aid no. 4.018 (Washington, D.C.: Small Business Administration, n.d.).

TABLE 1

Advertising as practiced by selected small businesses.

Type of Business	Average Ad Budget (% of Sales)[a]	Favorite Media	Other Media Used
Bars and cocktail lounges	1.0 to 1.2%	Newspapers (entertainment section), local magazines, tourist bulletins	Specialties
Bicycle shops	1.5 to 2.0%	Newspapers (sports section)	Fliers, *Yellow Pages*, cycling magazines, direct mail
Book stores	1.5 to 1.6%	Newspapers, shoppers, *Yellow Pages*	Direct mail
Building maintenance services	1.0 to 1.5%	Direct mail, door-to-door, *Yellow Pages*	Signs on company vehicles and equipment
Camera shops (independent)	2.0 to 3.5%	Direct mail, handouts, *Yellow Pages*	Newspapers (*except* large urban)
Drug stores (independent)	1.5 to 3.0%	Local newspapers, shoppers	Direct mail (list from prescription files)
Dry cleaning plants	0.9 to 2.0%	Local newspapers, shoppers, *Yellow Pages*	Storefront ads, pamphlets on clothes care
Equipment rental services	1.7 to 4.7%	*Yellow Pages*	
Gift stores	2.2%	Weekly newspapers	*Yellow Pages*, radio, direct mail, magazines
Hairdressing shops	2.0 to 5.0%	*Yellow Pages*	Newspapers (for special events), word of mouth
Home furnishing stores	5.0 to 6.0%	Newspapers	Direct mail, radio
Liquor stores (independent)	0.2 to 0.6%	Point-of-purchase displays	Newspapers, *Yellow Pages*
Mail order firms	15.0 to 25.0%	Newspapers, magazines	Direct mail
Pet shops	2.0 to 5.0%	*Yellow Pages*	Window displays, shoppers, direct mail
Plant shops	1.3 to 1.5%	Local newspapers, word of mouth	
Recreational vehicle and mobile home dealers	0.5 to 1.0%	Local newspapers, radio, *Yellow Pages*	Direct mail, television for multilot dealers
Repair services	1.0 to 1.6%	*Yellow Pages*	Signs on vehicles, direct mail, shoppers
Restaurants and food services	4.0%	Newspapers, radio, *Yellow Pages*, transit, outdoor	Television for chain or franchise restaurants
Shoe stores	3.0%	Newspapers, direct mail, radio	*Yellow Pages* (especially for specialty shoe vendors)
Small job printers	0.5 to 1.0%	Salespeople in the field	Direct mail

Source *Small Business Reporter* (San Francisco: Bank of America, 1978).

[a]Slightly higher in new establishments.

The expenditure reduction is the result of the cooperative advertising plan that calls for the manufacturer to pay 50 percent of the advertising, but percentages vary. Sometimes the participation rate is 25 percent, and, under special circumstances, the manufacturer may pay 100 percent. National manufacturers also supply the retailer with materials that are used in the advertisements. Small firms with limited funds for advertising can certainly benefit from cooperative advertising.

SALES PROMOTION

Another technique of promotional strategy is **sales promotion.** Sales promotion includes "those marketing activities other than personal selling and advertising, and publicity, that stimulate consumer purchasing and dealer effectiveness, such as displays, shows and expositions, demonstrations, and various nonrecurrent selling efforts not in the ordinary routine."[7]

Sales promotion techniques are designed to give added sales push for products. The promotional events take place within the store as well as outside. A number of sales promotion techniques suitable to the needs of the small business owner are discussed in the following sections.

Point-of-Purchase Displays

Owners should plan their store layout to encourage **impulse purchases. Point-of-purchase displays** strategically located throughout the store represent an effective method of generating impulse purchases. Usually, these displays are prepared by manufacturers or distributors of products and made available to small firm owners. Typical forms of display are wall or shelf displays, interior or overhead signs, and counter displays.

While shopping, consumers may find their attention attracted by a point-of-purchase display sign that describes the merits of a product. After reading the sign and examining the product, customers frequently decide to try the product. Consequently, a sale is made.

Point-of-purchase displays may be used effectively to remind customers of a product they need but had forgotten to include on their shopping lists. Another purpose of these displays is to suggest additional uses of a product. This technique is often successful in influencing a customer to buy a product.

A point-of-purchase display sign on a bargain table full of hardware items may remind the customer of the need for another hammer. And the display sign stresses that the items are on sale now at a special low price. Another point-of-purchase display suggests the usefulness of an electric grass trimmer

---

[7]Committee on Definitions, *Marketing Definitions: A Glossary of Marketing Terms* (Chicago: American Marketing Association, 1960), p. 20.

A point of purchase display often provided by the manufacturer can encourage impulse buying.

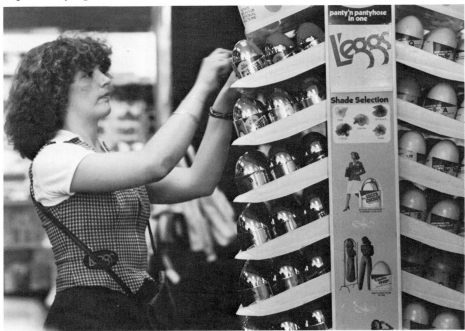

with a long handle, which eliminates the need for bending over to trim around trees or fences. Placing umbrellas or other rain apparel near the checkout counter of the store during a rainstorm is an excellent merchandising plan for stimulating impulse purchases. Many point-of-purchase displays are strategically located at the store's checkout counter. For example, razor blades, chewing gum, and flashlight batteries are just a few of the convenience goods displayed where consumers can purchase them on impulse.

Show Windows

Merchandise displays or signs in the show window should be appealing to the customer as well as attention getters. Show window displays should be designed for the purpose of presenting merchandise in such a way that the passerby stops, looks, enters the store to find out more about the merchandise, and is encouraged to make a purchase. Show windows can be effectively used to stimulate impulse buying. Show window displays should be changed regularly to make them most effective. If the same people pass your store daily, window displays should be changed more frequently.

Samples

One sales promotion technique is to distribute free samples of a product to customers. In this way, the small business puts the product in the hands of the customers for the purpose of getting them to try it. The expectation is that they will like it and become regular users. A sample tube of a new toothpaste, a sample box of a new detergent, or a sample jar of a new brand of freeze-dried coffee is given to customers to try. When a new food item is to be introduced, such as a new breakfast sausage, samples may be prepared in a grocery store. Customers are offered a sample, and its unique characteristics are explained. Customers who like the item then are encouraged to buy the product. An advantage of this sales promotion technique is that consumer acceptance or nonacceptance of the product is known as soon as it is tried.

Trading Stamps

Trading stamps offer the customer an extra value for each purchase in that the stamps can be redeemed for cash or merchandise. By offering stamps as a sales promotion technique, store owner–managers attempt to provide customers with an additional incentive to patronize their store. Or they may give stamps to gain a competitive edge over stores not offering stamps. By getting customers to save stamps, store owner–managers hope to build repeat patronage of the store.

Premiums

Premiums are products that are offered free or at minimal cost to the customer. Consumers may receive a dish, glass, or other merchandise free if they purchase another product or make a purchase in excess of a stated dollar amount, such as over $10.00. A retailer may offer one pair of shoes at the regular price and the second for 1 cent more.

Coupons

A frequently used sales promotion technique is coupons. Coupons are intended to stimulate sales by offering the consumer a discount on purchases. For example, a retailer may offer a series of coupons that are redeemable during a specified week. Or a service firm may offer a coupon that provides a discount for carpet cleaning.

Contests

Some contests are intended to attract new customers to use a product already in existence or to introduce a new product. Other contests attempt to get customers into the store to register for a cash prize or merchandise to be presented at a drawing held in the store. For example, a small grocery store may have a contest or a drawing for a free turkey to be given away at Thanksgiving.

SUMMARY OF KEY POINTS

1. Promotional strategy is the means that small business owners utilize to communicate information about their firm and its products and services to potential customers.

2. Advertising is any type of sales presentation that is nonpersonal and is paid for by an identified sponsor.

3. Two general objectives of advertising are promotional and institutional.

4. Promotional advertising has many purposes, such as increasing sales, creating an awareness of products or services, attracting new customers, or promoting a special sale or special offer.

5. Institutional advertising is intended to create goodwill toward the company and to create a positive image of the firm in the community.

6. Small business owners should recognize that advertising has a number of limitations.

7. The small business owner must choose the proper advertising media for the firm from among newspaper, radio, television, handbills, direct mail, transportation, magazines, and specialty items. The store sign is also important for identifying the small company.

8. Great care and diligent planning should go into the planning of the advertising program of the firm.

9. The advertising budget may be prepared using either a percentage of sales method or a unit of sale method as the guideline for the ad appropriation.

10. Sales promotion includes the marketing activities other than personal selling and advertising and publicity that stimulate consumer purchasing and dealer effectiveness, such as point-of-purchase displays, shows, and demonstrations.

DISCUSSION QUESTIONS

1. Explain the difference between advertising and sales promotion.

2. What are some of the purposes of promotional advertising?

3. Discuss the difference between publicity and institutional advertising.

4. Specify some of the limitations of advertising.

5. Discuss two advertising media that are suitable to the needs of small business owners.

6. Outline the procedure for designing an effective advertising program for the small business.

7. Explain the difference between the percentage of sales method and unit of sale method for advertising budget preparation.

8. Explain the role of point-of-purchase displays in sales promotion.

9. Discuss several sales promotion techniques.

STUDENT PROJECTS

1. View local television programming, listen to local radio stations, observe transportation ads and outside signs, read newspaper and magazine ads, and, if possible, collect direct mail ads and handbills of local small business firms. Make notes of the advertising messages and types of stores using the various advertising media. Also note how many different advertising media are used by the same stores.

2. Consult the *Standard Rate and Data Service* (available in most libraries), and determine the cost of advertising by means of radio on a station in your geographical area.

CASE A

Oakmont TV Sales and Service

Bill Griffith purchased Oakmont TV Sales and Service four months ago from Bob Andrews. When Bill bought the business, the products sold were two major brands of televisions, radios and stereos, videocassette recorders, and videodiscs. Since the business was purchased, Bill has decided to add a product line of household appliances (washers, dryers, refrigerators, freezers, and microwave ovens). The firm continues to offer full service for television repair. Bill is aware of the value of advertising and advertises regularly in the local newspaper. However, he plans to intensify his advertising effort now that he is adding another line of products.

Sales representatives from two local radio stations have visited the shop this week. Each has attempted to sell Bill on the idea of purchasing advertising time on their station. Both stations broadcast into the same geographic area. The demographic data for each station has been shown to Bill by the respective sales representatives.

Demographics for Radio Stations A and B

	Station A	Station B
Age		
Under 18	40%	6%
18–25	27	7
26–35	16	23
36–50	8	42
Over 50	9	22
Income		
Under $5000	16	5
$5000–$10,000	64	8
$10,000–$20,000	9	27
Over $20,000	11	60
Education		
High school graduate	55	12
College graduate	42	65
Graduate school	3	23
Occupation		
Student	35	5
Unemployed (nonstudent)	10	1
Clerical	12	8
Skilled	10	7
Unskilled	12	7
Technical	8	27
Managerial	6	26
Professional	7	19
Sex		
Male	46	73
Female	54	27

QUESTIONS

1. What are the demographic characteristics of each station's audience?
2. Which station would you recommend to Bill? Why?
3. Would television advertising be recommended for Bill's shop?
4. How does cooperative advertising aid a small business owner such as Bill?
5. What other advertising media would you recommend to Bill?
6. What sales promotion techniques, if any, should be recommended to Bill to further increase the public's awareness of Oakmont TV Sales and Service?

CASE B

Smith Lumber Company

Smith Lumber Company was formed in 1947 by Mr. and Mrs. J. T. Smith. They sold only one grade of lumber (#1) and a limited line of high-quality building accessories. Their main customers were building contractors and a group of customers who preferred quality and service over price. The Smiths carried on this tradition for 30 years until 1977, when Mr. Smith suffered a heart attack, and they were forced to sell the business.

The new owner, Mack Walls, purchased the physical plant, the inventory, and the company name. Shortly after the purchase, the business was relocated in a new, modern "Home Center" facility.

A chief objective of the new owner was to expand the offerings of products and services of the lumber company so as to serve building contractors as well as the "do-it-yourself" customers. Walls observed that there was a real need for this type of business in the area because none existed in the city. Walls also increased selling emphasis on hardware business, which he believed would aid in increasing sales and profits without sacrificing the personal touch of customer service for which Smith Lumber had become known.

All nine employees of the company were retained. Mr. Walls felt their knowledge and experience could help in the operations and decision making of the business. The former owner also agreed to serve as an adviser to the company, which aided the smooth transition of ownership.

A concern of Walls was the best type of advertising strategy to use to achieve the growth objective. Walls was undecided which combination of advertising media to use and their relative effectiveness in order to reach the "do-it-yourself" customer in the trade area and to maintain the image of service and quality.

Walls has considered the following alternatives.

1. Radio advertising—the town has one radio station.
2. Television advertising—television stations from two large metropolitan areas cover the city trade area.
3. Newspaper—two local biweekly papers are published on Thursday and Sunday. Both newspapers provided duplicate coverage of the trade area.
4. Circulars—direct mail circulars sent to all residents cost 11.7 cents per copy or newspaper inserts were available.
5. Miscellaneous sources—*Yellow Pages*, school programs, and so on.
6. No advertising.

QUESTION

What advertising strategy would you recommend for Mr. Walls in order for him to reach his objectives?

SMALL BUSINESS ADMINISTRATION PUBLICATIONS

Management Aids (Free)

Tips on Getting More for Your Marketing Dollar
Advertising Guidelines for Small Retail Firms
Signs in Your Business
Plan Your Advertising Budget
Do You Know the Results of Your Advertising?

Small Business Management Series (For Sale)

Small Store Planning for Growth

CHAPTER TWENTY

CONSUMER CREDIT

After reading this chapter, you will understand:

1. How important retail credit is to most small business firms.
2. How the traditional 30-day charge account operates.
3. How the revolving charge account functions and how small business firms use credit card companies to finance this credit.
4. How important bank credit cards are to small businesses and what functions they perform for them.
5. How installment credit functions.
6. How small business firms obtain credit information.
7. That the truth-in-lending law attempts to put credit on a more competitive basis and what information it requires business to disclose to customers.
8. The importance of the bad debt ratio and the system for collection of overdue accounts.

KEY WORDS

Credit

Mortgage credit

Consumer credit

Charge account credit

Thirty-day charge accounts

Revolving charge accounts

Interest

Credit cards

Bank credit cards

Installment credit

Retail credit bureaus

Truth-in-lending

Bad debts

Collections

SMALL BUSINESS PROFILE

Neal W. Thompson: Thompson Pulse-Purge Cooker

In Neal W. Thompson's case, dyspepsia was the mother of invention. His inability to digest fried food, which goes back to his Kentucky childhood, led him to invent a process that produces easily digested, low-fat fried food—the Thompson Pulse-Purge Cooker.

Thompson, a largely self-taught engineer and technician who had been working as an independent electrical and mechanical contractor, joined Kentucky Fried Chicken Corporation's engineering department as a technician in 1963. He developed his cooker on his own time because, he says, "I was determined to find a way to give everyone a good fried product that wouldn't cause indigestion. Everyone likes fried food, but a lot of people can't eat it."

His early experience gave him an idea. "The way to preserve food when I was a boy in rural Kentucky was to fry it and then store it in a tub of lard," he says. "The food was good if you could digest the fat, but I couldn't. So when my mother would heat up the preserved food and give us our portions, I'd put mine back in the hot skillet and add water. The steam took off the excess fat."

And that is the basic method he perfected. The Thompson cooker uses less oil to start with because it fries food faster than conventional fryers by using pulsing pressure. Then, when the cooking is complete, steam pressure blows the oil off the food and out of the cooking vessel through a filter, leaving the fried food virtually greaseless—yet still crispy.

Thompson began trying to market his cooker to commercial establishments as a complete unit, but the world did not immediately beat a path to his door. So he built a business converting conventional fryers to his method. He also used the cooker in a fast-food franchise he owned in Pittsburgh, where he moved in 1964.

One drawback to sales has been cost: His commercial cooker costs approximately $5,000, compared with a little more than $4,000 for a conventional pressure fryer. But Thompson's cooker has another advantage besides producing low-fat food and saving energy and oil. The high heat kills bacteria, thus extending the shelf life of perishable food in tropical countries lacking refrigeration.

Now that those advantages have been recognized, the cooker's time has come. Hospitals have ordered it, the government of Nigeria is checking it out for its sterilizing qualities, and leading fast-food chains, including Gino's and his former employer, Kentucky Fried Chicken, are taking a second look. At a recent National Restaurant Show in Chicago the lines to see the cooker were so long that Thompson's sales representatives could hardly get through with their clients.

Thompson, 58, is now turning to the home market, where concern over diets should ensure sales. "I'll have a small household unit on the market within six months," he says. "The price will be somewhat less than for a microwave oven."

Source   "All Steamed up over Fried Food," *Nation's Business,* October, 1981, p. 99. Reprinted by permission from Nation's Business, October, 1981. Copyright 1981 by Nation's Business, Chamber of Commerce of the United States.

Many small business firms extend either trade credit or retail credit. Manufacturers and wholesalers often extend trade credit to their customers. This trade credit usually exists in the form of supplying products to their customers on 30-, 60-, or 90-day accounts. Various forms of trade credit were discussed in Chapter 5.

Some sources consider credit extended to retail stores to be retail credit and credit extended by service firms to be service credit. However, for our purposes, retail credit will consist of **credit** extended to customers by both retail stores and service firms, that is, firms that conduct business directly with the ultimate consumer. This chapter is devoted to a discussion of various aspects of this retail credit.

IMPORTANCE OF CREDIT

Retail credit has been increasingly important in the United States since World War II. Today personal income has multiplied over 10 times what it was in 1950. **Mortgage credit** outstanding (credit that has a specific item mortgaged as security for the loan) has multiplied by 20 times what it was in 1950. During the same period **consumer credit** has multiplied by 18 times its 1950 amount. For the same period, the population only increased by 1.5 times. Figure 20–1 shows the rapid growth of various types of consumer credit between 1950 and 1980.

TYPES OF RETAIL CREDIT

Although there are many deviations in retail credit offered by firms to their customers, there are only two basic categories of retail credit—charge account credit and installment credit.

Charge Account Credit

The two primary types of charge account credit are the traditional 30-day charge accounts and the more modern revolving charge accounts. Neither type of **charge account credit** holds a chattel mortgage against a specific item purchased, as does installment credit.

FIGURE 20-1

Consumer credit: selected years.

Type of Credit	Amount (in billions of dollars)				
	1950	1960	1970	1980	1982
Total consumer credit outstanding	25.6	65.1	143.1	385.6	409.5
Installment	15.5	45.1	105.5	313.4	329.3
Automobiles	6.0	18.1	36.3	116.3	127.2
Revolving	NA	NA	5.1	59.9	58.6
Mobile homes	NA	NA	2.5	17.3	18.5
All other loans	9.5	27.0	61.6	119.9	125.6
Noninstallment	10.1	20.0	37.6	72.2	30.2
Single payment loans	3.6	9.1	19.3	39.9	44.4
Charge accounts	4.9	7.2	9.2	13.0	12.5
Service credit	1.6	3.7	9.1	19.3	23.3

Source *Statistical Abstract of the United States, 1984.*

Thirty-Day Accounts

The traditional **30-day charge account** extends credit to customers by allowing them to purchase merchandise on credit during the month and then pay the entire balance of the account at the end of the month. For example, a customer's record of charges and payments for three months might appear as follows.

	Credit Purchases During the Month	Payments at the End of the Month
September	$30	$30
October	44	44
November	68	68

Although it traditionally has been the practice of charge account creditors, both 30-day and revolving, to issue statements at the end of the month, many firms with large numbers of credit accounts have gone to cycle billing. Cycle billing is used in order to reduce the pressure of billing at the end of the month and to better utilize billing personnel by spreading the billing process over the entire month. Every two or three days, a different part of the accounts is billed, usually in alphabetical order of the customers' last names. Instead of the account's being due at the end of the month, it is due in a specific number of days after the billing date shown on the statement (usually in 10 days).

The customer is usually not required to pay any interest on his credit if he or she pays it off by the due date. Some stores give their customers credit cards as a means of identifying them as credit customers. However, this is not the most common practice. Most stores offering traditional 30-day charge accounts use some form of credit slip, which lists purchases and dollar amounts and is signed by the customer.

Retail stores that use 30-day charge accounts usually carry the credit accounts themselves. These stores sometimes borrow money against their charge accounts from banks or factors as a means of financing them (a discussion of factoring is contained in Chapter 5).

Revolving Charge Accounts

The **revolving charge account** method is similar to the traditional 30-day charge account in that customers may purchase merchandise on credit and pay off all or part of it at the end of the monthly billing period. It differs from the traditional 30-day charge account in that customers are not required to pay off all credit purchases on a monthly basis. The revolving charge account method requires the customer to pay only a part of the total amount owed. The minimum amount customers are required to pay is based on the total amount they owe. Customers are charged **interest** based on the daily average balance of the account. A customer's revolving charge account for three months might appear as follows:

	Purchases During the Period	Interest Charged	Payment	Balance After Payment
January				$368.28
February	$54.60	$6.93	$50.00	379.81
March	0	6.65	50.00	336.46
April	35.38	6.20	30.00	348.04

Firms that issue **credit cards** place a maximum amount that may be purchased using the card. The most common limit of credit cards is one that does not allow the cardholder to exceed a balance of $500. If requested, higher credit card limits may be established for individuals, depending primarily on their record and income.

Most retail firms charge interest based on the average daily balance. The average daily balance is calculated by totaling the balance outstanding for each day of the month and dividing by the number of days in the billing period. The most common rate of interest charged on revolving charge accounts is 1.75 to 2 percent per month, which amounts to an annual percentage of between 21 and 24 percent.

Almost all revolving charge accounts are set up to use credit cards. Firms sometimes carry their own accounts, but most small businesses accept credit cards issued by other companies. Some of the credit cards they accept may be from firms who produce a product and whose primary function is acting as something other than a financial institution. For example, many petroleum firms have their own credit cards and allow motels and other selected types of business to accept their credit cards for a fee.

Bank Credit Cards

Financial institutions also issue credit cards that may be used to purchase a wide range of merchandise and services. Visa and MasterCard are the principal bank-issued credit cards. In addition, Diners Club and American Express are two firms that specialize in consumer credit for many products and services.

Bank-issued credit cards have been a real boon to small businesses. Several years ago it was common for the authors to hear a small business owner say the firm's biggest problem was credit and collections. Many small businesses have gone out of business in the past owing to improper control of credit and inability to collect customer credit accounts. The **bank credit cards** have largely eliminated this problem for most small businesses. The cards have become so common that most small businesses do not offer credit except on the credit cards.

The small business does have to pay a percentage of all charges to the bank. The percentage ranges from 2 percent to 6 percent of the amount charged. The percentage charged each small business is determined primarily by the average amount of sales charged on each ticket. For example, the small business that usually turns in charge tickets that only amount to a few dollars is charged a much higher percentage than the firm that turns in charge tickets amounting to several hundred dollars each.

Although small businesses do have to pay a fee for the service, they have usually found it well worth the cost. Every charge ticket they receive they enter on their bank deposit slip, and the amount is immediately added to their account. The bank then bills them for the cost of their tickets. The small business, in a sense, can count bank credit charges as cash to their business. In general, they run no risk of bad debts. The cards also allow them to function on much less working capital, which is a cost to them. They do not have to process credit applications, and they maintain no credit or collection records.

One risk the firm runs is to fail to check the card against the invalid card list issued by the credit card company or to fail to telephone about all purchases over a specific amount. The small business must sustain the loss in these cases. Usually, credit card companies will pay a reward, usually about $25, to a clerk who calls the credit card company and takes up a card that appears on their invalid lists. This helps the small business by motivating clerks to be more diligent in checking the list in hopes of receiving a reward. Another risk is that the clerk does not properly imprint the charge ticket with the card machine. If the credit card company can not trace the customer, they will not accept the credit ticket.

Customers using bank credit cards are charged interest on the average daily balance. The current rate is 1.75 to 2 percent per month. Some firms, such as Diners Club and American Express, not only charge the customer interest and the business a percentage fee but they also charge the credit cardholder an additional yearly fee to receive the card.

The United States government has passed several laws concerning credit cards. One requires that no one can be sent a credit card unless he or she has requested the card. Another limits the liability of the card holder to $50 if the card is lost or stolen provided the customer notifies the credit card company as soon as possible. A court decision also allows the small business to offer the customer a discount for cash without the danger of losing the bank credit card service. A law passed in 1975 prohibits discrimination in credit owing to sex or marital status, and another passed in 1977 prohibits discrimination in credit owing to race, national origin, religion, age, or receipt of public assistance. The Fair Credit Billing Law allows customers to withhold payment to the credit card company if the merchant refuses to help with defective products. Also, in this law the customer may refuse to pay the first $50 of a disputed bill if his or her written complaint is not responded to within 30 days or ruled on within 90 days or both, regardless of who wins the billing argument.

Credit cards are important to some customers not only because of the deferred payment but also because they provide information for their income tax returns. For example, some salespersons use credit cards as a record and means of proof of travel and customer entertainment expenses.

The small business can also use bank credit cards to allow employees away from the business to purchase needed items, such as gasoline, meals, and lodging for salespersons and truck drivers.

Installment Credit

Installment credit is primarily used when customers purchase items of merchandise that costs several hundred or thousands of dollars, such as appliances, automobiles, boats, and homes. Interest is calculated on the amount that is financed after the down payment if there is a down payment. The balance due plus the interest charge is then divided by the total number of months over which the purchase is to be financed to determine monthly payments.

The number of years allowed for the installment purchase to be repaid varies by item and financial firm. Some of the more common lengths of financing periods are: large appliances, 1 to 3 years; automobiles, 3 to 4 years; boats, 1 to 4 years; and homes, 20 to 30 years.

Customers who obtain merchandise by installment purchases usually are required to sign an installment sales contract. This contract contains such information as total amount to be financed, interest rate, interest amount, repayment period, and an agreement in which the purchaser pledges the item purchased as security against repayment of the loan (installment credit is mortgage credit; legal aspects of different types of installment contracts are discussed in Chapter 21).

Some firms finance their own installment credit; however, most small busi-

FIGURE 20–2
Characteristics of charge account and installment credit.

Charge Account Credit		Installment Credit
Traditional 30-Day Accounts	**Revolving Charge Accounts**	**Installment Credit**
1. Nonmortgage credit	1. Nonmortgage credit	1. Mortgage credit (chattel mortgage)
2. Store financed (may factor)	2. May be financed by store other producing companies (such as oil company credit cards) financial institutions (such as bank credit cards)	2. May be financed by store bank sales finance company
3. No interest charged		
4. Paid off in full each month	3. Interest charged on balance	3. Interest added to amount financed
5. May or may not use credit card	4. Only a minimum amount must be paid each month and balance carried forward	4. Monthly payments for several months or years
	5. Usually involves credit card	5. Sometimes requires down payment

nesses use financial institutions to carry their installment credit. They usually sign customers to installment sales contracts and then sell or discount the contracts to banks or sales finance companies. (Banks and sales finance company credit operations are discussed in Chapter 5.)

See Figure 20–2 for a comparison of the characteristics of charge accounts and installment credit.

SOURCES OF CREDIT INFORMATION

Small business firms that carry their own customer credit have two basic sources of credit information about their customers: (1) credit application forms and (2) **retail credit bureau** reports.

The small business firm that does carry its own credit should require all credit customers to complete a credit application form. The small business may create its own application form or use a standardized application form.

Most cities have a local retail credit bureau to which the small business firm may belong to aid in credit decisions. These local credit bureaus are usually cooperatives owned by the local merchants. All local members supply the credit bureau with copies of all their credit applications. In addition, each month each member also supplies the local credit bureau with information on customer purchases, payments, and delinquencies. By collecting this information, the bureaus are able to obtain extensive credit files on large numbers of people in the community. Members of the local credit bureau are then able to telephone the bureau about new credit applicants and obtain credit ratings in a matter of two or three minutes. The bureau will also provide the small business with a more detailed report by mail if requested. In addition, if a small business has a delinquent account, he or she is able to obtain a "trade clearance" report, which summarizes the customer's more recent credit purchases and payments to other stores.

Most local credit bureaus also belong to Associated Credit Bureaus, which is a national organization. Thus the small business can obtain information on a nationwide basis.

Although local credit bureaus provide a valuable service to small businesses that grant credit, there have been some abuses. In some cases, information that was wrong or biased inadvertently found its way into the files of a few customers and created unwarranted problems for them. Federal law has been enacted that allows a customer to see his or her file on request and makes provisions for having the file corrected.

Although this chapter is devoted primarily to retail credit, another source of credit information is used to such an extent by businesses that it seems practical to mention it at this time. Dun and Bradstreet sells to subscribers a publication that contains credit ratings of several million business firms in the United States and Canada. Dun and Bradstreet also prepares detailed reports on many of the companies listed in its reference publications.

THE "TRUTH-IN-LENDING" LAW

In 1969, the United States Congress passed the Consumer Credit Protection Act, which is popularly called the **truth-in-lending** law. This law was intended to put credit on a more competitive basis by helping consumers more easily know what credit costs them. Small businesses that offer credit must be familiar with the law in order to comply with its provisions.

The most important of the disclosure items are the finance charge and the annual percentage rate. The business firm must advise the customer of these two credit expenses in writing that is the equivalent of 10-point type, 0.075-inch computer type, or elite-size typewritten numerals. The finance charge is the total of all costs paid by the consumer for credit. It includes all interest, carrying charges, cost of insurance premiums if required for credit protection, and credit investigation costs. The annual percentage rate is the percentage interest rate charge on a yearly basis. This annual percentage rate must be reported to the nearest quarter of 1 percent.[1]

The truth-in-lending law requires specific information be disclosed for re-

---

[1] Computations on installment sales can be complex for most people. To assist you, *Annual Percentage Rate Tables* is available from the Federal Reserve System in Washington, D.C., for $1.00.

volving charge accounts (called open-end transactions in the law) and installment contracts (called closed-end transactions).

Revolving Charge Accounts

The following information must be disclosed before the account is opened.

1. Conditions under which a finance charge may be made and the period within which, if payment is made, there is no finance charge (such as "30 days without interest").
2. The method of determining the balance upon which a finance charge may be imposed.
3. How the actual finance charge is calculated.
4. The periodic rates used and the range of balances to which each applies as well as the corresponding Annual Percentage Rate—for instance, a monthly rate of 1.5 percent (APR, 18 percent) on the first $500, and 1 percent (APR, 12 percent) on amounts over $500.
5. Conditions under which additional charges may be made, along with details of how they are calculated. (This applies to new purchases when charges are added to the account.)
6. A description of any lien (secured interest) you may acquire on the customer's property—for instance, rights to repossession of a household appliance.
7. Minimum periodic payment required.[2]

The following information must be included on each and every monthly statement sent to the customer in the correct terminology, which is indicated in boldface type in the following quoted material.

1. The unpaid balance at the beginning of the billing period (**previous balance**).
2. The amount and date of each purchase or credit extension and a brief description of each item bought if not previously given to the customer.
3. Customer payments (**payments**) and other credits, including those for rebates, adjustments, and returns (**credits**).
4. The finance charge expressed in dollars and cents (**finance charge**).
5. The rates used in calculating the finance charge and the range of balances, if any, to which they apply (**periodic rate**).

---

[2]*Understanding Truth-in-Lending* (Washington, D.C.: Small Business Administration, November 1969).

6. The annual percentage rate, which must be expressed as a percentage after January 1, 1971 (**annual percentage**).

7. The unpaid balance on which the finance charge was calculated.

8. The closing date of the billing cycle and the unpaid balance as of that date (**new balance**).[3]

Installment Contracts

Installment credit must also provide certain information to the buyer under the truth-in-lending legislation. This information must be disclosed on a printed form (usually an installment sales contract) before the credit is extended. It must also be provided in the terminology, specified by the law, which is indicated as follows.

1. The cash price (cash price).

2. The down payment including trade-in (cash down payment, trade-in, or total down payment—as applicable).

3. The difference between the cash price and down payment (unpaid balance of cash price).

4. All other charges, itemized but not part of the finance charge.

5. The unpaid balance (unpaid balance).

6. Amounts deducted as prepaid finance charges or required deposit balances (prepaid finance charge) or (required deposit balance) or both.

7. The amount financed (amount financed).

8. The total cash price, finance, and all other charges (deferred payment price).

9. The total dollar amount of the finance charge (finance charge).

10. The date on which the finance charge begins to apply (if this is different from the date of the sale).

11. The annual percentage rate, which must be expressed as a percentage after January 1, 1971 (annual percentage rate).

12. The number, amounts, and due dates of payments.

13. The total payments (total of payments).

14. The amount you charge for any default, delinquency, and the like, or the method you use for calculating the amount.

15. A description of any security you will hold.

16. A description of any penalty charge for prepayment of principal.

---

[3] Ibid.

17. How the unearned part of the finance charge is calculated in case of prepayment. (Charges deducted from any rebate must be stated.)[4]

BAD DEBTS AND COLLECTIONS

Small business owners would like to collect all their credit accounts, but this is not possible. The amount of bad debts they sustain on credit accounts will depend mostly on how effective they are in selecting people to whom they will grant credit and in the efficiency of their collection methods.

Small business owners should keep good records of credit accounts. By dividing **bad debts** by sales, they are able to compute the bad debt ratio. They should calculate this ratio on a periodic basis in order to check the adequacy of their credit program. Once they have decided what is a realistic bad debt ratio for the firm, any significant shift in the bad debt ratio should be a signal that something is wrong. Small business owners should try to balance their credit policy so that they are not too restrictive and eliminate good customers or too lenient and have excessive bad debts.

Collection of overdue accounts requires considerable skill to balance effective collection without harming customer goodwill. If the small business firm initiates action too soon and with too firm a hand, it may lose many good customers. On the other hand, if it moves too slowly, while giving an impression of a lax attitude, it may never collect the account.

Collection timing and methods should vary to some degree with the credit record of the customer. However, a process of stages of collection methods should be employed in collection efforts. These stages should move from a soft approach to a final stern, legal approach.

Collection Messages

The four steps in **collection** messages are (1) reminder, (2) stronger reminder, (3) inquiry and appeal, and (4) legal ultimatum.

Reminder

Most overdue accounts are collected with the first letter and are probably due to customers' oversight or procrastination. These people are valuable customers, so the reminder is intended to collect the money while retaining the goodwill of the customer. Consequently, the first message must start with the assumption that the customer fully intends to pay the bill but has overlooked it. The message must be very soft and must reassure the customer that the firm does not feel the individual is purposefully failing to pay the bill. The message should be a short note that includes something like "Have you overlooked us this month?"

---

[4]Ibid.

SPECIAL INTEREST FEATURE

Fair Debt Collection Practices Act

Some debt collection firms used rather drastic methods of collecting debts in the past. Telephone calls in the middle of the night, banging on the door and yelling in a loud voice that the debtor would have to pay the debt, making repeated telephone calls to the debtor at his or her work, and threatening drastic actions they could not legally take were some of the common abuses. In 1978 the federal government passed the Fair Debt Collection Practices Act to eliminate these abuses.

The Federal Trade Commission summarized the act as follows.

How May a Debt Collector Contact You?

A debt collector may contact you in person, by mail, telephone or telegram. However, it can't be at inconvenient or unusual times or places, such as before 8:00 A.M. or after 9:00 P.M., unless you agree.

A debt collector may **not** contact you at work if your employer disapproves.

Can You Stop a Debt Collector from Contacting You?

Yes, you may stop a debt collector from contacting you by saying so in writing. Once you tell a debt collector not to contact you, the debt collector can no longer do so, **except** to tell you that there will be no further contact. Also, the debt collector may notify you that some specific action may be taken, but only if the debt collector or the creditor usually takes such action.

May a Debt Collector Contact Any Other Person Concerning Your Debt?

A debt collector may contact any person to locate you. However, the Debt Collector Must:

Only tell people that the purpose is to try to contact you.
Only contact your attorney if you have an attorney.

The Debt Collector Must Not:

Tell anybody else that you owe money.
In most cases, talk to any person more than *once*.
Use a post card.
Put anything on an envelope or in a letter that identifies the writer as a debt collector.

What Is the Debt Collector Required to Tell You about the Debt?

Within 5 days after you are first contacted, the debt collector must send you a **WRITTEN NOTICE** telling you—

- the amount of money you owe;
- the name of the creditor to whom you owe the money; and
- what to do if you feel you do not owe the money.

If You Feel You Do Not Owe the Money, May a Debt Collector Continue to Contact You?

The debt collector must not contact you if you send a letter within thirty days after you are first contacted saying you do not owe the money. However, a debt collector can begin collection activities again if you are sent proof of the debt, such as a copy of the bill.

What Types of Debt Collection Practices Are Prohibited?

A debt collector may not *HARASS*, *OPPRESS* or *ABUSE* any person. For example, a debt collector cannot:

> Use threats of violence to harm anyone or anyone's property or reputation.
> Publish a list of consumers which says you refuse to pay your debts (except to a credit bureau).
> Use obscene or profane language.
> Repeatedly use the telephone to annoy anyone.
> Telephone any person without identifying the caller.
> Advertise your debt.

A debt collector may *not* use any *FALSE* statements when collecting any debt. For example, the debt collector cannot:

> Falsely imply that the debt collector represents the United States government or any State government.
> Falsely imply that the debt collector is an attorney.
> Falsely imply that *you* committed any crime.
> Falsely represent that the debt collector operates or works for a credit bureau.
> Misrepresent the amount of the debt.
> Represent that papers being sent are legal forms, such as a summons, when they are not.
> Represent that papers being sent are *not* legal forms when they *are*.

Also, a debt collector may not say:

- That you will be arrested or imprisoned if you do not pay your debt.
- That he will *SEIZE*, *GARNISH*, *ATTACH* or *SELL YOUR PROPERTY* or *WAGES*, *UNLESS* the debt collector or the creditor intends to do so and it is legal.
- That any *ACTION* will be taken against you which *CANNOT LEGALLY* be taken.

A debt collector may not:

- Give false *CREDIT INFORMATION* about you to anyone.
- Send you anything that looks like an *OFFICIAL* document which might be sent by any *COURT* or *AGENCY* of the *UNITED STATES* or any *STATE* or *LOCAL* government.
- Use any false name.

A debt collector must *not* be *UNFAIR* in attempting to collect any debt. For example, the debt collector cannot:

- Collect *any amount* greater than the amount of your debt, unless allowed by law.
- Deposit any postdated check before the date on that check.
- Make you accept collect calls or pay for telegrams.
- Take or threaten to take your property unless there is a present right to do so.
- Contact you by post card.
- Put anything on an envelope other than the debt collector's address and name. Even the name cannot be used if it shows that the communication is about the collection of a debt.

What Control Do You Have over Specific Debts?

If you owe several debts, any payment you make must be applied as you choose. And, a debt collector cannot apply a payment to any debt you feel you do not owe.

What Can You Do If the Debt Collector Breaks the Law?

You have the right to sue a debt collector in a State or Federal court within 1 year from the date the law was violated. You may recover money for the damage you suffered. Court costs and attorney's fees can also be recovered.

A group of persons may sue a debt collector and recover money for damages up to $500,000.

Source   *Fair Debt Collection Practices Act*, Federal Trade Commission.

Stronger Reminder

The second stage of the collection messages should, **like the first, still assume** the failure to pay is the result of oversight or procrastination. The firm is still trying to collect the bill but also keep the person as a customer. However, the message should be a little firmer. The phrase "overlooked" is still used but a definite request for payment should be included in the message.

Inquiry and Appeal

The third stage of the collection messages assumes that the failure to pay is not an oversight, but there is something wrong. The firm is still trying to collect the debt and retain patronage of the individual. The firm does not, at this point, assume the customer is a customer it does not want on a credit basis. Consequently, the message should try to find out what is wrong and at the same time increase the pressure to pay. It should contain such phrases as "What is the difficulty?" and "Your credit rating is valuable."

Legal Ultimatum

The small business must at this stage assume that the customer is not going to pay the bill unless force is applied. The firm also reaches the stage at which it must assume the customer is no longer a valuable credit customer but a "cash-only" customer. The message must have urgency and outline the action the firm will take if the debt is not paid at once. Phrases such as "turned over to a collection agency" and "This action will destroy your credit rating" should be included. The small business should then follow the action threatened if payment is not received.

Timing of Collection Messages

Credit customers differ, and so should the timing of the collection messages. The person who has a good credit record should be given a longer period in the four stages of the collection process. On the other hand, the person who has a record of slow payment should receive the messages over a much shorter interval. In general, the first reminder should be sent when the debt is 4 weeks overdue. The Inquiry and Appeal message should be sent when the debt is 6 weeks overdue and the Legal Ultimatum when the debt is 10 weeks overdue. The debt should be turned over to a collection agency or attorney for legal action after five to six months.

SUMMARY OF KEY POINTS

1. Retail credit has increased rapidly since World War II and is very important to small business firms.

2. Charge account credit consists of 30-day charge accounts and revolving charge accounts.

3. Credit cards are issued by many business firms and by financial institutions.

4. Revolving charge accounts charge the consumer interest on the average daily balance, and the selling firm pays between 2 and 6 percent of the purchase amount when bank cards are used.

5. Credit application forms and retail credit bureaus are the two major sources of credit information.

6. The "truth-in-lending law" requires several things to be disclosed to the customer.

7. Small business owners who grant credit must make sure their credit policies are not so restrictive that they lose customers and not so lenient that they have excessive bad debts.

8. Collection messages should progress through four stages from reminder to legal ultimatum.

9. The Fair Debt Collection Practices Act specifies what rights the debtor has and what the collection firm may do to collect debt.

DISCUSSION QUESTIONS

1. Why is retail credit important to most small business firms?
2. How are traditional 30-day charge accounts different from revolving charge accounts?
3. How does installment credit differ from charge account credit?
4. What are some of the ways small business firms finance 30-day accounts, revolving charge accounts, and installment credit?
5. How does a small business obtain information about potential credit customers?
6. What was the reason why Congress passed the truth-in-lending law?
7. How does the truth-in-lending law attempt to achieve its goal?
8. What is a bad debt ratio, and how is it used?
9. Should the collection system for overdue accounts be the same for all customers?

STUDENT PROJECTS

1. Identify a store that uses
   a. 30-day charge accounts.
   b. Revolving charge accounts.
   c. Installment credit.
2. Obtain a copy of a revolving charge account statement and an installment sales contract, and check them to see if they meet the requirements of the truth-in-lending law.
3. Obtain a copy of a credit application form, and analyze it to determine if you feel it does a good job of obtaining credit information.
4. Find out if your community has a Retail Credit Bureau and, if so, who owns it.

CASE A

The Computer Store

John Harris has rented a space in a local shopping center and is currently installing display equipment. The store will offer a line of the most popular game computers and an extensive line of game software for them. He also plans to market one popular make of small business microcomputers with several software packages.

He plans to sell the game computers and software to individuals on a cash or charge account basis. The business computers will be sold for cash or on a two year installment basis which he will finance.

John needs some information and you have been asked to advise him.

QUESTIONS

1. What would you advise in terms of sales to individuals on a charge account basis?
2. What are the major two items that John must disclose to his credit customers?
3. Will John have to pay any fees for any of the credit methods he will use?
4. Generally, how should John go about collecting overdue accounts on the installment sales?

CASE B

Lance Brian's Cozy Carpets

Lance Brian is the sole owner of Cozy Carpets, which has been selling carpet and other floor coverings to building contractors for two years. He extends credit to these contractors and has had some problems in the past; however, he now has separated customers into those who are reliable in paying their accounts and those whom he requires to pay in cash. He feels there is very little he can do to improve his credit and collection practices.

Lance recently moved his business to a new location in an attractive building. It is on a major thoroughfare and surrounded several miles in each direction by residential housing that is about 4 to 10 years old. Lance has had few retail sales to individual home owners in the past, but now he feels the surrounding residential neighborhood could produce considerable retail sales. He realizes that he must have some kind of retail credit available because each sale represents several hundred dollars and even a thousand plus dollars. Lance has the capital to offer retail credit if he desires.

Lance has asked you to help him set up a retail credit plan.

QUESTIONS

1. Would you advise him to offer 30-day charge or revolving charge credit?
2. Would you advise him to use bank credit cards? Explain your reasons.
3. Would you advise him to offer installment contracts? Should he finance them himself?

SMALL BUSINESS
ADMINISTRATION PUBLICATIONS

Free

Credits and Collections
Retail Credit and Collection

For Sale

Credit and Collections for Small Stores
Consumer Credit
Credit and Collections: Policy and Procedures

THE
GOVERNMENT
AND
SMALL
BUSINESS

SECTION SIX

CHAPTER TWENTY-ONE
LEGAL CONSIDERATIONS

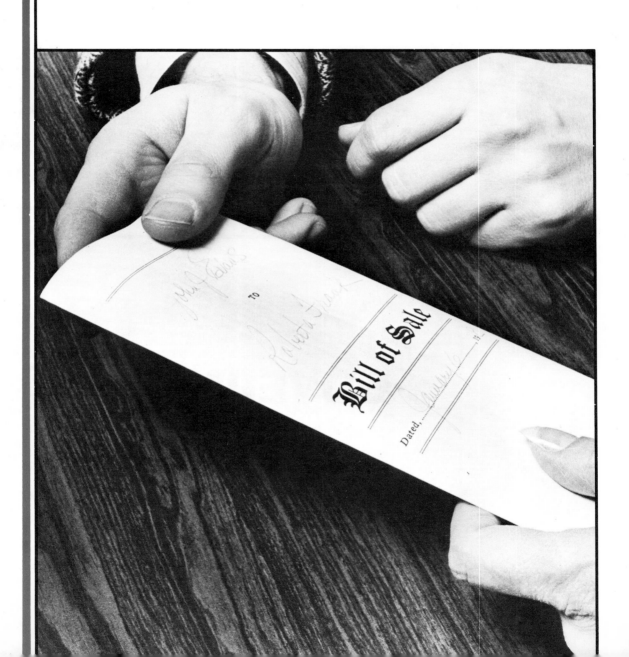

LEARNING GOALS

After reading this chapter, you will understand:

1. What the requirements are for a contract to be valid and enforceable in a court of law.

2. The various legal recourses available to a person when there is a breach of contract.

3. Why there is a Uniform Commercial Code, what it attempts to do, and what areas of commercial law it covers.

4. The different types of checks, how to minimize bad checks, and what to do when you receive a bad check.

5. How small businesses might use other negotiable instruments—certificates of deposit, money orders, letters of credit, and bills of lading.

6. That there are three different types of installment sales contracts, which of these are the best in terms of repossession, and how one should go about repossessing merchandise.

7. That small businesses must have various types of permits and licenses in order to operate.

KEY WORDS

Contracts	Money orders
Duress	Letters of credit
Fraud	Bills of lading
Breach of contract	Chattel mortgage
Uniform Commercial Code	Conditional sales contract
Checks	Lease-purchase contract
Certificates of deposit	Licenses

SMALL BUSINESS PROFILE

Gary Gabrel: Pente Games, Inc.

Gary Gabrel loved games so much while he was in college that he invented one. Now, at age 30, Gabrel is president of Pente Games, Inc., a company that grossed $3 million in 1981. He was named Oklahoma Small Business Person of the Year in 1982.

Friends introduced Gabrel, then a sociology student at Oklahoma State University, to two ancient Oriental board games, Go and Go-Moku, in 1973. Go exceeds chess in complexity; Go-Moku is relatively simple. Both are played with stones on the same board, a grid.

Gabrel began designing a version that would incorporate the profound strategy of Go and the speed and simplicity of Go-Moku.

At that time he was working his way through school at a pizza parlor, where he later became manager. "If friends came by, we'd play on the checkered tablecloths," he says. As they played, they refined the game.

But when he offered the idea to 10 leading manufacturers, he was turned down. So he decided to produce it himself. To do that, he needed a name and a border design. "I was looking for a design that would fit the nature of the game, so I was looking primarily at Oriental designs," he says. "But Oriental themes were not popular then because of the Vietnam War. In the library I came across a drawing of Achilles and Ajax, the boldest of the Greek heroes in the Trojan War, seated in full battle dress across a tablecloth board game." The design would give the game the Western flavor he wanted, but he still needed a name.

"I compiled a long list of Greek gods, goddesses, places names and wars," he says, "but none seemed right." Then, with an appointment with a printer coming up, he turned to the dictionary. "I looked up the Greek work for *five*, since the object is to get five stones in a row or five captures, and Pente became the name of the game."

Production was tougher. "I worked with local printers," Gabrel says. "They were patient with me. It was difficult because I wanted small quantities of a custom job, and it's hard for printers to do that kind of work profitably."

The games were sold mostly to friends and at craft fairs until 1979, when Gabrel incorporated and hired an employee. "The first profit came with the Christmas season of 1980," he says. And it has been steady ever since.

Gabrel now has 20 salaried employes and 20 more who work part-time or on an hourly basis. About 140 sales representatives promote the game, which is sold all over the United States and in Australia and Canada.

"A lot of people dream about inventing a game and getting rich," says Gabrel. "The reason I was successful was that I had an idea that was right—I don't know whether it was insight or luck—and I persevered." He also credits his game-loving friends with giving him good suggestions along the way.

He has little time to play Pente now. "A lot of my free time is spent playing games sent in by other inventors who want to get their games on the market," says Gabrel. "It's also frustrating because in many cases I have to mete out the same kind of rejections I faced when I was trying to get started. I try to give inventors encouragement."

The game, which was first made only with a wooden board, now also comes with more portable vinyl boards and a glass board. Prices range from $15 to $90. "I'm shooting for a gross of $8 million or $9 million this year," says Gabrel, who hopes Pente gives backgammon a run for its money.

Source "The Game Plan of a Gamester," *Nation's Business*, September, 1982, p. 90. Reprinted by permission from Nation's Business, September, 1982. Copyright 1982 by Nation's Business, Chamber of Commerce of the United States.

Small business firms exist in an environment governed by laws. In fact, business of any size could not exist without laws to set standards and requirements of conduct. Daily, the small business engages in activities that are governed by law. If the small business owner is to succeed, he or she must know his or her rights and responsibilities under the law.

CONTRACTS

The small business owner deals almost daily with some form of **contract**—written or verbal. (See Fig. 21–1.) For example, if a customer orders a sandwich in a restaurant, he or she and the business are entering into a verbal contract. The restaurant is agreeing to provide a sandwich, and the customer is agreeing to pay the advertised price for the sandwich. Examples of contracts in written form would be leases, deeds, warranties, and installment sales contracts. Because small business owners are engaged in contracts on a continuing basis, they must know what is required for a contract to be valid and enforceable. They must also be aware of their rights in case the other party does not honor the terms of the contract.

Requirements of a Valid Contract

Each state establishes its own laws concerning contracts. As a result, there are some variations in legal requirements for valid contracts in various states. However, the states do have the same basic requirements.

In order for a contract to be valid and enforceable in any state, it must meet the requirements of (1) competent parties, (2) consideration, (3) legal purpose, (4) mutual assent, and (5) legal form.

Competent Parties
All parties to a contract must be competent parties under the law. The law defines parties that are not competent as drunkards, convicts, insane persons, and persons who are below the legal age. Laws in the 50 states vary

FIGURE 21–1
Sections of a contract (a standard lease form).

A 185—Blumberg's Improved Gilsey Form Lease

JULIUS BLUMBERG, INC., LAW BLANK PUBLISHERS
80 EXCHANGE PLACE, AT BROADWAY, NEW YORK

This Agreement BETWEEN

as Landlord

and

as Tenant

Witnesseth: The Landlord hereby leases to the Tenant the following premises:

for the term of

to commence from the   day of   19   and to end on the

day of   19   to be used and occupied only for

upon the conditions and covenants following:

1st. That the Tenant shall pay the annual rent of

said rent to be paid in equal monthly payments in advance on the   day of each and every month during the term aforesaid, as follows:

2nd. That the Tenant shall take good care of the premises and shall, at the Tenant's own cost and expense make all repairs

and at the end or other expiration of the term, shall deliver up the demised premises in good order or condition, damages by the elements excepted.

3rd. That the Tenant shall promptly execute and comply with all statutes, ordinances, rules, orders, regulations and require- ments of the Federal, State and Local Governments and of any and all their Departments and Bureaus applicable to said premises, for the correction, prevention, and abatement of nuisances or other grievances, in, upon, or connected with said premises during said term; and shall also promptly comply with and execute all rules, orders and regulations of the New York Board of Fire Underwriters, or any other similar body, at the Tenant's own cost and expense.

27th. Landlord shall not be liable for failure to give possession of the premises upon commencement date by reason of the fact that premises are not ready for occupancy or because a prior Tenant or any other person is wrongfully holding over or is in wrongful possession, or for any other reason. The rent shall not commence until possession is given or is available, but the term herein shall not be extended.

And the said Landlord doth covenant that the said Tenant on paying the said yearly rent, and performing the covenants aforesaid, shall and may peacefully and quietly have, hold and enjoy the said demised premises for the term aforesaid, pro- vided however, that this covenant shall be conditioned upon the retention of title to the premises by the Landlord.

And it is mutually understood and agreed that the covenants and agreements contained in the within lease shall be binding upon the parties hereto and upon their respective successors, heirs, executors and administrators.

In Witness Whereof, the parties have interchangeably set their hands and seals (or caused these presents to be signed by their proper corporate officers and caused their proper corporate seal to be hereto affixed) this day of   19

Signed, sealed and delivered

in the presence of

....L. S.

....L. S.

....L. S.

between 18 and 21 in terms of minimum legal age. Generally, persons under the legal age specified by the state can enforce contracts against adults, but adults cannot enforce contracts against them. An exception exists in many states when the contract is for necessities, such as food, shelter, clothing, and ordinary education.

The small business owner should be aware that, although the law declares that drunkards and insane persons are not competent parties, it does not automatically mean that the person who appears intoxicated or acts abnormal cannot be a party to a valid and enforceable contract. In general, a person must be adjudged by the courts to be a confirmed drunkard or insane before he loses his status as a competent party. Intoxication and abnormal actions are usually not a defense against a valid contract unless the actions are so extreme as to prohibit intelligent action.

Consideration of Both Parties

Both parties to the contract must give some form of consideration for it to be a valid, enforceable contract. For example, a relative creates a contract in which he promises a young man that he will give him $5000 on his twenty-first birthday. This would not be an enforceable contract because the young man did not give any consideration in the contract. However, consideration does not have to be in the form of money or tangible goods. For example, if this relative promised to give the young man $5000 on his twenty-first birthday if he would refrain from drinking intoxicating beverages, it would be an enforceable contract because the young man would give consideration by not drinking intoxicating beverages.

A Legal Purpose

Contracts must be for a legal purpose to be valid and enforceable. In other words, the law will not enforce a contract requiring an act that the law itself declares illegal. For example, if a political candidate agreed to pay a person to break into his opponent's home for material to use in the campaign against her, the burglar could not force payment of the fee because it was for an illegal purpose and, therefore, not a valid contract.

Mutual Assent

In order for a contract to be valid and enforceable in a court of law, it must have mutual assent from both parties to the contract. The law recognizes four areas that violate the concept of mutual assent: (1) duress, (2) fraud, (3) mistake, and (4) undue influence.

Duress   **Duress** exists when a person is forced by threat to enter into a contract against his or her will. For example, if a person threatens bodily harm to another person unless he or she signs a contract, the resulting contract would not be valid and could not be enforced under the law.

Fraud   **Fraud** exists when there is intentional misrepresentation of fact. If fraud is present in a contract situation, then the contract is not valid and enforceable. For example, if a person intentionally turns back the speedometer of an automobile that she is selling and intentionally represents it to have a lower mileage, she is intentionally misrepresenting the automobile. A contract signed under these conditions would not be valid and enforceable. However, it should be pointed out that, though the law declares fraud illegal, proving intentional misrepresentation in court is not always an easy task.

Mistake   When one party to a contract makes an obvious mistake and the other party to the contract is aware of the mistake and takes advantage of it, the contract is not valid and enforceable. For example, if a contractor bid on a job and in listing costs added them together incorrectly, the other party could not take advantage of it and make him or her perform the job at the miscalculated price.

Undue Influence   If one party to the contract has undue influence on a person because of their relationship and causes the other party to contract to his or her harm because of this relationship, it cannot be a valid and enforceable contract. For example, an agent who has his or her client sign a contract to perform in a nightclub the agent owns at an unreasonably low fee could not enforce the contract because of the undue influence the agent had as a result of their relationship.

Legal Form
Contracts may be in either verbal or written form with certain limitations specified by the states. Some states specify that all contracts involving real property (real estate) must be in writing. Some other states specify that all contracts involving sums of more than a specified amount ($500 is a common amount) must be in writing. Some require both to be in writing. For example, if one person verbally tells another he will sell him his golf clubs (personal property) for $200 and the other person accepts, it is a valid contract. On the other hand, if one person verbally offers to sell another person her home for $20,000 and the other person accepts, it is not a valid contract in states that require real property contracts to be in writing.

Most contracts are of the verbal variety, such as the earlier example of the person ordering food in a restaurant. Though verbal contracts are valid and enforceable (with the exceptions noted earlier), they are sometimes difficult to prove in courts of law because of their verbal nature. Consequently, the small business owner should always insist on contracts of a significant value to be in the form of writing regardless of state requirements for legal form. (See Fig. 21–2.)

Recourse for Breach of Contract

When one party to a contract does not fulfill his part of the contract **(breach of contract)**, the other party to the contract has certain rights of recourse under law. In courts of law, he or she may (1) force performance of the contract, (2)

FIGURE 21–2

Requirements for a valid contract.

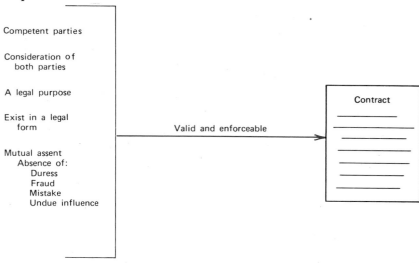

cause the contract to be discharged, or (3) collect damages resulting from nonperformance of the contract (see Fig. 21–3).

Performance of the Contract

One party to a contract may go to court to force the other party to the contract to fulfill his or her part of the agreement. For example, Joe sold Don land and received payment for it. Then he changed his mind, tried to give the money back, and kept Don from entering the land. Don could go into court, prove his claim, and the courts would direct Joe to turn the land over to Don. If Joe

FIGURE 21–3

Recourse for breach of contract.

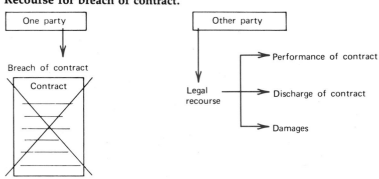

still refused, he would be declared in contempt of court and liable for criminal actions.

Discharge of the Contract

If one party to the contract fails to perform his or her part of the contract, the other party is not obligated to fulfill his or her part. For example, if one person agrees to sell another an automobile and then does not give this person the automobile, this other person is under no obligation to pay the purchase price.

Collect Damages

If one party to a contract suffers loss or damages as a result of the other party's not fulfilling his or her part of the contract, the injured party may recover damages in a court of law. For example, if a school hires a football coach and signs a contract for one year of employment and the coach is released from his or her duties after six months, the school must pay this coach wages for the remaining six months if he or she cannot find an equal position at another school.

UNIFORM COMMERCIAL CODE

Each individual state establishes its own laws (within the limits set by the U.S. Constitution and its state constitution) governing *intrastate* commerce (commerce within the state). The federal government establishes rules governing *interstate* commerce (commerce between the states).

Because each state establishes its own laws governing intrastate commerce, the early years of the United States witnessed a wide range of state statutes and judicial rulings. Conflicts and confusion were common because of the difference in state laws. In 1890 a move was initiated to encourage the states to adopt uniform laws governing commerce. By 1945 over 60 uniform statutes were formulated and adopted by a large number of states. In 1945 work was begun to combine all these uniform acts into a code encompassing the field of commercial law. In 1952 the **Uniform Commercial Code** was first published and then revised in 1958 to its present form. With the exception of the state of Louisiana, all 50 states have adopted the Uniform Commercial Code.

The general areas of law and some of the major provisions of each area that are included in the Uniform Commercial Code are these.

1. *Sales.* Requirements of contracts—rights of seller and buyer.
2. *Commercial paper.* Requirements of negotiable instruments including time, liability, acceptance, alteration, and delivery.
3. *Bank deposits and collections.* Banking practices such as cutoff time for posting.
4. *Letters of credit.* Rights and duties of bank, receiver, and customer.

5. *Bulk transfers*. Provisions preventing dishonest merchants from buying large quantities of goods without paying for them and selling them to third parties.

6. *Warehouse receipts, bills of lading, and other documents of title*. Regulates documents of title to personal property entrusted to others for various reasons.

7. *Investment securities*. Regulates registered and bearer bonds, stock certificates, and other investment paper.

8. *Secured transactions, sales of accounts, contract rights, and chattel paper*. Legal aspects of pledges, assignments, chattel mortgages, liens, conditional sales contracts, leases, and so on.

CHECKS AND OTHER NEGOTIABLE INSTRUMENTS

Some of the negotiable instruments a small business is likely to come in contact with are (1) checks, (2) certificates of deposit, (3) money orders, (4) letters of credit, (5) bills of lading, and (6) warehouse receipts.

Checks

Almost all small businesses receive and issue **checks** drawn on banks almost every day. Businesses that receive checks usually have a problem with bad checks. Retail and service firms usually suffer more than other businesses from bad checks, but manufacturers and wholesalers also find them a problem. Good check cashing procedures and collection practices help reduce losses from bad checks.

Types of Checks

The basic types of checks are (1) personal checks, (2) two-party checks, (3) payroll checks, (4) government checks, (5) counter checks, and (6) traveler's checks.

Personal checks A personal check is a check made out by the individual signing the check and made directly to the small business. A small business should require positive identification on all personal checks. If the state issues driver's licenses with photographs, this is one of the best means of identification. If not, the store should require the driver's license and note carefully the signature and description of the person. Additional identification should also be required in the form of credit cards, government passes, or identification cards. Signatures on these should also be compared to the driver's license and the check.

Two-party checks A two-party check is a check made out by one individual to another individual who endorses it so it can be cashed by the small business.

Generally, a small business should not accept two-party checks. The possibility of its being a stolen check or forgery is too great a risk.

Payroll checks Payroll checks are issued by a business to an employee for his or her salary. They usually have the word *payroll* printed on them and often have the amount imprinted on the check by a machine. The small business should require identification as described earlier. In addition, it generally is not a good policy to cash out-of-town checks. Thieves sometimes steal blank payroll checks from firms and then pass them to small businesses in other towns.

Government checks Government checks are checks issued by the local, state, or federal government. They may be for such purposes as wages, tax refunds, pensions, social security payments, welfare allotments, and veterans' benefits. It is not at all uncommon to find thieves who specialize in stealing government checks from mailboxes. In fact, in some metropolitan areas, stealing has become so common a practice that some banks will not accept government checks unless the person has an account in the bank. The small business firm should follow the same cautious identification procedure it uses with personal checks when accepting government checks.

Counter checks Banks usually have checks with the bank's name on them placed on counters in the bank so depositors may use them to withdraw funds from their accounts without having to have their personalized checks with them. Unless the small business knows the customer well, he or she should not honor a counter check.

Traveler's checks A traveler's check is a check sold by firms through banks to persons who do not wish to carry large sums of cash with them when they travel. The buyer signs each traveler's check in the presence of the bank teller and then must sign below the original signature when he or she cashes the check. A comparison of the two signatures identifies him or her as the owner. The small business employee or owner who accepts traveler's checks should *always* require the second signature in his or her presence and carefully check the two signatures.

Money orders may also be cashed as checks. Private firms, banks, and the United States Postal Service issue money orders for a fee. Small business firms should not cash money orders because they are usually purchased to send in the mail and not for direct transactions.

In addition to careful identification, the small business owner or employee who is cashing the check should look for

1. A difference in the written and the numerical amount on the check.
2. Proper endorsements.
3. Old dates or postdated checks.
4. An address of the customer and the bank.
5. Erasures and written-over amounts.

Types of Bad Checks
Checks may be bad because of (1) insufficient funds, (2) no account, (3) a closed account, or (4) forgery.

Insufficient funds Checks that are returned from the bank marked insufficient funds should be redeposited a second time after the customer is notified. Most of these checks are collected. State laws and bank practices vary, but, generally, if the check does not clear the second time, the bank will no longer accept it, and it is the small business owner's responsibility to collect it.

If the small business owner is unable to collect the check and resorts to prosecution in the courts, he or she should check state law to determine what actions must be taken to prosecute. Most states require the business owner to send the check writer a registered letter and wait from 5 to 10 days for payment before suit is filed.

No account When a check is returned from the bank marked "no account," there is almost no chance of collection. This is usually evidence of intentional fraud by the check writer. However, before notifying the police, the small business owner should make an attempt to contact the check writer just in case he or she has changed banks and inadvertently written the check on the wrong bank.

Closed account A returned check marked "closed account" is usually the result of a person's changing banks and forgetting he or she has a check outstanding. Also, the bank may have closed the account because of too many overdrafts. It may also be fraud on the part of the check writer. Collection should be attempted first and then prosecution begun if collection fails.

Forgery The police should be notified immediately in cases of forgery. Forged checks are worthless, and it would be rare indeed for collection attempts to be of any value. If the forged check is a U.S. government check, the small business should notify the nearest local field office of the U.S. Secret Service.

Small business firms should automatically stamp on the back side of all checks received the notation "for deposit only" and the name of the business. This prevents the checks from being cashed if stolen. (See Fig. 21–4.)

Certificates of Deposit

Certificates of deposit are documents that certify that a person has on deposit with a bank or savings and loan association a certain sum of money. The document also states the time the individual has agreed to leave the money on deposit until it matures. A person or business might have $1000 on deposit with a bank drawing 6.5 percent interest and might have agreed to leave it on deposit for six months minimum time. It can be withdrawn, with the bank's agreement, before the six-month period is up, but the person will pay a substantial penalty.

FIGURE 21-4
Types of checks and reasons for bank not accepting.

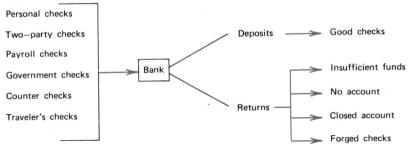

Money Orders

In a sense, a **money order** is a check drawn up by a post office, bank, or express office and purchased by an individual. It is a promise the institution will pay a specific amount of money on demand to specific persons. Money orders are often used to avoid the delay in clearing a regular check because the receiver knows the post office, bank, or express office checks are good. The person or business pays the institution the amount of the check plus a small fee.

Letters of Credit

A bank may issue a **letter of credit** requesting that money or credit be given to a specific person. The bank then guarantees payment of the debt. Letters of credit are often used in international markets and markets outside the usual business area of the firm.

Bills of Lading

Freight carriers, such as railroads and truck lines, issue **bills of lading** to certify certain merchandise is in their possession and is being transported. Only special types of bills of lading are negotiable, and they are called "Order Bills of Lading." The person or business whose name appears on the order bill of lading can endorse the shipment to another person. One way bills of lading are used is in the circumstance of a business that ships goods but does not have a warehouse, starting a carload of freight across the country and then selling it before it reaches the original destination. The firm endorses the shipment over to the buyer and diverts the car to him or her. Order bills of lading are often used by middlemen in farm products. They purchase carload lots of farm products and then sell them while they are in transit.

Warehouse Receipts

When goods are placed in a public warehouse (a warehouse that stores goods for business firms and individuals), the owners receive a warehouse receipt for the goods. If they wish to sell the goods, all they have to do is endorse the warehouse receipt over to the buyers, who then may claim the goods. Warehouse receipts are also used when a business borrows money and uses the warehoused goods as collateral. The warehouse receipt is signed over to the creditor until the debt is paid.

INSTALLMENT CONTRACTS AND REPOSSESSION

Installment sales contracts may exist in three basic types: (1) chattel mortgage, (2) conditional sales contract, and (3) lease-purchase.

Chattel Mortgage

Under the **chattel mortgage** contract, the title of the merchandise passes to the buyer at the time of the purchase. The contract is secured by the seller's having a lien against the merchandise.

Conditional Sales Contract

The **conditional sales contract** is the most common type used today. As the name implies, the sale of the merchandise is conditional on the buyer's making payments on time and meeting other conditions. These contracts usually require the purchaser to insure the merchandise and pay all maintenance costs until the merchandise is paid for. The title to the merchandise does not pass to the buyer until all provisions of the contract are completed.

Lease-Purchase

Under the **lease-purchase contract,** merchandise is rented to purchasers until they have made a specific number of payments. After they have made the specific number of payments, they receive title to the goods. Some small business firms that specialize in lease-purchase types of sales try to appeal to persons who have poor credit ratings.

The conditional sales contract and the lease-purchase arrangement are superior to the chattel mortgage in terms of repossession of merchandise. State laws governing repossession of merchandise under all three types of contracts vary widely. However, the chattel mortgage contract is more time-consuming and more expensive than the other two types of contracts in terms of repossession in most states. (See Fig. 21–5.)

The authors have known small business owners who repossess merchan-

FIGURE 21–5

Types of installment sales contracts.

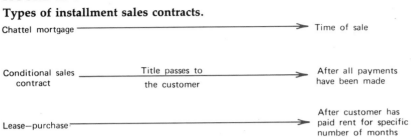

dise by going to the person's home, telling him or her they are there to repossess the merchandise, and then going into the house to take it back. *No small business owner should ever use this method of repossession.* Not only does it violate the rights of the customer, which can result in legal problems for the small business owner, but it can be very dangerous. Any small business owner who repossesses merchandise should first consult an attorney to learn the requirements of the state's laws and then carefully follow the requirements of the law.

SPECIAL INTEREST FEATURE

Legal Requirements Cause Headaches for Small Business

One of the more common complaints for small business owners is about the time and paperwork that are spent meeting various laws of city, county, state, and the federal government. The experience of two people amply illustrates the problem.

One entrepreneur, whom we will call Joe, wanted to build an auto parts store on a major road in a city of a population over 300,000. Joe found what he considered the best location for his store. After considerable negotiations, Joe obtained an option contract with the owner and deposited $5000 earnest money with a title company.

Joe then spent half a day talking to various people at the city trying to verify the zoning. He finally discovered that the zoning had never been finalized and that the property was zoned for single-family residence. Joe obtained all the information needed to try to get the zoning changed (it would take three months). Joe hired an architect to draw up a site plan taking into consideration all the various requirements of the city. Joe took his site plan to the city and was told he would have to see Planning to determine if it was a legal lot, Water Shed Management to determine the 100-year flood plain, Urban Transportation to determine parking requirements, Building Inspection to determine setbacks from the streets, and Landscaping to determine landscaping requirements. The second day while Joe was processing his application through these departments, he discovered that the city had an ordinance that required the property to have a 200-foot frontage on the main road to obtain direct access if there was another road next to the property. The property only had 180 feet of frontage and did have access to another road, thereby denying access, which made the property unsuitable for his store.

Another entrepreneur, whom we will call Sam, set up a business (in the same city) in which he bought a large barbecue cooker on wheels from a firm that had obtained the right to sell barbecued food in a supermarket chain's stores on the weekend. The meat was cooked on the cooker in the parking lot and sold by an employee at a table in the supermarket. The table was equipped with a glass guard, heat lamps, and equipment to keep the meat and equipment clean. Sam had to obtain a health permit. The employee at the health department said Sam had a choice. He could permanently affix his table and cooking equipment to the barbecue cooker, or he had to build restrooms next to his cooker in the parking lot. The official agreed there was no health problem with the way it was done in other cities. It took an appeal to a city council member to get the official to change his mind.

Sam had to go to the state controller to obtain a sales tax permit. He had to fill in a rather lengthy form and place a specific amount of money on deposit, which he could not withdraw as long as he had his tax license. Sam collected sales tax, kept a record of it, filled out a form each month, and remitted the tax collected.

Sam obtained an employer identification number from the Internal Revenue Service (he had one employee). Sam withheld income tax and FICA tax from his employee's salary each week and filled out a form (he had considerable trouble understanding it) every quarter and remitted the money. He was required to pay an equal amount of the FICA tax. Sam also was required to pay a federal unemployment tax on his employee and fill out a form reporting this tax.

Sam also had to acquire a number from the state employment commission, fill out report forms, and pay a state unemployment tax.

Sam also was required to fill out several reports each year for various government bodies, such as the Economic Censuses Report for the Department of Commerce and the personal property tax forms for the city, county, and school district.

LICENSES AND PERMITS

Most states and many local governments require businesses to obtain various types of **licenses.** In addition, state and local governments often require employees of small businesses to obtain permits, for example, health permits. Some of the licenses are for control purposes, as is the case of a health permit. However, many are for taxation purposes, such as city business permits.

Individuals interested in starting a small business should first check and determine what licenses and permits are required for the business. In some cases, these may result in their not being able to operate a business. For example, if an individual built a tavern and then could not obtain a liquor license for some reason, he or she could not operate the business. Persons buying a business should also make sure the licenses and permits of the business will transfer to them or that they will be able to acquire them after they have bought the business.

From this chapter, it can be easily seen that legal aspects of small business can be complex and differ from state to state. The small business entrepreneur would be well advised to contact an attorney when he or she is starting a business.

SUMMARY OF KEY POINTS

1. The requirements of a valid contract are (a) competent parties, (b) consideration, (c) legal purpose, (d) mutual assent, and (e) legal form.

2. Recourse for breach of contract may be requiring performance of the contract, discharge of the contract, or collection of damages.

3. The Uniform Commercial Code was created because widely differing state laws were causing problems in interstate commerce.

4. Checks may exist in the form of personal checks, two-party checks, payroll checks, government checks, counter checks, and traveler's checks.

5. Checks may be bad because of insufficient funds, no account, a closed account, or forgery.

6. Other forms of negotiable instruments are certificates of deposit, money orders, letters for credit, bills of lading, and warehouse receipts.

7. Installment contracts may exist in three basic forms: chattel mortgage, conditional sales contract, and lease-purchase contract.

8. City, county, state, and federal governments have numerous requirements that are placed on small business that require considerable time.

9. A new business must obtain various types of licenses.

DISCUSSION QUESTIONS

1. Who are competent parties in terms of a contract?

2. Does a contract have to be in writing, or may it be verbal?

3. What can a person do if another party does not honor a contract?

4. Do you consider the Uniform Commercial Code to be a good idea? Explain.

5. What types of checks would you advise a small business owner to accept?

6. How may a small business owner minimize bad check losses?

7. Which type of bad check returned by the bank is the most likely to be collected?

8. If you owned a department store, how might you use (a) certificates of deposit, (b) money orders, (c) letters of credit, and (d) bills of lading?

9. If you were a small business owner, which type of installment sales contract would you use? Explain.

10. How should a small business owner go about repossessing merchandise?

11. Why should a prospective small business owner investigate licenses and permits before he or she starts or purchases a small business?

STUDENT PROJECT

Obtain a copy of an installment sales contract (blank or completed). If it is a blank contract, fill in the contract with fictitious information as if you were buying an appliance.

1. Determine if the installment sales contract meets the various requirements of a valid contract.

2. Determine if it is a chattel mortgage, a conditional sales contract, or a lease-purchase agreement.

CASE A

The Sound Store

Marco Lucio is in the process of opening a stereo store. He plans to sell only high-priced, top-of-the-line equipment. Because Marco is going to offer only high-quality equipment, he knows he must offer some sort of finance plan other than bank cards. He plans to finance as much of his installment sales as possible.

Marco has asked your help.

QUESTIONS

1. What can Marco do to make sure his installment contracts are valid and enforceable?

2. What can Marco do if someone defaults on his or her contract?

3. What type of installment contract would you recommend?

4. What kind of checks should Marco accept, what kind of identification should he require, and what should he do if any are returned from the bank?

CASE B

Redell's Appliance Store

The Redell Appliance Store is owned and operated by Coy Redell. The store sells a well-known line of appliances—stoves, refrigerators, dishwashers, and others. It also has a complete service department for all the products it sells. Coy has been in business for 15 years and has been very successful.

Coy has been using a local bank to finance installment purchases for his customers. Because the business has been so profitable, Coy has quite a large sum of money accumulated in certificates of deposit in a local savings and loan association, and he has been looking for some place to invest it to earn more money. One day while filling in a loan application for a customer, Coy realized that the interest rate on the installment contract was considerably higher than the amount he was earning with his certificates of deposit. He decided that he would start financing his own installment contracts with his savings.

Coy has asked you to help him. He has several questions he needs answered.

QUESTIONS

Coy's questions are the following.

1. What should I do to make sure I have valid contracts with my customers?
2. What can I do if a customer does not make his or her payments on the installment contract?
3. What kind of installment contracts should I use?
4. A banker friend told me the other day that my certificates of deposit are one form of negotiable instruments. Are there other negotiable instruments I can use?

SMALL BUSINESS ADMINISTRATION PUBLICATIONS

Free

Outwitting Bad-Check Passers

CHAPTER TWENTY-TWO

GOVERNMENT CONTROL AND ASSISTANCE

KEEP REFRIGERATED

HOMOGENIZED   PASTEURIZED

VITAMIN D MILK

NUTRITION INFORMATION
Per Serving

SERVING SIZE .... ONE CUP
SERVINGS PER CONTAINER 8
CALORIES 150
PROTEIN .... 8 GRAMS
CARBOHYDRATE .... 11 GRAMS
FAT .... 8 GRAMS

Percentage of U.S. Recommended
Daily Allowances (U.S. RDA)

PROTEIN	20	VITAMIN D	25
VITAMIN A	 4	VITAMIN B₆	... 4
VITAMIN C	 4	VITAMIN B₁₂	...15
THIAMINE	 6	PHOSPHORUS	.20
RIBOFLAVIN	..25	MAGNESIUM	.. 8
NIACIN	*	ZINC	4
CALCIUM	30	PANTOTHENIC	
IRON	*	ACID	 6

*Contains less than 2% of the
U.S. RDA of these nutrients

INGREDIENTS: MILK & VITAMIN D
Dist. By Elmhurst

LEARNING GOALS

After reading this chapter, you will understand:

1. Which are the primary controls of business legislative acts, what they prohibit, and what agencies administer them.
2. What the Occupational Safety and Health Act is and how it affects small businesses.
3. What effect consumer protection laws have on small business firms.
4. That the Small Business Administration is the main governmental agency providing assistance to small business.
5. That the Small Business Administration helps small business firms with loans, management assistance, training, set-aside contracts, and publications.

KEY WORDS

Sherman Antitrust Act

Clayton Act

Federal Trade Commission Act

Robinson-Patman Act

Food, Drug, and Cosmetic Act

Occupational Safety and Health Act

Cooling-off periods

Fair Packing and Labeling Act

Federal Garnishment Law

Magnuson-Moss Warranty Act

Unordered merchandise

Small Business Administration

ACE

SCORE

University Small Business Institutes

Set-aside contracts

Office of Advocacy

SMALL BUSINESS PROFILE

Gordon Crane: Apple & Eve

If you are a David among Goliaths in the highly competitive food business, how do you survive and grow? "Be first with a product and be able to turn on a dime," says Gordon Crane, 32, president of Apple & Eve, Great Neck, N.Y., a leading marketer of pure, unsweetened apple and apple-cranberry juices.

Every day, in food stores from Maine to Florida and westward as far as Chicago, consumers make 25,000 purchases of Apple & Eve products. Other firms market natural apple juice, but Apple & Eve claims first place when it comes to sales in the dairy case. Its total sales this year are expected to top $10 million—$1 million for each of the 10 people in the company.

Gordon Crane's career objective was to be a lawyer, but when he graduated from the University of Rhode Island in 1972, he elected to take a year off before plunging into law school. He started a natural food distribution company in New York and got hooked on the joys of entrepreneurship. By 1975 he had found what he thought would be a good prospect for supermarkets— natural, unfiltered apple juice.

Crane developed a distinctive logo for his product—an apple with a bite taken out of it—and with a capitalization of less than $3,000 contracted with a processor for a supply of juice. To reach retailers he hawked his product at 5 in the morning at area farmers' markets.

By the time he had obtained his first big order from a major retailer in 1975, he had enrolled at Hofstra University's law school. Apple & Eve's office was the Crane home, and Gordon's mother, Ruth, offered to sit in when her son was attending classes. Soon, however, it was a full-time job. Older brother Alan joined the firm to head up the sales effort, and younger brother Cary joined after studying marketing at the University of Buffalo.

Gordon Crane got his law degree in 1978 and passed the bar, but he applies his legal training only to the business.

Until recently Crane was the buyer for the firm, visiting apple growers from Georgia to New England, but now Apple & Eve has a full-time buyer and also turns to the spot market. Growers turn their apples over to pressing plants, which then ship the juice to one of two processing plants in New Jersey. There the juice is blended with that of other varieties of apples, or cranberries if a mixture, and packaged for Apple & Eve in glass jars, cardboard cartons or Brik Paks, the new aseptic containers that employ a cold-pack process.

Being small allows the firm to turn on a dime, Crane says. He points out that Apple & Eve was first to hit the market—by several months—with aseptic packaging for juice, a process that relies on flash pasteurization. Products need not be refrigerated. The rectangular packaging allows retailers to accommodate 30 percent more stock, and transportation costs much less than for bottles.

Apple & Eve is now testing a pure juice made from fresh vegetables. "You've got to be first," Gordon Crane contends.

Source "Young Firm's Sales: $1 Million per capita," *Nation's Business*, September, 1982, p. 90. Reprinted by permission from Nation's Business, September, 1982. Copyright 1982 by Nation's Business, Chamber of Commerce of the United States.

Many states have social control of business legislation, but the more important pieces of legislation regulating business are federal laws that apply to interstate commerce. Major federal social control of business legislation exists in the form of the (1) Sherman Antitrust Act, (2) Clayton Act, (3) Federal Trade Commission Act, (4) Robinson-Patman Act, and (5) Food, Drug, and Cosmetic Act.

SHERMAN ANTITRUST ACT, 1890

The **Sherman Antitrust Act** prohibits restraint of trade and monopoly in business.

The two main sections of the act read as follows:[1]

Sec. 1 Every contract, combination in the form of trust or otherwise, or conspiracy, in restraint of trade or commerce among the several states, or with foreign nations is hereby declared to be illegal. . . .
Sec. 2 Every person who shall monopolize, or attempt to monopolize, or combine or conspire with any other person or persons, to monopolize any part of the trade or commerce among the several states, or with foreign nations, shall be deemed guilty of a misdemeanor. . . .

The restraint-of-trade section of the Sherman Antitrust Act has usually been applied to price-fixing arrangements between firms. One of the more famous cases of application of the Sherman Act was the conviction of several electrical manufacturers in the 1960s. For the first time in the history of the Sherman Act, several executives of the electrical manufacturers were sent to prison under criminal prosecution of violations of the act.

The section of the Sherman Act prohibiting monopoly has been greatly eroded by the courts. In 1911, the Department of Justice (which is responsible for administering the act) brought suit against Standard Oil Company of New Jersey and the American Tobacco Company. The government asked for and received a judgment that dissolved both companies into several smaller companies. (It is interesting to note that both Standard Oil of New Jersey and American Tobacco are larger companies today than were their parent com-

---

[1]United States Code, Title 15, Section 1-8.

panies before the 1911 dissolution decree.) However, the courts, in reaching their decision, established what is known as the "rule of reason." The rule of reason held there was cause for dissolution of monopoly only when "alarming and ungentlemanly conduct" and an overwhelming percentage control of the industry existed. The Department of Justice brought suit against the United States Steel Corporation (which then controlled 75 percent of the steel industry) in 1912, asking for dissolution. In 1920, the United States Supreme Court ruled in favor of United States Steel, claiming the Department of Justice had failed to prove unworthy motives, predatory acts, and overwhelming percentage control of the industry. The rule of reason has, for all practical purposes, eliminated the use of the monopoly section of the Sherman Act.

As mentioned earlier, the Sherman Act is administered by the Department of Justice. The Department of Justice may use either criminal prosecution or civil injunction under the law. Under criminal prosecution, persons may be subject to fines not to exceed $100,000 (corporations $1 million) or imprisonment of no more than one year or both. Civil injunctions involve asking the courts to issue a decree correcting the violation of the Sherman Act. In addition, individuals or businesses may institute civil proceedings to recover three times the amount of damages proved plus attorneys' fees from persons or firms guilty of violations of the Sherman Act.

CLAYTON ACT, 1914

The **Clayton Act** was intended to strengthen antitrust action by the federal government. It was intended to provide more specific legislation than was contained in the Sherman Act. The Clayton Act prohibits four practices of business: (1) price discrimination, (2) exclusive and tying contracts, (3) intercorporate stockholding lessening competition, and (4) interlocking directorates in competing corporations.

Price Discrimination

The Clayton Act prohibits price discrimination between different purchasers "where the effect of such discrimination may be to substantially lessen competition or to tend to create a monopoly in any line of commerce." This section was intended to prohibit a company from eliminating competition by selling at or below cost to selected customers. For example, one suit brought by the government charged that a manufacturer was selling spark plugs to automobile manufacturers at below cost in order to gain a large share of the replacement market (the government lost the suit because of the good faith provision discussed in the next paragraph).

The Clayton Act contained a provision that allowed price discrimination "when made in good faith to meet competition." The inability of the government to disprove good faith allowed almost a complete defense of this section of the Clayton Act. The inability of the Clayton Act to deal effectively with price discrimination led to the passage of the Robinson-Patman Act in 1936 (discussed later in this chapter).

Exclusive and Tying Contracts

The Clayton Act prohibits the following practices when their effect "may be to substantially lessen competition or tend to create a monopoly."

1. *Tie-in sales*   For example, the case of a mortgage company compelling home buyers to sign a contract to ensure their homes with a subsidiary of the mortgage company in order to obtain a home loan.
2. *Exclusive dealerships*   These arrangements require the dealer to agree not to sell products of the seller's competitors.
3. *Requirement contracts*   A contract that requires a customer to agree to buy all future needs from the seller.
4. *Full-line forcing*   The practice of selling a customer a product only if he or she agrees to purchase other lines of merchandise from the seller.

Intercorporate Stockholding Lessening Competition

This section of the Clayton Act prohibits a corporation from holding stock in another corporation when it would substantially lessen competition. For example, General Motors was forced by the courts to sell its stock in DuPont because DuPont supplied large amounts of paint to General Motors. The courts felt this intercorporate stockholding had the effect of lessening competition in the paint industry because General Motors used such vast amounts of paint.

Because the Clayton Act prohibited acquiring stock and not assets, many companies simply bought out the assets of competitors as a means of avoiding the act.

Interlocking Directorates in Competing Corporations

The Clayton Act prohibits a person from serving on the board of directors of two or more corporations that are or have been in competition if the effect could be to lessen competition. This section excludes banks, common carriers, and companies with capital of less than $1 million.

This section of the Clayton Act has not been as effective as intended by Congress because another person, such as a relative or employee, may serve on another board of directors and achieve the same results.

The Clayton Act is administered by the Federal Trade Commission with the following exceptions.

1. The Interstate Commerce Commission administers the Clayton Act when carriers are involved.
2. The Federal Reserve Board administers the act when banks are involved.

FEDERAL TRADE COMMISSION ACT, 1914

When the courts interpreted the Sherman Antitrust Act, they condemned unfair competition but declared the act did not make it illegal. Small business owners were concerned and demanded action from Congress. In response to public and small business pressure, Congress enacted the **Federal Trade Commission Act,** which contained the following provisions.

1. The Federal Trade Commission (FTC) was established to be comprised of five members appointed by the President for 7-year terms. No more than three members may be from the same political party.
2. Any unfair methods of competition were declared illegal.
3. The Federal Trade Commission was given power to issue cease-and-desist orders. These orders could be challenged in court by the defendant.
4. The Federal Trade Commission was empowered to collect information about a business and its conduct that was to be made available to the President, Congress, and the public.

The most important sections of the Federal Trade Commission Act were the section declaring unfair methods of competition illegal and the section giving the FTC the power to issue cease-and-desist orders. The broad nature of the provision declaring unfair competition illegal provides legal authority for the Federal Trade Commission to deal with all types of business activity that injure competition.

Before the passage of the Federal Trade Commission Act, any individual or business suffering loss because of antitrust violations had to proceed directly through the courts under the Sherman or Clayton acts or both. This often proved to be a long and expensive process. Under the Federal Trade Commission Act, individuals can file a complaint with the FTC, and the commission has the power to issue a cease-and-desist order.

The Federal Trade Commission has become the primary agency enforcing antitrust legislation. Since it was formed, it has been empowered to administer the following acts.

1. The Clayton Act of 1914.
2. Parts of the Wheeler-Lea Act of 1938, which dealt with false advertising of food, drugs, cosmetics, and devices.

3. The Wool Products Labeling Act of 1939, which requires that all wool products except carpets, rugs, mats, and upholstering have a label attached that describes the kind and percent of fiber contained in the product.

4. Parts of the Lanham Trade-Mark Act of 1946, which allows the Federal Trade Commission to apply to the commissioner of patents for cancellation of trademarks that are deceptive, immoral, obtained fraudulently, or in violation of the Lanham Trade-Mark Act or a combination of these.

5. The McCarran Insurance Act of 1948, which regulates various activities in the insurance industry.

6. The Fur Products Labeling Act of 1951, which requires manufacturers to show on labels attached to garments the type of animal fur, country of origin, and specified processing information.

7. The Flammable Fabrics Act of 1953, which prohibits sale of highly flammable wearing apparel.

8. Part of the Food, Drug, and Cosmetic Act of 1938 (discussed later).

ROBINSON-PATMAN ACT, 1936

The **Robinson-Patman Act** was passed to close weaknesses of the price discrimination section of the Clayton Act. The Robinson-Patman Act prohibits (1) price discounts that cannot be fully justified by lower costs to the seller, (2) selling private brands of a product that are identical to regular brands at a lower price, and (3) giving buyers proportionally unequal advertising and promotional allowances. One of the major strengths of the act was that it placed the burden of proof for justifying price differences on the seller. In addition, the act not only makes the seller guilty under the act in cases of price discrimination, but it also makes the buyer guilty if he or she knowingly accepts a discriminating price.

The Federal Trade Commission may issue a cease-and-desist order when the seller is unable to show cost justification for price discrimination. The parties judged guilty may be subject to fines under civil proceedings and even subject to criminal action in certain instances. In addition, the act provides for any person injured by violation of the act to recover treble damages in civil actions.

FOOD, DRUG, AND COSMETIC ACT, 1938

Over 100 pieces of legislation to protect consumers from impure foods and drugs were turned down by Congress before the first one, the Pure Food and Drug Act, was passed in 1906. The Pure Food and Drug Act of 1906 was passed only after extensive publicity of abuses in the food and drug industry. The Pure Food and Drug Act of 1906 prohibited (1) the sale of food and drugs unsafe for human consumption and (2) false information from manufacturers concerning their product. The Department of Agriculture was responsible for administering the act. The act was weak and ineffective in protecting the consumer.

In 1937 a drug manufacturer sold a drug contaminated with poison, which resulted in 93 deaths. The resulting publicity and public reaction caused Congress to pass the **Food, Drug, and Cosmetic Act** in 1938. The Food, Drug, and Cosmetic Act of 1938 was considerably stronger than the 1906 act. The 1938 act prohibits (1) adulterated products, (2) misbranding, and (3) false advertising.

The Federal Trade Commission administers and enforces the false labeling and misbranding sections of the 1938 act. The Federal Trade Commission also has power to administer the prohibition of adulteration and false advertising; however, it has generally left these functions to the Food and Drug Administration of the Department of Health, Education, and Welfare, which also has enforcement power.

Figure 22–1 shows major business legislation.

FIGURE 22–1

Major government control of business legislation.

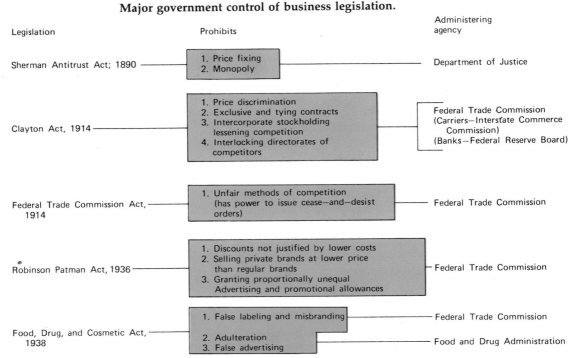

OCCUPATIONAL SAFETY
AND HEALTH ACT

There are about 13,000 deaths per year in the United States owing to occupational accidents. In addition, there are about 2.2 million workers who sustain disabling injuries on the job. In an attempt to reduce deaths and injuries related to work, Congress passed the **Occupational Safety and Health Act,** which is administered by the Occupational Safety and Health Administration (OSHA). The act requires that all workers must be free from recognized hazards that could cause death or serious injury.

OSHA has considerable power to enforce compliance with the law. The law allows fines of up to $1000 for each violation and fines of up to $1000 per day unless the violation is corrected within a prescribed time. Also, if an OSHA inspector finds a violation he or she feels could cause death or serious injury, the inspector can obtain a court injunction and have the business shut down until the violation is corrected.

Employers of more than 10 people must keep a log and summary of occupational injuries and illnesses. All employers, regardless of size, are required to report within 48 hours accidents involving a fatality or hospitalization.

Prior to 1978, safety inspectors could enter a firm without advance notice to make safety inspections. However, in 1978, the Supreme Court ruled (*Marshall* v. *Barlow's, Inc.*) that OSHA inspectors must obtain a warrant to gain entry to a workplace when the owner demands it.

Some businesses have maintained that some inspectors are overly zealous to the point of absurdity or do not have the knowledge necessary to perform their jobs realistically or both. In fact, many people in business have accused many of the government agencies of the same weaknesses. For example, one OSHA inspector ordered a manufacturer of pet sanitary litter to give all its employees a 2-week mine safety course, at company expense because it also owned a mine. Another agency was going to fine a person for flying a homemade helicopter 6 inches off the ground even though it was tied to the ground. The agency claimed he had failed to get FAA clearance. Publicity caused them to drop the case.

The small business owner should be aware of OSHA and the requirements for his or her type of business. The regulations cover, almost without exception, every type of business, even retail businesses. The requirements of OSHA can be very strict and most often are expensive. For example, the law requires any business that uses hydraulic jacks to have them inspected and serviced every 6 months by a certified dealer.

CONSUMER PROTECTION LAWS

The number of so-called consumer protection laws has been growing in recent years. The small businessperson must be aware of these laws and regulations in order not to violate their provisions. Some of the more important ones for small businesses are now discussed.

Cooling-off Periods

This Federal Trade Commission regulation requires a **cooling-off period** in door-to-door selling if the purchase exceeds $25. The buyer has 3 business days to cancel a purchase by written notification. The salesperson is then required to pick up the goods or make arrangements, at his or her expense, for the return of the goods within 20 days, or the customer can keep the goods. The salesperson must return in full any payment or trade-in received in the sale. The salesperson must also cancel any credit note or mortgage involved in the sale.

This regulation also makes provision for cooling-off periods in cases where the buyer's home is used as security in a credit transaction (not original purchase). Major repairs and remodeling often involve a second lien on the home. The 3-day period is required in these transactions, and the creditor must give the buyer written notice of his or her right to cancel. Written notification is also required to cancel the purchase.

There are certain exceptions—purchases made entirely by phone or mail, purchases made in relation to earlier negotiations at a retail store, purchases of stocks and bonds from registered brokers, purchases of insurance, the rental of property, and parts and labor for maintenance and repair.

Fair Packaging and Labeling Act

The **Fair Packaging and Labeling Act** of 1969 requires that any manufacturer or distributor of a consumer product must display prominently on labels the true net weight or volume of the contents. The law also prohibits such terms as *giant quart* or *jumbo pound*. Under the law, a manufacturer can only advertise coupon offers or "cents-off" sales if the price is below the regular price.

This famous product meets the new government regulations for safety seals.

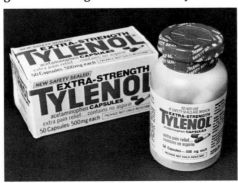

Any commodity labeled "economy size" or any other such term must be sold at a price that is at least 5 percent less than the per-unit of weight or volume price of all other sizes of the same product sold at the same time. Introductory price offers can last no longer than 6 months and may be used only for new products, products that are substantially changed, or products being introduced for the first time in a particular marketing area. Manufacturers who elect to show the number of servings on their label must also show the amount of each serving.

This law also requires manufacturers to list on the label all of the ingredients of the product in decreasing order of weight for any nonstandard foods. The common name of the product and the name and address of the manufacturer must appear on the label of all goods except prescription drugs.

Federal Garnishment Law

The **Federal Garnishment Law** of 1968 deals with an individual's wages being withheld for the payment of a debt. The federal law prohibits garnishments of more than 25 percent of an employee's disposable earnings (gross pay minus all deductions required by the law) in any one week or 30 times the federal minimum wage in effect at the time, whichever is less. The law also prohibits the employer from firing an employee because of one debt. The law does not prohibit firing if there are garnishments for two or more debts. If there is a state law covering garnishment of wages and it gives the debtor the better break, it is used instead of the federal law. Some states have laws prohibiting garnishment of wages and the federal law has no meaning in these states.

Magnuson-Moss Warranty Act

The **Magnuson-Moss Warranty** Act of 1974 provides that

1. No company can be forced to offer a written warranty.
2. Every term and condition of the warranty must be spelled out in writing.
3. All warranties must be written in ordinary language instead of in "legalese."
4. Any written warranty must be labeled either "full warranty" or "limited warranty."
5. Full warranties require that
   a. Defective products will be fixed or replaced free including removal and installation if necessary.
   b. They will be fixed in a reasonable time.
   c. The customer does not have to do anything unreasonable.
   d. The warranty covers any owner, not just the purchaser.
   e. If the product cannot be fixed, the customer has the choice between a new one or his or her money back.

6. Warranties that do not meet all these requirements must be labeled "limited warranties."

Merchandise, Mail Order and Unordered

Mail order firms must fill orders from customers within 30 days or offer the customers their money back. They must send customers a postcard allowing cancellation and the return of their money. If customers want their money back, it must be returned promptly. This regulation does not apply to magazines.

Free samples and merchandise mailed by charitable organizations soliciting contributions are the only **unordered merchandise** that can be sent through the mails. Other than these two categories, any merchandise that is unordered may be considered a free gift by the receiver. It is illegal for the business to bill or dun the person receiving unordered merchandise.

SPECIAL INTEREST FEATURE

The Increasing Burden of F.I.C.A. Tax on Small Business

F.I.C.A. (Federal Insurance Contribution Act) tax is familiar to most people through their payroll checks and W-2 forms. Social Security was instituted in 1934 as a mandatory insurance program. The program was extended in 1956 to provide benefits for disabled workers, and Medicare was added in 1965.

The benefits of the program have increased considerably since the start of the program, but the amount of contribution by worker and employer has also increased dramatically. The first tax rate was 1 percent for the employee, which was matched by the employer on wages up to $3,000—a maximum of $30 each. The following chart shows the increase for selected years:

Year	Percent Tax Rate	Maximum Income Taxed	Maximum Tax Amount
1976	5.85	$15,300	$ 895.05
1977	5.85	16,500	965.25
1978	6.05	17,700	1,070.85
1979	6.13	22,900	1,403.77
1980	6.13	25,900	1,587.67
1981	6.65	29,700	1,975.05
1982	6.70	32,400	2,170.80
1983	6.70	34,800	2,331.60
1984	6.70	37,200	2,492.40
1985	7.05	39,900	2,812.95

In addition to the F.I.C.A. tax, the small business must pay a 3.4 percent Federal Unemployment Tax on wages up to $6,000. The burden of payroll taxes to the small business firm has become an increasing concern.

Moreover, the small business owner must also pay a F.I.C.A. tax on his or her earnings. The rate has the same maximum income that is taxed; however, the rate is nearly ¾ of the combined amount the employees and employers pay. For example, the tax for self-employed persons in 1983 was 9.35 percent of all income up to $34,800.

GOVERNMENT ASSISTANCE TO SMALL BUSINESS

Many agencies of the federal government offer various forms of assistance to small business. For example, the Commerce Department will provide information and assistance to small businesses to help them engage in international trade. The Department of Labor has sponsored programs that provide assistance to businesses in poverty areas for training workers. The Office of Minority Business Enterprise in the Department of Commerce has sponsored programs designed to increase the number of minority small business firms. However, the bulk of government assistance to small business has come from the Small Business Administration of the Department of Commerce.

The **Small Business Administration** (SBA) was established by Congress in 1953 to "help small businesses grow and prosper." The SBA strives to achieve this goal by offering various services to small business firms. Without a doubt, the most important function of the SBA has been in its loan programs discussed in Chapter 5. The SBA also performs other valuable services to small businesses in the form of (1) management assistance, (2) training, (3) set-aside contracts, (4) the Office of Advocacy, and (5) publications. (See Fig. 22–2.)

Management Assistance

The SBA provides management assistance to small business firms in the form of (1) their own field representatives, (2) grants to consultants, (3) the ACE program, (4) the SCORE program, and (5) university Small Business Institutes.

Field Representatives

The SBA has 98 field offices spread out over the United States, Guam, and Puerto Rico. These field offices have field representatives whose primary function is to administer assistance to small businesses, particularly those with SBA loans. Although usually understaffed, these field offices provide valuable guidance in all phases of operations to small firms.

FIGURE 22–2

How the Small Business Administration helps small business (excluding loans).

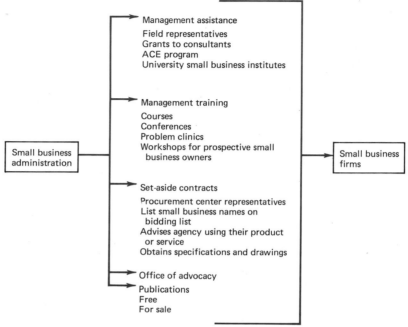

Grants to Consultants

The SBA provides funds, when they are available, to various types of consulting firms to assist loan recipients and other small businesses. The type of consulting sometimes varies from year to year, with such services as accounting and general business consulting being offered. The amount of funds made available for this type of service has been relatively small when compared to the amount of loans the SBA has outstanding. The SBA feels the program more than pays for itself in terms of improving the ability of loan recipients to repay their loans.

ACE Program

The **ACE** (Active Corps of Executives) program is one of the ways the Small Business Administration attempts to provide management consulting to small businesses. The SBA recruits persons actively engaged in small business, trade associations, major industry, professional fields related to small business, and educational institutions to join its ACE program. These volunteers provide free consulting (except for expenses that are paid for by the small business) to small business firms.

SCORE Program

The SBA forms **SCORE** (Service Corps of Retired Executives) chapters in cities and towns, consisting of persons who are retired from careers in business and business-related fields. These chapters include such persons as retired accountants, lawyers, engineers, economists, bankers, retailers, wholesalers, manufacturers, and educators. When a small business feels it needs help in solving problems or increasing efficiency of the business, it contacts the SBA field office, which in turn contacts the nearest SCORE chapter. The SCORE chapter then sends out one or more of its members who are best suited to help the small business. Today there are more than 4000 SCORE volunteers across the country helping small business firms. SCORE services are free to the small business except that the small business pays the out-of-pocket travel expenses of the volunteer.

University Small Business Institutes

The SBA contracts with colleges to provide business consulting to small firms through **University Small Business Institutes.** The SBA pays the school a small sum (currently, $400 each) for each business consulted. The methods of providing the service varies from school to school. Sometimes the instructor is directly involved in the consulting with his or her students. Sometimes the consulting is provided entirely by students. The school is required to provide periodical reports to the SBA and provide both the business and the SBA copies of the consulting recommendations. The service is entirely free to the small business. This program is designed to provide assistance to small business firms and give students exposure to real business firms and their problems. Both authors are involved in this program at their colleges and feel the program is very beneficial to both students and small businesses.

Management Training

The SBA provides management training through (1) courses, (2) conferences, (3) problem clinics, and (4) workshops for prospective small business owners.

Courses

The SBA cosponsors training courses for small business owners with educational institutions, SCORE chapters, and other civic organizations. Instructions are given by teaching staffs of colleges or other professionals. The small business owners who attend pay a small fee to cover expenses of the course, which usually consists of one day a week for several weeks.

The course may vary from general courses on policy and goals of small business to such specialized courses as bid preparation on government contracts or how to engage in export trade.

The SBA provides mailing envelopes and postage and helps with the publicity of the course. The institution provides the speaker and the room for the course.

Conferences

Conferences sponsored by the SBA are intended to help the small business owner with specific problems. They usually last only one day and cover such specialized topics as taxation. The SBA usually cosponsors these conferences with colleges, chambers of commerce, trade associations, and other civic groups. These conferences usually consist of a professional speaker, panel discussions, and question-and-answer sessions. The SBA provides mailing envelopes and postage for advertising the conference and helps with publicity.

Problem Clinics

The SBA also joins with cosponsoring institutions to offer problem clinics for small business owners. SBA contribution to the clinic is the same as for courses and conferences. The group of small business owners is led in a discussion of a common problem by a leader well versed in the specific problem. Problem clinics help small business owners exchange knowledge of a common problem and help them share in various methods of dealing with the problem.

Workshops for Prospective Small Business Owners

The SBA establishes workshops in cooperation with civic organizations in an attempt to help prospective small business owners understand the need for preparation before starting a new venture. SBA personnel or professionals hold a 1-day session or several evening classes to instruct prospective small business owners in how to start a new business. Training materials are provided by the SBA to both the instructor and the prospective small business owners.

Set-Aside Contracts

The federal government contracts with private business for billions of dollars worth of goods and services each year. The various purchasing agencies of the federal government **set aside contracts** on which only small businesses may bid in an effort to promote small business. The SBA has Procurement Center representatives in major government procurement agencies to review and recommend additional set-aside contracts for small business. The Procurement Center representatives also provide lists of small business sources to the procurement agencies and often recommend relaxation of restrictive specifications so that small firms may bid on them.

SBA field offices have personnel who help small firms in government contract bidding by performing such functions as advising which agency uses their products or services, helping them get their firms on bidding lists, and helping them obtain bidding specifications and drawings.

Office of Advocacy

"In recent years, high interest rates, inflation, and excessive government regulation have inhibited the performance of the small business sector."[2] Complaints from small business owners to the federal government are well summarized in this statement. In 1976, Congress created the **Office of Advocacy** within the Small Business Administration. The office was created to protect, strengthen, and represent small business within the federal government.

Its mandate from Congress is to

- *Act as the primary spokesperson for small business and represent its views and interests before Congress and other Federal bodies.*
- *Serve as a conduit through which suggestions and policy criticisms are received.*
- *Inform the small business community of issues that affect it, and assist the entrepreneur with questions and problems regarding Federal laws, regulations, and assistance programs.*
- *Examine the role of small business in the American economy with regard to competition, innovation, productivity, and entrepreneurship.*
- *Measure the impact of Federal regulation and taxation on small entities and make policy recommendations that may enhance the performance of small businesses.*
- *Evaluate the credit needs of small business, particularly with regard to the free flow of capital to minority and women-owned enterprises.*[3]

Publications

The SBA offers a wide range of both free and for-sale publications designed to help the small businessperson in a wide range of problems. Publications that are for sale are sold by the Government Printing Office at cost. Almost all free publications and some of the for-sale publications can be obtained from SBA field offices. A list of Small Business Administration publications and SBA field office addresses is presented in the Appendix.

SUMMARY OF KEY POINTS

1. The Sherman Antitrust Act prohibits restraint of trade and monopoly.
2. The Clayton Act prohibits price discrimination, exclusive and tying contracts, intercorporate stockholding lessening competition, and interlocking directorates in competing corporations.

---

[2] *SBA Advocacy: A Voice for Small Business* (Washington, D.C.: Small Business Administration).
[3] Ibid.

3. The Federal Trade Commission Act prohibits unfair methods of competition.

4. The Robinson-Patman Act prohibits price discounts that cannot be fully justified by lower costs to the seller, selling private brands of a product that are identical to regular brands at a lower price, and giving buyers proportionally unequal advertising and promotional allowances.

5. The Food, Drug, and Cosmetic Act prohibits adulterated products, misbranding, and false advertising.

6. The Occupational Safety and Health Act requires that all workers must be free from recognized hazards that could cause death or serious injury.

7. Cooling-off periods, fair packaging and labeling, the Federal Garnishment Law of 1968, the Magnuson-Moss Warranty Act, and regulations about unordered merchandise are some of the more important consumer protection laws.

8. The Small Business Administration aids small businesses with management assistance, training, set-aside contracts, the Office of Advocacy, and publications.

DISCUSSION QUESTIONS

1. What does the Sherman Antitrust Act prohibit, and how effective is it?
2. Who may sue for violations under the Sherman Act?
3. What does the Clayton Act prohibit, and is it effective?
4. What are the two most important parts of the Federal Trade Commission Act?
5. What are the major provisions of the Robinson-Patman Act?
6. Who administers the Food, Drug, and Cosmetic Act?
7. If you were a small manufacturer, would you be concerned with the Occupational Health and Safety Act? Explain.
8. Name at least one type of small business that could be affected by the following "consumer protection laws," and tell how it could be affected.
    a. Cooling-off periods.
    b. Fair Packaging and Labeling Act.
    c. Federal Garnishment Act.
    d. Magnuson-Moss Warranty Act.
    e. Mail order merchandise.
    f. Unordered merchandise.
9. What forms of management assistance does the Small Business Administration offer small firms?
10. How does the Small Business Administration assist small businesses in terms of government contracts?

STUDENT PROJECT

Take the list of Small Business Administration publications to a small business, and find out which the owner–manager thinks would be of interest to most small businesses.

CASE A

The French Bakery

George and Linda McCoy opened their French Bakery one year ago in a small shopping center. They offer French bread and a wide assortment of French-style pastries. They have a small but loyal number of customers.

Their rent is rather high, and they have lost money from the very day they opened the business. They can't understand why they don't have more customers because everyone who tries their products seems to like them very much. They feel part of the problem might be the fact that their shop is not very visible from the street. Their only advertising has been in the restaurant section of the local newspaper.

They need immediate help and have asked you where they might get help. Their funds are so low that they cannot afford to pay someone for assistance.

QUESTION

What type of help is available to George and Linda?

CASE B

Federal Trade Commission Expert

Recently, you graduated from college, and you have just accepted a job with the Federal Trade Commission. The first day on the job you had several letters on your desk. A description of each letter is presented as follows.

Letter A   A small businesswoman writes that she recently sent out bid requests and received three bids, each of which quoted exactly the same amount, $2,416.52.

Letter B   A small businessman writes that he is having to pay almost twice the amount for a product than paid by a large competitor who buys from the same firm.

Letter C   A small businessman writes that he was forced out of business by a competitor who sold his product at below what he could produce it for; then, after he went out of business, the competitor raised his price.

Letter D   An individual writes that she bought a product that, according to the label, was supposed to weigh 8 ounces, but it only weighed 7 ounces.

Letter E   An individual complains that he bought a vacuum cleaner from a door-to-door salesperson. He decided he didn't want it and asked for his money back. The company refused to refund his money.

Letter F   A worker writes that he was fired from his job because of a garnishment of his wages to pay a debt.

Letter G   A small businesswoman wants to know if her product warranty meets the full warranty or limited warranty requirements.

Letter H   A small businessman complains that he was sent equipment through the mail even though he had not ordered it. He does not want the equipment, and the company is sending him nasty letters threatening to ruin his credit.

Letter I   A small businessman writes that he has heard that the government provides assistance to small firms, and he wants to know whom to contact.

QUESTION

How would you answer each letter?

APPENDIX

FREE PUBLICATIONS

The **Management Aids (MAs)** recommend methods and techniques for handling management problems and business operations.

Small Business Bibliographies (SBBs) list key reference sources for many business management topics.

Starting Out Series (SOSs) are one-page fact sheets describing financial and operating requirements for selected manufacturing, retail, and service businesses.

Management Aids

Financial Management and Analysis
The ABC's of Borrowing
What Is the Best Selling Price?
Keep Pointed Toward Profit
Basic Budgets for Profit Planning
Pricing for Small Manufacturers
Cash Flow in a Small Plant
Credit and Collections
Attacking Business Decision Problems With Breakeven Analysis
A Venture Capital Primer for Small Business
Accounting Services for Small Service Firms
Analyze Your Records to Reduce Costs
Profit by Your Wholesalers' Services
Steps in Meeting Your Tax Obligations
Getting the Facts for Income Tax Reporting
Budgeting in a Small Business Firm
Sound Cash Management and Borrowing
Keeping Records in Small Business
Check List for Profit Watching
Simple Breakeven Analysis for Small Stores
Profit Pricing and Costing for Services

Planning
Locating or Relocating Your Business
Problems in Managing a Family-Owned Business
The Equipment Replacement Decision
Finding a New Product for Your Company

**General Management
and Administration**

Marketing

Improving Personal Selling in Small Retail Stores
Advertising Guidelines for Small Retail Firms
Signs in Your Business
Plan Your Advertising Budget
Learning About Your Market
Do You Know the Results of Your Advertising?

Organization and Personnel

Checklist for Developing a Training Program
Pointers on Using Temporary-Help Services
Preventing Employee Pilferage
Setting Up a Pay System
Staffing Your Store
Managing Employee Benefits

Legal and Governmental Affairs

Incorporating a Small Business
Selecting the Legal Structure for Your Business
Introduction to Patents

Miscellaneous

Association Services for Small Business
Market Overseas With U.S. Government Help

SBBs

Handcrafts
Home Businesses
Selling By Mail Order
Marketing Research Procedures
Retailing
Statistics and Maps for National Market Analysis
National Directory for Use in Marketing
Recordkeeping Systems—Small Store and Service Trade
Basic Library Reference Sources
Advertising—Retail Store
Retail Credit and Collection
Buying for Retail Stores
Personnel Management

Inventory Management
Purchasing for Owners of Small Plants
Training for Small Business
Financial Management
Manufacturing Management
Marketing for Small Business
New Product Development
Ideas Into Dollars

SOS

Building Service Contracting
Radio-Television Repair Shop
Retail Florists
Franchised Businesses
Hardware Store or Home Centers
Sporting Goods Store
Drycleaning
Cosmetology
Pest Control
Marine Retailers
Retail Grocery Stores
Apparel Store
Pharmacies
Office Products
Interior Design Services
Fish Farming
Bicycles
Roofing Contractors
Printing
The Bookstore
Home Furnishings
Ice Cream
Sewing Centers
Personnel Referral Service
Selling By Mail Order
Solar Energy
Breakeven Point for Independent Truckers

PUBLICATIONS FOR SALE

Small Business Management Series

The booklets in this series provide discussions of special management problems in small companies.

An Employee Suggestion System for Small Companies
Explains the basic principles for starting and operating a suggestion system.

Cost Accounting for Small Manufacturers
Assists managers of small manufacturing firms establish accounting procedures that help control production and business costs.

Handbook of Small Business Finance
Indicates the major areas of financial management and describes a few techniques that can help the small business owner.

Ratio Analysis for Small Business
The purpose of the booklet is to help the owner–manager in detecting favorable or unfavorable trends in the business.

Practical Business Use of Government Statistics
Illustrates some practical uses of federal government statistics.

Guides for Profit Planning
Guides for computing and using the breakeven point, the level of gross profit, and the rate of return on investment.

Profitable Community Relations for Small Business
Practical information on how to build and maintain sound community relations by participation in community affairs.

Small Business and Government Research and Development
Includes a discussion of the procedures necessary to locate and interest government markets.

Management Audit for Small Manufacturers
A series of questions about small manufacturing plant planning, organizing, directing, and coordinating efficiency.

Insurance and Risk Management for Small Business
A discussion of what insurance is, the necessity of obtaining professional advice on buying insurance, and the main types of insurance a small business may need.

Management Audit for Small Retailers
149 questions guide the owner–manager in a self-examination and a review of the business operation.

Financial Recordkeeping for Small Stores
Written primarily for the small store owner or prospective owner whose business doesn't justify hiring a full-time bookkeeper.

Small Store Planning for Growth
Included is a consideration of merchandising, advertising and display, and checklists for increase in transactions and gross margins.

Franchise Index/Profile
Presents an evaluation process that may be used to investigate franchise opportunities.

Training Salesmen to Serve Industrial Markets
Discusses role of sales in marketing program of small manufacturer and offers suggestions for sales force to use in serving customers.

Financial Control by Time-Absorption Analysis
A profit control technique that can be used by all types of businesses.

Management Audit for Small Service Firms
A do-it-yourself guide for owner–managers of small service firms to help them evaluate and improve their operations.

Decision Points in Developing New Products
Provides a path from idea to marketing plan for the small manufacturing or R & D firm that wants to expand or develop a business around a new product, process, or invention.

Management Audit for Small Construction Firms
Helps top executives of small construction firms to make a self-appraisal of their management practices.

Purchasing Management and Inventory Control for Small Business
Explains how to manage purchasing and inventory dollars.

Managing the Small Service Firm for Growth and Profit
This booklet aids you in developing a marketing strategy to improve services to assure growth as customer needs change.

Credit and Collections for Small Stores
Discusses credit plans to help owner–managers pick and run credit systems. Includes information on legal restrictions, recordkeeping, and trade credit.

Starting and Managing Series

This series is designed to help the small entrepreneur "to look before leaping" into a business.

No.   1   *Starting and Managing a Small Business of Your Own*
No. 101   *Starting and Managing a Small Service Firm*

Nonseries Publications

Export Marketing for Smaller Firms
A manual for owner–managers of smaller firms who seek sales in foreign markets.

U.S. Government Purchasing and Sales Directory
A directory for businesses that are interested in selling to the U.S. Government. Lists the purchasing needs of various agencies.

Managing for Profits
Ten chapters on various aspects of small business management, for example, marketing, production, and credit.

Buying and Selling a Small Business
Deals with the problems that confront buyers and sellers of small businesses.

Strengthening Small Business Management
Twenty-one chapters on small business management.

Small Business Goes to College
This booklet traces the development of small business management as a college subject and provides samples of courses offered at 200 colleges and universities.

The Best of the SBI Review—1973–1979
Management ideas for the small business owner–manager.

Business Basics

Each of the 23 self-study booklets in this series contains text, questions, and exercises that teach a specific aspect of small business management.

The Profit Plan
Capital Planning
Understanding Money Sources
Evaluating Money Sources
Asset Management
Managing Fixed Assets
Understanding Costs
Cost Control
Marketing Strategy
Retail Buying Function
Inventory Management–Wholesale/Retail
Retail Merchandise Management
Consumer Credit
Credit and Collections: Policy and Procedures
Purchasing for Manufacturing Firms
Inventory Management—Manufacturing/Service
Inventory and Scheduling Techniques

Risk Management and Insurance
Managing Retail Salespeople
Job Analysis, Job Specifications, and Job Descriptions
Recruiting and Selecting Employees
Training and Developing Employees
Employee Relations and Personnel Policies

SBA FIELD OFFICE ADDRESSES

Boston	Massachusetts 02114, 150 Causeway Street
Holyoke	Massachusetts 01050, 302 High Street
Augusta	Maine 04330, 40 Western Avenue, Room 512
Concord	New Hampshire 03301, 55 Pleasant Street
Hartford	Connecticut 06103, One Financial Plaza
Montpelier	Vermont 05602, 87 State Street, P.O. Box 605
Providence	Rhode Island 02903, 57 Eddy Street
New York	New York 10007, 26 Federal Plaza, Room 3100
Albany	New York 12210, 3100 Twin Towers Building
Elmira	New York 14901, 180 State Street, Room 412
Hato Rey	Puerto Rico 00919, Chardon and Bolivia Streets
Melville	New York 11746, 425 Broad Hollow Road
Newark	New Jersey 07102, 970 Broad Street, Room 1635
Camden	New Jersey 08104, 1800 East Davis Street
Rochester	New York 14014, 100 State Street
Syracuse	New York 13260, 100 South Clinton Street, Room 1071
Buffalo	New York 14202, 111 West Huron Street
St. Thomas	Virgin Islands 00801, Federal Office Building, Veterans' Drive
Philadelphia	Bala Cynwyd, Pennsylvania 19004, One Bala Cynwyd Plaza
Harrisburg	Pennsylvania 17101, 100 Chestnut Street
Wilkes-Barre	Pennsylvania 18702, 20 North Pennsylvania Avenue
Baltimore	Towson, Maryland 21204, 8600 La Salle Road
Wilmington	Delaware 19801, 844 King Street
Clarksburg	West Virginia 26301, 109 N. 3rd Street
Charleston	West Virginia 25301, Charleston National Plaza, Suite 628

Pittsburgh	Pennsylvania 15222, 1000 Liberty Avenue
Richmond	Virginia 23240, 400 N. 8th Street, Room 3015
Washington	D.C. 20417, 1030 15th Street, NW., Suite 250
Atlanta	Georgia 30309, 1720 Peachtree Road, NW.
Biloxi	Mississippi 39530, 111 Fred Haise Boulevard
Birmingham	Alabama 35205, 908 South 20th Street
Charlotte	North Carolina 28202, 230 South Tryon Street, Suite 700
Greenville	North Carolina 27834, 215 South Evans Street
Columbia	South Carolina 29201, 1801 Assembly Street
Coral Gables	Florida 33134, 2222 Ponce de Leon Boulevard
Jackson	Mississippi 39201, 200 East Pascagoula Street
Jacksonville	Florida 32202, 400 W. Bay Street
West Palm Beach	Florida 33402, 701 Clematis Street
Tampa	Florida 33602, 700 Twiggs Street
Louisville	Kentucky 40202, 600 Federal Place, Room 188
Nashville	Tennessee 37219, 404 James Robertson Parkway, Suite 1012
Knoxville	Tennessee 37902, 502 South Gay Street, Room 307
Memphis	Tennessee 38103, 167 North Main Street
Chicago	Illinois 60604, 219 South Dearborn Street
Springfield	Illinois 62701, 1 North Old State Capitol Plaza
Cleveland	Ohio 44199, 1240 East 9th Street, Room 317
Columbus	Ohio 43215, 85 Marconi Boulevard
Cincinnati	Ohio 45202, 550 Main Street, Room 5028
Detroit	Michigan 48226, 477 Michigan Avenue
Marquette	Michigan 49885, 540 West Kaye Avenue
Indianapolis	Indiana 46204, 575 North Pennsylvania Street
Madison	Wisconsin 53703, 122 West Washington Avenue
Milwaukee	Wisconsin 53202, 517 East Wisconsin Avenue
Eau Claire	Wisconsin 54701, 500 South Barstow Street, Room B9AA
Minneapolis	Minnesota 55402, 12 South Sixth Street
Dallas	Texas 75242, 1100 Commerce Street
Albuquerque	New Mexico 87110, 5000 Marble Avenue, NE.
Houston	Texas 77002, 1 Allen Center, 500 Dallas Street

Little Rock	Arkansas 72201, 611 Gaines Street
Lubbock	Texas 79401, 1205 Texas Avenue
El Paso	Texas 79902, 4100 Rio Bravo, Suite 300
Lower Rio Grande Valley	Harlington, Texas 78550, 222 East Van Buren
Corpus Christi	Texas 78408, 3105 Leopard Street
Austin	Texas 78701, 300 E. 8th Street
Marshall	Texas 75670, 100 South Washington Street, Room G12
New Orleans	Louisiana 70113, 1001 Howard Avenue
Shreveport	Louisiana 71101, 500 Fannin Street
Oklahoma City	Oklahoma 73102, 200 N.W. 5th Street
San Antonio	Texas 78206, 727 East Durango, Room A-513
Kansas City	Missouri 64106, 1150 Grand Avenue
Des Moines	Iowa 50309, 210 Walnut Street
Omaha	Nebraska 68102, Nineteenth and Farnam Streets
St. Louis	Missouri 63101, Mercantile Tower, Suite 2500
Wichita	Kansas 67202, 110 East Waterman Street
Denver	Colorado 80202, 721 19th Street
Casper	Wyoming 82601, 100 East B Street, Room 4001
Fargo	North Dakota 58102, 657 2nd Avenue, North, Room 218
Helena	Montana 59601, 301 South Park
Salt Lake City	Utah 84138, 125 South State Street, Room 2237
Rapid City	South Dakota 57701, 515 9th Street
Sioux Falls	South Dakota 57102, 8th and Main Avenue
San Francisco	California 94105, 211 Main Street
Fresno	California 93712, 1229 N Street
Sacramento	California 95825, 2800 Cottage Way
Honolulu	Hawaii 96850, 300 Ala Moana
Agana	Guam 96910, Pacific Daily News Building
Los Angeles	California 90071, 350 South Figueroa Street
Las Vegas	Nevada 89101, 301 East Stewart
Reno	Nevada 89505, 50 South Virginia Street
Phoenix	Arizona 85012, 3030 North Central Avenue
San Diego	California 92188, 880 Front Street

Seattle	Washington 98174, 915 Second Avenue
Anchorage	Alaska 99501, 1016 West Sixth Avenue, Suite 200
Fairbanks	Alaska 99701, 101 12th Avenue
Boise	Idaho 83701, 1005 Main Street
Portland	Oregon 97204, 1220 South West Third Avenue
Spokane	Washington 99120, Courthouse Bldg., Room 651

GLOSSARY OF
KEY WORDS

A

Accounting equation The equation that assets equal liabilities plus capital, on which accounting is based.

Accounts receivable Funds that are owed the business by customers.

Accrual accounting The accounting method by which transactions are recorded when they happen regardless of when money is received or spent.

ACE Active Corps of Executives.

Acid test ratio Cash plus accounts receivable plus marketable securities divided by current liabilities.

Advertising Any type of sales presentation that is nonpersonal and is paid for by an identified sponsor.

Advertising copy The written or spoken words of the ad or both.

Advertising media The total of the various types of advertising used by the small business owner.

Advertising medium A single source used for advertising.

AICDC principle The sales formula stressing attention, interest, conviction, desire, and close.

AIDCA principle The advertising principle that outlines the basic requirements of a good newspaper ad: attention, interest, desire, conviction, and action.

Analytical thinking The ability to analyze various problems and situations in order to effectively deal with them.

Application blank Written record of a job applicant's qualifications.

Apprenticeship training Formal type of training that combines formal classroom learning and on-the-job experience.

Assets Anything of value. Assets can be tangible or intangible.

Autocratic leader A leader who strives for maximum control with little delegation of authority and emphasis on one-way communication.

Automobile insurance Insurance that protects against loss related to an automobile.

B

Bad debts Debts of customers that are not collected.

Balance sheet An accounting statement in which all assets, liabilities, and capital are recorded.

Bank credit cards Credit cards issued by banks that allow customers to charge at a large number of businesses.

Bankruptcy Selling the assets of the business and dividing them among creditors and owners of the business when there are more liabilities than assets.

Batch processing Data that are accumulated for a period of time and then processed, such as payroll data.

Bid, cost, variance system A system of calculating various costs and profit in order to arrive at a bid price. If the bid is successful, the actual costs are recorded and compared to the bid.

Bidding Quotation of a price by a business firm to another firm for goods or services.

Bill of lading A certificate issued to shippers by transportation companies to show that certain merchandise is in their possession.

Bin tags A system of inventory control in which tags are attached to bins and withdrawals, receipts, and balance of the items are recorded.

Bona fide occupational qualification Means by which employers can discriminate on the basis of religion, sex, or national origin.

Bond A certificate of debt by a corporation. Bonds are not ownership and have an interest rate, maturity date, and amount.

Brand A name, term, sign, symbol, or design or combination of them that is intended to identify the goods or services of one seller or group of sellers and to differentiate them from those of competitors.

Breach of contract The act of not honoring all terms of a contract.

Budget A projected income statement for a future period of time. It shows estimated sales and expenses.

Burglar alarm systems Devices that warn if a burglar is breaking into a business.

Burglary The breaking into a business and stealing of merchandise or money by a person or persons.

Business format franchising A fully integrated relationship with the franchisee and the newer type of franchising.

C

Capital The part of the business that represents ownership. Assets minus liabilities equal capital.

Capitalization Multiplying the yearly profit of the business by some number to estimate the value of a business.

Cash accounting The accounting method in which transactions are recorded only when money is received or expended.

Cash discount Incentive offered the business owner for prompt payment of merchandise.

Cash flow statement An accounting statement that shows receipts and expenditures of cash.

Central Processing Unit (CPU) Contains the storage, control, and arithmetic-logic sections of the computer.

Certificate of deposit A document that certifies that a person or business has on deposit with a financial institution a certain sum of money.

Change fund The money that is retained from the previous day to make change for money transactions.

Channel of distribution The route that goods and services follow to the final user of the product.

Charge account credit Goods or services are bought on credit and paid for at a later time. This does not include installment sales contracts.

Chattel mortgage A mortgage obtained when something is sold on credit and a lien against the item is retained against whatever was sold. Title passes at the time of sale.

Check A negotiable instrument that instructs a third party (usually a financial institution) to pay a second party a specific sum of money that the first person has on deposit.

Civil Rights Act of 1964 The law designed to prohibit discrimination in employment practices of firms with 15 or more employees.

Clayton Act A law providing for social control of business that prohibits price discrimination, tying contracts, intercorporate stockholding lessening competition, and interlocking directorates in competing corporations.

Collection Collecting money that is owed by customers.

Commercial bank A bank that offers checking accounts and savings accounts, loans money, and provides other business services. Savings and loan institutions are not included.

Committee on Economic Development A body of people that has defined a business as small if management is independent, capital is supplied, and ownership is held by an individual or small group; if the area of operation is mainly local; and if the business is small when compared to the largest units in its field.

Common stock A certificate of ownership in a corporation, which usually does not have a fixed rate of dividend, is paid after preferred stock, and entitles the owner to a vote at shareholders' meetings.

Communications ability The skill to convey written and oral information effectively so that understanding is created between sender and receiver.

Community shopping center Consists of many shops in a community location. The shops offer shopping goods and serve a population of from 40,000 to 150,000.

Competitive pricing A pricing strategy by which a business tries to maintain lower prices than other businesses in the market.

Composition of population The distribution of various factors in the population of people in a given market, such as age, income, race, education, and so forth.

Computer hardware The computer and peripheral equipment.

Computer program The detailed set of instructions that outlines the specific sequence of operations the computer is to perform.

Computer service center A region where data for other firms are processed for a fee.

Computer software The languages, programs, and instructions used to communicate with the computer and direct its operation.

Conditional sales contract An installment sales contract in which title to the merchandise does not pass until the item is paid for.

Consignment purchasing A stockless purchasing system whereby the vendor's merchandise is displayed in the small business and the vendor is responsible for the merchandise display and ownership stays with the vendor until the goods are used or sold.

Consumer credit Money owed by ultimate consumers.

Contract A legal agreement between two or more parties.

Control The process of determining if current operations conform to established plans.

Convenience goods Goods that the customer needs immediately and that are usually purchased from the most convenient source.

Cooling-off period A cooling-off period required by law in door-to-door selling when the purchase exceeds $25.

Cooperative advertising An advertising plan by which the manufacturer shares in the cost of the advertising with the retailer, such as on a 50–50 basis.

Corporation A form of business ownership that must be chartered by 1 of the 50 states. It has 3 or more owners and issues stock certificates as evidence of ownership.

Corporation tax A federal income tax levied on corporation profit.

Cost of goods manufactured A section of an income statement of manufacturers that shows direct labor, raw materials, and factory overhead.

Cost of goods sold A section of an income statement of retailers and wholesalers that shows how much the merchandise they sold during the period cost them.

Counseling Direct, interpersonal communication between owner and employees, which may be either formal counseling or informal counseling.

Creative salesperson A type of salesperson who attempts to create a need for a service or merchandise in the mind of a customer.

Creative thinking The ability of the entrepreneur to adapt his or her actions to the needs of the business in various situations.

Credit Money owed; also, when liabilities, capital, or income is increased or when assets or expenses are decreased.

Credit card Plastic card that allows the customer to charge goods or services.

Current ratio Current assets divided by current liabilities.

Customer attitude survey A questionnaire survey of customers to determine what they think about the business relative to various factors.

Customer attitudes What the customers of a business think about the business concerning factors such as service, quality, price, and so on.

D

Debit Condition when assets are increased or expenses are incurred or when liabilities, capital, or income is decreased.

Debt capital Money that is put into a business that comes from borrowing.

Debt to net worth ratio Total liabilities divided by net worth less intangible assets.

Directing The supervision of employees on a daily, face-to-face basis.

Disbursement journal A basic accounting book in which all expenditures are recorded.

Discount prices A smaller than usual markup resulting in low prices.

Discretionary buying power The part of the income that is not required for the purchase of the basic necessities of life.

Disposable personal income The amount of money consumers have available to spend.

Dissolution Selling the assets of a business and dividing them among creditors and owners of the business. There are more assets than liabilities.

Dividend A payment of profits paid to stockholders in a corporation.

Domestic international sales corporation A corporation that can be set up that allows manufacturers to pay no tax on an export income up to $100,000 and defers taxes on 50 percent of the income above that amount.

Drive A person's motivation toward a task.

Duress Forcing a person to act against his or her will.

E

Emotional buying motive A purchase decision that involves little thought or deliberation.

Empathy The ability to put yourself in someone else's position and know how that person feels and perceives the situation.

Employee theft Theft of merchandise or money by employees.

Entrepreneur One who organizes a business undertaking, assuming risks, for the sake of profit.

Equal Employment Opportunity Act of 1972 Amendment to Civil Rights Act of 1964, also designed to prohibit discrimination in employment.

Equipment manufacturers and distributors Firms that sell equipment to businesses. They may make equipment or buy it for resale.

Equity capital Money invested in a business by the owners.

Exclusive agency contract An agreement that gives the distributor exclusive rights to sell goods or services within a designated territory.

Exclusive distributorship Agreement whereby a manufacturer gives the distributor exclusive rights to sell goods or services within a designated area.

Expenses Money that is spent.

Export Trading Company Act Law that permits companies to join with banks, ocean shipping companies, advertising agencies, distributors, and others to complete the distribution process necessary to handle a product from a U.S. factory to a foreign consumer while being exempt from antitrust prosecution.

F

Factors Firms that buy or discount accounts receivable.

Fair Labor Standards Act of 1938 Law that regulates the number of hours worked and provides for overtime pay in excess of 40 hours.

Fair Packing and Labeling Act Law that requires manufacturers to display the net weight or volume of the contents.

Fashion centers More suited for high-income areas, these centers consist of apparel shops, boutiques, and handcraft shops that sell high-price and high-quality merchandise.

Feasibility study A survey of the current information requirements of a firm, the areas of the company that would benefit the most from a computerized system, an evaluation of the computer systems that would meet the firm's requirements, the anticipated cost savings of the system, and a recommendation of the preferred system; also, a systematic study of the profit potential for a new business that has not been established.

Federal Garnishment Law A consumer protection law that prohibits more than 25 percent of an employee's disposable earnings from being garnished and prohibits an employee's being fired for only one garnishment.

Federal Trade Commission Act A federal law that established the Federal Trade Commission and prohibited unfair competition.

Financial condition The financial health of a business; the total monetary strength of the business.

Financial control Using financial records to record and analyze money transactions.

Fire insurance Insurance that insures loss due to fire and other damage.

Flexible markup Occurs when various percentages of markup are added to different types of merchandise.

Floor sample control An inventory control system used when large items are in stock in a warehouse area. Pads of numbers are pasted on the item, and each time one is sold, a number is removed, thereby showing how many are left in stock.

Flowchart Diagram of the activities needed to solve a problem by a computer.

F.O.B. buyer Title to goods passes when the merchandise is delivered to the buyer's place of business.

F.O.B. seller Title to goods passes as soon as the seller delivers the merchandise to the shipper.

Follow-the-market pricing A pricing strategy in which the business sets a price that is comparable to the going price charged by other firms.

Food, Drug, and Cosmetic Act A federal law that prohibits adulterated products, misbranding, and false advertising.

Franchise disclosure statement Detailed information about the franchise that the franchisor makes available to the franchisees, such as profit and franchise renewal.

Franchisee A licensed, affiliated dealer of the franchisor.

Franchising A continuing relationship in which the franchisor provides a licensed privilege to do business plus assistance in organizing, training, merchandising, and management in return for a consideration from the franchisee.

Franchisor The owner of a product, service, or method.

Fraud Intentional misrepresentation of fact.

Free-flow layout A store layout, which may be circular, octagonal, or U-shaped and has no uniform pattern of arrangement.

Free-rein leader A leader who emphasizes minimal contact with employees.

Fringe benefits Indirect payments to employees.

G

General partner A partner in a partnership form of ownership who has unlimited liability. There must be at least one in a partnership.

Grid layout Rectangular store arrangement that features a main aisle and secondary aisles that are located at right angles to the main aisle.

H

Hedging Shifting risk to others by buying and selling in the futures market.

Human relations ability The ability to work effectively with others.

I

Impulse goods "Spur-of-the-moment" purchases.

Impulse purchases Purchases made without preplanning.

Income Money that is received by the business.

Income statement An accounting statement that records income less expenses for a specific period of time.

Input data The data fed into the computer.

Installment credit Goods and services are bought and paid for on a regular installment basis. This does not include charge account credit.

Installment sales contract A contract in which a customer promises to pay for merchandise by making installment payments over a period of time.

Institutional advertising Advertising aimed at providing the general public with information about the company.

Insurance company A business that insures all sorts of risks in exchange for payment of premiums.

Interest The amount of money that is charged for debt.

Internal organization environment The climate of the firm, including the social, physical and economic factors.

International Franchise Association A nonprofit trade association that represents franchising companies in the United States and around the world.

Inventory Goods carried on hand by a firm.

Inventory turnover Cost of goods sold divided by beginning inventory plus ending inventory divided by two.

J

Job analysis Systematic investigation to collect all pertinent information about each task.

Job description Written record that defines the major and minor duties of each task.

Job evaluation The systematic and orderly process for determining the correct rate of pay for each job in relation to other jobs.

Job specification The qualities, knowledges, skills, and abilities an individual needs to perform a task satisfactorily.

Joint venture A form of a partnership that is created for a specific purpose and not for a regular day-to-day business; a foreign manufacturer is authorized to produce the products of the domestic company, but the domestic company also has an equity interest in the foreign company.

L

Layout The arrangement of selling and nonselling departments, aisles, fixtures, displays, and equipment in the proper relationship to each other and to the fixed elements of the building structure.

Lead time The time needed for delivery of materials so that they will be available when needed in the business.

Lease A contract between the property owner and the tenant.

Lease-purchase contract An installment sales contract in which the buyer or renter pays rent until an amount that equals the sale price is received. Title passes when the entire purchase price is paid.

Legal aspects   Matters of a business that relate to the laws of various governments.

Lessee   The tenant.

Lessor   The property owner.

Letter of credit   Letter issued by a financial institution requesting that money or credit be given a business or person and promising to pay up to a specific amount if defaulted.

Liabilities   All debt.

Liability insurance   Insurance that protects against being liable owing to acts of employees, conditions in the business, or products they sell or manufacture.

License   A certificate issued by a government agency allowing a business to do certain things.

Licensing   An arrangement whereby a foreign manufacturer is authorized to produce the products of a domestic company.

Life insurance   Insurance that pays for loss of life.

Limited partner   A partner in the partnership form of business ownership. This partner has liability only to the extent of the person's investment.

Line of credit   A commercial bank establishes a line of credit by agreeing to make loans automatically up to a certain established limit.

Long-term loan   A loan that has duration in excess of one year.

Loss of earning power   Insurance that protects against some event that causes the loss of ability to earn money.

M

Magnuson-Moss Warranty Act   A federal law that regulates warranties.

Management by objectives   A results-oriented approach to appraisal that involves employees in the goal-setting process.

Manager   One who supervises the work activities of employees in order to see to it that they accomplish their specific tasks.

Manufacturer's brand   A national brand advertised and sold in all or nearly all sections of the nation.

Market barriers   Psychological or physical barriers that define a market area. They limit customer access to the business.

Marketing   The performance of business activities that direct the flow of goods and services from the producer to the consumer or user to satisfy their specific needs.

Marketing concept   The objectives of the business are to identify the needs of customers and then use all resources of the firm to offer the goods and services that will satisfy consumer needs while earning a profit for the firm.

Marketing functions   The activities involved in the marketing process—buying and selling; transportation and storage; risk taking, standardization and grading, and financing; and market information.

Marketing mix   The strategy of the firm, which involves choosing the right mix of the four variables of products and services, promotional strategy, physical distribution, and pricing.

Marketing research   The process of collecting, recording, and analyzing data pertaining to the target market to which the firm caters.

Market segment   The target market of the firm, such as a particular age group.

Markup   The percentage added to the cost of goods to arrive at a selling price.

Mental ability   The overall intelligence (IQ), creative thinking ability, and analytical thinking ability of the entrepreneur.

Merchandising service establishment   Firms such as barber shops, beauty shops, and motels, which center on customer convenience and attractive physical appearance of the facility.

Microcomputer A small, personal computer with wide application for small businesses—often referred to as a computer on a chip.

Minicomputer A smaller computer introduced in the 1960s; the original small business computer.

Minimall A shopping center designed for customer convenience with major tenants being a junior department store; food, drug, or variety store; and a number of specialty and service outlets.

Money order A check drawn up by a post office, bank, and such, and purchased by an individual or business to be paid to some other party.

Morale The mental attitude of individuals and work groups toward their work environment.

Mortgage credit Credit on goods or real property that is secured by a lien against the goods or real property.

Motivation The inner drive that ignites behavioral actions to satisfy needs.

O

Occupational Safety and Health Act A federal law passed to reduce deaths and injuries related to work.

Office of Advocacy A division of the SBA that helps small businesses that have problems with the federal government.

100 percent location The optimum location for a retail store.

On-line processing Data that are processed as they are collected.

On-the-job training Training given on the job. It is the most often used technique for training in the small business.

Order getter A salesperson who attempts to recognize potential customers and to arouse their need for merchandise or services by providing them with necessary information.

Order taker The type of personal seller whose main activity is taking the orders of customers who have made up their mind with regard to a specific purchase.

Organization chart Graphical representation of the authority and responsibility relationships among personnel as well as the formal channels of communication in the company.

Organizing The coordination of the human, financial, and physical resources of the firm so that they follow the course needed to reach the firm's objectives outlined in the planning phase.

Output The final product of the computer.

P

Partial control system A system of inventory control in which the business maintains perpetual records on part of its inventory on a rotating basis.

Participative leader The leader who shares decision making with employees.

Partnership A form of business ownership in which there are two or more partners (owners) of the business. It is not a corporation that issues stock.

Par value The stated value of stock on the face of the stock certificate. It usually has no relationship to market value.

Patronage motives The factors that influence customers to return repeatedly to the same store to make their purchases.

Percentage of sales method The method used in preparing an advertising budget that maintains an ad budget in a consistent relationship to sales volume.

Performance appraisal The evaluation of each employee's job performance at periodic intervals.

Periodic inventory system A system of inventory control in which purchases and inventory levels are compared at reorder time.

Perpetual inventory system A system of recording inventory additions and reductions so that the balance of inventory on hand is known at all times.

Personal selling The process of personally informing customers about a product or service through personal communication for the purpose of making a sale.

Physical inventory count Inventory in stock is counted and compared to inventory records.

Physical facilities The plant or building of the business.

Planning The process of setting objectives and choosing the course of action that will enable the firm to reach the objectives.

Point of purchase displays Displays located throughout the store, usually prepared by the manufacturers or distributors of products, and made available to small firm owners.

Preferred stock A certificate of ownership in a corporation that usually has a fixed rate of dividend, must be paid before common stock, and does not give its owner a vote.

Price image How the customer perceives the business relative to the degree of price, such as a discount price image.

Prices The amount of money charged for merchandise or service.

Pricing for clearance Marking down the price of merchandise to get it out of stock.

Primary buying motive Awareness of the existence of the need to purchase a certain kind or general class of product or service.

Primary needs Basic needs such as physiological, safety, and security needs.

Private brand A distributor's brand or dealer's brand owned by an intermediary and advertised and sold in a more limited geographical area, such as a region or a state.

Private investor An individual who loans money or one who invests in business ventures.

Process layout The type of layout in plants where many different kinds of products are produced or are produced for customer specifications.

Processing-type service establishment Businesses that have processing operations separate from where customer orders are taken, such as print shops.

Product layout The type of plant layout used for mass production of goods.

Product trade name franchise The traditional type of franchising common among auto and truck dealers, gasoline service stations, and earth moving equipment as well as the soft drink industry.

Progressive discipline A disciplinary approach that applies a minimum of discipline to a first offense but that increases the degree of discipline for subsequent violations of rules or policies.

Promotional advertising Advertising to inform and remind the target market of the firm about its goods and services.

Promotional strategy The means that small business owners use to communicate information about the firm and its products and services to potential customers with the objective of influencing customers to purchase products or services that will satisfy their wants and needs.

Publicity A news item about a company reported by the media because the information has some apparent news value.

Punched card control An inventory control system in which punched cards are attached to merchandise and removed at the time of sale. They are then processed by equipment and recorded in perpetual inventory records.

Purchasing The process of buying the right quality of materials, products, and supplies in the appropriate quantity at the best price and at the proper time from the right vendor.

Q

Quantity discount Discount made available on larger purchases.

R

Rate of return The amount of profit generated by a business relative to the amount of money invested.

Rate of return on assets Profit divided by total assets less intangible assets.

Ratio A calculation that compares one or more category of income or expenses to other categories of income or expenses.

Rational buying motives A buying decision that involves a considerable amount of conscious thought and deliberation before a purchase is made.

Regulatory Flexibility Act of 1980 The purpose of this act is to require federal agencies to revise or drop excessive rules and regulations that are a burden to the small business.

Retail affinity Stores located near each other because they sell similar or complementary merchandise.

Retail credit bureaus An agency that is owned by participating merchants that keep and report credit records on customers.

Revolving charge accounts Goods or services are bought and paid for based on 30-day periods. Not all the money owed must be paid for at the end of the period, but some minimum amount is due.

Risk Exposure to injury or loss.

Robinson-Patman Act A law providing for social control of business that closed the weaknesses of the price discrimination section of the Clayton Act.

S

Safety factor The volume decided upon to be kept in inventory to meet the contingencies in the company.

Sales and cash receipts record A record that is kept each day to compare money received and what is on hand in the cash register.

Sales finance company Financial firms that purchase installment sales contracts from other businesses.

Sales journal A basic accounting book in which all sales are recorded.

Sales promotion The marketing activities other than personal selling or advertising and publicity that stimulate consumer purchasing and dealer effectiveness, such as displays, shows and expositions, and demonstrations.

Sales ticket control Part of an inventory control system in which all sales are recorded on sales tickets and posted to perpetual inventory control records.

Sample A part of the universe or total population.

SBA Small Business Administration.

SCORE Service Corps of Retired Executives.

Seasonal discount Discount on merchandise offered during off-seasons.

Secondary needs Higher order needs such as recognition and peer approval and status.

Section 8 (a) A program of the Small Business Act designed to provide assistance to small businesses owned and operated by economically and socially disadvantaged persons.

Selective buying motive The evaluation of possible alternative products or services that will satisfy a need.

Service salesperson A salesperson who primarily functions in the capacity of assisting the consumer in making a sale.

Set-aside contracts Government contracts that are offered only to small business.

Shelf space analysis An analysis that provides the amount of profit each item makes in terms of the number of inches required to stock it on shelves.

Sherman Antitrust Act A federal law that prohibits monopoly and price fixing.

Shoplifting Theft of merchandise by customers.

Shopping center A group of architecturally unified, commercial establishments built on a site that is planned, developed, owned, and managed as an operating unit related in its location, size, and type of shops to the trade area that the unit serves.

Shopping goods Goods sold through a select number of outlets; the cost is usually substantial so that consumers shop.

Short-term loan A loan that has a duration of less than one year.

Small business A business defined by the SBA as one that is independently owned and operated and not dominant in its field of operation.

Small Business Administration An agency in the Department of Commerce that helps small businesses obtain loans and also offers management assistance.

Small Business Investment Corporation A financial firm that borrows part of its capital from the SBA and lends or invests the funds in small business ventures.

Small business owner–manager The person in charge of the business where the owner is also the manager or where the manager is a paid employee.

Sole proprietorship A form of business ownership in which there is only one owner.

Source documents The original form of recorded data, such as sales orders or payroll time cards.

Specialty advertising Advertising that has the name and advertising message of the advertiser printed on useful items, such as pens or key rings.

Specialty centers A center that caters to unusual, special market segments and consists of many small specialty shops and restaurants.

Specialty goods Items that have a special quality or characteristic.

Staffing The activity of selecting and placing personnel in positions for which they are qualified.

Standard markup Markup that occurs when the same percentage of markup is added to all goods sold.

Stockholders Persons who own either preferred or common stock of a corporation.

Stress How people respond to events in the environment that pose a threat.

String street location Retail outlets located in an unplanned fashion along a heavily traveled street or highway.

Stub control Part of an inventory control system in which two or more part stubs are attached to merchandise and part of the stub is removed at time of sale for posting to perpetual inventory control records.

Subchapter S corporations Corporations meeting certain requirements that may elect to be taxed as a partnership, according to an Internal Revenue Service code.

Subcontracting Taking part of a job and paying someone or some other firm to complete the task.

Suggested retail prices Prices suggested by manufacturers that can be charged for the merchandise at the retail level.

Suggestion selling The sales technique of suggesting additional items after a customer has made an initial decision to buy or suggesting a better quality of merchandise.

Surety insurance Bonding to assure customers of the firm's ability to complete contracts.

T

Technical knowledge The ability to work with "things."

Theft insurance Insurance to insure loss due to theft.

Thirty-day charge accounts Charge accounts in which goods or services are bought and paid for at the end of a 30-day period.

Time management The systematic analysis of how the owner and employees are using time in performing job tasks.

Time-sharing center Many smaller firms share the computer time of a computer firm. The computer firm (the center) leases time to users and processes data for them.

Title Legal ownership to merchandise or property.

Trade area The geographic area that provides a major portion of the continuing patronage necessary to support the individual business or a larger shopping district.

Trade discount The discount available to purchasers on the basis of their trade classification wholesaler or industrial buyer or retailer).

Traditional bank loan A commercial bank loan in which the money is loaned for an entire period instead of being repayed in installments.

Traffic count A measure of the amount of pedestrian and vehicle traffic passing a site that represents potential customers.

Travel time The amount of time it takes to reach a business location from various points in the market area.

Truth-in-Lending Law A federal law that requires the disclosure of specific credit information to the customer.

Turnaround time The length of time it takes for data to be processed and returned to the user by the computer service center or the time-sharing center.

Turnover Total cost of goods sold divided by the average inventory.

U

Uniform Commercial Code A common legal code that covers areas of business law that was established and adopted by 49 states.

Unit of sales method The method used in preparing an advertising budget whereby a definite amount of funds is set aside for each unit of the product that is sold.

Universe The total population under study.

University small business institutes A joint effort between the SBA and universities to provide management consulting to small business.

Unordered merchandise According to law, unordered merchandise sent through the mail can be considered a free gift.

V

Value analysis The systematic study of a component or a product to determine whether any changes in parts or function can be made that will provide the same value to users at less cost or greater value at the same cost.

Vendors Firms that sell any type of goods or supplies to a business.

Visual inventory system A system of ordering inventory by looking at how much is on hand at regular intervals.

Volume of business The amount of sales over a specific period of time.

W

Word-of-mouth advertising Impressions of a firm that are passed from one person to another through conversation.

Workers' compensation Insurance for employees who suffer a job-related injury.

PHOTO CREDITS

I N D E X

Index